TOWARDS FREEDOM IN PONDICHERRY

Pondicherry had its own history due to its connection with the French. After delving deeply into social, cultural, economic aspects of the Pondicherry society, the study focuses on politics and the freedom movement as it developed there, using sources written in Tamil, English and French. But when the freedom movement gathered steam in British India, Pondicherry and its dependencies were caught between the ideas of joining the French Union, or the Indian Union.

Goubert's Socialist Party's strategy had always been to safeguard French India's special identity and interests. He and his party associates and supporters turned against the French offer to hold a referendum on the question of independence and decided to join the Indian Union, because Jawaharlal Nehru provided him a better guarantee to safeguard French Indian and Pondicherry interests. It was rather a very well planned move that took all his political adversaries including the French by surprise. Goubert actually won his battle without bloodshed, by accepting to bear a certain dishonor for that among the French. The French government finally chose to set aside the constitutional provisions of Article 27 of the French Constitution, which stipulated that no cession, or exchange or addition to the territories was valid without the consent of the concerned population.

Thus, they disregarded the population of French India deliberately and scuttled out of French India. Earlier, they had given away the *loges* to India even without consulting the parliament or the people concerned, but now they threw overboard the French constitutional provision to disengage themselves from India permanently, after obtaining some weak guarantees for their cultural presence.

Jean-Baptiste Prashant More (b.1955) is a reputed independent historian. He obtained his doctorate in history from the prestigious *Ecole des Hautes Etudes en Sciences Sociales* in Paris. He specialises in history, sociology and politics of southern India and colonial India. His latest books include *Pondicherry, Tamil Nadu and South India under French Rule: From François Martin to Dupleix 1674-1754* (Manohar, 2020) and *Bose and His Movement: From Nazi Germany to French Indochina* (Manohar, 2022).

Towards Freedom in Pondicherry

Society, Economy and Politics under French Rule (1816-1962)

J.B.P. MORE

LONDON AND NEW YORK

MANOHAR

First published 2023
by Routledge
4 Park Square, Milton Park, Abingdon, Oxon OX14 4RN

and by Routledge
605 Third Avenue, New York, NY 10158

Routledge is an imprint of the Taylor & Francis Group, an informa business

© 2023 J.B.P. More and Manohar Publishers

The right of J.B.P. More to be identified as author of this work has been asserted in accordance with sections 77 and 78 of the Copyright, Designs and Patents Act 1988.

All rights reserved. No part of this book may be reprinted or reproduced or utilised in any form or by any electronic, mechanical, or other means, now known or hereafter invented, including photocopying and recording, or in any information storage or retrieval system, without permission in writing from the publishers.

Trademark notice: Product or corporate names may be trademarks or registered trademarks, and are used only for identification and explanation without intent to infringe.

Print edition not for sale in South Asia (India, Sri Lanka, Nepal, Bangladesh, Pakistan or Bhutan)

British Library Cataloguing-in-Publication Data
A catalogue record for this book is available from the British Library

Library of Congress Cataloging-in-Publication Data
A catalog record for this book has been requested

ISBN: 978-1-032-37701-8 (hbk)
ISBN: 978-1-032-37702-5 (pbk)
ISBN: 978-1-003-34147-5 (ebk)

DOI: 10.4324/9781003341475

Typeset in Adobe Garamond 11/13
by Kohli Print, Delhi 110051

MANOHAR

Contents

List of Illustrations   7
Acknowledgements   9
Abbreviations   11
Introduction   13

1. Society, Land and Economy   29
2. Emergence of the Professional Class   55
3. Administration and Politics   76
4. British Indian Stalwarts in Pondicherry   113
5. From Revolt to Anti-Fascism, 1936-1945   135
6. Nationalist Awakening in Pondicherry   168
7. The Rise of Goubert   217
8. Goubert's Sway Continues   267
9. Towards Integration   295
10. Curtains Down on French Rule in India   333
11. Merger with India   358

Conclusions and Observations   385
Annexure   397
Biographical Notes   409
Bibliography   421
Index   447

Illustrations

(*between pp. 232-3*)

1. Edouard Goubert, Father of Pondicherry, in the 1970s, a few years before his death.
2. Edouard Goubert, Mayor of Pondicherry, 1963.
3. From left. Georges Sala, French Administrator of Yanam, Madhimchetty Satyanandam, Mayor of Yanam, Governor of the French territories in India, André Ménard and his wife, a French official, Kanakala Tataya in Yanam.
4. Muthu Komarappa Reddiar, Edouard Goubert and Muthu Poullé, September 1954, at the head of the Liberation Government in Nettapakkam.
5. Kewal Singh, Indian High Commissioner in Pondicherry, Muthu Komarappa Reddiar, R.K. Nehru and K.S. Venkatakrishna Reddiar at the residence of Muthu Komarappa Reddiar, in Nettapakkam, 1954.
6. In the photo could be seen Muthu Poullé (in the middle), Pakkirisamy Poullé, Jawaharlal Nehru, Edouard Goubert & Muthu Komarappa Reddiar, standing side by side, 1955.
7. In the photo could be seen Muthu Komarappa Reddiar (3rd from left), Edouard Goubert, Pakkirisamy Poullé of Karaikal and K. Kamaraj, standing side by side, 1955.
8. Leon Prouchandy of Pondicherry, last General Secretary of the Indian Independence League, Saigon, bidding farewell to Subhas Chandra Bose in his residence at 76, Hai Bha Trung Road in Ho Chi Minh city (Saigon), August 1945.
9. Plan showing French Pondicherry (striped) on the Bay of Bengal, June 1951
10. Plan of French Karaikal (striped), June 1951.

11. Plan of French Yanam (striped) on the Coromandel Coast, June 1951.
12. V. Subbiah, freedom fighter, Communist leader, with his wife Saraswathi.
13. Students manifesting for freedom in Pondicherry, 1948.
14. Lambert Saravane, Pondicherry personality during the freedom struggle.

Acknowledgements

In the year 2001, I authored a book on the freedom movement in Mahé, the former French colony on the Malabar coast. That was my second book. Six years later in 2007, I authored another book on the freedom movement that grew in Yanam, another former French colony on the Coromandel (Cholamandalam) coast. Since that time I have been collecting material to write an exhaustive history on the freedom movement in Pondicherry, which was the headquarters, or capital of French India or the French colonies in India, since the late seventeenth century. The present work fulfils this long-cherished objective.

I am greatly indebted to several prominent personalities who have been helpful directly and indirectly in the writing of this book. I have talked to and interviewed at length many of them regarding the freedom movement in Pondicherry and French India, and French Indian history. They came out frankly with their perceptions of French India and the freedom movement there.

The most prominent among them were Joseph Goubert, the son of the flamboyant French Indian politician, Edouard Goubert, Saraswati Subbiah, the wife of the late communist leader and freedom-fighter, V. Kailasa Subbiah, Mannar Mannan, son of the Tamil poet and politician Bharathidasan, Mr Radjanedassou and his brother Antoine Mariadassou, both freedom-fighters and student leaders of Pondicherry, Justice David Annoussamy, an experienced observer of French Indian politics, the late Professor M.P. Sridharan of Mahé, Palery Damodaran, a retired teacher in Mahé, Paramel Shatrughan, student leader in Pondicherry, P. Sisupalan, retired teacher and freedom-fighter of Mahé, Mangalat Raghavan, journalist and freedom-fighter of Mahé, Kanakala Tataya, Madhimchetty Betana, Madhimchetty Ziyana, Dr V. Nallam of Yanam, the late Ms Sai Kumari, daughter of Muthu Kumarappa Reddiar of Pondicherry, the late Mr Farook Marakkayar, former Chief Minister of Pondicherry, Chandra Varma, grandson of Sellane Naiker, Yves Perrier, former administrator of French India, Georges Sala, former administrator of French India, A. Arulraj and N. Marimuthu, freedom-fighters of Pondicherry, Mr Mathurakavy, retired Tamil teacher, Mr Kulasegaran, a social activist, Raman Reddy, spiritualist, and Cyril Antony, author of the *Gazetteer of Pondicherry*.

My special thanks are also due to my wife, Dr Leena, who has always been a source of encouragement to me, Professor K.S. Mathew, former head of the history department of Pondicherry University, Dr Murugaiyan, professor at the Community College of Pondicherry, Dr Ezhil Vasanthan, assistant professor of Tamil at Tiruvalluvar University College, M. Mubeen, a descendant of H.M. Cassime, former mayor of Pondicherry town and freedom-fighter, and many other well-wishers of Pondicherry. Besides, I am indebted to the staff of the various libraries and archives in India, France and the UK, who have been helpful to me all through my research in locating the relevant records and books. I am particularly thankful to the librarians Mrs Mohamed and Mrs Sundari Gobalakichenane of Inalco, Paris, Mrs Nalini Prasad of British Library, London, and Mr Ramamoorthy of Institut Français, Pondicherry.

It is never an easy task to write about the freedom movements and the rise of nationalism in the colonised countries. In my opinion, it is necessary to rise above the limitations imposed by national, linguistic, religious, ethnic and ideological affiliations in order to reconstruct the history of the freedom movement in Pondicherry without bias and prejudice and in the utmost impartial manner. This is what we propose to do in this work. If inspite of all my attention and care to portray the facts of history, in case the reader comes across any error of commission or omission, he can point that out to me frankly. I under-take to rectify those errors after due verification and cross-checking in the next edition.

Paris   J.B. Prashant More
20 December 2019

Abbreviations

AFP	Agence France Presse
Ann.	Annuaire des Etablissements Français dans l'Inde
AO	Asie Océanie
AOM	Archives d'Outre-mer, Aix en Provence, France
ADP	Archives Diplomatiques, Paris
BNF	Bibliothèque Nationale de France, Paris
EF	Etablissements Français
IF	Inde Française
JO	Journal Offciel des Etablissements Français dans l'Inde
NDF	National Democratic Front
Tél	Télégramme (telegram)

Introduction

In the course of this study, we intend to focus our attention on the development of nationalism and the growth of freedom movement in French India or rather the French pockets in India, with a special focus on Pondicherry, the capital of French India since 1701. Pondicherry is situated on the eastern coast of southern India, about 150 kilometres south of Pondicherry. The other four French territories, dependent on Pondicherry, were Karaikal, Yanam, Mahé and Chandernagore. Karaikal is situated about 150 kilometres, south of Pondicherry, while Yanam is situated hundreds of kilometres away from Pondicherry in the northern Coromandel Coast. Mahé is located on the western Malabar Coast.

My recent research has established that Pondicherry had come into existence during the fifteenth century. The Arab navigator, Sulaiman al Mahri had mentioned it as *Bandikari* in his navigational work at the turn of the fifteenth century. Before this period, there was no Pondicherry as there are no archaeological, inscriptional and literary evidence for that. For want of evidence Arikamedu, a seasonal port situated at about four kilometres south of Pondicherry some two thousand years ago, cannot be equated with the Pondicherry town, as it developed during French rule since 1673-4.[1]

Pondicherry region seems to have come under the sway of the Hindu Vijayanagara emperors by the end of the fourteenth century. Many Telugus had migrated and settled in the Tamil country including Pondicherry and Karaikal during Vijayanagara rule, as administrators, soldiers, priests, agriculturists and so forth. Muthu Krishnappa Nayakar, the Telugu vassal or chief of Senji, was the veritable founder of Old Pondicherry. It was he who allowed the Portuguese to establish godowns in Pondicherry in the early sixteenth century. Later, he allowed the Dutch and Danes to trade from there.[2]

As goods were brought to Pondicherry from outside in *vandis* or carts, Pondicherry seems to have acquired the name 'Vandichery' or

'Bandichery', which had been noted by Sulaiman al Mahri as *Bandikari* in his Arabic work, written at the turn of the fifteenth century. *Bandichery*, in the course of time, seems to have given rise to *Pandichery*, which is in vogue even today. *Pondicherry* of the English and *Pondichéry* of the French are merely corruptions of the Tamil *Pandichery*. However, as Pondicherry was a new town, it was also known as *Puduchery* to the Tamils, as noted by the Portuguese official historian, Joao de Barros in the sixteenth century. It must be noted here that *Pandichery* is as Tamil a word as *Puduchery*, and it had come into existence a little before Puduchery came into common usage among the Tamils.[3]

The Pondicherry region, where Tamil was spoken predominantly, came under the sway of the Bijapur Sultans during the second half of the seventeenth century. Sher Khan Lodi, the Pathan vassal of the Bijapur Sultan, ruled the region. With the successive retreats of the Portuguese, Dutch and Danes from Pondicherry, Sher Khan Lodi felt the need to revive trade in Pondicherry. Under his impulsion, the French, who were the latest Europeans to arrive in India, agreed to settle a trading outpost on behalf of the French East India Company in Pondicherry on the seaside under certain conditions.

The Frenchman, Bellanger de Lespinay, was the first to set foot in Pondicherry in 1673. Later, in 1674, François Martin, who had fled the French settlement at Masulipatnam, took over from him as director of the French settlement in Pondicherry. Under his guidance mainly, Pondicherry grew and expanded as a French colony, through acquisition of territories from the Muslim Sultans. In 1701, Pondicherry became the headquarters of all French colonies in India. A sovereign council, which later was known as the superior council, consisting only of European members, was created in Pondicherry and François Martin was nominated as the first governor of Pondicherry and all the French settlements in India.[4] Thus, the foundations of modern Pondicherry were laid.

Already, during François Martin's period, Christianity of the Roman Catholic variety had struck roots in Pondicherry. French Capuchin and Jesuit missionaries as well as the missionaries of the *Mission Etrangères de Paris* gradually converted a good number of Hindus from the 'lower' as well as 'higher' castes to Christianity. Sometimes force and coercion was used to spread Christianity in Pondicherry.

Nainiyappa Poullé, the *dubash* (interlocutor) of the French since 1708, was a victim of the excessive zeal of the missionaries and the colonisers to spread Christianity in the year 1717.[5]

Even before the arrival of the French in Pondicherry, there were Muslims in Pondicherry. They were the Tamil-speaking Sonagars. They had their own mosques in the southern part of the town near the seashore. Plans drawn during the Dutch and French rule in Pondicherry attest to this amply. We do not know if the Muslims of Pondicherry were descendants of migrants from the southern coastal towns or were descendants of local converts, with probably a sprinkling of Arab blood in them.

The Hindus, of course, were already present in the area since the time Muthu Krishnappa Nayakar developed Pondicherry into a trading port. Even before the arrival of the French, there were at least four or five Hindu temples, of which the most important were the Vedapuriswarar Temple, adjacent to the place occupied by the Jesuits in the Mission Street, the Ellaiamman (Border Amman) Temple towards the then southern limits of Pondicherry, the Manakula Vinayagar Temple (Poullaiyar) near the French governor's house, and the Thiruvakateeswarar Temple towards the west of Fort St. Louis (presently Bharathi Park). Other temples like the Perumal Temple and the Kalatiswarin Temple seems to have come up during the eighteenth century.

The Poullaiyar Temple was the only Hindu temple in the White town. During the ninetenneth century, the French politician, Montbrun, was much annoyed by the existence of the temple adjacent to his villa, as the priests and the devotees made a lot of noise with their rituals and ceremonies there. According to a prevailing legend, it seems that one day, Montbrun entered the temple, took the idol of Poullaiyar and threw it into the sea. He thought that in this way the temple would cease to exist. But the next morning, the idol was back at its place inside the temple. Montbrun repeated the operation two or three times. But every time the idol returned to its place miraculously. So Montburn was forced to abandon his attempt to get rid of the idol and the temple.[6]

However, in the year 1888, Montbrun wanted to cede 5- or 6-feet length of his property adjacent to the Poullaiyar Temple to the temple authorities. Negotiations went on between the temple and Montbrun with regard to the sale of this narrow piece of land. Montbrun asked for 12,000 rupees at that time in exchange.[7] I think the sale did not transpire for some reason and Montbrun himself died in 1905.

Finally, when the French left Pondicherry in the 1950s, Montbrun's descendants seem to have sold his house along with its furniture to Mirra Alfassa, the Frenchwoman who had become the Mother of the Sri Aurobindo Ashram. But legend has it that the Mother had a dream in which God Poullaiyar appeared and told her to cede some space adjacent to the temple to facilitate an extension to the temple as there was no space for his worshippers to go round the shrine for their ritual *parikrama* (circumbulation). So, it seems that the Mother called her manager the next day and all the arrangements were made to donate a long and narrow piece of the garden/courtyard to the Ganesh Temple, which Montbrun had wanted to sell to the temple in 1888.[8]

As in the rest of India, the Hindus were divided on the basis of castes. There were only three caste groupings in Pondicherry, viz., the Brahmins, the Shudras and the Parayas, known today as dalits or oppressed. These groupings were again subdivided hierarchically into several endogamous sub-castes. Among the Shudras, there were 'higher' and 'lower' caste Shudras. Before 1690, the French inhabited mostly the coastal areas, up to the point where the Upparu River (presently Petit Canal) flowing towards the east, joined the Ariyankuppam River, which flowed southwards. These areas were better planned and organised. The area beyond the Ariyankuppam River, which later became the Grand Canal, was inhabited predominantly by Tamils and Telugus. Every caste lived in a particular area of the town. By and large, the area inhabited predominantly by Indians towards the west came to be known as the Black town, while the area inhabited mostly by the French on the eastern side of the canal towards the seashore became the White town. It was not properly planned or organised, as could be seen in the map of Pondicherry drawn in 1690.

It appears that when the Dutch conquered Pondicherry in 1693, it was left to them to plan the entire town with straight roads intersecting at right angles. Thus, every caste grouping was allotted its own road or roads. The Dutch plans of Pondicherry drawn during the period of their occupation of Pondicherry amply prove this. When the French recovered Pondicherry in 1699, they simply adopted the town planning of the Dutch and improved upon it. What was planned by the Dutch in the 1690s is more or less in vogue even today.

With the Dutch fading away from the Indian horizon, the French were at loggerheads with the English all throughout the eighteenth century. However, in 1721, they had acquired Mahé on the Malabar Coast from the Rajah of Badagara. Malayalam was the spoken language in Mahé. In 1723, they acquired Yanam on the Andhra coast, where Telugu was spoken and in 1739, when Benoist Dumas was governor of Pondicherry, they acquired Karaikal, located at about 150 kilometres towards the south of Pondicherry on the coast, from the Maratha *Raja* of Tanjore. In Karaikal, Tamil was spoken predominantly. Earlier in 1690, Chandernagore, near Calcutta, was obtained. Here, the people spoke Bengali.

Joseph François Dupleix succeeded Dumas as governor of Pondicherry. During his tenure as governor, prodded by his *dubash*, Ananda Ranga Poullé, he tried his best to evict the English from the Carnatic, only to fail miserably. Besides, during his fight with the English, he committed the blunder of his life by giving orders to destroy the Vedapuriswaran Temple in September 1748, which earned him the displeasure of many Hindus. The English conquered Pondicherry in 1761 and razed the White town to the ground. Pondicherry was returned to the French in 1765. But the French were still intent upon evicting the English from nearby Fort St. David. The Frenchman, Lally Tollendhal, in his zeal to get rid of the English, forcibly enlisted the inhabitants of Pondicherry to participate in the siege of Fort St. David, without paying the least attention to the caste taboos of the Tamils. Thus, Brahmins, Shudras and Parayas were pressed into pulling the chariots side by side, which was a sacrilegious act for many Tamils. In spite of this, the English conquered Pondicherry in 1778 and returned it only in 1785.[9] The English conquered Pondicherry once more in 1793. But this time they saw to it that the French had no more means to wage war against them in India. Finally, the peace treaty of 1814-15 put an end to French ambitions in India. They were restricted by the treaty to just five small territories, viz., Pondicherry, Karaikal, Mahé, Yanam and Chandernagore, which were geographically separated from one another by hundreds of miles of British Indian territory. Pondicherry itself was an irregular stretch of land, with eleven enclaves surrounded by British Indian territory, cut off from the coastal stretch of Pondicherry, which included the Pondicherry town. Article 12 of the Treaty of Paris of 30 May 1814 forbade the French to raise an army in Pondicherry or fortify their settlements. But they could have policemen to maintain internal law and order.

The Upparu River (presently Petit Canal) which flowed from the west and joined the Ariyankuppam River in the east (presently Grand Canal) which usually flowed southwards, after flowing past the Jesuit Church, was lengthened northwards in July 1827, cutting the town conspicuously into two parts, viz., the White town on the eastern side of the canal where the French lived predominantly, and the Black town to the west of the canal, inhabited mostly by Indians. The very next year, the Cours Chabrol Road was established on the southern side of the seashore.[10]

Since 1701 a governor was appointed directly by the French government to rule over the Indians of these five territories. Pondicherry, of course, remained the capital of these territories. Thus began a new chapter in the history of Pondicherry and the French settlements in India. The French considered these settlements as their colonial possessions. Pondicherry, no doubt, held the greatest sentimental value for them, as it was one of their oldest possessions. They received orders from France about what to do in Pondicherry. They never severed their ties with France to melt into the Indian society. Instead, they were the colonial masters to the Indians. They were a projection of France, implanted in the Indian soil. The Indians/Tamils got accustomed to obeying these masters and carried on their lives, largely according to the will, policies and rules of their colonial masters.

When slavery was abolished, colonialism seems to have taken its place. In the colonies, the colonised people were not slaves. But they were subjected to the 'White man's rule'. They were rather their 'petted' slaves. Montesquieu wrote in his *Esprit des Lois*:

'The object of the colonies is to indulge in commerce in better conditions than what we do with the neighbouring peoples, with whom the advantages are reciprocal.'[11]

In the colonies, the colonial masters seem to have taken upon themselves the burden of civilising the colonised by introducing their system of education, their own concepts of landholding, their own economic system and their own administrative and political system. The colonised were, more or less, forced to conform to the dictates of their colonial masters.

The French had an especially high opinion of their civilisation. Wherever they went, they took their civilisation and values with them. Many Frenchmen and scholars, like Julien Vinson, thought that the Pondicherry people were fortunate to be under the benevolent French rather than the mercantile English.[12]

In 1925, Léon Blum, an ardent socialist who later became Prime Minister and President of France, declared:

'We accept the right and even the duty of the superior races to attract towards them, those who were not able to reach the same level of culture and to associate them with the progress that has been achieved thanks to the efforts of science and industry.'[13]

The French educationist, Jules Ferry, a convinced colonialist and promoter of free secular education in France had held the following:

'The superior races have a right towards the inferior races. I say that they have a right because they have a duty towards them. They have the right to civilize the inferior races.'[14]

In early 1947, the French Prime Minister, Paul Ramadier, confidently declared:

'Our task is to lead towards a modern political life, the people who had neither the taste nor the desire for it.'[15]

Thus, the French sought to justify their colonial adventures around the world, including those in India through their concept of the 'civilising mission'. They literally thought that they were indispensable to the non-White colonised people who, according to them, belonged to a lower degree of civilisation and culture and needed to be brought to a higher level through the intervention of the 'superior' White races, like the French. It is with this frame of mind that they introduced their own concepts and systems in the political, economic, administrative and educational fields to which the Indians and other colonised people became accustomed over the course of time. Even after the Independence of India in 1947, the French thought that colonisation was a part of their civilising mission and a service to humanity.[16]

There was no doubt a racial and cultural dimension to their colonisation. They thought that the introduction of their concepts and systems into the colonised countries constituted a great part of their civilising mission of the non-White races. The colonised people, including the Indians, had to evolve and function within the political, economic, legal, revenue, administrative, educational and intellectual frameworks put in place by the colonisers, which collectively may be termed as a total cultural invasion that thenceforth changed and determined the social relations between the people.

Any reaction to such colonisation by the colonised people with the objective of putting an end to it was bound thenceforth to be within the framework put in place by an outside agency, i.e. the colonisers themselves. This framework was not a product of consensus that rose from the concerned people. Instead, it was imposed from above without their consent or accord by the colonial French authorities, who wielded a certain power. It sought to control, shape and mould almost all facets of life of the people in India. Of course, the colonisers thought that that was the only way towards a certain progress, albeit one that had no end in sight, and many Indians, both in the French and British Indias, meekly accepted it or surrendered to it. So we have to determine in the course of this study the type of reactions in French India to colonial rule and impositions which can be classified broadly under the label of nationalist reactions or nationalism, which led to the growth of a certain freedom movement.

It needs to be borne in mind at the very outset that the growth of nationalism and freedom movement in Pondicherry against French rule was not totally independent of the happenings in British India. Let us first determine what nationalism is, before delving further into this study. There is no nationalism without a nation as there can be no tribalism without a tribe. Nation or nationalism does not exist factually like the sun and the moon or the earth. Instead, it is an idea born in the minds of men. It is an idea of oneness and equality on the basis of race, territory or language or some shared legacy, to the exclusion of others. The idea of nation is nothing but a thought or feeling of oneness in the mind. It does not exist otherwise. It needs to be noted that the principle of oneness or the feeling of oneness, which is the basis of a nation, is shared by eminent scholars and thinkers like Ernest Renan of France, V.D. Savarkar and B.R. Ambedkar of India. For the latter, 'nationality is a subjective psychological feeling of oneness', while for Savarkar people sharing many common features constitute a nation. In this, he was one with Muhammad Ali Jinnah. For the French thinker, Ernest Renan, nation is a soul, and he considers forgetfulness as one of the essential features in the creation of a nation.[17]

Generally, the priest functions within a religious framework. Similarly, the politicians need a framework to function. That framework is the 'nation'. The politicians depend upon the nation to exist and function. They are inter-dependent. One is not without the other. As the priests channelise and mobilise the religious feelings of the people, the politicians channelise and mobilise the national and political feelings of the people. They are the ones that stoke the fire of nationalism in the minds of the people and themselves for various reasons. We will go into this matter in the course of this work.

However, historians have always had different ways for interpreting and explaining the rise of nationalism in colonial India, which led to the freedom movement. R.C. Majumdar and Tara Chand are two pioneering nationalist historians of independent India. Both were profoundly nationalistic. But they did not attach any economic strings to explain the rise of Indian nationalism like D.D. Kosambi. Instead, their focus was on political, or rather socio-political, events and leaders that led to freedom movement in India. R.C. Majumdar profoundly believed that the Hindus and Muslims constituted two different nations, while Tara Chand batted for a composite Hindu-Muslim culture. While the former thought that religion or the feeling of religious oneness was the basis of nationalism, Tara Chand opted for a blend of Hindu-Muslim culture in his quest for a common national feeling.[18]

But Marxist historians of India, ranging from Palme Dutt to D.D. Kosambi and Irfan Habib or Bipan Chandra, did not subscribe to the cultural or religious theory to explain the rise of Indian nationalism. Instead, they considered material factors or economics as fundamental to the growth of Indian nationalism. While the focus of the

Indian liberal historians like Tara Chand was on Indian social and intellectual movements and on Indian political leaders, the Marxist historians concentrated on economic and class factors to explain Indian nationalism.[19]

Both types of historians run on parallel tracks that could never meet. But they were one when it came to running down the British imperialists. While Indian liberal historians accused the British colonialists of exploiting the divisions in the Indian society to their advantage, Indian Marxist historians dealt a body blow to the British by accusing them of exploiting India economically and draining India's resources for nearly two centuries.

Many British or British-influenced historians, conditioned largely by the British colonial past and the Western intellectual and political traditions and interests, naturally could not commit themselves either to the Indian liberal approach or the Marxist approach to explain the rise of Indian nationalism. But they were conscious of one thing, i.e. the British and their colonial policies and actions were at the receiving end in India. They were in a way under the obligation of reacting to this state of affairs intellectually. The well–thought-out reaction came eventually from a range of Cambridge scholars led by Anil Seal and the likes of John Gallagher.

These historians shifted the focus of their approach to explain Indian nationalism to British policies and institutional innovations in various fields, including politics. In the process, they downplayed the growth of nationalism under British rule. Instead, they sought to portray colonialism itself in a very favourable light. Their argument was that, without British innovations and institutions in the various fields like education and politics, there was no chance for Western-educated elite to emerge all over India and no chance of them competing and quarrelling with one another for power, prestige and social standing within the institutional structures put in place by British colonisers.

Besides, they argued that there was no chance for British colonial rule in India without the collaboration of the Indians. According to them the Western-educated Indian elite, being a British colonial product, were actually willing collaborators in the colonial enterprise. They sought to portray colonialism itself as a sort of joint British-Indian

Introduction

enterprise. They even held that it was when the Indian elite, in its quest for power and position, was not satisfied with its standing under the British that it took to the nationalist track and turned anti-British. Otherwise, Indians would have remained mere passive collaborators to British rule.

Indian nationalism was put down as a sort of competitive race among Indians in their quest for power, profit and prestige at the central, provincial and local administrative structures put in place by the British, and not motivated by any lofty nationalistic ideas, ideologies and principles at all. The nationalist movement itself was seen as a product of competition in the quest for power, profit and prestige within the economic, administrative, educational and judicial institutions of the colonial government. Besides, according to Seal, Indian nationalism did not spring from any class demand or sharp changes in the economic structure. It was even held that the competition between the various elite groupings based on caste and religion led to friction and conflict in the Indian society which ultimately ended in the Partition of India. Thus, the Cambridge scholars bypassed the Marxian class concept and the British bashing of the Indian liberal historians for their policy of 'divide and rule', by putting forward the concept of 'elitism' and the 'collaboration theory' to explain Indian nationalism and British colonialism. This caught the Marxist as well as the Indian liberal historians unawares.[20]

As far as south India is concerned, scholars like David Washbrook and C.J. Baker have faithfully toed the line of the likes of Anil Seal and John Gallagher and underplayed the rise of nationalism among south Indians. Instead, they portray their elite as caught up in the pursuit of power and prestige within the competitive structure of the colonial institutions. C.J. Baker had gone to the extent of branding the leading south Indian politicians as 'job hunters' rather than men imbued with the spirit of nationalism.[21]

In the course of this work, we have the task of finding out how far the preceding approaches to Indian nationalism of the Cambridge scholars as well as the Marxist and Indian liberal historians are relevant with regard to the rise of nationalism in Pondicherry, the capital of French India. We have also the task of finding out if there were other factors that might have contributed to the growth of nationalism in

Pondicherry. We have also to enquire about the relationship between ideas/ideology and power or profit, and whether one can stand independent of the other.

Unlike the Western countries, where the nation is generally constituted on the basis of language, race and territory, the growth of a common national feeling in India was never based on language or race, for there was no dominant language in India, like French in France or English in Britain. Instead, there were several Indian languages, with their respective geographical regions where each was predominant. Language was never a uniting factor in India to form the basis of nationalism. Similarly, Indians, by and large, do not belong to a distinctive White or Black race. They are a mixture of several races. So, racial oneness could never be the basis of Indian nationalism. Indians were also divided on the basis of religion and caste. Therefore, a common religious and caste feeling could not be the basis for the development of a unified national spirit. Such a spirit never seems to have existed in the history of India, in spite of Muslim conquests and European penetration. There was never in the history of India the longing to be one nation in spite of certain common socio-cultural aspects like the caste system and the peculiar traditions, beliefs and customs of the Hindus throughout India.[22]

It will be misplaced to claim that Emperor Ashoka or Chandragupta or Rajendra Chola, or Akbar and Aurangzeb, were votaries of Indian nationalism, though they tried to unite India under them through force and violence. Emperor Aurangzeb was the most successful in this respect, as he more or less united the whole of India under his rule. After him, there was no unity. There is no way to claim that the Nawab of Travancore or the Nizam of Hyderabad stood for Indian unity and nationalism. Instead, it was left to the the British to unite India from north to south and from east to west, politically and administratively. They introduced English as the medium of instruction and thus very quickly brought forth Western-educated elite, speaking English, though they belonged to various Indian religions and spoke different native languages. This English-speaking elite was needed to administer British India. Thus, the Indian elite, divided on linguistic and religious and caste lines, could converse with one another in a common language, i.e. English. The British had left the

Introduction

five small territories, including Pondicherry, under French control. The French did almost the same in their territories, by introducing French as the medium of instruction.

Pondicherry was only a minuscule region located in the Tamil-speaking country in the south of India on the Cholamandalam or Coromandel Coast. Though the people of Pondicherry spoke Tamil as the people of Tamil Nadu, they were under French rule, unlike most of the rest of India. They had always evolved in isolation politically since they came under the French in 1673-4. Though they shared many cultural and social features, like the caste system and language, with the people of Tamil Nadu and the rest of India, their colonial masters were the French, and not the English. That is why the study of the growth of nationalism and freedom movement in Pondicherry becomes all the more difficult. However, we intend to pursue with this task to the best of our ability and ascertain if the approaches of the Marxists, Cambridge scholars and the liberal historians to study nationalism and colonialism and the growth of freedom movement in British India are pertinent to Pondicherry or French India.

Professor Jacques Weber's 'Les Etabissements Français en Inde au XIXe siècle' deals with five-volume work in French on the French territories in India with the period from 1816 to 1914. In 1996, he brought out a condensed volume of this work with some additional chapters on twentieth-century Pondicherry. But the main drawback of this work is that he had neglected vernacular sources in his reconstruction of the history of twentieth-century Pondicherry. Professor Ajit Neogy's work, *Decolonisation of French India*, too, neglects Indian/Tamil sources to a large extent. Cyril Antony's attempt to retrace the history and politics of Pondicherry in his *Gazetteer and Encyclopaedia of Pondicherry*, does not give much importance to Tamil and French sources, either.[23] In my opinion, the writing of a meaningful and exhaustive history of the freedom movement in Pondicherry is not possible without taking into account the Tamil and French sources. In this work of mine, I intend to make use of all relevant sources in Tamil, French and English, available in the various libraries and archives in India, France and England, including interviews with relevant personalities, to reconstruct the history of the growth of nationalism freedom movement in French India, with a special focus on Pondicherry, the capital of French India, and the growth of nationalism there. Earlier in 2001 and 2007, I have produced two books on the history and freedom movement in Mahé and Yanam, respectively.[24] But Mahé and Yanam were dependent territories of French India, located several hundred kilometres away from Pondi-cherry, encircled by British Indian territory, while Pondicherry remained the capital of all French Indian territories in India, right from 1701 until November 1954. By French India, we mean the scattered pockets of territories which were under the occupation of the French in the Indian sub-continent.

We have to find out in the course of this study what pushed the French to finally quit India? We must find out whether it was due to the rise of Indian nationalism among the people of French Indian and its elite or whether it was a unilateral decision of the French? We must ascertain, too, what prompted the various upper class members and leaders of French India to veer towards Indian nationalism and under what conditions they did so? We have to find out whether pecuniary and material reasons pushed at least some of them onto this path?

NOTES

1. G.R. Tibbetts, tr., *Arab Navigation in the Indian Ocean before the Coming of the Portuguese,* London, 1981, p. 467; J.B.P. More, *From Arikamedu to the Foundation of Modern Pondicherry,* Pondicherry, 2014, pp. 141-67.
2. More, *From Arikamedu to the Foundation of Modern Pondicherry,* op. cit., pp. 19, 61-2.
3. Joao de Barros. *Asia: Primeira Decada,* Lisbon, MCMXLX, pp. 360-1; More, *From Arikamedu to the Foundation of Modern Pondicherry,* op. cit., pp. 26, 66; Tibetts, loc. cit.
4. More, *From Arikamedu to the Foundation of Modern Pondicherry,* op. cit., pp. 72-82, 90, 92, 106, 107.
5. More, 'Hindu-Christian Interaction in Pondicherry, 1700-1900', *Contributions to Indian Sociology,* 1998, pp. 97-121.
6. *Sukapi Viruthini,* 15 August 1934.
7. *Le Progrès,* 8 April 1888, p. 116.
8. Legend prevailing in Pondicherry.

9. Gopaljee Samboo, *Les Comptoirs Français dans l'Inde Nouvelle de la Compagnie des Indes à nos Jours*, Paris, 1950, p. 36.
10. E. Sicé, *Annuaire Statistiques des établissements Français de l'Inde pour l'Année 1841*, Pondicherry, 1841, p. 273.
11. Magloire Larnine, 'Le Bon Temps des Colonies' (in) *Arya*, Le Mans, 15 December 1996, no. 2, pp. 42-3.
12. Cf. Julien Vinson, *Les Français dans l'Inde, Dupleix et Labourdonnais: 1736-1748*, Paris, 1894.
13. Larnine, op. cit., p. 41.
14. Ibid., p. 42.
15. l'*Aube*, 24 February 1947.
16. l'*Aube*, 23 July 1948.
17. Ernest Renan, *Qu'est-ce qu'une Nation?* Paris, 1882, pp. 25-7, 82-4; A. Appadorai. *Documents on Political Thought in Modern India*, I, London, 1973, pp. 488-9, 504, 524.
18. Tara Chand, *History of the Freedom Movement in India*, vols. I-IV, Delhi, 1961-72; R.C. Majumdar, *History of the Freedom Movement in India*, vols. 1-3, Calcutta, 1962-3.
19. Palme Dutt, *India Today*, Bombay, 1947; D.D. Kosambi. *An Introduction to the Study of History*, Bombay, 1956; Sumit Sarkar. *Modern India, 1885-1947*, Delhi, 1978; Bipan Chandra. *Nationalism and Colonialism in Modern India*, New Delhi, 1979; Irfan Habib. *Essays in Indian History—Towards a Marxist Perception*, New Delhi, 1995.
20. Anil Seal, *The Emergence of Indian Nationalism*, Cambridge, 1971, pp. 341-51; C.A. Bayly, *The Local Roots of Indian Politics*, Oxford, 1975; C.J. Baker, Johnson Gordon, Anil Seal, ed., *Power, Profit and Politics: Essays on Imperialism, Nationalism and Change in Twentieth Century India*, Cambridge, 1981; John Gallagher, Johnson Gordon, Anil Seal, ed., *Locality, Province and Nation: Essays on Indian Politics, 1870-1940*, Cambridge, 1973; F. Robinson, *Separatism among Indian Muslims-The Politics of the United Provinces' Muslims, 1860-1923*, Cambridge, 1974.
21. Baker, *The Politics of South India, 1920-37*, Cambridge, 1976; Baker, D. Washbrook, *South India: Political Institution and Political Change, 1880-1940*, New Delhi, 1975, p. 3; Washbrook, *The Emergence of Provincial Politics, 1870-1920*, Cambridge, 1976.
22. Sicé, *Un Mot sur la Représentation des Etablissements Français de l'Inde à l'Assemblée Nationale*, Pondicherry, 1848.
23. Jacques Weber, *Les Etablissements Français en Inde au XIXe Siècle (1816-1914)*, 5 volumes, Paris, 1988; Weber, *Pondichéry et les Comptoirs de l'Inde après Dupleix: La Démocratie au Pays des Castes*, Paris, 1996;

C. Antony, *Gazetteer of India: Union Territory of Pondicherry*, 2 vols., Pondicherry, 1982; Antony, *Encyclopaedia of India*, Pondicherry, New Delhi, 1994; Ajit Neogy, *Decolonisation of French India. Liberation Movement and Franco-Indian Relations 1947-1954*, Pondicherry, 1997.

34. More, *Freedom Movement in French India: The Mahé Revolt of 1948*, Tellicherry, 2001; More, *The Telugus of Yanam and Masulipatnam: From French Rule to Integration with India,* Pondicherry, 2007.

CHAPTER 1

Society, Land and Economy

DEMOGRAPHY AND SOCIETY

In the year 1769, the French astronomer, Guillaume Le Gentil, had observed that in Pondicherry town there were 60,000 people of whom 1,000 to 1,200 were Europeans.[1] A systematic attempt was made by the French administration in Pondicherry to count the population in its territories only since 1842, when the system of maintenance of birth, death and marriage registers were instituted. The registration of births, deaths and marriages was made compulsory from 1854 onwards and the statistics were regularly published in the *Annuaire des Etablissements Français de l'Inde*.

In 1816, when Pondicherry was handed over to the French by the English, the population of Pondicherry region was just 40,821. There had been a steady decline in the population of Pondicherry right from the days of Joseph François Dupleix's governorship due to the incessant wars in which the French in Pondicherry were embroiled until they were cut to size by the peace treaty of Paris, 1763. By 1823, the population of Pondicherry had risen to 76,759, while that of Karaikal stood at 33,286, of Chandernagore at 44,538, Mahé at 2,966 and Yanam at about 7,000. In 1830, the population of Pondicherry region stood at 75,323 of which nearly 87.6 per cent were Hindus, 10.4 per cent Christians and only about 1.9 per cent were Muslim citizens.[2]

On 1 October 1842, orders were passed for the registration of the birth, marriage and death of all Indians, belonging to all castes and residing anywhere in the territory of French India. Separate registers were set up for Muslim citizens. The population of Pondicherry alone steadily rose to 81,963 in 1850, 1,77,346 in 1900 and, at the outbreak of the First World War, it stood at 1,80,174. In 1900, Karaikal had 56,577, Chandernagore 25,253, Mahé 10,729 and Yanam 5,033 people. Thus, the total population of these five French settlements in 1900 stood at only 2,70,346 as compared to that of British India which ran into several millions.[3]

In 1875, the total population of French India was around 2,60,000 which included 1,600 Europeans. In Pondicherry alone, there were 1,21,186 people in 1866, 1,76,235 in 1891 and 1,74,456 in 1901. In 1886, of the total population, there were 1,28,562 or 85.6 per cent Hindus, 19,043 or 12.7 per cent Christians and 2,434 or 1.6 per cent Muslims. In 1926, there were 1,75,076 people of whom 1,58,146 or 90.3 per cent were Hindus and 4,499 or 2.5 per cent were Muslims, while 12,425 Catholics formed 8.2 per cent of the total population.[4]

The area of Pondicherry region was just 29,145 hectares. Karaikal was made up of 11,772 hectares, Mahé 5,909 hectares, Yanam of just 1,772 hectares and Chandernagore comprised only 940 hectares. The total area of French India was only 58,803 hectares and the total population was just 2,88,546 in 1929. In 1931, the total population of Pondicherry region alone was just 1,83,555. It rose to 1,87,870 in 1936.[5]

In the year 1929, there were 12,425 Catholics in Pondicherry region, besides 91 Protestants, 4,499 Muslims and 1,58,153 Hindus. The total population was 1,75,168 people. Among the Catholics were Indian Christian converts, European Christians, White Créoles and Black Créoles, both groups being of Indo European descent. By 1936, the total population of French India was 2,98,851. Pondicherry region alone had 1,87,870 inhabitants. On 1 July 1941, Pondicherry region alone contained 2,04,653 persons. It rose to 2,22,949 persons in 1948 (87 per cent Hindus, 9.5 per cent Christians and 3.5 per cent Muslims) and at the time of the *de jure* transfer of the settlements in 1962, it stood at 2,58,540. Karaikal had a population of just 60,555 in 1941, 70,541 in 1948 and 83,986 in 1961. In 1971, Pondicherry region contained 3,40,240 while in Karaikal there were 1,00,042 people. In 1981, the total urban population of Pondicherry, including Mudaliarpet, was 1,62,639, while the total population of Pondicherry region was 4,44,417. This increase in population may be attributed to migration from neighbouring states.[6]

As in the rest of India, the Hindu community in Pondicherry comprised of several castes, all ranked hierarchically. The Hindus were also divided into the followers of Vishnu and the worshippers of Shiva. In Pondicherry, the Shiva worshippers were predominant. While the 'higher' castes had their temples in Pondicherry and worshipped gods like Shiva and Vishnu, the 'lower castes', such as the Mukkuwas and the Valangas (or the Untouchables, or the Adi Dravidas of Pondicherry) worshipped Mariamman, the mother goddess. Brahmins officiated by tradition as priests at the Mariamman Temple of the fishermen at Virampatnam and various other such temples during feast days.[7]

The Brahmins were, no doubt, placed right at the top of the caste hierarchy, while the Valangas were at the very bottom. The four-fold caste system of the *Varnasrama Dharma*, made up of Brahmins, Kshattriyas, Vaishyas and Shudras, was absent in Pondicherry, as in the rest of the Tamil-speaking country. Instead, there were only the Brahmins and Shudras and the Valangas, who were again divided into various endogamous sub-castes. The Shudras were divided into the so-called 'higher' castes, like the Vellalas and Reddiars, and the 'lower' castes, like the Pallis or Vanniyars. Among the 'higher' castes, we find the Tamil-speaking Vellalas, the Telugu-speaking Kavareys, the Chettys, the Telugu Komuttys and the Reddiars, and the Idayars or Yadavals. Among the 'lower' castes were the Pallis or Vanniyars, who claim to be Kshatriyas and the Kammalars (artisans). The former was the most numerous in Pondicherry region. Below the Vanniyars, we find the fishermen, also known as the Pattanavas or Mukkuwas, and a whole network of Valangas, led by the Valluvars, the Shivaite priests. In the nineteenth century, there were twelve Mukkuwa villages in Pondicherry. The 'lower' castes, like the Mukkuwas in Virampattinam, had Mariamman as their principal goddess.[8]

It is quite surprising to note that, since the eighteenth century and earlier, the 'higher' castes alone were considered as *Tamizhars* (Tamils) and not the others. Ananda Ranga Pillai had clearly made this distinction in his diary. Even in the nineteenth century, this state of affairs did not change, as pointed out by E. Sicé. But ever since Pondicherry had been founded, the Valangas had inhabited the White town and, in the nineteenth century, they also resided in the heart of the Black town as well. Nevertheless, in the villages, they were still relegated to the *paracheris* (*margins*).⁹

Among the Christians, there were the *Tamizhar* (or caste Christians) and Valanga Christians. Before 1908, there was no discrimination in the 'Jenma Rakini' Mary Church or the 'Samba Kovil' in Pondicherry on the basis of caste. Trouble started with the construction of a new church near the railway station, called the 'Iruthi Andavar' Church. Thenceforth, the caste Christians refused to accept the Valanga Chrisitians on an equal footing at this new church. As a result, the church was closed by the government. There was friction in 'Samba Kovil', too. Many Valangas started to become Protestants. They refused to go to the church. This led to the closure of 'Samba Kovil' for six months. Then a French priest, A. Combes, was entrusted with the task of finding a solution, which he did. It was agreed that both groups would have separate spaces allotted to them in the church of 'Jenma Rakini' *Maatha* Mary, or 'Samba Kovil' of Pondicherry. This had the sanction of the French Archbishop of Pondicherry. According to the rules so devised, the *Tamizhar* Christians were given the centre, north and northern wing of the church while the Valangas could occupy the south and southern wing of the church. The Valangas could enter the church only through the side gates. If they did not respect these allotments and occupied the portion of the church meant for the 'higher' castes, they were to be excluded from the church.¹⁰

In the early 1930s, under Archbishop Auguste-Siméon Colas, permission was granted for Valanga marriages to be solemnised in the cental altar of the church. The first Valanga marriage that thus took place was that of the Francine family. Francine was a leading merchant of Pondicherry.¹¹ It is surprising to note that, even as late as the first quarter of the twentieth century, 'higher' caste people alone were considered as *Tamizhar* and not the Valangas, though they spoke the same language.

The French generally had a good opinion of the Muslims though they were small in numbers in Pondicherry and more numerous in Karaikal. Being highly urbanised, they were considered indispensable to the colonial economy. They were also seen as honest, keepers of their word and ones who had putatively sought to extirpate the monstruous customs and abuses born out of the system of castes and Brahmanism, such as human sacrifice, *Sati* and female infanticide.

Since 1841, when Paul de Nourquer du Camper was the governor, the French had permitted the celebration of Santhanakudu in honour of saint Ahmad Moula Sahib. During this period, Baderdine Sahib was the kazi of Pondicherry. The Muslims observed Jamsey over eight days in honour of the martyrs, Hassan and Hussain. Hindus usually took part in the processions and demonstrations connected with this feast. But when the Hindu feast of Ayudha Puja and Jamsey coincided in 1884 and 1885, there was serious discord between the two communities, causing many victims on both sides. Besides, in Pondicherry, the Sunnites confronted the Wahhabites in the year 1862, just after the British quelled the Great Revolt of 1857.

In 1870, Esquer, author of an essay on castes in India, had held that generally 'the Muslims were much superior (to the Hindus) from the point of view of moral qualities, and the distance which separated paganism from theism'. On the other hand, the Tamil doctor, Paramananda Mariadassou, of Pondicherry had judged the Muslim as 'more refractory than the Hindu to the innovations (and) has remained as immutable as his faith amidst so many changes and who does not hear or rather does not want to hear the voice of progress'.[12]

In 1740, when Dost Ali Khan, the Nawab of Arcot, was killed at Damalcheri by the Marathas, there was an influx of Deccani-and Urdu-speaking Muslims into Pondicherry. Many of them preferred to settle in Pondicherry for good. But their relationship with the Tamil-speaking Muslims of Pondicherry was never on an equal footing. Karaikal always had a high proportion of Muslims, especially in the urban areas. They were mostly Tamil speaking, belonging to the Marakkayar clan.[13]

There were sometimes clashes between the Muslims and the Hindus, as in 1853, during the celebration of Panguni Uthiram by the Hindus, and in 1884 and 1885, during Jamsey by the Muslims and the Ayudha Puja by the Hindus at the same time. But such clashes never spilt into the political domain. Traditionally, the Hindus participated in the Jamsey ritual procession organised with great pomp at the Place du Gouvernment (presently Bharathi Poonga) annually. Jamsey was observed to honour the memory of Hussain, son of Ali and grandson of Prophet Muhammad, killed at Karbala by the soldiers of Yazid.[14]

In Karaikal, the friction between Hindus and Muslims was quite acute from time to time. In 1904, there were clashes between Hindus and Muslims regarding the ownership of a rice field that had been adjacent to a temple as well as a mosque. Conflict also broke out during the marking of Kanturi festivities, in honour of Mastane Sahib in 1910, that went on to take the shape of Hindu-Muslim riots.[15]

LAND, AGRICULTURE AND REVENUE

In Pondicherry, land had always been the property of the king. When the Indian rulers ceded Pondicherry to the French, they became the absolute owners of the land according to the customs of the land. But Karaikal followed a different paradigm. Here, the land belonged to those who actually possessed it.[16] The concept that land belonged to the king dated back to Muslim rule in India. That is why the Pondicherrians transferred the land to the French without the least resistance back in 1673-4. Thus did the French became absolute owners of the land in all French settlements.

Scholars like Vijayaraghavachari had claimed that landownership existed in pre-Muslim India and that it was the tiller/cultivator who possessed the land. But the ownership of land as we know it today has not been established in a clearcut manner. Private property was never the norm in Indian society. For example, in the Malabar or Keralam, including Mahé, which hardly came under Muslim rule, it has been established unequivocally that there was no landownership before the British, and the French introduced the concept of private property there, converting the custodians of the land, called *jenmis*, who paid the taxes, into absolute landowners.

From the very beginning of colonisation, land was a chief source of revenue for the French Indian government. Land was farmed out periodically, mostly to Indians who paid the requisite taxes to the government. Other sources of revenue were the sale of betel, tobacco, alcohol and salt, which were also farmed out mostly to Indians. The government also earned an income by levying customs duties on goods that came into the French settlements by land and sea.

It was believed by the French that India needed to be civilised by the institution of private property as it prevailed in Europe. Already in 1793, the zamindars, who were mere tax collectors under the

Mughals, were made absolute owners of the land by the British. The decree of 2 June 1828 sought to organise property in French India. The decree of 16 January 1854 made the possessor or cultivator of the land who paid the stipulated taxes the absolute proprietor of the land. Some of the important personalties of Pondicherry who rose to defend the interests of the cultivators and agriculturists during this period were Rassendra Poullé, Vingatarayer, Vingadassariar, Moutoucomarassami Poullé, Venou Chettiar, Nadou Sidamabara Mudaliar, Caji Baderdine Sahib, P. Rangappa Chettiar, Soupraya Mudaliar, R. Arounassala Chettiar, S. Appasami Poullé, Annasami Ayer, Ramasami Sastriar, Ka. Sivasidambara Mudaliar, Rassou Nallatambi Odéar, Cojandé Dayrianada Mudaliar and Ponnou.[17]

The institution of landownership by the French introduced a fundamental change in French Indian society. This set in motion a scramble for owning lands and property in which the well-to-do sections had a clear advantage over the others. In this insitutionalised race for landownership, there emerged a few big landlords and proprietors, and many other smaller landlords and proprietors of varying statuses below them. The rest of the population was reduced to farm labourers (Pannaiyals), who were paid thenceforth by the landlords. Thus, the social relations between the people and castes underwent a profound change due to the introduction of landownership. Indians were recast in the European fashion at the core of their economic life. Evidently, Indians got accustomed to this new system of social relations, without much resistance. It is needless to say that the notion and institution of private property and landownership constituted one of the pillars of Western or modern civilisation. Even the French Revolution did not do away with it. Instead, it consecrated private property as one of its cardinal principles, on which the entire society revolved thereafter. It was this European principle or norm that was transplanted into India by the British and the French in their respective territories, so that it became the core of the Indian civilisation and culture. It undoubtedly resulted in the 'Europeanisation' or modernisation of Indian society at the economic level.

Thenceforth, the individual became the focus, rather than the collective. A scramble for power, prestige and postion was set in motion in the local society between individuals, and it brought about a clearcut hierarchical class society. The more land one possesed, the more powerful one became and the more the number of privileges he enjoyed in local society. The modern notion of private property and landownership did not exist naturally anywhere in the world. It is not a tangible fact, like the sun and the moon. It was originally an idea which was translated into a certain reality by the Romans. This idea travelled to India during the colonial period. Ideas and beliefs are always associated with power, security and prestige. That is why the Indians, both in the British and French Indias, were made to scramble for power or scrambled to acquire power during the colonial period.

Due to the introduction of the institution of private property, the number of *mirasdars* or landlords swelled from 1,513 in 1843 to 2,479 in 1880, while the number of tenants rose from 1,885 to 2,434 and the number of Pannaiyals from 1,676 to 2,437. The *mirasdars* had a complete authority and control over the Pannaiyals. The Pannaiyals were mostly Valangas at the service of the aristocratic Reddiars, serving on a hereditary basis. They had no land in their possession. In any case, the privatisation of land had contributed to a more effective collection of taxes from the cultivators and agriculturists and increased agricultural productivity in the French settlements.[18]

The *mirasdar* was a Persian term, which signified beneficiary or the rightful claimant. But it is unclear if it meant that the *mirasdar* was the absolute owner of the land or if he had only usufructuary rights over the lands during Muslim rule. In Pondicherry, the Telugu-speaking Reddiars held the best lands, though they constituted only two to three per cent of the cultivators. They accounted for one-fourth of the total harvests and paid one-fourth of the total taxes on land. Generally, land in Pondicherry was largely under the control of the 'higher' castes, like the Reddiars and Poullés. There were several landowners from the Vanniyar caste, too, in Nettapakkam, Oulgaret, Bahur and Ariyankuppam.[19]

Agriculture was the mainstay of the French Indian economy. During colonial rule, the French engineers had developed an efficient system of irrigation, based on canals (like the Bangaravaikal), dams (like the Suttukény Dam) and lakes (like the Great Bahur Lake and the Oussudu Lake), both natural and artificial, which had transformed the land into fertile fields in Pondicherry. But land in Pondicherry and Karaikal was limited and generally divided into small holdings, which prevented intensive cultivation. However, the percentage of cultivated lands was quite high—70 per cent in Pondicherry region, out of about 29,000 hectares, 90 per cent in Karaikal out of 13,500 hectares, 92 per cent in Mahé out of 6,000 hectares and 49 per cent in Yanam out of 1,500 hectares. Karaikal was the principal producer of rice and coconuts, while Pondicherry produced grains like maize, millet (*kambou*) and eleusine (*kevre*). Groundnuts, as well as coconuts (toddy and oil were manufactured from the coconuts) and indigo, were also produced in Pondicherry. All varieties of fruit were cultivated in Mahé. But the rice produced in Karaikal and Pondicherry regions was never sufficient for local consumption. As a result, rice was imported into Pondicherry from British India and even from faraway French Indochina. Women worked alongside men in the fields in Pondicherry, and the Tamil country.[20]

The French Indian government extended credit facilities for agricultural development which was beneficial to the entrenched wealthy landholders. There were still no pawnbrokers from northern India during French rule. The decree of 8 January 1934 instituted the Agricultural Bank (*Crédit Agricole*) in French India. The Agricultural Credit Society was started on 18 August 1948 in Pondicherry for the benefit of the farmers.

The Mont de Piété was a government organisation set up in Pondicherry in 1827 to help cultivators, petty merchants, and even labourers with loans in exchange for gold, silver, copper and jewels. The interests never exceeded seven per cent, and the time period of the loan was just one year. It was financed by the governor to the tune of 1,00,000 francs. The Banque d'Indochine, a private bank, also lent money on jewels. The Mont de Piété was created in order to relieve the cultivators and labourers from the compulsion to borrowing money from the Chetties, who charged exhorbitant rates of interest. There was also a Chamber of Agriculture instituted on 27 September 1888. It was reorganised by the decree of 7 March 1914. In 1934, the Frenchman, Robert Gaebelé, was the president of the Chamber of Agriculture, while the jurist, Gnanou Diagou Mudaliar, was the secretary and Mouhamed Hanif the treasurer.[21]

Thus, land in Pondicherry generally belonged to those who

cultivated it, provided they paid the annual land tax to the government. Some land, like that in Karaikal, were held in *adamanom*, i.e. land leased out in perpetuity provided a fixed amount was paid to the government. It was the Indians who cultivated the land who paid the taxes.[22]

It is nonetheless noteworthy that, during the French period, there emerged a distinct class of landowners. They owned the land though they never tilled it. The majority of the farmers who tilled the land were actually reduced to the status of agricultural labourers, who worked for the landlords on a meagre salary.[23] These landlords constituted an elite or upper class in Pondicherry society. The rest of the population was placed below them in a 'lower' class category. Notably, most landowners were Hindus belonging to the 'higher' castes, with the exception of a few Christians and Muslims. They were largely a product of French innovations in the field of landownership and private property. It created a class of landowners and a class of labourers, which were the two components of a class society. The former were part of the elite society of Pondicherry and French India put in place by French administrators and they wielded a certain power, prestige and status in society due to their new economic status. In short, it was within the economic framework put in place unilaterally by the French colonisers that all French Indians had to function and evolve thenceforth, whether they liked it or not. This framework was actually a closed system. All had to function within its boundaries. Private property and landownership of the Western type became the foundation stone on which a hierarchical class society was built thenceforth in Pondicherry and French India.

SOCIO-ECONOMIC PROFILE

Pondicherry was a planned town, with the beach road to the east and boulevards on the three other sides. It was neatly divided by a canal running between White town and Black town. Mostly Europeans lived in the White town while the Black town was inhabited largely by Indians. The decree of 23 July 1907 authorised the extension of the beach road (Cours Chabrol, presently known as Goubert Avenue) towards the north, upto Kurussukuppam.[23] Most of the roads in the White town, if not all, were christened with French names, while in the Black town, the roads retained their Indian names. A few rich people possessed cars or horse-drawn chariots. Bicycles were not numerous. Just beyond the west boulevard were the oil-pressing mills called the 'sekku medu'. Going beyond the boulevard was risky in those days due to the presence of ruffians and other anti-socials.

It was under the governorship of Vicomte Eugène Desbassyns since 1826 that the beach road, Cours Chabrol, was created. On 13 May 1856, an order was passed to name all roads of Pondicherry in French and Tamil, and number all the houses in the town. It was during this period that the idea of constructing a quay on the beach was mooted in order to prevent the invasion of the land by sea as well as for the internal security of Pondicherry. It was also during this period that the embankment slope of the canal that separated the Black and White towns, which was earlier made of mud, was relaid with maçonnerie stuqué.[24]

The roads of Pondicherry were made of mud and in a deplorable condition. Water filled with sewage stagnated on the roads and in the Grand Canal as well as Petit canal. The evacuation of excrement was always a problem. Even in 1947, the big streets of Pondicherry were lit dimly inspite of an electricity supply since about 1909. The Black town and the Grand Bazar were the most unhygienic. There were a huge number of lepers and beggars going about in the Pondicherry streets. Outside Pondicherry town, the streets were lit sparsely with kerosene lights. It was dangerous to walk on these roads after 7 p.m. There was a system of sanitation and garbage collection in place since 1849, as per which the public was invited to clean in front of the houses up to the middle of the road before five every evening and the garbage collected at specific places, so that they could be removed by government carts later in the evening. Karaikal, which was equally unhygienic, was electrified in 1934. Defecating on the Pondicherry beach was prohibited in 1934.[25]

Through a decree dated 21 March 1948, the Grand Bazar Road was renamed Barathy Street while the Madras Road was renamed as the Mahatma Gandhi Road. This was a concession to the nationalist sentiments of the Pondicherrians. The roads were muddy and the wastewater from houses flowed freely into the gutter running by the side of the streets. Sometimes, this water stagnated and became the breeding ground for mosquitoes and poisonous insects, leading to epidemics of smallpox, dysentery and cholera. Several Pondicherrians died due to lack of hospital facilities and medicines. The roads were tarred only after 1954.[26]

During the governorship of Vicomte Desbassyns, the Grand Bazar (Peria Kadai, presently known as Goubert Market) was established on 25 November 1826, towards the west of Pondicherry at the site were the church of the Missions Etrangères de Paris stood earlier, and in front of the Central Jail for Indians. The Petit Bazar (Chinna Kadai, presently known as Kassim Market) was situated at the intersection of the Madras Road and Bussy Street towards the south. In April 1912, Calvé Soupraya Chettiar donated some land for the enlargement of the Petit Bazar (Chinna Kadai) towards the west of Madras Road. Then there was the Pala Kadai, founded by a certain Palin, situated at the end of rue d'Orléans (presently Manakula Vinayakar Street) towards the north, and the Kitchi Kadai (Bazar St. Laurent), which existed since 1688 in the southern part of the White town and was located near the beach along the Bazar St. Laurent Road. The Central Jail for Indians was established in front of the Grand Bazar towards the north, in 1828. A hospital was created for the Indians on 12 July 1852, during the governorship of De Mellay. Before that, when Vicomte Desbassyns was governor, he founded a leprosy centre in Pondicherry. He also founded a Charity Workshop ('Atelier de Charité') for the needy on 24 July 1826.[27]

On 24 July 1852, a clock tower was erected in the Grand Bazar by Mr Dairiyanadin, in the name of his uncle, Diagou Mudaliar, at the cross-section of rue Couttia Poullé and the principal village. A similar clock tower, but of a smaller size, was erected at Petit Bazar, which had come into existence in 1890, thanks to the generous donations of Ku. Latchoumanasamy Mudaliar. The foundation stone for this tower was laid by the Maharaja of Mysore.[28]

According to a legend, engraved at the foot of the fountain erected in honour of the dancing girl, Aayi, at the centre of Bharathi Park, one evening, the King, Krishnadeva Rayar, was on his way back from the Villianur Temple with his minister, Appazhiayer, when he saw an illuminated house. Thinking that it was another temple, he bowed in respect. Upon realising that it was, in fact, the house of a dancing girl called Aayi, he ordered it to be torn down and a well dug in its place. Aayi obtained from the king the permission to do this work with her own men and funds and name it after herself. Thus, came into existence the well and the pond at Muthirapalayam known as Aayi Kulam.[29]

There was always acute drinking water scarcity in Old Pondicherry. Generally, people drank the water from the wells, that was not very pure. But since the discovery of the ancient wells of Muthirapalayam towards the west of Pondicherry, water began to be brought to the White town in bullock carts from Muthirapalayam. The early French governors and colonisers were conscious of this problem. It was Dupleix who conceived the plan of bringing the Muthirapalayam water to Pondicherry. But the project was not executed. It was taken up again only in 1854. Water was finally brought from Muthirapalayam through channels attached to the fountains and reservoirs at the Place du Gouvernment (presently Bharathi Park) and at the Grand Bazar clock tower during the governorship of Napoléon Joseph Louis Bontemps in April 1863. Several taps connected to the reservoirs distributed the water to Pondicherrians, both in the White and Black towns.[30]

Pondicherry was surrounded by several choultries, where the poor and travellers could find a temporary place of stay, free food and water. The choultries were created by some wealthy Pondicherrains. But the choultry (*chattiram* or inn) founded in the name of Sinna Supraya Poullé was the most important among these. Poullé had given the totality of his properties to the administration, running into several lakhs, so that it could use permanently, the interests to assist the poor with free food, money and rice. It was the most important charitable organisation in the whole of south India. Irregularities had often been reported in the management of this choultry. Besides such choultries, the government had its own charitable organisations, like the 'Comité de Bienfaisance' (Welfare Committee), 'La Société de Secours Musulman' (Society to Help Muslims), and so on. The Charity Workshop was also founded about this time. It was to function under the control of the Welfare Committee (Comité de Bienfaisance).

Several orphanages, asylums and shelters for the poor, the sick, the mentally deficient and the needy were established in various parts of French India by Catholic establishments with government help. Of these, the most important were the orphanage of Saint Louis de Gonzague and the Desbassyns Old People's Home.[31]

The port of Pondicherry was not a port as ships could not approach the coast. Goods and passengers were transported instead by chelingues (wooden boats) manned by rowers and, since 1866, through a metallic bridge on the beach road called the Pier, some distance into the sea and thereafter by chelingues up to the ship, which stood quite far away from the coast. The Pier was extended twice, in 1881-2 and in 1908-9. However, 90 per cent of the goods were loaded and unloaded from the beach through chelingues. The Karaikal port functioned in a similar fashion.

Most of the import-export trade in French India was carried on through these two ports. Four-fifths of the imports were from the British colonies and America, while France and the French colonies made up for the rest. Pondicherry imported from France wine, alcohol, metals, saccharine, perfumes, marble and cement. The Anglo-Saxon countries furnished consumer items like rice, areca, sugar, cotton, petrol, etc. But 60 per cent of the products exported were to France and its colonies, while the rest was exported elsewhere. Exports consisted of mainly, cotton textiles, yarn, groundnuts, rice, onions and bone powder. With the exception of yarn and cotton textiles made in Pondicherry, the Pondicherry and Karaikal ports were merely ports of transit. Groundnuts grown in British Tamil Nadu found their way to distant places through the port at Pondicherry, while Karaikal imported petrol for the needs of Tanjore district.[32]

Since 1878 at least, the port of Pondicherry exported groundnuts, also grown in Pondicherry, to France. This trade flourished until 1905. But, due to competition from British ports like Cuddalore and Porto Novo, where there were better facilities at a less cost, the export of groundnuts fell year after year. Besides, there was competition from Senegal where too, groundnuts were produced and exported to France. Further, local rivalries between the stevedores of Pondicherry, like Selvarajalu and Saravana Chettiar, were not conducive to this trade. Some of the important individuals and companies which exported groundnuts were Maison Dreyfus, Best and Co., East Asiatique and Kuppusamy Iyer.[33]

The port of Pondicherry was only a secondary port in India. Ships regularly plied to Madras, Calcutta, Bombay, Singapore and Rangoon from Pondicherry. These ships could not approach the shore. Instead, they anchored very far away from the coast and the chelingues assured the transport of goods from the coast or from the Pier to the ship and vice-versa. These chelingues were under the control of a few stevedores who received a commission for assuring this service.[34]

A railway line connected the Pier to Vizhupuram from 1879. This line, measuring 12 kilometres from Pondicherry to Vizhupuram, was inaugurated on 15 December 1879. Only 500 metres of this line was in Pondicherry territory. The train served the communes of Mudaliarpet, Ozhugarai, Villianur and Thirubhuvanai. Since 1898 Karaikal was connected to Peralam by another railway line which measured 15 kilometres. Of this, only 500 metres was in French Indian territory and the rest was in British India.

As a matter of fact, the railways, post office and the telegraph in Pondicherry were exploited by British India on the basis of contract. This rendered the French territories highly dependent on British India. The French Indian government received a sum of Rs. 50,000 annually from the Indian government for this service. A French printing press was inaugurated in Pondicherry in 1817. On 19 July 1828, a Tamil printing press was also started. A Tamil political press was created under a certain Vingatarayer in 1838. Later, on 1 June 1840, the first printing press was installed by the side of Jesuit Church, where the temple of Vedapuriswarar stood originally.

In 1849, the first newspaper in French, known as *Impartial*, was published from Pondicherry. In 1887, a telephone network was established in Pondicherry. A lighthouse was erected on the beach in 1836. Attempts were made to start a flight connecting Paris with Pondicherry and Saigon.[35]

It is noteworthy at this juncture that some Pondicherrians, as well as a few from Karaikal, who had migrated to French Indochina, had done extremely well in business. Among them, the most prominent were Darmanathan Prouchandy, Xavier de Condappa, Saverican Prouchandy and Mouhamed Said of Pondicherry, as well as Virapoullé and S. Abdul Karim, hailing from Karaikal. Incidentally, Darmanathan Prouchandy was the first Tamil and south Indian to enter the steam navigation business in Indochina, which was a monopoly of

European companies until then. He started a steam navigation enterprise in 1891 and owned two steamers that plied goods, passengers and postal items in the Mekong River and Delta for about 10 years—from 1891 to 1900. His application to the French authorities of Saigon to ply steamers from Saigon to Thailand by the South China Sea was rejected, most probably due to colonial bias against Indians.[36]

Following a convention, concluded on 7 March 1815 with the British government, the latter obtained the exclusive right to buy salt manufactured in the French settlements exceeding the needs of their consumers at a fixed price. As compensation, the British government agreed to pay the French government in Paris an annual rent of 4,00,000 rupees. Through a second treaty concluded on 13 May 1818, the British government even bought the right that the French settlements had to manufacture salt. Instead, an annual indemnity of 4,000 pagodas or 34,580 gold francs were to be paid to the French government. Besides, it was stipulated that the British government would provide the salt necessary for consumption in the French settlements. Through the sale of this salt in retail, the local administration in the French settlements did make some profits. But the colonial government authorities in Pondicherry wanted the annual rents to be paid directly to them, instead of to the government in France, so that they might make use of them for their own financial and developmental needs. This appeal was renewed from time to time, but it went unheeded. Finally, in 1930, Mahatma Gandhi launched the Salt March in British India demanding the abolition of the salt tax. A year later, the salt rent paid by the British to the French government in Paris since 1815 was directly paid to the colonial government in Pondicherry. However, it is necessary to note that the government derived its revenue also from the sale of alcoholic drinks like kallu and arrack which remained the principal source of revenue for the government, far exceeding other sources of revenue.[37]

There was also a custom dispute between the French and the British Indias. The British had imposed customs control of all goods transiting through the free ports of Pondicherry and Karaikal to British India. The Pondicherry merchants objected to this measure as they could not transport their goods freely to British India. Besides, the British relaxed or suppressed the import duties in their ports to discourage arrival of goods at the ports of Pondicherry and Karaikal. Many traders in Pondicherry wanted the imposition of sea customs.[38]

Customs around Pondicherry was abolished towards the end of 1936. As a result, Pondicherrians travelling to British India were subjected to hardships. The frontiers were encircled with barbed wires and guarded in a military fashion. Besides, a decree abolished the transport of parcels between the French territories. Instead, the British were given the permit to transport them. The traders of Pondicherry were not happy with this measure. They closed their shops on 6 and 7 June 1936 and held a meeting at Gaebelé Theatre, presided over by S.S. Varadaraja Mudaliar, one of the biggest merchants of Pondicherry, asking the government to cancel the decree.[39] Besides, when the British Indians who visited Pondicherry returned home, they sometimes carried personal belongings, like vegetables, etc., which were taxed unjustly by the British Indian customs. According to the quota agreement between the French and British Indias, the French subjects who visited British India had certain rights. With a *laissez passer*, from the 'Service des Contributions' (Tax Office), a French subject might wear a new suit and wristwatch and take with him half a bottle of brandy. But the British Indian customs officials did not respect this quota and stopped them. As a countermeasure, the French wanted to enact some restrictive measures for foreigners who visited French India through the decree of 5 November 1938. But they postponed it.[40]

The customs convention of April 1941 came to regulate more or less the transit of goods between French India and British India. The sea customs of wartime came to an end on 1 April 1941 and land customs were set up again on the borders of the settlements. British India made an annual payment of Rs. 6,20,000 to French India under the customs union agreement.[41]

The Indian Tariff Act of 10 March 1894 adopted by British India, which imposed a tax of five per cent on all products *ad valorem* that entered its ports, was not favourable to the growth of commerce and industry in French India. Pondicherry and Karaikal were, in fact, free ports. The consequences of the Act were not felt for 30 years since its adoption because of the increasing demand for products from French colonies in Asia and Africa until 1904. But increasingly, trade with

British India was difficult and unprofitable. The tax was increased to 7.5 per cent in 1919, and then it was increased further according to the type of products. It even rose to 30 per cent for luxury products. This situation seems to have encouraged smuggling of various goods into British India in the 1930s. Besides, Indian merchants imported goods from Singapore through the French ports, in order to escape duty.[42]

Industry was not very well-developed in Pondicherry due to the scarcity of natural resources. Most of the industries were concentrated in Pondicherry, except for a jute mill in Chandernagore employing 6,000 workers, a tinned food factory in Mahé and a rice husking factory in Karaikal. In 1930, Pondicherry accounted for 120 oil mills, 20 indigo factories, 28 rice husking factories, 2 ice factories, 1 factory to manufacture bone powder and 3 cotton mills, employing several thousand workers. They faced competition from industries based in British India.[43]

For more than 50 years the manufacturing of saylasses (colourful loincloth or *kaili*), made manually was a flourishing cottage industry in Muthialpet, just outside the northern limits of Pondicherry town, as well as in other areas of Pondicherry, like Lawspet and Kadirgamam, as also in Karaikal and Mahé. There were about 15,000 weavers and 1,000 handlooms, in all. Pondicherry was also known for the production of exquisite wood furniture, jewels, mats, handcrafted furniture and objects, and statues and dolls made of baked clay.[44]

However of late, due to competition from *kaili* produced in Japan at a cheaper price, the costlier Muthialpet *kaili* was no more wanted in foreign markets in Burma, Singapore, Saigon, Java, Sumatra and Penang. This had led to the destruction of the *kaili* manufacturing industry in Pondicherry. But neither the government nor the representatives of the people, or the exporters of Muthialpet, were worried about this state of affairs by which the labourers, who mostly belonged to the Kaikolar caste, were being driven to beg on the streets or do odd jobs to survive.[45] The misery of the weavers continued well into the 1930s and 1940s. In the 1930s, some local council members, like Marie Savary and R. Babilonne, asked for reductions of taxes for goods produced in French India, especially the saylasses, in order to compete efficiently with the cheaper Japanese goods which were flooding the Grand Bazar.[46]

The first cotton mill was started in Pondicherry in 1829. This mill was expanded in 1838 to include weaving and the production of blue cloth which was exported to the French colonies. Already in 1865, there were three cotton mills—G. Tardivel & Compagnie (Villianur road), Poulain & Compagnie (Ariyankuppam road) and Paget & Compagnie (Kosapalayam road). In 1864, Pagel & Co. had started a cotton mill at Kosapalayam. This mill passed into the hands of one Sababady Mudaliar, before it was bought by the Gaebelé brothers. In 1892, Henri Gaebelé had started the Mudaliarpet Cotton Mill. In 1898, the Anglo-French Textiles was started with English capital. It was popularly known as the 'Rodier Mill', because François Pierre Rodier was governor of Pondicherry at the time. These mills used the red cotton of Cocanada, and the white cotton produced in the Tuticorin region.[47]

The Savanna Cotton Mill belonged to the French company, Cornet & Cie. It was in existence since the nineteenth century. So, one could say that as far as the big industries like the cotton mills were concerned, it was mostly the preserve of the Europeans, as only they had adequate capital. The workers in these mills were drawn from the 'lower' castes, such as Vanniyars.

In 1954, the cotton mills employed about 7,000 to 7,500 workers of whom 4,000 worked in Rodier Mill, 2,000 in Savana Mill and about 1,000 in Barathi Mill (Gaeble Mill). About 35–40,000 people were dependent on them for their livelihoods. This population constituted one-sixth of the total population of Pondicherry. Cotton textiles produced in these mills were exported to British India and the French colonies. But the mills depended entirely upon raw cotton imported from British India.[48]

Frenchmen like Henri Gaebelé, Spielmann and Emile Gaudart also had oil-mills. Additionally, they exported groundnuts to countries as far apart as Philippines and France. This lucrative export trade was literally in French hands, with businessmen like Gallois-Montburn and Gaebelé in the lead. Pondicherry emerged as their principal port from which to export groundnuts. But very soon they had to face competition from nearby Cuddalore and Porto Novo in British India.[49]

Calvé Sangara Chettiar was an industrialist who had oil-mills and owned stakes in activities such as weaving, spinning and crushing bones in the beginning of the twentieth century.[50]

In the year 1902, the Frenchman Emile Gaudart founded the Sainte Elizabeth factory, which manufactured some machinery tools for the cotton mills of Pondicherry. In the same year, another Frenchman called Jules Guerre founded an ice factory in Pondicherry. Three years later, Henri Gaebelé and another Frenchman called L. Spielmann started a factory near the railway station to manufacture artificial fertilisers. Besides, there were tanneries, oil mills, indigo manufacturers and dye-works in Pondicherry. Indigo manufacturing and dyeing units were principally in the hands of Tamils. In 1929, there were 120 oil mills, 20 indigo manufacturing units, 38 factories to decorticate the rice, 2 ice factories and a foundry. The Standard Oil Company already established in Karaikal had a petrol reservoir in Pondicherry. However, Pondicherry was highly indebted at this time.[51]

From 1943, Pondicherry received electricity from the Mettur Hydro-Electric Power Station due to an agreement between Colonel Platts, chief engineer for electricity, Government of Madras, and R. Surleau, head of the Public Works Department, signed on 3 December 1943. In addition, there was the thermal station, Sainte Elizabeth, in Pondicherry to supplement or even replace the Mettur electricity. This agreement would end on 2 January 1954.[52]

A Chamber of Commerce functioned in Pondicherry since 1 September 1842. In 1845, mortgage registries were started in Pondicherry and its subordinate territories. Among the leading businessmen in 1865, there were Calvé Soupraya Chetty, Grindam Couroumourty Chetty and Goguilom Balagobalan.[53] During the first half of the twentieth century, we see the emergence of other businessmen and business houses in Pondicherry like Grindé R. Manikka Chetty & Sons, H.M. Cassime & Co, Mouhamed Said & Co, Govindasamy Mudaliar (Ananda Emporium), Mathru Café, Francine Shop, Selvarajulu Chettiar, Kuppusamy Iyer and Nanayya Bhagavathar & Sons. Some of them, like Mouhamed Said, Saverican Prouchandy and Xavier de Condappa, invested the profits that they made in their business ventures and industrial houses in Pondicherry, or in French Indochina, in buying land and properties.

In 1934, the Frenchman, Henri Gaebelé, was the president of the Chamber of Commerce and the vice-president was the lawyer, Gnanou Diagou. The treasurer was Mohammad Haniff. It had the botanical garden under its control. A branch of the French bank, Banque d'Indochine, was started in Pondicherry in 1875.[54]

From 1882, the French Indian government decided to promote the consumption of alcohol among Indians to raise revenue for the local budgets. Since then, arrack (local alcohol) and toddy played a decisive role in not only balancing the budget but also during election times. There was a distillery established in Pondicherry in 1903. It was in private hands until late 1933, when the government took it over.[55]

From the above, it is quite clear that there had emerged since the second half of the nineteenth century, some businessmen, merchants and industrialists in French India. They flourished within the framework of the economic structure put in place by the French colonialists, which was definitely capitalist in nature. Thus, there arose among Pondicherrians, both French and Indian, a few capitalists like Henri Gaebelé, Sababady Mudaliar and Calvé Sangara Chetty. There were also flourishing merchants like Nanayya Bhagavathar, Murugesa Poullé, Grindé R. Manikka Chetty & Sons, and H.M. Cassime. They belonged to the wealthy and privileged section of the French Indian society. It had emerged conspicuously and in a more organised manner during French rule. In other words, these capitalists became an important and influential segment of the elite society that emerged in Pondicherry during French rule.

NOTES

1. Jean Deloche, ed., *Le Papier Terrier de la Ville Blanche de Pondichéry, 1777*, Pondicherry, 2002, p. 15; Jacques Weber, *Les Etablissements Français en Inde au XIXe Siècle (1816-1914)*, vol. I, Paris, 1988, p. 6.
2. Ibid., vol. I, p. 482; vol. V, p. 2716.

3. Ibid., vol. V, pp. 2716-17; *Annuaire des Etablissements Français dans l'Inde*, 1854, p. 119; 1935, p. 112.
4. A.P. 720, D. 2 Recensements de 1926, Religions, AOM; Weber, op. cit., vol. IV, pp. 2254-5; vol. V, p. 2728; Raymond Delval, *Musulmans Français d'Origine Indienne*, Paris, 1983, pp. 141-2; Morachini, *Les Indigènes de l'Inde Française et le Suffrage Universel*, Paris, 1883, p. 8.
5. Ibid.; *Journal Officiel des Etablissements Français dans l'Inde*, vol. II, 1935, p. 655; Alfred Martineau, *Etablissements Français dans l'Inde*, Paris, 1931, p. 54.
6. Martineau, op. cit., p. 66 ; *l'Union Hindoue*, 3 June 1901, p. 21; *Annuaire des Etablissements Français dans l'Inde*, 1937, p. 459; *Hand Book of Statistics, 1960-1*, Pondicherry, p. 12; Weber, op. cit. vol. V, p. 27 (cf. Louis Bonvin, Intro.); *L'Inde Française dans la Guerre*, Pondicherry, 1942; *Union Territory of Pondicherry, Statistical Hand Book, 1972-3*, p. 5 and 1981-2, Government of Pondicherry, pp. 7, 10; Weber, *Pondicherry, et les Comptoirs de l'Inde après Dupleix: La Démocratie au pays desCastes*, Paris, 1996, pp. 34-40.
7. Weber, op. cit., vol. I, pp. 493, 502-3; Interview with the Head Priest of Virampatnam Temple; Maurice Maindron; *Dans l'Inde du Sud: Le Coromandel*, vol. I, Paris, 1992.
8. Weber. op. cit., vol. I, pp. 510, 515-6, 518-19, 520, 522-3, 527, 530; *Annuaire des Etablissements Français dans l'Inde*. 1850, pp. 159-60; *Desasevagan*, 22 January 1924; Beaujeu, *Inde Française, Etudes sur les Etablissements*, 1867, pp. 29-40, ADP.
9. Weber, op. cit., vol. II, p. 707; E. Sicé, *Un Mot sur la Representation des Etablissements Français de l'Inde à l'Assemblée Générale*, pp. 12-13.
10. *Frenchu Nesan*, 4 June 1913, p. 5 ; *Le Progrès*, 25 July 1886.
11. *Puduvai Murasu*, 8 December 1930, pp. 10-11.
12. J.B.P. More, 'Muslim Evolution and Conversions in Karaikal, South India', *Islam and Christian-Muslim Relations*, 1993, 4(1), pp. 65-82; More, 'A Tamil Muslim Sufi', *Islam and Christian-Muslim Relations*, Birmingham, 1999; Weber. op. cit., vol. I, pp. 555-6, 559, 571; vol. II, p. 718; vol. IV, pp. 2058, 2059f, 2060; More, 'A Tamil Muslim Sufi', op. cit., pp. 5-21; Généralités 674, D. 2997, Lettre de l'Evêque de Drusipare au Ministre, 21 December 1841, AOM; Cf. A. Esquer, *Essai sur les castes dans l'Inde*, Pondicherry, 1870; Paramananda Mariadassaou, *Moeurs Médicales de l'Inde et leurs Rapports avec la Médecine Européenne*, Pondicherry, 1906, p. 2; Nadour Sidam Barom, *Les Habitants Indiens de Pondichery à la Chambre des Deputés*, Nantes, 1846.

13. More, 'The Marakkayar Muslims of Karaikal, South India', *Journal of Islamic Studies*, Oxford, 1991; Weber, op. cit., vol. I, p. 554f.
14. Weber, op. cit., vol. I, 559; vol. IV, p. 2058; vol. V, p. 2771; Inde 345, D.176, *Lettre de Richaud au Ministre*, 18 April 1885, AOM.
15. Weber, op. cit., vol. IV, pp. 2061, 2062-8, 2101-5 ; Beaujeu, *Inde Française Etudes sur les Etablissements, 1867*, 218, ADP.
16. *Le Temps de l'Inde Française*, 8 September 1893, pp. 1-2; Beaujeu. Inde Française, Etudes sur les Etablissements, 1867, 119, ADP.
17. Weber, op. cit., vol. II, pp. 760-1; vol. V, p. 2805; Beaujeu. Inde Française, Etudes sur les Etablissements, 1867, p. 120, ADP; cf. *Mémoires adressés par les Cultivateurs français de Pondichéry, à l'Assemblée Nationale législative et à M. le Président de la République Française contre la Surtaxe Imposé sur les Terres à Adamanom des Aldées par Décret en Faveur des Etabliseements Français dans l'Inde*, 4 February 1851(*redigé par Ponnou*), Paris, 1851; Nadour Sidam Barom. *Les Habitants Indiens de Pondichéry à la Chambre des Députés*, Nantes, 1846; Pattabhi Sitaramayya, *The History of the Indian National Congress*, vol. I, Bombay, 1946, pp. 106-7; cf. More, *Freedom Movement in French India: The Mahé Revolt of 1948*, Tellicherry, 2001, Ch. 2; Adrian Mayer, *Land and Society in Malabar*, Oxford, 1952.
18. Weber, op. cit., vol. I, p. 678; vol. IV, p. 2197; Inde, 365, p. 347, Pondicherry, 27 February 1892, ADP; More, op. cit., Barry Nicolas, *An Introduction to Roman Law*, Oxford, 1962.
19. J.O. 1920, p. 423, Weber, op. cit., vol. II, pp. 757, 784-5.
20. *Inde Illustrée*, March-April 1933; Desobagari, 19 June 1937; Martineau, op. cit., 1931, p. 62; cf. also, Emmanuel Adicéam, *La Géographie de l'Irrigatin dans le Tamilnad*, Paris, 1966.
21. JO 1909, p. 278; Weber, op. cit., vol. I, p. 477, vol. III, p. 1735, vol. IV, p. 2199; JO 24 February 1934; *Dupleix*, 28 May 1934; *Ediroli*, 24 January 1938, p.1; More, *Freedom Movement in French India: The Mahé Revolt of 1948*, Tellicherry, 2001, p. 32; Ann. 1850, pp. 155-6; Ann. 1885, p. 265; *Le Temps de l'Inde Françasie*, 8 September 1893, pp. 1-2; Martineau, op. cit., 1931, pp. 62-3; Weber, op. cit., 1996, p. 339; JO 1934, p. 128.
22. Weber, op. cit., vol. I, p. 223; Ann. 1850, pp. 157-60.
23. *Suthanthiraam*, 1 February 1947.
23. JO 1909, p. 191.
24. *Impartial*, 2 June 1849; Ann. 1935, p. 118; Ann. 1937, p. 113.
25. *Dupleix*, 24 March 1934; 7 July 1934; *Impartial*, 28 July 1849; *l'Echo de Pondy*, 28 August; 4, 18 September 1887; *Suthanthiram*, 18 February

1939; *Desobagari*. 3 July 1937; *Indochine-Inde*, 28 May 1933; Weber, op. cit., 1996, pp. 342-3.
26. *Vennila*, 16 December 1947; Interview with Elenamma; *Suthanthiram*, 20 November 1934, vol. 6, pp. 6-7; JO 1948, p. 168.
27. Ann. 1841, p. 272; 1850, pp. 155, 157-8; 1937, pp. 112-13, 144; JO 1912, p. 368; Weber, op. cit., 1996, p. 57.
28. Ann. 1937, p. 149; 1938-9, p. 110; *Vikata Prathapan*, 16 February 1890, p. 1.
29. *Inde Illustrée*, August 1933; *Vennila*, 10 September 1947, p. 15.
30. *l'Union Hindoue*, 27 May 1901, pp. 17-18.
31. *Messager de l'Inde*, 8 August 1900, pp. 33-5; *Sukapi Viruthini*. 19 July l1935, p. 2; JO 1936, p. 629; Ann. 1938-9, p. 30.
32. Martineau, op. cit., p. 61; Ann. 1935, 23; *Desobagari*, 3 July 1937, p. 2; *Notes Documentaires et Etudes*, no. 735, Les Etablissements Français de l'inde, AO, IF 7, ADP; Weber, op. cit., vol. II, pp. 893-4.
33. *Inde Illustrée*, April 1933; Weber, op. cit., vol. IV, pp. 1975-6, 1980-1, 1983f, 1989-91; *Notes Documentaires et Etudes*, no. 735, Les Etablissements Français de l'inde, AO, IF 7, ADP.
34. Weber, ibid., vol. IV, pp. 1895f, 1919.
35. Martineau, op. cit., p. 59; A.P. 3184, D. 10, Report of 6 May 1914, Pondicherry, AOM; *Indochine-Inde*, 10 May 1936; Ann, 1841, pp. 272, 281, 283-4; 1935, pp. 19, 106; 1938-9, pp. 31, 101; *Sukapi Viruthini*, 15 November 1937; M. Barret, *Consul de France à Bombay à M. Stephen Pichon, Ministre des Affaires Etrangères*, Bombay, 24 August 1903, pp. 62-3, no. 35, *Indes Politique Etrangère II, 1907-9*, ADP Convention Postale Note p. 80, AO, IF 67, ADP.
36. More, *Indian Steamship Ventures, 1836-1910: Darmanathan Prouchandy of Pondicherry, First Steam Navigator from South India, 1891-1900*, Pondicherry, 2013; More, *Tamil Heroes in French India, 1870-1954. Their Role in Business, Social Reforms and in Netaji's Freedom Struggle from Vietnam*, Pondicherry, 2016; More, 'Commerçants Musulmans Tamouls en Indochine Française', Lettres du C.I.D.I.F., 16 March 2011.
37. Weber, 'La rente du sel', no. 22, *Lettres du C.I.D.I.F.*; Martineau, op. cit., p. 57; *Le Reveil Saigonnais*, 13 January 1923; *Messager de l'Inde*. 28 July 1900, pp. 21-2; *Le Democrate*, 21 January 1900, pp. 5-6; Weber, op. cit., 1996, pp. 340-1.
38. *Desobagari*, 11 February 1939; *Indochine-Inde*, 26 February 1933; *Inde Illustrée*, April 1933.

39. *Indochine-Inde*, 28 June, 20 December 1936; *Saigon Dimanche*, 17 May 1936; *Desobagari*, 30 July 1936.
40. Note of Government of India to British Embassy, Paris, 13 December 1938, p. 237; French Note of 18 January 1939 to British Embassy, p. 260, Ministère Affaires Etrngères, 1930-40, Indes Françaises, no. 4, ADP; *Ediroli*, 14 Febaruary 1938, p. 1; *Desobagari*, 10 April 1937, p. 2; 23 April 1938.
41. *Hindustan Times*, 19 November 1948; *Jeunesse*, 18 May 1949; *Notes Documentaires et Etudes*, no. 735, Les Etablissements Français de l'inde, AO, IF 7, ADP; *The Hindu*, 16 April 1954.
42. *Inde Illustrée*, May 1933; *Indochine-Inde*, 11 June 1933; Note of British Embassy to Ministry of Foreign Affairs, Paris, 28 December 1936, pp. 125-8, 146, MInistère Affaires Etrangères, 1930-40, Indes Françaies, no. 4, ADP.
43. *Notes Documentaires et Etudes*, no. 735, Les Etablissements Français de l'inde, IF 7, ADP.
44. Martineau, op. cit., 1931, p. 62; *Inde Illustrée*, May, October 1933.
45. *Suthanthiram*, 10 September 1934, pp. 2-4: *Sukapi Viruthini*, 15 September 1934, 3; *Taynadu*, 2, 9 March 1934.
46. *Dupleix*, 13 January 1934; 7 April 1934; Ministre des Affaires Etrangères au Ministre des Colonies, Paris, 30 May 1938, pp. 188-9, Ministère Affaires Etrangères, 1930-40, *Indes Françaies*, no. 4, ADP; *Libération*. 26 May 1949, p. 2; *Desobagari*. 17 July 1937, p. 1; 31 July 1937, p. 2; 25 February 1939.
47. Weber, op. cit., vol. IV, pp. 1932f, 1955, 1965; Ann. 1935, pp. 106-7; Ann. 1875, pp. 172-3; Beaujeu, *Inde Française, Etudes sur les Etablissements*, 1867, pp. 147-56, ADP.
48. Lettre de R. Massigli Ambassadeur de France à Londres à M. G. Bidault, ministre des Affaires Etrangères, Londres, 24 January 1945; Lettre de C. Monod, Chef de la Mission des Colonies à Londres à R. Masigli, Ambassadeur de France, Londres, 18 January 1945, pp. 2-6, IF, no. 61, ADP; Reprise des Négociations avec l'Union Indienne, Note de M. Delteil, Directeur Politique, 23 June 1954, p. 184, ADP.
49. Weber, op. cit., vol. II, pp. 1149-51; vol. IV, pp. 1949, 1985-6, 1989, 2006; Ann. 1850, pp. 144-5.
50. Weber, ibid., vol. IV, p. 1953.
51. Weber, ibid., 1996, p. 328; Weber, ibid. vol. IV, pp. 1941-3, 1941f.
52. Lettre du Commissaire de Pondichéry au Ministre de la France d'Outremer, Pondicherry, 11 July 1953, 28, AO, IF 69, ADP; Mission de M.

Crouzet, Direction des Affaires Economiques et Financieres, p. 2, AO IF 69, ADP; Convention between the Government of French India and the Government of Madras, 3 December 1943, pp. 6-11, AO, IFf69, ADP.
53. Ann. 1935, p. 113.
54. Ann. 1938-9, p. 36; Beaujeu, *Inde Française, Etudes sur les Etablissements*, 1867, p. 168, ADP; *Inde Illustrée*, February-March 1934, p. 8; Weber, op. cit., vol. I, p. 678; Interviews with the Descendants of Mouhamed Said, H.M. Cassime, Saverican Prouchandy and Xavier de Condappa.
55. *Dupleix*, 16 December 1933; Weber, op. cit., vol. IV, pp. 2202, 2214.

CHAPTER 2

Emergence of the Professional Class

EDUCATION AND EMPLOYMENT

Traditionally, education in Pondicherry and French India was never a state affair. Instead, it was based on caste and occupational lines, and had been, since time immemorial. Knowledge was transmitted from father to son. Every caste in the social fabric specialised in a particular occupation. As a result, there was a certain inter-dependence and co-operation between various castes in every village. This relationship was quite independent of the king or the state. The concept of mass education, imposed by an authority from above, simply did not exist. Coercion and compulsion to work by a superior state authority were also absent.

But the Europeans who came to India had developed their own system of education. According to this system, education needed to be organised and regulated by the state—the church or the government—to cater to the administrative and other needs of the society. Thus under French rule in Pondicherry, education became a state responsibility in the course of time. It was the French missionaries who had laid the foundations of modern education in the early part of the eighteenth century. They first opened schools to educate only European children. It was they who opened a missionary school in Pondicherry in 1787. In 1790, the school was thrown open for public instruction. Nevertheless, only the White children enrolled in it. After 1816, when the French had recovered Pondicherry from the English, it was reopened again as a missionary school.[1]

On 19 June 1826, Eugène Panon Desbassyns de Richemont, comte de Richemont (born in Paris on 27 March 1800) was appointed governor of Pondicherry. During his governorship, the preceding missionary school came to be known as the Royal College and was reopened on 6 October 1826 in a splendid colonial building. The very next year, the Pondicherry public library was inaugurated through the decree of 16 May 1827. It contained 20,000 volumes and 30,000 government records.

The Royal College was a primary and secondary school. But the students were mostly White. Some Créoles, i.e. people of mixed Indo-European descent, were also admitted over the course of time. The Tamils/Indians had to wait until 1879 to be formally enrolled in this school. Students aged 7 to 15 years were admitted to this school. Knowledge in secular subjects, like recitation, handwriting, counting, Latin, French, English, Hindustani, Tamil, mathematics, history, geography, drawing and mythology, was imparted. Scholarships and hostel facilities were provided for students of the Royal College from 20 March 1828 by the colonial treasury.[2] Thus, the modern system of education introduced by the French into Pondicherry contributed to the regimentation of students for more than 10-12 years of their youthful life on a competitive basis. In other words, students were trained to compete with one another in order to excel in their studies right from the beginning of their childhood.

The decree of 30 September 1843 sought to organise the various branches of education in French India. This decree dealt with primary and secondary education, public and private schools and also special or technical education. There were two types of primary schooling in French, elementary and superior. The primary schools or *ecoles primaires* were spread out in the rural and urban areas. Every commune had an *ecole centrale* or central school. After receiving primary schooling one could enter the *ecole centrale*. Following this was secondary school and college where one could obtain the Baccalauréat. After this, if one wanted to pursue higher studies, one had to go to France, for there was no university-level education offered in Pondicherry. French was the medium of instruction in all these schools, while Tamil, Telugu, Malayalam and English were taught as second languages. There were also facilities to study and pass the Tamil *Brevet*.[4]

The system of education was perfectly secular, accessible to everyone freely up to the secondary level. After passing the secondary level, one had to pay just a nominal fee. Deserving students suffering from financial constraints were awarded scholarships to pursue their studies, either in Pondicherry or in France. However, students got to learn more about France than India through this system of education begining at the primary level. The study of Indian history and culture was sometimes overlooked as the syllabus was based on course curricula taught in France.

On 30 December 1846, the management of the Royal College reverted to the Missionaries of the Congregation of the Holy Spirit. The Royal College was renamed the Colonial College. As mentioned before, the college was the preserve of the Whites and Créoles (or Franco-Indians).[5]

Already, the decree of 18 November 1863 permitted students from French India to appear for the diploma of Brevet de Capacité de l'Enseignement Secondaire. From 14 February 1872, they were allowed to exchange this diploma for the diploma of Baccalauréat in Pondicherry itself. From 1870 and 1898, Classical Baccalauréat and Modern Baccalauréat, respectively, could be obtained from Pondicherry.

It should not be forgotten that the *Collège Colonial* was thrown open to all Indians from all castes from 1877, despite opposition from the Créoles and others. In November 1905, the Baccalauréat as it prevailed in France was extended to Pondicherry. It was the last stepping stone to university education and it thus came into force in French India. However, as the French had established no university in Pondicherry, students had to go to France for higher studies or go to British India to study in the universities established there. The Colonial College was renamed *Collège Français* (French College) in 1945.[6]

On 10 February 1727, a girls' boarding school (*pensionnat*) meant only for Europeans was established in Pondicherry. Later, on 21 August 1829, a free school for Créole girls was opened. These two schools were managed by the sisters of St. Joseph of Cluny. On 14 February 1827, a free school for 'high' caste Tamils (Christians, Muslims and Hindus) was opened in Pondicherry. The very next year, on 28 July 1828, another free school was established for the 'lower' caste Untouchables in Pondicherry, as they could not attend the schools meant for the 'higher' castes due to caste taboos.[7]

In 1834, there were 650 students in all these schools. Besides these schools, there were the Tamil 'poyal' schools, run mostly by Brahmins. Later, a separate school was established for Muslim girls in the Old Hospital Road (rue Ancien Hopital). The proportion of girl students towards the turn of the nineteenth century and after in primary schools was very low as compared to boys. Around 1900, only 25 per cent of the total number of boys in Pondicherry were in primary schools. This figure was nine per cent for girls.

The distinction between the 'higher' and 'lower' castes in schools gradually disappeared by the first half of the twentieth century due to the non-discriminatory policies followed by the French government.[8]

Primary schooling was made available at the 'Pensionnat de Jeunes Filles' and the Colonial College. The latter school was organised on the lines of primary schools in France, save the fact that English was taught here to cater to local needs. In the beginning, these schools were meant only for White children. There was also primary schooling in local languages like Tamil, Telugu, Malayalam and Bengali. The syllabus of these schools was the same as those in other primary and elementary schools. This seems to have contributed much to the fight against illiteracy. These schools attracted more students and cost less because vernacular language teachers were paid less than the French teachers. A diploma in the local languages like the *Certificat de Langue Indigène* and the *Brevet de Langue Indigène* was awarded.[9] Thus there came into existence Tamil teachers in Pondicherry and Karaikal.

A special course in English was also conducted at 'Collège Calvé' of Pondicherry, 'Collège Dupleix' of Chandernagore and the branch of the Collège Calvé opened in Mahé. Collège Calvé was founded in 1877 by Calvé Subbaraya Chetty, a wealthy merchant of Pondicherry. It was a private caste Hindu establishment subsidised by the government. Muslims were admitted to this school. The syllabus followed in this school was recognised by the universities of Madras and Calcutta. The students could obtain the matriculation diploma here like their counterparts in British India. In 1885, the heirs of Calvé donated the school to the government. It was subsequently thrown open to children from all castes and religions.

In 1886, the Puduvai Hindu Union School was established where English and Tamil were taught. There existed in Pondicherry another primary and secondary school meant for Indians, known as the 'Petit Seminaire' (formerly known as *Collège Colonial des Missions Etrangères*). There was also a Petit Séminaire in Karaikal since the 1880s. Otherwise, following in the footsteps of Pondicherry, there came into existence in Karaikal the English-medium Hindu Union Middle School in January 1886 at the house of Savalai Manikka Mudaliar. It was started by P.S. Krishnasamy Iyer. A girls' school was started in 1889 in Bahur by the women teachers of the indigenous Christian mission called St. Coeur de Marie.[10]

The decision of the French Indian government to teach English and Indian languages like Tamil was to have its own long-term consequences. This decision seems to have sent a message to the Pondicherrians that their future was inextricably linked to British India and Tamil Nadu, something that the French might not have intended at all. The instruction in English and Tamil not only exposed some students to British Indian influence but also potentially woke up their linguistic consciousness. Thus in Pondicherry, there came into existence a section of people educated in French as the medium of instruction, while many others grew up learning English or Tamil.

Secondary education was imparted at the *Collège Colonial* of Pondicherry by trained university professors. The syllabus and methods of education in this school were similar to those in France. Students could appear for the exam of *Brevet de Capacité Colonial* which was equivalent to the Baccalauréat. Exams were also conducted for the *Certificat d'Etudes*, the ordinary and superior *Brevets* and the indigenous language *Brevet*. Professional courses could be availed of at the 'Ecole des Arts et Métiers' in Pondicherry. Valangas were admitted to the *Collège Colonial* only from 1878. In 1899, the *Collège Colonial* was taken away from the control of the missionaries and secularised. The number of government schools in 1915 was 65.[11]

On 17 July 1838, law studies were inaugurated by the French in Pondicherry. The decree of 24 February 1876, and that of 24 December 1910, created a law school in Pondicherry. A three-year course was instituted. The syllabus was in conformity with those followed in the faculties in France to obtain the degree of *Licence en Droit*. The students who passed out from this school could continue their studies in France. Those who obtained diplomas at the end of the second or third years would be granted the grade of *Bachelier* or *Licencié en Droit*, as appropriate, after passing a special exam in France. By the end of the 1930s, there were at least 30 Indian magistrates from French India serving in various French colonies.[12]

There functioned a medical school in Pondicherry from 1823. It was the oldest French medical school established outside France, older than those of Hanoi, Alger and Tannanarive. It was reorganised by an official decree in 1863. Local Tamil medical men called 'mestrys', belonging to every caste, operated during this period among the populations of French India. They were trained by French doctors. The French considered the introduction of modern methods in healthcare and disease prevention as part of their civilising mission in India.

One could become a health officer after completing a five-year course in the French medical school. One had to study for three years to become a midwife and two years to become a vaccinator. The professors in this school were generally French doctors. There were facilities for Indians of all castes and religions to become doctors, health officers, pharmacists and also male nurses. It appears that, due to the influence of progressive French values at that time, nobody questioned the caste origins of these early medical men, even while caste taboos were present in other fields of work. A pharmacy was opened in Pondicherry on 20 June 1829.[13]

Professional teaching was started as early as 1826, especially through the 'Ateliers de Charité', under the management of the Comité de Bienveillance. The decree of 15 January 1907, established a professional school called 'Ecole des Arts et Métiers' in Pondicherry. Skills like tailoring, repairing of machines, etc., were taught there. A library was established in Pondicherry on 16 May 1827. Another library came up in Karaikal on 17 February 1890.[14]

It appears that the French system of education comprised the primary schools (elementary and superior) in the urban and rural areas. Tamil was taught later in two superior primary schools—the Laporte School for Girls and the Calvé College. Beyond the primary schools were the ecoles sentrales or the central schools, known also as the superior primary schools. There was one central school in every commune. In Pondicherry The Ecole Centrale at Mission Street, near the church, was opened on 17 September 1885. During the nineteenth century, there was opposition to Parayars dispensing water to all students. Some orthodox 'upper' caste members wanted Brahmins to be employed who would distribute water only to the *Tamizhars* ('high' castes) and not the Parayars.[15] Around 1900, there were in French India, 50 public elementary primary schools, with 5,343 boys and 3,925 girls, and 222 private elementary primary schools, with 6,210 boys and 398 girls. In 1920, 68 per cent of the whole population of French India was illiterate. The number of public primary schools rose to 64 in 1936. But most of these schools did not have a building of their own. They were mostly located in rented houses which had inadequate space and were unhygienic most of the time, especially in the countryside. Besides, the classes were overcrowded. According to one account, from 1901 to 1936, the total number of students in public and private schools never exceeded 16,500 every year.[16]

There was no compulsory education at the primary level, yet education was free right up to the secondary level. Education in the French medium was open to all sections of the society without restrictions. In English medium schools and for undergraduate studies, the fees was nominal, so these institutions were therefore, accessible to practically everyone. Besides, scholarship was available to all deserving students, including the poor, on the basis of a competitive exam, so that they could pursue their studies without hindrance either in Pondicherry or in France.[17]

In 1936, of the 45,000 children of schoolgoing age, only 17,000 went to school. A total of 11,500 went to government school, while the remaining 5,500 went to private school. Pondicherry town had only a 14 per cent illiterate population, but Ariyankuppam had 75 per cent, Oulgaret 76 per cent, Villianur 80 per cent, Bahur 85 per cent, Nettapakkam 86 per cent, Mudaliarpet 87 per cent and Thirubhuvanai 90 per cent. Other territories like Karaikal, Chandernagore, Yanam and Mahé had 60, 48, 37 and 31 per cent illiterate populations, respectively. In the early 1950s, the southern French territories had a 35 per cent literate population, while in India, this figure was just 10 per cent. In 1935-6, there were only 150 students obtaining the *Certificat d'études Français et Indigene*, 27 passing the elementary *Brevet* and only 2 the superior *Brevet* while 8 had passed the Baccalauréat.[18]

Following the changes that were taking place in France at the beginning of the twentieth century in the relationship between religion and the state, education in Pondicherry was secularised to a great extent. Already in 1899, the Colonial College was taken over by the government from the control of the French missionaries. In 1945, the Colonial College was renamed as Collège Français or French College, as noted earlier.[19]

Apart from the aforementioned system of education put in place by the successive French governors of Pondicherry, an organisation called the Alliance Française saw its birth in the year 1889 through the efforts of a French marine captain by the name of E. Martinet when Armand Montbrun was the mayor of Pondicherry. Its object was to spread French civilisation and culture through the medium of the French language. Some of the first Indian members of the administrative council of this association were Shanmugam Velayudam Mudaliar (Vice-President), Bandé Sahib (General Council member), Calvé Sadasiva Chettiar (proprietor), Calvé Sangara Chettiar (proprietor), Murugesa Poullé (merchant, founder of the *Société Progessiste*) and Louis Rassendran (General Council member). Among the other members were Henri Gaebelé (industrialist), Louis Rassendran, A. Gnanadicom, Annusamy Modeliar (proprietor), Mariadassou Doraisamy, (Vice-President of the 'Société Progressiste' and deputy mayor of Pondicherry) and Narayanasamy Chettiar (proprietor). On 22 October 1890, a French government circular had sought to study the various other means to propagate the French language, civilisation and culture in French India. The result of this initiative was the birth of the Alliance Française in Pondicherry in April 1894.[20]

As a rule, more attention was paid in all the schools to the study of the history and geography of France rather than of India and Tamil Nadu. Students were made to learn that the Gauls were their ancestors. They were taught about Clovis and Charlemagne, but nothing about India, Tamil Nadu or Pondicherry.

In 1927, there was a students' strike in Calvé College against the rustication of six students. Out of this strike grew a youth movement, which led to the establishment of the French India Youth League in 1931. Some of these students came into contact with the workers and began advocating for their welfare.

Emergence of the Professional Class 63

In October 1936, there was again a students' strike in the Calvé College of Pondicherry. The students had several demands including augmentation of the infrastructure of the college. They also wanted the teaching of English and Tamil as well as the history and geography of India.[21]

In 1948, out of the total population of 3,17,222 in the four southern French territories, the number of illiterate persons was 2,13,762. In Pondicherry town, out of 59,835 persons, 33,478 were illiterate. The corresponding figures for Ouigaret was 35,311 and 28,407; for Mudaliarpet, this was 18,787 and 17,487; for Ariyankuppam, 18,797, and 15,425; Villianur 27,991 and 17,880, Bahur 20,591 and 17,108, and Nettapakkam 14,423 and 6,345. Of the total population of the Pondicherry region, 1,91,001 were Hindu, 7,077 Muslim and 25,281 were of the Christian faith.[22]

Historically speaking, from the time the French set foot in Pondicherry as colonisers there had always existed positive discrimination in favour of the Christians and those who had converted to Christianity, both in the fields of education and employment. The French needed educated people to run the colonial administration which was put in place in the early eighteenth century when the first governor of French India was appointed from France. Both the colonisers and the missionaries favoured the Christians. This has been amply demonstrated in one of my articles, titled 'Hindu-Christian Interaction during French Rule in Pondicherry', published in the journal, *Contributions to Indian Sociology*, in 1998.

The headstart that the Christians had enjoyed in education and employment continued to persist during the nineteenth century as well as the first half of the twentieth century. A perusal of the *Annuaires* and the *Journal Officiel* would amply demonstrate this fact.

This discrimination existed in government employment throughout French rule in Pondicherry, especially after 1840 when the administration was re-organised based on various departments like the general secretariat, treasury, public instruction, public works, tax, police, health, transport and ports, local administration, finance, agriculture and information. The governor was vested with all executive powers. All the top posts in the administration and education were held by White men from France, who were paid on a different scale. The Créoles, both 'White' and 'Chocolate', held the posts that were next in importance, while the Indians mostly occupied the lowest rungs of the administrative ladder though they might possess enough qualifications. Among the Indians, the Christians were better represented, the logic being that their community had been exposed to modern education right from the time when the missionaries started establishing schools in French India in the early eighteenth century. They had also been the ones who obtained higher education earlier and more frequently than any other community members. There were more doctors and lawyers as well as magistrates among Christians, than among the Hindus or Muslims. Even the Untouchable converts to Christianity and their descendants had progressed in education. Being more literate and more educated among the Indians, the Christians were represented more in government employment than the other communities. By virtue of their education, they also played a significant role in politics as it evolved in French India under French rule, as we are going to see in subsequent chapters.

This state of affairs evoked resentment against Christians from the Hindu populace. This feeling is reflected by the owners and editors of *Dupleix*, a popular newspaper published in the 1930s, in which articles appeared criticising the Christians for being over-represented, especially in the administration. It was thought that an anti-Christian movement was necessary for French India, similar to that in the British Madras Presidency. There an anti-Brahmin movement had begun in reaction to the preponderance of Brahmins in the administrative and education fields as well as in politics in the form of the Justice Party, founded in 1916. The Self-Respect Movement in Tamil Nadu was started in 1925 by E.V. Ramasamy Nayakar 'Periyar' who incidentally happened to be of Telugu/Kannada descent. Nevertheless, there was no anti-Christian party that came about to counter Christian domination in administration in French India.

One reason for the above could be that, unlike in Madras Presidency, there was no quota system or communal representation/reservation in the fields of administration and employment instituted by the French government for the various communities. There were, of course, some 'chery schools' established in the villages to cater to the specific needs of the Valangas and other 'lower' castes, but no measure were taken beyond that level. Besides, the Brahmins were simply conspicuous by their absence in the administrative and political life of French India and, therefore, there was no anti-Brahmin movement in French India. Education and employment were open to all Indians in Pondicherry on an egalitarian, competitive basis, at least on paper.

Thus, by the twentieth century, a professional class had emerged in French India, drawn from various communities. A perusal of the government *Annuaires* and the *Journal Officiel* will throw enough light on this aspect.

Very soon, many students of all castes and religions who had come out of the schools and colleges with diplomas found themselves without jobs. This forced many of them to migrate to the French colonies, like Indochina, in search of better job opportunities.[23]

However, there were students from a more modest background who took advantage of the scholarships and other facilities and pursued higher studies. Thus, many from the 'lower' and oppressed castes emerged as doctors, lawyers, teachers and professors, as pointed out by R. Babilonne. They were seen increasingly competing for jobs in the educational and administrative fields during the first half of the twentieth century, as attested to by the entries in the *Annuaires* and the *Journal Officiel*. They became part of the new professional class.

To conclude, one could ascertain that, with the introduction of modern secular education into French India, having the French language as the prime medium of instruction, especially in higher studies, there emerged over time a professional class among Indians of all castes and creeds. This class might not have been as well-to-do as the landlord, merchant or industrial capitalist classes, but it was quite preponderant throughout French rule, especially in the educational, administrative and political structures put in place by the French colonisers, who considered their modern methods in the educational and employment fields as being in themselves a great part of their grand civilising mission. It should not be forgotten that the professional class also consisted of members drawn from the landowning and merchant classes, alongside those from a more modest or ordinary background.

EDUCATION AND CULTURE: PRIVATE EFFORT

Apart from the Calvé College set up privately and then made over to the government, we have a few private schools established with the help of funds donated by a few wealthy men. In Reddiarpalayam, Ku. Lakshmanasamy Chettiar had donated a school, and Colacara Rangassamy Naiker had donated another school in Lawspet.[24]

As early as the 1890s, too, there was in Muthialpet a 'Tamizh Kalvi Sabhai' (Tamil Education Society) to promote modern education among Tamils. During this period, there was also the *Thanit Kalvi Koodam,* of which Mariadassou Doraisamy Poullé, deputy mayor of Pondicherry, was president. The Tamil magazine, *Vigadapradapan*, wanted the Tamils to learn their own language in schools and its study made compulsory exactly like French in government schools.[25]

In 1912, an association called 'Kalvi Kazhagam' (Education Centre) was founded to promote the Tamil language. It had a library containing 500 books.[26] In the early part of the twentieth century, Bangaru Patthar, the Tamil pundit who taught in Calvé College founded the magazine called *Kalaimakal* (*Daughter of Arts*) and an association called 'Puduvai Kalaimakal Kazhagam'(Pondicherry Daughter of Arts Association) to promote pristine Tamil. He claimed, probably following Rev. Robert Caldwell, that Tamil did not originate from Sanskrit. In April 1917, he founded the *Puduvai Tamizh Sangam* (Puduvai Tamil Sangam).

Tamil pundits and Brahmins, like Tirupulisamy Iyer and Thi. Venkatarama Iyengar were much involved in the activities initiated by Bangaru Pathar.[27] Later, we have journals like *Karpagam*, advocating the line of thought spelt out by Bangaru Pathar, which held that Tamil did not originate from Sanskrit. *Nyayabhimani* of Karaikal also stood for a separate Tamil culture and the purity of the Tamil language.[28]

The very next year in May 1918, another association called 'Tamizh Tallir' was founded in Pondicherry to promote Tamil. Gnanapragassam Gnany, professor at the Colonial College, was the president of this association till his death in July 1924.[29]

However, the French Indian government did not take any special measure to promote Tamil in Pondicherry, apart from teaching Tamil in schools and organising Tamil studies to produce Tamil teachers.

Students who received their education in French did not know how to speak Tamil without making mistakes. Their knowledge of India was next to nil, but they knew about the geography and history of France. Besides, though men above 21 years were given voting rights since 1871, they did not have sufficient knowledge to make use of it as only six per cent of the population was literate. The *Suthanthiram* and *Dupleix* newspapers held that there was a lot of confusion, commotion and corruption during elections due to illiteracy. They demanded that education should be made compulsory until the age of 15 or 16 years, like in England and France, to avoid these troubles. Other newspapers, like *Kudiarasu*, wanted education to be in the mother tongue, i.e. in Tamil, rather than in French.[30]

The Tamil, R. Babilonne, a member of the Pondicherry local council, and First World War veteran (sergeant chef), hailing from the depressed Valanga caste of Nellithope, demanded that students be taught more of Indian history and geography. He owned a book shop at No. 4, rue Surcouf, in a building belonging to another Pondicherry Tamil trader called Francine. Babilonne had married a girl of the Francine family that, too, had shops in Suffren Street and Bussy Street from 1883 to 1895. The French governor of Pondicherry, George Bourret, as well as the president of the general council, Sellane Naiker, and many other prominent personalities of Pondicherry attended the marriage. Babilonne was happy that such prominent personalities of Pondicherry had attended a 'low caste' marriage. This showed that French egalitarian values had permeated the caste-based Pondicherry society, and allowed all Pondicherrians to participate on an equal footing in the social life of Pondicherry. Babilonne was also the president of the Young Republicans' Association, while its secretary was another Pondicherrian called L. Mariannie.[31]

On 25 December 1880, Ponnou Murugesa Poullé, an agriculturist and proprietor, son of Purushotthama Ponnusamy Poullé and member of Brahma Madam, started the association called 'Cercle Progressiste' in Pondicherry, with the youngsters of the Madam. Its office was established in the first-floor room of the house of Kottaval Doraisamy Poullé in Muthu Mariamman Kovil Street. Later, Ponnou Murugesa Poullé was instrumental in founding the 'Société Progressiste' in Pondicherry in 1883 along with some prominent Tamils of the 'higher' castes for the promotion of Western (French)-style education. He, himself, was the general secretary of the Society. The Society had been set up to spread the French language and culture and ran a free school. K. Lakshmanasamy Chettiar, Siajy Krishnasamy Chettiar, Calvé Sangara Chettiar, Goquilon Sundiramurthy Chettiar, Annasamypoullé and, later, Madurai Nanayya Bagavathar were among those who donated for the upkeep of this Society. The Sangam functioned at 16, Kalatisparin Street, in the mansion belonging to Balappa Chettiar. Couttia Sababady Poullé was the president of Société Progressiste in 1925. In the year 1936, an association called 'Saraswati Sangam' was started by a certain S. Samou.[32]

In 1893, some prominent Valangas, who had renounced their personal laws, founded the Société Progressiste of the Valangamugattars to promote the Valanga community. Later other castes and religions, too, founded their own associations. These included the Alliance Educative des Vanniars, founded by the Vanniyar caste members in September 1919, the Anjuman Himayatul Islam, founded in 1910 by some Muslims. Another association was founded by the Yadavas or Idayars in 1924, the Sanror Kula Paripalana Sabhai founded in 1927 and the Arya Vaishya Samajam, founded in December 1933.[33]

Srinivasa Kavundan had contributed a lot to the awakening of the Vanniyars in Pondichery. Sellane Nayagar was the only Vanniyar who studied law during this period. There were movements, like the Vannikula Mithran, who called upon the Vanniyars to vote only for members of their own caste and send them to the municipal and other councils, instead of sending Mudaliars, etc.[34]

R. Babilonne and the *Suthanthiram* newspaper of V. Kailasa Subbiah were probably the first in Pondicherry who insisted on compulsory primary education all over French India. Babilonne was a veteran of the First World War. So he asked for the construction of a monument in Pondicherry in memory of those who died during the war. Babilonne was instrumental in the abolition of the appellation of certain 'low' caste schools like the 'chery schools' or the 'Valangamugattar' schools and replacing it with the name, 'Adi Dravida'. He even claimed that, in the Valangamugattar caste, there were administrators, magistrates, lawyers, professors, doctors, traders and large proprietors. It is worth noting here that the Pondicherrian, Francine Appasamy, of the

Valanga caste, was recognised as a distinguished magistrate in Pondicherry already in the 1870s, and another Valanga, Marcel Clairon, was a barrister of the Pondicherry high court in 1924.

The low caste Adi Dravida/Valanga population in Pondicherry accounted for more than 15 per cent of its total population at this time. Babilonne was at the forefront of the agitations against caste in the churches, burial grounds and theatres.[35]

The 'Reveil Social' (Social Awakening) was founded on 20 July 1907 to promote the interests of the 'lower' caste Valangas. It comprised prominent Pondicherrians, like the Clairon brothers, Mr Noel, M.A. Latour, Mr Lazare and François Lesel. This was the time that the French governor decided to give certain special treatment for the uplift of the Valangas. Money was spent by the government for their material and moral development. Special wells were dug for them in 54 localities in the Pondicherry region, as the 'higher' castes would not allow them to use their wells. Special schools were also opened.

The 'Reveil Social' was functioning in the building donated by Madame Lazare Lesel in 1936 with Gnanousamy Meyel as president. Some of its prominent members in 1936 were Clairon, H. Titus, G.A. Magnifique, G. Parmentier, and P. Charlemagne. It had 174 adherents in 1937. In Uppalam, there was the association called 'Etoile de Matin' with Mr Kesavan as president in 1931 and Mr Jone as secretary.[36]

During a function organised at the 'Reveil Social' in honour of Joseph Davidu, newly elected mayor of Pondicherry, E. Virasamy Saguerre, secretary of the 'Reveil Social', demanded from Mr Davidu to render primary education compulsory in Pondicherry. Davidu was an honorary member of this Sangam and had helped 20 poor students with books. The 'Cercle Sportif Pondichérien' also sought to develop education among the needy members of the oppressed castes by conducting a class of 45 students. The students were given clothes, food (twice a week) and oil for a head bath. The Créoles, or Franco-Indians, had their own association called 'Refuge', catering to the needs of Créoles alone. Louis Sinnaya Gnanapragasa Mudaliar organised literary and philosophical conferences in his mansion 'Mangalavasam' at Karadikuppam for the elite Tamils of Pondicherry.[37]

On their part, the Muslims started their own *sangams* to promote education among Muslims. There was the *Karai Muslim Sangam*. In February 1927, the *Muslim Vidya Sangam* was started in Karaikal. They also ran a middle school called the *Muslim Kalasalai*. For the first 10 years, only Muslims were admitted to this school. There was a 'Cercle Littéraire Musulman' (Muslim Literary Circle), with Haji Mougamadou Madar Sa Marécar alias Sinnamarécar as president and Seyadu Mougamadou as secretary. In 1938, this event was made open to all. There was also the *Neravy Muslim Educational Sangam*. All these *sangams* worked to promote women's education as well. Under the French governor's orders, an association called the Islamana Dharma Paripalana Sabha, functioned in the 1890s. It ran night schools for poor Muslim workers, particularly handloom workers. The *Anjumane Himayat Islam* of Pondicherry had its own school. There was also an association called *Madjmaoul-Mousinul-Mouminine* in Pondicherry since 1890 to assist the needy Muslims and probably also for promoting modern education among Muslims. There was a school for Muslim girls in the rue de l'Ancien Hopital (Old Hospital Road). In the late 1920s, there was a Pondi-cherry journal in Tamil, called *Jawaharul Islam*, run by Muslims like Kazi Abdul Rahman of Sultanpet, near Villianur. In 1939, another Muslim association was formed in Karaikal with 60 members, with Sahib Marécar as president.

Despite all these initiatives, the Muslims of French India seem to have remained largely indifferent to modern education. In 1910, the Muslims were far behind 'upper' caste Hindus and caste Christians as far as their numbers in schools were concerned. The Muslims were provided with Arabic teachers in the government schools and the Muslim girls had special schools.[38]

In May 1934, a 'Tamizhar Kalvi Kazhagam' was started to promote education among Tamils. On 26 January 1936, the *Saraswati Sangam* was started in Pondicherry with 22 members. Its objectives were to spread French culture and language, to unite all French Indians, to work for East-West meeting of minds, to create a study centre for the promotion of Hindu thought and civilisation and to develop Indian studies in France. A Youth League was also started by this *Sangam*. Conferences on the history of India were held by the *Sangam*.

M. Lambert Saravane, professor at the Colonial College, advocated a synthesis of Hindu heritage and the French rationalist and humanist values.[39]

A Society of the Ladies of Pondicherry functioned in 1936 with Madame Gnanou Tamby as president and Balalatchoumyammalle as vice-president. This Society had come into existence officially on 15 March 1931 through the efforts of Madame G. Tamby, Madame Joseph Davidu and a certain Ammaniammalle. The name of the association was *Nangayar Nalvazhi Sangam*. There were at least 100 Pondicherry women who were members of this association. Some prominent members were Ms L. Rassendran, Ms T. Saravane, Ms L.R. de Condappa, Louise Tetta, Susila Bai (wife of Selvarajalou Chettiar) and Juliette Annoussamy. It is worthwhile to note in this connection that Ms Queenie Radjou was the first Pondicherry girl to pass the Baccaluaréat exam. She subsequently pursued higher studies in English at Queen Mary's College in Madras.[40] A certain intellectual and social awakening was present among the Tamil women of Pondicherry during this period, due mainly to the French influence, stemming from their civilisational agenda.

On 8 August 1937, the *French Indian Madhar Aikya Sangam* was established through the efforts of Mayor Joseph Davidu, president of the Reveil Social, G. Meyel and its secretary, Titus Germaine, with Srimati Richard David as president and Mrs Richelieu as secretary, in the presence of the French governor, the mayor and the *Nangaiyar Nalvazhi Sangam* members. The meeting was presided over by Ms Meenambal Sivaraj. Joseph Davidu told the 150 people assembled that, to bring about equality, caste and religion must be set aside. He added that all communities had been given equal treatment in schools and in the villages, and that the 'chery schools' were now known as Adi Dravida schools.[41]

Another association called 'La Solidarité des Dames de l'Inde Française' was founded through the decree of 17 June 1937. Its founding was celebrated at the Hotel de Ville (municipal hall). This association had 156 members. It stood for the uplift of Tamil women in the presence of Mayor Davidu, Rathinavelu Poullé, vice-president of the Chamber of Commerce, Mr Meyel, president of 'Reveil Social', Clairon and Ms Meenambal Sivaraj, honorary magistrate. Joseph

Davidu told the gathering that the French Republic was based on the principle of equality.

Despite the establishment of these women's associations, the *devadasi* system continued to be in vogue in not only in Pondicherry but also the whole of south India. Girls aged 5-12 years were consecrated as devadasis in temples, even in the 1930s.[42]

Two exclusive clubs meant only for Europeans were opened on 4 December 1886 and 4 April 1899, respectively. This was, no doubt, racial discrimination. In 1936, the General Council of French India called upon the all white club, known as the 'Cercle de Pondichéry', to throw open its doors to people of all castes and colour.[43]

From the above facts, it becomes quite obvious that there was a certain awakening of the Tamil linguistic consciousness of Pondicherrians during French rule. There was also a definite social awakening of the 'lower' castes. like the Valangas and the Vanniyars, as well as of women.

Education was the key to employment in the French Indian administration. The well-to-do sections of Pondicherry society had an advantage over others in this respect. These sections consisted, mainly, of the landowning class and the merchant class. They formed the elite or privileged section of French Indian and Pondicherrian society. They were in a better position to avail themselves of the employment opportunities provided by the French administration. They took to teaching in schools and colleges and became lawyers or doctors. They, especially the lawyers among them, were the ones who took to politics as it emerged under French rule, within the framework of the political institutions put in place by the French. It was not very different in British India, where lawyers played a prominent role in politics.

NOTES

1. Ann. (by E. Sicé), 1841, pp. 258, 269; Valmary, *Rapport sur l'Enseignement dans l'Inde Française de XVIIIe siècle à nos jours*, Pondicherry, 1922.
2. *Indian Republic*, 29 March 1889, p. 22; Ann., 1841, p. 142; 1931, p. 127; Valmary, op. cit., pp. 9-13; Ann., 1850 (by E. Sicé) pp. 150, 154; Ann. 1841, pp. 143, 272; A. Martineau. *Etablissements Français dans l'Inde*, Paris, 1931, p. 65 .

3. Ann., 1841, pp. 142, 274.
4. A. Ramasamy, *History of Pondicherry*, Delhi, 1987, p. 195; *Notes Documentaires et Etudes*, no. 735, Les EF de l'inde, IF 7, ADP; Valmary, op. cit., pp. 19-20, 38; Jacques Weber, *Les Etablissements Français en Inde au XIXe siècle (1816-1914)*, vol. IV, Paris, 1988, p. 2274.
5. A. Ramasamy, op, cit., Ann, 1850, p. 154; 1935, p. 113; Ann. 1880, p. 54; Valmary, op. cit., p. 11; JO 1933, p. 1050; JO 1934, vol. I, p. 750.
6. Valmary, op. cit., pp. 19-20, 38; Jacques Weber, op. cit., vol. IV, p. 2274; Ann, 1927, pp. 117-18; Ann, 1935, p. 141; Ann 1938-9, pp. 131, 133; *Vikata Prathapan,* 12 January 1890, p. 1; Lafrenez, *Précis d'Histoire de la Mission de Pondichéry*, Pondicherry, 1953; *Notes Documentaires et Etudes*, no. 735, Les EF de l'inde, IF 7, ADP.
7. Ann. (by E. Sicé), 1841, pp. 144, 272-4; Valmary, op. cit., pp. 9-13; Ann. 1850. pp. 154-5.
8. Weber, op. cit., vol. IV, pp. 2051, 2261, 2264, 2274-5; JO 1936, p. 630.
9. Valmary, op. cit., pp. 56, 69-70; Ann, 1841, p. 144.
10. *Vikata Prathapan*, 6 February 1889, p. 64; 29 May 1889, pp. 145-6; 7 January 1891, p. 3; *Notes Documentaires et Etudes*, no. 735, Les EF de l'inde, IF 7, ADP; Ann, 1931, p. 128; Ann., 1935, pp. 127-8; *Inthiya Vikata Vinodhan*, 31 May 1889, p. 6; *Le Jeune Patriote*, 10 July 1897, p. 82; *l'Union Hindoue*, 3 June 1901, p. 23; *Le Jeune Patriote*, 16 April 1897, p. 34; *Hindu Nesan*, March 1891.
11. Weber, op. cit., vol. IV, pp. 2046, 2287; Ann., 1880, pp. 54, 56; Ann., 1938-9, p. 31; Valmary, op. cit., pp. 43, 55-7; *Notes Documentaires et Etudes*, no. 735, Les EF de l'inde, IF 7, ADP; Martineau, op. cit., 1931, pp. 64-5; Ann, 1938-9, p. 32.
12. *Saraswati,* Jan 1939; A. Martineau, op. cit., 1931, p. 59; Ann, 1841, p. 275; 1914-15, p. 123; Ann., 1931, p. 115; Valmary, op. cit., p. 21; Ann., 1880, p. 71; Ann., 1928, pp. 101-2.
13. Ann., 1938-9, p. 37; Martineau, op. cit., 1931, p. 64; *Saigon Dimanche/ Indochine-Inde*, vol. 8, 29 January 1933; Ann., 1931, p. 115; Valmary, op. cit., pp. 21, 44; JO 1936, vol. I, p. 1324.
14. Ann., 1938-9, p. 36; *Notes Documentaires et Etudes*, no. 735, Les EF de l'inde, IF 7, ADP; JO 1918, p. 259; Valmary, op. cit., p.13; *Ediroli,* 7 March 1938, p. 1.
15. *Vikata Prathapan,* 12 June 1889, p. 153; 3 July 1889, p. 163; *Indochine-Inde*, 9 August 1936; JO 1918, p. 80; Valmary, op. cit., pp. 42-4.
16. JO 1936, pp. 1330-3; Valmary, op. cit., pp. 25, 36, 41-2, 44, 53-4, 70-1;

Weber, op. cit., vol. IV, p. 2279; C. Guy, *Exposition Universelle 1900: Les Colonies Française, Les Etablissements Français de l'Inde*, Paris, 1900, p. 47; see for, e.g. JO 1918, pp. 596-7.
17. *Dupleix*, 27 January 1934; Ramasamy, op. cit., p. 196.
18. JO 1936, vol. I, pp. 1329-30; *Monographies sur Pondichéry par Mouzan*, p. 133, IF 89, ADP; JO, 1936, vol. I, pp. 1327-8.
19. Lafrenez, op. cit., Ann., 1914-15, pp. 148-53.
20. Ann., 1938-9, p. 421; Annousamy, 'l'Alliance Française de Pondichéry', le Trait-d'Union, April 1982; *Indian Republic*, 22 February 1889, pp. 6-7; 15 March 1889; *Vikata Prathapan*, 27 February 1889, pp. 82-4.
21. Interviews with elderly and informed Pondicherrians; *Ediroli*, 7 March 1938, p. 7; *Indochine-inde*, 11 October 1936; V. Subbiah, *Saga of Freedom Movement: Testament of my Life*, Madras, 1990, pp. 20-2; Ranganathan, *National Movement in French India*, Pondicherry, 1988, Sec. 2, p. 2; M.C. Vashist, 'Trade Union Movement in Pondicherry State with Special Reference to Mahé', M. Phil. Dissertation, University of Calicut, 1993, p. 35.
22. *Note Affaires Politiques*, June 1951, p. 88, IF 51, ADP.
23. *Note Affaires Politiques*, June 1951, pp. 88, IF 51, ADP; *Saigon Dimanche*, 7 August 1927; 18 November 1928; *Le Reveil Saigonais*, 30 January 1923; 12 February 1923; *Messager de l'inde*, 6 October 1900, p. 123; *Vikata Prathapan*, 26 June 1889, p. 159; J.B.P. More. 'Indians in French Indochina' (in) Mathew, K.S. (ed.), *Nationalism in French India*, vol. II, New Delhi, 1999; cf. also editions of *Dupleix* newspaper; More. *Rise and Fall of the 'Dravidian' Justice Party, 1916-1946*, Tellicherry, 2009.
24. Valmary, op. cit., p. 72.
25. *Vikata Prathapan*, 20 February 1889, p. 74; 9 October 1889, p. 1.
26. Mission dans l'IF par le Gouverneur H. Deschamps, November-December 1952, p. 126, IF 89, ADP.
27. *Kalaimakal*, April-May 1913; *Vidyabhivardhani*, May 1897; *Kalaimakal*, February 1913, pp. 2-3; May 1913, p. 25; JO, 1917, vol. II, p. 419; *Frenchu Nesan*, 7 May 1913; 2 July 1913.
28. *Nyayabhmani*, 20 April, 4 May 1934; *Karpagam*, February 1924.
29. JO, 1918, vol. II, p. 302; JO, 1912, p. 7; *Desasevagan*, 15 July 1924.
30. *Suthanthiram*, November 1934, vol. 6, pp. 7-8; *Dupleix*, 3 February 1934; *Kudiarasu*, 31 March 1938.
31. *Saigon Dimanche*, 16 October 1932; 12 May 1935; *Dupleix*, 30 June 1934; *Indochine-Inde*, 23 February 1936; *Puduvai Murasu*, 11 April 1932, pp. 20-1; *Inde illustrée*, September 1933; July 1934.

Emergence of the Professional Class 75

32. *Saigon Dimanche*, 20 November 1932; JO 1918, p. 184; JO 1917, p. 1173; *Le Jeune Patriote*, 1 July 1897, p. 75; *l'Union Hindoue*, 10 June 1901; 17 June 1901, p. 31; *Vikata Prathapan*, 6 March 1889, p. 91; 13 March 1889, pp. 97-8; 3 April 1889, p. 117; *Sree Soudjana Ranjini*, 2 April, 1925; *Sukapi Viruthini*, 15 November 1937; *Agni*, 9 March 2004; *Le Jeune Patriote*, 1 December 1897, p. 74; JO 1936, p. 632.
33. C. Antony, *Encyclopaedia of India, Pondicherry*, New Delhi, 1994, pp. 174-5; Ann., 1938-9, pp. 421-4; *Nadar Kulam*, February 1948, p. 4; JO 1896, p. 344.
34. *Desasevagan*, 17, 19, 22 January 1924.
35. Antony, op. cit., 1994, p. 174; *Saigon Dimanche*, 3 February 1935; *Suthanthiram*, 20 November 1934, vol. 6, p. 8; Inde 364, D. 344, *Lettre du Gouverneur*, 27 May 1874, AOM; *Desasevagan*, 4 February 1924; *Saigon Dimanche*, 10 July 1932.
36. *Puduvai Murasu*, 26 January 1931, p. 16; Weber, *Pondichéry et les Com-ptoirs de l'Inde après Dupleix: La Démocratie au pays des Castes*, Paris, 1996, pp. 132, 174, 302-3, 332; Antony, op. cit., 1994, p. 174; *Indochine-inde*, 12 April 1936; Ann., 1938-9, p. 424; *Desobagari*, 20 November 1937.
37. *l'Union Hindoue*, 6 May 1901, p. 6; 17 June 1901, p. 30; *Desobagari*, 14 August 1937; 20 November 1937; *Saigon Dimanche*, 24 March 1935.
38. *Kudiarasu*, 24 January 1938; 25 April 1938; 18 July 1938; *Taynadu*, 23 March, 13 April 1934; *Dupleix*, 20 January 1934; Valmary, op. cit., 1922, pp. 13, 40-1, 71; More, 'Muslim Specificities in French India during the Nineteenth Century', *Journal of the Institute for Research in Social Sciences and Humanities*, vol. 2, no. 1, January-June 2007, pp. 126-7; Ann., 1908, pp. 176-7; JO 1928-30, vol. I, p. 604; JO 1935, I, p. 230; JO 1928, p. 990; JO 1936, p. 630; *Rapport sur les Activités d'une Association Compose de Notables Musulamans*, June 1945-Police, Carton 450, Dossier 39, AOM; Kudiarasu, 24 January 1938.
39. *Saraswati*, January 1939, p. 27; November 1938, 8-11, 12, 13, 20, 23, 27-8; *Kudiarasu*, 13 February 1939; *Nyayabhimani*, 25 May 1934; *Hindu Nesan*, 22 May 1891.
40. *Inde illustrée*, March 1933; *Indochine-Inde*, 26 April 1936; *Saigon Dimanche*, 27 March 1932; *Desobagari*, 3 December 1938.
41. *Desobagari*, 14 August 1937.
42. *Dupleix*, 24 March 1934.
43. Antony, op. cit., 1994, p. 176; Ann., 1938-9, pp. 36, 122, 133.

CHAPTER 3

Administration and Politics

POLITICAL INSTITUTIONS AND EARLY POLITICS

Democracy of the representative type was born in France out of a clash between the monarchy, feudal aristocracy and the church on one side and the rising capitalist class and the peasantry on the other. It is a product of great tension and violence, if one takes into account the French Revolution of 1789. It was a time when the English and the French were at loggerheads in India. However, as a result of the French Revolution, an all-White General Assembly was held on 2 February 1790 in Pondicherry. The assembly wanted to submit its wishes and grievances to the National Assembly in Paris. An all-White Municipality was set up in Pondicherry in August 1791 with five members and a mayor. A new representative committee drawn from the various settlements was also set up. French India sent two Frenchmen as representatives to the National Assembly. But such institutions were meant only for the White men. No Indian or Créole was allowed to participate in them.[1]

Subsequently, the representative committee was replaced by a colonial assembly, consisting of 21 members, 15 from Pondicherry, three from Chandernagore and one each from Mahé, Karaikal and Yanam. All White Frenchmen above the age of 25 years were to elect these representatives. It appears that the colonial assembly had provided for the admission of four local Indian representatives, for presentation of data and views when matters related to Indians were to be discussed. But this measure was never implemented and was abrogated later. Indeed, a new constitution drawn by the colonial assembly went to the extent of rationalising and justifying the refusal of franchise and representation to Indians.[2]

As a matter of fact, it could be said that the French Revolution did not mean any change in the status of the French Indians with respect to their relationship with their colonial masters. There was no question of any sort of equality between the Tamils of Pondicherry and the French. There was no question of even a semblance of decolonisation. It appears that the Indians continued to remain the 'petted slaves' of the French who needed to be civilised further in order for them to be given any sort of representation in the political institutions of Pondicherry. In short, the Revolution was meant only for the White French and not for the Indians who were excluded from the movement or stood aloof as spectators.

Their five originally occupied territories were restituted to the French by the English in 1814-15. It was then that the French set about re-organising these territories in a more effective way.

In July 1826, the French Indian government under Vicomte Desbassyns prohibited all Indians, both male and female, of all religions, from wearing the dress of the *topas* or people who wore hats, i.e. the Europeans. Any Indian who transgressed this bar was fined 25 rupees and was caned 25 times.[3]

According to the decree of Count André Julien Dupuy, dated 6 January 1819, all Indians, Hindu, Muslim or Christian, were to be judged according to their personal laws, customs and caste. In 1827, a consultative committee on Indian jurisprudence was set up. In the committee, all castes were represented including the Valangas. It should be noted here that the population of French India was subject to most of the French laws in civil matters as well as in commercial, penal and criminal matters. But in matters relating to personal laws, like marriage and inheritance, they could follow the ancient laws of the land, based on custom and tradition.[4]

On 23 July 1840, a decree called the 'Ordonnance Organique' re-organised the French Indian administration. The French governor was vested with sweeping powers over all affairs of French India and the various government departments like the general secretariat, treasury, public instruction, public works, tax, police, health, transport and ports. He was answerable only to the Government of France. Thus the privy council, instituted in 1829, was replaced by an administrative council, which was just an advisory or consultative body with no executive or legislative powers.

The decree envisaged the creation of a General Council, and local or sectional councils, as well as the appointment of a delegate to Paris. An assembly of important personalities came into existence in Pondicherry, chosen by the governor. Most members of this assembly were European. The merchant, Balakrishna Poullé, was an Indian member of this assembly. This assembly elected 10 members to the General Council. In the General Council, Naniapa Appasamy Poullé was the Indian member. The Indians were not happy as they were grossly under-represented. Local councils were created in Karaikal and Chandernagore. The General Council was abolished in 1848 and the parliamentary representation accorded by the decree of 15 March 1849 to all Indians residing in Pondicherry for five years and more was held back, three months after its creation.[5] Thus the timid process of integration of the colonies with France was nullified.

However, the Third Republic instituted in France preferred the policy of assimilation of the colonised people with those in France. As a result, parliamentary representation was re-established by the decree of 1 February 1871. Thus, the French Indians became the first to enjoy democratic voting rights in the Indian sub-continent, irrespective of class, caste or religion, even while in British India nomination to the various councils was still the norm, even much after the turn of the nineteenth century. This was indeed a revolutionary step in a caste-ridden society.

In the elections to choose a delegate to the National Assembly, the great majority of the voters were Indians. All adults above the age of 21 had the right to vote, on the basis of equality. Thus the Brahmins, the land-owning castes, the professionals and merchants were put on a par with the ordinary labourer and worker through the introduction of democracy and the voting system. This was a revolution indeed in a caste-ridden society. Thus, all men belonging to the various castes and religions, elected the Frenchman, Alexandre Panon Desbassyns de Richemont, as their first delegate or deputy to the National Assembly in Paris. He defeated Ristelhueber, the ex-public prosecutor of Pondicherry as well as Sandouodéar, who was professor of Tamil in Paris University and who claimed equal rights for Indians on a par with the Europeans. Desbassyns had the support of the Créole, Emile Hecquet, as well as of the Tamil lawyer, Ponnuthamby Poullé, who wanted Indians to participate in managing the affairs of the colony. Ristelhueber was supported by a group of conservatives led by Gallois-Montbrun, who opposed the representation of Indians in the local assemblies and wanted to maintain the supremacy of the Europeans and Créoles.

Following the policy of assimilation, the decree of 14 June 1872 created local councils in Pondicherry and its dependencies, which gave more political representation to Indians. The local council in Pondicherry had 12 members, Karaikal had eight members, Chandernagore six, and Mahé and Yanam four each. They were elected for six years, on the basis of two distinct lists, one for Europeans and the descendants of Europeans, and the other for Indians. The list had equal representation in the councils. In this way, the predominance of the Europeans in the councils was assured. The local councils were merely consultative. A restricted Colonial Council was also created, composed of 12 members with the governor as head. Of the 12, five were Europeans, including the governor, and of the remaining seven, two were Europeans, with all the seven to be elected by the local council members. Thus, the European element predominated also in the Colonial Council. There was just one Muslim elected to the Colonial Council and it was Bandé Sahib, a merchant from Karaikal. Of the other two most important figures elected to the Colonial Council were Nadou Shanmuga Velayuda Mudaliar, a prominent Hindu landlord, who stood for defending Hindu custom, and the lawyer, Ponnuthamby Poullé of the Christian Vellaja community, who wanted not only political and administrative assimilation, but also cultural and moral assimilaton. Since the time Ponnuthamby Poullé won the right to wear shoes in the courts as did the Europeans, he wanted the abolition of castes through the fusion of castes, while his rival Nadou Shanmugam wanted the maintenance of medieval customs and traditions. Only a few intellectuals like the Frenchman, Jules Godin, and the Tamil, Louis Rassendran, supported the line of Ponnuthamby, who proudly and defiantly declared 'I am French and there is my caste'. It was argued at that time that all Indians of the French colonies in India were French and, therefore, had the right to elect their representatives.[6] However, Indians in their great majority preferred to follow the line of Nadou Shanmugam.

It is quite clear from the preceding that, apart from the Europeans, the three prominent Indians elected to the Colonial Council were from the privileged section of the Indians, having a mercantile, professional or landholding background. Thus, though the elections were held on an egalitarian basis, it was the elite section of the society that emerged as the dominant influence in the local assemblies and the Colonial Council. The democracy introduced by the French seems to have been tailormade for the coming about and existence of this influence.

The decree of 24 Februay 1875 allowed French Indians to elect a senator to the French Senate. Desbassyns de Richemont, son of the former governor, became the first senator. Both Europeans and Indians above 21 years of age had voting rights on an equal footing. In this way, the Republican Government of France sought to integrate French India (and all its other colonies) into the French political system, unlike the British. The process of assimilation of Indians within the French national orbit had begun with such measures. Strangely, the delegates elected to the French parliament from French India were all White Frenchmen from France, right up until the 1940s. Thus, though Indians had voting rights, they were never elected to the French parliament until the 1940s.[7]

The decree of 25 February 1879 created the General Council, in the place of the Colonial Council established in 1872. It consisted of 28 members—12 from Pondicherry, 8 from Karaikal, 4 from Chandernagore, 2 from Mahé and 2 from Yanam. Some of the first members elected to this council were Ponnuthamby Poullé, Nadou Shanmugam Velayuda Mudaliar, Govindassamynaiker and Bandé Saheb, along with another Muslim member from Karaikal called Agamadou Saib. These early members belonged to either the professional class like Ponnuthamby Poullé, the landowning class like Nadou Shanmugam or the mercantile class like Bandé Sahib. Thus, right from the start only the privileged classes, which included either the White men or the elites of the French Indian society, took advantage of the democratic political institutions put in place by the French.

A privy council was created to assist the governor. Indians were nominated to the privy council along with Frenchmen. In 1884, both Bandé Sahib and Agamadou Saib were re-lected to the General Council. Both were loyal allies of Nadou Shanmugam.[8]

In 1880, French India was divided first into 10 communes or municipal divisions. Then, through the decree of 25 December 1907, it was re-divided into 17 communes. These were—Pondicherry, Ariankuppam, Mudaliarpet, Oulgaret, Bahur, Nettapakkam, Villianur, Thirubhuvanai, Karaikal, Tirunallar, Nedunkadu, Cotchery, Grande Aldée, Neravy, Chandernagore, Mahé and Yanam. Every commune was to have its own municipal council with elected members. The commune members selected the mayor. All Indian and European men, who were 21 years old, had voting rights. The municipal councils and the mayors had specific rights and duties to perform. In the elections held to the municipal councils, contrary to all expectations, the progressive, assimilationist party led by Ponnuthamby was defeated everywhere. The party led by Shanmugam, which was essentially an alliance of the 'upper' castes and the Muslims won. This party stood for *mamoul* (custom and traditions). Shanmugam and the traditionalists then emerged as the most powerful factor in French Indian politics. Nadou had his men elected to all councils. Even Frenchmen sought his support to get themselves elected to the French parliament. Nadou Shanmugam thus came to be known as the 'Black King Louis XI' of Pondicherry. The reformist agenda of Ponnuthamby took a back-seat.

On 30 May 1880, the French lawyer, Léon Guerre, became the first elected mayor of Pondicherry. The French businessman, Armand Gallois-Montbrun, was mayor from 1884 to 1893. In 1887, when Armand Gallois-Montbrun of the conservative European Party was the mayor, Nadou Shanmugam (landlord), Louis Rassendran (agriculturist and notary), Cassimsaïb, Calvé Sadasiva Chettiar (merchant, landlord), etc., were municipal council members. Sababady Subbaraya Poullé was one of the early Tamil deputy mayors in 1880. Otherwise, there were few Muslims in the local and municipal councils, except in the communes of Karaikal and Grande Aldée.[9] Though they were generous enough to introduce these democratic reforms, at a time when nomination to the councils was the norm in British India, the French government sought to retain power in its own hands. We have seen that no Indian was elected to the French parliament until the 1940s. Now, if the same voting system were to be applied in the general, local and municipal councils as in the election of the parliamentary delegates, the Indians, due to their preponderant numbers, would naturally dominate them.

The French in Pondicherry sought to undermine this possibility on various pretexts. They created two lists of voters with equal representation in the councils. Thus, the Europeans, who were very small in numbers, even if the *topas* or Créoles were to be included in their list, had equal representation in the councils along with the overwhelming majority of Indians who accounted for about 98 per cent of the total number of voters. The Indians hardly objected to this discriminatory measure which had been formulated on the basis of race and ethnicity. This reinforces the notion that the Europeans were racially distinct and culturally superior to the Indians, the introduction of democracy notwithstanding. Thus, the two-list voter system came into vogue in French India, which was abolished only after the Second World War.[10] Through this discriminatory system, Frenchmen freely participated in local politics and dominated it until the late 1920s through alliances and adjustments, as in the case of Pondicherry town commune where hardly any Tamil could get himself elected as mayor until the 1930s. This was not the case in many rural communes where Indians, Tamil or Telugu, got themselves elected as mayor.

Meanwhile, at the insistence of Ponnuthamby, caste was symbolically abolished during a reception organised at the house of Rassendren. The decree of 21 September 1881 allowed Indians to renounce their personal laws and adopt the common French civil code.[11] As a result, some Pondicherrians with Ponnuthamby Poullé (who had adopted the French surname, La Porte) in the lead wanted to join the first list by renouncing their personal laws in favour of the French civil laws. Thus, came into existence the party of Renouncers. They were prevented, however, from joning the first list, as it was feared that the Renouncers might outnumber the Europeans there. Instead, a second list was created for the Renouncers, based on conditions, by the decree of 26 February 1884, due mainly, to the influence of the senator, Victor Schoelcher, who favoured the creation of such a list. The Renouncers were also not many in numbers but were given equal representation with the Europeans and Indians in the representative bodies. Many of the Renouncers were drawn from the 'lower' castes. Others were mostly government employees of the 'higher' castes.

The great majority of the Renouncers were Christians. On the whole, the Renouncers accounted for hardly 1,600 men in the five French territories in 1884-5 and just 2,861 in 1891.

Thenceforth, the Renouncers had their own political party called the 'Parti Libéral Renonçants' (Liberal Renouncers Party) and enjoyed preferential treatment in government employment reserved until then for the Indians who had not renounced their personal laws. They also filled in a good proportion of the jobs which were held previously by the Europeans. Besides, jobs were also created for them by reducing the diverse responsibilities of the salaried Europeans. There appeared judges, registrars, notaries, lawyers, councillors, etc., in the ranks of Renouncers. They sometimes enjoyed the same salaries as the Europeans. They also had their General Council, municipal and local council members. One of them was appointed to the privy council, and held the vice-president and the deputy mayor's posts. As such, the Renouncers, who were few and mostly Christian, enjoyed lucrative posts in government service and the administration. They joined hands with the first list politically. Despite its members forming the vast majority, this resulted in the overriding of the influence of the list of non-Renouncers. It was during this period that the foundation for a certain domination of Indian Christians in the administration and politics of French India was laid by men like Ponnuthamby La Porte, with the help of the Europeans.[12]

Very soon, due to pressure exerted, especially by Nadou Shanmugam, the Renouncers' list was abolished in 1899 by Governor François Pierre Rodier, which prevented, to some extent, the upward social mobility of the lower castes. However, a certain domination of Indian Christians continued even after the the Renouncer's list was abolished by the decree of 10 September 1899 and the Renouncers, whose numbers were always limited, were included in the first list of the Europeans, again under conditions.[13]

While Ponnuthamby La Porte, who himself belonged to the Poullé caste, was in favour of the fusion of castes and French civil laws, his rival, Nadou Shanmugam or Shanmuga Velayuda Mudaliar, wanted to uphold the caste system and the Hindu and Muslim personal laws. The latter was considered by some Frenchmen as being against progress and the French culture, civilisation and ideas. However, French political and economic institutions and culture of the capitalist democratic type had struck roots throughout French India by then, which the Hindus, including Nadou Shanmugham, and the Muslims hardly resisted. At the same time, it was felt that the lack of penetration of the French language among Hindus especially prevented them from being completely Europeanised or 'civilised'.[14]

The creation of the Renouncers list led some Muslims to petition the French government in 1892 for separate electorates, or a separate list for the Muslims, who numbered more than 28,000 in French India. They demanded equal representation with the Hindus in the various representative bodies. This was the first political demand of the Muslims. Neither Bandé Sahib, nor Ahamdou Sahib, the faithful supporters of the Tamil or Indian Party of Nadou Shanmugam were signatories to this petition. But the government refused to entertain the Muslims' demand, which had the potential to create a rift between Nadou Shanmugam and his Muslim supporters like Bandé Sahib.[15]

Already in the 1880s, there was Hindu-Muslim discord and even bloody riots in Pondicherry during the celebration of Jamsey in the *Place du Gouvernement* (presently Bharathi Park).[16] But, generally, the Muslims preferred to ally with Nadou Shanmugam, the protector of the caste system and custom. On the other hand, due probably to the creation of the Renouncers list, the Valangas or Untouchables of French India had never resorted to demanding a special list or reservation of seats for themselves as their counterparts did in British India. Many educated Valangas became part of the first list of voters when the Renouncers list was abolished in 1899. This situation could be attributed largely due to the relentless crusade of Ponnuthamby La Porte against caste and in favour of French egalitarian values and ideas.[17]

Nadou Shanmugam was a landholder and jurist who entered politics in the 1870s. Apart from his interventions in the debates at the General Council, he rarely appeared in public and lived in a modest house with his wife, supporters and astrologer.

Ponnuthamby, too, was a lawyer. Since 1868, the French allowed only the Valangas to wear shoes. But Ponnuthamby La Porte wanted this right to be extended to the Vellaja caste as well, to which he belonged. In short, Ponnuthamby was the anti-thesis of Nadou Shanmugam. However, when Ponnuthamby died in June 1886, there was opposition from some Europeans for his funeral ceremonies taking place in the Capuchin Church, reserved for the White community.[18]

Personal laws or French civil laws were manmade, on the basis of certain ideas and beliefs. Ponnuthamby staked his claim for power, equality (with the Europeans) and prestige on the basis of the French civil laws or ideas, which he considered as modern, progressive and rational. At the same time, Nadou Shanmugam asserted his power and mobilised the people on the plea of protecting the personal laws and ideas of the Hindus and Muslims. He earned the goodwill of the Muslims by intervening with the administrator of Karaikal in favour of them, so that the Hindus stopped playing music whenever their processions passed in front of mosques.

In both these cases, it is quite obvious that power was initimately and invariably related to an idea or a set of ideas. The French or European Party led by Armand Gallois-Montburn during this period stood, of course, for the supremacy of the French civil laws and ideas. It was considered as the party of the European industrialists (like Gaudart and Henri Gaebelé), Indian Christian professionals (like A. Gnanadicom of the Oulgaret commune) and rich Muslim traders. Gnanadicom was considered as the political agent of Gallois Montbrun during this period.[19]

After the sudden death of Ponnuthmaby, Nadou Shanmugam became the uncontested spokesman and leader of the overwhelming majority of Indians, who wanted to uphold custom. But, somewhat contradictorily, Shanmugam favoured secular education in the pure French tradition. He was a powerful landlord. He founded the Brahmanical Party, called also the Clerical Hindu Party or the Indian Party. In local parlance, it was known as Tamizhar Katchi or the Tamil Party. Some Frenchmen, like the magistrate, Gaston Pierre (mayor of Pondicherry in the 1890s), hailing from Lorraine, allied with this party to safeguard their position against the party of Ponnuthamby La Porte. Some 'higher' caste Tamil Christians like Louis Rassendran, agriculturist, notary, nominated member of the General Council from the second list and representative of the Renouncers of Karaikal, and

Saigon Louis Sinnaya Naidu, a printer and publisher, as well as the merchant of Karaikal, Bandé Sahib, also supported Shanmugam. Naidu was a very close associate of Shanmugam. So, he was called 'Mudaliar Naidu'.

At this juncture, it must nevertheless be conceded that French Indians above the age of 21 were exercising their franchise without any restrictions since the 1870s. They voted in parliamentary elections as well as the local and municipal elections and elected their own representatives, while nomination to the various legislative bodies was still the norm in British India. They were also trained in party politics since the 1870s, whereas in British India, the Indian National Congress was founded only in 1885 for all Indians. But unlike in French India, a party catering only to the Muslims, known as the All-India Muslim League was founded in 1906 in Dacca, which laid the ground for communal politics in British India. Shanmugham and other Indian candidates who contested in the elections were considered as Swadeshists or sympathisers of the Swadeshi Movement that grew in Bengal and northern India since 1905, when the Congress Party split into the moderate and extremist (Swadeshi) factions.[20]

Louis Rassendran was actually the successor of Ponnuthamby La Porte, according to the latter's wish. Rassendran contended that La Porte, through his efforts, united the Renouncers with the 'grand French family'. But it is strange to note that he was supporting Nadou Shanmugham of the third list. Therefore, it appears that he was not a worthy successor of Ponnuthamby.[21]

It is noteworthy that, even during this early period of electoral politics, members of different political parties and factions accused one another of corruption, goondaism and electoral frauds. It was as if the introduction of democracy into French India by the French had spawned corruption, goondaism and electoral fraud.[22] This is actually true to a great extent because democracy was an idea that existed in French India as implemented by the French. This idea was translated into a certain reality by conferring voting rights on people, who, in turn, elected their representatives to rule over them. Democracy was not just limited to this system. It also entailed a continuous competition for power and prestige on the basis of a certain set of ideas or ideology between individuals or groups of individuals called

Administration and Politics

political parties. The principle of competition was central to the type of democracy introduced by the French in Pondicherry. It was not at variance with the economic, educational and administrative systems put in place by the French, which also functioned largely on the basis of a certain competition. Right from the primary school classrooms, the students were trained to compete with one another. Competition was at the core of modern civilisation in most of its aspects. Competition for power and prestige was one of its aspects. It goes without saying that competition can never happen in a peaceful, stressless, tensionless and non-conflictual atmosphere. That is why we find the individuals involved in this competition for power, prestige and profits resorting to every possible means to acquire them, including corruption, goondaism and various frauds. It is actually the competitive democratic system put in place by the French which had produced all this. The individuals, left to themselves, would not have indulged in them.

Frenchmen got elected regularly to the National Assembly with the support of Nadou Shanmugam. Gaston Pierre became mayor of Pondicherry with his help. Certain French governors, like Louis Jean Girod, also supported Shanmugam. Shanmugam's power expanded with the abolition of the Renouncers list. But Shanmugam favoured the 'higher' castes for government jobs, even over the legitimate rights of the 'lower' castes and Europeans in the field. Besides, he was accused of favouring his own caste members in the selection of the commune mayors at the expense of Vanniyars, who were the most numerous in French India, especially in places like Villianur and Oulgaret. Shanmugam also enjoyed the support of some die-hard caste Christian Renouncers, like Louis Rassendran. In 1890, Rassendran was accused of forgery and imprisoned. Nadou Shanmugam had, in his possession, some documents to prosecute Rassendren. He did not use them against Rassendren. Instead, he got him out of prison in exchange for his support in the elections.[23] Thus, Nadou Shanmugam might be considered as the prinicipal inaugurator of electoral fraud, corruption and even goondaism in French India and Pondicherry.

It was generally believed that there was no chance for the 'lower' castes to climb up the social ladder as long as Shanmugam dominated politics, which assured the supremacy of the Vellajas and Reddiars, many of whom were landholders. As a result, some of the lower caste leaders like Nallava Sadasiva Naiker (hailing from Karaikal) broke away from Shanmugam. Thus, Shanmugam's out reach was weakened. Besides, in the 1890s, some Renouncers with the 'higher' caste Christian by the name of M.A. Gnanadicom (son-in-law of Ponnuthamby La Porte) in the lead, along with Sadasiva Naiker and his followers as well as Gnanou Diagou Mudaliar and Nandagobalu Chettiar (of the fishermen community), joined the French Party to counter the influence of Nadou Shanmugam.[24]

Among the Europeans, the industrialist Henri Gaebelé, hailing originally from Alsace in France, whose mansion was located at the present site of the Pondicherry general post office, emerged as the foremost leader of the first list and the French Party, succeeding Gallois Montbrun. Newspapers, like *Vikata Prathapan*, edited by Sinnasamy Poullé, supported Shanmugam and his associate Bandé Sahib in the elections, against Sadasiva Naiker, whom it dismissed as a puppet in the hands of the white Frenchmen, incapable and having passed the law diploma exam in Pondicherry only after several attempts. Other newspapers, like *Hindu Nesan*, opposed Shanmugam. He was accused of siding with the Renouncers, who were considered enemies of the Hindus. Sinnasamy Poullé also published the English weekly called *The Indian Republic* during this period.

There was a certain awakening of political consciousness among Indians in Pondicherry in the last decades of the nineteenth century itself, with the introduction of representative democracy in French India. This consciousness was represented by men like Nadou Shanmugam, Bandé Sahib and Sinnasamy Poullé in its early period. Nadou Shanmugam's power became almost absolute in politics as well as the administration with the abolition of the second list of Renouncers in the summer of 1899 by Governor Rodier. But during his ascendancy, it is generally admitted that there was economic stagnation, financial difficulties, postponement of infrastructural works and budget deficits, favouritism towards Indians belonging to the 'higher' castes, not to speak of electoral terrorism and muscle power.[25]

In spite of the creation of the preceding councils, the power of its members was extremely limited. The councils functioned more or less like consultative or advisory bodies and never had executive or legislative powers. Instead, by the decree of 1840, all powers related to the administration of French India was vested with the governor, who acted since 1879 in collaboration with the 'chefs de Services' or chiefs of the various government departments, ranging from the judiciary to the police and postal services, who were all Frenchmen. Besides, the implementation of the democratic ideal was impeded to a great degree by the two-list voter system.[26] Further, Karaikal, Mahé, Yanam and Chandernagore were placed under an administrator, who were also Frenchmen up until the 1940s. Administrators were directly answerable to the governor. The municipal and local councils were only consultative or advisory bodies.

PONDICHERRY POLITICS, 1901-35

In November 1901, Nadou Shanmugam was arrested for electoral fraud and extortion. Later, Shanmugam fled to Valavanur (in British India) due to the violence and insecurity prevailing in Pondicherry. In the General Council elections held in 1906, the French Party led by the industrialist, Henri Gaebelé, captured power. Shanmugam's party lost the elections. In 1907, the communes of Pondicherry were redesigned which liberated the low caste Valangas from the domination of the Reddy landlords to a considerable extent. In the municipal elections held in September 1908, the French Party, headed by the industrialist Gaebelé, routed its opponents in all municipalities except Nettapakkam (where the Reddy landed aristocracy dominated), Mahé and Chandernagore.[27] Gaebelé became mayor of Pondicherry on 19 September 1908, defeating Gaston Pierre, the French ally of Nadou Shanmugam. He remained in that position till 15 May 1928. However, electoral fraud and violence had become commonplace by then in Pondicherry. The henchmen of Shanmugam and Sadasiva Naiker fought violently during every election since 1891.[28]

In 1908, some Swadeshists of Pondicherry wanted to organise a meeting at Odiansalai to collect funds for the victims of the Tuticorin riots. Some supporters of Shanmugam wanted to participate in this meeting. But Mayor Gaebelé banned this meeting. At that time, there was a clash between the Muslims of Kottakuppam of British India and the fishermen of Pondicherry led by the merchant C. Nandagobalou Chettiar and others.[29]

Nadou Shanmugham died in exile on 9 December 1908. He had no heir, and his wife was blind. Louis Sinnaya Gnanapragassa Mudaliar, the *dubash* and sub-director of Savanna mill, was elected in place of Nadou Shanmugam to the seat left vacant by the latter, with the help of Henri Gaebelé and his son-in-law Paul Goubert as well as the Valanga and Vanniyar votes. He defeated the lawyer, Couttia Sababady Poullé, the successor and friend of Nadou Shanmugam. This happened in spite of the fact that Louis Sinnaya was believed to have worked against the Valanga Catholics' social ascension. But later Sinnaya's election was invalidated according to the law as he did not know to read or write French.[30]

It was during this period in September 1908 that Subramania Bharathi, accused of sedition in British India, sought refuge in Pondicherry, along with some other members of the extremist faction of the Congress Party like Mandayam Srinivasachari and Neelakanta Brahmachari. In 1910, the barrister, V.V.S. Iyer, joined them, too. Bharathi was an ardent promoter and defender of the nationalist cause even in Pondicherry through the newspapers. He promoted the Swadeshi Steam Navigation Company of Tuticorin founded by V.O. Chidambaram in 1906. However, he was unaware that Darmanathan Prouchandy of Pondicherry was already indulging in the steam navigation business on his own in French Indochina since 1891. Darmanathan owned two steamers by the names of *Alexandre* and *Prouchandy*, which plied passengers, postal items and goods in the Mekong delta. Besides, Prouchandy was refused permission by the French colonial rulers of Saigon to ply a steamer by the South China Sea from Saigon to Thailand during 1893-5.

We do not know if Bharathi had heard of Nadou Shanmugam before he stepped into Pondicherry. But when the latter died, he made an inflated statement characterising Nadou as one of the greatest men, who shaped 'the Indian mother country'. It is possible that Bharathi made this statement because Nadou Shanmugam had fashioned himself as the great defender of Hindu or Indian interests, culture and personal laws.[31]

Aravindha (Aurobindo) Ghose, the Bengali nationalist and journalist, knowing that the Tamil nationalists like Bharathi had found a safe haven in Pondicherry, made his way to Pondicherry, in his turn, in April 1910, as 'he did not feel called upon to surrender on the warrant for sedition'. Ghose stood for violent methods in politics in his early days to overthrow the British and was a prominent leader of the extremist faction of the Congress Party. Bharathi and other nationalists expected Aravindha Ghose to take over the leadership of the nationalists in Pondicherry. They had given him adequate publicity in their journals, like *India, Vijaya, Karma Yogi,* and *Dharumam,* printed and published from Pondicherry. But Aravindha Ghose was not interested in politics anymore. He rather veered towards philosophy and spirituality. He would discuss such matters with his Tamil nationalist friends rather than politics. Bharathi was disappointed with Aravindha Ghose. Bharathi seemed wedded to the French values of liberty, equality and fraternity from the time he stepped into Pondicherry. His writings and literary productions during his stay in Pondicherry, especially after 1911, stand testimony to the fact that Bharathi had emerged as an uncompromising egalitarian, a socialist and a secularist.[32]

Besides, Aravindha Ghose and his colleagues like Nolini Kanta Gupta had also befriended some young, educated men of Pondicherry like Joseph Davidu, Louis Rassendren, Du Tamby, Emmanuel Tetta, Adicéam, Le Vaillant de Pajanor, Sada Odayar and Marie Savary during their early years in Pondicherry.[33] In 1911, Lord Hardinge, the Viceroy of India, set at rest the rumour by which Aravindha Ghose was about to be extradited to Calcutta. At that time, some Pondicherry French newspapers like the *Indépendant* of the Dartnells supported Ghose's stay in Pondicherry alongwith a host of the Pondicherrians, in his capacity as a distinguished journalist. Some other newspapers, like *Suryothayam* of Saigon Chinniah Naidu and *Le Petit Pondichérien* (Puduvai Vasi) of Kasturirangan, were also supportive of the nationalist stand of Bharathi.[34]

Further, in the year 1910, the Frenchman, Paul Bluysen, was elected to the National Assembly in Paris with the support of the Tamil Party or Indian Party, and Nadou Shanmugam's allies Gaston Pierre, etc. Sadasiva Naiker had supported Paul Bluysen during this election. He emerged as the successor of Nadou Shanmugam, though he belonged to the 'lower' caste of Vanniyars. He had even allied with the powerful Reddiar and Vellala castes against the Valangas. He openly declared that he wanted Brahmanism to triumph over Catholicism. But Paul Bluysen did not consider his supporters of the Indian Party as Indian nationalists or Swadeshists, though it was obvious that the Swadeshi movement that started in Bengal in 1905 and the foundation of the All-India Muslim League in Dacca had had their influence in the French territories of India including Pondicherry. Paul Bluysen later switched sides and joined the 'French' Party of Gaebelé. When Sadassiva Naiker left the French Party, his place was taken by Sellane Naiker.[35]

Saigon Louis Sinnaya was one of the prominent Swadeshi faces during this period. His meetings were banned by the French governor. Subramania Bharathi used to write in his newspaper, *Suryothayam*, which was no doubt a Swadeshi newspaper and, therefore, seditious to the British. The British thought that Swadeshi terror emanated from Pondicherry. In Karaikal, there was the Tamil newspaper, *Kalamegam*, which was definitely nationalist and reformist in tone. It stood for Hindu-Muslim unity and the abolition of the caste system.[36] It was also in full praise of Muslim rule as 'there was no famine, no plague and no money that went out of India. Indian money remained in India. . . . There were intermarriages. There was no difference as black and white during Muslim rule. . . . Because of the English we obtained many benefits, we all became "Indians". . .'[36]

Bluysen refused to accept the accusation that the seven British Indians who had sought refuge in Pondicherry since 1908, including Bharathi and Aravindha Ghose, were anti-French. The convention of 1876 prevented the extradition to British India of these political refugees.[37] Paul Bluysen was opposed by Henri Gaebelé, Gnanou Diagou (proprietor, jurist, General Council member and mayor of Ariyankuppam), Vallabhadassou (jurist related to J. David) and M.A. Gnanadicom (proprietor).[38]

Electoral violence, arson, robbery and murder was the order of the day during that period, as it was during the time of Nadou Shanmugam. Nandagobalu Chettiar, the Mukkuwa (fishermen's caste) leader, merchant and deputy of Henri Gaebelé, Sadasiva Naiker, Manjini

Kavundan, Paul Goubert, Pierre Gaston, Couttia Sababady Pajanirassa Poullé, Louis Sinnaya, Narayanasamy Naiker of Kosapalayam were largely involved in this violence with their respective 'bandes' or gangs of anti-socials.[39] But the French Party triumphed in most of the subsequent elections to the various councils against the Opposition, led by Gaston Pierre and the Tamil Party, or the Indian (Hindu) Party. Couttia Sababady Poullé became the chief of this party after May 1913 when Sadasiva Naiker died. Couttia thus emerged as a sort of Indian nationalist who wanted to defend Indian or Hindu interests following the departures of Nadou Shanmugam and Sadasiva Naiker. He then admitted the lawyer, Joseph Davidu Poullé, into the party. Gnanou Diagou Mudaliar also finally opted to join the party of Couttia Sababady Poullé. Together, they countered the French Party, led by Henri Gaebelé in the elections.[40]

In the election to the National Assembly held peacefully in April 1914, Gaebelé, mayor of Pondicherry, revised his position and supported Paul Bluysen against another Frenchman, Lemaire, who had the support of Gaston Pierre and the Indian (Hindu) Party under Couttia Sababady. In this election, the French philosopher and lawyer, Paul Richard, who had freshly come from France with his wife, Blanche Rachel Mirra Alfassa, also contested. There were two Tamil candidates, a certain Rajamanickam and the lawyer, La Porte, son of Ponnuthamby La Porte. It appears that at first Subramania Bharathi canvassed for Paul Richard, along with his aide, Venugopala Naiker. But very soon, realising the mood of the people, he extended his support to Paul Bluysen. Paul Richard was squarely defeated by Paul Bluysen. Bluysen obtained 33,155 votes, while Lemaire got 5,628, La Porte 372, Paul Richard 233 and Rajamanickam 2 ballots.[41]

Paul Richard stood for an East-West philosophical synthesis and the advent of the supra-nervous man. He also wanted to 'normalise' the Hindus. He had enjoyed the support of Subramania Bharathi, who, it is believed, introduced Paul Richard and his French wife of Jewish descent, who dabbled in occultism, to Aravindha Ghose. But the latter did not remember with certainty the person who brought Paul Richard to him.[42]

Later in the early 1920s, Ghose himself (as well as James H. Cousins) translated some of Paul Richard's French books into English under the titles, *To the Nations, Wherefore of the Worlds* and *The Dawn over Asia*.[43] Paul Richard seems to have parted company with his wife, Mirra Alfassa, in the early 1920s. He left Pondicherry for good, due to the misunderstandings that developed between him and his wife with regard to the latter's relationship with Ghose, now known as Rishi Aurobindo.[44] Paul Richard was never known to have divorced Mirra Alfassa.

In the First World War that followed, Pondicherry participated by sending 786 men to the theatres of the colonial wars in Europe and Africa. Pondicherrians also contributed gold coins and money to the war treasury. Most of the Pondicherry soldiers belonged to the Créole, Renouncer and Valanga groups.[45] Thomas Arul Poullé, General Council member and proprietor of Karaikal, contributed generously to the war fund. Other prominent contributors were Calvé Soupraya Chettiar, Ibrahim Isaack Sait, 'Chevalier' Saverican Prouchandy, Manjini Naiker, Gnanou Diagou, M.P. Virapoullé (Karaikal), Kader Sultan Maricar (Karaikal) and Louis Sinnaya.[46] It is noteworthy that Subramania Bharathi who was in exile in Pondicherry at that time was overjoyed at the fact that Tamil soldiers were being sent to Europe to fight in the war. Later, on 3 April 1934, when Jospeh Davidu was mayor of Pondicherry a war memorial was erected on the beach front to commemorate the memory of the Frenchmen and Pondicherry Tamils who had fallen in the battlefields of France and Africa.[47]

Some Pondicherrians who excelled on the war front were honoured and decorated by the French state. Of them, the most prominent was Abdul Cader of the 4th Regiment of French Colonial Infantry of Morocco, who fought the Germans in Morocco and was severely wounded on 10 June 1916. Among other prominent Tamil Pondicherrians who were victims fighting the Germans in France and/or were honoured for their bravery and valour were Roc Victor Simonel, a civil engineer in the French army, Gnanousamy Ludovic, Brigadier in the 83rd Heavy Artillery Regiment (awarded *Croix de Guerre* for his bravery), and Marie Joseph Faife.[48]

It was during the First World War that Mohandas Karamchand Gandhi joined the Congress Party and entered British Indian politics. He introduced the concept of satyagraha in his agitations against British colonialism. He and the Ali brothers, Shaukat Ali and

Mohamed Ali Jauhar, jointly launched the Non-Cooperation and Khilafat Movements against the British in 1920. This forced Muhammad Ali Jinnah to quit the Congress. He remained a leader of the Muslim League. The influence of the Gandhian Movement was hardly felt in Pondicherry and Karaikal. The people in these territories were busy with their own politics.[49] During this period, there was a French periodical called *Le Collégien*, run by some old students at the Colonial College of Pondicherry, like Léon Saint Jean, who wrote about the Indian motherland and the soul of India. It looked forward to an Indian Renaissance and autonomy for India.[50]

The ascendancy of the French Party under Gaebelé in French Indian politics contributed to the awakening of the 'lower castes' to a great extent. Valangas (Parayars) were admitted thenceforth into the police force. They also benefitted from loans for the first time. In the year 1907, an association called 'Reveil Social' (Social Awakening) was founded to promote the interests of the Valangas. In 1908, the Sacred Heart Church was inaugurated. Valanga Christians contributed greatly for its construction. But Hindu Valangas were not admitted entry into the various temples in Pondicherry town during Nadou Shanmugam's period. Shanmugam even prevented the French governor from entering the ancient Villianur temple. The lack of a temple for the Valangas was remedied when, through the efforts of Tandu Chandra Subbaraya Poullé, a temple for the Valangas/Parayars came into existence. This temple was called the 'Tandu Mariamman' temple.

The French Party enjoyed the support of the numerous Valangas and Vanniyars. Thus, there was present a political cleavage between the 'lower' and 'higher' castes during this period. The former had actually thrown in their lot with the French Party led by French capitalists like Henri Gaebelé against the domination of the 'higher' castes in French Indian politics during Nadou Shanmugam's period and even afterwards. With the death of Shanmugam, and the ascendancy of Gaebelé, the alliance forged by the former with the Muslims and Muslim leaders like Bandé Sahib broke down and there were increasing instances of conflicts between Hindus and Muslims, especially in Karaikal.[51]

In 1918, Henri Gaebelé, mayor of Pondicherry, opposed the extradition of Aravindha Ghose to British India.[52] In 1922, Gaebelé was elected senator and in 1924 re-elected as president of the General Council. But due to ill-health, he renounced these posts. Gnanou Diagou had been the pillar of Gaebelé's party for the past 18 years.[53]

Nandagobalu Chettiar remained the henchman of Gaebelé. In September 1919, he declared that the administration, police and justice was in his hands. The Frenchman, Robert Goubert-Gaebelé, the adopted son of Henri Gaebelé, also assisted the latter in all his enterprises during that period. He succeeded Henri Gaebelé as president of the General Council. Father and son were accused of corruption and embezzlement in the work related to the consolidation of the harbour. Not only that, Gaebelé was also accused of nepotism, unlike Shanmugam. Gaebelé's family members controlled the political institutions and the economic life of Pondicherry.

In February 1924, Gnanou Diagou left the French Party of Gaebelé and somehow got Couttia Poullé to his side. The latter being ailing and old, Gnanou Diagou virtually led the party against Gaebelé's. Couttia Poullé died in 1924. Louis Sinnaya always remained an indefatigable opponent of Henri Gaebelé, until he died on 17 May 1925.[54]

Joseph Davidu (son-in-law of advocate M.D. Vallabhadassou, editor of *Sree Soudjana Ranjani*, who died in 1926), was earlier with Couttia Poullé's's party. He had entered politics in 1919, with the help of the French Créole leader, Gallois Montbrun. He then joined Gaebelé's French Party. These were the two great parties of French India. As for Couttia Poullé's party, it was a diluted version of Nadou Shanmugam's Hindu/Tamil Party.[55]

In December 1927, Rathina Sellane Naiker, a former ally of Gaebelé, joined the Hindu Party of Couttia Poullé after the latter's death. Thomas Arul of Karaikal, too, joined the Hindu Party. Thus Davidu, Diagou, Thomas and Sellane as well as Benjamin Thiroux were all in the same party. The party was renamed as the Franco-Hindu Party. In the election to the General Council, Thomas Arul succeeded in capturing the post of president of the General Council. On 13 May 1928, this party won the municipal elections against Gaebelé's party. On 9 December 1928, the French candidate, Dr Eugène Le Moignic, of the Franco-Hindu Party was elected as senator, while Pierre Dupuy was elected to the National Assembly with the support of the same party. Very soon, Gnanou Diagou broke off with the clan of Davidu and Thomas and was evicted from the party.[56]

Datchinamurthy Chettiar, deputy mayor of Pondicherry and chief of the fishermen, as well as Edouard Goubert, the court registrar, along with Selvarajulu Chettiar and Robert Goubert Gaebelé, had backed Henri Gaebelé in the elections. The latter refused to admit that a Catholic, Thomas Arul, who, he said, owed everything to him joined with the Hindu, Sellane Naiker, to oppose him. On the other hand, he told Virapoullé that, as a Hindu member of the General Council from Karaikal, he must not support Thomas Arul as he was a Catholic. It is worthwhile to note at this juncture that Datchinamurthy Chettiar, was a leader of fishermen, merchants and proprietor of the charcoal park at the southern end of the Cours Chabrol. He was related to both Nandagobalu Chettiar and Selvarajalu Chettiar.[57]

In the municipal elections held in French India in May 1928 to elect the mayors and deputy mayors, the Frenchman Jules Guerre was elected mayor of Pondicherry, with K. Rathinavelu Poullé and Joseph Davidu as deputy mayors. R. Sellane Naiker was elected mayor of Oulgaret, while the landlord, Thomas Arul Poullé, was elected mayor of Karaikal and the merchant Virapoullé became his deputy. In the same year, on 19 April, the Frenchman, Jean Coponat, was elected deputy of French India to the National Assembly, with the support of Sellane Naiker, Thomas Arul and Joseph Davidu's Franco-Hindu Party. Rathinavelu Poullé and Gnanou Ambroise were prominent members of this party. Gradually, Joseph Davidu became the uncontested leader of the Franco-Hindu Party.[58] Thus the rout of Gaebelé's party was complete.

During this period, the Tamil weekly, *Niyayabhimani*, published from Karaikal, was one of those rare papers that adopted a deliberately nationalist tone. It gave prominence to the confiscation of Bharathi's patriotic songs at several places in British India. It stood for Swarajya (self-rule) in everything. We have also the *Desasevagan*, which was definitely nationalistic, advocating against some aspects of Western civilisation, but also against Untouchability and dowry, and in favour of Hindu, Muslim and Christian unity. The paper also took up the cause and defence of Pondicherrians. It complained that at least 8 out of 10 clerks, writers and *mestrys* in the Rodier mill were outsiders and wanted those jobs to be given to Pondicherrians who knew English. Besides, more than 4,000 workers in the mills were outsiders, too, not to speak of the businessmen and traders who had come to Pondicherry from Madurai, selling their goods at a higher price and draining the income of the Pondicherrians. These migrants who were poor when they came some 15 years ago were now rich, having houses, farms, cash, etc., and were a hindrance to the prosperity of local businessmen. The paper suggested taxing of every migrant at the rate of one rupee per person to turn Pondicherry into a wealthy city, or 'Kubera Pattanam'. It also complained that there were fewer and fewer farmers in Pondicherry.[59]

The nationalist journal, *Deshabandhou*, opined that Sellane Naiker followed in the footsteps of Nadou Shanmugham and Sadasiva Naiker and wanted to protect and promote the interests of the Tamils/Hindus. The paper considered Gnanou Diagou Mudaliar as the enemy of Tamils and Tamil rule since 1901.[60]

On 11 September 1928, Paul Bluysen, who was then senator, died. At the end of November 1928, there was election to the General Council. Joseph Davidu was elected to the council. Subsequently, Thomas Arul became the president of the General Council. Rathinavelu Poullé and Joseph Davidu were secretaries to the council. Some other members of the council were Rathina Sellane Naiker, P. Danaraja Poullé, Henri Gaebelé, S. Perumal Naiker, Gallois-Montbrun Lucien, Joseph Rassendran, Gnanou Diagou Mudaliar and P. Ramachandra Naiker. One could say at this juncture that the General Council was almost entirely in the hands of Tamils.[61]

In the elections to decide a senator from French India held in December 1928, once again, a Frenchman by the name of Eugène Le Moignic was elected with the support of the Franco-Hindu Party, and its leader Sellane Naiker, against the French Jewish billionaire, Le Dreyfus. It was the habit of French aristocrats and millionaires of France who had no chance of getting elected in France to the French parliament, to get themselves elected from French India, sometimes even without setting foot there. Right from the time of Shanmugam to the period when Sellane Naiker and Joseph Davidu gained prominence in French Indian politics, this remained the dominant trend.[62]

The Franco-Hindu Party held sway in Pondicherry politics, assembly and municipality for about 10 years, starting from 1928. Sellane Naiker was not hostile to the French at that time. But there was already a rift in the Franco-Hindu Party, with Thomas Arul joining hands with Davidu, on caste basis, it was said, against Sellane Naiker.[63] Sellane Naiker insisted that the system of two lists must be abolished, while Davidu and Thomas wanted its maintenance at least temporarily as they were elected easily from the first list of Europeans, Créoles and Renouncers, with just a few voters. They seem to have been convinced that they would lose this advantage if the two lists were to be merged. Besides, it is noteworthy that the Muslims of Karaikal, for their own reasons were not in favour of the abolition of the two-list system.[64]

In 1930, Gandhi launched the Civil Disobedience Movement in British India. Many Congressmen and nationalists fled to Pondicherry to escape arrest and persecution. There were many sympathisers of the Gandhian Movement and the Congress Party during this period in French India. It was during this period that labour and farmer unrests started.[65]

As a matter of fact, the year 1928 was the beginning of the decline of the clan of Henri Gaebelé and Nandagobalu/Selvarajalu Chettiar. The latter monopolised the transit of goods by chelingue in the port of Pondicherry and had enriched himself in the process. Already in 1927, Selvarajalu had men under his orders who indulged in violence against and exerted political pressure on the candidates of the Franco-Hindu Party. In 1929, the High Court of Pondicherry had ordered Selvarajalu Chettiar, son of the Kurusukuppam stevedore Nandagobalu Chettiar, to pay 200 francs in damages and spend two months in jail for having threatened and manhandled Sellane Naicker and 13 other members during the council meeting. Selvarajalu's friends, Subbaroyan and Rajagopal, were imprisoned for one month. However, during that period, the Gaebelé-Selvarajalu combine had the support of the French governor as well as that of the lawyer, Gnanou Diagou Mudaliar.[66]

In the riots of November 1931, C. Dakshinamurhty Chettiar's boats were attacked by the boats of the Saravana Chettiar group. All those arrested in the attack were condemned to two-three months in prison and slapped a fine of 16 to 25 francs. Dakshinamurthy Chettiar was related to Selvarajalu Chettiar. Saravana Chettiar, a rival of Sevarajalu, hailed from Vamba Keerapalayam, though his house was located in the town at the intersection of Gandhi Road and the Tillé Maistry Street.[67]

In 1932, Selvarajalu dabbled in Karaikal politics. He was accused of trying to buy the support of a Karaikal member at a sum of 10,000 rupees. He was also criticised for allying with Europeans like Henri Gaebelé and Gallois Montbrun against the interests of the Tamils and committing atrocities at their behest as also having connections with known criminals like Zainulabidin, Pulikuti Natesan and Arumuga Padayachi. It is surprising to note that Gnanou Diagou Mudaliar was in the company of Selvarajalu Chettiar when they met Zainulabidin in Villianur. Gnanou Diagou also defended Zainulabidin in a criminal case. Robert Gaebelé, too, was in touch with the latter. In the power politics that existed in Pondicherry during this period, there was a certain alliance and convergence of interests between Gaebelé, Gnanou Diagou and Selvarajalu against the ruling combine of Sellane Naiker, etc. It is believed that the former had the support of the French governors.[68]

There were frequent clashes between the boatmen owing allegiance to Selvarajulu Chettiar of Kurusukuppam in the northern coastal part of Pondicherry and Saravana Chettiar, stevedore of Vamba Keerapalayam. J. Davidu defended the interests of the latter in the courts. There were also frequent clashes between Chettiar's Pattinava men and the other castes, like the Vanniyars, especially in the coastal villages. As a matter of fact, Selvarajalu Chettiar and Saravana Chettiar monopolised the transport of goods by chelingue, to the detriment of small boat-owners and traders.[69] Selvarajulu Chettiar was a dark, plump man. He had two large diamonds adorning his ears. His brother's name was Krishnaradja Chettiar. Dakshinamurthy Chettiar, paternal uncle of Selvarajulu, was the chief of the Mukkuwa community.[70]

In 1931, Selvarajulu Chettiar wanted to strike out on his own. He organised a labour conference on Odiansalai ground in September. It was attended by influential leaders from Tamil Nadu like P. Subbaroyan, barrister and landlord, K.S. Kannappar, as well as C.R. Srinivasan, the editor of the nationalist daily, *Sudesamitran*. It seems he had the blessings of the then French governor, François Adrien Juvanon.[71]

One of the major achievements of the Franco-Hindu Party which was in power was with regard to the Salt Rent which was paid by British India directly to the French government in Paris. From 1931, this rent, which amounted to Rs. 4,00,000 was paid to the colonial government in Pondicherry. This was a great financial relief to the Pondicherry budget.[72]

In 1933, Rathina Sellane Naiker was the president of the General Council. He was the first Tamil Hindu to hold that position. He was considered as a 'young Tamil strongman' by *Dupleix* newspaper. The paper accused Thomas Arul and Davidu of favouring Christians when the former was holding that post to the detriment of the Hindus. *Dupleix* considered Sellane Naiker and Selvarajalu Chettiar as having brought honour to the Hindus.[73] It is noteworthy at this juncture that C. Dakshinamurthy Chettiar was the owner of *Dupleix*. He was the paternal uncle of Selvarajulu Chettiar. Bharathidasan's articles were regularly published in *Dupleix*.

But in the course of time, Sellane Naiker seems to have meddled with European officials working for the French Indian administration. He thought that their numbers were more than necessary. Besides, they were drawing huge salaries, much more than the Indian officials, being paid out of the colonial budget. Naturally, the French officials were not happy with Sellane and seem to have considered him as pro-Indian nationalist.[74]

However, Sellane seems to have had the reputation of never coming to the help of the mill workers. He was at loggerheads with Davidu. In spite of Sellane being the president from the second list, nothing practically changed with regard to the quasi-monopoly enjoyed by the first list, which included Europeans, Créoles and Renouncers, who were mostly Christians, in government posts, especially at the higher level, while smaller and lower paid posts were left to the second list voters. Besides, all the presidents of the various councils and the Chambers of Agriculture and Commerce, and the privy council were under the influence or in the hands of the first list men, who also managed the income and expenditure of the colony. It was the same in Karaikal where all important posts were occupied by Christians. It was to remedy this situation that Sellane had always stood for the abolition of the two lists and the creation of a common list. But

Thomas Arul and Davidu would not accept that. It was, therefore, openly said that about 600 people of the first list who were mainly Christians ruled over 60,000 people of the second list.[75]

This gave rise to resentment against the Christians, who styled themselves as 'French Indians' and dominated administration and politics in French India. Some demanded communal representation for Hindus, Muslims and the 'low' castes in education and the administration, as it was in Madras Presidency of British India where non-Brahmins enjoyed communal representation in the services, education and government employment. The French governors were accused of showering favours on Christians. Papers like *Dupleix* crticised Hindus and those like *Baradam* supported Christians like Davidu and Thomas Arul. *Dupleix* called for the establishment of a non-Christian movement to protect the interests of the Hindus and Muslims and the 'low' castes, on the lines of the non-Brahmin movement of Madras. In its turn, *Baradam* accused Dupleix of trying to create a rift between Christians and the Hindu Valangas.[76]

Dupleix even criticised the Nangaiyar Nalvazhi Sangam, which it said, was controlled by the family members of Davidu. It accused the Sangam of never submitting its accounts inspite of receiving large amounts of money from the government to help widows and the poor. It also maintained that the Sangam was used by Davidu's family members to get government jobs.[77]

But Davidu took the initiative to adopt a new law as per which a maximum of at least 50 votes were necessary in every commune, instead of the usual 20, for the maintenance of the first list. As in Chandernagore, Mahé and Yanam, there were just 20 or 30 votes on the first list, the election to the first list was abolished, whereas in Pondicherry and Karaikal, the first list continued to function.[78]

As a result, during the assembly and municipal elections held in 1934, it seems that the French administration wanted to defeat Sellane Naiker at all costs. It also seems that the police, goondas and officials unleashed a reign of terror and arson in Pondicherry to frighten the voters and rig the election in favour of Davidu's party. During that period, sub-inspector Raphael Dadala had claimed to have been supportive of Sellane Naiker, in spite of threats from the French officials, and confronted the police and the goondas with their own men. The police chief, Aziz Khan, was a supporter of Joseph Davidu.[79]

Since 1928, Selvarajulu had emerged as a great shipping magnate, respected in Pondicherry and south India. He had also earned a name as a philanthropist. In 1922, he had taken over the business of his father Nandagobalu Chettiar when he was just 20 years old. Very soon, he extended it with offices at Madras, Pondicherry, Nagapattinam, Cuddalore, Masulipatnam, Vishakapatnam and Kakinada. Selvarajulu Chettiar and C. Balasubramanian were General Council members from Yanam in 1934. Selvarajulu helped some students in Yanam financially to pursue their studies. Later, he agreed to donate land in Tirubhuvanai for a hospital. He even helped some harbour workers to build houses in Vemba Keerapalayam.

Selvarajulu Chettiar also involved himself in the celebration of Hindu religious festivals. He patronised the famous Macy Magam festival of the Pondicherry region. Macy Magam was a Hindu festival celebrated since very early times at Tirukanji river, near Villianur. But since 1905, Macy Magam was celebrated in Pondicherry itself. The idol of Subramanya was brought down from Mailam which was about 25 kilometres towards the west of Pondicherry, with the permission of the chief of the Bommiarpalayam Mutt, who was the administrator of the Mailom temple. The idol of Subramanya was brought down in a procession with twenty of his divine consorts. The procession used to stop at Vanur, Mortandi, Sarom and Pudupalayam, before it reached the Balaya Swamigal Mutt's premise in Mission Street (Pondicherry) from where the idol was taken to Vaithikuppam for a ritual bath in the sea. Selvarajulu Chettiar whose magnificent mansion stood near the seashore used to throw a grand feast on the occasion to the personalities of the town, both French and Tamil. The next day God Subramanya, seated on a silver peacock, was taken in procession through the streets of the town before it wound its way back to Mailom by the same route.[80] The participation of Selvarajulu Chettiar in such festivals earned him a very good name among the people of Pondicherry.

In 1934, Joseph Davidu was again elected to the General Council. When Lucien Gallois Montbrun, mayor of Pondicherry, died in 1934, Joseph Davidu became the interim mayor. Henri Gaebelé being old and ill, Davidu became mayor of Pondicherry in February the very next year, with the patronage of the French governor Léon Solomiac. Even then, he was accused of being against the workers. However, an

Indian/Tamil had at last become mayor of Pondicherry. Davidu had Rathinavelu Poullé, the businessman of Pondicherry, as his deputy. In 1936-8, Thomas Arul of Karaikal was the president of the General Council. In 1934, there were no municipal elections and the system of conducting elections every three years was changed to holding polls every six years. But in 1936, Sellane Naiker was defeated in the elections and that left the field clear for the Davidu-Thomas combine to dominate politics in Pondicherry and Karaikal. On 12 July 1936, B.A. Muthukumarappa Reddiar, was elected mayor of Nettapakkam and his deputy was C.T. Gurusamy Reddiar. He was already municipal councilor in 1914. Muthukumarappa Reddiar hailed from a modest background. He became mayor with the help of Joseph Davidu in compensation for the services he had rendered to him. Later, he was appointed as president of the municipal commission. He held that post until 1942. Davidu had also got him elected to the local council of Pondicherry. In 1934, Muthu Poullé, the brother of Rathinavelu Poullé, entered politics as a lieutenant of Joseph Davidu. He got himself elected to the local council of Pondicherry.[81]

It is quite obvious from the above that French Indians, especially from Pondicherry, were embroiled in their own internal politics, disconnected from what was happening in British India. Apart from rare occasions, when Pondicherrians showed their sympathy to the Gandhian Movement, into which we shall go into briefly in the next chapter, they were least influenced by the Freedom Movement that was developing in British India under Gandhi. Primarily, there was a rift between the first and second list voters, which led to the growth of an anti-Christian movement in Pondicherry on the lines of the anti-Brahmin movement in Madras Presidency among certain Hindus, especially in the 1930s, who resented the domination of Christians in the administration and politics of French India. The most prominent among them were Sellane Naiker, Bharathidasan and C. Dakshinamurthy Chettiar. But all these three men seem to have had different agendas and never unified to launch a full scale anti-Christian movement in French India. Bharathidasan's actions were particularly motivated by the influence exerted by the Self-Respect Movement, founded in 1925 by E.V. Ramasamy Naiker in Tamil Nadu. However, the anti-Christian movement did not gain momentum and petered out in the course of time with the outbreak of the Second World War and the subsequent abolition of the two-list system. The Chrisitian leaders were certain that their domination would end if the two lists were abolished in favour of a common list of voters. Therefore, they delayed or resisted as much as they could the adoption of a common list.

The preceding pages have also brought to fore, the fact, that Frenchmen were freely participating in French Indian and Pondicherry politics and even dominating it for a considerable period of time due to the existence of the two-list voting system. Opposition to their dominance never arose as long as Nadou Shanmugam, the defender of Hindu and Muslim personal laws, and Henri Gaebelé, the French industrialist wedded to French values and culture, were alive. But with their disappearance from the political scene, men like Sellane Naiker dared to challenge their dominance as well as the dominance of the Tamil Christian Renouncers, who were one with the former group, belonging as they did, to the same list. It must not be forgotten that it was during the period of dominance of Europeans in French Indian politics that 'lower' caste men, like Sellane Naiker and Selvarajalu Chettiar, could rise to prominence in Pondicherry politics, while the Brahmins, the topmost among the Hindu castes, were simply conspicuous by their absence in politics and also the administration, unlike in the Madras Presidency of British India. This also facilitated to a considerable extent the rise of the Valangas in the educational, employment and political fields of Pondicherry.

It is nevertheless noteworthy that it was the French who introduced democracy in the Indian soil, though it was vitiated to a great extent by the two-list voter system. It was they who also gave Indians of all castes and religions the opportunity to adopt a Uniform Civil Code right from the 1880s. But the great majority of Indians, both Hindus and Muslims, preferred to stick to their own personal laws rather than adopt the Uniform French Civil Code by renouncing them. The French Uniform Civil Code was generally misunderstood by both Hindus and Muslims as an attempt by the French colonisers to de-Indianise them and make them full-fledged French citizens. Nadou Shanmugam and his Tamil Party became the champions of maintenance of Hindu and Muslim personal laws, while there arose other Tamils, mainly Christians, who preferred to adopt the Uniform French Civil Code and its values. These were the two ideas—the Tamil or Indian idea, represented by Nadou Shanmugam and the French idea, whose foremost representative was Ponnuthamby La Porte. It was around these that politics revolved and evolved, in one way or another, until the two-list voter system was abolished in 1945. Nadou Shanmugam, or rather some of his supporters like Saigon Chinniah, might have been sympathetic to the Swadeshi Movement that developed in Bengal, but never did the Swadeshi Movement, nor the later Gandhian Movements in the 1920s and 1930s, gain momentum in Pondicherry or French India, and become a mass movement, until well after the abolition of the two-list voter system. Otherwise, both Nadou Shanmugam and Ponnuthamby La Porte, as well as Henri Gaebelé and their successors preferred to operate within the economic, educational and administrative framework put in place by the French colonisers.

Nadou Shanmugam and his supporters and successors were the representatives and spokespersons of a certain Indianess or Tamilness. They were the protectors of certain Tamil values, customs and traditions. In fact, Nadou Shanmugam upheld the Tamil Hindu's caste system. His party was founded upon such ideas. But Ponnuthamby La Porte stood for the fusion of castes and upheld the French-inspired values of egalitarianism and fraternity, along with Frenchmen like Henri Gaebelé. No politician could set aside these ideas in the competition for power, prestige and profits within the political, economic and other frameworks put in place by the French. It was on the basis of such ideas and ideologies that politicians scrambled for power in French Indian politics. Ideas cannot be separated from the struggle for power and prestige, as Cambridge scholars like Anil Seal, Gordon Johnson and C.J. Baker note. They are one and the same process.

Before proceeding any further into the evolution of society and politics in Pondicherry leading towards the Freedom Movement, we would have to look into the influence exerted by certain stalwarts of British India, who visited Pondcherry or sought refuge there, on Pondicherry and French Indian society and politics.

NOTES

1. A. Martineau, *Inventaire des Anciennes Archives de l'Inde Française*, Pondichéry, 1931, pp. 18-19; Sridharan, *Papers on French Colonial Rule in India*, Calicut, 1997, pp. 87-8; Ann., 1841 (by E. Sicé), p. 258; Ann., 1938-9, p. 27.
2. Martineau. *Etablissements Français dans l'Inde*, Paris, 1931, pp. 46-7; Sridharan, op. cit., pp. 88, 90-1; Ann., 1935, p. 95; Mss.inde, c^2 214, ff. 7-156 and c^2 242, ff. 217-225, AN; Ann., 1938-9, p. 29.
3. Ann., 1841 (by Sicé), p. 272.
4. Jacques Weber, *Les Etablissements Français en Inde au XIXe Siècle (1816-1914)*, vol. I, Paris, pp. 479, 625; Morachini, *Les Indigènes de l'Inde Française et le Suffrage Universel*, Paris, 1883, pp. 9, 11, 15, 17-18.
5. Lettre d'un natif Indien aux Chambres Françaises, sur l'Exécution de l'Ordonnance Royale, 23 July 1840, concernant la représentation coloniale dna sles établissements français dans l'Inde, Paris, 1841; Weber, *Les Etablissements Français en Inde au XIXe siècle (1816-1914)*, vol. I, Paris, 1988, pp. 218-21, 674, 685; vol. III, p. 1507; J.B.P. More, *Freedom Movement in French India: The Mahé Revolt of 1948*, Tellicherry, 2001, pp. 50-1; Morachini, op. cit., p. 4; Ann., 1885, p. 34; Ann., 1841, pp. 119, 283-4; Sicé, Un Mot sur la Représentation des Etablissements Français de l'Inde à l'Assemblée Nationale, Pondicherry, 1848; Lettre d'un natif Indien—Concernant la Représentation Coloniale dans les Etablissements Français dans l'Inde, Pondicherry, 1840.
6. Weber, op. cit., vol. IV, p. 2059f ; Weber, *Pondichéry et les Comptoirs de l'Inde après Dupleix: La Démocratie au pays desCastes*, Paris, 1996, pp. 217-18, 221, 227-9.
7. More, op. cit., Ann., 1931, pp. 71-6, 161-2; Morachini, op. cit., p. 7; Weber, op. cit., 1988, vol. III, p. 1334; Ann., 1885, p. 307; Ann., 1935, p. 121.
8. Weber, op. cit., vol. IV, p. 2059f; vol. III, p. 1589.
9. Ibid., vol. IV, p. 2059f; Etablissements Français de l'inde, Textes et documents, p. 64, no. 5, AO, ADP; Antony, *Encyclopaedia of India*, Pondicherry, New Delhi, 1994, p. 100; Ann., 1885, pp. 34, 309-13; Ann, 1880, pp. 38-9; 289-91; Ann., 1935, pp. 130-1; Ann., 1938-9, p. 123; *l'Echo de Pondichéry*, 3 April 1887, p. 2; Weber, op. cit., 1996, pp. 246-7.
10. Martineau, op. cit., 1931, pp. 54-5; M.V. Pylee, *Constitutional History of India, 1600-1950*, Calcutta, 1967, p. 46.
11. Morachini, op. cit., p.11; Weber, op. cit., 1996, p. 235; Gnanadicom, *L'Inde Française, sa régénération*, Toulon, 1894.

12. *Le Progrés*, 1 April 1888, p. 118; *Le Patriote*, 15 March, pp. 1-3; 28 May 1898, pp. 47-9; *l'Indépendant*, 25 June 1897, p. 61; More, 'Muslim Specificities in French India during the Nineteenth Century', *Journal of the Institute for Research in Social Sciences and Humanities*, vol. 2, no. 1, January-June 2007, p. 126; Weber, op. cit., 1996, p. 243.
13. Martineau, op. cit., 1931, p. 55; Weber, op. cit., 1888, vol. III, pp. 1520, 1689; vol. IV, p. 2046.
14. Ibid., vol. IV, p. 2007; *l'Echo de Pondichéry*, 8, 29 May 19, 26 June 1887.
15. Ibid., vol. IV, pp. 2059-60; More, op. cit., 2007; Pétition des Musulmans Relative au Régime Électoral de l'Inde au Ministre de la Marine et des Colonies et aux Membres du Conseil Supérieur, 14 September 1892, Pondicherry.
16. Weber, op. cit., vol. IV, 2058; vol. I, 557-9; More, 'A Tamil Muslim Sufi', *Islam and Christian-Muslim Relations*, Birmingham, 1999; Inde 345, D. 176, Lettre de Richaud au Ministre, 18 October 1885, AOM.
17. *Le Progrés de l'Inde Française*, 7 November 1881, pp. 74-5.
18. *Vikata Prathapan*, 12 June 1889, p. 153; Weber, op. cit., vol. III, pp. 1403, 1410-12, 1712.
19. *Le Patriote*, 18 June 1898, p. 56; Lettre de Chanemougavelyoudamodélier à l'Administrateur de Karaikal, 4 June 1904 - Cultes, Police. Aff. Pol. Carton 231, Dossier 1, AOM.
20. *Madras Mail*, 30 November 1906; *Annales Coloniales*, Hebdo, 4 June 1908.
21. *Vikata Prathapan*, 24 February 1889, pp. 130-1; 19 June 1889, p. 155; *Le Jeune Patriote*, 16 May 1897, p. 47; 1 July 1897, p. 69; 1 September 1897, p. 98; 16 October 1897, p. 120; C. Antony, *Encyclopaedia of India*, Pondicherry, New Delhi, 1994, p. 101; Weber, op. cit., vol. III, pp. 1589, 1639, 1641, 1698-9; vol. IV, p. 2059; JO 1918, p. 184 *Sudesa Vartamani*, May 1909, no. 3; JO 1915, p. 465; JO 1915, I, p. 20; *Desasevagan*, 4 March 1924, 15; *l'Union Hindoue*, 17 June 1901, p. 31; *Le Progrès*, 1 April 1888, p. 118.
22. *Le Jeune Patriote*, 16 May 1897, p. 47; 1 July 1897, p. 69; 1 September 1897, p. 98; 16 October 1897, p. 120; 1 January 1898, pp. 2-4.
23. *Vikata Prathapan*, 6 April 1890 (supplement); 26 October 1890; 16 November 1890; Antony, op. cit., 1994, pp. 101-2; Weber, op. cit., vol. III, pp. 1647, 1734; JO 1935, p. 643; *l'Independant*, 25 July 1897; *Hindu Nesan*, April, May 1891; Jacques Weber, *Pondichéry et les Comptoirs de l'Inde après Dupleix : La Démocratie au pays des Castes*, Paris, 1996, p. 252.

24. *Sukapi Viruthini*, 15 March 1934; Antony, op. cit., 1994, pp. 102-4.
25. Martineau, *Etablissements Français dans l'Inde*, Paris, 1931, p. 51; Weber, op. cit., vol. IV, pp. 2008, 2010; vol. III, pp. 1622, 1639, 1734; *Vikata Prathapan*, December 1890; 26 October 1890, p. 1; 25 February 1891, p. 2; 7 December 1890, p. 2; 14 December 1890, p. 2; *The Hindu*, Metro Plus Pondicherry/Miscellany, 'A House with a History', 25 April 2007; *The Indian Republic*, 1889; Weber, op. cit., 1996, pp. 270-322.
26. Martineau, op. cit., pp. 51, 55-6.
27. *l'Union Hindoue*, 6 December 1901, p. 117; *Bulletin Officiel des EF de l'Inde.*, 1908, pp. 792-3; A.P. 723, D.4, Lettre d'Angoulvant, 19 June 1907, no. 30c, AOM.
28. Weber, op. cit., vol. IV, p. 2081; Antony, op. cit., pp. 104-6; Weber, op. cit., vol. IV, pp. 2033, 2041; Interview with Jean Kessavaram and Helene Prouchandy.
29. From Arthur Lawley, Political Department, to Governor of Pondicherry, Government House, 6 October 1909, p. 242; *Siècle*, 13 October 2008, p. 113; *Indes-Relation avec la France, Loges et Possessions Françaises*, 1907-9, no. 35, ADP; *Annales Coloniales*, Hebdo, Paris, 4 June 1908.
30. JO 1916, p. 619.
31. More, *Indian Steamship Ventures, 1836-1910: Darmanathan Prouchandy of Pondicherry, First Steam Navigator from South India, 1891-1900*, Pondicherry, 2013; *Suryodhyam*, 28 March 1909; *India*, 12 December 1908.
32. *Vijaya*, February 1910; *India*, 19 February 1910; P. Heehs, *The Bomb in Bengal. The Rise of Revolutionary Terrorism in India, 1900-10*, New York, 1993; More, *L'Inde Face à Bharati: Le Poète Rebelle*, Tellicherry, 2003.
33. Documents in the Life of Sri Aurobindo, *La Lettre du CIDIF*, no. 20, 1998, p. 87; Archival Notes: *Sri Aurobindo and the Mother, 1914-20*, pp. 85-6; Interview with N. Marimuthu, Jean Kessavaram; Sri Aurobindo, *Autobiographical Notes and Other Writings of Historical Interest*, Pondicherry, 2015, pp. 264-70; *The Hindu*, 8 November 1910.
34. *Le Petit Pondichérien*, 19, 26 August 1911; see *Suryothayam* issues; *l'Indépendant*, 8 June 1911.
35. *Sukapi Viruthini*, 15 March 1934; Weber, op. cit., vol. IV, pp. 2112, 2150; *Desasevagan*, 4 March 1924, p. 15.
36. *Kalamegam*, 23 September 1912, pp. 2-3; 9 January 1913; *Madras Times*, 7, 9 July 1911; 12 August 1912, pp. 4-5; 19 August 1912, pp. 2-3.

37. Antony, op. cit., 1994, p. 106; Weber, op. cit., vol. IV, pp. 2019-21, 2085, 2088, 2092-3, 2096, 2112; F. Falk, *Situation Politique de l'Inde Française*, s.l., s.d.; A.P. 1278, D. 4, Letter of 9 June 1909, no. 355, AOM; JO 1920, p. 177; JO 1920, vol. II, p. 561; *Desasevagan*, 22 April 1924.
38. Antony, op. cit., 1994, p. 106; Weber, op.cit., vol. IV, pp. 2019-21, 2085, 2088, 2092-3, 2096, 2112; A.P. 727, D.1, Lettre du gouverneur par interim Rognon, 12 April 1908, AOM; F. Falk. *Situation Politique de l'Inde Française*, s.l., s.d.; A.P. 1278, D. 4, Letter of 9 June 1909, no. 355, AOM; JO 1920, p. 177; JO 1920, vol. II, p. 561; *Desasevagan*, 22 April 1924.
39. A.P. 1278, D. 4, no. 355, AOM; A.P. 1271, D. 2, no. 166-7, AOM; Jacques Weber, op. cit., vol. IV, pp. 2081, 2086, 2095-6, 2098, 2113-15, 2121; A.P. 717, D. 8, no. 35 bis c; A.P. 1278, D. 6, no. 52, c, AOM; *Le Matin*, 13 April 1914; A.P. 1271, D. 2, Report of 4 May 1910, AOM; JO 1920, p. 299; *Le Pionnier*, 17 February 1910, pp. 3, 10; 12, 19 May 1910.
40. *Sukapi Viruthini*, 15 March 1934, pp. 2-4; Weber, op. cit., vol. IV, p. 2172.
41. *Inde-Politique Etrangère-Relation avec la France, 1913-15*, no. 38, p. 36, ADP; A.P. 1271, D. 3, March-April 1914, AOM; Weber, op.cit., vol. IV, pp. 2175, 2179; P. Richard, *Le Corps du Christ Après sa Résurrection, Essai Métaphysique*, Montauban, 1900; P. Richard, *Les Dieux*, Paris, 1914; P. Richard, *L'Ether vivant et le Réalisme Supranerveux*, Paris, 1911; Vennila, 10 September 1947.
42. Sri Aurobindo, op. cit., 2011, p. 28.
43. JO 1914, p. 426; A.P. 1271, D.3 Elections Legislatives du, 26 April 1914, AOM and *Lettre de Martineau du* 9 April 1914, no. 7c, AOM; Heehs, *Sri Aurobindo. A Brief Biography*, Delhi, 1989, p. 80; Richard, *The Lord of the Nations*, Madras, 1923, p. 8; cf. also Richard, *The Wherefore of the Worlds*, tr. by Aurobindo Ghose, Madras, 1923.
44. Heehs, *The Lives of Sri Aurobindo,* Columbia University, 2008; *Makkal Manasaatchi*, 12-18 May 2010; JO 1914, p. 426.
45. JO 1915, vol. II, p. 1011; JO 1916, vol. I, pp. 74-5; *Desobagari*, 20 November 1937.
46. JO 1918, vol. II, p. 775; JO 1917, vol. II, pp. 127-8; More, *Tamil Heroes in French India, 1870-1954: Their Role in Business, Social Reforms and in Netaji's Freedom Struggle from Vietnam*, Pondicherry, 2016; JO 1918, vol. II, p. 590; JO 1914, vol. II, p. 1017.
47. *Desobagari*, 9 April 1938; More, *Puducheri Valartha Bharathiar* (Tamil),

Pondicherry, 2016; More, *Subramania Bharathi in British and French India, Nationalist, Revivalist or Thamizh Patriot?*, Chennai, 2017.
48. JO 1917, vol. II, p. 884; JO 1920, p. 462; *Suthanthiram*, 2 April 1938; JO 1917, vol. I, p. 267; D. Gressieux, *Les Troupes Indiennes en France, 1914-18*, Tours, 2007.
49. Situation dans les Etablissemets par le Gouverneur, Pondicherry, 3 March 1921 (in) Ministère des Affaires Etrangères, Direction des Afaires Politique et Commerciales, no. 14, p. 87, ADP.
50. Situation dans l'IF, par le Gouverneur, Pondicherry, 10 February 1921, p. 53 in Asie 1918-29 Indes Françaises, no. 1, ADP.
51. Weber, op. cit., vol. IV, pp. 2041-43, 2046-7, 2050, 2072; Antony, op. cit., 1994, p. 174; *Indochine-inde*, 12 April 1936; Weber, op. cit., 1996, pp. 313-14.
52. Weber, Ibid., vol. IV, p. 2309.
53. Ibid., Antony, op. cit., 1994, p. 107; *Desasevagan*, 18 March 1924, p. 17.
54. Ibid., p. 17; 8 April 1924, p. 11; 20 May 1924; *Inde Nouvelle*, pp. 64-5, 73-4; *Sree Soudjana Ranjani*, 21 May 1925; Weber, op. cit., 1996, pp. 329-30.
55. *Desasevagan*, op. cit., p. 17; *Sree Soudjana Ranjani*, 3 September 1925; 16 December 1926; Les Partis Politiques de l'IF, 1944—Inde G 28, AOM.
56. Weber, op. cit., vol. IV, p. 2309; *Baradam*, 15 January 1933; Weber, op. cit., 1996, p. 330; Les Partis Politiques de l'IF, 1944—Inde G 28, AOM.
57. *Inde Nouvelle*, January 1928, no. 4 bis-supplement, vol. II, pp. 104-7; Weber, op. cit., 1996, p. 330; JO 1938-9, p. 127.
58. *Indochine-inde*, 11 October 1936; Weber, op. cit., vol. IV, p. 2309; *Saigon Dimanche*, 17 June 1928; JO, 1918, p. 1011; *Saigon Dimanche*, 19 August 1928; 30 December 1928.
59. *Desasevagan*, 8 January, 27 May 1924; *Nyayabhimani*, 20 April 1926; 3, 17, 24 October 1928; 17 October 1928, 24 October 1928; *Desasevagan*, 29 January 1922, p. 7; 29 April 1924; 3, 6 May 1924.
60. *Deshabandhou*, 17 May 1929, p. 3; 31 May 1929.
61. Ann., 1931, p. 73; *Desasevagan*, 22 April 1924; *Nyayabhimani*, 20 April 1926; *Saigon Dimanche*, 18 November 1928.
62. R. Dadala, *My Struggle for the Freedom of French India*, Pondicherry, n.d., p. 3; *Saigon Dimanche*, 30 December 1928; Weber, op. cit., vol. IV, p. 2309; *Deshabandhou*, 7 December 1928, p. 4; 3 May 1929, p. 2.

63. *Taynadu*, 2 March 1934; JO 24 April 1934; *Sukapi Viruthini*, 15 June 1934.
64. Ibid.
65. Jacques Weber, op. cit., vol. IV, p. 2309.
66. *Saigon Dimanche*, 15 May 1932; *Deshabandhou*, 3 May 1929, p. 4; *Djothy*, 13 August 1929.
67. Interview Jean Kessavarm; Dupleix, 5 May 1924.
68. *Baradam*, 25 December 1932, pp. 2-3; 15 January 1933, p. 4; 26 March 1933; 30 April 1933, p. 4; *Djothy*, 13 August 1929; *Dupleix*, 31 March 1934.
69. *Suthanthiram*, 3 March 1938; *Saigon Dimanche*, 8 May 1932; *Sukapi Viruthini*. 15 November 1937; 14 October 1933.
70. *Saigon Dimanche*, 8 May 1932.
71. *Puduvai Murasu*, 14 October 1930; 14 September 1931, pp. 15-19; M.C. Vashist, 'Trade Union Movement in Pondicherry State with Special Reference to Mahé', University of Calicut, M. Phil dissertation, 1993, pp. 24-35; *Sree Soudjana Ranjini*, 15 October 1931.
72. Weber, op. cit., 1996, p. 331.
73. *Dupleix*, 25 November 1933.
74. Dadala, op. cit., pp. 3, 4; *Taynadu*, 25 May 1934.
75. *Taynadu*, 16 March 1934; *Dupleix*, 2 December 1933; *Sukapi Viruthini*, 15 March 1934, 15 March 1939; *Desobagari*, 23 October 1937, 20 November 1937.
76. *Dupleix*, 28 October, 4, 18 November 1933; 9, 23, 30 September, 7 October 1933.
77. *Dupleix*, 11 November 1933.
78. *Taynadu*, 20 April 1934; *Dupleix*, 5 May 1934.
79. Dadala, op. cit., pp. 4-6; *Desobagari*, 12 March 1938, p. 2; *Dupleix*, 27 January 1934; 10 March 1934.
80. *Dupleix*, 23 December 1933; *Saigon Dimanche/indochine-inde*, 7 January 1934; 7 March 1937; 16 September 1939; Ann., 1934, p. 197; *Desobagari*, 3 December 1938; *The Hindu*. 17 December 1938.
81. JO 1936, p. 821; *Baradam*, 23 April 1933, p. 4; *Dupleix*, 14 April 1934; JO 1935, vol. I, p. 138; Ann., 1936, p. 247; Ann., 1938-9, p. 221; JO 1936, pp. 284-5; JO 1914, vol. II, p. 902; Note sur Mouttoukomarapparettiar, Membre de l'Assemblée Représentative—Inde H 22, AOM; Note sur Mouttousamy Poullé—Inde H 22, AOM; Note à M. le Chef de Service et de la Police—Inde G 28, AOM; Les Partis Politiques de l'IF, 1944—Inde G 28, AOM.

CHAPTER 4

British Indian Stalwarts in Pondicherry

MAHATMA GANDHI AND JAWAHARLAL NEHRU

In the year 1930, Mahatma Gandhi and the Congress Party launched the Civil Disobedience Movement against foreign rule in India. The Congress stood for total freedom from foreign rule. This development naturally had its influence in French India, too, though Pondicherrians hardly participated in this new Gandhian Movement. There were, however, some newspapers like *Baradam,* which came out in support of the non-cooperation movement of Gandhi. There were other newspapers which had adopted a nationalistic tone, like *Niyayabhimani* of Karaikal, and *Desasevagan* and *Deshabandhu* of Pondicherry, but never did they clamour for Independence or freedom. *Desasevagan* was founded by Saigon Louis Chinniah as early as 1922 and criticised British and French colonialism. Chinniah was also attracted by Gandhian principles.[1]

As far as I know, no Pondicherrian resigned from his job in Pondicherry heeding the Civil Disobedience call of Gandhi. But in faraway French Indochina, there was one man from Pondicherry, called Léon Prouchandy, who held a lucrative job in a French credit bank in Saigon. Prouchandy voluntarily gave up his job in support of Gandhi's call. This was reported in *L'Inde Illustrée*, a Pondicherry French newspaper. It is worthwhile to note that Léon Prouchandy belonged to the prominent Prouchandy landed family of Pondicherry and French Indochina/Saigon.[2]

Nevertheless, due to the impetus given by Mahatma Gandhi, several youth organisations were formed in Pondicherry in 1931-2. The Ramakrishna Reading Room came into existence at that time at the cross-section of the Bussy Street and Madras Road in the space that was given by the wealthy Arokiasamy Mudaliar. It was actually founded by V. Kailasa Subbiah. It was due to the initiative of the youth organisations that the Harijan Sevak Sangh, founded by Gandhi earlier, was launched in Pondicherry on 6 December 1933 by the lawyer, Jean Savarinathan Poullé (hailing from Karaikal, and a relative of Joseph Davidu), Maurice Clairon and R. Dorairaj. Valanga stalwarts, following the call of Gandhi gave a call to do away with Untouchability and let the Valangas enter the caste Hindu temples. Clairon and Dorairaj had officially formulated the demand for the founding of this *sangam*. Some of the early members of this *sangam* were R.L. Purshotthama Reddiar of Bahur, H.M. Cassime, V. Subbiah Naidu, Ghouse and L.J.X. Doraisamy. V. Subbiah and his associates founded the *Puduvai Valibar Aikya Sangam* on 13 July 1934.

On 18 January 1934, Savarinathan, who belonged to the Poullé caste and was a Christian, organised a meeting at Odiansalai in which Swami Sahajananda spoke. The office of the Harijan Sevak Sangh was situated at the National Café on the first floor in Dupleix Street. The Indian National Congress saw its birth in Pondicherry here. Later, the office was shifted to the Ansari Café building in the same street.[3]

There were complaints from some Hindu quarters about why some Hindus like Subbiah Naidu, who was a life insurance company employee then, were supporting Saverinathan and about why a Christian was worried about Hindu Valanga welfare, when there was a caste problem among the Christians in Pondicherry festering for a long time. In Nellithope Church, there was then a raging controversy over a stone wall separating 'high' and 'low' caste Christians. Besides, it was pointed out that Maurice Clairon, a Valanga Christian of Pondicherry, was financing the *Hindu Harijan Sevak Sangam*. What was forgotten is that Untouchability existed also in Christianity, as a vestige of Hindu culture and, therefore, according to some quarters like the *Dupleix* paper, Christians had the right to participate in the anti-Untouchability campaign for this reason.[4]

However, all such controversies did not prevent top personalities of Pondicherry from attending the marriage of R.P. Babilonne, the local councillor, with a girl of the Francine family in June 1934. They belonged to prominent Christian Valanga families of Pondicherry.

Among the personalities who attended the wedding was the French governor of Pondicherry, M. Bourret, Sellane Naiker, president of the General Council, Emmanuel Tetta, Jean Saverinadin and many others. They also took part in a grand lunch held at the residence of Babilonne.[5] Such was the solidarity and mutual respect that had developed between the various castes and religious groups during French rule and under French influence.

Gandhi as a politician thus indulged freely in reforming Hindu society, which was fast decreasing in numbers due, mainly, to the conversion of 'low' caste Hindus and Untouchables to Islam and Christianity. The youth organisations of Pondicherry were much influenced by Gandhi's philosophy. Many reading rooms and night classes were started by them. Under their influence, the mill workers, who were quite numerous in Pondicherry, began to organise themselves into trade unions. Men like V. Subbiah, S.R. Subramanian, R. Dorairaj, R.L. Purushotthama Reddiar and Gabriel Annussamy were active in these organisations.[6] Subbiah, Subramanian and Dorairaj were often found with the mill workers of Mudaliarpet, trying to organise them. It has been admitted by Subbiah himself that it was due to his acquaintance with the 'low' caste Valangas in the villages during this period that he came in contact with the cotton mill workers of Pondicherry. G. Annoussamy was a French teacher of Calvé College. He served also as interim assistant director of the Dupleix College of Chandernagore.[7]

In faraway Saigon, Léon Prouchandy of Pondicherry, albeit supporting the Gandhian Movement against Untouchability and even contributing to his Harijan fund, did not take to Gandhian reforms. Instead, he started his own Social Reform Movement among the Indians and Pondicherrians of Indochina. He started the 'Dress Reforms Movement' through which he asked the Indians settled in Indochina and Indians travelling abroad to cut off their *kudumis* (tuft of hair on the crown), shed their *veshtis* and *kailis* and take to European dress. Many prominent Tamils settled in Indochina, like J.M. Mohammad Ismail and the wealthy Nattukottai Chettiars, heeded to the call of Prouchandy and took to westernwear. Prouchandy even wrote to Selvarajulu Chettiar, the wealthy stevedore of Pondicherry, to intervene with his boatmen on the Pondicherry coast so that they take to wearing short trousers instead of the loincloth that hardly hid their genitals and that was an embarrassment to women and foreigners. He even wrote to his journalist friends in India as well as to Mahatma Gandhi and E.V. Ramasamy Periyar to come out in favour of his dress reforms which, according to him, would go a long way in modernising Indians, and changing their social outlook.[8]

In pursuit of his all-India campaign against Untouchability, Mahatma Gandhi decided to visit Karaikal first on 16 Febraury 1934. In Karaikal, the Harijan Sevak Sangh was headed by Ilayangudi Arangasamy Naiker. He was known as the 'Gandhi of French India'. Through his journal, *Kudiarasu*, he relentlessly espoused the causes of farmers, workers, the poor and the downtrodden. He also called for the abolition of Untouchability. Gandhi received donations. He auctioned off the presents he received. Karaikal mayor Thomas Arul and Arangasamy Naiker were among those who bought the presents in the auction. Gandhi spoke at a meeting against Untouchability.[9]

It seems that initially Gandhi wanted to meet Sri Aurobindo in Pondicherry. He wrote to him in this respect. But Sri Aurobindo refused to meet Gandhi on the pretext that he had retired into silence and meditation and could, therefore, receive no one. He also stated that the Ashram Mother, Mirra Alfassa, could not receive Gandhi either, owing to her tight schedule. As a result, Gandhi is believed to have cancelled his visit to Pondicherry. But others claim that Gandhi did not want to come to Pondicherry because the Harijan Sevak Sangam was headed by a Christian. No politician or stalwart of Pondicherry, be it Sellane Naiker, Joseph Davidu or Bharathidasan, dared to invite Gandhi to Pondicherry. Instead, it was left to the youngsters of the Harijan Sevak Sangam, like V. Subbiah and S.R. Subramanian, to go to Coonoor in the Nilgiris, where Gandhi had come, in the car of the prosperous Tamil wine merchant, Maurice Clairon. With the help of Gandhi's lieutenant, C. Rajagopalachari, and another Congress leader, T.S.S. Rajan, they met Gandhi and invited him to Pondicherry. V. Subbiah told Gandhi that he must not refrain from coming to Pondicherry just because Sri Aurobindo had refused him an appointment. Gandhi finally arrived in Pondicherry at 7 a.m. on 17 February 1934, accompanied by Rajagopalachari, his daughter, Rajan, and Miraben. He was garlanded by Jean Savarinathan and given a warm welcome by the Pondicherrians. Gandhi spoke in English about the necessity of abolishing Untouchability, etc., at a grand meeting at Odiansalai ground in Pondicherry, in the presence of Saverinathan and the prominent merchant of Pondicherry, Nanayya Bhagavathar.[10] He collected funds for the Harijan movement in Pondicherry. He said:

> I don't have much time to talk in length, as you have asked, because I have to go to other places. As Pondicherry is French nation, there is equality and brotherhood here. For this, so many people had given their lives. . . . I think probably there will be responsibility regarding anti-Untouchability. We have to give all help to the Untouchables. . . .[11]

Though Gandhi praised France for its great ideals of liberty, equality and fraternity, yet he carefully avoided asking for Independence for French India. Sellane Naiker who was president of the General Council when Gandhi visited Pondicherry, excused himself for not being able to meet him as he had some urgent work. He sent a small sum of money for Harijan uplift to Gandhi. Gandhi replied on 21 February 1934 thanking Sellane for his donation and telling him that he would have been happy to meet him.[12] Once in Pondicherry, Gandhi never sought to pay a visit to Sri Aurobindo. It was rumoured that the latter was so under the influence of the Mother of the Ashram, who was promoting him as a universal prophet, that it was quite possible that he was not aware of Gandhi's presence there. Others hold that Sri Aurobindo was prevented from meeting Gandhi by the Ashram Mother.[13]

It was after Gandhi's arrival in Pondicherry that V. Subbiah, active in the youth organisations, started the weekly journal called *Suthanthiram* which literally meant 'freedom', on 1 June 1934. The official authorisation to run the journal was granted on 15 January 1935. Subbiah belonged to the Telugu-speaking Balija caste. Subbiah's paternal ancestors belonged to Tamil Nadu, where his grandfather was village munsiff. But his father was a merchant, born just outside Pondicherry. Subbiah's family seems to have settled in Pondicherry when Subbiah was still quite young. They had some land in Villianur.[14]

The *Suthanthiram* paper had the avowed objective of fighting for the liberation of the poor and downtrodden, and the workers. It was not founded to fight for the liberation of French India from colonial rule. It was sympathetic to Mahatma Gandhi and Nehru in its initial issues. It also carried essays and articles by Subramania Bharathi in favour of social justice and equality. It was critical of the French governors who took sides in local politics. It was also critical of the group of educated people who held high offices as representatives of the people but cared little for the welfare of the common man and workers.[15]

In February 1936, the Harijan Sevak Sangh president was R. Dorairaj. Maurice Clairon and Appasamy Chettiar were vice-presidents. Among the committee members and sympathisers were R.L. Purushottama Reddiar, Jean Saverinadin, V. Subbiah and H.M. Cassime.[16]

Later, on 17 October 1936, the Congress leader, Jawaharlal Nehru, visited Pondicherry. He was the guest of Selvarajulu Chettiar and stayed in his grand mansion in Kurusukuppam on the seaside. During his stay, he did not meet Sri Aurobindo. The latter had refused to meet him on the pretext that Nehru's mission was political and neither he nor the Ashram Mother was interested in politics.[17] Nehru was later informed by his English friend Prof Edward Thompson, a lecturer at Oxford University, that Aurobindo, whom he knew well, was once a fine intellect and patriot, but in Pondicherry he was indulging in mumbo jumbo along with a Frenchwoman, claiming to be Shiva or the Supreme Soul himself, and styling his companion as the reincarnation of Parvati. He further shared that Aurobindo provided darshan three days in a year to his devotees who were shepherded to glimpse him only momentarily. Nehru did not pay much attention to Edward Thompson's letter and dismissed Aurobindo's predilections as of minor importance. However, Nehru had always nurtured a great sympathy for France, its culture and values. He understood the French language and spoke it fluently.[18]

Nehru did not stay for long in Pondicherry. He addressed a meeting on 17 October and left Pondicherry on the same evening.[19]

The Catholic Christian journal of Pondicherry, *Sarva Vyapi*, stood against Gandhi's attempt to uplift the Harijans. It accused Gandhi of fasting for Harijan uplift only to save Hinduism and maintain Hindu dominance. It held that Gandhi knew that if Harijans leave

Hinduism, the Hindu religion would be weakened. It claimed that Christians had done more to uplift Harijans, whereas Gandhi was just collecting money and making speeches. In Pondicherry, too, he did the same, it said. The Hindus were reforming themselves and allowing Untouchables to enter temples without his help, it averred. It wanted the Pondicherry Christians to do the same and abolish caste in Christianity. *Sarva Vyapi* also attacked the Madras magazine, *Ananda Vikatan*, for criticising Christianity and its attempts to convert the Untouchable Hindus.[20]

PERIYAR E.V. RAMASAMY IN PONDICHERRY

E.V. Ramasamy Naiker of Erode, of Telugu-Kannada descent, started his political career as a Congressman. He was famous for organising the Vaikom Satyagraha in Travancore state. He was a rising leader of the nationalist Congress Party in Tamil Nadu, which was then under the leadership of C. Rajagopalachari. He was arrested and released on 21 June 1924 for his participation in Vaikom satyagraha.[21]

As a Congressman, E.V. Ramasamy Naiker came out in favour of Hindi as the national language of India. But very soon, unable to countenance the dominance of the Tamil-speaking Brahmins in the Congress Party of Tamil Nadu, some of whom accused him of corruption when he was secretary of the Tamil Nadu Congress, he left the Congress Party. He immediately founded the apolitical Self-Respect Movement in 1925. Thereafter, he trained his guns against the Brahmins, the Hindu gods and the brahmanical or Aryan culture way of life and philosophy, which had penetrated south India a long time ago. He considered all south Indians, except Brahmins, as Dravidians. Thus, he propounded a simplistic racial theory that all south Indians were Dravidians by race, while the Brahmins and north Indians were Aryans.[22]

E.V. Ramasamy first visited Pondicherry in 1926. He seems to have addressed a meeting at Muthialpet. He again visited Pondicherry in 1931. This time, he addressed a meeting at Gaebelé Theatre (presently a commercial complex) which was in Dupleix Street. His revolutionary ideas against religion, Brahmins and God attracted many young Pondicherrians. The Tamil teacher, Subburathinam, who had styled himself as Bharathidasan out of his admiration for Subramania Bharathi, soon became one of his ardent followers in Pondicherry. Bharathidasan took a position against the caste system prevailing among the Christians of Pondicherry, in spite of the conversions. By then, E.V. Ramasamy was increasingly becoming known as 'Periyar' or the Elder to his followers. In Pondicherry, Mr Noel was one of the founders of the Periyar movement.[23]

It is interesting to note that the Left-leaning V. Subbiah also subscribed to the Aryan-Dravidian theory of Periyar during the 1930s. Journals like *Puduvai Murasu* trained its guns against the Brahmins. It considered the Congress Party as an organisation working for the domination of Brahmins. It insisted that Brahmins should rewrite the Puranas and reform their customs. It endorsed the standpoints of the Self-respect movement. The *Dupleix* paper took a position against Hindu religious rituals and superstition in favour of rationalism. It blamed the Hindu laws for the present low status of women. Since the time it was started in 1933, *Dupleix* had adopted a frankly pro-Self-Respect Movement stand.[24]

In Karaikal, there were newspapers, like *Suravali* and *Periyar*, which wrote in favour of Periyar's movement. They were published by Techena.[25]

The opposition to Periyar's movement was given a voice by newspapers like *Baradam*. *Baradam* asked its audience not to discriminate between people on the basis of caste.[26] Some other papers, like the pro-Brahmin monthly, *Karpagam,* stood for the abolition of Untouchabliity, the greatness and promotion of Tamil and considered Aryans and Dravidians as brothers born of one Indian mother. They did not directly attack the Periyar movement. But *Karpagam* wanted the Brahmins to adhere to the *Brahmana Dharma*, if they did not want to be treated as 'Karma Sandalai'. There was no point in claiming to be a Brahmin if one did not follow the *Brahmana Karma*, according to its editorials.[27]

Until about 1925, Bharathidasan was a congressman who wore only *khaddar* clothes. He started as a believer in God. He wrote poems in praise of God, especially Murugan. Bharathidasan, under the influence of Periyar, described the Harijan movement of Gandhi as a Vaishnava movement and criticised V. Subbiah and other

Pondicherrians like Maurice Clairon who were involved in its propagation. Bharathidasan denounced the caste system. His colleague, Mr Noel, one of the earliest followers of Periyar in Pondicherry, started the weekly journal, *Puduvai Murasu*, which came down heavily on Christian priests and caste discrimination in the churches of Pondicherry. Some of those who were involved in running the journal were S. Gurusamy, K. Ramakrishnan, S. Sivaprakasam and Ponnambalam. Bharathidasan himself took an anti-Christian stance during that period. He denounced the domination of the Christians in Pondicherry and Karaikal. He equated them with the Brahmins of the Tamil country.[28]

In faraway Indochina, the Pondicherrian social reformer and philanthropist, Léon Prouchandy, who launched dress reforms among Indians, was attracted towards the radical ideas of Periyar. He wrote in the French journals in favour of his ideas. Like Bharathidasan, Prouchandy condemned the caste system prevailing in Pondicherry society among Indians. He thought, like Subramania Bharathi and Periyar, that the Brahmins were responsible for the degradation of Hindu society and Hinduism which, he nevertheless conceded, was a 'beautiful religion'. He called upon the caste Christians of Pondicherry to give up caste following Ponnuthamby La Porte. He also called upon the Indians and Tamils to follow the teachings of Periyar and considered the Self-Respect Movement as a great revolutionary movement.[29]

The nationalist journal of Pondicherry called *Deshabandhou* criticised Periyar and his followers. It accused them of being patronised by the government, i.e. the non-Brahmin Justice Party. It opined that E.V. Ramasamy was involved in the Self-Respect Movement only to earn money. It further held that just because he had problems with some Brahmins, it was not right on his part to accuse all Brahmins of bigotry. It lamented that some Pondicherrians, who do not know how to exercise their voting rights, have decided to follow E.V. Ramasamy. At that time, a certain A. Lebrian had circulated a tract under the signature of 'Oru Paraiyan' (a Paraya) criticising the Hindu religion. *Deshabandhou* warned critics like Lebrian not to meddle with religion.[30]

On 21 January 1929, E.V. Ramasamy Naiker visited Pondicherry.[31] After a subsequent tour of Russia, Periyar switched over to the socialist ideology and started preaching it. One of his followers, A. Ponnambalam, preached the egalitarian ideology in Mudaliarpet and Muthialpet in early 1933. He was expelled from Pondicherry by the French government. *Baradam* accused Periyar of joining the Bolshevik Party for money. It asked the Tamilians not to believe in Periyar's anti-God, anti-Brahmin and anti-religious philosophy. It lamented that some Pondicherrians and Christians like S.M.A.D. La Hache were attracted to Periyar.[32] In May 1933, Periyar attended the *Suya Mariyathai Vaibhavam* feast at Muthialpet in Pondicherry. Drawing inspiration from him, some Pondicherrians had started the *Samayocitha Sabhai* in Pondicherry. In Uppalam, the *Than Mathippu Kazahagam* (Self-Respect Movement) was started by men like Pon. Ramalingam. They celebrated the 69th birthday of Periyar at the Reveil Social Hall.[33]

Baradam wanted the workers to cooperate with capitalists instead of trying to destroy them. It criticised Bharathidasan for earning money by using the Self-Respect Movement and writing about it in *Dupleix* newspaper, owned by Dakshinamurthy Chettiar, related to Selvarajalu Chettiar, and *Puduvai Murasu*. The paper also accused Bharathidasan of trying to create a rift between Christians and the Valanga caste.[34] Another newspaper called *Sri Soudjanarandjani* was also critical of the Self-Respect Movement. It held that the author of the *Ramayana*, Valmiki, and that of *Mahabharata* and the 18 Puranas, Vyasa, were not Brahmins. Therefore, it held, that it was not the Brahmins who recounted irrational superstitious stories and cheated the others.[35]

Periyar and his movement did have some influence and following in Pondicherry. Newspapers like *Vennila* wrote extensively in favour of Tamil and Dravidian separatist politics, especially after Independence in August 1947. But Periyar wanted a separate Dravidanadu for Dravidians. He did not want south Indians to be subjected to the rule of north Indians. He wanted the abolition of the caste system which he considered as Aryan and proposed inter-caste marriages to get rid of it. Pondicherry, Karaikal, Mahé and Yanam were thought to be part of his Dravidanadu idea.[36]

Thiru V. Kalayanasundaram, C.N. Annadorai and Bharathidasan, too, highlighted the need to safeguard Tamil and avoid north Indian domination through secession. They supported Periyar's demands.

Bharathidasan viewed Barathiar, whom he knew personally in Pondicherry, as an egalitarian and revolutionary poet, unlike Sri Aurobindo, while Annadorai, the Dravidian Party leader thought that the Brahmins ignored Bharathi because he was critical of them and their so-called values.[37]

Some nationalist journals, like *Pittan*, opposed the Dravidian parties as well as the *Tamizharasu Kazhagam* of M.P. Sivagnanam and favoured Hindi. Others like *Vennila* favoured the Dravidian and Tamil nationalist movements. It opposed the Telugus demanding the city of Madras for their Andhra state.[38]

Bharathidasan proved to be an indefatigable opponent of Hindi and Brahmanism. He spoke and wrote extensively in favour of a separate Dravidian state and Tamil. He refused to accept Agastya as having written the first book in Tamil, denounced the caste system as un-Dravidian and called for the unity of all Dravidians, irrespective of caste, religion or class. However, some of his contemporaries whom I spoke to held that Bharathidasan never practised what he preached or wrote.

In 1945, E.V. Ramasamy again visited Pondicherry. He and his collaborators were taken out in a procession from the house of Subburathinam/Bharathidasan to the Odiansalai ground. A meeting was organised at Sami Palace cinema hall. S. Perumal of Pondicherry and Mrs Satyavani spoke in this meeting, along with Bharathidasan. Some people then protested against the release of a portrait of Bharathidasan. Congressmen, like Paul Latour and Albert Velu, raised pro-Nehru slogans, along with Murugasamy Udayar of Kosapalayam and Kannan of Orléanpet. In their turn, Lambert Saravane and Ansari P. Duraisamy demonstrated against E.V. Ramasamy.[39]

Bharathidasan, who had the sympathy and support of Edouard Goubert, wrote in *Kuyil* the following on 1 January 1948:

> Not today or yesterday, but for hundreds of years the northerners tried to destroy the Dravidian land, through the trick of the *Manu Shastras*. Many sages came from the north to capitivate Dravidanadu.
>
> Stories denigrated Dravidians and made them to believe such stories. 'We belong to God's race', the Dravidians were told—the kings were intoxicated. . . . They attracted Dravidians by saying that the Hindu religion was being submerged by Mughals and other invaders.

By saying it is God's language, they tried to lift up their language in Dravidian land.

They obtained all the benefits from the foreigners and now they act as if they are against them in the name of patriotism.

The English left the power to the northerners; They told there is no race as Dravidians. They say that Tamil is born from the northern language. What arrogance!

Dravidandu has become a market for northern products. They indulge here in usury.

We should not have difference between Dravidians. Some Dravidians are acting against our interests. If they don't realise it today, they will realise it tomorrow. . . . We have to relieve Dravidians from northerners.

Of all newspapers in Pondicherry, the Catholic journal of Pondicherry, *Sarva Vyapi*, was in the forefront of the opponents of Periyar E.V. Ramasamy and his Self-Respect Movement, alongside its press organs like *Kudiarasu, Pakutharivau, Puduvai Murasu* and *Puratchi*. It rejected Periyar's atheism and defended Christianity and the priests. It called upon Christians to organise meetings against the Self-Respect Movement, boycott their journals and send petitions to the government against the atheist movement. It defended the priests from the attacks of the self-respecters by declaring that the priests had helped the development of many villages, opened schools, shelters and hospitals, unlike the self-respecters, who had done nothing. Following the atheist exhortations of Periyar. It asked the Harijans not to leave Christianity, and attack it. Instead, it called upon 'high' caste Christians to abolish caste. Lahache of Pondicherry and Gurusamy, editor of *Puduvai Murasu*, were great critics of Christianity.[40]

SRI AUROBINDO OF BENGAL IN PONDICHERRY

We have seen earlier that Bharathi had introduced Mr & Mrs Paul Richard to Aravindha Ghose. We have seen, too, that Aravindha Ghose was friendly with some young Pondicherrians like Louis Rassendran, Joseph Davidu and Emmanuel Adicéam. These young men, who were still students at the Colonial College, had come into contact with Blanche Rachel Mirra Alfassa, wife of Paul Richard, the French philosopher and lawyer. She seems to have given this group of students the name of 'l'Idée Nouvelle' or New Idea. An association was registered on 3 May 1914 in the name of this group. February 1920 onwards, some members of this group edited a monthly journal called *Collégien*.[41]

Paul Richard and Sri Aurobindo, on their part, started on 4 July 1914 a magazine of philosophical synthesis called *Revue de Synthèse Philosophique* or, in short, *Arya*. We have also seen that Ghose was friendly with Tamil nationalists like Subramania Bharathi. During that period, Ghose and the nationalists discussed a lot of philosophy. Ghose was a liberal. He freely smoked cigarettes and drank wine, available cheaply in Pondicherry.[42]

It seems that Sri Aurobindo refused to go to Africa, unlike Subramania Bharathi who was willing to go to Algiers to escape from being deported to British India.[43] Around 1916, Ghose is believed to have become a 'Superman', accomplishing his spiritual nirvana.

The monastery or Ashram in the name of Sri Aurobindo was founded by Mirra Alfassa and Aurobindo in 1926. It was registered later as a charitable trust. Mirra Alfassa was a wealthy woman, being the daughter of a banker called Maurice Alfassa. She had the material means to set up the Ashram. Aurobindo alone could not have done it, as he had no money and had come to Pondicherry as a penniless refugee. Besides, Mirra Alfassa had high connections with the colonial establishment. Her brother was a French governor of colonies. It was she who installed Aurobindo as the Master or Lord of Yoga, according to his biographer, Srinivasa Iyengar.[44] The main building of the Ashram or the *samadhi* building, where Mirra Alfassa and Sri Aurobindo started to live in the 1920s was a palatial mansion. It seems to have originally belonged to a Muslim.[45]

It seems that in the 1920s it was simply impossible to meet Sri Aurobindo as he had taken a vow not to see anyone. In 1924, Manavai R. Tirumalaisami of *Swadesamitran*, a popular Tamil nationalist daily, had tried to meet him without success. Aurobindo would not come out of his garden. It seems that the police had followed Manavai from the railway station to Sri Aurobindo's house. He was taken to the police station and searched before being let off. He met a certain Ashramite called Amudan, but he refused to allow him to meet Sri Aurobindo. Manavai held that there was a sort of fortress around Sri Aurobindo.[46] It seems that Sri Aurobindo went into total retirement in the year 1926, when the Ashram was founded. Some papers, like the *Lokabhakari* of Tamil Nadu, considered Pondicherry as a sort of despotic police state during that period.[47]

Within a few years, the Ashram became popular, attracting devotees from mainly western India and Bengal. Tamil devotees were quite few. In the 1930s, there was an influx of Hindu Bengalis from the Bengal Presidency where the Bengali Muslims were a majority. There were at least 500 adepts of the Ashram during this period. By the 1940s, when there was another influx of Bengalis due to Netaji Subhas Chandra Bose's Indian National Army knocking on the doors of Bengal. The Ashram had grown into an important sectarian community in Pondicherry, consisting of Indians and Europeans. It preached certain universal values and wanted to work out an East-West synthesis, with Mirra Alfassa, on one side, and Sri Aurobindo, on the other. The Ashram members conducted business and bought properties in Pondicherry, especially in the White town, for the benefit of the Ashram. It enjoyed the patronage of the French authorities in Pondicherry due to the fact that the Ashram Mother herself was a Frenchwoman.

Due to the steady influx of Bengalis and others to Pondicherry since the 1930s, there was a housing crisis in Pondicherry. The rent shot up in the town as more and more disciples of Sri Aurobindo arrived. It seems that the French administration in Pondicherry, as well as the governor, were not happy with this situation, in which the locals and French officials suffered due to the rise in rent and the buying of houses by the Ashram. It seems that Sri Aurobindo intervened personally through his 'Inner Force' with the French Foreign Ministry in Paris to get a governor favourable to the Ashram. Sri Aurobindo himself claimed that he succeeded in this attempt as in 1935 a new governor was appointed in Pondicherry who favoured the Ashram. However, even this governor asked the Ashram not to rent or buy houses but to build instead.[48]

Mirra Alfassa was married twice before she joined hands with Sri Aurobindo in what is said to be a common spiritual endeavour. She had a son called André through her first marriage with Henri Morisset. Mirra Alfassa and the Ashram enjoyed French colonial patronage and sympathy due to the fact that she was an influential and wealthy

Frenchwoman, given that her father was a banker and her brother the French governor of colonies. Mirra Alfassa styled herself as The Mother, in the Christian European fashion, for the Ashram mates who had come to Pondicherry in their quest to become 'supermen'. Her name 'Mirra', which was a Hebrew name meaning Miryam, was modified to Mira or even Miradevi, i.e. Goddess Mira after the Indian fashion, so that it became acceptable to the Hindus. Sri Aurobindo spent much of his time in Pondicherry writing in English, while Mirra Alfassa saw to it that French was taught in the Ashram. There was no question of the promotion of any Indian language in the Ashram right from the start. Critics hold that Sri Aurobindo's philosophy, too, was a mixture of the ideas of Nietszche, Paul Richard and the Tamil saint, Thirumoolar. They also hold that the Ashram organisation was totally in the grip of the Mother due, mainly, to her financial muscle. Witnesses attest that she was a showy woman who always went about decked in gold and diamond ornaments.[49]

This Ashram cannot be deemed as a traditional Hindu ashram, as its founders had never claimed that it was one. Though its members were mostly drawn from Hinduism, there was never any question of worshipping the Hindu gods and goddesses in the main premises of the Ashram like the *samadhi* (burial site) or the dining hall (Villa Aroumé). Instead, the focus was on Sri Aurobindo and the Mother. Even the 'superman' philosophy developed by Sri Aurobindo and the Mother does not resemble the traditional Hindu philosophies, centred around the *karma* and rebirth theories. For them, the next stage of human evolution was towards the production of a series of supermen or divine beings, for which task the Ashram seems to have been founded.[50]

French governors freely participated in the activities of the Ashram. For instance, on 4-5 December 1936, the Ashram organised an exhibition of the paintings of the beautiful landscapes of Pondicherry, like the beach and the Ushuteri Lake, by some Ashram mates like Jayantilal and Champaklal from Gujarat and Romen from Bengal. The French governor of Pondicherry, Léon Solomiac, along with other high French officials like the Commandant Morizon, chief of the governor's council, as well as Joseph Davidu, the Tamil Christian mayor of Pondicherry, were present at the inauguration of this exhibition by the Ashram.[51] In 1938, Sri Aurobindo came out of total retirement into a sort of modified retirement.[52]

On 23 October 1940, Mirra Alfassa and Sri Aurobindo jointly wrote a letter to the consul of Britain in Pondicherry, to make known their position that they were not in favour of the government at Bordeaux and that they placed their community at the service of England. The date of the letter proved that they did not rally immediately behind Charles de Gaulle after his call of 18 June 1940.[53] It is quite surprising to note that Sri Aurobindo, who it is believed to have lived as a spiritual recluse and 'superman', refusing to participate in any political activity, committed a sudden political act through the letter. This seems to be largely due to the influence exerted by Mirra Alfassa. Sri Aurobindo openly supported the British and the Allies in the War against Axis powers. He donated Rs.1,000 to the Viceroy's War Fund. He contributed also Rs. 500 to the Madras governor's war fund and 10,000 francs to the *Caisse de Défense Nationale* in France (National Defence Fund of France).[54]

However, it is noteworthy that one of the important members of the Ashram community, by the name of P. Barbier Saint Hilaire (born on 16 January 1894), who was an engineer at the service of the French administration in Pondicherry, had written a letter to the consul of Britain on 5 July 1940 itself, notifying that he did not endorse the government of Maréchal Pétain, put in place by the Germans, and that he rallied behind de Gaulle. Probably it was due to Saint Hilaire's influence that Mirra Alfassa and Sri Aurobindo decided to pen their letter to the consul of Britain.[55]

Later, in March 1942, when Sir Stafford Cripps proposed a formula to break the constitutional deadlock in British India, Sri Aurobindo, who had always claimed to have abandoned politics, and had been forgotten by the Indian people for a very long time, was quick to endorse Cripp's offer. He even sent a long telegram to Cripps himself supporting his plan. He even contacted some Congress and Hindu Mahasabha leaders like C. Rajagopalachari and Moonje through his representative, Duraisamy Iyer, asking them to accept the Cripps offer. But both the Hindu Mahasabha and the Congress under Mahatma Gandhi, Maulana Abul Kalam Azad and Vallabhbhai Patel and even Subhas Chandra Bose in exile refused to accept the

Cripps offer. Rajagopalachari alone wanted the Congress to accept the Cripps Mission. Gandhi is believed to have asked Sri Aurobindo to go to Bengal to express his views.[56] Later, Sri Aurobindo came out in support of the Wavell Plan in June 1945. He also thought it not fit to reject the Cabinet Mission proposals in March 1946.[57] There is no explanation as to why Sri Aurobindo suddenly took an interest in Indian politics from Pondicherry since 1942.

By 1946, it appears that the Ashram had become quite influential in the political and administrative circles of Pondicherry. It possessed already several beautiful houses in the White town of Pondicherry and was in the process of buying many more.[58]

Some Pondicherry Tamil journals, like *Pittan*, held Sri Aurobindo in great esteem.[59] Suddhananda Barathiar of Telugu descent was a yogi, ascetic, writer, poet and Tamil nationalist from Panaiyur, Tamil Nadu. He had stayed and meditated in the shrine complex of the Ashram in the 1940s, giving all his property to the Ashram. He had translated many works of Sri Aurobindo into Tamil and written books on him and the Mother in Tamil. It seems that he left the Ashram due to the opposition he faced from the Bengali clique surrounding Sri Aurobindo. He also disliked the domination of the Ashram by the Mother.[60]

According to official sources, Sri Aurobindo died of kidney failure in 1950. The historian from Mahé, M.P. Sridharan, was present in Pondicherry and was at the shrine complex when Sri Aurobindo passed away. It was then believed that Sri Aurobindo would get back to his body in a few days and come back to life. But when that did not happen, he was buried in the compound of his residence on the fourth day, without the performance of the usual Hindu rites and ceremonies. The burial spot assumed all the trappings of a West Asian saintly tomb. Permission for this burial to take place within the White town and in his own mansion at that, was granted by the French Administrator and Governor, Charles François Marie Baron, who became a devotee of the Ashram.[61]

It becomes obvious from the preceding that Mahatma Gandhi was more influential among the people of Pondicherry than any other British Indian stalwart who had visited or found refuge in Pondicherry. The Harijan Sevak Movement saw its birth in Pondicherry due to his influence. Many, like Savarinathan, H.M. Cassime, V. Subbiah,

R.L. Purushotthama Reddiar, Maurice Clairon and Léon Prouchandy, were drawn towards the Gandhian Movement. However, there was no attempt to establish a branch of the Congress Party in Pondicherry or Karaikal during the 1930s. Gandhi stood for the uplift of the Harijans. But he never derided the *Varnasrama Dharma* or the fourfold Hindu caste system, very much like Nadou Shanmugam. In fact, he upheld it in his own way.

Periyar E.V. Ramasamy, after he broke away from the Congress and started the Self-Respect Movement, seems to have wielded a certain influence in Pondicherry and Karaikal. There were various associations set up to propagate his ideas and ideals against God, Brahmins and the caste system. After his tour of Russia in 1931, he even became an avowed socialist. He and his movement propagated socialist ideas and ideals for some time in Tamil Nadu as well as in Pondicherry. It could be said that it was he and his movement which sowed the seeds of socialism in Pondicherry. Bharathidasan, who knew Subramania Bharathi when he came to Pondicherry, was already influenced by his egalitarian, revolutionary writings, before he came into contact with Periyar and his movement's egalitarian philosophy. Bharathidasan was naturally inspired by Periyar's revolutionary ideals, which finds a prominent place in his writings. V. Subbiah, too, seems to have come under Periyar's influence to some extent during this period. But the fact that Subbiah regularly published the writings of Subramania Bharathi in his journal, *Suthanthiram*, from 1934 proves that he was more enthused by Bharathi's sociological writings than by the theology of Periyar.

As for Sri Aurobindo, his influence on Pondicherry politics and society was limited. Most of his followers and disciples came from western and eastern India. As his objective was to produce a race of 'supermen' or divine beings on earth, his interaction with local society and politics was always very little. In fact, the expansion of the Ashram founded in his name in the material plane, under the supervision of Mirra Alfassa by the acquisition of various colonial buildings in the White town had created a lot of suspicion and ill-will towards the Ashram as such. This was reinforced by the fact that Sri Aurobindo had preferred not to meet Gandhi and Jawaharlal Nehru when they visited Pondicherry but had no inhibitions talking with Frenchmen like Schumann and Baron. This had sent a wrong message to the Pondicherry people that Sri Aurobindo was against Gandhi and Nehru, who were fighting for India's freedom non-violently. Instead, many in Pondicherry believed that he was actively collaborating with the French to keep Pondicherry in bondage. Generally, the people of Pondicherry never understood him or his philosophy or the motives of the Ashram, as Sri Aurobindo or his Ashram stayed aloof from Pondicherry society in their own spiritual world, hardly interacting with the local society at large.

NOTES

1. *Baradam*, 22 October 1933; see also issues of *Nyayabhimani, Deshabandhou* and *Desasevagan*.
2. J.B.P. More, *Tamil Heroes in French India, 1870-1954. Their Role in Business, Social Reforms and in Netaji's Freedom Struggle from Vietnam*, Pondicherry, 2016; More, 'Léon Prouchandy. Réformateur Social de Pondichéry en Indochine Française, 1930-9', *La Lettre du C.I.D.I.F*, Paris, November 2009.
3. *Sukapi Viruthini*, 15 February 1934, p. 4; Interview with A. Arulraj; *Podujanam*, 17 April 1948, p. 10; *Taynadu*, 26 January 1934; Note à M. le Chef de Service et de la Police—Inde G 28, AOM.
4. *Dupleix*, 16 February 1934; *Taynadu*, 19 January 1934, p. 3; Nara, 'Puthuvai Desiya Iyakka Varalatru Nikazhchikalin Kalakurippukal', in *Suthanthiram Pon Vizha Malar, 1934-84*, Pondicherry, 1987, pp. 41-6.
5. *Inde Illustrée*, July 1934.
6. C. Antony, *Encyclopaedia of India, Pondicherry*, New Delhi, 1994, p. 109; Jacques Weber, *Les Etablissements Français en Inde au XIXe Siècle (1816-1914)*, vol. IV, Paris, 1988, p. 2309; JO, 1933, p. 1050; G. Annoussamy,'Thunbankallukku Tholvi Thanthavar', *Va. Subbiah Pavala Vizha Malar*, 1988, pp. 63-4.
7. JO 1935, p. 796; JO 1936, p. 283; *Dupleix*, 16 February 1934; J.B.P. More, *The Political Evolution of Muslims in Tamil Nadu and Madras, 1930-1947*, Hyderabad, 1997; S. Subramanian, S. 'Ninaivuk Kovai', *Va. Subbiah Pavala Vizha Malar*, Pondicherry, 1988, pp. 134-8; V. Subbiah, 'Puduvaiyin Pazham Perum Varalatru Pinnani', *Suthanthiram Pon Vizha Malar*, 1987, pp. 37-41; Subbiah, *Puduvaiyin Viduthalaiai Vendradutha Thozhilalarkalin Veera Varalaru*, Puduchery, 1986, p. 7.

8. Cf. More, op. cit., 2016.
9. *Dupleix*, 24 February 1934; see also issues of *Kudiarasu*, Karaikal.
10. *Inde Illustrée*, February-March 1934, no. 11, p. 7; *Va. Subbiah Pavala Vizha Malar*, Pondicherry, 1988, vol. I; S. Subramanian, op. cit., pp. 134-5; *Sukapi Viruthini*, 15 February 1934, p. 4; Sri Aurobindo, *Autobiographical Notes and Other Writings of Historical Interest*, Pondicherry, 2015, pp. 442-4.
11. *Dupleix*, 17 February 1934.
12. *Dupleix*, 24 February 1934; *Sarvavyapi*, 21 February 1934, p. 14; Antony, op. cit., 1994, p. 176.
13. Interview with Paramel Shatrugnan and Paul Radjanedassou.
14. Interview with Saraswati Subbiah; *Sukapi Viruthini*, 15 June 1934; JO 1934, p. 34; E. Divien, 'V. Subbiah' in *Va. Subbiah Pavala Vizha Malar*, 1988, pp. 39-40; JO 1934, p. 44.
15. *Suthanthiram*, 10 September 1934, pp. 6-7; Interview with Paul Radajanedassou; cf. *Suthanthiram*, 20 November 1934, vol. 6, pp. 2-5; 'Subramania Bharathiyar Charithra Surukkam' by V. Subbiah in *Suthanthiram*, 10 September 1934.
16. *Saigon Dimanche*, 9 February 1936.
17. Sri Aurobindo, op. cit., pp. 447-8.
18. Lettre de Henri Roux, chargés d'affaires à Delhi au Ministre des Affaires Etrangères, Delhi, 26 May 1947, p. 100, IF 6, ADP; Jawaharlal Nehru. *A Bunch of Old Letters*, Delhi, 1986, pp. 212-13.
19. Tel de Crocicchia au Ministre des Colonies, Pondicherry, 18 October 1936, p. 114, Ministère Affaires Etrangères, 1930-40, Indes Françaies, no. 4, ADP.
20. *Sarvavyapi*, 24 July 1935, pp. 58, 237, 239; 31 July 1935, pp. 241, 248, 251, 253; 14 August 1935, pp. 257, 263; 10 January 1934, p. 10; 16 March 1934; 17 January 1934, p. 18; 21 February 1934, p. 19; 10 January 1934, pp. 11; 24 January 1934, p. 28.
21. *Desasevagan*, 8 January 1924, p. 3; 24 June 1924, p. 10; 27 May 1924.
22. More, *Rise and Fall of the 'Dravidian' Justice Party, 1916-46*, Tellicherry, 2009.
23. Antony, op. cit., 1994, 175; *Suthanthiram*, 10 September 1934, pp. 18-19.
24. *Dupleix*, 18 November 1933; 28 April 1934; 5 May 1934; *Puduvai Murasu*, 11 September 1931, pp. 14-15; 12, 26 January 1931, pp. 14-15.
25. JO 1948, p. 2.
26. *Baradam*, 15 January 1933; 22 October 1933.

27. *Karpagam*, July 1925, p. 209; February 1924, pp. 37-8; September 1924, p. 214; October 1927, pp. 278-82.
28. V. Subbiah, 'Nan Arintha Pavendar Bharathidasan', *Suthanthiram Pon Vizha Malar*, 1987, pp. 100-1; cf. issues of *Puduvai Murasu*; Weber, op. cit., 1996, p. 332; Su. Velmurugan, *Puduvai Sivamum Marumlarchiyum*, Pondicherry, 2009, pp. 24-5; Interview with Dorassamy Naiker, former student Congress leader; Interview with Mannar Mannan, son of Bharathidasan.
29. More, op. cit., 2016; More, *Subramania Bharathi in British and French India, Nationalist, Revivalist or Thamizh Patriot?*, Chennai, 2017.
30. *Deshabandhou*, 3 and 31 May 1929, p. 3.
31. Lena Tamilvanan, ed., *Pandichery Manilam*, Madras, n.d., p. 160.
32. *Baradam*, 19 February 1933; 26 March 1933; 23 April 1933; 7 May 1933.
33. *Vennila*, 9 October 1947.
34. *Baradam*, 21 May 1933; 22 October 1933; 12, 19 November 1933.
35. *Sree Soudjana Ranjini*, 19 March 1931; 2 April 1931.
36. *Vennila*, 6 August 1947; 23 September 1947.
37. Barathidasan & Annadorai, *Mahakavi Bharathiar*, Pondicherry, 1948, pp. 5, 9, 17-18, 29, 36, 37; *Vennila*, 28 October 1947, 1 December 1947.
38. *Vennila*, 10 September 1947; *Pittan*, 16 September 1948.
39. *Kuyil*, 1 January, 1 February, 1 March, 15 July, 15 August, 15 July 1948; *Mouvement Self-respect de Pondichéry, 1945*—Inde H 22, AOM; Interview with Doressamy Naiker, former student Congress leader.
40. *Sarvaviyapi*, 13 June 1934, pp. 47, 189; 28 February 1934, p. 18; 3 January 1934, p. 5; 28 February 1934, p. 18; 12 September 1934, pp. 73-4; 19 April 1935, p. 49; 10 July 1935, p. 35; 17 January 1934, pp. 6, 24; 14 March 1934, p. 22; 1 April 1934, p. 27; 11 April 1934, pp. 113, 24.
41. Documents in the life of Sri Aurobindo, *La Lettre du CIDIF*, no. 20, 1998, p. 87; *Mother India*, October 1981; P. Heehs, *Sri Aurobindo, A Brief Biography*, Delhi, 1989, p. 80; JO 1914, p. 492.
42. *Makkal Manasatchi*, 23-9 June 2010; Heehs, *The Lives of Sri Aurobindo*, Columbia University, 2008; JO 1914, pp. 575, 579.
43. A.B. Purani, *The Life of Sri Aurobindo*, Pondicherry, 1978, p. 152.
44. S. Iyengar, *Sri Aurobindo. A Biography and a History*, I. Pondicherry, 1972, pp. 974, 1023, 1051, 1250; Sri Aurobindo, op. cit., pp. 102-3.
45. *Makkal Manasaatchi*, 23-9 June 2010; Agnès De Place, *Dictionnaire Généalogique et Armorial de l'Inde Française, 1560-1962*, Paris, 1997, p. 30.

46. *Desasevagan*, 18 March 1924.
47. Sri Aurobindo, *Letters on Himself and the Ashram*, Pondicherry, 2011, p. 36; *Le Patriote*, 2 September 1924; *Desasevagan*, 2 September 1924.
48. Sri Aurobindo, op. cit., 2011, pp. 31-2; *Saigon Dimanche*, 6 October 1935.
49. cf. Peter Heehs, op. cit., 2008; *Makkal Manasaatchi*, 16-22 June 2010; Agbes de Place, op. cit., p. 30; Interview with Jean Kessavaram and M.P. Sridharan.
50. cf. Sri Aurobindo, *The Life Divine*, Pondicherry, 1970.
51. *Saigon Dimanche*, 9 October 1932; 19 January 1936; *Inde Illustrée*, October 1933, p. 21.
52. Sri Aurobindo, op. cit., 2011, p. 36.
53. Comités, Inde française, vol. 374, pp. 7-8, ADP.
54. Sri Aurobindo, op. cit., 2015, pp. 104, 453-68.
55. Comités Inde française, p. 8, ADP; JO 1935, II, p. 1171.
56. *Makkal Manasatchi*, 23-29 July 2010; Sri Aurobindo, op. cit., pp. 104, 469-70.
57. Sri Aurobindo, op. cit., pp. 471-2.
58. Lettre de Henri Roux, chargé d'affaire à Delhi au Ministre des Affaires Etrangères, Georges Bidault, Delhi, 16 May 1946, p. 95, IF 6, ADP.
59. *Pittan*, 4 September 1948.
60. Interview with Dr Selvaradja; *Parada Sakti*, annual supplement, 1947, pp. 13-20; September 1947, pp. 194-6; cf. also Suddhananda Barathiyar. *Keerthanjali*, Pondicherry, 1947.
61. Interview with M.P. Sridharan, Antoine Mariadassou and Doressamy Naiker; More, 'Hindu-Christian Interaction in Pondicherry, 1700-1900', *Contributions to Indian Sociology*, 1998, pp. 97-121; According to a few like M.P. Sridharan, an acquaintance of P. Counouma, and Doressamy Naiker, former student Congress leader of Pondicherry, Sri Aurobindo died of liver cirrhosis.

CHAPTER 5

From Revolt to Anti-Fascism, 1936-1945

During the 1930s, the administration of Pondicherry was riven by factions. One faction was led by the mayor of Pondicherry, Joseph Davidu and his ally Selvarajulu Chettiar, while the other was led by V. Subbiah, who had become a labour leader. A third faction was led by Sellane Naiker.

Davidu was a liberal. He was praised by one and all for beautifying Pondicherry during his tenure as mayor, given that earlier the roads were in a very pitiable condition. In certain social aspects, Davidu had followed the principles of Ponnuthamby La Porte. He was very enamoured with the French principle of equality and he preferred to set aside caste and religion in the affairs of the state. He did away with the appellation 'chery schools' meant for the oppressed castes. He was not in favour of naming the roads with caste names. When there was a demand to change the name of Komutty Street to Vaishyal Street, he preferred to name the road 'Calvé' Road. He did away with the name Vellala Street, as it was a caste name. He renamed Tanga Salai (rue de la Monnaie) after Victor Simonel, a Tamil who died in the war front in France during the First World War. He also took steps to abolish the practice of mentioning caste in public documents like birth certificate, etc. It was a revolutionary step to do away with caste altogether, which was in line with Ponnuthamby La Porte's ideals.[1]

However, when Davidu was in charge of the affairs of Pondicherry and French India, there was a revolt brewing among the mill workers of Pondicherry. Though Davidu was aware of the mill problems for more than a decade, he did not have much influence then in the mills.

WORKERS' REVOLT OF 1936

From the time the cotton mills had come into existence in Pondicherry, there were problems between the workers and the management or mill owners on various issues, such as working conditions, working hours, hygiene, subsidies, bonus, wages and strikes, and housing. Right from 1906, the French Parliament was aware of the miserable working conditions in the cotton mills of Pondicherry, where workers toiled for 14 hours to earn a pittance. Child labour was also rampant in these mills. The employees worked for 11 hours a day for a miserable salary. Strikes seem to have started in 1908 itself to obtain salary increment.[2]

Since 1918, the workers had been asking for 48 hours work weeks. It is asserted that it was Joseph Davidu who had negotiated with the mill owners in 1919 and obtained facilities for the workers like bonus, Deepavali *inam*, rice and cloth at a cheap rate.[3] During this period, a certain Balu Pillai and Singaravelu Pillai were in the forefront protecting and promoting workers' rights in the Mudaliarpet Gaebelé Mill. Balu Pillai had obtained, through negotiations, some facilities for the workers like one month's bonus and a building for workers to eat in the shade and not in the open under the sun, and he had also asked for another building and a bank (Sahaya Nidhi) for helping workers financially in times of need. But later, when Balu Pillai was fired by the management, it seems that he wanted to start a labour union in the 1920s with the help of Joseph Davidu. But this attempt did not bear fruit.[4]

In 1921, the workers of Gaebelé Mill went on strike as the bonus was not paid to them that year. They also demanded the reduction of working hours to eight daily, instead of 12, from 6 a.m. to 6 p.m.[5] There were also problems in the Rodier Mill (Anglo-French Textiles), owned by the British firm Best, since 1919 and in the Savana Mill, as the workers demanded more salary and other concessions. The Rodier Mill alone employed about 4,000 workers. In the agitations that followed, one worker of Rodier Mill drowned in the lake nearby while fleeing the police. Newspapers like *Sukapi Viruthini* and *Sree Soudjana Ranjini* denounced the working conditions of workers in the Pondicherry mills, which was much worse than those in British India.[6]

There were attempts to introduce the French labour code in French India as early as the 1920s. A commission under Sellane Naiker, in which there was no representative of the workers, recommended some labour legislation as was prevailing in British India. But it was turned down in 1928.[7] During this time, the workers normally put in 11 hours of work every day. Whenever the mills closed for one reason or the other, the workers and their families suffered. In Rodier Mill alone, there were 5,000 workers at that time, including women and children, who came from villages like Tavalakuppam, Vilvanallur and Muthialpet. They complained that they had left their traditional occupations of agriculture and trade out of ignorance and come to work in mills for a meagre salary.[8]

Child labour was prevalent in the mills. Small boys working in the mills were used by the *mestrys* like Apee Mohideen Sahib to do their domestic chores. Poverty seems to have driven the parents into sending their children to work in the mills.[9]

In the early 1930s, those who were active in the youth organizations of Pondicherry, like V. Subbiah, S.R. Subramanian, R.L. Purushotthama Reddiar, S. Perumal and G. Annusamy, took an interest in the problems of the workers. Most of them like V. Subbiah were not mill workers, but still took an active part in the course of time in organising workers, who were mostly drawn from the very 'low' castes. Some newspapers of Pondicherry, like *Puduvai Murasu,* extended their support to the workers. Pondicherrians, like M. Noel, Bharathidasan, Gurusamy, S. Sivapakasam, and La Hache, were involved in the editing, publishing and printing of this journal, which leaned towards the Self-Respect Movement of E.V. Ramasamy. *Sukapi Vridhini,* edited by N. Vengadasala Naiker, also favoured the workers and their agitations against the mill owners.[10]

In March 1931, workers in the Savana Mill went on strike as their salaries were reduced. The Savana Mill workers were again on strike in February 1935. For 10 or 12 hours of exhausting work per day, the worker earned a meagre salary of just one or one-and-a-half *fanam.* Mr Valet was the director of the Savana Mill, which employed about 2,000 workers.[11] To frighten the striking workers, a French overseer, Petit-Dommange, shot in the air. But he fled as the workers went after him. The French govenor, Léon Solomiac, intervened to pacify the workers. An agreement was reached between the workers and the mill owners which allowed the workers to resume their work in April 1935.[12]

The mill workers in Savana Mill were ill-treated in the most inhumane manner. They were sometimes kicked with boots when they made mistakes. There was no bonus in this mill in 1934 and no holidays for festivals or death of a relative. In the Rodier and Gaebelé Mills, where the workers had no comforts, they had even to bribe *mestrys* or writers in the weaving department in order to be employed. Generally, in the mills there was no provident fund (Sahaya Nidhi) to survive even for six months, even if the worker had put in 40 years of service. Women had no holidays for pregnancy or delivery. During the working hours there was no time for them to give breast milk to their children.[13]

The mill workers of Pondicherry went on strike from June 1936 demanding eight-hour workdays, increase in wages, annual holidays and the right to form trade unions. It was at that time the Left-leaning Popular Front had won the elections in France. The Pondicherry workers, like their counterparts in France, demanded eight hours work, increment in salary, paid holidays, the right to form trade unions and a labour convention.

The workers went on strike again in the last week of July 1936. In August 1936, the workers of Savana Mill held the European directors of the mill as hostages. Governor Solomiac and the new mayor of Pondicherry, Joseph Davidu, were supportive of the mill owners and the management, and wanted to break the strike. The police and the troops intervened to release the directors. There were pitched battles between the armed police and striking workers in which 12 to 20 people died and 65 people were hurt. It seems that it was the French governor, Solomiac, who gave orders to open fire on the strikers. The Savana Cotton Mill was set on fire by some workers and the fire destroyed almost the entire mill. The damages amounted to Rs. 20,00,000. Even the public prosecutor, Mondragon, was hurt in the commotion.[14] The French governor, Solomiac, was called back to France due to the shooting and mishandling of the strike.

The Gaebelé Mill at Mudaliarpet, which employed about 1,200 workers, went on strike on 25 July 1936, while the Savanna and Rodier (founded in 1898) Mills struck work from 28 July. The Rodier Mill belonged to some Englishmen. The director of the Gaebelé Mill was Ehny, while its new owner was Kessoram Poddar & Co of British India. It appears that 20 European British subjects, including 11 women and children, were sequestered in the mill by the labourers. All of them were released in a week. All these events took place at a time when the French Socialist Party, the *Front Populaire*, had won the elections in France.[15] The new French governor, Horace Valentin Crocicchia, discussed the matter with V. Subbiah and L.J.X. Doraisamy, who were the labour leaders.[16]

Later, an arrest warrant was issued against V. Subbiah, the director of the journal, *Suthanthiram*. This journal, which was founded on 16 March 1934 by Subbiah, was banned in 1936. Subbiah was accused of being one of the instigators of the workers against the mill owners. Some workers were arrested as well. L.J.X. Doraisamy was the secretary of the workers' committee of French India at this time.[17]

Labour leaders, V.V. Giri and Gurusamy from Madras, had met the French governor and discussed the situation on 5 August 1936. The French governor took some measures to alleviate the sufferings of the workers. He called a meeting of the directors of the various mills and the mayors of the different affected communes to thrash out measures in favour of the workers without jobs, who were French nationals or residing in Pondicherry. A committee was formed for this purpose, especially to distribute food aid. The Colonial Commission allotted Rs. 20,000 to help those who were affected.[18]

A meeting was organised in Madras, the capital of the Madras Presidency of British India, in favour of the striking Pondicherry workers, in which leaders of the Congress Party as well as the members of the working class participated. The labour leaders, S. Ramamurthi, presided over the meeting. S.R. Subramanian and D. Jeevarathinam of Pondicherry spoke in this meeting. S.R. Subramanian was an excellent orator in Tamil. The speakers criticised vehemently the French and Indian overseers of the mills for their brutality towards the workers.[19]

As a consequence to the workers' revolt in Pondicherry, there was an attempt on 30 July 1937 to murder the mayor of Pondicherry, Joseph Davidu, who had always been supported by the French governor Crocicchia, who had succeeded Solomiac. Davidu had tried to mediate between the mill owners and the workers. This seems to have infuriated some leaders like L.J.X. Doraisamy, V. Subbiah and G. Annusamy. Subsequently, Davidu was fired upon at the 'Samba Kovil'. He sustained an injury on his right thigh, while a 17-year-old Pondicherrian by the name of Duprat died in the hospital of bullet wounds. V. Subbiah and his colleague, Doraisamy, were summoned by the judge. Subbiah, as well as a certain Nadanam, were accused of instigating the shooting. Mayor Davidu named Nadanam as the person who shot him. The missionary journal, *Le Semeur*, wrote that the attempted assassination had been a Communist plot.[20]

As a result of the agitations and commotions, the Savana Mill was closed for six months. The Rodier Mill was closed indefinitely, while the decision on the functioning of the Gaebelé Mill was awaited. As many as 12,000 workers were without work. The Rodier Mill alone accounted for about 5,000 workers.[21]

The Rodier Cotton Mill would reopen again on 16 November 1936. After 30 July 1936, the workers were on forced strike. An agreement was reached on 31 October 1936 between the directors of the mill and labour leaders like L.J.X. Doraisamy and V. Subbiah. Work in the mill resumed and 3,400 workers went back to work. A new strike began in the Mudaliarpet Cotton Mill towards the end of 1936. André Ménard, the French chief of cabinet, who went to the mill to negotiate, was taken hostage by the workers. It seems that sub-inspector, Raphael Dadala, intervened with his men and got Ménard released. But the French governor, Crocicchia, who had succeeded Solomiac on 9 October 1936, mediated between the workers and the mill owners. As a result, the workers went back to work. The Savana Mill was to reopen in March 1937 after the end of the workers' revolt.[22]

R.L. Purushottama Reddiar, a representative of the workers and employee at the Pondicherry radio station, claimed that there were 10,000 workers without jobs and 40,000 people were dependent on them at that time.[23]

Towards the end of 1936, the French government decided to send a senator by the name of Justin Godart to enquire into the grievances of the labourers in the fields and towns, and workers in the factories. He came to Pondicherry as a special envoy of the Left-oriented *Front Populaire* government in France. Justin Godart heard the grievances of the various sections of society. He heard the grievances of the poor farm labourers who slogged in the fields. He heard the grievances of the fishermen of Vamba Keerapalayam, Virampatnam, Vaithikuppam, Solatandavankuppam and Kurusukuppam. They complained about their inactivity over three months as the loading and unloading of goods at the port was monopolised by just two entrepreneurs, Selvarajulu Chettiar and Saravana Chettiar. They held that for every voyage into the sea, each boatman earned just a meagre three annas. Those who worked in the shops had their own set of grievances. They wanted to reduce their working hours from twelve to eight. They also wanted 15 days of holidays in a year and preference to be given to native Pondicherrians in such jobs. The artisans of the Viswakarma caste and the weavers had their own grievances. Demands for compulsory primary education and the creation of a single list of voters were also placed before the senator by the mayor, Joseph Davidu and others.[24]

It needs to be noted here that a broad agreement was reached between the workers and the mill owners due to the intervention of Justin Godart.[25] According to the agreement, from 1 November 1936, the workers would work 9 hours per day and 54 hours a week and be paid the same salary as they were when they worked 10 hours a day. A total of 100 workers would be laid off of whom 50 would enjoy a pension and the remaining 50 would be attached to the public works under Mr Girod. Those who had worked for 25 years would have the right to pension at four per cent of their salary. If a worker died during service, he might be replaced by his son. The old workers who had been hurt while working would get free medical treatment and their full salary. A doctor would be present during work at the mill. Young workers would not have a salary less than 4 *anas* and 3 *caches*. Any supplementary work during the day would be paid at 150 per cent and supplementary work during the night would be paid at 200 per cent of the original salary. The workers would have the right to five weeks of paid holidays in a year. The annual bonus would not be paid in 1936, but in 1937 every worker would have the right to get a bonus equivalent to one month's salary. The cloth badly woven would be given back to the worker who wove it at three-fourth of its real value. Lastly, at the request of the worker, the owners might affect a deduction of 5 per cent of the salary which would bear interest at 0.50 per cent.[26]

This agreement seems to be the outcome of the strikes and agitations in which the workers indulged during 1936 and the activities of the labour leaders like V. Subbiah and L.J.X. Doraisamy. But the Franco-Hindu Party, under J. Davidu, accused Subbiah of not belonging to the labour movement using the labourers for his own self-interest. It also accused others like G. Annousamy who were not workers, of provoking the workers to agitate. They accused Subbiah of enriching himself with workers contributions, owning as he did a press and a car. He was also accused of mobilising the traders against the Franco-British customs agreement of 1936.[27]

It is worthwhile to note at this juncture that the mill workers generally did not observe any caste distinctions among themselves at the workplace. A Valanga or a Vanniyar worker could work by the side of a 'higher' caste labourer in the workplace without any problems or discrimination. The European mill owners never tolerated any discrimination within the mill. By the decree of 16 June 1937, the caste names were thenceforth dropped from the official certificates. It is also worthwhile to note that the original French owner of the Mudaliarpet Mill, Henri Gaebelé, died in the year 1936 in Pondicherry.[28]

In October 1936, Jawaharlal Nehru came to Pondicherry. He spoke at a public meeting at Odiansalai ground. It seems that Subbiah explained to Nehru the problems of workers in Pondicherry. On its part, the government with the collaboration of the mayor, Davidu, and the governor, prepared a draft called 'Workers' Protection Laws' and sent it to the French Overseas Minister for consideration.[29]

Heeding the advice of Nehru, Subbiah went to France on 6 March 1937, with a recommendation letter from him, to talk about the labour problems of Pondicherry with French ministers. French reports maintained that Nehru had entrusted another letter with Subbiah addressed to a certain Frenchwoman, Louise Morin, residing at 5, Rue Marie Davy, Paris 14. He was accompanied by the veteran lawyer, Jean Savarinathan, as Subbiah did not know the French language. Subbiah was delivered a French passport. It appears that Selvarajalu Chettiar financed Subbiah's trip to France. He went to France on behalf of the Workers' Committee of French India.

However, Justin Godart had by then submitted his report of the needs of the French Indians which resulted in the decree of 6 April 1937 according to which the workers obtained further redressal of their grievances with regard to their working hours, salary, holidays, hygiene, safety, etc., on the lines of what was prevailing in France. As a matter of fact, their working hours were reduced a second time to their sought-for eight-hours-per-day schedule. Besides, workers and farmers obtained the right to set up trade unions and the right to strike. The grievances of the other sections of society were also addressed. Compulsory primary education was introduced, and child marriages were also forbidden.[30]

The decree of 6 April 1937 had come about due to the efforts of the Frenchman Justin Godard, without Subbiah intervening in it or its drafting in any way. The decree was published in the *Gazette* only on 18 April 1937. V. Subbiah reached Marseille on 5 April. However, he had claimed that he had sent the new labour decree to Pondicherry from France. According to him, it was Bharathidasan who translated it into Tamil, though it seems that others, like G. Annusamy and Ku. Sivaprakasam, might also have helped with the translation. We do not know exactly the consequences of Subbiah's trip to Paris and what he did there. Subbiah was still a Congressman at that time. He was not a Communist as the French India Communist Party came into existence only in 1942. On the other hand, L.J.X. Doraisamy and his men had somehow published a tract on 5 April 1937 in Tamil claiming victory for the workers due to the arrival of Subbiah in France and his decisive influence.[31]

When the mill labourers organised a workers' meeting in May 1937, the Indian labour leader, V.V. Giri, was prevented from entering Pondicherry and participating in the meeting by the French governor as well as by Mayor Joseph Davidu and his men. V.V. Giri wrote about this incident to the socialist French Prime Minister, Léon Blum. It seems that Blum expressed regrets for the incident to V.V. Giri through a letter to him in French.[32]

When Subbiah and Jean Savarinathan returned to Pondicherry on 6 July 1937, a mammoth meeting of 30,000 workers was held at the Dupleix statue ground at the beach, to greet them for their actions and achievements in Paris in favour of the workers. There were 400 workers to control the crowd, apart from the police. A large congregation of 2,000 women workers was also present. Even before the return of Subbiah, a labour union saw the light in Rodier Mill on 23 June 1937 itself.[33]

As a result of the preceding labour decree, several trade unions came into existence in Pondicherry which was grouped under the French Indian Labour Federation.[34] Thus men like V. Subbiah and L.J.X. Doraisamy acquired a vast following among the labourers. The attempts by Selvarajulu Chettiar to organise the labourers behind him since 1931 failed. Instead, he set up the powerful Fishermen and Boatworkers' Union on communal lines to break the unity of the labour unions and the workers under the influence of V. Subbiah and L.J.X. Doraisamy. Similarly, a Vanniyar Labour Union and a Christian Labour Union were set up to weaken the workers' unions.[35] This led to frequent clashes between Selvarujulu Chettiar and his men, who by then had allied themselves with Joseph Davidu's Franco-Hindu Party, and the labourers of the cotton mills.

In August 1937, the Mudaliarpet Mill was still on strike and the factory occupied by workers. In the ensuing years, intermittent strikes continued in the various mills on various grievances. Conflicts between the workers and the management were the order of the day. In October 1937, French troops were dispatched from French Indochina to maintain law and order as the local police was not sufficient to handle the violence.[36]

The Franco-Hindu Party led by Joseph Davidu had been always patronised by the French governors. Trade union leaders and workers had always been the target of the hooligans at the service of this party. The police took the side of the Franco-Hindu Party against the workers. Governor Crocicchia took no action inspite of complaints against these hooligans. These were some of the allegations levelled by labour leaders, V. Subbiah and L.J.X. Doraisamy, and the opponents of the Franco-Hindu Party at that time. Joseph Davidu invited his supporters among the workers to demonstrate that Subbiah and Doraisamy did not command much influence among the workers. Even Crocicchia was of the view that Subbiah and Doraisamy did not represent all workers and were not the originators of the labour movements. According to him, they exploited the workers for their personal gains and ambition in politics. As they also lacked funds, the governor himself blocked attempts by them to collect funds through the Puduvai Valipar Aikya Sangam, presided over by Savarinathan. Other members of this *sangam*, which was originally founded on 13 July 1934, included R.P. Babilonne, V. Subbiah, Rathina Vinayagam (secretary), Gabriel Anussamy, a teacher, and L.J.X. Doraisamy.

French records maintain that, before the strikes, Subbiah was on the payroll of the railway workers of Trichinopoly, while L.J.X. Doraisamy was unknown. Both of them did not speak French and were not highly educated. But the records affirmed that Subbiah did not lack intelligence and he was in the forefront of all activities, unlike Doraisamy who took the back seat. Subbiah was already in touch with the Communist Party of British India.[37] The fact that needs to be noted at this juncture was that Subbiah had actually gained a certain following among the working class of Pondicherry. But at that time, he was still sympathetic to the Congress Party of British India.

MAHAJANA SABHA PARTY

In December 1936, it seems that V. Subbiah, G. Anussamy, L.J.X. Doraisamy and a certain Narayanasamy Naidu met Selvarajalu Chettiar to persuade him to contest the municipal elections due in May 1937. There was no agreement on this matter. Besides, on 24 January 1937, there was an attempt to assassinate Davidu. Subbiah and his friends were suspected of being involved in the conspiracy. This created tensions in the town. Meanwhile, it seems that the lawyer, Marie Savary, along with G. Anussamy, met Selvarajalu Chettiar to persuade him once again to contest the municipal elections. Their attempt was not successful.[38]

Gandhi's visit to Pondicherry seems to have spurred some persons to find a party with more radical views and to counter the outrightly pro-French Franco-Hindu Party. The new party came into existence on 21 September 1937 (but was made official on 20 March 1938). It was known as the Mahajana Sabha Party. Marie Savary (nominal head), Dorairaj, S.R. Subramanian, Joseph Latour and R.L. Purushothama Reddiar, as well as men like Arangassamy Naiker and Léon Saint Jean of Karaikal and I.K. Kumaran of Mahé, were its members. V. Subbiah was the most active Leftist member of the party. The party had the support of the workers right from the beginning. The head office of the Mahajana Sabha Party was first located at 51, Rangapillai Street, Pondicherry.

Unlike the Franco-Hindu party, the Mahajana Sabha Party stood for a radical change in the political system of French India. It wanted a reduction in unemployment and taxes and free primary education. First of all, it wanted to abolish the absolute powers conferred on the governor by the decree of 1840. Besides, it wanted to democratise the elections by abolishing the two-list voter system. In April 1937, the government banned all public meetings, processions and demonstrations in all of French India.[39]

Municipal elections were to be held on 2 May 1937. Until then, the first list voters, which included the Renouncers, had prevented the second list voters who were the majority of traders, workers and farmers from capturing power and electing a General Council president from amongst themselves, except in 1932. This time, the workers, farmers and traders were believed to support the Mahajana Sabha Party. But the Franco-Hindu Party under Davidu claimed to have given seats to workers, traders, Adi Dravidas and other backward classes. Davidu was, as noted earlier, very much wedded to the principle of equality, and he preferred to set aside caste and religion in the affairs of the state.[40]

In the municipal elections of 2 May 1937, the Franco-Hindu Party led by Joseph Davidu and Selvarajulu Chettiar won. Marie Savary who contested from the second list lost. It appears that the elections had been rigged with the help of the French governor of Pondicherry. Large-scale violence was unleashed by the Franco-Hindu Party supporters. Even the house of Subbiah and those of the candidates were attacked by the *goondas* of Davidu. Davidu used the police force and the government machinery to suppress the Mahajana Sabha Party. The Opposition retaliated.

The municipal elections were followed by the General Council elections on 10 October 1937. Marie Savary and R.L. Purushotthama Reddiar were defeated in the elections once again. In Karaikal, Thomas Arul Poullé, an ally of Joseph Davidu, was defeated in the General Council elections. A certain Pakkirisami Poullé, who was a rice merchant, seems to have contributed very much to his defeat. After the death of Thomas Arul, Pakkirisamy started preaching against the dominance of Catholic Christians in Karaikal and later even founded a party to counter Karaikal personalities like J. Savery and Léon Saint Jean.

By then, V. Subbiah had returned from France. He once again persuaded without success Selvarajalu Chettiar to contest the General Council elections. It seems that Marie Savary, in his turn, pleaded with Selvarajalu to contest the elections as a Mahajana Sabha candidate. But Selvarajalu preferred to ally with Davidu, due to the intervention of Crocicchia.[41] The Franco-Hindu Party led by Davidu won in Pondicherry, with the help of Selvarajalu Chettiar. But in Karaikal, the Mahajana Sabha Party won. The Franco-Hindu Party, led by Thomas Arul Poullé in Karaikal, lost. Thomas Arul had been dominating Karaikal politics for the last 20 years. He had always had the support of the Karaikal Muslims.[42] Thomas Arul was re-elected as president of the General Council, with Rathinavelu Poullé as vice-president.[43]

These elections were followed by extreme violence, in which the police were also involved. Many police stations were attacked. Mill workers were attacked in places like Mudaliarpet, Muthialpet, Odiansalai and Ariyankuppam by men believed to belong to the Selvarajulu-Davidu camp, with the connivance of the police and the governor. There were at least two deaths due to police firing in Muthialpet. Franco-Indian Party supporters were attacked in their turn. Some people fled Pondicherry due to the attacks.[44]

In November 1937, the printing press of *Suthanthiram* newspaper edited by V. Subbiah was attacked. On 20 April 1938, the printing press of *Ediroli*, the pro-Selvarajalu newspaper, was attacked and destroyed. A group of 22, supposed to be belonging to the Selvarajalu camp and involved in this attack, were arrested. Three lawyers, Marie Savary, Gnanou Diagou Mudaliar and C. Balasubramnian (a disciple of Gnanou Diagou), defended the accused, while Gnanou Ambroise was the lawyer for Selvarajalu's men. The magistrate, Edouard Goubert, of Franco-Tamil descent, issued a prison sentence to all of them, apart from fines.[45] Goubert's father was a Frenchman, but his mother was a Tamil Harijan woman.[46]

In their turn, the workers and Mahajana Sabha Party supporters retaliated and attacked the boatmen and Franco-Indian Party men in Ariyankuppam, Puranamkuppam, Manaveli, Mudaliarpet, Nellithope, Oulgaret, Kadirgamam and Muthialpet. The houses of Selvarajalu, Rathinavelu Poullé and Gnanou Ambroise were targets of hooligans. On the trade front, the export of cloth came to a standstill. Pazany, Pulykutty, Raghavan and Nelly Krishnan were believed to be the principal lieutenants of V. Subbiah. On 22 January 1938, both Selvarajalu Chettiar and Davidu, mayor of Pondicherry, had gone to Keerapalayam and promised to provide water, electricity and road repair, in order to pacify the people there.[47]

The French government in Paris sent a high official called Texier to Pondicherry to enquire about the riots and violence. Among those who were subject to this enquiry were L.J.X. Duraisamy, V. Subbiah and S.R. Subramanian. G. Anussamy used to write letters in French to the French Prime Minister in defence of Subbiah and others during this time.[48]

Nevertheless, the Mahajana Sabha Party went for a Gandhian style Non-Cooperation Movement. They refused to pay taxes, disregarded the orders of the police and the judiciary, substituted themselves to these institutions in some places, and set up village panchayats. Naturally, the government came to a standstill and was forced to negotiate with the Mahajana Sabha Party leaders. But political dynamics in France at that time was favourable to the Franco-Hindu Party. The government, instead of organising fair and free elections as demanded by the Mahajana Sabha Party, confronted the workers and sought to suppress their movement. Davidu and Selvarajulu were party to this attempt.[49]

The continued unrest and the Non-Cooperation Movement of the Mahajana Sabha brought about an administrative stalemate. The Mahajana Sabha Party was not completely non-violent. In 1938, a 20-year-old youngster from Karaikal known as Arul Marie Joseph had set up a bicycle brigade in Pondicherry, on behalf of the party. This brigade struck terror in Pondicherry. Joseph Davidu complained that men on bycycles were threatening municipal members, Saravana Chettiar, Mohamed Haniff, Ambroise, and Rathinavelupoullé, asking them to resign. Under pressure, the members of the town municipality and the mayor resigned on 4 April 1938. Governor

Crocicchia finally dissolved all the municipal councils of Pondicherry and appointed municipal commissions, whose members were generally not drawn from the Franco-Hindu Party.[50] Some attribute the dissolution to the effort of V. Subbiah. Davidu and Thomas had thus lost power. However, the governor did not dissolve the General Council and local councils.[51]

Earlier, in January 1938, Subbiah participated in the Congress conference at Haripura. Subbiah was still a Congressman. At that time, Selvarajalu Chettiar was appointed as the president of the Colonial Commission. During the Haripura conference, Subbiah struck a good relationship with Left-wing elements of the Congress Party, including Jawaharlal Nehru. On 28 May, he even attended a meeting of the farmers' (kisan) party and the Communist Party.[52] In April 1938, the Popular Front Government, led by Léon Blum, fell and was succeeded by a government headed by Edouard Daladier. Under him, a new round of repressive policies seems to have been unleashed in Pondicherry. During this period, there was a clash between Selvarajalu Chettiar's men (Mukkuwas) and the workers (Vanniyars and Valangas) who loaded the goods in boats. The latter wanted an increment in their salary, but all the boats in the harbour belonged to Selvarajulu Chettiar, who, it was alleged, had the support of Governor Crocicchia. It was believed that Subbiah's men attacked the Franco-Hindu Party workers and created problems in and around Pondicherry during that period.[53]

Governor Crocicchia dissolved the existing municipal commissions and appointed new ones, with its members mostly sympathetic to the Franco-Hindu Party. Periodicals like *Suthanthiram* and *Kudiarasu* were banned from 19 May 1938 onwards. Public meetings and processions were banned. All periodicals, newspapers and leaflets were censored. Labour leaders like R.L. Purushotthama Reddiar and R. Dorairaj as well as many others, including students, were arrested. The police even opened fire in Muthialpet killing two. Many took refuge in neighbouring villages of British India. The 11th French regiment from Indochina landed in Pondicherry in November 1938 to bolster the repressive actions of the government. The French governor, it is believed, propped up men like Selvarajulu Chettiar and Thomas Arul vigorously during this period.[54]

It seems on the whole that the French governors, since the institution of democratic political institutions in French India, had never striven energetically to put an end to the internecine quarrels and clashes between the political parties and their rowdy elements. They never had a plan or policy to even restrict them. Instead, they seem to have taken the side of one party against the other and thus contributed to the misery and insecurity, especially in Pondicherry society. In fact, it had become an intrinsic part of colonial culture as far as Pondicherry was concerned. This colonial culture also created the illusion among some French Indians that they were part and parcel of the great French family, though France was thousands of kilometres away from minuscule Pondicherry, which was just a point in the vast Indian sub-continent.[55]

On 23 September 1938, Louis Bonvin took over as governor from Croccichia. The Indian press held that it was Nehru and V.K. Krishna Menon, who influenced the recall of Crocicchia. In any case, it had a salutary effect on the general situation prevailing in Pondicherry. People who had left Pondicherry (about 10,000, according to one estimate) out of fear started to return. Workers' grievances were addressed and cases against them were withdrawn. Even the French troops were withdrawn. It seems that Marie Savary was instrumental in bringing about this process of reconciliation.[56] Generally speaking, the Muslims of Karaikal, like those of Pondicherry, were split between the Franco-Hindu Party and the Mahajana Sabha Party. In Karaikal, the Mahajana Sabha leader, N. Ahmad Naina Maracair, declared: 'There is no religious, cultural difference between British India and French India. Both belong to one nation. Both are slaves'.[57]

However, due to the unrest in Pondicherry, Subbiah had gone to Madras during the first week of December 1938. Later, due to an understanding with Selvarajalu Chettiar, Subbiah acceded to return to Pondichery and present himself to the magistrate there on 17 December. Subbiah returned to Pondicherry early on 16 December. On the same day, at 4.30 p.m., Selvarajalu Chettiar, who was then president of the Colonial Commission, was shot dead by a 21-year-old Left-leaning mill labourer called Ramiah, belonging to the Vanniyar caste, hailing from Kumbakonam, who worked in the Savana Mill. He shot Selvarajalu at the Government Finance Department building, just in front of the rear gate of the governor's palace in Dupleix Street, while he descended the staircase. Selvarajalu died in the Colonial Hospital, while Ramiah shot himself dead.[58]

Riots broke out at the death of Selvarajalu in the town, especially in the Grand Bazar area. Shops belonging to the sympathisers of the Mahajana Party were looted. The *Suthanthiram* press was attacked. Marie Savary's house and Subbiah's driver were attacked. Police entered Subbiah's house without warrant. Lawyer Gnanou Ambroise took the place of Selvarajalu as president of the Colonial Commission.

The chief of the bicycle brigade, Arul Marie Joseph, was arrested on 23 December 1938. But he was released in April 1939, as there was no evidence to implicate him in Selvarajalu's murder. In the very same year, Subbiah nominated him as the manager of his paper, *Suthanthiram*. L.J.X. Doraisamy, a close associate of Subbiah, was also arrested and kept in custody for three months following Selvarajalu's murder. He then broke away from Subbiah, declaring that the latter was a parasite of the workers, who made a living by exploiting them for his own political development. He denounced Subbiah and his clan as parasites and hailed Marie Savary as an honourable leader.[59]

According to some, Ramiah sold Communist newspapers like *Janasakti* and *Suthanthiram*, for which he was beaten up by Sevarajalu's men and imprisoned. This led Ramiah to enact his revenge on Selvarajalu. Whether he planned the attack all by himself or whether he had accomplices was never known. In any case, it is certain that Subbiah knew Ramiah as the latter visited his house quite often. On the other hand, Ramiah also knew Marie Savary. Ramiah was seen travelling in his car, while Subbiah was a refugee in Madras. In fact, on the day of Selvarajalu's assassination, Marie Savary's car was stoned by some miscreants.

There was a general feeling in the town that Subbiah had instigated the murder of Selvarajalu. Subbiah was thus implicated in the murder of Selvarajalu Chettiar. His house in Pondicherry was searched. He was arrested in Madras and kept in custody. At that time, V. Radja Bangarammal, Subbiah's mother, who was then in Madras, wrote to Governor Louis Alexis Étienne Bonvin asking him to give adequate protection to her son. Subbiah had already been wanted by the French police for some time. The British handed Subbiah over to the French, who imprisoned him for six months. Governor Bonvin had nursed a visceral hatred for Subbiah, and he banished him from French India on 18 August 1941. It was believed then in French official circles that Subbiah lived on the money extorted from the workers. Other labour leaders like S.R. Subramanian, R. Dorairaj and Purushottama Reddiar were also arrested and imprisoned in Pondicherry. To ease the tensions and stop clashes and find a way for the return of refugees, Governor Bonvin called an all-party meeting on 8 February 1939. Marie Savary, Davidu, along with C. Balasubramanian, the Samuga Democratic Party leader and some Karaikal leaders, like Leon Saint Jean, were invited for talks. Davidu, however, withdrew from the talks, while Subbiah never attended them.[60]

Subbiah was released on bail on 16 June 1939. The other leaders were also released. S.R. Subramanian was released after about one-and-a-half years in jail in March 1940. *Suthanthiram* was restarted in March 1939 as a bilingual paper with Mariappan and Lebaud as editors. The case against Subbiah was dropped as there was no evidence against him in the murder of Selvarajalu Chettiar. He came back to Pondicherry in 1940. Further, at that time, the joint magistrate's court of Tindivanam had sentenced Subbiah to six months imprisonment on 20 November 1940, under the Defence of India Rules.[61]

During this period, Joseph Davidu continued to be the president of the General Council, though his party was in decline. Besides, on account of continued violence and conditions of unrest in Pondicherry, the economy was also in decline as during Nadou Shanmugam's period. When things were thus, the Second World War broke out in September 1939. Bonvin did not think it fit to consult Joseph Davidu before declaring that French India was at war, too, against the Fascists. Initially, Bonvin was in favour of Philippe Pétain who had allied with Hitler. But due to British pressure in India, he revised his position and supported Charles de Gaulle's Free French government in exile in London. Bonvin came down heavily on Leftists like Subbiah once again, following the clampdown on Communists in British India. However, Subbiah and his men continued to be active not only among the mill workers, but also among the agricultural labourers, toddy tappers, teachers and government servants of Pondicherry, organising them in unions and fighting for their rights. French records maintain that they were nationalistic and Communist, and against the Europeans.[62]

DURING SECOND WORLD WAR, 1939-45

On 1 September 1939, the Second World War broke out. Subbiah was prohibited from speaking in meetings in French and British India. At that time, A.K. Gopalan, a Malayali leader of the Communist Party of India was hiding at Muthupettai under Dharmalinga Thevar's protection. S.R. Subramanian had admitted that he, along with Subbiah and Ilayankudi Arangasamy Naiker, wanted to launch an armed revolution in Tamil Nadu, taking advantage of the war situation. But it seems that A.K. Gopalan who came to Karaikal dissuaded them from doing so, as Russia would help them at the appropriate time. Subsequently, Subbiah was arrested on 12 January 1941 in Tanjore on the Karaikal border, when he was with a certain Ramanathan Chettiar and was kept in Vellore Central Jail till September 1942. He was then still a Congressman and a Mahajana Sabha Party member. All shops were closed in Pondicherry in reaction to the arrest of Subbiah. Subbiah went on a fast in Vellore jail. A French note tells us that Subbiah was at that time an agent of the Imperial Insurance Company of New Delhi. His mother V. Bangaramal wrote once again to the governor of Pondicherry, from her residence at 7, Velalja Street (Pondicherry), requesting him to intervene and free Subbiah as he 'was the only bread-winner in the family'. Marie Savary also wrote to the governor, petitioning for the release of Subbiah.

The British Indian government lifted the ban on the Communist Party of India in July 1942. Subbiah launched the Communist Party of French India after his release from Vellore jail, along with men like S.R. Subramanian. Some Mahajana Sabha Party members joined him or supported him in this venture. Subbiah had always had the support and sympathy of some oppressed caste Christian stalwarts, who were actually Renouncers, like Joseph Latour and Murugasamy Clemenceau, since the 1930s. Murugasamy Clemenceau was a retired war veteran.

In 1940, after the 18 June declaration of Charles de Gaulle and his subsequent call to the French people in the East, Bonvin, after some hesitation, rallied behind De Gaulle, though, largely, owing to British pressure in India. Thus, he chose the camp of De Gaulle, in the place of Pétain, who sided with Germany quite early during the Second World War. In February 1941, a Franco-British agreement was signed which established a customs union between French and British India. It had its disadvantages for the French settlements. Above all, they had hereafter the right to sell their products in the huge British Indian market, at a time when there were difficulties in selling them in France and its colonies due, mainly, to the war conditions.[63]

Later, in 1940, the Communist Party of France extended its support to the Free France Movement of De Gaulle, and the ban on Communists was lifted also in French India, which allowed men like Subbiah to participate in politics. In July 1942, when Russia supported the allies, the ban on the Communist Party was lifted in British India.

The General Council of Pondicherry, presided over by Joseph Davidu, passed a unanimous resolution in favour of *France Libre* (Free France) and sent it to De Gaulle. De Gaulle was reminded of the sacrifices made by the Pondicherrians during the First World War. The resolution affirmed that French India was not a colony but a continuation of French territory and its institutions.

French Indians of all classes contributed profusely to the war fund. The amount collected rose to more than 1,00,000 rupees. Many young men of Pondicherry voluntarily enrolled in the French army to fight the Germans. De Gaulle acknowledged Governor Bonvin and the French Indians' support to the Resistance Movement. Charles François Marie Baron, the future governor of Pondicherry, was sent to Singapore from Pondicherry to represent De Gaulle in 1941. Baron had played a crucial role in rallying French India behind the Free France Movement of De Gaulle.[64]

When Mahatma Gandhi launched the Quit India Movement in British India, the response to it was generally muted in Pondicherry. There was still no Congress Party in Pondicherry. It seems that Ambady Narayanan and Lambert Saravane, both professors at the Colonial College, used to deliver lectures to students at the Pier in favour of

From Revolt to Anti-Fascism, 1936-1945 155

the Quit India Movement. Subbiah did not come out in support of the movement launched by Gandhi on 9 August 1942, as the Communist Party of India was against it. At that time, Subbiah got married to Saraswati of Madras from his own Telugu Balija caste.

From 1939 to 1945, Subbiah spent most of his time underground and was wanted by the French police. Much of this time he spent in Tamil Nadu. At other times, he stayed in disguise at the motor pump shed in the lands of Chandrasekhara Reddiar of Pandasozhanallur. He was a persona non grata in Pondicherry until 6 September 1945.

Pondicherrians who had settled and prospered in French Indochina, especially Saigon, also contributed liberally to the war fund. Mr Prouchandy and Madame Prouchandy of Pondicherry donated 100 *piastres* each to the war fund in October 1939. Another person from Pondicherry who had prospered in Indochina and who donated to the war fund during the two World Wars was Mohamed Said. In November 1943, he donated 110 rupees to the fund. Earlier, in 1918, he had also subscribed to the national loan scheme of the French government. In Pondicherry itself, Professor Mohamed, who taught at the Colonial College, contributed to the war fund. There was even a street called Ruelle Mohamed Said in Hanoi. Sri Aurobindo is believed to have spiritually invested in turning the tide of the Second World War in favour of the Allies.[65]

Indians settled in France as students, both from French India and British India, were arrested and interned in the Nazi concentration camps for some time before being released. Many of them participated in the French Resistance Movement against the Nazis and thus fought for the liberation of France. A student who had studied in the *Collège Français* of Pondicherry, called Mouchilotte Madhavan, was pursuing his higher studies in Paris. He, too, had joined the Resistance Movement and was arrested by the German Gestapo. He was shot dead by the Nazis along with 40 others at Mont Valérien outside Paris. He gave up his life for freedom and France.

It is noteworthy at this juncture that in the year 1942, the exiled Indian leader, Subhas Chandra Bose, who wanted to drive the British out of India by raising an Indian army with German help, had met Pierre Laval, a minister in Vichy France. He seems to have broached the topic of Independence for the French colonies in India with Laval.

But Laval, though he was allied with the Nazis, was not interested. It was a time when the Japanese had conquered Singapore. It was rumoured then that Japan was eyeing Pondicherry and taking Aurobindo Ghose hostage. At that time, Edward Thompson suggested that the British should take Pondicherry under their protective custody.[66] In February 1943, Subhas Chandra Bose made his way to Japan and Southeast Asia to fight for Indian Independence from there, with Japanese help.

Governor Bonvin declared on 6 November 1944 that the French Indian population had donated a total of Rs. 8,12,200 to the war effort. Besides, much money was donated to the Red Cross which was sent to France, apart from 580 parcels and 10 tons of goods, worth more than Rs.1,50,000. To this amount must be added the Rs. 38,000 donated in cash to the Red Cross and the subscriptions for the Red Cross that amounted to more than Rs. 80,000. Besides, the Marakkayars of Karaikal had contributed considerable cash for the war effort. A sum of Rs. 20,000 was collected from the Karikal Muslims alone in one go for the armaments fund. On the whole, Bonvin concluded that French Indians had given nearly one million and 10,000 rupees or 16 million francs.

French records maintain that Joseph Davidu, when he was mayor, made use of Muthu Kumarappa Reddiar to extort money from the rich Reddiar landlords who did not support him. During his tenure as president of the General Council, he was accused of indulging in corruption and abuse of power. While he was president of the General Council in 1943 after the death of Marie Savary, his lieutenants were Gnanou Ambroise, head of the Commission of Finance, and Rathinavelu Poullé, who headed the Colonial Commission. During this period, Davidu was tried for corruption, abuse of power and misappropriation of funds. He was prosecuted, convicted of the charges and sentenced to prison. But taking into account his social ranking, he was left in liberty. He was succeeded by the Frenchman, Paul Le Faucheur, as president of the General Council. It was then that the demand was raised in the General Council for the abolition of discrimination on the basis of colour and race which was in vogue in the European Club of Pondicherry. But Davidu's influence as well as that of the Mahajana Sabha Party was on the decline. In April

1944, his membership of the Municipal Commission of Pondicherry was cancelled by the governor. Joseph Davidu died in 1944 and the Franco-Hindu Party became irrelevant after him. It was the time when the Fourth Republic had come into existence in France.

'Combat' was a Resistance Movement of France born in the year 1941. It rallied behind Charles de Gaulle during 1942, when it established itself firmly in the French colony of Algeria in North Africa. *Combat* was part of what was known as the *France Combattante* or Fighting France. Maurice Schumann was the spokesman of the *France Combattante*.[67] It was realised then that France alone, without its colonies as members of the same family, would not be considered as a superpower in future. It was also held that, as there was a Catholic France and a Protestant France, there was also a Muslim France. French India and Pondicherry were to be parts of this French federation or empire. In a conference in Washington on 9 July 1944, the idea of French Federation or Union was endorsed.[68]

On 25 May 1942, the French under General Koenig fought the Germans at Bir Hakeim in Algeria (*Combat*, 5 June 1943). Volunteers from different parts of the French colonies went to take part in this battle. Some Tamil and Franco-Tamil Pondicherrians, too, went there to fight the Germans under General Koenig. In April 1944, Bonvin received the *Croix de la Libération* from General De Gaulle himself during his visit in Algiers. On 5 October 1944, the secretary of the *Comité Redressement Inde Française* (Recovery Committee of French India), Joseph Latour, sent a telegram to General De Gaulle, affirming the support of the people of French India in his efforts to renovate France and the French empire.[69]

On 29 February 1944, there was a workers' meeting at the choultry of Tirumudy Nadaraja Chettiar (proprietor), presided over by V. Subbiah. There were 20 people attending the meeting. They were— V. Subbiah, Mr Durand, Mr Laloum, Mr Prigent, Saravane Lambert, Tambuchetty, Dorairadjou, H.M. Cassime, Muthu Poullé, Ribeiro, R.L. Purushothama Reddiar, Murugasamy Clémenceau, Paul Latour, Sainte Rose, Mrs Tetta, Mrs Prigent, Ms Paulpont, Gnana Vennemani and Daniel. During the meeting, Subbiah said that Emmanuel Adicéam, a history teacher and relative of Davidu, wanted to join them.

Subsequently, two delegates from Pondicherry were present at the meeting of the colonial section of the *Combat* in Alger. They were D. Jeevarathinam and Emmanuel Adicéam.[70] The latter was a French teacher of history at the high school of Oran in Algeria. He hailed from Pondicherry and was a cousin of Mayor Joseph Davidu. He was sent on a three-month mission to Pondicherry to establish the *Combat* in December 1944. The *Combat* in Pondicherry was actually started by Emmanuel Adicéam, and it seems to have functioned right from February 1944. A branch of *Combat* was also started in Karaikal through the efforts of Adicéam and Subbiah. Among the participants in a meeting organised in Karaikal for the purpose were Subbiah, Adicéam, lawyer J. Xavéry, councillor Arangassamy Naiker, Léon Saint Jean and his father Saint Jean, his relative and lawyer De la Flore, cultivator Ganapathy Iyer and 13 others of the Mahajana Sabha Party. It seems then that some of Subbiah's friends in Karaikal were turning against J. Xavéry and Léon Saint Jean. However, in the beginning, Governor Bonvin himself welcomed the efforts of Emmanuel Adicéam to promote *Combat*.

Emmanuel Adicéam left Pondicherry in April 1944. By then, *Combat* had 28 members. The head office of *Combat* was in Subbiah's house at No. 7, Vellaja Street, which had earlier served as the head office of the Mahajana Sabha Party. V.Subbiah, who was then the labour leader, was made the president of *Combat* by Adicéam himself according to some, while Frenchmen like Commandant Auge and Prof Prigent were the vice-presidents. Prof Lambert Saravane, Dr Sainte Rose and Madame Paul Pont of Karaikal were the general secretaries, while H.M. Cassime/Muthu Poullé was the treasurer.[71] The *Combat* consisted of a wide variety of people ranging from government officers, students, workers, farmers, friends of Davidu and Communists. It did not include leaders of the local political parties but took the support of the Communists. Some of the others who sympathised with *Combat* were Muthu Kumarappa Reddiar and Edouard Goubert. The *Combat* in Pondicherry was supposed to be a pro-French Patriotic Organisation. French records maintain that men like Lambert Saravane, Sainte Rose, Tetta, and Adicéam wanted Subbiah to lead *Combat* in Pondicherry. Bonvin disliked the Communists, especially Subbiah. So, he gradually revised his position and turned against *Combat*.

Bonvin, an ardent protagonist of the two-list system in French Indian politics, now no longer saw the activities of the *Combat* in Pondicherry in a favourable light, though he was its honorary president. He thought that there were no fascists in Pondicherry and men like Saravane and the other *Combat* members had no role to play in the French Resistance Movement.[72] Bonvin disliked Subbiah above all, whom he accused of taking orders from the Communist Party of British India. Subbiah was accused of running down the French administration and conspiring the removal of Bonvin. Hence, Bonvin passed orders to actually banish Subbiah from Pondicherry in April 1944. He claimed that Subbiah was not a French national from Pondicherry and did not speak a word of French. Subbiah protested, but in vain. The governor accused the Communists for their defence of the proprietors in French India, as Subbiah inspite of being a Communist was on good terms with the leading merchants and landlords of Pondicherry, like Tirumudy Nadaraja Chettiar, H.M. Cassime and Muthu Poullé. Men like Muthu Poullé being prosperous merchants, helped Subbiah financially and gained his sympathy. They defended the causes of Subbiah. Marie Savary also came to the defence of Subbiah in the nationality case. He protested against the claim that Subbiah was born of British Indian parents. Subbiah's supporters held several meetings to press with their claims to cancel the order outlawing Subbiah. Bonvin ended up banning all meetings and censored the press and postal services. He even held that the *Combat* was an illegal group.

Subbiah, in his turn, unleashed propaganda against Bonvin in the frontier areas by qualifying him as a fascist and a Nazi and comparing him with Marshal Pétain and his collaborator Laval, with the intention of getting rid of him as governor. He also filed a case in the Karaikal court against the orders of Bonvin. The judgement of the Karaikal court delivered on 25 September 1944 ruled that Subbiah was a 'foreigner', in spite of him being born in French India on 7 February 1911 of a French mother. Subbiah appealed against this judgement in the higher court of Pondicherry. But by 6 September 1945, Subbiah's expulsion was rescinded by the interim governor, Jeandin. Thus, Subbiah was able to return to Pondicherry. Another *Combat* member, Emmanuel Tetta, who was transferred by Bonvin to Yanam as administrator, was brought back to Pondicherry as *chef de service des contributions* (head of the tax assessment department). Lambert Saravane was reinstated as professor in the Colonial College.[73]

Emmanuel Tetta was at the head of a sporting association in Pondicherry called 'Cercle Sportif de Pondichéry'. The other two heads of this association were Mariadassou, the son-in-law of Joseph Davidu, and the magistrate, Tamby. All the three were related to one another. The association had 210 members of which the majority were 'higher' caste Catholic Chrisitians. However, this sporting club was not exclusively meant for 'high' caste Christians as was the European Club, the membership of which was open to Europeans only.

During the period when Subbiah was in exile, the labour movement was kept alive by men like Murugasamy Clemenceau. Murugasamy is known to have spent much of his money for the Communist Party in Pondicherry. In February 1945, an Anti-Fascist Conference was organised in Pondicherry in which Pondicherry stalwarts like Murugasamy Clemenceau, Lambert Saravane, G. Annusamy and Paul Latour participated. However, some 200 workers of Rodier Mill broke off with Subbaya at that time. They started a short-lived journal called *Puduvai Thozhilali*. Later, on 5-6 October 1945, a meeting took place in a room on the first floor where the head office of the association called Saraswati Sangam was located in Ranga Poullé Street, Pondicherry. The head office of *Combat* was then on the ground floor of the same building. The participants in the preceding meeting were Emmanuel Tetta, Lambert Saravane, Subbiah, Kali Charan Ghosh, and Murugasamy Clémenceau, an intimate colleague of Subbiah. The Congress-minded nationalist, P. Duraisamy, who ran the Ansari Café (presently Indian Coffee House in Nehru Street) at that time, vehemently criticised Subbiah for his purportedly nonnationalist political stance during this period. P. Duraisamy later came to be known as Ansari Duraisamy.[74]

It is worthwhile to note at this juncture that the Muslims of French India highly favoured remaining in the French Union. They never participated in the Muslim League conferences organised in British India. But in Karaikal, a small number of young Muslims founded the French India Muslim League, with Syed Kamal as president. It supported the policies of the All-India Muslim League of Muhammad Ali Jinnah. But they had very little influence on the local Muslim society. They even started a newspaper called *Balyan (Young Man)* as the organ of the party. But in Pondicherry the ideology of the Muslim League did not find adherents.[75]

NOTES

1. *Desobagari*, 8 May, 28 August 1937, p. 2; *Indochine-Inde*, 23 March 1937; 4-5 April 1937; *Saigon Dimanche*, 28 May 1935.
2. *Sukapi Viruthini*, 15 August 1935, p. 3; M.C. Vashist, 'Trade Union Movement in Pondicherry State with Special Reference to Mahé', University of Calicut, 1993, p. 30; *Puduvai Murasu*, 11 September 1931, pp. 20-1; *Puduvai Murasu*, 26 January 1931, p. 15; Jacques Weber, *Pondichéry et les Comptoirs de l'Inde après Dupleix: La Démocratie au pays desCastes*, Paris, 1996, p. 333.
3. *Desobagari*, 8 May 1937, pp. 3, 4; *Sukapi Viruthini*, 21 January 1921.
4. *Desobagari*, 3 July 1937; *Puduvai Murasu*, 14 September 1931, p. 17; *Dupleix*, 25 August 1934; Siva ilango, *Pirachintiyavum Dravida Iyakkamum* (Tamil), Puduchery, 2000, pp. 17-21.
5. *Sree Soudjana Ranjini*, 19 February 1921.
6. Lettre du Gouverneur de l'IF au Ministre des Colonies, Pondicherry, 9 February 1922, p. 112; Asie 1918-29, IF, No. 1, ADP; Ilango, op. cit., pp. 26-9.
7. Vashist, op. cit., pp. 30-4; *Gazetteer of India: Union Territory of Pondicherry*, Pondicherry, 1982, vol. II, pp. 243-4; *Puduvai Murasu*, 14 September 1931, p. 18; Manifeste du Parti Communiste de l'IF-Inde G 29, AOM.
8. *Desasevagan*, 29 January 1924, p. 15; 4 February 1924, p. 17.
9. *Dupleix*, 25 August 1934; *Suthanthiram*, 10 September 1934, pp. 2-3; *Puduvai Murasu*, 19 January 1931, p. 17; *Puduvai Murasu*, 19 January 1931, p. 17; *Dupleix*, 2, 23 June 1934.
10. Vashist, op. cit., p. 34; V. Subbiah, 'Naatu Viduthalai Poratathil Thozhilalar Pangum Kadamaiyum' in *Suthanthiram, Suthanthira Thina Sirappu Malar*, Pondicherry, 1980, p. 10; Ilango, op. cit., pp. 18, 33-41; *Puduvai Murasu*, 19 September 1931.
11. *Indochine-inde*, 16 August 1936; *Saigon Dimanche*, 24 February 1935, 30 October 1932; *Inde illustrée*, October 1933; *Sukapi Viruthini*, 15 August 1935, pp. 3-4; *Sree Soudjana Ranjini*, 19 March 1931; 23 April 1931.

12. *Saigon Dimanche*, 7, 14 April 1935.
13. *Dupleix*, 25 August 1934; 4 November 1933, 13 January 1934, 14, 28 April 1934.
14. *Indochine-inde*, 9, 16 August 1936; 8 November 1936; Weber, *Les Etablissements Français en Inde au XIXe Siècle (1816-1914)*, vol. IV, Paris, 1988, pp. 2201, 2309; *Suthanthiram Pon Vizha Malar*, 1987, Editorial; *Suthanthiram*, 1 December 1938; *Sukapi Viruthini*, 2 May, 1 September 1936.
15. *Indochine-inde*, 9 August 1936; *Saigon Dimanche*, 24 February 1935; *Inde illustrée*, March 1933; *Ministre des Colonies au Ministre des Affaires Etrangères*, Paris, 3 August 1936, p. 95, in Ministère AE, 1930-40, Indes Françaies, no. 4, ADP.
16. Tél Crocicchia au Ministre des Colonies, Pondicherry, 18 August 1930, Ministère Affaires Etrangères, 1930-40, Indes Françaies, no. 4, p. 113, ADP.
17. *Saigon Dimanche*, 23 August, 6 September 1936; JO 1934, I, p. 34.
18. *Indochine-inde*, 16, 23 August 1936; *Sukapi Viruthini*, 1 September 1936.
19. *Saigon Dimanche*, 23 August 1936; Interview with Paul Radjanedassou.
20. *Indochine-Inde*, 7, 21 February 1937; 17 June 1937.
21. *Indochine-inde*, 12 July 1936; *Sukapi Viruthini*, 1 September 1936.
22. *Indochine-inde*, 14-15 March 1937; Tél Crocicchia au Ministre des Colonies, Pondichéry, 2 November 1936; MInistère Affaires Etrangères, 1930-40; Indes Françaies, no. 4, p. 116, ADP; *Indochine-inde*, 10 January 1937.
23. *Indochine-inde*, 10 October 1936; *Saigon Dimanche*, 29 November 1936.
24. Aff. Pol. Missions en Inde, 1936, AOM.
25. JO 1936, pp. 1342-5.
26. *Indochine-Inde*, 15 November 1936.
27. *Desobagari*, 8 May 1937; 7, 21 May 1938.
28. *Indochine-inde*, 8 November 1936; Jacques Weber, op. cit., vol. IV, p. 2051; V. Subbiah, 'Nan Arintha Pavendar Bharathidasan', *Suthanthiram Pon Vizha Malar*, 1987, p. 101; Aff. Pol; Missions en Inde, 1936, AOM.
29. *Desobagari*, 8 May 1937; *Va. Subbiah Pavala Vizha Malar*, vol. II; Subbiah, V. 'Puduvaiyin Pazham Perum Varalatru Pinnani', *Suthanthiram Pon Vizha Malar*, 1987, p. 40; V. Subbiah, *Saga of Freedom Movement: Testament of my Life*, Madras, 1990, pp. 105-32.
30. *Suthanthiram Pon Vizha Malar*, editorial, 1987; Interview with A. Arulraj; Ediroli, 28 February 1938, p. 6; Lettre du Service de la Police et de la Sûreté aau Gouverneur de l'IF, Pondichéry, 10 June 1938-Inde G 29, AOM; Lettre du Gouverneur de l'IF au Ministre des Colonies, Pondi-

cherry, 20 May 1935 – Inde G 28, AOM; Dossier Comité Ouvriers de l'IF, -Inde G 28, AOM.
31. Subbiah, op. cit., p. 101; Aff. Pol; Missions en Inde, 1936, AOM; *Suthanthiram*, 5 April 1937; Ilango, op. cit., pp. 87-149; Lettre du Gouverneur de l'IF au Ministre des Colonies, Pondicherry, 25 April 1937—Inde G 28, AOM.
32. *Suthanthiram Pon Vizha Malar*, pp. 10-11; V.V. Giri's speech in Pondicherry on 14 September 1969, when he was President of India; M.P. John, 'Employer-Employee Relationship', *Suthanthiram Pon Vizha Malar*, 1987, pp. 16-17; R. Dadala, *My Struggle for the Freedom of French India*, Pondicherry, n.d., pp. 39-40.
33. *Sukapi Viruthini*, 1 August 1937; Weber, op. cit., 1996, p. 334.
34. Subbiah, op. cit., 1990, p. 135.
35. *Suthanthiram*, 11 January 1939, 1 December 1939; Lettre du Gouverneur de l'IF au Ministre des Colonies, Pondicherry, 20 May 1935—Inde G 28, AOM.
36. Ministre des Colonies au Ministre des Affaires Etrangères, Paris, 27 October 1937, p. 104, Ministère Affaires Etrangères, 1930-40, Indes Françaises, no. 4, ADP; *Desobagari*, 14 August 1937, p. 2; 22 December 1937; *Suthanthiram*, 2 July 1939; 5 December 1939.
37. *Suthanthiram*, 10 March 1937; *The Hindu*, 29 October 1936; Lettre du Gouverneur de l'IF au Ministre des Colonies, Pondicherry, 25 October 1932—Inde G 28, AOM; Lettre du Chef de Police au Gouverneur, Pondicherry, 22 March 1937, AOM.
38. *Ediroli*, 28 February 1938, p. 6; Lettre du Gouverneur de l'IF au Ministre des Colonies, Pondicherry, 26 March 1937—Inde G 28, AOM.
39. JO 1938, pp. 485, 522; E. Divien, 39; Subbiah, op. cit., 1990, p. 147; Interview with Paramel Shatrughnan; Les Partis Politques de l'IF—1944, Inde G 28, AOM.
40. *Desobagari*, 28 August 1937, p. 2; 8 May 1937.
41. *Ediroli*, 28 February 1938, p. 6; *Desobagari*, 8 May 1937, 23 October 1937; Weber, op. cit., 1996, p. 335; Note KY 559 Copie—Inde G 28, AOM.
42. *Kudiarasu*, 7 February 1938; 7, 14, 21 March, 23 May 1938; *Nyayabhimani*, 26 April 1937; *Suthanthiram*, 6 June 1938.
43. *Nyayabhimani*, 1, 22 November 1937; *Desobagari*, 23 October 1937, 4 December 1937.
44. *Suthanthiram*, 20 May 1938.
45. *Desobagari*, 5 November 1938; *Suthanthiram*, 22 December 1937; Lettre

du Gouverneur à M. le Procureur Général, Pondicherry, 30 May 1938 – Inde Série G 27, AOM.
46. Interview with A. Arulraj and Jean Kessavaram.
47. *Ediroli*, 24 January 1938, p. 5; *Sukapi Viruthini*, 1 November 1937; *Desobagari*, 23 October 1937, p. 2; 4 December 1937; 23 April 1938; 21 May 1938; 1 June 1938; 5 November 1938; 25 February 1939; *Suthanthiram*, 20 May 1938.
48. S. Subramanian, 'Ninaivuk Kovai', *Va. Subbiah Pavala Vizha Malar*, Pondicherry, 1988, pp. 136-7; Subbiah, op. cit., pp. 115, 153-5, 157-8, 165-6; *Suthanthiram*, 10 February 1937, 1 December 1937, 6 June 1938, 15 December 1938; *Ediroli*, 17 January 1938, p. 4; *Sukapi Viruthini*, 15 May 1938.
49. Weber, op. cit., vol. IV, p. 2309; Vashist, op. cit., pp. 47-8; Subbiah, op. cit., 1986, p. 19.
50. B. Krishnamurthy, *Pirench Intiya Viduthalai Porattam* (Tamil), Pondicherry, 1991, p. 44; *Sukapi Viruthini*, 15 April 1936; *Suthanthiram*, 2 April 1938; Rapport du Commandant de la Brigade de Grand Bazar, Pondicherry, 12 May 1947—Inde G 29, AOM.
51. *Samuga Mithiran*, 13 April 1938, p. 3; *Kudiarasu*, 28 March 1938; 4, 11 April 1938; *Sukapi Viruthini*. 15 April 1938; Lettre de M. David au Procureur de la République, Pondicherry, 19 March 1938—Inde Série G, AOM.
52. *Ediroli*, 28 February 1938, p. 6; Lettre du Service de la Police et de la Sûreté aau Gouverneur de l'IF, Pondicherry, 10 June 1938—Inde G 29, AOM.
53. *Kudiarasu*, 25 April 1938; *Ediroli*, 4 April 1938, p. 4; 18 April 1938, pp. 1,5; Subbiah, op. cit., 1986, p. 21.
54. *Kudiarasu*, 28 November 1938; *Desobagari*, 5 November 1938; Subbiah, op. cit., 1990, pp. 188-91; B. Krishnamurthy, op. cit., p. 45; *Kudiarasu*, 2 May 1938; C. Antony, op. cit., p. 245; Dossier Remaniement des Commissions Municipales—Inde G 28, AOM.
55. D.K. Ramanujam, 'Liberation Movement In French India: Its Significance, Historic Importance and Special Features,' paper presented at the Historical Society Seminar on 28 February 1998, p. 4.
56. *Suthanthiram*, 1 December 1938; Antony, *Encyclopaedia of India*, Pondicherry, New Delhi, 1994, p. 109; Vashist, op. cit., pp. 51-2; Weber, op. cit., 1996, p. 336.
57. *Suthanthiram*, 1 December 1938; Renseignements Généraux sur les Activités Islamiques en Inde Française et dans les Indes Britiannques, September 1945, Aff. Pol. Carton 2109, Dossier 16, AOM.

58. Ibid., 1 January 1939, Rapport de la Police—Inde Série G 27, AOM, *The Hindu*, 17 December 1938.
59. Ibid., 3 April 1939; *Desobagari*, 10 April 1937, p. 3; 17 July 1937, p. 3; *Suthanthiram*, 1 January, 18 February 1939; Rapport du Commandant de la Brigade de Grand Bazar, Pondicherry, 12 May 1947—Inde G 29, AOM; Lettre de L.J.X. Doraisamy au Gouverneur, Pondicherry, 1 January 1941—Inde G. 29, AOM.
60. *Kudiarasu*, 6 March 1939; *Desobagari*, 3 December 1938, 25 February 1939; *Suthanthiram*, 16 March 1939; Interview with Doressamy Naiker; Lettre du Procureur Général au Gouverneur de Pondichéry, Pondicherry, 24 December 1938; Lettre du MDL Riche, Commissaire de Police, Grand Bazar à M. le Commissaire Général, Pondicherry, 12 January 1939; Letter from V. Bangarammal to the Governor, Madras, 9 January 1939— Inde Série G 27, AOM; *The Hindu*, 27 December 1938; Renseignements sur V. Subbiah, 10 June 1947—Inde G 8, AOM.
61. *Indochine-inde*, 8 July 1939; S. Subramanian, op. cit., pp. 135-6; *Suthanthiram Pon Vizha Malar*, pp. 34-5, 44; Krishnamurthy, op. cit., p. 45; Subbiah, op. cit., 1990, pp. 196-8; Antony, op. cit., vol. I, p. 246; *Suthanthiram*, 3 February 1940; *Janada*, 20 April 1945, pp. 4-5; Rapport du Capitaine Bouhad, Pondicherry, 19 August 1947—Inde G 8, AOM.
62. *Suthanthiram*, 1, 10 February 1947; 12 April 1947; 12, 24 May 1947; C. Antony, op. cit., 1982, vol. I, pp. 246-7; Weber, op. cit., 1996, p. 336; Les Partis Politques de l'IF—1944, Inde G 28, AOM.
63. Notes Documentaires et Etudes, no. 735, EF de l'Inde, IF 2, ADP; Ramanujam, op. cit., p. 3; Arrestation de Subbiah—Inde G 29, AOM; *The Hindu*, 29 January 1941; *Sudesamitran*, 23 January 1941; Rapport du MDL chef, Pondicherry, 24 January 1941; *Lettre de Labatut, Commisaire de Police de Modeliarpeth à M. Le Chef du Service de l'Information*, Modeliarpet, 18 April 1941; *Bulletin de Renseignements*, 3 August 1940, EF de l'Inde—Inde G 29, AOM; *Lettre de V. Radja Bangarammalle au Gouverneur de l'Inde Française*, Pondicherry, 18 September 1941—Inde G 29, AOM; Marie Savary, Avocat, Pondicherry, 5 April 1944—Inde G 29, AOM.
64. V. Graf, *Les Partis Communistes Indians*, Paris, 1974, p. 32; Vashist, op. cit., p. 53; *France-Orient*, July 1941, pp. 5-6, 105-8; *Combat*, 9 April, 1944; *Note de Renseignments par le Vice-Amiral Auboyneau, Commandant des Forces Navales à l'Extreme Orient, Marine Nationale*, 13-16 July 1946, p. 4, IF 51, ADP; Gabriel Monod Herzen à un ami, 9 March 1941, vol. 372, p. 68, ADP; Gabriel Monod Herzen was the

manager of the government distillery, vol. 374, Inde Française, p. 7, ADP.

65. S. Iyengar, *Sri Aurobindo: A Biography and a History*, vol. II, Pondicherry, 1972, p. 1270; E. Divien, 'V. Subbiah' in *Va. Subbiah Pavala Vizha Malar*, 1988, pp. 39-40; A. Arunagiri, 'Viduthalai Velviyil Pudamitta Pon', *Va. Subbiah Pavala Vizha Malar*, 1988, pp. 107-8; Subramanian, op. cit., 137-8; *Janada*, 20 April 1947, p. 5; Interview with Adhimoulame and Ahmed Syed, Pondicherry, son of Mohamed Said; Lettre du G. Mohamed Said à Monsieur le Résident Maire de la ville de Haiphong, Hanoi, 16 February 1932 (copy in the possession of the author); *Indochine-inde*, 15, 26 October 1939.

66. Interview with Serge Choumoff of Paris; More, 'A Mahesian in the French Resistance', in K.S.Mathew (ed.), *Maritime Malabar and the Europeans*, Gurgaon, London, 2003; Extract of *Hindustan Standard*, 24 October 1944, p. 6, no. 6, AO, ADP; Balachandran Vappala, *A Life in Shadow: The Secret Story of A.C.N. Nambiar. A Forgotten Anti-Colonial Warrior*, New Delhi, 2016, p. 165; Ceylon Daily News, Special London Cable, 11 May 1942—Inde Série H 16, AOM.

67. *Combat*, 14 November 1943; *Grand Larousse Encyclopédique*, 3 vols., Paris, 1960; *Combat*, 13 March 1943; F. Knight, *The French Resistance*, London, 1960, p. 230; Discours Prononcé par le Gouverneur des Colonies, Louis Bonvn le, 6 November 1944, Brochure, no. 6, ADP; Weber, op. cit., 1996, p. 358; Note de J.L. Affaire David, Joseph—Inde Série G 32, AOM; Note sur Mouttoukomarapparettiar, Membre de l'Assemblée Représentative—Inde H 22, AOM; JO 1944, 15-21 April; Revendication de la Communauté Musulmane de Karikal, 1952—Aff. Pol. Carton 2274, Dossier 10, AOM.

68. *Combat*, 23 July 1944; *Combat*, 19 December 1943; 30 January 1944; 20 February 1944; Les Partis Politques de l'IF—1944, Inde G 28, AOM.

69. Tél au Ministre Affaires Etrangères, Paris, de Joseph Latour, Secrétaire, Comité Redressement Inde Française, Pondicherry, 5 October 1944, p. 2, no. 6, AO, ADP; *Combat*, 9 April 1944; Gabriel Monod Herzen, ibid., p. 69.

70. *Combat*, 4 June 1944; Rapport de Brigadier en chef, Murugappa, Grand Bazar, 29 February, 1944—Inde G 32, AOM.

71. Interview with Saraswati Subbiah; Antoine Mariadassou. 'History of the Freedom Struggle of the French India Students Congress', *La Lettre du CIDIF*, no. 20, 1998, p. 55; Note pour M. Le Ministre, Directeur des Affaires Politiques, 23 March 1948, p. 82, IF 51, ADP; Ordre de Mission, Inde G 32, AOM; Lettre du Gouverneur à Alger, Pondicherry,

29 February 1949—Inde G 32, AOM; Rapport de l'Adjudant chef, Le Parc, Commandant à Karikal sur la Venue de Subbiah à Karikal, 22 February 1944—Inde G 32, AOM; Renseignements Généraux, Pondicherry, 10 August 1945—Inde H 22, AOM.

72. Subbiah, op. cit., p. 215; *Suthanthiram*, 10 December 1945; Interview with A. Arulraj; Lettre de Louis Bonvin au Ministre des Colonies, 1 March 1945, Pondicherry, Affaires Politiques—Inde E 23, AOM; JO 1944, p. 430; Mission Adicéam—Inde G 32, AOM; Lettre du Gouverneur à Alger, Pondicherry, 28 February 1944—Inde G 32, AOM; Le Combat de Pondicherry—Inde H 22, AOM.

73. Subbiah, op. cit., 1986, p. 25; Indochine, *Nouveau Fonds*, Carton 121, Dossier 1102. *Bulletin de Renseignement*, no. 2515, 31 July 1945, Rapport de M. Adicéam sur la Section de l'I.F. AOM; Brochure, discours prononcé par le Gouverneur des Colonies, 6 November 1944, pp. 3-6, no. 6, ADP; *Note pour le Ministre, Directeur des Affaires Politiques*, 3 March 1948, pp. 82-6, IF 51, ADP; Ajit Neogy, Decolonisation of French India, Pondicherry, 1997, p. 13; Tél de Bonvin à Alger, Pondichéry, 18, 27 February 1944—Inde G 32, AOM; Tél de Bonvin à l'Administrateur de Karikal, Inde G 32, AOM; Note sur la nationalité de Subbiah –Inde G 8, AOM; Note sur Mouttousamy Poullé—Inde H 22, AOM; Marie Savary, Avocat, Pondicherry, 5 April 1944—Inde G 29, AOM; JO 1944, 15-21 April; *The Hindu*, 22 April 1944, 8 August 1944.

74. N. Ranganathan, 'Suthithirap Poril Saka Poralikalum Naanum., *Suthanthiram*, 24 May 1947 (copy in my possession); Asssemblée Nationale, 25 May 1949, AO, 1944-5, no. 28, p. 2, ADP; Resignments Généraux, Pondicherry, 9 October 1945—Inde Série G 8, AOM; *Sudesamitran*, 15 August 1945; Renseignements Généraux, Pondicherry, 24 May 1945—Inde H 22, AOM; Renseignements Généraux, Pondicherry, 5 July 1945—Inde H 22, AOM.

75. Renseignements Généraux sur les activités islamiques en Inde française et dans les Indes britiannques, September 1945, Aff. Pol. Carton 2109, Dossier 16, AOM.

CHAPTER 6

Nationalist Awakening in Pondicherry

The decree of 23 August 1945 of Charles de Gaulle's Fourth Republic abolished the system of two voters' lists and created a unified list of voters. Women, too, were given the right to vote, which paved the way for some Pondicherry women entering the political arena. The creation of the common list of voters clearly signalled the eventual demise in the course of time of Christian domination in French Indian politics, with the Hindus constituting the vast majority of the French Indian population.

In the elections held to decide upon a member for the provisional national consultative assembly in Algiers at that time, D. Jeevarathinam, the son-in-law of Muthu Poullé, contested, as a candidate of the party that he founded, against Lambert Saravane. Jeevarathinam was elected as the representative of French India by the General Council. Pakkirisamy Poullé of Karaikal as well as the members of the Muslim Association of Karaikal, headed by Sahib Marécar and Ibrahim Marécar, supported him. Earlier during 1930-3, Jeevarathinam was administrator and interim magistrate in Yanam. His tenure there was terminated due to abuse of power in conjunction with Kamichetty, Sri Venugopalarao Naidu, a fugitive from British India. They together used to participate in parties where wine from Pondicherry flowed and dancers from Kakinada graced the occasion. French records maintain that Jeevarthinam extorted money from the Yanam zamindar, Maniam Canacaya, and even sent bandits to attack his mansion, which forced the zamindar to flee to nearby Kakinada in British India. As a result, he was recalled from Yanam and barred from becoming magistrate.

When he was elected member of the consultative assembly,

Nationalist Awakening in Pondicherry 169

Jeevarathinam was sent off at the railway station by some supporters of Subbiah as well as Dr Amaladassou, Robert Gaebelé, Mr and Mrs Colambani, Cojandé Diariyanathen, lawyer and son of Gnanou Diagou, Abel Clovis, Mohamed Ismail and members of *Combat* like Lambert Saravane, Gnana Vennemani and Paul Latour. But the consultative assembly was dissolved in six months and Jeevarathinam lost his status as delegate. However, it seems that Jeevarathinam was instrumental in getting the two-list voting system cancelled. Jeevarathinam spoke in the assembly in favour of one list. As a result, the decree of 23 August 1945 created a unified list of voters, when Jeandin was still the acting governor.

In October 1945. as a sort of reward, Jeevarathinam was elected to the first Constituent Assembly of France. He obtained 22,171 out of 43,414 votes.[1] But before we proceed still further into the evolution of politics in Pondicherry and French India, it is necessary to take a look into the participation or non-participation of French Indians, especially from Pondicherry and Karaikal, in the Indian freedom struggle led by Netaji Subhas Chandra Bose who had fled to Southeast Asia in February 1943 from Germany to Japan.

THE NETAJI-PROUCHANDY EPISODE

Very soon after his arrival in Southeast Asia and Japan, Bose revived the Indian National Army and the Indian Independence League. Branches of the Indian Independence League were set up in all the countries of Southeast Asia, including in French Indochina, which was a French colony then like Pondicherry. Bose's intention was to invade India from the East, with Japanese help, and plant the Indian flag on the Red Fort by defeating the British in the battlefield. He even set up the Provisional Government of Free India or Azad Hind Government in Singapore, with Cabinet Ministers and various government departments. Bose, of course, was at the head of this government, recognised by Japan and few of its allies. But no French Indian was given a post of responsibility in the Azad Hind government of Bose, due to the fact that most of the Indians settled in Southeast Asia were in Malayasia, Singapore and Burma, which were British colonies captured by the Japanese since 1942, while in French

Indochina which was also taken over ultimately by the Japanese, Indians were quite a few in number. Their population was estimated then to be around 6,000 people, of whom the majority were settled in Saigon in the Cochinchina province of Indochina. Of them, only about 2,000 actually hailed from French India, especially from Karaikal and Pondicherry. The majority of them were concentrated in Saigon, while there were some others operating in Hanoi, north Indochina, Cambodia and Laos.[2]

Archival records attest the fact that the great majority of the French Indians settled in French Indochina were pro-French in their attitude, though they were under Japanese influence and rule. They never wanted to identify themselves with Bose's Freedom Movement. Instead, they pre-ferred to be loyal French citizens. However, branches of the Indian Independence League were established in Saigon and Hanoi, with Japanese sponsorship. Besides, when Vichy France held sway over Indochina, there was a prohibition on French Indians from participating in the freedom struggle of Bose. French Indians actually wanted to be identified as French and treated like the French. Very rarely did French Indians show their sympathy to Bose's movement at the time.[3]

The only notable exception seems to be the stand taken by the social reformer and philanthropist, Léon Prouchandy, who hailed from Pondicherry. He had been writing in French journals during the 1930s asking the Indians to emulate the Japanese and modernise themselves in order to be at par with the Europeans. But with Bose visiting Saigon in August 1943, he seems to have thrown in his lot with his movement for the freedom of India. When Bose rode past the main road of Saigon called rue Catinat (presently Don Khoi Road) in an open car, Prouchandy stopped the car and garlanded him with a gold necklace. Since then, Prouchandy became a close associate of Bose in Saigon and had been helping the Indian Independence League in Saigon financially from behind the scenes.[4]

In March 1945, the Vichy France government in Indochina was done away with and the Japanese assumed full control of Indochina. This provided the opportunity for Prouchandy to come out in the open and participate in the Indian Independence League activities in Saigon. He had already given his mansion situated at 76, rue Paul

Blanchy (presently Hai Bha Trung), free of rent to Bose, so that the general secretariat of the Indian Independence League might function there. He was now included as an executive council member of the Indian Independence League of Saigon. Many French people and soldiers were imprisoned by the Japanese forces. This included Symphorien Lamy as well as Yves Perrier, a French Indian administrator and barrister. Yves Perrier was a Créole, related to Edouard Goubert, who was conversant in Tamil, French, English and Vietnamese. He was released after the Japanese surrender in August 1945. He was aware of the identity of those Indians who were pro-Japanese and pro-Bose at that time. He cited to me the name of Prouchandy when I interviewed him in Paris in the closing years of the twentieth century, while I was preparing my book on the freedom movement in Mahé. Yves Perrier had been the French administrator of Mahé in 1948.

By that time, the Indian National Army, along with the Japanese, had been defeated on the Burmese front. Bose, himself, was on the run with a good amount of the war treasure that had been collected from the Indians in Southeast Asia to fight the British. In the course of his flight, Bose came to Saigon on 17 August 1945. All available records and testimonies establish that he went straight to the secretariat of the League, which was in Prouchandy's mansion, from where he disappeared to an unknown place next day. At that time, Prouchandy had become the general secretary of the Indian Independence League, Saigon, as his predecessor, Ramanathan had fled Saigon. It was in that capacity that he welcomed Bose to Saigon. Prouchandy did not flee Saigon after the Japanese debacle.[5]

In the third week of September the French recovered the Netaji war treasure at the IIL secretariat. Prouchandy was arrested and held at Bot Catinat French prison, where he was tortured for three months before being let off in an amnesiac state. It is quite probable that Prouchandy was aware of some secrets regarding Bose's whereabouts and also Netaji's war treasure. Possibly, he gave out these secrets under severe torture. Yves Perrier was aware of the fact that Léon Prouchandy was arrested by the French forces in Saigon. He seems to have conveyed this message to Edouard Goubert, his relative, when he returned to Pondicherry.

Prouchandy was subsequently taken to Pondicherry by his wife and family. He spent the rest of his days at Villa Selvom, No. 5, Nehru Street, Pondicherry, always in an amnesiac state until he passed away unknown and unsung by his countrymen in 1968, in spite of the great sacrifice he had made for the freedom of his countrymen. There is a lone classified file tucked away in the defence archives in France, closed to the public for 100 years, that must contain information of what actually happened to Prouchandy, Subhas Chandra Bose and some of his associates in Saigon after 17 August 1945. The author was not allowed to access this file by the French archival authorities.[6] That this man who gave his wealth and life for his countrymen hailed from Pondicherry was unknown to the Pondicherrians, except for a few like Yves Perrier, Edouard Goubert and N. Marimuthu, a freedom fighter of Pondicherry. Prouchandy was the first French Indian from Pondicherry who gave the call to drive the British out of India. He was no doubt an Indian nationalist of the first order, while his countrymen in Pondicherry and French India were still unsure about their then status and future and had not yet started any movement to liberate themselves from French rule.

THE FOUNDATION OF NATIONAL DEMOCRATIC FRONT

V. Subbiah returned to Pondicherry on 27 June 1942. While he was in jail, the Ramakrishna Vasaka Salai, founded about ten years back by him, still functioned in Pondicherry at the cross-section of Madras Street and Tille Maistry Street. One Ellapoullé, a teacher, was the president. Gabriel Anussamy was the honorary member. The earlier members of this association were suspected of having been involved in the murder of Selvarajalu. These members, along with Marie Savary, Lambert Saravane and Dorairaj were the principal supporters of Subbiah in Pondicherry while the latter was in jail. Subbiah took part in various labour union activities in Pondicherry. A manifesto of the Communist Party of French India, signed by Subbiah, Nandagobalu (president of the Rodier Labour Union) and a certain Vaithialingam was published. Subbiah was banished from Pondicherry on 18 April 1944.

On 9 September 1945, Subbiah returned from exile. He was given

Nationalist Awakening in Pondicherry

a rousing welcome at Odiansalai ground. A new party called the National Democratic Front was formed in September 1945, by the amalgamation of two groups one led by the Frenchman Gallois Montbrun, which consisted of lawyers like Sellane Naiker, C. Balasubramanian (of the Democratic Union Party) and P. Danaraja. In the absence of Gallois-Montbrun, the party came under the influence of Edouard Goubert, a Créole who then held the post of Pondicherry chief court registrar. Goubert, thus, entered politics by the side of V. Subbiah. Karaikal Pakkirisamy Poullé also joined this front. Units of the front came up in the five settlements. On the whole, the front consisted of socialists and Communists like Subbiah, former Franco-Hindu Party members and members of the *Combat*. It also had the support of stalwarts like Lambert Saravane, S.R. Subramanian and D. Jeevarathinam.

The name of this new party was itelf ambiguous. Whether the word 'national' in the party's name would imply inclusion of the whole of India or only French India or whether French India belonged to the Indian nation or the French nation or if it were to be an independent French Indian nation was not known. The name may also be attributed to the fact that various parties, individuals and groups were part of this party.

Actually, it was the support of Saravane to this new front, which brought C. Balasubramanian into it. Balasubramanian was instrumental in bringing all the various parties and groups together. The party demanded full self-governance within the French Union, abolition of the excessive powers of the governor and greater representation for French India in the representative bodies in France.[7] Subbiah was the most powerful political personality in Pondicherry at that time. When the minister for colonies, Marius Moutet, visited Pondicherry in 1946, Communist flags and not French flags greeted him, all along the roads that led to the governor's palace from Kottakuppam.

The French Indian government, including the French governor, did not like the emergence of this new party under the leadership of Subbiah. They held that crime was quite common in the Pondicherry of those days, due partly to the dominance of the Communist Party under Subbaish inside the National Democratic Front.[8]

In February 1946, A. Karunendra Mudaliar, the Pondicherry landlord, founded the 'Union Socialiste Républicaine Démocratique de l'Inde Française' (Republican, Democratic Socialist Union of French India). G. Anussamy, the French teacher from Bahur, founded the 'Union Nationale et Démocratique de l'Inde Française' (National Democratic Union of French India) in May 1946.[9] But these organisations were individual attempts without having much of a following.

On 20 March 1946, François Baron, the ex-Inspector of labour and administrator of French India, was appointed governor of Pondicherry. It was a time when France and the French empire had emerged from the war, extremely enfeebled economically, politically and financially, and Britain was contemplating granting Independence to India in the near future. Jawaharlal Nehru was heading an interim government in British India. He was increasingly hostile to French policy in Indochina. It was necessary for the French to mollify him. Besides, separatist tendencies were becoming more marked in Chandernagore rather than in Pondicherry during this period.

Right from the beginning of Baron's governorship, he wanted to create a Franco-Indian cultural centre in Pondicherry. He was reputed to be socialist-minded. He developed close contacts with Mirra Alfassa and, through her, with many local stalwarts like Lambert Saravane and Counouma. At that time, the French writer, Alexander David Neel, believed Sri Aurobindo's philosophy to be lacking in originality. But Governor Baron thought that the Ashram in his name could incorporate the French Institute of his conception, whereas Jean Filliozat, secretary of the Asiatic Society, Paris, mooted the idea of an Institute of Indian Civilisation in Pondicherry, outside the Ashram. Baron became a disciple of Sri Aurobindo. He thought that Aurobindo's philosophy was a synthesis of Hinduism and Western rationalism. Sri Aurobindo communicated with the outer world through Mirra Alfassa. Baron eventually joined the Sri Aurobindo Ashram. The French Foreign Ministry, for reasons we do not know, always thought that the Ashram was a sect.[10]

Lambert Saravane met the Prime Minister, Jawaharlal Nehru, and explained to him the structure of democratic governance in French India. Nehru then assured him that the integration of the French territories with India would not be immediate and would be decided after ascertaining the wishes of the people. Governor Baron, however, thought that a society of three lakh would not stand to benefit from joining 40 crores of India as it would lose its identity and uniqueness. He never thought of severing the French connection with India. On 6 April 1946, he declared that all men and women were free and equal in the new French union of which French India would be a part.[11]

The National Democratic Front swept the municipal elections held in June 1946. Its candidates were elected mayors in all the municipal councils of French India. In Pondicherry, Muthusamy Poullé, known popularly as Muthu Poullé, became the mayor. Muthu Poullé was a merchant who engaged in the import and export of groundnuts. Vanniyars and Valangas were elected as members to the various municipal councils, in spite of the fact that there were no reservations, especially for the latter, as in British India. However, French records maintain that Subbiah wielded immense power on the municipalities, and it was he who made Muthu Poullé the mayor of Pondicherry. The latter had been of no influence until then in Pondicherry politics.

In 1942, Muthu Kumarappa Reddiar had broken off with Joseph Davidu. From then, he drew closer to Muthu Poullé and ended up joining the NDF. He also cultivated the friendship of Dr André Zeganathan, related to Lambert Saravane, as well as Vengadasubba Reddiar of Madukarai. French records maintain that the latter was a rich landlord but not very sophisticated. Later, it seems that it was Muthu Kumarappa Reddiar who made Vengadasubba Reddiar the mayor of Nettapakkam. French records also maintain, that when Kumarappa Reddiar was mayor and even afterwards, he indulged in selling goods meant for the municipality in the blackmarket. As for André Zeganathan, he earned wealth by practising his medical profession. He was at the service of the rich Reddiars. The preceding persons, except Muthu Poullé, were all of Telugu ancestry. André never went to Indochina to enrich himself unlike his Catholic relatives or compatriots like Saravane, Dumont and Delafon, who were all of Telugu ancestry.

The National Democratic Front (NDF), mainly under the influence of V. Subbiah and his lieutenants, put forward the demand to replace the General Council with a representative assembly. It seems that Governor Baron in collaboration with Lambert Saravane, an ardent proponent of French India remaining in the French Union, hatched a new set of reforms, under pressure from the National Democratic Front, which clamoured for more autonomy. Accordingly, a decree was adopted on 25 October 1946 by which a new representative assembly consisting of 44 members came into existence, instead of the General Council. A total of 22 of the members were from Pondicherry region, 12 from Karaikal region, 5 from Chandernagore, 3 from Mahé and 2 from Yanam. It was again just a consultative and advisory body, with no legislative powers, which were vested with the governor as usual.

Elections were held on 15 December 1946 to elect the members of the assembly on the basis of universal adult suffrage. The National Democratic Front won 34 seats out of 44. Of the 34, two belonged to the Praja Party of Yanam, affiliated to the NDF. Edouard Goubert, Saravane, Muthu Poullé, Balasubramanian, Venkata Subba Reddiar, and others, were elected as the Front's members. Subbiah was the driving force in these elections. Most of the members elected to the Representative Assembly owed their candidacy to him. This included even educated men like C. Balasubramanian, Dr André, Edouard Goubert and Ambroise. They were obedient to him. The French accused Subbiah of indulging in smuggling cotton yarn and other products meant for local consumption to British India and blackmailing the traders and merchants using the power that he wielded on the mayors and the elected representatives.

Padmanabhan Counouma was elected from Mahé, along with Nalporeil Sahadevan, and Valiavittil Govinin. In January 1948, A. Karunendra Mudaliar resigned his job in the Charity Workshop and was elected to the Representative Assembly from Villianur. The assembly had the power to vote the budget. The governor gave an oral assurance that the assembly decisions would be implemented, except in certain cases as when they were against the law or undermined law and order.[12]

Jean Savarinathan, the original Congress sympathiser and leader of Pondicherry, preferred to sever his ties with the Congress Party during the war in the early 1940s. His place was taken by R.L. Purushotthama Reddiar of Bahur, formerly a political lieutenant of

Subbiah, who was sympathetic to the Quit India Movement launched by Mahatma Gandhi. Thus, was born the French India National Congress on 14 June 1946. R.L. Purushotthama Reddiar was assisted by men like S.R. Subramanian, who was the secretary of the party, Ansari Doraisamy, K. Sivaprakasam, a good orator, Sethurama Chettiar (son of Tirumudy Nadaraja Chettiar), La Hache, André Selvanadin and Mahesian, Ambady Narayanan, professor at the Colonial College who was associated with the Ashram. Its office was located on the first floor of Ansari Café building (Indian Coffee House building in the present Nehru Street), right in front of Gaebelé Theatre. The Café belonged to Ansari Doraisamy. It is quite noteworthy that both R.L. Purushotthama Reddiar and S.R. Subramanian were previously close associates of Subbiah during the 1930s in the youth organisations and labour movements. In the same year, Baron also permitted the foundation of the All-Indian Muslim League in French India by Abdul Haji Sahib Levé.

At about the same time, the French India Students' Congress was started in June 1946 at a meeting on the first floor of Ansari Café, attended by over 100 students. It was born out of the Saraswati Sangam which had ceased to exist by then. Antoine Mariadassou, whom we spoke to, was the first president of the Sangam. Dorai Munisamy was chosen as the secretary of the Students' Congress. Among the other members of the organisation was Sebastian and Arumugam. Another student leader, Paul Radjanedassou, brother of Antoine Mariadssou, maintained that the Students' Congress was the brainchild of R.L. Purushotthama Reddiar. The latter actually used it to launch the Independence movement in Pondicherry. Doressamy Naiker, Students' Congress president in 1949 maintained that the veteran politician, Sellane Naiker, contributed much to the development of the Students' Congress.[13]

Later, on 7 October 1946, the All-French India Congress was started by Thirumudi N. Sethurama Chettiar and Muthu Venkatapathi Reddiar, with the patronage of Congress leaders from Tamilnadu like K. Kamaraj Nadar and Bhaktavatsalam. The Socialist Party Wing of the Congress party was led by S.R. Subramanian in Pondicherry from January 1947. S.R. Subramanian had parted company earlier with Subbiah and had become a revolutionary socialist. The Congress, in general, and R.L. Purushotthama Reddiar, in particular, then wanted Pondicherry and Karaikal to be integrated with Tamil Nadu, without referendum, though Nehru had earlier favoured a referendum to decide upon the issue. Then there came into existence the Congress Youth Wing in Pondicherry. Some of its leading members were A. Arulraj, Dorai Munisamy and K. Karunanidhi. The precedence established that the Congress or the nationalist camp was split between various organisations in Pondicherry, with no unity in sight. Thus, it was left to the Students' Congress to spearhead the agitations for freedom. Among its ranks were eloquent speakers like Dorai Munisamy and Paramel Shatrughnan.[14]

Antoine Mariadassou, the first president of the Students' Congress, met Governor Baron in early 1947 to talk about self-rule. But Baron dismissed Mariadassou as a mere student. He asked him to meet his propaganda secretary, Bernard Ingenger, a young man in his 20s who was the information officer then. Later Ingenger became a devotee of the Ashram under the name 'Satprem', following in the footsteps of Baron. Mariadassou claimed that Ingenger wanted the students to work for French India to remain in the French Union and even proposed government scholarships to the student leaders after their Baccalauréat so as to pursue their studies in France.[15]

In April 1946, the National Democratic Front held a two-day conference in Pondicherry in the presence of Governor Baron and V. Subbiah, its undisputed leader. The demand for autonomy for French India within the French Union was stressed during this conference. Governor Baron was able to take stock of the strength of the Front and its capacity to demand Independence, in case British India obtained freedom. His colonial interests began to ponder on this eventuality. During this conference, Governor Baron praised Lambert Saravane profusely, though V. Subbiah was the top man of the Front.[16]

In June 1946, Saravane Lambert contested in the elections held to send a delegate to the French Constituent Assembly, as a National Democratic Front candidate. He was supported by the Pondicherry Communists and the moderates. Saravane was a professor then in the French College and an ardent social worker. He had the support of workers and farmers. He opened private schools and reading rooms for them. He vehemently criticised his opponent, D. Jeevarathinam, as a miser and an enemy of the workers. Jeevarathinam, in his turn, accused men like Saravane, J. Xavery and Léon Saint Jean, who were Christians like the late Joseph Davidu, of seeking power in order to exploit the Hindu masses. Nevertheless, the voters were not swayed by the communal propaganda of Jevarathinam and Saravane won with a thumping majority. He won against a host of candidates like Gabriel Annussamy, Jean Saverinadin, S. Perumal and D. Jeevarathinam who lost their deposits. In November 1945, Saravane declared that he intended to procure autonomy for French India.[17]

In November 1946, Lambert Saravane was elected to the French National Assembly, trouncing his opponent Jean Savarinathan by a wide margin. This would not have been possible without the connivance of Governor Baron, who had become an ardent patron of Saravane by then. The French journal, *Franc-Tireur*, found fault with the irregular manner by which Saravane was elected. Saravane had the support of the Communists and Subbiah, who had unleashed a reign of terror in Pondicherry during that period. The Muslim Association of Karaikal under Sahib Marécar also supported Saravane. Unlike Bonvin, Baron had adopted a conciliatory policy towards Subbiah during that period.[18] Baron seems to have counted upon Saravane to maintain French India within the orbit of the French Union or empire at that time, more than on anybody else, probably because like himself, Saravane was close to the Ashram and its Mother, Mirra Alfassa. By coming out in favour of Saravane, Baron probably thought of keeping in check his potential rivals like Subbiah, Jeevarathinam and C. Balasubramanian.

Jean Saverinathan who was defeated in the elections still believed that the four southern settlements could be maintained in the French Union, with a few more reforms, especially those administrative in nature. Earlier, Saravane had asked for 100 million francs to develop education in Pondicherry.[19]

At that time, Professor Emmanuel Adicéam, a delegate of the Alliance Française of Pondicherry, received a cold welcome in Mahé, where he had talked of the greatness of French culture. The Mahesians denounced French culture as a cloak for French imperialism. The Mahesians even submitted a letter to the French Inspector of Colonies, Tezenas du Montcel, asking him for the date of departure of the French from Mahé.[20]

Baron imposed press restrictions and prevented the nationalist newspapers of Tamil Nadu from being sold in French India. But Nehru had already said in August 1946, that only the French Indian population would decide whether or not they wished to join the Indian Union. Besides, he was not averse to the idea of Pondicherry becoming a French cultural centre. Certain newspapers of Paris had reported at the same time that even Baron, the governor of Pondicherry, held an opinion similar to Nehru's on the future of French India. But Baron had also held that the Franco-Indian community were at the service of both India and France and was a link (*trait-d'union*) between two civilisations and two cultures. He maintained that the French Revolution of 1789 had sounded the death knell of colonialism. This could not, however, mean that Baron wanted to renounce the French territories in India. On its part, the Parisian journal, *Franc-Tireur*, accused Baron of trying to create a principality like Monaco out of Pondicherry under the influence of India.[21]

In the elections held to the Representative Assembly on 15 December 1946, the National Democratic Front emerged victorious. It won 30 seats out of 44. Two members elected from Yanam joined the Front later. In Mahé and Yanam, the pro-Indian nationalists won. In early 1947, the National Democratic Front adopted a resolution in favour of Independence for French India at its meeting. This was naturally not to the liking of Governor Baron. C. Balasubramanian was elected as the president of the Representative Assembly. Prof. Gabriel Annusamy demanded autonomy and the setting up of a constituent assembly for French India to frame a Constitution. Though, initially, the Representative Assembly had adopted a resolution for the immediate integration of the French settlements with India, to the great surprise of New Delhi, it was recognised later that the problem of transfer of power was more complex than earlier thought of.[22]

However, on 26 January 1947, V. Subbiah and Pakkirisamy Poullé of Karaikal of the Front got themselves elected to the French Senate (*Conseil de la République*), in spite of their party's resolution favouring Independence. Subbiah had the support of Commissioner Baron this time. Pakkirisamy Poullé seems to have had the support of Edouard Goubert.

On 20 May 1947, the Pondicherry court confirmed the Karaikal court's judgment that Subbiah was a 'foreigner'. But he still became senator. It was Commissioner Baron who countered the judgment saying that Subbiah was already enrolled in the voters' list in 1945, which was never contested. Besides, Subbiah was allowed to be a senator by the French Senate as he had taken the case of his nationality to the appeal court of Pondicherry.[23]

Thus, three French Indians, one Tamil and two other Tamils of Telugu ancestry, from Pondicherry were elected to the French Parliament from French India for the first time.

In the very first meeting of the Representative Assembly held on 11 January 1947, the unanimous desire of the members was to have a sovereign assembly, enjoying complete autonomy. What they wanted in fact was a small parliament. Subbiah personally seems to have wanted only autonomy for French India within the French empire, as he was a senator. This was the reason why Baron supported him at that time, eventhough he was a Communist. Surprisingly, Lambert Saravane came down on the French government's policy towards the freedom movement in Indochina at that time, which naturally created doubts about Saravane's adherence to the French Union.[24] Pakkirisamy Poullé and V. Subbiah hardly spoke in the French Parliament about French India, its Independence or autonomy.

On 22 March 1947, Lambert Saravane made one of those memorable speeches in the French National Assembly, which was acclaimed by one and all. He was a sort of spokesman for the entire overseas French territories in the French Parliament. While claiming that the idea of French Union was a revolutionary idea, he went on to explain the conditions for this union to come about. Mutual respect and brotherhood, and not war and hatred, could bring about this union, he told the French parliamentarians. This speech was delivered in the context of suppression of rebellions in Vietnam and Madagascar under the French regime.[25]

Even the French Indian Communist party press organ, *Suthanthiram*, praised Saravane's speech. But very soon by August 1947, V. Subbiah accused Saravane, following Governor Baron's reforms, of attempting to adopt a resolution in the French Parliament to make French India an autonomous unit within the French Union. He stated that if the French really believed that they had the support of the French Indians, they should prove it by organising a referendum.[26] It was at that juncture that eight mayors of the Pondicherry region, K. Muthusamy Poullé of Pondicherry town, S. Muthu Venkatapathi Reddiar of Tirubhuvanai commune, Venkata Subba Reddiar of Nettapakkam commune, Vaithiyalingam of Mudaliarpet commune, Govindasamy of Oulgaret commune, Viswanatha Padayachi of Ariyankuppam commune, Ramakrishna Reddiar of Bahur commune and Kuppusamy Kavundar of Villianur commune passed a resolution in favour of joining the Indian Union and made it known to Jawaharlal Nehru.[27]

The All-India Students' Congress decided to celebrate Vietnam Day on 21 January 1947. The French India Students' Congress followed suit. They refused to jointly celebrate Vietnam Day with the Communist-oriented French India Students' Union. Dorai Munisamy was particularly against it. On that day, the Students' Congress took out a procession, in spite of a ban, from Nehru Vanam through Madras Road up to Saint Thérèse Street, where they were blocked by policemen. Eight student leaders were arrested. They were Antoine Mariadassou (Students' Congress president), Dorai Munisamy (secretary of Students' Congress), Annamalai (secretary of French Indian National Congress), Haridas Valiavittil (student leader, son of the notary, Valiavittil Govinin of Mahé, and brother-in-law of Ambady Narayanan, orator in French, married to Françoise, daughter of Mme Lernie of Pondicherry), Marie Antoine, B. Rangapillai, Venugopal and Arumugam. Workers' Union leaders, like Saminathan and Nawab Jan, condemned the actions of the police. V. Subbiah and the mayor of Pondicherry came to the place to calm the tensions. It also seems that R.L. Purushotthama Reddiar and Ambady Narayanan intervened with the French authorities and got all the eight released. A meeting took place eventually, presided over by Antoine Maraiadassou, in the presence of S.R. Subramaniam.[28]

Vietnam Day was celebrated also by the French India Students' Union and French India Workers' Union. Their meeting was presided over by the secretary of the Students' Union, Arumugam. Student leader Srinivasan and Kalicharan Ghosh of Chandernagore who was secretary of the Communist Party of French India participated. V. Subbiah came out in support of the Communists in Vietnam and denounced European imperialism and colonialism.[29]

S.R. Subramanian was a convinced nationalist and mill worker. He declared that the Alliance Française had been started in Pondicherry to maintain French imperialism and spread French culture in French India, with the help of the power-hungry local men. He alleged that the labour unions too, were in the hands of power-seekers. This was an indirect attack against his former colleague, Subbiah. He further said that V. Subbiah, G. Annusamy and N. Ranganathan were never workers themselves though they came to be leaders of the workers. He accused Subbiah of monopolising power in the party, by getting rid of all his rivals. He accused him of becoming senator by using the workers' support, though he had earlier disparaged such political posts as 'bones thrown by White men to Indian slave dogs'.[30]

In April 1947, K. Kamaraj Nadar spoke at a meeting in Senji Salai ground, in the presence of R.L. Purushotthama Reddiar and Ku. Sivaprakasam and asked the French to leave India. Reddiar came down heavily on the economic and cultural sops being offered by Governor Baron, like the promise to open a university and some colleges in Pondicherry, even as he kept quiet on the issue of political freedom.[31]

While Subbiah was in France, a massive procession of 5,000 factory workers was organised by the French Indian Communist Party and the National Democratic Front in Pondicherry on 17 February 1947 as a show of strength. All shops and schools were closed, except Ansari Café (presently Indian Coffee House), belonging to a die-hard Congressman called Doraisamy, in Dupleix Street (presently Nehru Street). The Ansari Café and the Congress office, which were in the same building, were attacked in broad daylight with stones by the pro-cessionists. It was claimed that one of the processionists called Rajagopal was shot dead from the Ansari Café. That was the end of Ansari Café. It was completely destroyed and looted by the pro-cessionists. The Congress office was shifted elsewhere, and Ansari escaped death somehow. It seems that Governor Baron was behind the Communists then, as they attacked the pro-Congress and pro-merger elements in Pondicherry.

During that period and until June 1947, the Communists were with Lambert Saravane, Edouard Goubert, Muthu Poullé and others under the National Democratic Front banner. It was they who perse-cuted and harassed the Congressmen, whose lives and properties were endangered, as they stood for union with India. Newspapers and pamphlets against the governor were proscribed. This tense situation continued more or less from 2 October 1946 to 17 August 1947. Communists openly ran the government with the support of Governor Baron. The Mudaliarpet, Ariyankuppam and Oulgaret communes were under their control. The supply of yarn and rations (rice, oil, cloth) were in the hands of the Communists. Money was collected from the shopkeepers for the labour movement.[32]

The British decision in February 1947 to quit India by 30 June 1948 changed the entire political scenario in French India. But the French Foreign Minister, Marius Moutet, insisted on 3 March 1947, that British withdrawal from India would have no consequence in French India as the latter was an overseas territory of the French Union. Baron, too, thought on similar lines.[33]

Strangely, while Subbiah was in France, the Pondicherry High Court confirmed the 1944 judgement of the Karaikal court that Subbiah was not a French Indian. In July 1947, Subbiah returned to Pondicherry from France. He claimed that he was French citizen, i.e. born in Pondicherry. He said his father had been born in a frontier village of British Indian territory, adjacent to the French territory. He claimed that he had a French passport to go to France in 1937 and that he ran a journal since 1934 as he was a French citizen and only they were allowed to run journals in Pondicherry. He added that his name was on the electoral list and that he was member of local representative assemblies. He declared that he would appeal against the judgment.

But the judgment seems to have infuriated Subbiah very much. In British India things were moving very fast, under the new Viceroy, Lord Louis Mountbatten, who was determined to quit India on a short notice. Besides, many mayors of the Pondicherry communes had passed a resolution in favour of merger with India. Given these developments, Subbiah, who was until then in favour of remaining in the French Union and had also got himself elected to the French Senate on account of this with Governor Baron's support, was all of a sudden pushed to make a declaration against the imperialistic attitude of the French and the necessity for them to quit India. He claimed that Marius Moutet, the French Foreign Minister, had told him that the French government would give full administrative and financial autonomy to Chandernagore alone. Subbiah made it known to the minister that he was against such partial reforms. Subbiah then revealed that he had received a letter from Prime Minister Nehru to meet him to discuss French India.[34]

On 14 August 1947, Subbiah claimed to have met Nehru in Delhi and discussed with him freedom of French India. Meanwhile, some of his supporters raised the slogan, Quit India, in Pondicherry. At that time, the governor categorically rejected the project of double nationality put forward by some inhabitants of French India.[35]

It should be noted that many in the National Democratic Front still stood for complete Independence for French India and an eventual merger of Pondicherry and Karaikal with Tamil Nadu, Mahé with Kerala, Yanam with Andhra and Chandernagore with Bengal. But the British decision to quit India by 15 August 1947 seems to have had its effect in Pondicherry, where the National Democratic Front continued to press for more autonomy.

Through two decrees dated 12 April and 12 August 1947, Governor François Baron created a 'Council of Government' or rather a 'Council of Ministers' to replace the privy council. It consisted of 6 members, 3 drawn from the Representative Assembly members and the other 3 appointed by the governor. It was actually a veritable government with ministers. They had the power to vote the budget. But their opinion was still not binding on the governor in matters related to the republican laws, police, and justice. However, Baron himself admitted that the Representative Assembly was sovereign, with independent powers to manage the finances of the territories. In the same year, by the institution of the decree of 20 August 1947, the title of governor, which had been in effect since 1701, was replaced by the title of 'Commissioner of the Republic of French India'. French India would, thenceforth, be represented in the French Parliament by a deputy and two counsellors of the republic.[36]

The public opposition to these reforms came from Chandernagore, Mahé and Karaikal and not so much from Pondicherry. In Karaikal, the National Congress under Srikanta Ramanujam, the Communist Party, the All-India Muslim League and the Dravida Kazhagam joined together to oppose Baron's reforms.[37]

The 6 members or ministers of the Council of Government were

Dr André, Agriculture Minister, Padmanabhan Counouma, Education and Finance Minister, Deivasikamani Kramany, Revenue Minister, Sivasubramania Poullé, Food and Rations Minister, Lakshmanasamy Reddiar, Health Minister, and Edouard Goubert, Industry and Public Administration Minister. All 6 were well-versed in the French language. The police department had always been under the control of the French governor.[38] Dr André was related to Lambert Saravane and was quite intimate with the Ashram. Of the 6, 4 were government employees, of whom Goubert was one. Goubert had very little political experience then. Among the 6 ministers, two were Christian, 3 were Hindus of the 'higher' castes, while one was from Mahé. Chandernagore and Yanam were not represented in the Council. There was no Muslim. Goubert was of mixed Valanga-French origin while Dr André was of Telugu ancestry. The Assembly had had 44 members since January 1947, who had all been elected.[39] Among the members, the Hindus were in a great majority. This was the result of the introduction of a common list of voters. Christian, including European, influence in politics was diminishing very fast in French Indian and Pondicherry politics since 1945. Christians and Europeans had no more the first list advantage that they enjoyed previously. Edouard Goubert seems to have been quite conscious of this fact, that the power equations had tilted towards the majority community.

The French government sent Tezenas du Montcel to make an on-the-spot study of the situation in French India. Chandernagore wanted to steer clear of Pondicherry and clamoured for more financial and administrative autonomy. They seem to have developed by then a visceral dislike for being under the dominance of Pondicherry and hurriedly took steps to achieve complete Independence. In Mahé, too, some clamoured for immediate Independence. But in the other territories, including Pondicherry, the capital of French India, things moved at a slower pace.

On 9 August 1947, the government banned public meetings from being organised by the Students' Congress in order to deliver an ultimatum to the French to leave India. On the same day, Subbiah's supporters, who consisted mainly of workers, picketed government offices, arms depots and police stations. Due to official intervention, they later stopped the picketing. However, all shops remained closed and workers struck work. A massive procession was organised by the Students' Congress. Several students were arrested. On 10 August, a meeting was held in Odiansalai ground and a resolution adopted to bring down the French flags on 15 August and raise the Indian flag instead. This was done by all National Democratic Front municipalities and government offices. Commissioner Baron was told to leave French Indians to join the Indian Union, if he wanted unity between India and France. During that period, Paul Radjanedassou, brother of Antoine Mariadassou, had become the president of the Students' Congress, while Dorai Munisamy continued to be the secretary.[40]

But the Representative Assembly meeting held on 15 September adopted a resolution in favour of Baron's constitutional reforms. G. Annusamy, secretary of the National Democratic Front, spoke against Baron's reforms in the Assembly.[41]

When the call for Independence and merger by the Congress was becoming more and more strident, Subbiah raised his voice more vigorously in favour of the Independence of French India. In some quarters, it was said that the Communists wanted French India to leave the French Union and be independent like the princely states. This turned Commissioner Baron against the Communists.[42] In the course of time, Murugasamy Clémenceau, member of the Representative Assembly, Vaidyalingam, mayor of Mudaliarpet, and Vasudevan, president of the Rodier Labour Union, along with N. Ranganathan (hailing from Villupuram), D.K. Ramanajum, Ayyamperumal (hailing from Villupuram) and many other Communists, were arrested. In his turn, Subbiah declared that the skeletal reforms of Baron would not prevent French India from joining the Indian Union. Thus, the Communists were at loggerheads with Baron. Subbiah was at the pinnacle of his power at that time. When Marius Moutet came to Pondicherry, he was welcomed by the Communists, waving Communist flags all along the 15 km route that led to the governor's palace. Significantly, there was no one to wave French flags along the route.[43]

Some members of the National Democratic Front felt at that time that it was not necessary to join the Indian Union as it would result in the loss of Pondicherry's identity as a separate political unit that had evolved for nearly three centuries under French rule. They thought that they need not break away from the French Union to get dissolved in the Indian Union. But they could come to an amicable arrangment with the Indian Union so that French India could serve as a cultural link between France and India.

Of those belonging to this line of thinking, the most prominent were Lambert Saravane, Dr André, Joseph Latour, Padmanabhan Counouma and Karunendra Mudaliar, all under the influence of the Ashram and Mirra Alfassa in varying degrees. Lambert Saravane had formed a group along with Dr André, Karunendara Mudaliar and Counouma. This group had close contact with the Ashram Mother. Subbiah was angry that Saravane had abandoned him. His supporters attacked Saravane with shoes and chappals at a students' demonstration. But the Saravane group did not command the necessary following among the people. This was when Edouard Goubert, who was a French-educated lawyer, formerly the government registrar in Chandernagore and the then chief court registrar of Pondicherry, entered the fray. Goubert was of mixed Franco-Tamil descent. According to French records, his father was a Frenchman of pure blood called Berchin de Fontaine Goubert and his mother was a Paria (Pariyar or Valanga) servant. Edouard Goubert was until then fond of cockfights, a game with heavy stakes that he played with his wealthy Muslim friends. He was nicknamed as 'Kozhi Goubert' (Cock Goubert). Some others called him 'Lakhadi Goubert' (Rowdy Goubert).[44]

FOUNDATION OF SOCIALIST PARTY OF FRENCH INDIA

Unhappy with the stand of the National Democratic Front in favour of Independence, Edouard Goubert, too, broke away from the Front in July 1947, along with some of his supporters like Deivasikamani, an agriculturist and landlord, who was earlier awarded the Chevalier du Mérite Agricole, Lakshmanaswamy Reddiar, Dr André and Padmanabhan Counouma (of Mahé) as well as Muthu Kumarappa Reddiar, the Nettapakkam landlord and K. Muthu Poullé, the Pondicherry merchant, to form the Socialist Party of French India. It was only socialist in name, as its leadership was mainly composed of landlords, merchants and professionals. All the six ministers joined Goubert's party. It had no connection with the Socialist Party of France. In fact, Goubert and his followers were neither socialist nor nationalist at that stage. Commissioner Baron seems to have played a great role in the creation of this party to counter the National Democratic Front. In other words, he propped up Goubert to counter V. Subbiah. Goubert and the Socialist Party were naturally accused of being protected by their 'White masters'.[45]

In any case, it appears that it was then the turn of Goubert to unleash his own brand of terror, called the 'Terreur Blanche' (White Terror), against his former colleague Subbiah, and the Communists in general. It was then that the cry *Français Quittez l'Inde* or 'French Quit India' was heard for the first time on the roads of Pondicherry raised by some Communist workers sympathetic to Subbiah. The lawyer, Gnanou Ambroise, a close associate of Subbiah, got in touch from Cuddalore with the Chief Minister of Madras, Omandur Ramasamy Reddiar, and agreed to work for the Indian cause.[46]

Commissioner Baron followed the precedent set by his predecessors in meddling with French Indian politics, probably better than any of them. He, patronised the Socialist Party, against the Communists, who turned against the government. Goubert then became the cornerstone of French Indian politics. The French and Baron counted more and more on him to defend French interests in India. Thus, Goubert literally became the 'right hand' of France in India. In a way, he had the support of France, and Commissioner Baron could do nothing about it. Goubert drove many of his Communist opponents in exile with the connivance of Baron and the administration.[47]

The Socialist Party's programme was published in June 1947. Sri Aurobindo himself seems to have drafted it. This implied that the Sri Aurobindo Ashram had also played its part, along with Baron, to create the Socialist Party. The party programme wanted Pondicherry to join the French Union freely with the people's consent as an autonomous territory but demanded the immediate transfer of powers to the Representative Assembly to manage the affairs of French India. It also demanded local legislative powers and the restriction of powers of the commissioner and the bureaucracy. It wanted the commissioner to be appointed by the French government in consultation with the Pondicherry assembly. The commissioner as head of the administration would be assisted by an executive council of ministers but would have no powers to rule by decree and the administration would be accountable to the elected assembly.[48]

Sensing, however, that the Socialist Party leaders were being accused of being 'slaves' of French imperialism, Muthu Poullé released a tract, dated 28 July 1947, that stated that they would ultimately join the Indian Union under a certain plan and at the right moment. This seems to have been taken note of by the French administration.[49]

At that juncture it could be said, nevertheless, that neither the Congress nor the Communists had a plan to agitate for the freedom of French India. Instead, the Communists had started to clash with the socialists of Goubert. S.R. Subramanian of the Congress Socialist party accused the government of spending 20 lakh rupees in 1946 without any debate in the assembly. He said that, except for one or two persons like advocate Balasubramanian, no member of the Assembly understood the budget. Subbiah never went to the Assembly. Besides, neither Subbiah nor Pakkirisamy Poullé, who were members of the Senate, ever spoke in the National Assembly for the Pondicherrians. According to S.R. Subramanian, none of the members had the capacity to understand anything about the budget presented in the assembly.[50]

It is believed by some that Goubert had the support of Commissioner Baron for the preceding plan, though there was no evidence for it. But it is quite possible that Baron was more sympathetic to Goubert's moves at that time, as V. Subbiah and some others of the National Democratic Front were clamouring for complete Independence. But Baron had never given the slightest hint that he approved the entire programme of Goubert's Socialist Party regarding devolution of power.[51]

It seems also quite possible that Mirra Alfassa, the Ashram Mother, might have had a hand in the drafting of the preceding programme of the Socialist Party of French India, along with Sri Aurobindo, as the pamphlet explaining the programme was printed at the Sri Aurobindo Ashram Press. However, it is not at all certain that Goubert had played into the hands of Commissioner Baron or Mirra Alfassa, as he seems to have wanted a very large autonomy for French Indians in order for Pondicherry to remain in the French Union. Goubert's supporters, like Dr André, Saravane and Counouma, were known to be close to the Ashram Mother. They had played their role in the creation of the French India Socialist Party. Antoine Mariadassou, Students' Congress leader, told me this fact. Besides *Baratha Sakthi*, a newspaper edited in reality by Suddhananda Barathiyar who was in the Ashram at that time, came out in support of the French India Socialist Party government.[52] It is, however, clear from the preceding that Sri Aurobindo and Mirra Alfassa did play a part in the politics of French India and favoured the position taken by the Socialist Party.

In any case, it was the Socialist Party of French India under Goubert which spelt out first very clearly the future of the French Indians in the form of a programme. It stressed that the Indians of French India, though they were Indians ethnically, religiously and linguistically, had developed a peculiar identity of their own due to their long historical association with France. The party stood for safeguarding this identity of French India, as an autonomous territory of the French Union, with wide legislative powers. This was quite unlike other parties like the Congress, the Communist Party and their leaders who wanted complete Independence and merger with India, without spelling out in concrete terms their desire to protect the special interests and identity of the French Indians. Goubert and his party were no doubt responsible for the development of a certain French Indian consciousness or sub-nationalism in French India, in the face of the rising tide of Indian nationalism. It must be noted here that Goubert was a Pondicherrian by virtue of him being born there, though his father was a Frenchman, while some other leaders like V. Subbiah, S.R. Subramanian or their parents were actually migrants to Pondicherry and had relatives in Tamil Nadu and were, therefore, not in a position to develop a purely French Indian consciousness like Goubert and his supporters.

Besides, Goubert's writ ran throughout Pondicherry and even within the government council. All opposition to him was quashed or silenced. Commissioner Baron, too, started feeling the heat of Goubert's politics when the latter literally threatened to get him recalled to France. Goubert even threatened the commissioner with the prospect of Pondicherry joining the Indian Union, if he contradicted him. The French commissioners, right from 1947 up until 1954, lived under the illusion that Edouard Goubert being a Créole would never go against France. As a result, they allowed him to act according to his wishes. However, the Congress Party as well as the students' organisations, both Congress and Communist, stridently clamoured for immediate integration of the French territories with free India.[53]

Sensing that things might get out of hand in French India as Indian Independence was round the corner, the French commissioner, François Baron, went all the way to Delhi where he conferred with Nehru and the French chargé d'affaires, Henri Roux. He also met other leaders like Rajendra Prasad, Maulana Abul Kalam Azad, Vallabhbhai Patel and Muhammad Ali Jinnah and explained to them his plans for Pondicherry. He seems to have said during these meetings that the only objective of the French was to make the people benefit from French culture. But Pondicherry Communists, like N. Ranganathan, thought that converting Pondicherry into a French cultural centre would only strengthen French imperialism. Baron also went to Calcutta later where Gandhi was camping. It seems that during the prayer meeting of 12 August 1947, Gandhi declared the following:

The Indians in the Portuguese and French possessions are destined to join Independent India at the right time. But the Indians of these territories should not take the law into their own hands.

It also seems that Governor Baron had assured Gandhi in person that the French would quit India in peace. Gandhi as well as the other political leaders whom he met in Delhi felt that the future of French India was in the hands of its population. Baron promised that Indian government servants could visit Pondicherry on a study tour in order to better understand the French culture and language, until the time when a French university would be created in Pondicherry.[54]

But Baron's meeting with Nehru in Delhi, in the presence of Henri Roux, when the Customs Union Affair was broached, was not a big success. Nehru appears to have cold-shouldered Baron. This was reported in the press. As for Roux, he later expressed his opinion that there was no other alternative for France except to quit India. According to him, the French settlements in India were insignificant and unprofitable and could become an embarrassment in future. He held the view that it was better to give them to India at once in exchange for some cultural, linguistic and educational advantages. In any case, the settlements were doomed to be lost according to Roux.[55] Roux seems to have realised that the unilateral calling off of the Customs Union Agreement of 1941 by New Delhi would put the French settlements almost immediately in economic distress, which could never be remedied.

Commissioner Baron's idea regarding the future of French India was different. He wanted to buy more time. Roux did not know or realise that Baron had already propped up Edouard Goubert and the Socialist Party which stood for autonomy within the French Union with the collaboration of even Sri Aurobindo and Mirra Alfassa. As a result, he proposed to give a large autonomy to the settlements and then organise a referendum to decide its future. Baron had no intention of abandoning the French settlements like Roux. In fact, the French government, too, had declared that French India's sovereignty was vested with the people, who might then, in accordance with democratic principles, choose to form a government reflecting their aspirations and establish freely international relations designed to promote the independence and institutions of French India.[56]

In fact, the decree of 8 July 1947 provided for a large administrative and financial autonomy of the settlements. Baron's idea was to give the settlements the status of 'Associated State' within the French Union. This had the support of Lambert Saravane, deputy of French India.[57] The French President, Paul Ramadier, was in favour of finding a solution with New Delhi on the basis of a condominium. Roux was actually against the idea of double nationality of Baron, by which the settlements would be attached to the French Union as well as India. This was an idea born due to his closeness with the Aurobindo Ashram, which had its own interests in mind, as most of them, including Sri Aurobindo and Mirra Alfassa, were settlers in Pondicherry and not its original inhabitants. Henri Roux dismissed Baron as not practical and being too idealistic. He, too, was not in favour of a referendum as the Indian government could refuse to accept the result if it was not favourable to them. So, he wanted to give up the *loges* immediately as wanted by Nehru and open negotiations with the Indian government to transfer the settlements to India in exchange of some cultural advantages.[58]

As for Jinnah, he had already invited Roux to send an ambassador of French India to Karachi. According to certain press organs, Sri Aurobindo seems to have approved the reforms of Baron. The Ashram was besieged in consequence. There was one person killed and several injured in the agitations against the Ashram which had supported the reforms of Baron, led by pro-mergerists.[59] One could conclude at this juncture that Baron was not inclined to give up the settlements to the Indian Union as Roux had wanted, due partly to the influence exerted by the Ashram Mother and Sri Aurobindo on him. On the other hand, Emmanuel Tetta, a respected government officer wanted to proceed by stages. He first sought a special status for the settlements as a French dominion, before realising the national unity.[60]

When Baron returned to Pondicherry, he got Mahatma Gandhi's conciliatory words related to the French settlements printed in leaflets and distributed among the Pondicherrians. Congressmen in Pondicherry were caught unawares by this position of Gandhi and its exploitation by Baron. The statement of Gandhi or rather the exploitation of it by Baron somewhat calmed down the nationalist passions.[61]

As a sort of goodwill gesture towards free India and the Congress Party, the French government under Georges Bidault decided unilaterally to transfer the eight *loges* (Calicut, Surat, Masulipatnam, Balasore, Goretti, Dacca, Jougdia and Cassimbazar) covering an area of three to four square miles, belonging to France to the Indian Union. Jawaharlal Nehru accepted this transfer or donation without hesitation. There were 2,000 French citizens in these *loges*, of which two, Dacca and Jougdia, were in Pakistan. The transfer happened without a vote in the French Parliament or without consulting the inhabitants of these *loges*, who were French citizens, as required by the French Constitution. Thus, the transfer of the *loges* to India was unlawful, as per French law. But nobody cared about it at that time. In any case, there were no means to defend them as they were virtually surrounded by Indian territory and dependent on the latter economically and materially. The transfer of these *loges* to India was done in the most undemocratic manner in order to be in the good books of Nehru and buy time to find an amicable settlement for the other French territories.

On 6 October 1947, the *loges* were duly transferred to the Indian Union without any formality during a brief ceremony at Masulipatnam in the presence of P.A. Menon, joint secretary of Foreign Affairs, representing India and Mr Fouchet, representing France. Rashid Ali Baig, Indian consul general at Pondicherry since September 1947, was also present. Fouchet brought down the French flag while the Indian flag was raised by Menon. Strangely, the inhabitants of the *loges* were hardly represented during the ceremony or the transfer of power. Thus, power in these *loges* was transferred by France to India without involving the local inhabitants of these *loges*. This, in a way, showed what was in store for the remaining French territories and its people, if they were to be integrated with the Indian Union. But nobody, especially in Pondicherry, including Edouard Goubert or V. Subbiah, was prepared or had the far-sightedness to take note of it.[62] On the Indian side, there was room to assume that the rest of the French territories could also be transferred amicably to India.

However, Commissioner Baron would not give any commitment on the integration of the remaining five French outposts in India with the Indian Union. Instead, he resorted to delaying tactics by announcing more and more constitutional reforms like the concept of Free towns, or a complete fiscal and administrative autonomy, without really addressing the issue of Independence of French India or the merger of French India with the Indian Union. Instead, we see him pronouncing the following words during the inauguration of a French cultural centre in Madras on 7 November 1947:

Thus, the cultured part of humanity, those who believe in the highest values of the spirit and who think that man has to accomplish the Divine Design, i.e. the civilization, remain threatened by barbarity. However, nothing is lost.
 ... If France and India unite fraternally, as wanted by the men here endowed with good will ... if the best minds of the Orient and the Occident, i.e. of France and India, work together for human friendship, then this civilisation which is so much threatened will be saved and beautified and it will last as long as there are Frenchmen and Indians in this world.[63]

The above statement established the extent to which François Baron was influenced by Sri Aurobindo and Madame Mirra Alfassa's universal idea and philosophy of East-West synthesis. Left to himself, Baron could not have made such a statement. Besides, in France, too, the opinion gained ground that the French empire should be replaced by the French Union. In fact, the French Union was considered as another generous French concept and a gift to the colonised people. The president of France, Vincent Auriol, proclaimed:

> Yes, French Union is an ideal community, the same respect for the dignity of man and the same will to raise their condition in the diversity of their beliefs and civilisations. And as this ideal reflects the vocation of France that around her are freely associated people, nations and the men of all parts of the world. This is the meaning of French presence in all the continents. . . . France does not oppress, she liberates.[64]

Thus, the French strove to safeguard their empire, by inventing the idea of French Union, where the colonised people can become 'free' citizens under France. But it proved to be a belated attempt to safeguard the colonies under the label of overseas territories, as there were revolts and rebellions against French rule in many French colonies stretching from Africa to Indochina which had large populations over which the French could never exercise their control indefinitely. In a report by Tezenas du Montcel, inspector of colonies, dated 15 January 1948, it was clearly stated that the various reforms introduced by Baron would pave the way for a unified referendum in the four settlements to be defined by the Representative Assembly and not separate referendums in the various settlements as wanted by the Indian government.[65]

As a result, it was clear that the French were not ready to leave Pondicherry. Naturally, there was opposition to their rule. The *Vennila* newspaper of Pondicherry was among those who were against their rule. Accusations were hurled on the French republic for trying to promulgate reforms that were favourable to maintain their rule and keep the Tamils/Indians under subjection like 'dogs' which were well-fed and dressed. They were critical of the power of the French commissioner. The paper exhorted the French to leave India and allow the French Indians to join the Indian Union according to the wishes of the people.⁶⁶ A. Lahache of *Libération* and *Jeunesse* of Dorai Munisamy came down heavily on what they termed as the the neo-colonialist and imperialist attitude of the French, masked by a certain generosity, in the name of the French Union.⁶⁷

Jeunesse was the journal founded by the Students' Congress in November 1947 at the residence of Antoine Mariadassou in Candappa Street. It was started when the Youth Congress was founded with Dorai Munisamy as president in the same month, with the sole aim of merging French India with the Indian Union. It was banned by May 1949 by the French authorities. Even the *Jeunesse* was banned on account of the virulently anti-French articles appearing in it.⁶⁸

Emmanuel Tetta, in a pamphlet titled 'Le Problème de l'Inde Française' wanted the constitution of a constituent assembly, which would decide about the integration of the French settlements with India and which would fix a transitional period with the agreement of the Indian government. On his part, Jawaharlal Nehru, the Prime Minister of India, dismissed Baron's reforms as insufficient, as it did not address the core issue of Independence. Nehru also dismissed the idea of double allegiance of French India to the Indian and French governments, spawned by Baron and Robert Schumann of the French Ministry of Foreign Affairs, in conjunction with the Sri Aurobindo Ashram.⁶⁹

The French, however, wanted India's neutrality, in their conflict in Vietnam, rather than a hostile India. For that, it was thought that France must strike a good relationship with New Delhi, especially because Pondicherry was an essential transit point between France and Indochina.

Krishna Menon, ambassador of India in Great Britain and trusted lieutenant of Nehru, met Ramadier, the President of France and the French Foreign Minister, Georges Bidault. Ramadier and Bidault stressed on the successive reforms that gave administrative and municipal autonomy to the French Indian settlements. Ramadier also insisted on the presence of French culture in the territories. Bidault, on his part, ruled out a referendum in the territories as it would create a precedent for other territories of the French Union. Krishna Menon welcomed the reforms and French culture, though he seems to have felt that it did not address the core issue of Independence. Krishna

Menon wanted the local populations of French India to choose immediately for themselves whether to remain with France or join India.[70]

When the British gave Independence to India, by partitioning India into India and Pakistan, Sri Aurobindo decried it and made a political statement that the Partition will cease to exist one day.[71] But as far as Pondicherry was concerned, Sri Aurobindo maintained a studied silence, while the Communist leader, V. Subbiah, opted to join India after meeting Jawaharlal Nehru in Delhi on 13 August 1947. Strangely, he did not resign his post as member of the French Senate. In fact, he remained a member of the French Senate until 1948, which diluted very much his nationalist stance and even rendered it ambiguous. However, this membership afforded him parliamentary immunity. Later, in November 1947, he was accused of having inspired a group of armed miscreants led by Vaidyalingam and Vassudevan, who were arrested. During an inquiry, the latter two told authorities that they had acted under the orders of Subbiah, who was the head of a committee of which they were members. Therefore, there was a demand in the French Parliament to cancel the parliamentary immunity of Subbiah.[72]

STUDENT AGITATIONS, ASHRAM AND RELATED EVENTS

On 14 August 1947, the Students' Congress of Pondicherry took out a procession. Antoine Mariadassou rode a horse dressed like Nehru and wearing his trademark cap. The next day, they wanted to hoist the Indian national flag at Nehru Vanam (presently an Ashram property) to celebrate Independence Day for India. Some leaders of the Students' Congress and the National Congress met the Sri Aurobindo Ashram authorities to request them to send a contingent of young Ashramites to participate in the procession and flag-hoisting. The Ashram authorities refused to participate on the pretext that their youth would take part only under the Ashram's banner of 'Lotus'. The Congress leaders considered this as an insult to the national flag and opined that the refusal of the Ashram to share in the jubilation of the people for India's Independence was a shame.

On 15 August 1947, the Aurobindo Ashram inmates celebrated the 75th birth anniversary of Sri Aurobindo, instead of the freedom of India. They never raised the national flag. It seems that some nationalists and Communists were infuriated by this attitude and attacked the Ashram inmates. The Dravidian nationalist, Bharathi- dasan, was critical of the Ashram in some of his Tamil works. *Suthanthiram* asserted that there was a tacit understanding between the Ashram Mother and Baron to maintain French India within the French Union in order to safeguard the properties of the Ashram and the agenda of French imperialism in India. It alleged that it is with these objectives that they had spawned the French India Socialist Party.[73]

The Ashram secretary dismissed the attack on them as the work of some 'professional *goondas* of the town hired and organised for the purpose' by those 'who are violently opposed to the existence of the Ashram, the advocates of *Dravidisthan*, extreme Indian Catholics and the Communists'. He maintained that Sri Aurobindo was not a citizen of French India, though he supported the programme of the Socialist Party and that he wanted French India to remain in the French Union under certain conditions.[74]

However, Congressmen refused to join the Communists in the Independence Day celebrations. The Students' Congress organised its own celebrations and processions, in which retired militarymen, 3,000 women, students and Muslims participated. In the meeting held on the occasion, Mohan Kumaramangalam, the Indian Communist Party politburo member said that Baron was trying to rule over Indians in the name of culture.[75]

The Congress procession on 14 August was led by the founder- president of the Students' Congress, Antoine Mariadassou, riding a white horse, followed by Paramel Shatrughnan holding aloft the Congress tri-colour flag. On 15 August early morning, the national anthem of India was sung by a host of girl students from the Colonial College (renamed then as Collège Français), after R.L. Purushotthama Reddiar, president of the National Congress of Pondicherry, hoisted the national flag. National and Congress flags fluttered all over Pondicherry and its neighbourhood. The Indian flag was raised even on the municipality building of Pondicherry as well as in the eight municipalities of the Pondicherry region. But it was brought down immediately in Pondicherry. At Odiansalai, Emmanuel Tetta, president of the *Cercle Sportif de Pondichéry* (who had married the daughter of Paramananda Mariadassou, the granduncle of the student leader Antoine Mariadassou), hoisted the national flag before a huge crowd. A huge public meeting took place at Nehru Vanam. All these events seem to have taken place without any obstruction from the government or other parties.[76]

It seems that some pro-French groups attacked the people celebrating Indian Independence. On 24 September 1947, 3,000 students went on srike in the Colonial College and other schools against Baron's reforms. Traders closed their shops in support of the students. Students of Mahé and Karaikal supported the students' strike in Pondicherry. On 24 September 1947, Paramel Shatrugnan spoke in a student meeting organised against Baron's reforms and also against Lambert Saravane, who was labelled as a 'traitor'. At a meeting at Nehru Vanam, student leader, Dorai Munisamy, spoke against Baron's reforms. It seems that at that time, rowdies attacked Paramel and sought refuge in Goubert's house. S.R. Subramanian denounced Goubert and dismissed him as having been just a government servant before Subbiah brought him into politics. On 1 October, two workers were killed in Mudaliarpet, allegedly by Communists.[77]

Mudaliarpet mayor and Rodier Labour Union secretary, Vaidhyalingam, labour leader of Rodier Mill, D.K. Ramanujam, as well as N. Ranganathan, member of the All-India Labour Congress General Council, were arrested. G. Annusamy, secretary of the National Democratic Front in the Assembly, denounced Goubert's intention to tax the handloom weavers and his penchant to award gifts to policemen who served to bolster French imperialism. Later, Annusamy moved a resolution in the Assembly to restrict the house rents which had increased in Pondicherry due to Sri Aurobindo Ashram's acquisition of properties. This resolution was defeated by Goubert's Socialist Party and Saravane, devotee of the Ashram.[78]

As many as 500 students went in a procession to Cuddalore to meet O.P. Ramasamy Reddiar, the Chief Minister of Madras province, and submitted their grievances. Even Prime Minister Nehru was apprised of the plight of the students in Pondicherry. Student

Congress leaders even demanded the arrest of Goubert, whom they considered as the mastermind behind the attacks against them.[79]

On 7 October 1947, the student leader of the Colonial College, Dorai Munisamy (Students' Congress secretary), went on fast to register the students' protest against the French government's political reforms of 24 September 1947. The students had indulged in sit-ins since 26 September 1947 to protest against the reforms. Many merchants and traders participated in their protests. Even some women students of Colonial College like Jacqueline Lernie participated in some of the students' actions like fasts, etc. The Students' Congress secretary, Dorai Munisamy, decided to go on fast indefinitely as the government would not provide adequate protection to the students and would not redress their grievances. At the same time, he asked the students to attend the classes.

Dorai Munisamy's fast lasted for 16 hours. The Indian consul general of Pondicherry, Mirza Rashid Ali Baig, assured the students that their grievances would be redressed and persuaded Dorai Munisamy to break his fast by offering him fruit juice. Pondicherry personalities like Karunendra Mudaliar, Emmanuel Tetta, Dr Srinivasan, D. Jeevarathinam, Mariappan, Selvanathan, Victor Mariadoss, H.M. Cassime, V.K. Pazhanisamy Mudaliar, R.L. Purushotthama Reddiar, Ambady Narayanan and even Sellane Naiker persuaded Munisamy to stop the fast.[80]

On 9 October 1947, Kamaraj Nadar, Congress leader of Tamil Nadu, spoke in Pondicherry during the Gandhi Jayanthi meeting thus:

In French India 3 lakh people are slaves. French imperialism has not yet left. Many are planning for those Whites to stay here. They have fabricated a party to support them. These dramas won't succeed. It is natural that the Whites do like this. But it is regretful that Indians are supporting them. It is shameful that Tamilians behave in this manner.[81]

Earlier, on 1 November 1947, Mahatma Gandhi had declared that French Indian people belonged to the Indian Union.[82] The Congress high command replied to a letter written by K. Muthu Poullé, the close associate of Goubert, in favour of dual citizenship for French Indians, through its representative Dr. N.V. Rajkumar, secretary, Foreign Department, Congress Party, in the following terms:

... You want dual citizenship ... You do not want to join the Indian Union. But we cannot accept your arguments. In Vietnam, French is indulging in atrocities. Why not realize it? There is no doubt about union with India. Now, news comes that France will accept dual citizenship. Vietnam delegates have explained to us about French tricks. You have to look to them. Only God can save French Indians and you, if you think you can prolong French rule.[83]

On 2 November 1947, the Netaji Kazhagam (Association) was opened in Mudaliarpet with the participation of Ansari Doraisamy, Purushotthama Reddiar, Ambady Narayanan, B. Rangapillai and Ku. Sivaprakasam. But they knew nothing of the role played by the Pondicherrian, Léon Prouchandy in the Netaji Movement in Saigon at that time, alongside Subhas Chandra Bose.

The decree of 7 November 1947 created the Free Town of Chandernagore, with a certain administrative and financial autonomy. It was also endowed with an administrative Council and an elected municipal assembly, with a president and vice-presidents. On 17 November, a similar decree was passed which created the Free towns of Pondicherry, Karaikal, Mahé and Yanam, under the same conditions as in Chandernagore, without consulting the Representative Assembly. It was the new ambassador of France in India, Daniel Levi, who invented the name 'Ville Libre' or Free Town. Paul Ramadier, the president of France, endorsed it. There was heavy opposition to the Free Town concept in the southern French Indian territories, as it was feared that it would strip the council of government of its powers. The concept discriminated between Hindus and Muslims and reserved eight seats for the latter in Karaikal. Subbiah denounced the concept of the Free Town of Chandernagore as a 'simulacre'. The Congress Party as well as Saravane were against it. But the secretary of the French India Muslim League, S. Mohamed Dawood, pointed out that there was no Muslim representative in the government Council, though they constituted about one-third of the population in Karaikal, Chandernagore and Mahé. The Representative Assembly members threatened to resign if the Free Town concept was implemented in southern French India. This forced Baron to backtrack, hence, Chandernagore alone embraced his Free Town project. Subbiah considered the other reforms of Baron, like the decrees of 12 August

1947 and 8 November 1947, as an eyewash to perpetuate French domination and imperialism in the settlements.[84]

On 18 November 1947, a meeting of the Students' Congress took place at Odiansalai, under student leaders, Dorai Munisamy, Subbu (president of Tamil Nadu Students' Congress) and Paramel Shatrughnan, attended by 1,000 persons. During his speech, the latter came down heavily on Lambert Saravane whom he tagged as a 'traitor'. Subbu took to task the Sri Aurobindo Ashram. He said that the Ashram Mother and Sri Aurobindo were collecting money in the name of religion and philosophy. He asked Sri Aurobindo to run to Bengal to save his (Bengali) countrymen from killing one another, instead of living in opulence in Pondicherry. He considered Commissioner Baron and Lambert Saravane who were disciples of the Ashram as 'quislings' who want to perpetuate French imperialism in India.[85]

Ravindra Varma, president of the All-India Students' Congress, also attended this meeting. In the course of his speech, he came down heavily on France, Commissioner Baron and the Sri Aurobindo Ashram. He declared that Aurobindo was a 'traitor' and 'coward' who had deserted the battlefield of Independence a long time back and claimed himself as God in Pondicherry. He proclaimed that Aurobindo left Bengal as he feared British incarceration. He also said that his place was not in Pondicherry in a palace, well-lit, well-ventilated, and with all the modern conforts of the Westerners, but in Bengal where Hindus and Muslims were killing each other. He opined that Aurobindo should not live-in idleness and indolence, under cover of yoga, but go to Bengal to re-establish order there. Instead of doing this, he was in the hands of a 'foreign woman' and a handful of Frenchmen, a docile instrument to maintain his compatriots in misery and in slavery. This was shameful indeed, said Ravindra Varma. He added that Aurobindo who had asked (the Congress) to accept the Cripp's Mission in 1942, would now have no other alternative except 'to ask us to accept the reforms of Baron, too'. He told Baron not to consider the Hindus as degenerate, alcoholics or consumers of opium that they would go and prostrate themselves in front of this 'living corpse' which was Aurobindo. He dismissed Baron during his speech as an uncultured 'small' man without virtue, a hypocrital comedian, a human parasite and a salaried mercenary. Varma also came down heavily on the 'so-called socialists like Lambert Saravane, who wanted to remain French. He asked Saravane to sell his properties in Pondicherry and go to France.[86]

As a result of the above speeches, Commissioner Baron decided to prohibit entry into Pondicherry of Ravindra Varma and Subbu of the Congress Party. He accused them of coming to French India to insult France, its representatives and elected members. Rachid Ali Baig, the consul general, countered Baron saying that Varma and Subbu had come to Pondicherry only on the invitation of local organisations.[87] It is, however, interesting to note that the student leaders of Pondicherry never spoke against the Ashram or Sri Aurobindo during the above meeting. It was rather 'outsiders' like Ravindra Varma and Subbu who slammed Sri Aurobindo.

When India became Independent, the position of Sri Aurobindo and Mirra Alfassa with regard to the Independence of Pondicherry became ambiguous. On 24 November 1947, there was the annual *darshan* in the Ashram, when Sri Aurobindo and Mother Alfassa appeared to the public. That very evening, there was a procession of students, workers and the public passing through the streets of Pondicherry shouting slogans against Mirra Alfassa, accusing her of playing politics in Pondicherry, instead of practising yoga. They organised an 'Ashram Opposition Day' condemning her purportedly anti-Indian activities and labelling her as 'foreign imperialist agent'. They asked the Ashramites to liberate themselves from the Mother's conspiracies! There was also opposition to the Ashramites' elitist attitude. It was said that when all men were equal, it was not right on their part to declare themselves as 'supermen' or unique. Earlier, when Subramania Bharathi was in Pondicherry, he had denounced the purportedly elitist attitude of Sri Aurobindo.[88]

Besides, it was maintained by *Suthanthiram*, that Sri Aurobindo had spent 35 years in Pondicherry peacefully and the people of Pondicherry have put up with the expansion of the Ashram which had created a housing scarcity for the Pondicherrians. But presently, the paper claimed, Sri Aurobindo had left spirituality and entered politics. He had refused to meet Mahatma Gandhi as he had taken a vow of silence. But when the French leader Maurice Schumann, came to Pondicherry after Independence in 1947 as head of a cultural mission, he talked with him for hours together. *Suthanthiram* also opined that all the plans of French imperialism were hatched in the Ashram, with the connivance of Sri Aurobindo and Mirra Alfassa.[89]

Lambert Saravane, who was close to Mother Alfassa, met the leaders of the anti-Ashram procession of 24 November near the government distillery on the Kurussukuppam seashore and tried to dissuade them from going ahead with their protests. He was shouted down and forced to retreat. On the other hand, some nationalist newspapers, like *Dinamani*, owned by Ramnath Goenka, misreported the incident as favourable to the Mother and the Ashram. The paper was accused of supporting the Mother who was branded as a French imperialist agent who wanted French India to remain with France. Paramel Shaturughnan attacked Lambert Saravane in no uncertain terms and branded him as a 'traitor'.[90]

It was the Congress Party which stood for complete merger of French India with the Indian Union right from the beginning. R.L. Purushotthama Reddiar, president of the Congress, criticised Baron's reforms and his concept of 'Free Towns'. On 8 November, Chandernagore was declared a 'Free Town'. The decree of 17 November 1947 theoretically gave this status to the remaining four southern French territories. The Samuga Democratic Union Party, which included men like the lawyer, S. Perumal, declared at that time its intention to join the Indian Union. However, it is noteworthy at that juncture that the French India Congress Party was always wary of the Communists and there was hardly any collaboration between them.[91]

Following the Congress Party, on 10 December 1947, V. Subbiah, the leader of the Communist Party of French India, made it clear that the objective of his party was complete Independence and merger with the Indian Union. He affirmed that the Socialist Party of French India wanted the maintenance of French sovereignty over the five outposts. However, neither Subbiah nor Reddiar spelled out in clear terms how they were going to protect the historical interests and identity of French Indians after Independence when the territories would be merged with the Indian Union. It is quite strange to note that *Suthanthiram*, the official organ of the Communist Party of French India, frequently accused Nehru and the Congress Party as being favourable to capitalists and imperialists and held that it would, therefore, not be freedom for the French Indians to join the Indian Union.[92]

But, in the same month, Lambert Saravane declared that it was not practicable to incorporate immediately the French terriotires in India as the outcome would be detrimental to both the Indian Union as well as the French Indian population. He considered India as a boat caught in the midst of a rough sea. Therefore, it was not judicious for him (as well as the French Indian ministers) to join the Indian Union when Nehru did not know how to solve the problems of India. Saravane was, in fact, in favour of the 'Etat Associé' (Associated State) status for French India within the French Union, though he denounced the rule by decrees. On his part, Pakkirisamy Poullé refused to accept the status of 'Free Town' for Pondicherry and Karaikal.[93]

Karunendra Mudaliar, member of the council of government and a landlord who belonged to the Socialist Party, wanted French India to be part of the French Union. He, along with R.P. Babilonne and Mohamed Ismaêl of the information service, was reputed to be staunchly pro-French at that time. Lambert Saravane and Senator Pakkirisamy Poullé were not lagging behind either, in their enthusiasm to remain in the French Union.[94]

In January 1948, the Karaikal nationalist, Arangasamy Naiker, passed away at the age of 65. On 17 January 1948, Commissioner Baron declared that talks would take place between France and India regarding the future of French India.[95] This statement had crucial implications as, for the first time, Baron had made it known that the merger of French India with the Indian Union was not the problem for the French Indian leaders to deal with. Instead, it would be decided by the new Indian government and France. This made it increasingly clear that the French Indians could not aspire for outright Independence like Pakistan. Instead, they had to choose between remaining in the French Union or joining the Indian Union.

However, Baron wanted to keep French India with France by all means. So he and the French colonialists, in general, resorted to various means and methods to achieve this objective. They distributed posts and titles to anti-mergerists. They told the Valangas that their lot would not improve if they joined India. They argued that Pondicherry was peaceful, unlike India. They put forward the cultural argument that Indians stood to benefit from French culture. They said that French India would be an 'Etat Associé' (Associate State) of the French Union. Besides, there was a rumour at that time that Pondicherry would become an American military base.[96]

The National Congress of French India, led by R.L. Purushotthama Reddiar, still wanted a complete withdrawal of France from French India without any conditions. The French India *Mahasabhai* conference of 25 January 1948, presided over by R.L. Purushotthama Reddiar, in the presence of Kamaraj Nadaar, decided that French India should join India without condition. They rejected a referendum to decide the future of French India.[97] Congressman Ansari Doraisamy was frequently fined for asking the French to get out of Pondicherry in meetings held at Ariyankuppam and Villianur. When the judge asked Ansari his profession, he replied that his profession was to get rid of French Imperialism. On the whole, the Congress wanted to find a negotiated settlement for French India, without really resorting to large scale agitations for freedom.[98]

Towards the end of December 1947, Nehru declared:

Pondicherry can and must be a link between India and the French culture. It is a natural window of France on India, and I will be happy if it was a window of India on France.[99]

When the situation was such, Gandhi was shot dead by Nathuram Godse, a Marathi Brahmin on 30 January 1948. Congressmen, especially the students, were shocked by this incident. A little of Gandhi's ashes were brought to Pondicherry and kept at the Congress office at Kalatiswaran Kovil street for people to pay their respects. Prayer meetings were held at the beach and also at the Nehru Vanam (presently Ashram Paper Mill) located just beyond the intersection of the Gingy road and North Boulevard. The ashes were finally mingled with the sea water at Vaithikuppam. It is interesting to note at that juncture that the assassination of Mahatma Gandhi was celebrated by some at the Sri Aurobindo Ashram by distributing sweets. As a result, Ashram buildings were attacked by Congressmen. Ansari Doraisamy pacified the agitators. But the consul general of India, Rashid Ali Baig, organised a meeting to condole the death of Gandhi. One Indian government official read the Gita, while Professor Mohamed, who taught at the Colonial College read the Quran and Sriman Dasappa read the Bible.[100]

NOTES

1. Brochure, Discours prononcé par le Gouverneur des Colonies, 6 November 1944, pp. 3-7, no. 6, ADP; Dramond. *France under de Gaulle*, London, 1970, p. 92; Krishnamurthy, *Pirench Intiya Viduthalai Porattam* (Tamil), Pondicherry, 1991, p. 50; Jacques Weber, *Pondichéry et les Comptoirs de l'Inde après Dupleix: La Démocratie au pays desCastes*, Paris, 1996, p. 358; Note de J.L.1943-5-Inde Série G 32, AOM; Lettre du Gouverneur au Ministre des Colonies, Pondicherry, 19 October 1944, Renseignements de la brigade, Pondicherry, 17 October 1944-Inde G 32, AOM; Rapport sur les activités d'une association compose de notables musulmans, June 1945-Police, Carton 450, Dossier 39, AOM.
2. J.B.P. More, *Tamil Heroes in French India, 1870-1954. Their Role in Business, Social Reforms and in Netaji's Freedom Struggle from Vietnam*, Pondicherry, 2016, pp. 23-4.
3. L'Occupation Japonaise, 10H80(1); L'Indochine sous l'Occupation Française, 10H78(1), Service Historique de l'Armée, Paris; More, op. cit., pp. 117-18.
5. Interview with Yves Perrier, former French administrator of Mahé, related to Edouard Goubert; Interview with Elenamma, stepdaughter of Léon Prouchandy; Lettre de Yves Perrier à M. le Ministre de la France d'Outre-mer, Pondicherry, 4 July 1949, Inde Série H 29-Dossiers sur Yves Perrier, Archives d'Outre-mer, Aix en Provence; J.B.P. More, op. cit., pp. 122-3.
6. Interview with Yves Perrier and Elenamma; More, op. cit., pp. 129-31. For more details see J.B.P. More, *Bose and His Movement: From Nazi Germany to French Indochina*, New Delhi, Manohar, 2022.
7. Weber, *Les Etablissements Français en Inde au XIXe Siècle (1816-1914)*, vol. IV, Paris, 1988, p. 2309; *Va. Subbiah Pavala Vizha Malar*, Pondicherry, 1988, vol. III; C. Antony, *Gazetteer of India: Union Territory of Pondicherry*, vol. I, Pondicherry, 1982, p. 248; V. Subbiah, *Saga of Freedom Movement: Testament of My Life*, Madras, 1990, pp. 227-30; Krishnamurthy, op. cit., 51; V. Subbiah, 'Naatu Viduthalai Poratathil Thozhilalar Pangum Kadamaiyum' in *Suthanthiram, Suthanthira Thina Sirappu Malar*, Pondicherry, 1980, p. 11; Antoine Mariadassou, 'History of the Freedom

Struggle of the French India Students Congress', *La Lettre du CIDIF*, no. 20, 1998, p.55; *The Hindu*, 15 September 1945; Notes Documentaires et Etudes, no. 735, Les EF de l'inde, IF 7, ADP; Lettre du gouverneur p.i. de l'IF à Ministre de la France d'Outre-mer, Pondicherry, 4 June 1946, pp. 12-13, IF 51, ADP; *l'Intransigeant*, 21 April 1954; Association Ramakrishna Vasaka Salai, Pondichéry, 4 September 1942 and Lettre du MDL Chef Anantarayer au Commmandant de la brigade de Gendarmerie, Pondicherry, 27 June 1942, Inde G 29, AOM; Arrêté du, 18 April 1944, Pondicherry-Inde G 29, AOM; *The Hindu*, 25 November 1944.

8. Critique du Rapport de Paul Devinat, Deputé sur le Projet Tendant à Autorisé le Président de la République Française à Ratifier le Traité de Cession, signed on 28 May 1956, p. 129, no. 326, AO 1956-67, ADP.
9. JO 1946, pp. 234, 240.
10. Note pour la Direction d'Asie, Affaires Etrangères, Paris, 5 November 1946, p.17, IF 80, ADP; Note pour M. Henri Roux, AO, 27 March 1947, p. 18, IF 80, ADP; Subbiah, op. cit., pp. 234-5; Ranganathan, *The Ashram in Politics*, Pondicherry, 1982, pp. 12-18; *Podujanam*, 5 February 1948, p. 7; Lettre du Gouverneur de l'IF au Ministère de la France d'Outre-mer, Affaires Politiques, Pondicherry, 23 July 1946, C 368. D3, AOM.
11. *Podujanam*, 5 February 1948, p. 7; Lettre du Ministre de la France d'Outre-mer au Ministre des Affaires Etrangères, Paris, 17 September 1946, pp. 2-4, IF 80, ADP; Lettre du gouverneur p.i. de l'IF au Ministre de la France d'Outre-mer, Pondicherry, 23 July 1946, p. 9, IF 51, ADP; Ministre France d'Outre-mer au Gouverneur, Pondicherry, Paris, 17 September 1946, pp. 14-19, IF 51, ADP; Ajit Neogy, *Decolonisation of French India*, Pondicherry, 1997, pp. 18, 20.
12. JO 1946, p. 619; Renseignements sur V. Subbiah, 10 June 1947-Inde G 8, AOM; Note sur Mouttoukomarapparettiar, Membre de l'Assemblée Représentative-Inde H 22, AOM; Note sur Mouttousamy Poullé-Inde H 22, AOM; Note sur André Zeganathan-Inde H 22, AOM.
13. Interview with Paul Radjanedassou and M.P. Sridharan; Antoine Mariadassou, op. cit., p. 56; Interview with Antoine Maraidasou; Renseignements Généraux, Pondicherry, 5 July 1945-Inde H 22, AOM; Purushothama Reddiar papers, Pondicherry National Archives; Interview with Doressamy Naiker, Students' Congress leader.
14. Antoine Mariadassou, op. cit., p. 56; *Podujanam*, 5 February 1948, p. 7; 17 April 1948, p. 10; *Podujanam*, 5 February 1948, p. 7; 17 April 1948, p. 10; A. Arulraj, *Puducheri Suthanthira Poratathin Kalachuvadukal*, Pondicherry, 2005, p. 98; JO 1946, p. 406.

15. Mariadassou, op. cit., Enginger, Information Officer of French India, p. 178, IF 9, ADP; Neogy, op. cit., pp. 27-8; *Franc-Tireur*, 1 November 1946.
16. Interview with Saraswati Subbiah; *The Hindu*, 14 June 1947; 7 October 1946; Assemblée Nationale- 2ème séance, 25 May 1949, p. 2, AO 1944-55, no. 28, ADP; *Suthanthiram*. 27 April 1946.
17. JO 1946, p. 512; Lettre du gouverneur p.i. de l'IF au Ministre de la France d'Outre-mer, Pondicherry, 4 June 1946, pp. 12-13, IF 51, ADP; *Indian Express*, 22 November 1945; Renseignements Généraux, Pondicherry, 5 July 1945-Inde H 22, AOM.
18. *Franc-Tireur*, 20 October 1946 ; JO 1946, pp. 512, 789; *Le Monde*, 19 August 1954; Rapport sur les Activités d'une Association Compose de Notables Musulmans, June 1945-Police, Carton 450, Dossier 39, AOM.
19. Note de l'Ambassade de France à Londres, au Ministère des Affaires Etrangères, Londres, 28 May 1947, p. 128; Ministre de la France d'Outre-mer au Gouverneur, Pondichéry, Paris, 17 September 1946, pp. 14-19, IF 51, ADP; Neogy, op. cit., p. 14.
20. Lettre de Henri Roux, Chargé d'Affaires au Ministre des Affaires Etrangères, Delhi, 16 May 1946, pp. 98-9, IF 6, ADP.
21. *Franc-Tireur*, 20 October 1946; JO 1946, p. 837; M.C. Vashist, 'Trade Union Movement in Pondicherry State with Special Reference to Mahé', M. Phil dissertation, University of Calicut, 1993, p. 58; Note, Ambassade, AO, 21 September 1950, no. 43, p. 115, ADP; Lettre du Ministre de la France d'Outre-mer au Ministre des Affaires Etrangères, Paris, le 14 June 1946, p. 23, IF 6, ADP; Lettre de Christian Fouchet, Consul Général de France à Calcutta, à M. Georges Bidault, Ministre des Affaires Etrangères, Calcutta, 12 July 1946, IF 6, p. 45, ADP.
22. *The Hindu*, 8 January 1947; Subbiah, op. cit., pp. 248-9; Lettre de Levi à Bidault, Ministre des Affaires Etrangères, New Delhi, 7 May 1947, p. 187, IF 8, ADP.
23. Assemblée Nationale- 2ème Séance, 25 May 1949, p. 2, AO 1944-55, no. 28, ADP; JO 1947, p. 140; Note pour le Ministre, Directeur des affaires politiques, 23 Mars 1948, pp. 82-6, IF 51, ADP; AFP, Pondicherry, 14 December 1948, AO, 1944-55, no. 53, p. 21.
24. Anonymous note, 8 May 1947, p. 117, IF 6, ADP; Communication au Conseil du Ministre, Ministère de la France d'Outre-mer, Paris, 19 May 1947, p. 113, IF 6, ADP; Lettre du Minsitre de la France d'Outre-mer au Gouverneur de l'IF, Paris, 1 April 1947, C 370. D1, AOM; *Hindustan Times*, 9 May 1947; E. Divien, 'V. Subbiah' in *Va. Subbiah Pavala Vizha Malar*, 1988, p. 40; A. Sebastien. 'Nan Kanda Imayasikaram', *Va. Subbiah*

Pavala Vizha Malar, Pondicherry, 1988, p. 100 (Sebastien was a French teacher known to Subbiah); Antony, op. cit., vol. I, pp. 248, 250; Interview with Saraswati Subbiah, A. Arulraj and Paul Radjanedassou; JO 1947, p. 140; *The Hindu,* 8 January 1947; Neogy, op. cit., pp. 31-2.
25. *l'Humanité,* 24 March 1947; 5 April 1947; *Suthanthiram,* 12 April 1947.
26. *Suthanthiram,* 2 August 1947.
27. Ibid.
28. *Janada,* 9 February 1947; Suthanthiram, 1 February 1947.
29. *Suthanthiram,* 1 February 1947; Weber, op. cit., 1996, p. 261.
30. *Janada,* 6, 20 April 1947, pp. 4-5.
31. *Janada,* 13, 27 April 1947.
32. *Samudayam,* 14 September 1947; Mariadassou, op. cit., p. 57, Asie-Océanie, Inde 1956-67, Critique du Rapport de M. Paul Devinat, Deputé du Traité de Cession, New Delhi, 28 May 1950, no. 326, ADP; Tél de Massigli au Ministère des Affaires Etrangères, Londres, 15 March 1947, p. 43, IF 51, ADP; Interview with Saraswati Subbiah and A. Arulraj; Tél de Pondichéry au Ministère de la France d'Outre-mer, 27 February 1947, Affaires Politiques, C 368, D3, AOM.
33. *The Hindu,* 3 March 1947; Tél du Secrétaire Général Pacha au Ministère de la France d'Outre-mer, Pondicherry, 5 March 1947, Affaires Politiques, C 370. D1, AOM.
34. *The Hindu,* 15 July 1947.
35. Tél d'Ange au Ministère des Affaires Etrangères, Canberra, 12 August 1947, p. 51, IF 51, ADP; V. Subbiah, 'Naatu Viduthalai Poratathil Thozhilalar Pangum Kadamaiyum' in *Suthanthiram, Suthanthira Thina Sirappu Malar,* Pondicherry, 1980, p. 11; *Suthanthiram.* 24 May 1947; AFP E 81 1-Une declaration de Subbiah, Conseiller de la République de l'IF, Paris, 5 June 1947, p. 44, IF 51, ADP; Tél de Henri Roux au Ministère des Affaires Etrangères, New Delhi, 22 July 1947, p. 46, IF 81, ADP.
36. G. Samboo, op. cit., p. 51; *Suthanthiram,* 31 May 1947; 14 June 1947; Circulaire no. 203 IP, Paris, 14 August 1947, Ministre des Affaires Etrangères, Service d'info et de Presse, p. 36, no. 5, AO, ADP; *Suthanthiram,* 27 September 1947; Circulaire no. 916-IP, Paris, 26 November 1947, Affaires Etrangères, Service d'Info et de Presse, no. 5, AO, ADP; A. Ramasamy, *History of Pondicherry,* Delhi, 1987, pp. 152-3; Weber, op. cit., 1996, p. 360.
37. *Suthanthiram,* 23 August 1947; 4, 20 October 1947.
38. *Baratha Sakthi,* November 1947, AO, No. 53, pp. 258-60, 281-4, ADP; JO 1948, pp. 144, 155, 163, 269, 278.
39. *Podujanam,* 13 April 1948, pp. 3-4; Interview with David Annoussamy

and Dr Selvaraja; AO à Amba France, New Delhi, Paris, 13 May 1950, p. 47, AO 1944-55, no. 26, ADP; Circulaire no. 916-IP, Paris, 26 November 1947, Affaires Etrangères, Service d'Info er Presse, pp. 26-35, no. 5, AO, ADP.
40. Mariadassou, op. cit., p. 59; *Samudayam*, 7 September 1947; JO 1947, p. 787; B. Mayandi, 'Subbaiyavum Suthanthiramum Onru', *Va. Subbiah Pavala Vizha Malar*, Pondicherry, 1988, p. 47; Bazin, Administrateur de Chanderngore au Gouverneur des EF dans l'Inde, Chandernagore, 28 May 1947, C 369, D1, AOM.
41. *Suthanthiram*, 4 October 1948; V. Subbiah, op. cit., 1980, p. 11; *Samudayam*, 11 September 1947; Note sur Pakkirisamy Poullé-Inde H 22, AOM.
42. *Samudayam*, 14 September 1947; *Suthanthiram*, 2 August 1947.
43. Asie-Océanie, Inde 1956-67, Critique du Rapport de M. Paul Devinat, Deputé du Traité de Cession, New Delhi, 28 May 1950, no. 326, ADP; Tract of Parti Communiste de l'Inde Française, 6 September 1947, Pondicherry; *Indian Express*, 24 August 1947; *Suthanthiram*, 16 April 1948; *Dinamani*, 26 August 1947; Rapport du Capitaine Bouhard, Pondicherry, 19 August 1947 et Renseignements sur le nommé Ranganadin-Inde G 8, AOM.
44. Mariadassou, op. cit., p. 58; Interview with Antoine Mariadassou, Paramel Shatrugnan and Paul Radjanedassou; Letter of Aurobindo to Surendra Nath Ghosh, 1 April 1949 in Sri Aurobindo, *Autobiographical Notes and Other Writings of Historical Interest*, Pondicherry, 2015, p. 494 ; Problème de l'I.F. s.d. Dactylographié, AO, 1944-55, pp. 5-6, no. 53, ADP; Asie-Océanie, Inde, 1956-67, no. 326, Critique du rapport de Paul Devinat, Deputé sur la ratification du Traité de cession, New Delhi, 28 May 1956, no. 326; ADP; *l'Intransigeant*, 21 April 1954.
45. Mariadassou, op. cit., p. 58 ; Problème de l'I.F. s.d. dactylographié, AO, 1944-55, pp. 5-6, no. 53, ADP; *Jeunesse*, 15 June 1949; V. Subbiah, *Puduvaiyin Viduthalaiai Vendradutha Thozhilalarkalin Veera Varalaru*, Pondicherry, 1986, pp. 28-9.
46. Asie-Océanie, Inde-1956-67, no. 326-Critique du Rapport de M. Paul Devinat du Traité de Cession, New Delhi, 28 May 1956, ADP.
47. Asie-Océanie, Inde-1956-67, Critique du Rapport de Paul Devinat, Depute du Traité de Cession, New Delhi, 28 May 1956, no. 326, ADP; *Samudayam*, 14 September 1947; *Nadar Kulam*, November 1947, p. 13; *Le Monde*, 19 August 1954; *Suthanthiram*, 9 December 1947; *Le Monde*, 19 August 1954.
48. The Future Union, A Programme (in) *Sri Aurobindo*, op. cit., pp. 481-91.

49. Avis à la Population, par le Maire de Pondichéry, K. Muthu Poullé, 28 July 1947 (tract).
50. *Samudayam*, 14, 21 September 1947.
51. Krishnamurthy, op. cit., p. 56; Antony, op. cit., p. 248; JO 1947, p. 787; *The Hindu*, 14 August 1947; V. Subbiah, *Saga of Freedom Movement: Testament of My Life*, Madras, 1990, pp. 257, 259; *l'Humanité*, 11 August 1947; l'Union de l'Avenir (programme), Juin 1947, Pondicherry.
52. *Podujanam*, 4 January 1948, p. 3; Mariadassou, op. cit., p. 58; Interview with Antoine Mariadassou.
53. Asie-Océanie, Inde-1956-67, no. 326-Critique du Rapport de M. Paul Devinat du Traité de Cession, New Delhi, 28 May 1956, ADP; Weber, op. cit., 1996, p. 363.
54. *The Hindu*, 14 August 1947; 27 August 1947; *Suthanthiram*, 14 June 1947; AFP, Pondicherry, 7 June 1947; AFP Service Special outre-mer, 2 June 1947, pp. 140-1, IF 6, ADP.
55. Lettre du Ministre des Affaires Etrangères au Ministre de la France d'Outre-mer, Paris, 10 June 1947, pp. 143-4, IF 6, ADP; Henri Roux, Ambafrance, New Delhi au Ministère des Affaires Etrangères, 5 July 1947, pp. 161-2, IF 6, ADP.
56. Lettre de Henri Roux à Bidault, Ministre des Affaires Etrangères, New Delhi, 5 July 1947, pp. 163-7, IF 6, ADP; *Statesman*, (probablement début May 1948), p. 223, IF 8, ADP.
57. JO, 8 July 1947, p. 170, IF 6, ADP; Note pour M. Chauvel, Asie Oceanie, 28 July 1947, p. 171, IF 6, ADP; Note pour le Ministre, AO, sur le Statut de l'IF, 31 July 1947, pp. 192-6, IF 6, ADP.
58. Note pour le Ministre, AO, 13 August 1947, pp. 265-7, IF 6, ADP; Lettre de Henri Roux au Ministre des Affaires Etrangères, New Delhi, 18 July 1947, IF 6, ADP; Neogy, op. cit., pp. 39-43.
59. Tél de Roux, New Delhi, 19 August 1947, p. 256, IF 6, ADP; Tél de Roux, 18 April 1947, New Delhi, pp. 243-4, IF 6, ADP; Lettre de Henri Roux à M. Baudet, Ministre des Affaires Etrangères, New Delhi, 18 July 1947, IF 6, ADP.
60. 'Le Sort de l'IF' par Emmanuel Tetta, Citoyen de l'IF, 15 July 1947, Pondicherry, pamphlet, p. 180, IF 6, ADP.
61. Note sur la situation politque des EF dans l'Inde, Ministère de la France d'Outre-mer, 15 January 1948, p.3, IF 8, ADP.
62. AO, 1944-55, Inde fr. Loges française en Inde, no. 23, pp. 1-65, ADP; Tél de Roux au Ministère des Affaires Etrangères, New Delhi, 27 August 1947, no. 4, p. 9, ADP; cf. also Hughes Jean de Dianoux, *Les Loges Françaises dans l'Inde et au Bangladesh et les îles Spratly*, Paris, 1986.

63. *France-Asie*, January 1948, pp. 187-9; JO 1947, pp. 1202, 1311, 1440; *Suthanthiram*, 23 August 1947; *Indian News Chronicle*, 18 September 1947.
64. *Le Populaire*, 30 April 1948; *Le Populaire*, 11 February 1948.
65. *Le Figaro*, 14 May, 8 June 1954 ; Note sur la situation politique des EF dans l'Inde, Ministère de la France d'Outre-mer, 15 January 1948, pp. 3-7, IF 8, ADP.
66. *Vennila*, 22 August 1947; 1 December 1947.
67. *Libération*, 26 May 1949; *Jeunesse*, 20 April 1949.
68. Mariadassou, op. cit., p. 59.
69. Tél de Roux au Ministère des Affaires Etrangères, New Delhi, 11 October 1947, IF 7, ADP; Note de M. Daniel Levi, 8 November 1947, IF 7, ADP; Emmanuel Tetta, 'Le Problème de l'Inde Française', pamphlet, Pondy, 30 January 1948, p. 19, IF 8, ADP; Tél de Roux au Ministère des Affaires Etrangères, New Delhi, 9 October 1947, IF 7, ADP.
70. Tél de Roux au Ministère des Affaires Etrqangères, New Delhi, 13 October 1947, IF 7, ADP; Note pour le Ministre, EF, AO, 11 October 1947, IF 7, ADP; Entretien de M. Ramadier avec M. Krishna Menon, Ambassadeur de l'inde à Londres, Paris, 20 October 1947; Entretien de M. Bidault avec Krishna Menon, 20 October 1947, IF 7, ADP.
71. S. Iyengar, *Sri Aurobindo. A Biography and a History*, vol. II, Pondicherry, 1972, p. 1287.
72. La Demande de levée de l'Immunité Parlementaire de M. Subbaya, AFP, 22 November 1947, IF 7, ADP.
73. *Suthanthiram*, 2 August 1947; Interview with Paul Radjanedassou and M.P. Sridharan; *The Hindu*, 21 August 1947; *Makkal Manasaatchi*, 13 July 2010; Interview with Anne Marie Legay.
74. Letter of the Secretary of the Ashram to the Editor of the Statesman, 20 August 1947, in *Sri Aurobindo*, op. cit., pp. 491-2, 495-6.
75. *Suthanthiram*, 23 August 1947; 23 January 1948.
76. Mariadassou, op. cit., pp. 60-1; Interview with Antoine Mariadassou; Tél de Roux au Ministère des Affaires Etrangères, New Delhi, 20 August 1947, p. 53, IF 51, ADP.
77. *Samudayam*, 25 September 1947; 2, 9 October 1947; *Vennila*, 9 October 1947; Interview with Antoine Mariadassou, student leader.
78. *Suthanthiram*, 6 May 1948; 4 October 1947; 20 October 1947.
79. *Samudayam*, 2 October 1947; *Suthanthiram*, 20 October 1947; *Vennila*, 9 October 1947.
80. *Suthanthiram*, 13 October 1947; *Vennila*, 9 October 1947; *Samudayam*, 16 October 1947; Interview with Anne Marie Legay.

81. *Samudayam*, 16 October 1947; *Suthanthiram*, 13 October 1947.
82. *Samudayam*, 20 November 1947.
83. *Samudayam*, 13 November 1947.
84. JO 8 November 1947; Note, EF de l'inde, New Delhi, IF 7, ADP; Télégramme, Reuter, 10 November 1947, IF 7, ADP; Commission d'études de l'Union Française. Procès-verbal de la Séance, 6 November 1947, IF 7, ADP; Lettre de Baron à Tézenas du Montcel, Pondicherry, 29 November 1947, Affaires Politiques, C 437, D1, AOM; 'Revendication politiques des Musulmans de l'IF'; Affaires Politiques, C 368, D3, AOM; Lettre du Ministre de la France d'Outre-mer au Ministre des Affaires Etrangères, 4 February 1948, AO, IF 8, ADP.
85. *Extrait d'un discours pronouncé en tamoul par M. Subbu*, president of Students' Congress of Tamil Nadu, November 1947, IF 51, ADP.
86. *Compte-rendu d'une réunion politique du Congrès sous la présidence de M. Varma*, president of All India Students' Congress, Pondicherry, 19 November 1947, pp. 84-7, no. 24, AO, ADP; Discours pronouncé en angalis par M. Ravindra Varma, president of All India Students' Congress, 18 November 1947, IF 51, ADP ; *Suthanthiram*, 24 November 1947.
87. Gouverneur Baron au Conseil du Gouvernement, Pondicherry, 21 November 1947, pp. 69-70, IF 51, ADP; Rashid Ali Baig au Gouverneur, Pondicherry, 25 November 1947, p. 71, IF 51, ADP.
88. *Podujanam*, 4 January 1948, p. 8; cf. More, *Subramania Bharathi in British and French India, Nationalist, Revivalist or Thamizh Patriot?*, Chennai, 2017.
89. *Suthanthiram*, 1 December 1947; *Vennila*, 1 December 1947; Neogy, op. cit., pp. 65-6.
90. *Samudayam*, 4 December 1947; *Suthanthiram*, 1 December 1947; *Vennila*, 1 December 1947; *Samudayam*, 20 November 1947.
91. *Suthanthiram*, 1, 21 December 1947; *Samudayam*, 4 December 1947; *Podujanam*, 4 January 1948, p. 3; *Suthanthiram*, 23 January 1948; 26 April 1948; Circulaire no. 916, Paris, 26 November 1947, Affaires Etrangères, Service de la Presse, no. 5, p. 26, AO, ADP; Saravane Lambert, 1945-1950-Inde G 8, AOM.
92. *Suthanthiram*, 26 April 1948; 11 June 1948; Samboo, op. cit., p. 121; *Suthanthiram*, 24 November 1947; 22 February 1948; 29 February 1948.
93. *Suthanthiram*, 23 January 1948; Samboo, op. cit., p. 124; *Suthanthiram*, 26 October 1947; 4 November 1947.
94. *Suthanthiram*, 20 October 1947; Samboo, op. cit., p. 124; *Libération*, 26 May 1949, pp. 3, 5; *Jeunesse*, 26 March 1949.
95. *The Hindu*, 18 January 1948.

96. *Podujanam*, 4 January 1948, pp. 4-5; *Suthanthiram*, 23 January 1948; 30 March 1948; *Sudesamitran*, 26 March 1948.
97. *Jeunesse*, January-February 1948; *Samudayam*, 12 January 1948; 5, 19 March 1948; 27 February 1948; *Lettre de R.L. Purushotthamma Reddiar*, Président Congrés National de l'IF au Ministre des Affaires Etrangères, pp. 79-80, IF 51, ADP.
98. *Suthanthiram*, 11, 22 February 1948; 30 March 1948; *Samudayam*, 19 March 1948.
99. Lettre de M. Bernard H., Ministre Plenipotentiare en Espagne au Ministre des Affaires Etrangères, Madrid, 30 December 1947, IF 7, ADP.
100. *Podujanam*, 22 January 1948; Interview with Husain, Kazy of Pondicherry; The 'Reveil Social' also condoled Gandhi's death; Interview with M.P. Sridharan; Saraswati Subbiah; A. Arulraj; A. Arulraj, *Puducheri Suthanthira Poratathin Kalachuvadukal*, Puduchery, 2005, pp. 110-11.

CHAPTER 7

The Rise of Goubert

According to the Census of 1948, the population of Pondicherry was 2,12,572, of which 1,94,997 were Hindu, 6,382 Muslim and 21,137 of the Catholic faith. A total of 1,70,162 were born in Pondicherry while 50,900 were born in India. The population of Karaikal was 70,541, of which 55,399 were Hindu, 6,815 Muslim and 8,327 Catholic. The total population of the five French settlements was 3,62,042, of which 2,68,570 were Hindu, 23,144 Muslim and 30,368 Catholic. A total of 2,60,124 were born in the settlements, while 1,00,446 were born in India. The total area of French India was 30,238 hectares. Pondicherry (29,145 ha.) was divided into 8 communes: Pondicherry, Oulgaret, Ariyankuppam, Mudaliarpet, Villianur, Thirubhuvanai, Bahur and Nettapakkam. Karaikal region (13,515 ha.) had six communes.[1]

REFERENDUM AND ELECTIONS

In the month of March 1948, Jawaharlal Nehru, the Prime Minister of India, announced in the Parliament that a referendum would be held in the French settlements to ascertain the wishes of the people about joining India. The French had already opted for a referendum in the settlements. By April 1948, R.L. Purushotthama Reddiar, the president of the French India Congress Party, who had earlier rejected referendum, also came out in favour of a referendum to know the wishes of the people as soon as possible. He would not take a position against the wishes of Nehru and the Congress high command.[2]

By then, the French businessman, Mr Godard, who was the president of the Chamber of Commerce of Pondicherry, wanted the replacement of François Baron as Commissioner, as he thought that Baron was increasingly antagonising the local elements and populations. He thought that maintaining him as governor would ruin the chances of retaining the French territories for France.[3] It was true that Baron was on a collision course with the local forces including Edouard Goubert due to his ideas related to the maintenance of French India within the French Union and his overt intimacy with the Sri Aurobindo Ashram, which had its own interests and agenda to defend, which were unrelated to the concerns of the Pondicherry population.

Commissioner Baron and the Inspector of Colonies, Tezenas du Montcel, were in favour of consulting the members of the Representative Assembly before entering into an agreement with the Indian government with regard to referendum. Mr Iyengar of the Indian Ministry of Foreign Affairs was in favour of a combined referendum in all the five French settlements while the Indian officers like Girija Shankar Bajpai, secretary in the Ministry of External Affairs, were for separate referendums in the five settlements. In any case, the plan for holding a referendum was almost settled between the governments of India and France.[4]

On 10 April 1948, Muthu Poullé, the mayor of Pondicherry, made a declaration on behalf of French Indian Socialist Party that the time had come to liberate French India from French rule. But he did not specify whether French India would stand alone or join the Indian Union. The Congress Party steadfastly stood for the merger of Pondicherry and Karaikal with the Tamil districts of Madras province. On his part, Léon Saint Jean, general secretary of the Congress grouping in the Representative Assembly, declared that French India would be integrated with the Indian Union immediately.[5]

Exasperated by the increasing support for the Congress Party even among the government servants, who enjoyed fat salaries, the First World War veteran, Abdul Cader, who had been awarded the title of Chevalier de la Légion d'Honneur, took a strong position in favour of French India remaining in the French Union. Many Karaikal Muslims, too, were not in favour of joining the Indian Union. Some others like the Pondicherrian, Arthur Annasse, worked for the maintenance of the French settlements in the French Union. It is interesting to note that during this period, the pro-Dravidian revolutionary poet of Pondicherry, Bharathidasan, had started a pro-French organisation on 25 July 1948 for French Indians to remain in the French Union. A conference of this organisation was held at Swami Picture Palace Theatre called the 'Thakara Kotta' theatre (presently Kamban Kalai Arangam). Periyar E.V. Ramasamy participated in this conference. But due to attacks by pro-Indian *goondas*, the conference was suspended and its organisers fled the scene. The 'Dravidian' Pondicherrians, led by Bharathidasan joined with some Communists under the Progressive Democratic banner to oppose joining the Indian Union.[6]

On 30 April 1948, the Representative Assembly rejected the resolution of Léon Saint Jean which asked for immediate integration of French India with the Indian Union. A total of 27 members voted against the resolution, while 10 voted in favour of it. Lambert Saravane, in his turn, put forth a resolution which was against integration with the Indian Union. This resolution obtained 34 votes in its favour and only 3 votes against it. Strangely, the Communists voted in favour of both the resolutions. That shows the confused state of mind of the Communist Party of French India as well as its leader, V. Subbiah, at that juncture.[7]

In May 1948, the Students' Congress called for a general strike at the *Collège Colonial* to protest against the swearing-in ceremony of Goubert's Socialist Party. It seems then that Paramel Shatrughnan, (who became president of the Students' Congress in August 1948) was assaulted by some *goondas* within the college premises in front of the professors. The students sat on a dharna on the road. At that time, students of the Communist Students' Union joined the agitation. They all took part in a procession and a meeting at Nehru Vanam. This was the time when Charles Chambon had replaced Baron as commissioner. It was also the time when a new French consulate was opened in Madras.[8]

During a public meeting organised by the Communists of Pondicherry in June, Communist speakers spoke against integration of French India with the Indian Union and against French imperialism. They held that the government of India was in the hands of the capitalists. Therefore, it would be preferable for French Indians to remain a separate state completely independent and free of either French or Indian tutelage. On 15 August 1948, in a meeting attended by 600 persons in the quai of Gingy ground, Subbiah once again affirmed Communist opposition to integration with the Indian Union.[9] However, by September, Lambert Saravane, too, sang the song of integration with India without referendum, following the Congress, abandoning his old friend, Subbiah.[10]

After the Independence of India, France was in a quandary with regard to its possessions in India. The French realised very soon that it would be immoral and impossible to hold on to these minuscule territories indefinitely without the concurrence of its inhabitants. Therefore, after several high-level discussions, they proposed holding a free and fair referendum in the settlements to decide about joining with India or remaining with France. An agreement to this effect was signed on 8 June 1948 with the Indian government in Delhi led by Jawaharlal Nehru, who had always had great admiration for French values and culture. He and the French ambassador, Daniel Levi, exchanged letters on 29 June 1948, confirming the referendum. It was also decided that the modalities of this referendum would be finalised by the municipal councils of these territories. Bajpai, the secretary at the Indian Ministry of External Affairs, reminded the French that the referendum should be held at short notice and in no way could it be put off by the local assemblies by 10 or 20 years.[11]

Sellane Naiker was probably the first Pondicherry leader to denounce this referendum as a trick by the French to dupe Nehru's government. The Communists and Subbiah, who were in favour of referendum earlier, revised their position and denounced the referendum. They were also against holding of separate referendums in the five enclaves. This was mainly because the Indian government was turned against the Communists at that time.[12]

But the Pondicherry Representative Assembly adopted the Delhi agreement. Both Mr Balasubramanian, president of the Representative Assembly, and Edouard Goubert welcomed the agreement, hoping that it would pave the way for a good relationship and unity between France and India.[13] It was expected, especially, by the Indian government that the referendum would be held under the supervision of a Franco-Indian team. In any case, Nehru announced that there would be Indian observers during the referendum. If the Indians insisted on having their observers, the French thought it would be better to have neutral observers.[14]

At that time, the French considered the holding of the referendum as very favourable to French interests. The French decision to hold the referendum was generally welcomed in India. But some Congressmen, with the likes of C. Rajagopalachari, the governor general of India at that time, in the lead, denounced the referendum as 'madness' and the elections in Pondicherry as 'fraudulent', though earlier in April 1914 in an article in *Modern Review*, Rajagopalachari had recognised the French citizenship of the Pondicherrians. Thus, Rajagopalachari was at loggerheads with Jawaharlal Nehru with regard to the holding of the referendum. Some other Congressmen thought that when British India could obtain Independence without referendum, why not French India? Others would not accept the idea of co-sovereignty being floated at that time by Frenchmen like Daniel Levi, the French ambassador in India, who toed more or less the line of Commissioner Baron, as well as the Aurobindo Ashram and Mirra Alfassa.[15]

Baron had passed orders on 25 July 1948 that in Pondicherry no liquour shops would be kept open after 8 p.m., no tea or tobacco stall after 10 p.m., and no restaurant or entertainment after midnight. With effect from 18 July and until further orders all public meetings, processions, campaign of notices and tracts, propaganda by vehicle, bicycle or by loudspeakers, had been banned in Pondicherry. Baron also announced that breach of the above orders was liable for prosecution under the French Penal Code. Baron wanted the French ambassador, Daniel Levi, to visit Pondicherry. He also wanted the dispatch of a French warship to the shores of Pondicherry during the elections for law and order. But inspite of such orders, processions by Indian students from the neighbouring Indian territories passed through Pondicherry during 15 August, the day of Indian Independence. The French Indian authorities did not block such processions.[16]

The date of the new elections to the municipal councils was fixed on 10 October 1948. It was postponed due to the demand of Rachid Ali Baig, the Indian consul in Pondicherry. N.R. Pillai, in charge of the Indian embassy in Paris, in his meeting with Robert Schuman, French Minister of Foreign Affairs, demanded the presence of observers even during the municipal elections, though it was a purely internal affair of Pondicherry.[17] The elections were finally held on 24 October.

During September 1948, the French administration adopted a high-handed attitude towards some pro-Congress student agitators of Pondicherry who clamoured for Independence. In that month, a large procession was organised without permission by pro-Congress students, from the Congress office to *Chinna Kadai*, through Dupleix and Gandhi roads. Police dispersed this procession. Some student leaders and activists like Antoine Mariadassou (b. 10 September 1928), Tamby Evariste (b. 10 July 1924), Paramel Shatrughnan (b. 12 September 1927) and Manickam (b. 10 November 1928) were fined and sentenced to prison for one month for participating in an unauthorised meeting. They were dumped in a dingy and dark cell with other deadly criminals. Top lawyers of Pondicherry like D. Jeevarathinam, S. Perumal, Abel Clovis, P. Danaraja and C. Balasubramanian defended the students, while advocate Mohamed Ismail pleaded for the French administration. The students appealed against this sentence.

Dorai Munisamy was also arrested a few days later for publishing a 'seditious' article in his journal, *Maanilam*, asking the people to revolt against the French. However, all the arrested students were later let off by the high court judge, Jerome Simonel (a Tamil of Pondicherry), under certain conditions. B. Rangapillai asked the French to leave India following the English and alleged that those who wanted the French to stay were 'traitors'. In the same month, processions and meetings, except electoral ones, were banned in Pondicherry and the other French territories.[18]

According to Paramel Shatrughnan, Dorai Munisamy was a true patriot, who strove for the liberation of Pondicherry tirelessly, but was never given his due. Many student leaders like Paramel Shatrughnan, Antoine Mariadassou, Haridas Valiavittil (as well as others like Ambady Narayanan Maligavittil, *Licencié és Lettres* and *Licence en Droit*), adopted French nationality and gradually disengaged themselves from politics thenceforth, probably because the problem of French India was being taken up by Nehru himself as well as due to other personal reasons like the pursuit of studies in France. Of these leaders, Paramel Shatrughnan and Antoine Mariadassou never opted for French nationality, even after the merger of French India with the Indian Union. This established their strong Indian nationalist credentials.[19]

On 21 September 1948, the French government approved in principle the project for an autonomous status for French India within French Union, promoted by Goubert and his Socialist Party. But in the same month, the Indian government set in process the annexation of the principality of Hyderabad through the employment of force.[20]

Earlier on 28 August 1948, Mr Nandagopal, a labour leader of Rodier mill, was shot dead by the Communists. Such violent actions were quite common in Pondicherry under Goubert's regime. Around that time, it has been reported that Gabriel Annusamy, member of the Representative Assembly, was attacked allegedly by pro-Congress *goondas*. Annusamy was incarcerated during 1948-9 and he was suspended from his job as teacher. There were also attempts to remove the parliamentary immunity of V. Subbiah during this period. Pro-mergerists like the Congressman Srikanta Ramanujam of Karaikal, Paramel Shatrughnan and Dorai Munisamy, student leaders in Pondicherry, I.K. Kumaran of Mahé and many others were prosecuted for disobeying prohibitory orders.[21]

On 28 September 1948, V. Subbiah declared at a meeting at Senji Salai ground that the Nehru government was a puppet of British imperialism, and it would not be freedom but more slavery for French Indians to join Indian Union. He asked French Indians not to be cowed down by threats that India would cut off electricity to French India or would suspend the train services to French India. He affirmed that Pondicherry was not Hyderabad for Indian troops to enter, as the French government was a superpower and India could not withstand an attack by the French naval force. Subbiah even vowed that the French territories would remain in the French Union and asked the French Overseas Ministry to postpone the referendum.[22]

By then, a warrant of arrest had been served on the Communist leader, V. Subbiah, by the government of India. In 1948, the Indian government banned the Communist Party of India. It seems that the French government also cracked down on the Communists and wanted to arrest Subbiah. Anti-Communist forces led by the dreaded ruffian Nelli Krishnan, numbering more than 400, paraded through the Madras Road and passed through Subbiah's house shouting slogans like 'Down with the Communists' and 'Down Subbiah'. Subbiah is believed to have returned to Pondicherry during this period but remained underground most of the time.[23] As a result, he did not take part directly in the elections, which left the field free for Goubert's Socialist Party.

On the eve of the municipal elections in Mahé, a general uprising took place under the leadership of I.K. Kumaran of the Mahajana Sabha Party. The French administrator of Mahé, Yves Perrier, a Franco-Indian related to Goubert surrendered. The Indian government under Nehru was asked to take over the administration of Mahé. But as the government had already agreed to hold a referendum to ascertain the wishes of the people, they refused to accede to the demand. As a result, the French recovered Mahé by sending in troops. Commissioner Baron, himself, visited Mahé to put the house in order. It is to be remembered at this juncture that I.K. Kumaran, as well as the Indian Socialist Party led by Jayaprakash Narayan, later stood for the merger of Mahé with a united Socialist Kerala state, unlike Goubert and his colleagues who wanted to safeguard the individuality of French India. This event, however, sent a strong message that the future of French India did not depend entirely on the referendum. Even Padmanabhan Counouma, ex-minister and member for the Representative Assembly from Mahé, regretted that Commissioner Baron had sent in cruisers to re-establish French authority in Mahé.[24]

On 21 October 1948, the councillors (ministers) of the government, Padmanabhan Counouma (Minister for Finance), Dr André Zeganathan (Minister for Agriculture) and Lakshmanasamy Reddiar (minister for health) resigned their membership in the council in protest against the holding of the municipal elections. They were supporters of Saravane. The former two were sympathetic to the Ashram causes. On 24 October, Karunendra Mudaliar, Haji Mohammad Ismail and Muthu Kumarappa Reddiar were, respectively, named as members of the Council of Government in their place. Karunendra was in charge of Finance and Public Instruction, Ismail was entrusted with Health and Information, while Muthu Kumarappa Reddiar was put in charge of Public Works and Agriculture. Edouard Goubert was Minister for General Administration, Deivasikamani was minister for Taxes and Sivasubramania Poullé was Minister for Supplies during that period.[25]

However, before the elections, Commissioner Baron who had previously contributed to the rise of Goubert in French Indian politics, thinking that he would be subservient to him, had put himself on a collision course with Goubert. A few days before the elections, Baron tried to prop up a new party called the Progressive Democratic Party led by Dutamby and Dr F. Bleicher. This was not an intelligent move, for thenceforth Goubert became wary of Baron's veritable intentions to cut him down in French Indian politics.[26]

By this time, Lambert Saravane, French Indian deputy at the National Assembly, who was like a weathercock in French Indian politics, sensing that the merger movement with India was gaining ground and wanting not to be left out, dissociated himself from the Ashram line in politics and opted for Independence and merger with India.[27] However, when Daniel Lévi, ambassador of France in India, visited Pondicherry in October 1948, Saravane changed colours once again and veered towards co-sovereignty and tripartite talks between France, India and the French Indian representatives. Levi was sympathetic to this idea, though it had been ruled out by Nehru earlier. While in Pondicherry, Lévi met and exchanged views with the Archbishop of Pondicherry, Mgr Colas, as well as the French Mother of the Ashram, Mirra Alfassa, apart from a few local personalities.

Pro-Congress students raised anti-French slogans during his visit. Seven of them were arrested. Lévi seems to have understood that at that time the French could count only on two forces—the Communists and the Dravidian separatists, as Goubert was no more in the good books of Baron and so could not be relied upon. As a matter of fact, on 25 July 1948, an 'Anti-Merger Association' was started by the Dravidians of Pondicherry. It had the support of the Dravida Kazhagam of Tamil Nadu and its leader, E.V. Ramasamy Periyar. Bharathidasan was at the head of this movement in Pondicherry. They praised French rule in Pondicherry and wanted their rule to continue. Bharathidasan wrote in his journal, *Kuyil*, in favour of a separate Dravidian state, the Tamil language and against Hindi. The nationalist Tamil newspapers like *Dinamani* wrote against Bharathidasan and the Dravidians. They wanted the amalgamation of Pondicherry and Karaikal with the Madras province as a taluk.

Ambassador Levi finally proposed to the French Ministry of Foreign Affairs to send a unit of the French navy to Trincomalee to maintain law and order during the forthcoming elections. The French government refused to have external observers to monitor the municipal elections as demanded by Nehru. Daniel Levi is known to have made then the following memorable declaration:

'Whether observers come from the Indian Union or the Sun or the Moon we would set an example to the whole world by conducting the elections and the referendum with absolute fairness and in the best democratic manner'.[28]

Prior to the elections, there appears to have been four distinct political groups in Pondicherry. The Socialist Party led by Goubert seems to have had the backing of the administration. This was the biggest and most influential party. Then we have the Ashram group of politicians led by Saravane, Dr André Zeganthan, P. Counouma and others like Joseph Latour, who then clung to the idea of Independence for French India after the French had left. N.V. Rajkumar claimed that the Independence move was inspired by the Sri Aurobindo Ashram and had the backing of some French authorities. The third was the Congress Party, led by R.L. Purushotthama Reddiar, which was organisationally weak in Pondicherry. It was actually spearheaded by the Students' Congress, dominated mainly by some Christian student leaders of the 'higher' castes of a Franco-Indian cultural background. These student leaders most certainly, according to Monod Herzen, chief of public instruction, thought of inheriting power after the departure of the French in local administration and politics. Last of all, there was the new Democratic Progressive Party which was a mushroom anti-merger party formed at the eve of elections, on the initiative of the administration and Baron. This was a conglomerate group consisting of the Communists, (who had earlier opted for Independence, now wanted a continued connection with France, probably because they were hunted in India), the Dravida Kazhagam Party which wanted a separate Dravidian state, including Pondicherry and

Karaikal, and some other dissident groups. Besides, the Muslims, especially of Karakal, were anti-merger for their own reasons. Pakkirisamy, the senator from Karaikal, who hardly spoke French, had veered towads the Congress position of joining the Indian Union, though he got himself elected subsequently to the municipal council as a Socialist candidate. Earlier, he had belonged to the NDF group.[29]

In the elections held to decide the members of the municipal councils of French India on 24 October 1948, the members of the Socialist Party of French India, led by Edouard Goubert, who were reluctant and ambiguous supporters of the French Union, obtained 83 seats out of the total 102 in Pondicherry region. It won 64 seats in Karaikal region leaving just 10 to the Congress Party and in Yanam the 12 seats were won by pro-Goubert or pro-French Union elements. In Pondicherry commune, among the Socialists elected to the municipal council were H.M. Cassime, Edouard Goubert, K. Mouttoussamy (Muthu Poullé) and Virasamy Saguerre, C. Balasubramanian, V. Deivasikamani, Emmanuel Tetta, R. Doréradjou and Karunendra Mudaliar. R.P. Babilonne got himself elected to the Mudaliarpet municipality as a Socialist. Lambert Saravane and his Republican Party did not contest the elections.

Among those who lost miserably were the Democratic Progressive Party candidates, Paul Radjanedassou, Annasse Arthur Evariste Tamby, Joseph Latour, and V. Subbiah, and the Congress candidates, Ansari Dorai Munissamy, Ambady Narayanin, M.T. Annamalai, Dorai Munissamy, Samy Lourdes, D. Mariappin, Srimathi Marie Lernie, Srimathi Marie Thérèse Condappa, and Purushotthama Reddiar. The latter had dismissed Goubert and his associates as well as Subbiah and his men as 'local mercenaries' who gambled with the future of French India. In Karaikal, R.M.A.S. Pakirissamy Poullé was among the most prominent people who had won. The Congress, under Mr Venkatachalapathy, boycotted the elections. In Nettapakkam commune, Goubert's men, Ba. Muthu Kumarappa Reddiar and Vat. Vengadasouba Reddiar had won. They were both influential landlords in that area.[30] Among those who lost, many of them like Radjanedassou and Dorai Munisamy were students. It is noteworthy that the Communist Party did not contest in these elections officially. But it supported the Progressive Democratic Party, led by Dutamby and Bleicher. However, later, the Progressive Democratic Party joined the camp of Goubert.[31]

In Mahé, the elections were postponed due to a revolt by the Mahesians against French rule. But after the revolt was suppressed, the municipal elections were held on 27 February 1949. In Chandernagore the municipal elections were held on 25 July and 1 August 1948.[32]

Mr Laugenie, a spokesman of the French government and political advisor of Commissioner Baron, told a press conference, that he gave without the concurrence of Governor Baron, that the municipal elections held then did not signify anything and the presence of Indian observers during the elections could not be considered as an external pressure on voters. Further, he wanted negotiations to be opened between the French and the Indian governments and the representatives of French India. Commisioner Baron was not happy with the declarations of Laugenie and accused him of being under the influence of Saravane.[33]

It is noteworthy at that juncture that the Pondicherry women with a nationalist bent of mind, Srimathi Marie Lernie and Srimathi Marie Thérèse Condappa, belonging to the landed Condappa family, had contested as nationalists and lost the elections. They were nevertheless the pioneers among women who entered politics in Pondicherry, though they were defeated in the elections by Goubert's men.

Attacks against the nationalists and Communists by Goubert's henchmen multiplied at that time. P. Subbaroyan, president of the Madras provincial Congress, and N.V. Rajkumar, secretary for Foreign Affairs of the Congress Party, had come to Pondicherry as observers of the municipal elections, with the permission of the French, who were under pressure from Nehru. Rachid Ali Baig was the consul of India in Pondicherry at that time. They witnessed the aggression of the pro-French *goondas*. The overwhelming influence of Goubert and his men saw to it that the Indian nationalist spirit was completely muted. P. Subbaroyan and N.V. Rajkumar had the opportunity to witness from close quarters the impossibility of the Indian nationalists to win a referendum in French India under the prevailing conditions. They reported the matter to Jawaharlal Nehru. Dr N.V. Rajkumar as well as others like C.E. Barathan, a leader of the Mahajana Sabha

Party of Mahé, and Lakshmanaswamy Reddiar, one of the three ministers who resigned some time back from the French Indian government, accused the French administration of rigging the elections and pressuring the local populations to vote in favour of the Socialist Party.[34]

V. Subbiah got just one vote. This lends credence to the accusation that the voting was rigged to a considerable extent. But the Communist Party did not participate in the elections officially. It is, however, noteworthy that neither Subbaroyan nor Rajkumar refused to accept the verdict of the elections, nor did they advise the Indian government not to accept it. Rajkumar simply dismissed the French Indian elections as a 'prostitution of democracy'.[35]

However, Rajkumar also affirmed that, after the municipal electons in which the Socialist Party emerged victorious, he had met Goubert, the leader of the Socialist Party, as well as K. Muthu Poullé, the new Socialist mayor of Pondicherry. His talks with them revealed that they wanted a tripartite conference of the representatives of the Indian government, the French government as well as the representatives of the people of French India, i.e. the Socialist Party leaders, to find a solution for the future of French India. He affirmed that neither Goubert nor Muthu Poullé were in favour of a referendum. Instead, they wanted to send a delegation to Delhi to open preliminary discussions.

Rajkumar further held that the Socialist leaders were actually 'sitting on the fence'. They did not fight the elections on clearly defined issues like merger or no-merger. Hence, the results of the elections did not reveal the real wishes of the people.[36] However, what seems to be obvious is the fact that the Socialist Party had contested on the autonomy plank and the people seem to have supported it.

The municipal elections paved the way for Goubert to rise to undisputed power in French India. The merchant, Muthu Poullé, and the landlord, Muthu Kumarappa Reddiar, were his staunchest collaborators. Those who opposed them had even to flee Pondicherry. The Communists held that during their rule the workers, weavers and farmers and small traders were at the receiving end, while the new ruling trio amassed immense wealth by fraudulent means. The Indian government hesitated to accept these elections as valid, as the voters were under pressure and were terrorised by the dispatching of a French warship to Pondicherry during the elections.[37]

On 31 October 1948, Edouard Goubert, leader of the Socialist Party, declared in the course of an interview that the French Indians must negotiate and come to an agreement which had the support of the Indian and French governments, in order to establish their future status, which would preserve the interests of the French Indians of south India. He thought that the French Indians must cultivate a good relationship with the Indian Union, without forgetting that they have their own political and cultural heritage. He opined that, personally, he felt that a referendum was not the best means to decide on the future status of French India. He added that at the forthcoming assembly of the municipal council members of French India to fix a date for the referendum, he would submit a resolution regarding the future status of French Indians which, with the approval of the assembly, could be sent to the Indian and French governments so that they might study it.[38]

The declaration established the mindset of Goubert. His only objective and ideology were based on the defence of the interests of all French Indians ranging from merchants to pensioners and the protection of the historical Indo-French identity of French Indians by all means available. He never seems to have swerved from this ideology right from the time he entered politics or rather from the moment he established the Socialist Party of French India. It was on the basis of this ideology that he sought power, while the Congress leaders, like R.L. Purushottama Reddiar, sought power on the basis of merger with India, and the Communists and Saravane as well as the Sri Aurobindo Ashram kept alternating their position from remaining with France to Independence of French India to co-sovereignty or double nationality, to a merger with India, according to the prevailing and evolving circumstances.

On 16 November 1948, the French businessman Maurice Gaudart, related to Goubert, was elected to the assembly of the French Union. He was the candidate of the French India Socialist Party. Goubert whole-heartedly supported him. He defeated the Tamil P. Joseph Latour of the Communist Party and Paul Latour, supported by Lambert Saravane. It seems that the Congress Party had sympathised with

Gaudart, against the Communists during that period. Later, Saravane seems to have preferred to join the Indian Union, if complete Independence for French India was not forthcoming.[39]

In December 1948, at its Jaipur meeting, the Congress declared its policy to incorporate all foreign enclaves in India within the Indian Union. It maintained that it would allow the people of these areas who had evolved in a different manner historically, administratively, judicially and in education, some time to adjust themselves gradually to the realities of the rest of India. The Congress also favoured the preservation of the cultural heritage of these areas if the people of these areas so desired. The Congress promised a measure of autonomy to the foreign enclaves, wherever possible, so that the people of these areas could safeguard their culture and institutions. Jawaharlal Nehru threw his weight behind the Jaipur resolutions and called for a gradual, peaceful absorption of foreign possessions due to political, economic, geographical and defence reasons. He affirmed in parliament that the union of these areas with India need not involve any immediate merger in the neighbouring province or other unit of India. Instead, their incorporation would take into account the wishes of the people concerned.[40] The Jaipur resolution and the declaration of Nehru obviously went to a considerable extent to meet the demands and aspirations of Goubert and his Socialist Party who clamoured to retain the individuality of French India. The Congress Party led by R.L. Purushotthama Reddiar welcomed the Jaipur resolution.

As a matter of fact, the Representative Assembly, in its meeting of 19 December 1948, welcomed the Jaipur resolution. In France, too, leaders of the Socialist Party of France (SFIO), like Charles Dumas, were veering towards the idea of the incorporation of French India with the Indian Union. However, at that juncture, the French Indian Communists accused Nehru and the French of trying to find a negotiated settlement without referendum. At that time, the *Suthanthiram* paper was prevented entry into India by the Madras Chief Minister.[41]

In January 1949, P.A. Menon, political director in the Indian Ministry of External Affairs, known to be a champion of immediate integration of the French enclaves with India, and an agent of Vallabhbhai Patel, the uncompromising Home Minister, came to Pondicherry and had discussions with the mayor of Pondicherry,

Muthu Poullé, the president of the Representative Assembly, C. Balasubramanian, and the councillors of the Assembly, which included Edouard Goubert. He also met the leaders of all political parties, including the Congress. There were four main parties at that time—the Indian National Congress, the Socialists, the Progressive Democrats and the Communists. The latter two were pro-France, the Congress was pro-India, and the Socialists were sitting on the fence.

It seems that Menon obtained the consent of the Socialist Party of Goubert to maintain Pondicherry and Karaikal as autonomous units within the Indian Union, under an Indian high commissioner. It was also agreed at that time that there would be tripartite negotiations between India, France and French India to find a lasting solution to the French territories in India, instead of holding a referendum according to the Franco-Indian treaty of June 1948. Besides, it was agreed that Yanam, Mahé and Chandernagore were to be integrated immediately with India as they were dependent on India economically.[42] It also appeared that Goubert altered his position somewhat due to the rumour that Commissioner Baron, an ardent supporter of Pondicherry remaining with the French Union, was to be recalled and replaced.[43]

At that time, Nehru insisted in the Parliament that the holding of the referendum needed to be reconsidered. He also held that geographical, political, commercial and defence reasons would naturally lead to a political union with India of the foreign territories in India. He also ruled out any merger of these territories with the neighbouring provinces, without ascertaining the wishes of the people concerned. This again sent a clear message to Goubert that the unique identity of Pondicherry and French India would be safeguarded and there would be no merger with the neighbouring provinces, as sought by some Congress leaders of south India and French India, like R.L. Purushotthama Reddiar and Kamaraj Nadar.[44] Besides, the Madras Congress Party denounced the idea of referendum and there were demands in Pondicherry for the postponement of the referendum. By June 1949, Saravane, too, considered referendum as unnecessary. He said, 'We are all Indians and we belong to India'.[45]

On 17 February 1949, the Indian government proposed to the French government to renew the 1941 Customs Agreement until the

Figure 1: Edouard Goubert, Father of Pondicherry, in the 1970s, a few years before his death. *Source*: Author's personal collection.

Figure 2: Edouard Goubert, Mayor of Pondicherry, 1963. *Source*: Author's personal collection.

Figure 3: From left. Georges Sala, French Admiinstrator of Yanam, Madhimchetty Satyanandam, Mayor of Yanam, Governor of the French territories in India, André Ménard and his wife, a French official, Kanakala Tataya in Yanam. *Source*: photograph given to me by Kanakala Tataya in Yanam.

Figure 4: Muthu Komarappa Reddiar, Edouard Goubert and Muthu Poullé, September 1954, at the head of the Liberation Government in Nettapakkam. *Source*: Photo given to me by Ms. Sayikumari, daughter of Muthu Komarappa Reddiar.

Figure 5: Kewal Singh, Indian High Commissioner in Pondicherry, Muthu Komarappa Reddiar, R.K. Nehru and K.S. Venkatakrishna Reddiar at the residence of Muthu Komarappa Reddiar, in Nettapakkam, 1954. *Source*: Photo given to me by Ms. Sayikumari, daughter of Muthu Komarappa Reddiar.

Figure 6: In the photo could be seen Muthu Poullé (in the middle), Paakkirisamy Poullé, Jawaharlal Nehru, Edouard Goubert and Muthu Komarappa Reddiar, standing side by side, 1955. *Source*: photo given to me by Ms. Sayikumari, daughter of Muthu Komarappa Reddiar.

Figure 7: In the photo could be seen Muthu Komarappa Reddiar (3rd from left), Edouard Goubert, Pakkirisamy Poullé of Karaikal and K. Kamaraj, standing side by side, 1955. *Source*: Photo given to me by Ms. Sayikumari, daughter of Muthu Komarappa Reddiar.

Figure 8: Leon Prouchandy of Pondicherry, last General Secretary of the Indian Independence League, Saigon, bidding farewell to Subhas Chandra Bose at his residence at 76, Hai Bha Trung road in Ho Chi Minh city (Saigon), August 1945. *Source*: www.pressreader.com/INDIA/the-hindu/20160725/ 282690456551258. Accessed on May 2020.

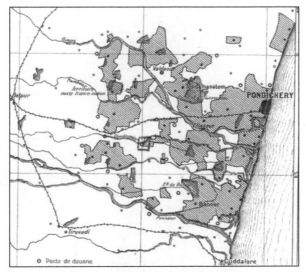

Figure 9: Plan showing French Pondicherry (striped) on the Bay of Bengal, June 1951. *Source*: Bibliothèque Nationale de France, Paris

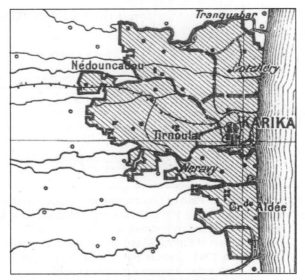

Figure 10: Plan of French Karaikal (striped), June 1951. *Source*: Bibliothèque Nationale de France, Paris.

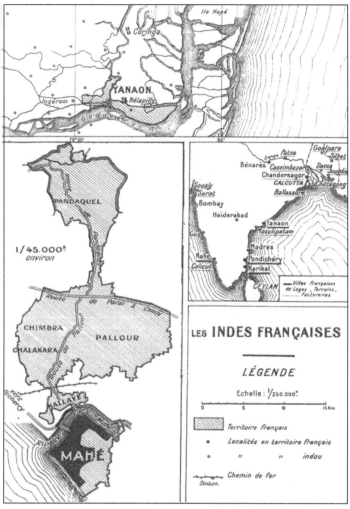

Figure 11: *Above*: Plan of French Yanam (striped) on the Coromandel coast, June 1951. *On the right*: Map showing the French territories (underlined) in India, June 1951.
On the left: Plan of French Mahé on the Malabar coast (striped), June 1951. *Source*: Service Géographique du Ministère des Affaires Etrangères, BNF.

Figure 12: V. Subbiah, freedom fighter, Communist leader, with his wife Saraswathi. *Source*: Puducherryheritage.blogspot.com.

Figure 13: Students manifesting for freedom in Pondicherry, 1948. Antoine Mariadassou, student leader (with a cap). *Source*: Given to me by Elfriede Mariadassou, his wife.

Figure 14: Lambert Saravane, Pondicherry personality during the freedom struggle. *Source*: http://www2.assemblee-nationale.fr/sycomore/fiche/(num-dept)/6287.

referendum. The French government agreed to renew the agreement with some modifications. The Indian government refused to consider this and wanted either a resigning of the 1941 agreement as it was or its abrogation. At that time, the French government made known its intention of having neutral observers to supervise the referendum.[46]

THE ASHRAM ANGLE

In March 1949, the municipal councils of Pondicherry adopted a resolution asking for a transitory period of 30 years before they could join the Indian Union. They also insisted that those enrolled already in the electoral lists alone could participate in the referendum.[47] At that time, a spokesman of the Ashram, probably the Frenchman, Bernard Ingenger, who had come to Pondicherry as a French government employee, announced that Sri Aurobindo Ghose also wanted the French settlements to join India.[48] However, this was not confirmed by the 77-year-old Aurobindo himself. He had never made any declaration to this effect before he passed away. It should be noted that, in June 1947, he had exerted his influence on the drafting of the Socialist Party programme, which provided for French India to remain in the French Union under certain conditions.

Besides, it was almost certain that the 48-year-old Mother of the Ashram, Mirra Alfassa, was in favour of remaining in the French Union. It was said that she accepted blind loyalty from the 600-odd Ashramites, while Sri Aurobindo himself was a 'voluntary prisoner' in his own spiritual colony and had retired from the public eye. The Ashram, where French was the language spoken, celebrated many French festivals, like the Storming of the Bastille, and was intimate with the French government. The Ashramites were enthusiastic participants in the Bastille Day procession organised by the French government, but they were quite conspicuous by their absence from the funeral cortege that the whole population of Pondicherry joined when Gandhi was assassinated on 30 January 1948.

However, they seem to have later celebrated Indian Independence Day on 15 August, as it happened also to be the birthday of Sri Aurobindo. Since 1927, the latter had become the mystic par excellence, who lived on a sealed upper floor of the main Ashram building in the northern part of the White town. No devotee, including the Ashramites, could meet him, except during the four *darshan* days a year when they could get a glimpse of him and the Mother, and worship them from a certain distance. Only the Mother and a few trusted lieutenants had access to him. Communication with the mystic took place only through the mediumship of the Mother, who not only issued his communiqués, but also interpreted his philosophical works in her occult classes. Ashramites thought and believed that he was the personification of the great supramental force who would come down to save mankind.[49]

The Ashram was the biggest property owner in Pondicherry town, drawing the envy of the local Tamil population. The inmates, who were mostly from eastern and western India, were lodged in these properties in a room or in a small house, according to their needs and their importance in the eyes of the Mother. Every inmate had to surrender himself and all his worldly goods to the Mother before he could be taken into the Ashram and taken care of by the Mother. This was how wealth and property accumulated in the hands of the Mother and Sri Aurobindo. Every Ashramite was assigned to do some work in the Ashram, beneficial to the collective. Behind its grey walls, the Ashram was actually described as an area of 'collective selfishness' by the journal, *India*.

The Mother, though considered a divine being alongside Sri Aurobindo, had a staunch preference for finery and her 20 personal assistants spent months of devoted labour making the most exquisite gold, silver and coloured embroidery on the choicest chiffons and silks for her to wear on a daily basis. Her shoes and footrests were lined with velvet while her morning robes were of nylon and Benares brocade. She also sported an elaborate headgear with a costly jewel dangling from its centre. The assistants would wash and iron her clothes. She applied make-up to her lips and cheeks. At 68, she played ping-pong. According to *India*, she was a little old woman, with big teeth and hypnotic eyes, gorgeously dressed and standing in her power. She exercised her influence over the smallest details of her 600 subjects' lives. And Sri Aurobindo, whatever he uttered or did not utter with regard to politics or French India, was only through the Mother or her spokesmen.[50]

There existed a school in the Ashram up to the secondary level with 400 students. The students comprised mostly Bengalis and Gujaratis. Most subjects in this school were taught in French. The ex-polytechnician, Bernard Ingenger, who was information officer in Commissioner Baron's office, was the secretary general of the Ashram by the 1950s.[51]

CUSTOMS UNION AND ECONOMIC BLOCKADE

There was a Customs Union Convention containing 24 articles between British India and the French since 28 January 1941. Before that, Pondicherry and Karaikal were free ports, and these two territories were surrounded by British Indian customs. All products transiting between these two territoires and India had to pay duties on the frontier. But the Convention of 1941, established by Governor Louis Bonvin and the British consul general, Lt Col Reginald Schonberg, had created a customs Union between Pondicherry/Karaikal and British India, while Mahé, Yanam and Chandernagore already had a customs union with British India. It was a wartime measure.

On 13 March 1948, the government of India sprang a surprise. It gave final notice to the French government of their desire to put an end to the Custom Union Agreement of 1941. There was no mention of a possible new Customs Agreement in this notice. But the Indian government called it off unilaterally on 30 March 1949, as provided by Article 23 of the aforesaid agreement, though it expressed its desire to continue with it until the holding of the referendum. Goubert, at that time, wanted the renewal of the Customs Union Convention. But the French administration did not want to renew the customs convention, probably in order to demonstrate that French India was not dependent on India economically, and with the objective to turn the French Indians against India. It was also feared that a customs union would lead to political union with India.[52]

On 1 April 1949, the French government allowed imports into the French territories without any restrictions. Pondicherry became a free port. The Indian maritime customs did not function any more off Pondicherry and Karaikal. For the traders and industrialists of Pondicherry and Karaikal, the advantages of a free port were obvious. It encouraged vast smuggling of goods from Pondicherry into India. The Indian government took countermeasures.

The Indian government reverted to its earlier stand and re-imposed customs control and payment at the frontier from 1 April 1949. Indian troops were deployed on the frontier for this purpose. This aggravated the economic pressure on Pondicherry and, especially Karaikal, which depended on India for its goods and provisions. Goods could not transit even between the enclaves in the Pondicherry region through Indian territory though this measure violated the Barcelona Convention of 1921 of which India was a signatory and the agreement of June 1948 between the Indian and French governments. All previous licences for the transit of goods between the French settlements through Indian territory were cancelled. All export licences of goods to the French settlements from Indian territory were cancelled, too. A permit system was also established by the Indian government for persons to transit between the settlements as well as between the enclaves of a settlement. Besides, the reduction or suspension of the frequency of goods and passenger trains between the French settlements and to the French settlements from India was put in practice due to the customs and security formalities introduced since the terminantion of the Customs Union. Vehicles from the French settlements could no more travel to India. They created customs houses and checkpoints all over the frontier and insisted on passports with photographs obtained from the Indian authorities to travel to and fro. If the passengers had a French Indian passport, they could stay in Indian territory for 15 days. They also prevented transit of goods between Pondicherry and Karaikal. French Indian vehicles were stopped from entering Indian territory. Even medicines and milk powder for children were barred from transiting to the enclaves from Pondicherry.

On 25 May 1949, 26 prominent traders of Pondicherry, such as Grindé R. Manikka Chetty & Sons, Nanayya Bagavathar & Sons, Mathru Café, Ananda Emporium, Sankara Iyer and Ebrahim Essack Sait & Co, petitioned the French embassy in New Delhi and the French Ministry of Foreign Affairs. They complained that the imposition of the customs made it difficult to procure essential items for the population of Pondicherry from India and elsewhere. They wanted the immediate re-establisment of maritime customs.

All such Indian measures had amounted to an economic blockade. They were also vexatious in character. For example, private and official letters were opened by a censorship bureau. A foreign diplomat was obliged to fill up the customs declaration despite the presence of their diplomatic passports. Fines were collected without the delivery of a receipt. A great majority of the population made up of workers, farmers, artisans, shopkeepers, sugarcane and betel growers as well as vegetable hawkers were affected by all these measures.[53]

On its part, the French government requested the vice-president of the International Court of Justice on 26 April 1949 to send at once neutral observers to report on the condition in Karaikal and Pondicherry. But the Indian government responded on 30 April by once again offering to continue the 1941 agreement until the referendum. On 23 May 1949, the French government refused to consider the proposition of the Indian government under duress. On the same day, the French government informed the Government of India of the appointment of two neutral observers—Holgar Anderson and Castro—during the period of the referendum. Within a week, the two observers arrived in India.[54]

Earlier, on 16 February, the Government of India wanted to renew the Customs Union Agreement of 1941. But the French government would not have it. On 2 June 1949, the Government of India once again expressed its desire to renew the Custom Agreement of 1941 with slight modifications. At the same time, it was announced that the Indian government would waive the restrictions put in force for the transit circulation between the French settlements and its enclaves. The French Inspector of Colonies, Tezenas du Montcel, came out with a counterproposal in favour of a mixed administration, which was rejected by the Indian government.[55]

Whatever goods were imported into Pondicherry by ships, cotton from Pakistan, rice, coal and petrol from Indochina, iron and bricks from France were not enough to control the spiralling prices of the essential items. This affected the workers and farmers very much. Many of them from Muthialpet, etc., were forced to migrate into

Indian territory.[56] Of the three cotton mills, only one, i.e. the Savana Mill, was under the control of the French, while the Gaebelé Mill had become the Barathy Mill and was owned by Indians and the Rodier mill the Anglo-French Mill, owned by the British. All the three mills depended on the cotton imported from Pakistan. Unemployment and rise in the cost of living threatened the people.[57]

The blockade had particularly affected the communes of Mannadipet, Nettapakkam and Bahur. Their mayors, Vengadasouba Reddiar, Vengadasamy Reddiar and R. Reddiar, respectively, petitioned the Ministry of Foreign Affairs to relax or stop the economic blockade and vexatious measures adopted by the Government of India against the French enclaves.[58]

D. Jeevarathinam of the Congress Party, in a meeting at Nehru Vanam held on 8 May 1949, asked the French government to accept the generous offer of the Indian government in favour of renewing the old Customs Convention without any modification for some time. But the French government would not agree to renew the Customs convention under pressure exerted by the Indian government. Paramel Shatrugnan, leader of the Students' Congress, denounced the Socialist Party leaders as the puppets of colonialists and declared that the economic situation in Pondicherry could not be dissociated from the political situation. But he would not denounce the Congress Party and the Indian government which was orchestrating the blockade.[59] Henri Roux, the predecessor of Daniel Levi, had forewarned about the difficulties that the settlements would face, and the hopelessness of the French intention of continuing to stay in India, if the customs union was called off. But Levi and the French commissioners in Pondicherry, starting from Baron, had no time to listen to this advice, as they had something else on their agendas.

On 30 May 1949, Goubert's party leaders signed a memorandum accusing India of isolating French India by imposing an economic blockade which was not conducive to the holding of a free and fair referendum. This memorandum was submitted to Tezenas du Montcel, Inspector of Colonies, who was sent on a mission to Pondicherry. The two observers of the International Court of Justice, deputed to Pondicherry to study the economic situation were also informed of the memorandum. It is strange to note that the expenses of Tezenas du Montcel which amounted to Rs. 8,000 per month was borne by the Pondicherry budget.[60]

The French thought that Rachid Ali Baig, the consul general of India in Pondicherry, had a part to play in the decision to impose the economic blockade on French India and asked the Indian government to recall him and his six security agents, four from Madras and two from Cuddalore. In an official communiqué of New Delhi dated 4 June 1949, it was expressly declared that the French territories would be administered like the autonomous units of a chief commissioner's province. All changes in the administrative structure would be affected after consultation with the people and their special linguistic and cultural rights would be preserved. It was a time when India refused to agree to hold a plebisicite in Kashmir as per the resolution adopted at the United Nations. Pakistan was in favour of holding a plebiscite.[61]

However, there were two tendencies with regard to French India emanating from New Delhi. One was the inflexible attitude of Vallabhbhai Patel, the Home Minister, while the other was that of Nehru who was more open to adjustments. On 11 June 1949, the Indian government accepted the following recommendations made by P.A. Menon, who was believed to be under the influence of Patel:

1. Goods carried between enclaves be exempted from import and export regulations and customs duties;
2. No identity certificate required of persons moving between enclaves;
3. Goods in transit between Pondicherry and Karaikal by rail be exempted from import and export regulations and customs duties if conveyed under customs seal; and
4. All goods to Pondicherry and Karaikal for which contracts had been signed before 1 April, when the customs convention was terminated, be exempted from new rules.

These decisions put an end to the economic blockade put in place since 1 April 1949. It was also stated that the government of India was considering a new customs agreement slightly different from that of 1941.

Meanwhile, a conference of the municipal members of the four

French territories of the south took place on 20 March 1948, as Chandernagore had decided to go its own way.[62] The municipal members of Chandernagore failed to participate in it. It was decided in this conference to hold the referendum on 11 December.

The Chandernagorians, led by the nationalist Karma Parishad party, were always in a hurry to join the Indian Union, as they never relished the prospect of being under Pondicherry. So, they decided to take the matters into their own hands. They did not want to follow Goubert's Socialist Party policies. As a result, a referendum was organised in Chandernagore on 19 June 1949. This referendum was held in accordance with Article 27 of the French Constitution which stipulated that 'no cession, no exchange, no addition of territory is valid without the consent of the population concerned'. But earlier the *loges*, which was also French territory, was transferred in an irregular unlawful manner without consulting the population of those *loges*, in flagrant violation of Article 27 of the French Consitution. Nobody took note of this contravention at that time.

The overwhelming majority of the Chandernagorians, pushed by feelings of nationalism of the Indian kind, voted to join the Indian Union. Chandernagore, which was land-locked and made up of only 3 square miles, was reduced to the status of a small municipality within the province of Bengal in no time. If Chandernagore had stood unified in its demand, along with the rest of French India, and had pressed for a joint referendum, such a situation would not have come about.[63] But Baron's policies of creating autonomous 'Free Towns', etc., had allowed the Chandernagorians to go their own way, cutting themselves off completely from Pondciherry and finally opting to join the Indian Union. As a matter of fact, Commissioner Baron's policies, which were sponsored by his higher-ups, had laid the pathway for the dismantling of the French settlements. On 2 May 1950, the de facto transfer of Chandernagore took place. A treaty of cession was signed in Paris on 2 February 1951, which was followed by the de jure transfer in June.

In June 1949, the pro-Congress National Liberation Front, led by Lahache, organised a meeting at Odiansalai in Pondicherry to celebrate Chandernagore Day. They were attacked by pro-French groups, who staged anti-Indian demonstrations. Lahache, Jeevarathinam, who was president of Pondicherry Congress, D. Mariappan and Ambady Narayanan were attacked. On 16 July 1949, the National Liberation Front of French India adopted a resolution expressing its desire to merge with the Indian Union. This resolution was transferred to the executive committee of the Indian National Congress in New Delhi.[64] With the accession of Chandernagore, the Indian government gradually reversed its policy of holding a referendum in Pondicherry. It appears that they developed cold feet at that juncture. They were not sure if the Indians would opt for joining the Indian Union in other settlements, too, if they were allowed to vote in a referendum.

Even a reputed professor of *Collège Colonial*, Emmanuel Adicéam, came out in a long letter to the French governor against the holding of the referendum. According to him, the memory of Dupleix did not create a right for France over its Indian territories. Instead, he wanted to find a solution which satisfied the Indians and the Indian Union, without lowering the prestige of France or sacrificing its interests. He stressed in the letter the desires of certain local Pondicherry politicians and interests, like the Sri Aurobindo Ashram, which clamoured for an independent territory, or a Franco-Indian condominium or even double citizenship, as impracticable.[65]

TRIP TO PARIS AND DELHI, AND ITS AFTERMATH

In a meeting of the municipal councillors of French India on 2 July 1949, it was decided to send a delegation of the members of the Representative Assembly consisting of Mr Balasubramanian (president of the Representative Assembly), as well as Edouard Goubert, Emmanuel Tetta and Karunendra Mudaliar, to find a solution to the constitutional deadlock. There was no Muslim in the delegation. Pakkirisamy Poullé accompanied the delegation. In the meantime, in Pondicherry, a blanket ban was imposed on public meetings and demonstrations of a political nature.

The delegation arrived in Paris on 12 July 1949. Goubert had personally met the French ambassador, Daniel Levi, and had a long talk with him before flying to Paris. During their stay in Paris, they met the president of France, the president of the French Union, the

Minister for Overseas Affairs and other top French personalities and put forward their plan of autonomy for French India within the French Union. Their demand was accepted in principle by the Minister for Overseas Affairs and also the French Council of Ministers. But the Foreign Minister, Coste-Floret, submitted to them an imprecise text of an autonomy project in favour of the four towns being constituted into a federation. On his part, Daniel Levi unofficially wanted the creation of a new state, comprising of the French settlements whose autonomy would be guaranteed by both France and India and approved by the French Indian population.[66] But Nehru or even Goubert was never in agreement with the idea of co-sovereignty or co-suzerainty of Daniel Lévi. Nevertheless, Goubert admitted that the treatment meted out to them in France was far from satisfactory.[67]

On 23 July, the delegation left Paris for Delhi. In Delhi, the delegation was joined by five French Indian ministers, the president of the French Indian Congress and the president of the Municipal Assembly. Among them were Deivasikamani, Muthu Poullé, Pakkirisamy Poullé and Muthu Kumarappa Reddiar. The delegation talked with Girija Shankar Bajpai, secretary general, Ministry of External Affairs, in the presence of K.P.S. Menon, P.A. Menon and Rachid Ali Baig, the Indian consul in Pondicherry. The Indian government treated the hosts courteously but was uncertain of the degree of autonomy that they would grant to the four territories, though it was more or less willing to accord an autonomous status to French India, which could not be changed without consulting the people, for a period of one or two years, after which the southern territories would be integrated with the Madras province. Besides, it was made clear that there was no question of autonomy guaranteed by France and India. On the other hand, the Indian government, including Prime Minister Nehru, made a veiled threat regarding the difficulties that the territories would face if they joined the French Union.

The delegation with Goubert in the lead had met Prime Minister Nehru, Governor-General C. Rajagopalachari and other top Indian officers during their stay in Delhi. Goubert talked to Nehru for 45 minutes. Both of them were Francophiles. Nehru subsequently told the delegation that even if the people of French India voted to remain with France, the issue of integration will not be settled, and it will be reopened at some future date. However, Girija Shankar Bajpai seems to have assured Goubert and his friends that considerable autonomy would be granted to the French settlements.[68] Curiously enough, N.V. Rajkumar, who had earlier denounced the municipal elections as the 'prostitution of democracy', warned the Indian government about the 'mercenary' and haggling attitude of the Pondicherry delegation.[69]

It appears on the whole that the delegation had tried both in Paris and Delhi to obtain maximum autonomy and concessions for French India. They actually wanted complete autonomy for French India for five years, after which the question of integration with India could be decided through a referendum.[70] In the National Assembly in Paris, Pakkirisamy Poullé had spoken in favour of granting a large autonomy for the territories to remain in the French Union. Goubert clarified that his Socialist Party had nothing to do with the Indian Socialist Party and admitted that it was formed to check the 'increasing menace of Communists in French India'. On his return to Pondicherry, Goubert declared that the referendum would be held on 11 December 1949. Commissioner Baron considered this delegation of no value, while the French Foreign Ministry was in no mood to grant a large autonomy to the French territories as demanded by Goubert and his colleagues, though the French Council of Ministers did contemplate a restricted form of autonomy subsequently.[71]

However, the French ambassador, Daniel Levi, warned that that if France did not give a large autonomy to the settlements, Goubert might turn against the French during the referendum. This was also the opinion of the French Ministry of Foreign Affairs. In spite of this situation, the French Foreign Minister, Paul Coste Floret, refused to heed to the invitation of the Council of the Government of French India and visit Pondicherry, while on his way back to Paris from Saigon. Instead, he declared in Calcutta where he was met by Goubert and his colleagues that he would want to know the opinion of Goubert through the French commissioner regarding the autonomy project that he had submitted to him in Paris. He added that Goubert had asked for financial assistance from France for the settlements, which, according to him, would go some way in influencing the voters in the referendum to be held on 11 December. This sent a strong signal to

Goubert that the French government was not interested in him and his overtures for more autonomy. As a result, it appears that, from October 1949 onwards, Goubert and his colleagues decided to delay the holding of the referendum, as nothing had been concretely offered to Pondicherrians and French Indians as far as autonomy was concerned.[72]

It was a time when Lambert Saravane had veered towards joining the Indian Union. During this period, Goubert and his Socialist Party were not openly pro-French, unlike the Progressive Democratic Party of Dutamby and Dr Bleicher, and the Association of Patriots of Arthur Annasse, who had lately broken away from the former. Arthur Annasse who was serving the French administration as Chief of Direct Taxes in Cameroon, was induced to join Pondicherry politics during this period by none other than the Inspector of Colonies, Tezenas du Montcel. The Progressive Democratic Party was inclined, however, towards the Communists and V. Subbiah, who were being hunted by New Delhi. The latter, however, did not command the allegiance of the influential castes and counted mostly upon the support of the 'lowest' castes, Franco-Indians and Muslims. H.M. Cassime was associated with Subbiah right from the time that the Harijan Sevak Sangh was founded in Pondicherry. Subbiah also enjoyed the sympathy of some merchants like Nanayya Bhagavathar. On the other hand, the Socialist Party, though led by the Franco-Indian Goubert, was constituted mainly of the 'higher' Brahmanic castes of landlords, merchants and professionals. France had no other alternative but to count upon Goubert and his party for the ensuing referendum for one year.[73] But Goubert was a slippery customer. His insistence on autonomy unsettled the French. It seems that Goubert and his men like Balasubramanian had a more sypmpathetic hearing in support of their position in New Delhi rather than in Paris.

Meanwhile, Charles Chambon had succeeded Baron as the new French commissioner in Pondicherry. Baron was actually recalled to France due to what was believed to have been his faulty policies, which had allowed French Indians to turn increasingly against French rule. Baron was accused of supporting and propping up Subbiah and then Goubert. The economic and financial woes of French India increased during his period. Students of Pondicherry were agitated and restless under him. To sum up, Mr Godard, the president of the Chamber of Commerce of Pondicherry, held that he had done incalculable harm to French interests in India that had cost the sympathy of the people towards the French. He demanded his removal. His closeness to the Sri Aurobindo Ashram might have also cost him his post, according to Ajit Neogy.

However, Chambon put himself in touch with Goubert very soon to thrash out an autonomy project. But the French were no longer sure of Goubert's support for the French cause. Besides, Chambon was not very favourable towards holding the referendum.[74]

According to the terms of the exchange of letters dated 29 June 1948, the Municipal Councils of the French settlements should meet in a single assembly to examine the methods of conducting the referendum. As a result, a conference of over 200 Municipal Council members of French southern India took place on 17 and 18 October 1949. They had to decide on the conditions for the holding of the referendum with regard to the presence of neutral observers during the referendum, the quorum, etc. But among those present, there was not much or open enthusiasm in favour of merging with India. They complained that the Indian authorities were putting pressure on the French enclaves surrounded by Indian territory which threatened the freedom to exercise the voting rights of Pondicherrians. They also complained of blockade of the enclaves preventing the circulation of goods and persons. They were forced to produce passports with photographs, which were particularly difficult, especially for women and Muslims.[75]

The conference decided to postpone the referendum, instead of examining the methods to conduct the referendum. This decision might have been prompted at least partially due to the violence that ensued after the referendum in Chandernagore and the continued economic blockade of the territories, in spite of the agreement reached by P.A. Menon earlier. The conference also rallied behind the autonomy project of Edouard Goubert and the Socialist Party without really going into the details. But this autonomy project was not exactly the same as envisaged earlier by the Socialist Party. Instead, the idea was to create a federation of autonomous towns within the French Union under the authority of a president, assisted by a council of ministers, owing responsibility to a federal assembly. However, strangely, the powers of the autonomous towns and the federal assembly as well as the council of ministers were not broached upon during the conference. The Council of Government, or rather the council of ministers, had approved the autonomy project within the French Union on 21 September 1949, though the French government had not still given its consent to it. The French government further feared that the refusal to accept the postponement of the referendum had the potential to drive Goubert and his supporters to join the pro-merger camp. But the French commissioner, Chambon, continued to think that the referendum would not solve the problems of the settlements. This was favourable to Goubert's moves for postponing the referendum. Besides, the agreement of June 1948 had stipulated that there will not be any important modification in the structure of the French settlements before the referendum.[76]

The decisions of the municipal conference sent shock waves into the ranks of the pro-mergerists as well as the Indian government. On 27 October, the government of India issued a communiqué that, if the French settlements decided to join the Indian Union, they will be administered as autonomous units in direct relation with the central government and that no changes would be made in the administrative set up without consulting the public opinion. The Communists under V. Subbiah opposed the autonomy project of Edouard Goubert tooth and nail. They preferred to join the Indian Union. But in India, there was repression of Communists during this period which rendered Subbiah's position very ambiguous. Besides, some Muslims, especially of Karaikal did not want to join the Indian Union.[77] A resolution was adopted by the Representative Assembly, most probably under the influence of Goubert, on 10 December 1949. It declared pro-mergerists like V. Subbaya, and his Communist associates Gabriel Anussamy and Murugasamy Clémenceau as having resigned officially from their membership of the Assembly.[78]

Actually, Rachid Ali Baig, supported by his political friends in Pondicherry like Emmanuel Adicéam and Emmanuel Tetta as well as Léon St. Jean of Karaikal, secretary of the Congress Party in the Representative Assembly of Pondicherry, was expecting Goubert to join the Indian Union. Rachid Ali Baig worked to rope in Goubert and his group, which was the most dominant in Pondicherry at that time, to favour merger with India. But the Indian government had not come out with a concrete project of autonomy for French India. As a result, Baig and his friends were deeply disappointed at Goubert's decision to remain with the French Union. Further, it is held by Ajit Neogy that Rachid Ali Baig was critical of the Aurobindo Ashram. Instead, he was thought to be in favour of the Catholic group, led by men like Tetta, which dominated the administration. It was believed that this dominance was disliked by men like Muthu Poullé, Muthu Kumarappa Reddiar and Balasubramanian. None of them belonged to the Congress. It seems they had confided with Rajkumar that they would want to get rid of it at the opportune moment by joining the Indian Union, provided Rachid Ali Baig was recalled. At this juncture, it is good to remember right since the early 1930s, there was an anti-Christian movement, spear-headed by the likes of Bharathidasan and Sellane Naiker, in reaction to the dominance of Christians in administration and politics.

Besides, Rachid Ali Baig had consistently neglected the Congress Party led by R.L. Purushotthama Reddiar, which did not have popular support, and also its students' wing. According to the Students' Congress, Baig's actions served to promote and consolidate Goubert's group to the detriment of the Congress Party. When the Municipal Assembly Conference refused to join the Indian Union and chose to remain in the French Union, it became quite obvious that Rachid Ali Baig had failed in his strategy of courting Goubert for the Indian cause. This infuriated the Students' Congress. Its members sent telegrams to Pattabhi Sitaramayya, president of the Congress Party, Vallabhbhai Patel, the Home Minister, Raj Kumar and Gopalaswamy Iyengar, Minister (interim) for External Affairs, about the nature and outcome of the municipal conference which was not favourable to India. They held that the conference wanted to postpone the referendum indefinitely. They said that the conference did not want the re-establishment of the maritime customs union. They clamoured for the free transit of goods. They said that the conference wanted the promulgation of the autonomy promised by the French government on 27 July 1949 and rejected the referendum as it was adopted by France without the consent of the people of French India or their representatives. They maintained that the conference also wanted a quorum of 60 per cent of the enrolled electors for the election to be valid, which was impossible in the then prevailing conditions. They accused Baig of creating this situation for two years by hobnobbing with Goubert and asked for his immediate recall and the institution of an inquiry. Besides, they stuck posters in French, Tamil and English all over Pondicherry town including the Indian consulate denouncing Rachid Ali Baig and Emmanuel Tetta as 'traitors'. The posters asked Baig to go back to Pakistan or Paris. Baig accused Dorai Munisamy of the Students' Congress and Ansari Doraisamy of having orchestrated this campaign against him. He was extremely saddened by this development and told D. Jeevarathinam and Léon Saint Jean that he had failed in his attempt to rally Goubert for the Indian cause, but denounced the young student nationalists as mere 'agitators'.[79]

It seems that the Pondicherrian Papusamy, vice-consul at the French embassy in New Delhi, had played a role in persuading Goubert to remain with the French Union. Papusamy himself was convinced that Goubert by his origin, his education, his political antecedents and the advantages he enjoyed under the present regime would not opt to join the Indian Union. This unexpected situation took even Chambon, the then commissioner, by surprise. On 9 November 1949, he declared in Madras that there was not enough time to meet all the necessary conditions to hold the referendum and, therefore, the referendum had to be postponed to a future date to be decided by the Indian and French governments. Thus, he toed the line of Goubert.

The Chief of the Foreign Affairs Department of the Congress Party declared, in his turn, that if the French government wanted to retain its territories in India, the Indian government would cut off all the advantages and facilties that they received from India. As a matter of fact, heeding the request of the Students' Congress, N.V. Rajkumar was sent to Pondicherry. He mobilised the pro-merger forces without much obstruction from the French commissioner or government at that time both in Pondicherry and Karaikal, independently of Rachid Ali Baig, the Indian consul, whom he refused to meet. This naturally seems to have sent a message to the French Indians that the French government was gradually abandoning them.[80]

On 15 December 1949, Edouard Goubert, Minister for General

Administration and Labour, declared during the meeting of the Council of Government, in the presence of the French commissioner, that there could be no viable referendum if it did not have a definitive irreversible character and if Nehru kept declaring that he would reopen the issue, even if he did not win the referendum in India's favour. Besides, those who were in favour of France had no guarantee of their security even if the people voted to remain with the French Union. Goubert accused Nehru of being 'illogical' when, after agreeing to hold a referendum, he declared in the same breath that the question of integration with India will remain open if the pro-mergerists did not win the referendum. He demanded the French government denounce the agreement of 29 June 1948, if the Indian government did not respect the verdict of the referendum. But the French government was not helpful to Goubert at this juncture. Moreover, the Indian government was annoyed by the tactics adopted by the French Indian administration in Pondicherry, which not only insisted on a quorum of 60 per cent of the voters, but also wanted to revise the electoral rolls before the referendum without the supervision of the neutral international observers. The Council of Government also wanted a free transit of goods and persons between the enclaves before the organisation of the referendum, as restrictions had been renewed since the agreement with P.A. Menon earlier.

Goubert and his other ministerial colleagues like Deivasikamani, Minister for Taxes, and Muthu Kumarappa Reddiar, Minister for Public Works, wanted the Indian and French governments to conclude a treaty with regard to the political, economic and social situation of the French territories after the referendum, as the agreement of 29 June 1948 did not address this problem. This demand was a serious strategic error made by Goubert, probably under the influence of his colleagues like Muthu Kumarappa Reddiar.[81] In fact, the demand implied that the French and Indian governments could decide about the future of French Indians in future. Most certainly, Goubert and his colleagues were unaware of the implications of such a demand at that time, by which they were ruling out French Indian participation in the negotiations to determine the future of French India. The demand indirectly implied that the French and Indian governments can negotiate together the future of French India, without involving the French Indians. But this error was not apparent at that time and did not come out into the open. Earlier, the referendum was decided by an agreement between the French and Indian governments, without the involvement of the French Indian representatives as stakeholders. It was only later that the French Indian representatives endorsed this agreement, only to retract about a year later.

It is noteworthy at this juncture that in Chandernagore there were more Indian citizens (24,000) than French citizens (19,000), when the referendum was held there. However, they were all included in the electoral list. But in the four southern territories, there were 60,000 Indian citizens living in the French territories while the French citizens numbered 2,49,000. The French government was not inclined to allow the Indian citizens to be registered on the electoral list, probably because they thought that they will vote to merge with India as they did in Chandernagore.[82]

A good number of Muslims, especially from Karaikal, were not in favour of joining the Indian Union and preferred to be with the French Union. Besides, the Karaikal Committee for Union with France claimed that the vast majority of the Karaikal people were in favour of remaining with France. They claimed that they were 'French belonging to the Tamil race'.[83]

However, the French government was still undecided about conducting the referendum. André Morisset, the son of the Ashram Mother, Mirra Alfassa, and her first husband, Henri Morisset, had told the French Overseas Minister that India would renounce holding the referendum. But the local Pondicherry politicians, including Goubert, did not want the French government to open any negotiations with India in case the referendum was favourable to France. They anticipated that France, once it had won the referendum, would try to obtain India's support in the case of Vietnam, by agreeing to negotiate on Pondicherry. On the other hand, some Indian journals seem to think that France was intent upon postponing the referendum by adopting some dilatory tactics.[84]

On his part, N.V. Rajkumar, after a visit to Pondicherry where he, Goubert and the president of the Representative Assembly, C. Balasubramanian among others, declared that a fair and impartial referendum was impossible in the settlements due to the conditions of tension and intimidation prevailing there, implying the absolute control that Goubert had in the territories. Rajkumar further wanted the presence of Indian police in the French settlements during the referendum as he had no confidence in the French Indian administration. He also expressed himself for an immediate transfer of power and the cessation of the French Indian administration. But the new French commissioner, André Ménard, declared that the referendum was a purely internal affair of France. Others, like the National Liberation Front of Pondicherry, wanted the referendum to be held under the surveillance of both the French and Indian governments. At that time, Goubert had openly come out once again in favour of remaining with France.[85]

Meanwhile, Jawaharlal Nehru declared in Parliament that the Government of India had been negotiating with the French government regarding the various arrangements and modalities in connection with the forthcoming referendum. Nehru also declared that, though every Pondicherrian was an Indian, yet from the strictly legal point of view they were not Indian nationals till they became part of India.[86]

Besides, the Government of India did not want government servants to take part in the preparation of the electoral rolls or in the electoral campaign as they were politicised as being against the merger. On 24 February 1950, the French National Assembly held a debate and adopted a decree authorising its government to organise the referendum in the four southern territories.[87]

In December 1949, the French India Central Merger Committee was established at Manjakuppam, outside Pondicherry, near Cuddalore, with Sellane Naiker as president. Gnanou Ambroise was the vice-president. Many, like A. Lahache, D. Jeevarathinam, S. Perumal and André Zeganathan, sympathised with or joined the Committee. In Karaikal, Xavéry became the president of the Merger Committee, while Léon Saint Jean was vice-president.[88] Sellane Naiker was a veteran politician of the previous generation. In the 1930s, he was known for his grudge against the European employees of the French government in Pondicherry, who were paid more than their Tamil counterparts. He had also been against the two-list system which favoured the Europeans and Christians. Besides, he was reputed to be caste minded. Edouard Goubert, V. Subbiah and Lambert Saravane as well as R.L. Purushotthama Reddiar were all his juniors in politics. However, in the changed political situation and circumstances, he was no more a force to be reckoned with and had no popular support. He preferred to run his own show in politics as he never joined the nationalist Congress party, led then by R.L. Purushotthama Reddiar or the Communist Party led by V. Subbiah. He also disliked Goubert and his Socialist Party. Nevertheless, he styled himself as a nationalist, quite belatedly, by establishing the Merger Committee. However, Naiker, in spite of being an experienced lawyer, was not a wealthy man, unlike Muthu Poullé or Muthu Kumarappa Reddiar or Vengada Subba Reddiar.

During this period, there was a group in Pondicherry known as 'l'Union Républicaine de l'Inde Française', with the Pondicherrian H.D. Saint Jacques as president. This group claimed to represent the Vanniyar caste, which made for about three-fifth of the total population of French India, and the Harijans, who made up another one-fifth of the total population. They complained to the Minister for Overseas Territories that their castes were not represented in the Council of Government, which was monopolised by the 'higher' 'capitalist' castes, though they were fewer in numbers. They, however, declared their allegiance to the French Union, and asked for the nomination of ministers from the Vanniyar and Harijjan castes.[89] Incidentally, Sellane Naiker belonged to the Vanniyar caste and was one of its leading figures since the death of Sadasiva Naiker.

In 1948-9, French records attest that Muslim political activities were non-existent in Pondicherry, Yanam and Chandernagore. But in Karaikal, where Muslims were more numerous, and more generally in Pondicherry and other French territories, Muslims were reticent towards joining either the Indian Union or Pakistan. Rather, they were more favourable to the French. Meanwhile, Rachid Ali Baig was replaced by Sarat Kumar Banerjee as consul general of India towards the end of 1949. Within a year, Banerjee was replaced by Raj Krishna Tandon of the Punjab civil service, as the former, being a Bengali, was spending most of his time at the Sri Aurobindo Ashram.[90]

In January 1950, Lambert Saravane, the deputy of French India in the National Assembly in Paris, put forward certain proposals in France to solve the deadlock with regard to the French Indian settlements.

He wanted the French government to open negotiations with the Indian government to chalk out a special constitutional plan for the four French Indian towns and submit that plan to the people of those towns for approval.[91] Léon Saint Jean, the influential lawyer from Karaikal and vice-president of the pro-merger French Indian Congress, came out in support of Saravane. He, however, added that no fair referendum could take place in the conditions prevailing then in the French Indian settlements.

On his return from Paris to Madras, Saravane affirmed that the French parliamentarians were not in favour of a referendum and that they would prefer to settle the problem amicably through negotiations. Saravane was also of the view that the French government did not desire to keep the French Indian territories attached to France.[92]

Strangely, a high colonial administrator of France known as Mr Dairien who was of Pondicherry Tamil origin met some high Indian officials and personalities like Rajkumar and Bajpai. He ascertained from his conversations that the Indian authorities were not sure of winning the referendum and, therefore, wanted to abandon it. But they could harm the interests of the local people by imposing customs restrictions. This message he communicated to the higher authorities in France. He was also of the view that the plebiscite needed to be held so that the final verdict could be pronounced by the people. He maintained that the people of French India shared all the rights and privileges as French nationals, but they were economically linked with India. However, he thought that if the referendum was not held, an agreement needed to be made with the Indian government to maintain French sovereignty over the settlements.[93]

It was the turn of Léon Saint Jean of Karaikal to meet the Indian authorities in Delhi. Following Saravane and Dairien, he, too, was of the opinion that the Indian government wanted to shelve the referendum and enter into a direct understanding with the French government for an amicable settlement of the issue. The government of India wanted the restoration of peaceful conditions in the settlements before the referendum could be held. It wanted, above all, the resolution of the economic difficulties and an end to pressure on the settlements, exercised by itself, as well as the return of the refugees to the settlements to take part in the consultation.[94]

On the other hand, Lambert Saravane, in his capacity as deputy of the French Parliament and leader of the Republican Party that he had newly created and that had hardly any following, declared that he would move a resolution in the National Assembly in favour of the integration of the French territories with India without referendum on 17 October 1950. He dismissed Article 27 of the French Constitution as invalid as the French territories were only rejoining the 'mother country' and so the move could not be termed as a cession of French territory. He claimed in the same breath that he had the assurance of New Delhi that French culture would be protected in the settlments for at least 15 years. Saravane was confident that his resolution would be adopted by the French Parliament.[95]

Opposition to Saravane's moves in favour of integration with India came from the ruling Socialist Party, the mayors, the Representative Council members and the French Indian officials in Pondicherry. It was expected that Goubert himself would go to Paris to counter the proposition of Saravane. At that time, Robert Schuman, the French Minister of Foreign Affairs, declared that since Goubert was court registrar as well as member of the Council of Government, he could not be stopped from participating in the electoral campaigns.[96]

Opposition to Saravane's intended resolution also came from Pondicherrians settled in the French colonies. For example, the president of the *Amicale des Français* Association in Saigon, Symphorien Lami, who was a Créole like Goubert, shot a letter to Robert Schuman as well as the French Minister for Overseas Affairs, asking them not to accept the proposition of Saravane who had lost all mass support. Instead, he asked them to go ahead and conduct a fair and free referendum in French India as stipulated by the French Constitution. Mr. Mitterand of the French Overseas Affairs proposed the elaboration of an autonomy project by the Local Assembly in Pondicherry, in case the referendum was favourable to France.[97]

But Saravane went ahead in putting forth his proposition in the National Assembly in December 1950. He promoted the idea that, in order to be in conformity to Article 27 of the French Constitution, the French and the Indian governments had to first enter into a treaty, which would define the modalities for the transfer of sovereignty to the territories to India and then the population could be asked in a referendum to approve the treaty. This was unlike his earlier proposition where he had ruled out a referendum. It is interesting to note that the judicial advisor of Saravane's party was the veteran politician Sellane Naiker.[98]

Nationalist papers like *The Hindu* and *The Times Of India* considered Saravane's proposition as judicious. But his proposition did not find favour with the parties in the French National Assembly. Besides, Commissioner Ménard had gone to Paris with his own proposition of autonomy for the four French settlements in favour of the status of an 'Associated State' within the French Union, like Laos and Camboddia.[99]

At that time, Mr Keskar of the Indian Ministry of Foreign Affairs, who was a student of the Orientalist Sylvain Levi, professor at Collège de France, met Lambert Saravane in Pondicherry. The French government never prevented him from coming to Pondicherry. Saravane wanted the immediate transfer of sovereignty of the French territories to India. However, Keskar did not denounce the 1948 agreement on referendum. Like Rajkumar, he held that the atmosphere in the settlements was not conducive to the holding of the referendum. In fact, both Keskar and Rajkumar were toeing the line of Nehru who declared at the plenary session of the Congress in Nasik that there coud be no referendum if the situation did not change on the ground. At the same time, he added that all French settlements were integral parts of India. The intention, thus, of the Indian government seems to be one of delaying the holding of the referendum or avoiding it on various pretexts.[100]

Meanwhile, the economic blockade was resumed in late 1949 and no goods could enter Pondicherry. Electricity was cut off and no foodgrains could arrive in Pondicherry. Besides, since 1 January 1950, there was a blockade on transport of goods from Pondicherry to the enclaves through Indian territory. This forced the Pondicherrians to think seriously about joining the Indian Union.[101]

However, in the year 1950, the French considered the Socialist Party of Goubert as pro-French. Goubert's party had a certain hold over the workers and the labour union due to the fact that the president of the Federation of the Workers' Syndicate was a paid employee of the French Indian government. Goubert had practically eliminated Communist influence in the textile mills by setting up Socialist labour unions. The French counted a great deal on the Socialist Party for their continued stay in India. The new party founded by Saravane was pro-merger. But it had very little popular support. The Congress Party was not very active, though it was pro-Indian. Besides, Commissioner André Ménard had created a pro-French faction in Pondicherry at that time called 'La République Française'. During this period several 'nationalist' papers saw the light of the day in Pondicherry and Karaikal. Some of them were the *Podujanam* of Dr Srinivasa Iyer, *Libération* of A. Lahache, *Barathy* of Mani Iyer and *Karai Mail* of A. Manikkam.[102]

NOTES

1. *Notes Documentaires et Etudes*, no. 735, Les EF de l'inde, IF 7, ADP; Recensement Général mai 1948, pp. 91-2, IF 8, ADP.
2. AFP, Pondicherry, 2 April 1948, p. 111, IF 8, ADP; *Indian Express*, 4 March 1948; *Hindustan Times*, 1 March 1948; Mission d'Information aux Indes de Daniel Lévi et Tezenas du Montcel, December 1947-January 1948, pp. 47-8, IF 8, AO, ADP.
3. Visite de M. Godard, président de la Chambre de Commerce et Français de Pondichéry à la Direction d'Asie, 8 April 1948, p. 112, IF 8, ADP.
4. Téll de Lévi au Ministre des Affaires Etrangères, New Delhi, 3 May 1948, p.175, IF 8, ADP; *The Hindu*, 17 April 1948; Téll de Lévi au Ministère des Affaires Etrangères, New Delhi, 14 April 1948, p. 191, IF 8, ADP.
5. *Podujanam*, 27 April 1948; *Jeunesse*, 20 April 1948.
6. Annasse, *Les Comptoirs Français de l'Inde, Trois Siècles de Présence Française, 1664-1954*, Paris, 1975; Interview with Paramel Shathrugnan and Mannar Mannan.
7. AFP, Pondicherry, 30 April 1948, p. 93, IF 51, ADP.
8. Antoine Mariadassou, 'History of the Freedom Struggle of the French India Students Congress', *La Lettre du CIDIF*, no. 20, 1998, p. 61; Interview with Antoine Mariadassou, Paul Radjanedassou et Paramel Shathrugnan; AO, 1944-55, Letter of 28 May 48, IF 1, ADP.
9. Lettre du Gouverneur au Ministre de la France d'Outre-mer, 28 August 1948, p. 120, if 51, ADP; AFP, 1 June 1948, Pondichéry, p. 94, if 51, ADP.
10. AFP, Pondicherry, 30 September 1948, p. 134, IF 51, ADP.

11. Tél de Levi au Ministre des Affaires Etrangères, New Delhi, 19 August 1948, p. 152, IF 9, ADP; R. Dadala, *My Struggle for the Freedom of French India*, Pondicherry, n.d. pp. 8-9; *Libération*, 26 May 1949, p. 4; *Suthanthiram*, 15 March 1948; *Hindustan Times*, 2 July 1948; JO 1948, p. 780; N.V. Rajkumar, *The Problem of French India*, Delhi, 1951, p. 23; *The Hindu*, 12 June 1948.
12. Note pour M. Boissier, AO, 8 July 1948, p. 94 IF 9, ADP; Interview with Chandra Varma; S. Lastick, 'The Role of Sellane Naicker in the Freedom Struggle of Pondicherry', M. Phil. Dissertation, University of Pondicherry, 1998; *Suthanthiram*, 14 July 1948.
13. Tél de Balasoupramanien, Président de l'Assemblée Réprésentative au Ministère de la France d'Outre-mer, 10 June 1948, p. 27, IF 9, ADP; Déclaration de Goubert au sujet de l'IF, p. 36, IF 9, ADP; *Statesman*, 13 June 1948; AFP, 9 June 1948, Pondicherry, p. 25, IF 9.
14. Tél de Levi au Ministre des Affaires Etrangères, New Delhi, 18 June 1948, p. 60, IF 9, ADP; Aide Mémoire, Ministry of External Affairs, New Delhi, 1 July 1948, p. 85, IF 9, ADP; Reuter, New Delhi, 30 August 1948, p. 160, IF 9, ADP; Note pour Schuman, Ministre des Affaires Etrangères, AO, Paris, 13 November 1948, IF 9, ADP.
15. *Times of India*, 10 June 1948; *Statesman*, 13 June 1948; *Hindustan Times*, 12 June 1948; Tél de Levi au Ministre des Affaires Etrangères, New Delhi, 24 October 1948, p. 112, IF 9, ADP; Note pour Schuman, Ministre des Affaires Etrangères, AO, Paris, 13 November 1948, p. 187, IF 9, ADP; Tél de Du Montcel au Ministère de France d'Outre-mer, New Delhi, 18 June 1948, p. 62, IF 9, ADP; Notes pour M. Boissier, AO, 8 July 1948, pp. 94-5, IF 9, ADP; Lettre de Levi à Bidault, Ministre des Affaires Etrangères, 23 July 1948, pp. 107-11, IF 9, ADP; Lettre de Levi à Schuman, Ministre des Affaires Etrangères, New Delhi, 5 November 1948, p. 190, IF 9, ADP; *Modern Review*, April 1914, p. 463.
16. Note, Ministre Affaires Etrangères, AO, Paris, 5 October 1948, pp. 161-4, IF 9, ADP; *The Hindu*, 25 July 1948; Compte-rendu d'une reunion tenue le 4 Aôut 1948 à AO au sujet de l'IF, Paris, 10 August 1948, IF 9, p. 145.
17. JO 1948, p. 784 ; Entretien de M. Schuman avec le Chargé d'affaires des indes, Pillai, Paris, 23 October 1948, p. 169, IF 9, ADP; Tél du Ministre des Affaires Etrangères à Ambafrance, Paris, 19 July 1948, p. 105, IF 9, ADP.
18. JO 1948, p. 256; Antoine Mariadassou, op. cit., pp. 64-5; Interview with Antoine Mariadassou, Paramel Shathrugnan and Paul Radjane-

dassou; Audience Publlique correctionelle extraordinaire du Tribunal Supérieur d'appel de l'Inde Française du samedi, 9 Octobre 1948, (in) *La Lettre du Cidif*, no. 20; *Maanilam*, 11 September 1948.
19. Interview with Paramel Shatrugnan and Antoine Mariadassou; Représentation française à Pondichéry, January 1955, p. 140, no. 3, AO, ADP; *HindustanTimes*, 1 October 1948.
20. *Le Populaire*, 14 September 1948; G. Samboo, *Les Comptoirs Français dans l'Inde Nouvelle de la Compagnie des Indes à nos Jours*, Paris, 1950, p. 82.
21. *Suthanthiram*, 29 February 1948; 11 June 1948; *l'Humanité*, 21 July 1948; *Suthanthiram Pon Vizha Malar, 1934-84*, Pondicherry, 1987, p. 48; *Maanilam*, 11 September 1948; *Indian Express*, 17 August 1948; *The Hindu*, 27, 28 September 1948; Ajit Neogy, *Decolonisation of French India*, Pondicherry, 1997, pp. 98-9.
22. *Suthanthiram*, 29 September 1948; *Indian Express*, 5, 20 July 1948; cf. also Affaires Politiques, C428, D2, AOM; Lettre de Subbiah au Ministre de la France d'Outre-mer, 24 September 1948, Affaires Politiques, C 436, AOM.
23. S. Arumugam, 'Perumithathin Thiru Uruvam', *Va. Subbiah Pavala Vizha Malar*, 1988, p. 96.
24. *Indian Express*, 31 October, 1 November 1948; Translation of (Indian) Socialist party leaflet explaining party position; *l'Epoque*, 25 October 1948; Lettre de Daniel Levi à Schuman, Ministre des Affaires Etrangères, New Delhi, 12 November 1948, p. 11, no. 40, ADP; *Indian Express*, 23 September-8 October 1948.
25. JO 1948, pp. 144, 155, 163, 269, 288 ; JO 1948, p. 341; Tél de Comrep au France d'Outre-mer, 24 November 1948, AO, 1944-55, situation locale, no. 53, p. 3, ADP; l'*Aurore*, 22 October 1948; JO 1948, p. 376.
26. Communicaton du Ministre de la France d'Outre-mer sur la situation politique dans les EF de l'inde, 16, 17 September 1949 par Paul Coste Floret, AO 1944-55, Inde-fr, no. 28, pp. 229-35, ADP.
27. *Daily Mail*, 8 October 1948, AO 1944-55, no. 52, p. 18, ADP.
28. *Kuyil*, 14 September 1948; *Dinamani*, 21 September 1948; C.S. Murugesan, *Viduthalai Velviyil Puduchery*, Chennai, 2004, pp. 118-32; A. Ramasamy, *A History of Pondicherry*, Delhi, 1987, p. 163; Tél de Lévi au Ministre des Affaires Etrangères, New Delhi, 9 October 1948, pp. 20-1, no. 52, ADP; Note of Embassy of India to Minister of Foreign Affairs, Paris, 22 October 1948, no. 52, p. 90, ADP; Lettre de Levi à Robert Schuman, Minstre des Affaires Etrangères, New Delhi, 13 October 1948, AO, 1944-55, pp. 42-60, no. 52; A. Arulraj, *Puducheri*

Suthanthira Poratathin Kalachuvadukal, Puduchery, 2005, pp. 112-14; Interview with A. Arulraj; *The Hindu*, 27 September 1948.
29. *India*, 28 November 1948, AO, 1944-55, no. 53, p. 27, ADP; *Le Monde*, 9-10 January 1949; Lettre du chef de service de l'Instruction Pubique au Gouverneur, Pondicherry, 24 November 1948, pp. 69-70, no. 53, ADP; *Kuyil*, 14 September 1948.
30. *l'Aurore*, 26 October 1948; JO 27 November 1948, pp. 366-8; JO 1948, pp. 247-84; *l'Epoque*, 26, 28 October 1948; *Le Monde*, 26 October 1948; *Le Figaro*, 25 October 1948; JO 27 November 1948, p. 366.
31. *Suthanthiram*, 19 February 1949; 3 October 1948; 17 November 1948; cf. JO, 1948, 1949 and R.L. Purushotthama Reddiar papers, National Archives of India, Pondicherry.
32. Note of 20 July 1949, Les Etablissements français de l'Inde et les rapports franco-indiens, no. 11, p. 6, AO, ADP.
33. Tél de Baron au Ministre des Affaires Etrangères, Paris, 27 October 1948, p. 183, IF 9, ADP; Tél de Levi au Ministre des Affaires Etrangères, New Delhi, 26 October 1948, p. 175, IF 9; ADP; Note, 26 October 1948, p. 178, IF 9, ADP.
34. G. Samboo, *Les Comptoirs Français dans l'Inde Nouvelle de la Compagnie des Indes à nos Jours*, Paris, 1950, pp. 111, 118, 124f; *Indian Express*, 27 September-9 October 1948; *l'Aurore*, 26 October 1948; *Le Populaire*, 23 September-4 October 1948; R. Dadala, *My Struggle for the Freedom of French India*, Pondicherry, n.d., p. 9.
35. *India*, 28 November 1948, AO, 1944-55, p. 28, no. 53, ADP; Aide Mémoire, 3 February 1950, no. 12, pp. 168-70, AO, ADP.
36. *Indian Express*, 1-2 November 1948; Note of Embassy of India to Minister of Foreign Affairs, Pondicherry, 27 October 1948, AO, 1944-55, no. 52, p. 182, ADP.
37. Tél de Levi au Ministre des Affaires Etrangères, New Delhi, 26 October 1948, p. 175, IF 9, ADP; B. Mayandi, 'Subbaiyavum Suthanthiramum Onru', *Va. Subbiah Pavala Vizha Malar*, Pondicherry, 1988, p. 47.
38. Samboo, op. cit., p. 124.
39. Lettre du Ministre des Affaires Etrangères au Ministre de la France d'Outre-mer, 24 January 1949, AO, no. 53, p. 48, ADP; JO 1948, p. 369; *l'Aube*, 17 November 1948; *Suthanthiram*, 24 November 1948.
40. *Indian Express*, 4 February 1949; *Jeunesse*, 26 January 1949; *Indian Express*, 18-20 December 1948.
41. *Suthanthiram*, 11 December 1948; *Jeunesse*, 26 January 1949; *Le Populaire*, 3 December 1948; *Suthanthiram*, 11 December 1948; *Jeunesse*,

26 January 1949; cf. R.L. Purushottama Reddiar papers, National Archives of India, Pondicherry.
42. Asie Océanie, 1944-55, Dossier General, AFP, Pondicherry, 8 January 1949, p. 2, IF 10, ADP; Tél de Levi, New Delhi, 11 January 1949, IF 10, ADP.
43. Tél de Levi à Ministre des Affaires Etrangères, New Delhi, 18 January 1949, 20 January 1949, IF 10, pp. 12, 14, ADP; Tél de Bertrand au Ministère des Affaires Etrangères, New Delhi, 25 May 1949, IF 10, AO, p. 116, ADP.
44. Nehru's answers in Parliament, 3 February 1949, 57-8, IF 10, AO, ADP; Tél de Levi au Ministre des Affaires Etrangères, New Delhi, 4 February 1949, p. 23, IF 10, ADP.
45. *Statesman*, 15 June 1949, in AO, no. 53, p.107, ADP; Lettre de Levi à Robert Schuman, Ministre des Affaires Etrangères, New Delhi, 24 March 1949, p. 64, no. 53, ADP; AFP, Pondicherry, 25 May 1949, p. 94, no. 53, AO, ADP.
46. IF 10, AO, p. 207, ADP; IF 10, AO, p. 208, ADP.
47. *The Hindu*, 24 March 1949.
48. *Statesman*, 15 June 1949; *The Hindu*, 15 June 1949, AO, no. 53, pp. 107, 113, ADP.
49. *India*, 12 June 1949, AO, no. 53, p. 126, ADP; Lettre de Levi à Robert Schuman, New Delhi, 21 June 1949, no. 53, AO, p. 111, ADP.
50. *India*, 12 June 1949, AO, no. 53, p. 126, ADP.
51. Monographies sur Pondichéry par Mouzan, pp. 131-2, IF 89, ADP.
52. Convention du 28 Janvier 1941(JO 1941) IF 10, AO, p. 207, ADP; Text of the note presented by Minister of External Affairs and Commonwealth relations, India to Ambassador of France, New Delhi, 29 March 1948.
53. Tél de Comrep au Ministère de la France d'Outre-mer, Pondicherry, 28 June 1949, no. 53, AO, p. 120, ADP; JO 1941, p. 62, etc; Note du 20 Juillet 1949, Les Etablissements français de l'Inde et les rapports franco-indiens, IF no. 11, pp. 41-2, AO, ADP; Aide Mémoire, Ministry of External Affairs, New Delhi, 30 April 1949, IF 10, AO, ADP; IF10, AO, pp. 208-9, ADP; *Le Monde*, 13 April, 19 August 1954; *Jeunesse*, 21 March 1949; 18 May 1949; Copy of a note dated 13 May 1949 from the French Embassy in New Delhi to the Ministry of External Affairs, New Delhi, IF 10, pp. 107-8, AO, ADP; *Le Monde*, 22 May 1949; *Libération*, 26 May 1949, p. 6; La situation politique et économique de l'IF par RMAS Pakkirisamy Poullé, 1949, AO, no. 53, pp. 96-7, no. 53, ADP; Note du 20 Juillet 1949, Les Etablissements français de l'Inde et les rapports franco-indiens, no. 11, p. 6, AO, ADP;

From the pro-tem Commissioner of the Republic of French India to the Minister for Overseas France, Paris, 27 April 1949, AO, IF 42, ADP; Tél au Ministre des Affaires Etrangères, 23 May 1949, Pondichéry, p. 45, IF 61, ADP; *Combat*, 19 April 1949 ; Tél de Bertrand au Ministre des Affaires Etrangères, New Delhi, 28 May 1949, pp. 130-4, IF 10, AO, ADP.
54. IF 10, AO, p. 210, ADP.
55. Note EF May 1954, p. 163, IF 18, ADP; IF 10, AO, p. 211, ADP.
56. *Libération*, 26 June 1949, p. 5; *Suthanthiram*, 20 October 1948.
57. *Le Monde*, 7 August 1954; *Jeunesse*, 21 March 1949; 18 May 1949; Note, Les EF de l'Union Indienne et les rapports franco-indiens, 20 July 1949, p. 152, no. 53, AO, ADP.
58. Maires des communes de Mannadipeth, Nettapacom, Villenour, Bahour, Oulgaret à M. Ministre des Affaires Etrangères, October 1951, pp. 249-53, IF 66, ADP; It is noteworthy that these three mayors were big landlords.
59. *Jeunesse*, 18 May 1949; Note entretien de M. Baeyens avec M. Chambon, Paris, 19 March 1949, p. 104, IF 10, AO, ADP.
60. *Jeunesse*, 15 June 1949; 26 March 1949, 15 June 1949.
61. Tél de Bertrand au Ministre des Affaires Etrangères, New Delhi, 29 May 1949, pp. 135-6, IF, 10, AO, ADP; Lettre de Levi à Robert Schuman, Ministre des Affaires Etrangères, New Delhi, 23 May 1949, pp. 17-18, no. 4, ADP; Copy of a note dated 23 May 1949 from the French Embassy, New Delhi to the Ministry of External Affairs, n.d., IF 10, AO, pp. 107-8, ADP; Tél de New York à Ministère des Affaires Etrangères, 9 June 1949, p. 184, IF 10, AO, ADP; *Libération*, 10 June 1949, p. 4; *The Hindu*, 4 June 1949.
62. Tél de Levi au Ministre des Affaires Etrangères, New Delhi, 20 March 1949, p. 106, IF 10, AO, ADP; IF 10, AO, p. 211, ADP.
63. *The Hindu*, 22 June 1954; Note du 20 Juillet 1949, Les Etablissements Français de l'Inde et les Rapports Ffranco-Indiens, no. 11, p. 6, AO, ADP; Jacques Weber, *Pondichéry et les Comptoirs de l'Inde après Dupleix: La Démocratie au pays des Castes*, Paris, 1996, p. 365; *The Hindu*; 21, 22, 23 June 1949.
64. Samboo, op. cit., p. 115; *Hindustan Standard*, 28 June 1949 (in) no. 53, AO, p. 121, ADP.
65. Lettre de E. Adicéam, Professeur au Collège Colonial au Gouverneur, Pondicherry, 28 June 1948, IF 10, AO, pp. 219-25, ADP.
66. *L'Aurore*, 2 August 1949; JO, 24 October 1935; AO, no. 53, pp. 274-79, ADP; *The Hindu*, 25 July 1949.
67. Extrait d'une lettre de M. Lévi à M. Baeyens, no. 11, pp. 56-7, ADP;

Note pour le Ministre-AO Paris, 7 September 1949, p. 113, no. 11, ADP; Projet de Statut de ville libres, 1 September 1949, p. 100, no. 11, ADP; AFP Special Outre-Mer, 2 July 1949, p. 6, IF 11, ADP; *The Hindu*, 19 October 1949.
68. Note pour le Secretaire General, Asie Océanie, 22 August 1949, p. 96, no. 11, ADP; AFP, New Delhi, 19 October 1949, AO, no. 53, p. 234, ADP; AO, 1944-55, Inde. fr. no. 43, pp. 11-12, ADP; *Indian New Chronicle*, 24 July 1949, 1 August 1949; *Sunday Statesman*, 30 July 1949, pp.168, 170-2, no. 53, AO, ADP; AFP, Special Outre-Mer, 2 July 1949, no. 11, p.6, ADP; Levi à Robert Schuman, Ministre des Affaires Etrangères, New Delhi, 20 September 1949, p. 122, no. 11, ADP; *The Hindu*, 25 July 1949.
69. Lettre de Chambon au Ministre de la France d'Outre-mer, Pondicherry, 8 November 1949, no. 11, pp. 232-4.
70. *The Hindu*, 29 July 1949; Levi à Robert Schuman, 2 August 1949, no. 53, pp. 165-7, ADP.
71. AFP, Bombay, 2 August 1949, no. 53, p.163, ADP; Note pour le Ministre, AO, 18 August 1949, p. 80, no. 11, ADP; Note Ministre des Affaires Etrangères, Paris, 12 November 1949, pp. 195-6, no. 11, ADP; Débat à l'Assemblée Nationale sur le referendum, 2e séance du 25 May 1949, p. 51, no. 43, ADP; AO, 1944-5, no. 41, pp. 6-7; Tél de Levi au Ministre des Affaires Etrangères, 30 July and 3 August 1949, New Delhi; *Hindustan Times* Weekly, 31 July 1949, no. 53, p. 169, AO, ADP; AFP, Bombay, 2 August 1949, no. 53, p. 163, ADP.
72. Tél de Levi au Ministre des Affaires Etrangères, New Delhi, 5 October 1949, p. 136, no. 11, ADP; Tél de Levi au Ministre des Affaires Etrangères, New Delhi, 27 August 1949, p. 91, no. 11, ADP ; Le Ministre des Affaires Etrangères à Ambafrance, Paris, 2 September 1949, no.11, p. 118, ADP; Levi à Robert Schuman, Ministre des Affaires Etrangères, New Delhi, 6 September 1949, p. 111, no. 11, ADP; Note pour le Ministre, AO, Paris, 7 September 1949, pp. 113-16, no. 11, ADP.
73. Interview with Saraswati Subbiah and G.S. Mubeen; Communicaton du Ministre de la France d'Outre-mer sur la situation politique dans les EF de l'inde, 16, 17 September 1949 par Paul Coste Floret, AO 1944-55, Inde fr. no. 28, pp. 229-35, ADP; Tél du Ministre des Affaires Etrangères à Amba France, New Delhi, Paris, 25 July 1949, no. 53, p. 150, ADP; Communication du Ministre de la France d'Outre-mer sur la situation politque dans l'IF, 12 September 1949, p. 84, IF 89, ADP; *Lettre de M.A.Annasse du*, 31 March 1955, p. 130, no. 3, AO, ADP; Une note par M. Jacquier, Conseiller de l'Union Française sur

Arthur Annasse, 14 January 1955, pp. 131-3, no. 3, AO, ADP; Arthur Annasse was an ardent supporter of Union Française. He came to Pondicherry and thus lost three years of his service. He later asked the French government to nominate him as the bureau chief of the French representation in Pondicherry as a sort of compensation.

74. Communicaton du Ministre de la France d'Outre-mer sur la situation politique dans les EF de l'inde, 16/17 September 1949 par Paul Coste Floret, AO 1944-55, Inde fr. no. 28, pp. 229-55, ADP; Ministre de la France d'Outre-mer au Ministre des Affaires Etrangères, Paris, 7 April 1949, pp. 82-3, no. 53, ADP; Extrait d'une lettre de M. Lévi à M. Baeyens, no. 11, pp. 56-7, ADP; Neogy, op. cit., pp. 129-32.

75. Samboo, op. cit., p. 89; *Jeunesse*, 15 June 1949; Motion des Assemblées des Conseils Municipaux de Pondichéry, séance du 18 October 1949, pp. 166-8, no. 41, ADP; Circular no. 299, Information and Press Service, Ministry for Foreign Affairs, Paris, 20 October 1949, p. 143, no. 11, ADP.

76. Reuter, Pondicherry, 7 November 1949, p. 185, no. 11, ADP; Samboo, op. cit., p. 82; Note pour le Secrétaire Général, Asie Océanie, 25 October 1949, pp. 151-2, no. 11, ADP; AO, pp. 158-9, no. 11, ADP; *The Hindu*, 19 October 1949.

77. Rapport fait au nom de la Commission de la France d'Outre-mer sur le projet de loi, adopté par l'Assemblée nationale; autorisant le gouvernemnt à organiser par décret un refrendum dans les EF par M. Marius Moutet, Sénateur, pp. 201-32, IF 42, AO, ADP; C. Antony. *Gazetteer of India: Union Territory of Pondicherry*, vol. I, p. 260.

78. JO 1949, p. 60; *The Hindu*, 25 July 1949.

79. Lettre de Chambon à Ministre de la France d'Outre-mer, Pondicherry, 8 November 1949, pp. 232-7, no. 11, AO, ADP; Renseignements Généraux de Pondichéry, 23 December 1949, Affaires Politiques, C 2270. D2, AOM.

80. Lettre de Chambon à Ministre de la France d'Outre-mer, op. cit., pp. 232-7; Lettre du Ministre de la France d'Outre-mer au Ministre des Affaires Etrangères, Paris, 15 November 1949, p. 202, no. 11, ADP; Tél du Commissaire au Ministre des Affaires Etrangères, Pondicherry, 12 November 1949, p. 201, no. 11, ADP; Samboo, op. cit., p. 85; Tel de Comrep au Ministère de la France d'Outre-mer, Pondicherry, 19 October 1949, AO, no. 53, p. 237, ADP; Lettre de Levi à Robert Schuman, Ministre des Affaires Etrangères, New Delhi, 26 October 1949, no. 53, p. 253, ADP; Note de Papoussamy sur son voyage à Pondichéry, AO, no. 53, pp. 255-61, ADP; *The Hindu*, 24 October 1949; Reuter,

Madras, 9 November 1949; AFP 9 November 1949, no. 11, pp. 190-1, AO, ADP; AFP, Special Outre-mer, 6-7 November 1949, no. 11, p. 184, ADP.
81. *The Hindu*, 20 December 1949; *Indian Express*, 21 December 1949; Procès-verbal de la Séance du Conseil du Gouvernement du 15 Décembre 1949, pp. 268-72, no.11, ADP; Note sur 'Le Problème des Etablissements Français dans l'Inde', Affaires Politiques, C 449, AOM.
82. Note pour le Séc. Gén. Paris, 22 February 1950, IF 42, AO, ADP.
83. Ibid.; Samboo, op. cit., p. 95; Comité de l'Union Française Karikalaise, 10 January 1950, pp. 31-3, no. 12, ADP.
84. Lettre de Levi à Robert Schuman, Ministre des Affaires Etrangères, New Delhi, 2 May 1950, pp. 208-9, no. 12, ADP; Procès verbal de la session du 2 June 1950 au Ministère des Aaffaires Etrangères sous la Présidence de Robert Schuman, no. 12, pp. 149-68, ADP.
85. Tél de Belle, New Delhi, 3 June 1950, p. 241, IF 12, ADP; Lettre de Belle, Chargés d'Affaire à New Delhi, à Robert Schuman, New Delhi, 4 June 1950, no. 12, ADP; Tél de Belle à l'Asie Océanie, New Delhi, 30 May 1950, pp. 239-40, no. 12, ADP; Lettre de Henri Bonnet, Ambassadeeur de France aux Etats Unis à Robert Schman, Washington, 24 June 1950, p. 248, no. 12, ADP.
86. *Statesman*, 10 February 1950; Tél de Levi au Ministre des Affaires Etrangères, New Delhi, 7 February 1950, no. 12, p. 114, ADP.
87. Tél du Ministère des Afffaires Etrangères à Ambafrance, New Delhi, 25 February 1950, p. 181, no. 42, ADP; Embassy of India to Ministère des Affaires Etrangères, Paris, 18 February 1950, IF 42, ADP.
88. *The Hindu*, 10 July 1949; 26 August 1949; 28 December 1949; 6, 7 January 1950; S. Lastick, 'The Role of Sellane Naicker in the Freedom Struggle of Pondicherry', M. Phil. Dissertation, University of Pondicherry, 1998, p. 23; Dadala, op. cit., pp. 12-13; Tél de Pondichéry au Ministère de la France d'Outre-mer, Pondicherry, 1 November 1950, Affaires Politiques, C 437, AOM.
89. H.D. Saint Jacques, Président de l'Union Républicaine de l'Inde Française à Ministre de la France d'Outre-mer, Pondicherry, 22 December 1949, pp. 71-6, IF 12, ADP; Interview with Doressamy Naiker, former student leader in the 1950s.
90. Embassy of India, Paris to Ministry of Foreign Affairs, Paris, 11 May 1950, p. 93, no. 4, AO, ADP; Tél du Commissaire, Pondicherry, 18 May 1950, p. 87, no. 4, AO, ADP; Embassy of India, Paris to Minister of Foreign Affairs, Paris, 14 December 1949, p. 74, no. 4, AO,

ADP; Aff. Pol. Carton 1122, Dossier 5, Rapport sur les activités islamiques dans les colonies durant 1948 (1948-9).
91. Motion adoptee le 4 Janvier 1950 par la Commission des TOM sur la proposition de Lambert Saravane, Paris, AO, no. 12, p. 3, ADP.
92. *Times of India*, 7, 8 February 1950; Tél de Levi au Ministre des Affaires Etrangères, New Delhi, 7 February 1950, p. 114, no. 12, ADP.
93. Lettre du Ministre des Affaires Etrangères à Ambafrance, Paris, 4 May 1950, no. 12, pp. 215-16, ADP ; Tél de Levi à Ministre des Affaires Etrangères, New Delhi, 11 February 1950, pp. 123-6, no. 12, ADP; *The Hindu*, 27 February 1950.
94. Tél du Ministère des Affaires Etrangères à AmbaFrance, New Delhi, Paris, 17, 20 February 1950, pp. 128-33, no. 12, ADP; Lettre de Levi à Robert Schuman, Ministre des Affaires Etrangères, New Delhi, 2 November 1950, pp. 208-13, no. 12, ADP.
95. Lettre de Belle au Ministre des Affaires Etrangères, 10 October 1950, pp. 75-6, IF 13, ADP.
96. Procés verbal de l'entretien du 1 March 1950 entre Robert Schuman et Sardar Malik, Ambassade de l'inde, p. 199, no. 42, ADP; Telegram, Reuter, Paris, 6 November 1950, pp. 99-101, IF 13, ADP; Tél de Levi, Amba france au Ministre des Affaires Etrangères, New Delhi, 2 March 1950, p. 219, no. 42, ADP.
97. Lettre de S. Lami, Président de l'Amicale des Français de l'Inde, Saigon, 10 November 1950, pp. 87-9, IF 13, ADP; Lettre du Président de l'Amicale des Français de l'Inde à Ministre de la France d'Outre-mer, Saigon, 2 November 1950, IF 13, ADP; Procés verbal de la reunion interministérielle, tenue dans le bureau de M. Robert Schuman, en la presence de Danièl Levi et M. Mitterand de la France d'Outre-mer, IF 13, pp. 91-6, ADP.
98. Proposition de Resolution de M. Saravane à l'Asssemblée Nationale, session de Déc 1950, IF 13, pp. 140-1, ADP.
99. *The Hindu*, 4, 5 December 1950; *Times of India* 2, 3 December 1950.
100. Note Ministre des Affaires Etrangères, Paris, 21 September 1950, pp. 57-60, IF 13, ADP; Communiqué pour France d'Outre-mer du Commissaire, Pondicherry, 6 September 1950, p.38, IF 13, ADP; Lettre de Christian belle, chargés d'affaires de France à Robert Schumann, Ministre des Affaires Etrangères, New Delhi, 9 September 1950, pp. 43-50, IF 13, ADP; Commissaire au Ministre des Affaires Etrangères, Pondicherry, 23 September 1950, p. 54, IF 13, ADP.
101. Communicaton du Ministre de France d'Outre-mer sur la situation

politique dans les EF de l'inde, 16-17 September 1949 par Paul Coste Floret, AO 1944-55, Inde fr. no. 28, p. 229, ADP; Ministre des Affaires Etrangères à AmbaFrance, New Delhi, Paris 13 January 1950, p. 63, IF 13, ADP.
102. Note sur la situation dans les établissements français des Indes, s.d., IF 13, pp. 23-37, ADP; French India Settlements by V.A. Pannikar, Government of India Information Service, 31 August 1950, pp. 36-7; Lettre du Commissaire au Ministre France d'Outre-mer, Pondichéry, 27 September 1950, pp. 208-10, IF 13.

CHAPTER 8
―――――
Goubert's Sway Continues

TOWARDS ELECTION VICTORIES

At a meeting in Murungapakkam on 8 January 1950, there was an attempt made on Eduoard Goubert's life. A bomb was thrown at Goubert, but he escaped unhurt. Two bombs were also thrown at Keerapalayam on Socialist Party workers. The Socialist Party offices were attacked by the Communists. This time, the cycle of violence was started by V. Subbiah's men. There was immediate retaliation by Goubert's men against their rivals, especially the Communists. The events set in motion a whole new cycle of violence. Meanwhile, three Communist members of the Representative Assembly, including Subbiah, were disqualified from their membership.[1] They fled to Indian territory.

Violence was unleashed against Communists by hundreds of *goondas*, starting 11 January 1950, to quell the rising support that the pro-mergerists like Subbiah and Lambert Saravane enjoyed among Pondicherrians. The French police failed to intervene. The *Suthanthiram* press and the cooperative store of the labourers were looted and destroyed. On 15 January 1950, Subbiah's only house at 7, Nidarajapayer Street, which served as the Communist Party office, was attacked and set on fire by Goubert's men, with the connivance of the police force led by its French chief Bouhard. Earlier, on 3 July 1950, Saravane's house had been attacked. There were also attacks perpetrated on the Indian consul general's staff. Even the refugees in Indian territory were not spared, while French citizens were manhandled in Indian territory. Goubert came down heavily on the Indian press for its false and malicious propaganda about French repression in French India. He claimed that the labour force in French India was behind the French India Labour Federation controlled by the Socialist Party of which he was president.[2]

It was generally believed that the attackers had been the pro-French Goubert's men. Even the merchant Nanayya Bhagavathar's garage was destroyed because he was a steadfast supporter of Subbiah. Several of Subbiah's supporters, especially among the workers, weavers and farmers, had to flee Pondicherry in the face of increasing violence against them. Some of their houses were set on fire. The houses of Lambert Saravane, Murugasamy Clemenceau and Gabriel Annusamy were vandalised in July 1950. Nanayya Bhagavathar's and Rathina Mudaliar's shops were looted. Subbiah, too, fled from the violence and sought refuge in the farmlands of Shanmuga Chettiar of Valavanur for some time and then left for Madras. The French Indian government sought to arrest Subbiah by all means. Communist leaders, N. Ranganathan, D.K. Ramanujam and Ayyamperumal, were also expelled from Pondicherry. It seems that the attacks on the Communists and Saravanists continued in spite of Commissioner André Ménard's warning Goubert not to perpetrate such terrorism.[3]

At that juncture, the French government wanted to involve Goubert in finding a solution regarding the terms of the referendum to be held in Pondicherry. These included the presence of neutral observers during the referendum and the quorum or percentage of voters required to validate the referendum.[4]

Goubert ruled Pondicherry like a 'dictator' during this perod. He was feared even in Karaikal, where Senator Pakkirisamy Poullé revised his stand in favour of merger and rallied behind Goubert. Poullé, it seems, was an opportunist of the first order who, according to Tezenas du Montcel, looked to the 'highest bidder who paid him the best'. But the French still counted upon Goubert to buttress their sagging fortunes. During this period, Goubert was accused of indulging in smuggling gold, diamonds and mercury to Indian territory from Pondicherry, where gold was cheaper. A total of 450 kg of gold was imported into Pondicherry in 1949. But in 1952, this rose to 11 tonnes. Of this, the French Bank, *la Banque d'Indochine* imported 70 per cent. Much of the gold was passed into British India through four Muslim merchants.[5] It was believed that Goubert even accepted commission when alcohol and toddy shops were leased out. People from British India came to drink cheap liquor in Pondicherry manufactured by the local government distillery. Besides, liquour was smuggled to India as there was prohibition in the Madras province.[6]

Goubert lived in a rented house when he was registrar at the Pondicherry court. By 1951-2, he was believed to be owning at least 10 houses. However, this was never substantiated. All his associates around him too, enriched themselves during this period. In 1951, when he contested the deputy election against Saravane, the worst methods of intimidation and corruption was employed. In 1952, the Pondicherry government treasurer complained that Goubert received salaries for being member of the parliament and registrar at the same time. Very soon, the news of his activities reached the ears of the Parisian government. They were becoming increasingly doubtful of Goubert's intentions.[7] As a matter of fact, Goubert had a income revenue of Rs. 5,500 at that time, which included the parliamentary indemnity paid by the State Bank of France (Rs. 1,500), parliamentary indemnity paid by the local budget (Rs. 1,000) and his salary as court registrar (Rs. 3,000).

Besides, the budget of French India had always been an autonomous local budget. The local revenues were enough to meet the expenditure. Metroplitan France did not subsidise the budget. Goubert controlled this budget and was believed to have manipulated it. However, when I interviewed his son, Joseph Goubert, more than two decades after his father's death, he was living a precarious and unknown life in a rented house. If Goubert had really amassed wealth when he was in power, he would not have left his children in such a sorrowful state, he said. Various witnesses, including his son, confirmed to me that he never pocketed public money while he was in power, unlike some of his associates,

The pro-Congress newspaper *Jeunesse*, edited by Dorai Munisamy, accused Muthu Poullé, who had no means to repay a debt of Rs. 7,000 before he became mayor, of amassing more than two lakh rupees in two years after he was appointed to the post. Muthu Poullé was accused of obtaining a contract through illegitimate means for the supply of cement in favour of his son-in-law, one for the supply of molasses in favour of Muthu Kumarappa Reddiar (total profits from which amounted to more than Rs. 50,000) and several contracts for supply of materials to the Public Works Department in favour of the latter's relatives. But according to French records, Muthu Poullé's father was already wealthy. Muthu Poullé had inherited some of that wealth. Besides, Muthu Poullé was a merchant in his own right. He had a friendly relationship with the French industrialist and merchant, J.M. Colombani. Poullé sold his groundnuts to J.M. Colombani and, according to French records, the latter obtained information regarding the activities of Saravane through Poullé. Sivasubramania Poullé, Food Minister in Goubert's Cabinet, who was a rival of Pakkirisamy Poullé in Karaikal, indulged in smuggling to amass wealth, according to R.K. Tandon, the Indian consul general. It was admitted even by the Indian consul general that the ministers and other members of the Socialist Party were steeped in graft, smuggling and corruption and misused public funds. It was through this route that men of little means amassed huge wealth within a short period, building houses and buying motor cars.

From 1946, Muthu Kumarappa Reddiar entered business in a big way. He started to buy and sell oil engines. Later, he imported gold and diamonds with H.M. Cassime as an intermediary and was also partner in Muthu Alagananda Oil Mills. He also imported ten thousand tonnes of Cuban sugar and sold it in Pondicherry. He took to the moneylending business from 1950 to 1954. By his own admission, he had accumulated enormous wealth from his various business deals.[8]

As far as the organisation of the referendum was concerned, Goubert was unhappy that French Indians had not been sufficiently consulted. He also wanted the Indian and French governments to enter into a formal agreement regarding the future of French India before organising the referendum. In this, he toed almost the line of Saravane Lambert. He was also not sure if the Indian government would accept the verdict of the referendum if it favoured remaining in the French Union. He nevertheless subjected the holding of the referendum to the relaxation of the customs regulations by the Indian government.[9] However, it is quite surprising to note that Goubert who stood for safeguarding French Indian interests by all means, was willing to allow the French and Indian governments to thrash out a settlement without the participation of French Indians.

On 5 September 1950, Dr B.V. Keskar, Minister of the Indian

Government, opined that the verdict of a referendum under the present circumstances and conditions prevailing in Pondicherry and Karaikal would not be binding on the Indian government. N.V. Rajkumar, too, sang the same tune. Commissioner André Ménard and the French embassy in New Delhi were also not sure about the result of the referendum.[10]

A little earlier, Edouard Goubert, had been awarded the grade of Chevalier de la Légion d'Honneur for his services as chief registrar and councillor. Even his men like Muthu Poullé and Karunendra Mudaliar had been awarded the title of Chevalier de la Légion d'Honneur.[11] The French government decided to bestow such prestigious awards to Goubert and his men, knowing fully well that some of them were steeped in corruption. These medals were pinned on their chest during a public ceremony by none other than the French commissioner. This was deliberately done by the French government in order to keep Goubert and his men loyal to the French and the French Union. Goubert was even sent to Saigon by Commissioner Ménard to procure rice for Pondicherry during the economic blockade.

But Goubert was an extremely slippery customer. By January 1951, the French Ministry of Foreign Affairs realised that Goubert could switch sides and demand the integration of the French settlements with India. At that time, Goubert insisted on the re-organisation of the council of ministers. He wanted it to be invested with greater powers. He also wished that all the six ministers be elected by the French India Representative Assembly and the duty of allocation of portfolios to the ministers be vested with the leader of the party and not the commissioner. Of course, Ménard would have none of it and insisted on holding the referendum.[12]

In any case, the French government or the Pondicherry administration never minded the corruption prevailing in French India when Goubert's sway was absolute, probably because that was the custom that existed there since the introduction of democracy and the emergence of party politics under men like Nadou Shanmugham. This seems to suggest that the type of competitive democracy or the political and economic system introduced by the French spawned or had the potential to spawn corruption. Men who indulged in corruption since the time of Nadou Shanmugam upto Goubert were victims of this competitive system and environment, wherein there was a scramble for power. In this, they were mostly aided and abetted by the French establishment who had put the system in place.

On 17 June 1951, Goubert organised an election to send a deputy to the National Assembly in Paris. He himself contested the election against Lambert Saravane, who had founded the Republican Party. Saravane's popularity had waned by then. He demanded immediate merger without referendum. He also had his own *goonda* brigade to counter the ruffians of Goubert. Goubert won the election. Of the total number of votess which added up to 90,667, Goubert got 90,053 votes and Saravane obtained just 149 votes. It was admitted even in certain French circles that the elections had been rigged on a massive scale in favour of Goubert's party. Doubts lingered about Goubert's victory. But Saravane did not contest Goubert's victory. In fact, he did not have any conspicuous mass support in his favour. Neither did the French establishment contest the victory, as it was favourable to France. Goubert was considered by the French as the champion of the French cause at that juncture.[13]

Goubert just went once to the National Assembly to validate a vote. Otherwise, he was always in Pondicherry. He had consolidated his power. He had put his men at the head of all departments of the administration. He had control over the textile unions as well as the workers. He was all-powerful in the absence of a solid pro-French opposition which could be used by the French commissioner against him. Goubert literally thought that the French were at his mercy.

Using his position, it was believed, that Goubert and his men were making immense amounts of money through fraudulent or questionable means. The French administration, including the governors until then, had preferred to close their eyes on such activities of Goubert, thinking that Goubert being a Créole would not challenge French supremacy in the settlements.[14] At that moment, neither the French nor the Indian government could antagonise Goubert, who without any personal fortune to boot, was nevertheless solidly supported by rich merchants and landlords like Muthu Poullé and Muthu Kumarappa Reddiar. He also had the popular mandate. The merchants among others had enriched themselves by smuggling goods into India that included gold, diamonds, liquor, watches, bicycles, etc. In many ways, the future destiny of French India more or less depended upon the actions of Goubert. He was out of control of both the French and Indian governments. The French, though, decided to stick to their demand for referendum.[15]

Saravane was no more a force to be reckoned within Pondicherry politics. He was no more the deputy. His confrontation with Goubert had cost him a lot. The French dismissed him as a crypto-Communist. He had earlier put forward a project at the National Assembly by which the French and the Indian governments would first come to an agreement to transfer the territories to India and then organise a referendum asking the people to ratify the agreement.[16] This project was an ingenious method to solve the constitutional deadlock in Pondicherry. He did not, however, abandon the principle of referendum. His project was emulated later by others, including Jawaharlal Nehru.

R.K. Tandon was the consul general of India in Pondicherry at that time. He took note of the serious law and order situation prevailing in Pondicherry. Raphael Dadala, the sub-inspector of police in Pondicherry, established contacts with Sellane Naiker and Tandon. The French police chiefs, Bouhard and Lagisquet of Pondicherry, were suspicious of the anti-French activities of Dadala. Dadala resigned from his job as sub-inspector in September 1950 and fled to Cuddalore (an Indian territory bordering Pondicherry), on the advice of Sellane Naiker and R.K. Tandon, as claimed by none other than himself. He then founded a 'French India Liberation Volunteer Corps' to fight the police and the *goondas* of Goubert.[17] Dadala organised the resistance against the French regime and Goubert from Cuddalore and the outlying areas of Pondicherry. This seems to have created confusion and panic in Pondicherry. Dadala's intention was to get the referendum cancelled, as he was probably sure that the people at large would not vote to join India and because he feared that the referendum could be rigged as usual in favour of the pro-French elements in Pondicherry like Goubert. The consul general of India was accused of patronising Dadala.[18]

Since 1951 itself, Sellane Naiker had developed a certain animosity towards the high commissioner, R.K. Tandon. He was also against

Goubert. In 1951, Sellane had unsuccessfully approached Omandur Ramasamy Reddiar, the Chief Minister of Madras, on behalf of his merger committee asking him to intervene to further the cause of the merger. Already in early 1951, it seems that he had got the Cuddalore police arrest Saigon Rajamanickam, a Pondicherry labour union leader and the editor of the journal, *Urimai*. In 1952, Naiker wrote a letter to C. Rajagopalachari, the new Chief Minister of Madras, asking him to help the mergerists. Rajagopalachari curtly replied that he had no time or chance to think of such problems and that Sellane must take up the matter with Tandon and the External Affairs Department in Delhi.

At that time, the French government refused to grant amnesty to the rioters of Mahé. But the Indian government insisted that they should be allowed to vote in the ensuing referendum. Besides, the Government of India would not allow Goubert, the head of the Socialist Party, to have the control of the police.[19]

Tandon was subjected to severe criticism in some local pamphlets, tracts and newspapers like *Urimai*, as he continued the same policy as Rachid Ali Baig as far as the economic blockade was concerned. The papers, in fact, claimed that Tandon had prevented food items like rice entering Mahe, Karaikal, Yanam and even enclaves like Bahur, Kalapet and Tirubhuvanai. He was accused of rationing food like in India.[20] Tandon got rid of Pondicherrians like the pro-consul Papourayen, who was the right hand of his predecessors. Instead, he surrounded himself with nationalists like Ramanujam and Krishna Rao. Tandon communicated with several local personalities like Dorai Munisamy, Mariappan, Saravane and others. He did not accord much importance to local Congressmen like Sami Lourdes and La Hache of the National Liberation Front and R.L. Purushotthama Reddiar and Ansari Duraisamy of the National Congress of French India. Instead, he turned towards Sellane Naiker, Lambert Saravane, S. Perumal, Raphael Dadala, Venkatarama Iyer, and lawyer, Ambroise. These persons derided Goubert, who was in power, as the 'Créole dog' (*sattakara naaye*). But they feared Goubert nonetheless. They had no mass following.

Sellane Naiker and his assistants, Dadala and S. Perumal, operated from the frontier towards Cuddalore, while Lambert Saravane and his men like Gnana, Latour and Doréadjou controlled the roads to Madras at Mortandi and Mudharatravady. All these people were in contact with Tandon. They were financed most probably by the Indian collector of south Arcot and secretly by Tandon himself. They indulged in propaganda and vindictive actions against Goubert's Socialist Party and some of his men like Rajamanikam, editor of *Urimai* and president of the Workers' Federation of French India, and anti-Indians like Raouf Sahib of Villianur. Sellane was considered to be the number one enemy of the 'Whites', while Muthu Poullé, a majority of the Catholics and a fraction of Congressmen considered him to be sectarian. Raphael Dadala was a former policeman-turned-gang leader, while Venkatarama Iyer was furiously anti-Ashram and had actually been expelled from the institution which was controlled by Mirra Alfassa, due to his political activities.[21] The French considered Raphael Dadala as a 'deserter' and wanted him to be extradited. But Nehru as well as the Chief Minister of Madras Presidency, C. Rajagopalachari, did not pay attention to the French demand. Instead, Dadala, along with Sellane Naiker and advocate S. Perumal, submitted a memorandum to Nehru regarding the troublesome situation in Pondicherry under Edouard Goubert, asking him to intervene.[22]

All such activities of pro-mergerists infuriated the French very much. They wanted the United Nations to intervene in the matter as the atmosphere was increasingly becoming impossible to hold the agreed referendum due to the activities of forces ranging from Dadala and his gangs to Subbiah operating on the frontiers of Pondicherry and others like the pro-Indian Congress Party operating within Pondicherry.[23] The French probably thought that the United Nations would rule in their favour after conducting an inquiry in the French territories of India through a team of neutral observers. Thus, the French government wanted to internationalise the problem, instead of settling it bilaterally through talks and negotiations.

In response to the French petition, the International Court of Justice sent five neutral observers to ascertain the general situation including its economic and political aspects in the French territories of India. The Indian government, after some hesitation, agreed to receive these observers, though they were not obliged to do so.

However, the government also made it clear that their report would not be binding on them. The observers were Holgar Anderson of Holland, Baron Rodolpho Castro of Spain, Perreard of Switzerland, Mr Chan of Phillipines and Mr Krabbe of Denmark. They arrived in Pondi-cherry in March 1951.

After touring the various territories and gauging the situation prevailing there through field studies and interviews with various leaders and personalities of French India like the pro-French Edouard Goubert, Muthu Poullé, the mayor of Pondicherry and Pakkirsamy Poullé and also pro-mergerists like Léon Saint Jean of Karaikal, Shamsul Islam Sangam of Karaikal and Raphael Dadala, former inspector of police hailing from Yanam and accepting petitions from various organisations including the Pondicherry Youth Congress led by men like A. Arulraj and K. Karunanidhi, the observers' committee submitted a report. Goubert told the observers that there was no goondaism in Pondicherry and that he had crushed Communist terror. Muthu Poullé held that the Socialist Party was neither for nor against merger. Saravane, like the Congress, pleaded that merger should happen without referendum. The observers denounced the economic blockade imposed by the government of India to pressure the voters to opt for merger. They denounced the smuggling activities between Pondicherry and British India. They held that the elections so far held in Pondicherry were never fair or free. They finally claimed in their report that the general situation in French India was not conducive to holding a fair and impartial referendum.[24]

The French government did not accept the report, though it was on its own request that the international observers had made their visit. It was an error on their part to bring in foreign observers to mediate between India and France. It is noteworthy that the Indian government had earlier in 1948 asked for neutral observers during the referendum which was refused by the French government. Besides, the electoral rolls were revised without their presence, with the help of anti-merger government officials, in spite of the assurance given by the French government. It was held that, unless such drawbacks were rectified, the government of India need not honour the 1948 agreement. At that time, the secretary for foreign affairs in the Congress Party published a book called *French Pockets in India*. In this book, he retraced the history of the negotiations between the French and the Indian governments, before concluding in favour of a denunciation of the Agreement of 1948. He wanted first an agreement on the principle of transfer and then later the details could be worked out for a transfer without much difficulty.[25]

However, in spite of the report, the French government still harped on holding a referendum in Pondicherry to decide the issue of merger with the Indian Union. But the opinion of not holding the referendum had been gaining ground in Indian circles since 1949. Others asked for the revision of electoral rolls before organising the referendum. The Government of India wanted the quorum for the referendum to be fixed at 51 per cent, while the French wanted it to be 60 per cent.[26]

It should not be forgotten that the Government of Nehru, in the context of the Cold War between Communist Russia and the capitalist USA, had tilted somewhat towards the Soviet Union in international affairs through the Non-Aligned Movement. At the same time, Nehru's government dealt with the Communists, especially in south India, with great ferocity. They were hunted and suppressed. Subbiah being a Communist, the Indian government wanted to arrest him as well. He still had some following within Pondicherry, unlike Saravane or Sellane or the pro-mergerists of Karaikal like J. Xavery and Léon Saint Jean who were never all that active.

The Indian government realised that, of all the French Indian leaders, Subbiah alone could counter Goubert. So, it decided to prop him up in August 1951. The Indian government revised its attitude towards Subbiah as it needed more support to press forward its claim for the integration of French Indian territories with India, when Goubert's control over Pondicherry was absolute. The government of India abruptly cancelled the arrest warrant on Subbiah. But Subbiah still could not enter Pondicherry. Instead, he waged a relentless struggle against French rule from the border areas like Kottakuppam, while Dadala operated from Cuddalore.[27]

Thus, Subbiah was, thenceforth, free to move about in the frontier areas of Pondicherry in Indian territory and activate the movement against French rule. This was a headache for the French Indian government and Goubert, who hated the Communists. The move, however, had bolstered the pro-mergerists against Goubert and his party as well as the French government. Goubert was, of course, conscious of the fact that all leading Pondicherry leaders from Saravane to Sellane and then Subbiah had become pro-mergerists and that they had the support of the government of India. He realised that the pro-Indian forces were gaining in strength, while he remained isolated. He was the lone man fighting to remain with France, with some ambiguity, of course, in his stance. His associates like Muthu Poullé did not command the respect and sympathy that Goubert had among the people all over French India. His landlord associates like Muthu Kumarappa Reddiar or Vengadasubba Reddiar had influence only in their constitutencies. They did not wield any influence elsewhere. They were leaders because they were associated with Goubert. Without the latter, they could do nothing. Goubert himself was conscious of this fact. There was a rumour then that Goubert wanted to set up a pro-merger group with C. Balasubramanian, Muthu Poullé, Tetta and Léon Saint Jean to counter Subbiah.

The Communists had literally been pushed out of Pondicherry by then, as admitted by Goubert himself. They re-assembled under Subbiah in Cuddalore and Kottakuppam, near the Pondicherry frontier. The French Indian government had issued arrest warrants against him. But the Indian government would not arrest him, as they probably thought of using him against Goubert and the French.[28]

On 2 October 1951, the French Indian government under André Ménard and Edward Goubert banned the celebration of Gandhi's birthday and cancelled the public holiday on that day. Pro-Congress students in Pondicherry and Karaikal were infuriated by this act. They took out anti-government processions with Congress flags to condemn the move. Many were arrested. During that period, Doressamy Naiker, related to Sellane, was active in the Students' Congress.[29]

The Congress Party was extremely weak in Pondicherry. But in Karaikal it had a stronger presence under the leadership of Léon St Jean and J. Xavery. Nehru was not for a showdown with the French at that time. He preferred to wait. Many Pondicherry Congressmen, taking the cue from Nehru, chose not to contest in the ensuing elections for the Representative Assembly of Pondicherry against the Socialist Party of Goubert. They also did not want to ally with Lambert

Saravane, who was running his own little show and creating disorder on the frontier at Mortandi with the help of Indian police. Neither did they seek to ally with Sellane Naiker.[30]

The elections took place peacefully on 16 December 1951 in Pondicherry and the other French settlements, in spite of the attempts of Lambert Saravane, V. Subbiah, Sellane Naiker and other pro-Indian and pro-merger forces to disrupt it. But the pro-merger groups were not united. The Congress Party disliked Saravane. Subbiah moved towards the anti-Congress separatist Dravidian parties. The Socialist Party of Goubert won a spectacular victory unopposed in Pondicherry and its dependant territories. The 'nationalist' pro-merger parties had boycotted the elections for reasons of insecurity prevailing in the settlements. But it seems that they feared losing the elections, given the pro-French trend especially in Pondicherry and Karaikal.

The Socialist Party did not take any stand on the future of the settlements during these elections. Goubert won the elections nonetheless. Some of those elected then to the Representative Assembly from Pondicherry were C. Balasubramanian, H.M. Cassime, P. Danaraja, Gaudart, Arthur Dartnell and Virasamy Saguerre. From Karaikal, among those elected were S.M. Ibrahim Maricar and Aboubaker Siddhick Maricar, who were related to one another and Léon Saint Jean. The French, of course, were not happy with the election of H.M. Cassime in Pondicherry, as he was not educated in French, unlike his predecessor Haji Mohammad Ismail, who was a lawyer and minister well-versed in French. However, Muslims generally thought that they were under-represented in the Karaikal and Pondicherry communes.

According to a French report, this situation could not be remedied without the creation of separate electorates for the Muslims and attributing a fixed number of seats in the various councils for Muslims. The status of Free Towns, proposed earlier by François Baron, sought to grant reservations of seats to Muslims, which was opposed by the Congress and the Representative Assembly. Even the Christians were not enthusiastic about it, though it had the support of some groups like the 'Associatiion de la Jeunes Musulmane'. Some of the other influential Muslim personalities who supported the Free Town status for Pondicherry with separate electorates and reservation of seats were

K.E.M. Mohamed Ibrahim Maricar, Karaikal municipal councillor, O.A. Haniffa, director of the journal, *Balyan*, A.M. Salih Maricar, president-founder of the Muslim League of French India, M.M. Aly, president of the association 'Jeunesse Musulmane' of Karaikal and Salah Maricar, president of the association called 'Shamsul Islam' of Karaikal. However, in Pondicherry such demands were not forthcoming. For example, H.M. Cassime, keeping with his nationalist trend since the 1930s, never entertained such ideas, as far as I know of.

However, Goubert's power and that of his colleagues had been consolidated for another five years. Naturally, they preferred the status quo to continue so that they could focus on the governance of the territories. The lawyer, C. Balasubramanian, was to continue as the president of the Representative Assembly.[31] The French commissioner, Ménard, had nothing to worry about the absolute power of Goubert as the latter was not hostile to the French. Besides, Goubert's father was a Frenchman. However, Ménard doubted very much the continued allegiance of Goubert and his colleagues towards France at that juncture, probably due to the overwhelming power enjoyed by Goubert in French Indian politics and the increasing activities of Subbiah as well as Sellane's group at the borders. But, for reasons we do not know, he never tried to maintain a good relationship with Edouard Goubert. Instead, he maintained his distance from Goubert, without realising that if he handled Goubert in an appropriate manner, in spite of all his drawbacks, he could be of great use in maintaining the French Indian settlements within the orbit of the French Union. This was a strategic error on his part, and on the part of the French establishment at that time.[32]

ECONOMIC PRESSURE AND REFERENDUM

Many people had started to leave Pondicherry due to the insecurity and penury prevailing there since 1950. In 1951 alone, 5,000 tons of rice was imported from Indochina to meet the needs of Pondicherrians. An equal quantity was also imported from Burma. Besides, about 600 tons of wheat was imported from Pakistan, 7,000 tons of cotton mostly from Pakistan, 8,000 tons of coal from India, 1,150 tons of cement from India and England, and so on.[33] Later, the Indian authorities constructed barbed wire fences on the borders to prevent smuggling of gold and diamonds and imposed further restrictions such as licences and permits on transporting food items to Pondicherry. Even Indian currency was made unavailable in Pondicherry so that Pondicherrians could no longer buy any goods without exchanging French Indian money for Indian money by paying a commission. Essential goods could not be transported from Pondicherry to the other enclaves. The French commissioner, Ménard, wanted the French ambassador in New Delhi to protest against the government of India for violating French sovereignty in the territories by not allowing goods to be transported from Pondicherry to the enclaves.[34]

On 4 June 1952, Jawaharlal Nehru condemned the 'method of gangsters' prevailing in Pondicherry, which prevented the holding of a decent referendum. On 1 August, the Communist Party had defined its strategy to liberate Pondicherry. On 4 August 1952, a refugee conference was held at Cuddalore. In the same month, the French authorities with the concurrence of Goubert and his ministers banned the celebration of Indian Independence Day in French India.[35]

In March 1952, the French government had already rejected the customs union proposed by the Government of India. In July 1952, the French government had tried to open negotiations with the Indian government to find a solution to the economic problems of Pondicherry. In August 1952, Mr De Pimodan, delegate of the Ministry of French External Affairs who was sent to French India to study the economic situation, re-affirmed that the French Constitution did not permit any part of the French territories to dissociate from France without consulting first the will of the people of that territory.[36]

Very soon, the Indians radicalised their stand and started a violent campaign against the retention of 'colonial enclaves' in India. Even French police was attacked by Dadala's men in Bahur. Naturally, the French government feared that the Indian government would oppose the aerial connections with Indochina through Pondicherry. At that time, the French government still thought of transferring power gradually to the local executive, which would negotiate directly with the Indian government, on the basis of the agreement of June 1948. The French ambassador and the French commissioner in Pondicherry were in favour of this solution.[37] But Goubert was not aware of such thoughts doing the rounds in French circles, which would have put him in a very strong position to negotiate directly with Nehru with regard to the future of French India. But these thoughts were never translated into acts and never came to the notice of Goubert.

An all-party meeting was held in Cuddalore by certain nationalists and Communists at that time. Some Youth Congress members participated in it. Suddhananda Bharathiar, who was previously in the Sri Aurobindo Ashram, also took part in it. There was a French India Refugees Association established at Villupuram, with Murugasamy Clemenceau as president, and V. Nara and N. Ranganathan as secretary and vice-president, respectively. They adopted 16 resolutions at the meeting held in Cuddalore on 1 August 1952.

On 29 August 1952, some hooligans entered Sellane Naiker's house in Mahatma Gandhi Road (formerly Madras road), in front of *Amudhasurabhi* and shot at him. He escaped with two bullet wounds in his thigh. It seems that Saigon Rajamanickam, one of Goubert's men, led the attack. No action was taken against the culprits and Sellane Naiker himself retreated to Madras, without even lodging a police complaint. Prime Minister Nehru took note of the assassination attempt in Pondicherry. Nehru also extended his help to the refugees who were fleeing Pondicherry. Goubert was held accountable for the attempt on Sellane's life, as Rajamanickam was his man, though there was no evidence.[38]

But this attack, if at all orchestrated by Saigon Rajamanickam, seems to have been more personal than political, due to his arrest earlier in Cuddalore at the prodding of Sellane Naiker. At the same time, Antoine Maraidassou of the Students' Congress had asserted that Sellane Naiker was shot because he had some incriminating documents against Muthu Poullé and Edouard Goubert regarding their involvement in smuggling activities.[39] Whatever might be the truth, the Indian consul general, R.K. Tandon, was at the receiving end from some local quarters due to his ambiguous stand in Pondicherry politics during this period. It seems that he had a good relationship with Goubert and his associates at that time.[40]

Following the attack on Sellane Naiker, there was some commotion in Bahur. Some pro-merger workers were also forced to leave

French India leaving behind their belongings. Houses of pro-merger leaders in the French enclaves were attacked by *goondas* and there was an exodus of French Indians to Arcot. Among those who exited Pondicherry was also the editor of a frankly anti-Indian journal called *La République Française*, known as Jean Emmanuel Sarcey. Until October 1952, he was pro-French. But suddenly he switched sides and wanted the French settlements to join India. Earlier, in the elections to send a deputy to the French Parliament, he had not supported Goubert, the candidate who was backed by the government. It seems that goondas were unleashed against him by anti-mergerists, and he had to flee Pondicherry altogether. At that time, K. Todatry Ramanoudjadassane, a Left-leaning citizen of Pondicherry, wrote that the French presence in India was nothing more than a pure and simple occupation. This was reported in the Parisian newspaper, *Le Monde*.[41]

Meanwhile, Dadala, who had deserted the French police force, and his men, like Kichenane of Kottakuppam and Salam of Sultanpet, were harassing French Indians at Valavanur on the route to Villupuram and also at Kizhur. They appear to have attacked and injured French Indians travelling from one French enclave to another and to the Indian territory. The Indian consul general in Pondicherry defended Dadala and asserted that the refugees from Pondicherry were carrying on peaceful propaganda for merger in places like Vinayagapuram. On the other hand, Subbiah and the Communists were also present in the frontier areas like Valavanur. They disliked the activities of Dadala's men and complained that the Indian government was not taking action against him. They also said it did not address the real issues related to the future of the settlements. All the same, they did not respond favourably to the demand for the extradition of Dadala.[42]

As a matter of fact, since November 1951, there were 98 incidents in the frontier areas, in which one was killed and 70 were hurt. A pro-mergerist municipal councillor of Bahur, Venkatesa Padayachi, died in a Cuddalore hospital due to a wound reportedly caused by anti-mergerists. E. Thangavelu Gounder, deputy mayor of Bahur, asked the French to quit India without referendum. He was harassed by the police. He was the first person in Bahur region to boldly raise his voice against French presence in India.

Many of these incidents were caused by Dadala and his men. Dadala was dead against the trio which held Pondicherry, i.e., Goubert, Muthu Poullé and Muthu Kumarappa Reddiar, aside from their supporters like the senator, Pakkirisamy Poullé, and the minister, Sivasubramaniapoullé. Dadala and his men operated at the frontier from Bahur to Kottakuppam. Dadala was taking great personal risk in attacking, humiliating and threatening French Indians favourable to France. Among those attacked were municipal councillors and even police commandants. They included Sinnassamy Iyer, Chief of the police of Bahur. Some pro- and anti-French leaflets and anti-Indian leaflets were also distributed widely in Pondicherry during this period. On one side, Tandon was accused of being responsible for the arrest of Rajamanickam. On the other, he was accused of supporting Raphael Dadala and Lambert Saravane. Sinnasamy Iyer was also accused of manhandling pro-mergerists. But Subbiah who, too, harassed the French Indians, did not appreciate the activities of Dadala and his men. A record of all the atrocities committed against pro-mergerists since 1949 termed the 'Goonda raj in Pondicherry' was submitted to journalists in October 1952.

The Government of India, on its part, issued a communiqué on 26 October, citing 350 cases of aggression in the French settlements since 1951 with the complicity of the French police. It claimed that there was a criminal class of smugglers and *goondas* in the settlements. Besides, more than 1,000 families in Pondicherry and 80 per cent of the population of Mahé had sought refuge in Indian territory due to the regime of terror prevailing there. This situation had rendered the holding of the referendum impossible, according to the communiqué.[43]

On 5 October 1952, Subbiah united six pro-merger groups in Cuddalore to form a single group, with eight committee members. This group wanted the political parties of India to help them morally and materially to achieve their objectives. However, even Sellane Naiker did not join Subbiah, and he was left all alone to steer his way most of the time. Commissioner Ménard feared that if the French abandoned the Socialist Party, the Communists would get the upper hand once again in Pondicherry and the integration of French settlements with India would become unavoidable. This implied that the French should support Goubert whatever his excesses or failings.[44]

Due to continued organised arson and robbery in Pondicherry, Prime Minister Jawaharlal Nehru developed cold feet regarding the holding of referendum in French India. On 9 October 1952, he put an end to the 'plebiscite business' in Pondicherry. He made it clear before a gathering of 1,00,000 in Madras that the integration of the French settlements with India was non-negotiable. He also referred to the attack on Sellane Naiker during the meeting in Madras.[45] He later declared in the Council of States that India had no intention of declaring war on France over this issue. He averred that the only way forward was through negotiations. On 23 October 1952, Rajagopalachari, the influential Chief Minister of Madras, also opined that France had no alternative other than returning its territories to India. On 24 October, the embassy of India in Paris declared that the Indian government was no more bound by the agreement of 8 June 1948 to hold a referendum and that the principle of transfer of these settlements should be accepted first. Srikanta Ramanujam, president of the pro-merger movement in Karaikal, came out openly in support of the declarations of Nehru in Madras.[46]

Towards the end of December 1952, the French ambassador, Count d'Ostrorog, opined that France should not stick to judicial values, but should take into consideration the ground reality in Pondicherry, But the French establishment in Paris still held that there could be no transfer without a referendum, as it was a requirement of the French Consitution. Besides, they were annoyed at Nehru's continued insistence for Independence of the French colonies in Indochina and North Africa. They still believed that the territories could be part of the French Union. A French report of August 1952 brings out the fact that the French largely relied on the Christian and Muslim minorities, especially in Pondicherry and Karaikal, to counter-balance the Hindu bloc, made up of many immigrants. They still thought that the Muslim population was still loyal to France as they were since the days of Dupleix and Tipu Sultan. Besides, since August 1947 and the massacre of Muslims during the Partition of India, Muslims generally were favourable to remain in the French Union. They had made known this position to the body of neutral observers earlier. They had contributed a lot to the war efforts of De Gaulle. The French literally thought that they would win the referendum with the help of the Christians and Muslims. Besides, Goubert was still with them.

In the face of French intransigence in favour of respecting the Constitution regarding transfer of territories, the Government of India affirmed that it will maintain the cultural and other rights, including language, laws and customs, of the inhabitants of these territories. It added that any change in such and like matters would be made only with the consent of the people of these territories and that it would welcome the continuation of these territories as a Centre of French Language and Culture. It was also hoped that the French government would agree to open negotiations regarding the transfer of French territories to India. On its part, the Government of India refused to enter into negotiations to normalise economic relations between India and the French territories. It also refused to accept neutral observers to monitor the terror and tension prevailing in and around the French settlements.[47]

At the end of 1952, the French Ministry of Finance and the Overseas Ministry sent two of their agents, Mr Rivain and Mr Henry, to enquire into the economic situation in Pondicherry. They submitted a report stressing the need to restore the customs union under the prevailing conditions in order to solve the present economic difficulties, though there was the risk that a customs union would lead to political union with India. The report also said that a Franco-Tamil Cultural Centre in Pondicherry was out of question as it would face opposition from New Delhi, who feared Tamil separatism. Instead, it was suggested that the Alliance Française be developed in the main towns of India.[48]

In any case, by 1953, Mahé and Pondicherry had survived artificially due to the infusion of massive funds from France. Five million pounds sterling was pumped into Pondicherry to keep it afloat.[49] On 29 and 30 November 1953, two decrees issued by the French commissioner banned the exchange of Pondicherry rupees for Indian rupees and suspended temporarily all transactions in gold. Besides, the latest devaluation of *piastres* had rendered futile all monetary smuggling between Pondicherry and Saigon. Further, the attempt to make Pondicherry a free trade zone since 1949 was not practicable as Pondicherry was completely dependent on India for the supply of its essential commodities and its economic survival. Under these conditions, Mr Rivain wanted to restart the conversations between the Indian and French governments suspended for about six months.[50]

The balance of trade between French India and India was highly favourable to the latter, in spite of restrictions on Indian currency and the smuggling of French goods into India. It is nevertheless noteworthy that the amount of gold alone imported into French India and then smuggled to India was quite enormous. Local interests were involved in this smuggling.[51]

The suggestion of restoring the Customs Union would not find favour with certain local mercantile interests in Karaikal and Pondicherry enjoying the support of Goubert, who still represented Pondicherry in the French Parliament. Goubert was all powerful in Pondicherry. He enjoyed popular support and had his *goondas* and even the police under his control. He would not tolerate any measure that would undermine his personal influence. There was a widespread belief in Pondicherry at that time that Goubert and some of his colleagues and subordinates as well as many of his wealthy supporters like Muthu Poullé and Pakkirisamy Poullé made immense profits out of smuggling. Goubert was capable of plunging Pondicherry into chaos and anarchy if a measure was adopted against his interests. Not even the imposition of a duty of two to three per cent on gold imports and other restrictive measures by the French government could stop the smuggling.[52] The people of Pondicherry had, in general, benefited from the non-existence of the Customs Union since 1949. Their standard of living was superior to that of the people of the Indian Union. They were also largely pro-French. On no account would they want to alter this situation by restoring the Customs Union with India which, it was feared, would lead, ultimately, to the integration of French territories with India.[53]

During this period, Goubert was particularly favourable towards France and wanted the French Indian territories to remain as part of France. He even said that 2,000 Pondicherrians were fighting for France in Indochina against the Communists and that this number could be further increased. But for reasons that were unclear, the officials in the French embassy in New Delhi, including the Ambassador Count d'Ostrorog, were unfavourable towards Pondicherry and especially towards Goubert. The ambassador, who was on a tour of southern India, failed to visit Pondicherry, the capital of French India, where he could have met Goubert and discussed the situation with him and Commissioner Ménard. Instead, he preferred to ignore Pondicherry and Goubert, the strongman of Pondicherry, which was taken note of by the latter. Goubert actually felt slighted by the French ambassador, when the latter had had all the time in the world to mollify him and consolidate his pro-French line by just talking to him and giving him his due importance.[54] Goubert was the only power to be reckoned with inside Pondicherry at that time. Subbiah was banished. Sellane Naiker and Lambert Saravane did not command much of a following in Pondicherry and Karaikal. The Congress was inactive with not much popular backing. But the French ambassador, probably heeding the advice of Commissioner Ménard, somehow preferred to ignore Goubert. This was a real diplomatic blunder of the highest order, committed by the French ambassador and Commissioner Ménard, who still operated with a colonial frame of mind that looked down upon whatever that was indigenous. It did not matter if Goubert was a Créole with a French father. They simply did not want to deal with a so-called subordinate like him on the basis of equality.

Goubert was a sensitive man. He would not tolerate the condescending attitude of the French ambasador and Commissioner André Ménard towards him. In fact, Goubert got along better with his Indian colleagues than with his French counterparts. However, it is true that at that juncture Goubert kept his cards close to his chest that created doubts about his intentions regarding the future of French India in the minds of men like Ménard. This in spite of the fact, that Goubert on and off gave signals of his intention to remain in the French Union. Ménard remained a proud and haughty Frenchman who would not bend before Goubert who wielded absolute power and influence in Pondicherry and French India. Goubert, too, was a proud Pondicherrian who would not bend to please Ménard or act according to his wishes. Instead, he desired to strike out on his own in politics, which displeased many a Frenchman posted in Pondicherry from France.

NOTES

1. *Note pour le Séc Gén*, AO, 13 January 1950, p. 17, IF 71, ADP; Interview with A. Arulraj; *Lettre du Commissaire à Ministre de la France d'Outre-mer*, Pondicherry, 27 September 1950, pp. 208-10, IF 13, ADP.
2. *Ministère des Affaires Etrangères à Ambafrance*, Paris, 14 January 1952, p. 48, IF 71, ADP; *Statesman*, 3 August 1950; *Dinamani*, 31 October 1951; *Lettre d'Ostrorog au Ministère des Affaires Etrangères*, New Delhi, 28 November 1951, pp. 31-4, IF 71, ADP; Tél, Pondicherry, 30 November 1951, p. 42, IF 71, ADP; Ajit Neogy, *Decolonisation of French India*, Pondicherry, 1997, p. 168; *Franc-Tireur*, 19 January 1950.
3. *Lettre du Commissaire au Ministre de la France d'Outre-mer*, Pondicherry, 27 September 1950, pp. 208-13, IF 13, ADP; *Va. Subbiah Pavala Vizha Malar*, vols. II, III; S. Arumugam, 'Perumithathin Thiru Uruvam', *Va. Subbiah Pavala Vizha Malar*, 1988, pp. 93-7; Arumugam was a former secretary of the Communist Party of Pondicherry from 1948-50, close to V. Subbiah; *The Hindu* 14 January 1950; Lettre de Yves Chataigneau, Ambassadeur de France en URSS à Robert Schumann, Ministre des Affaires Etrangères, Moscou, 3 August 1950, pp. 10-11, IF 13, ADP; V. Nara, 'Varalatru Nayakanin Siraivasamum Thalaimaraivu Vazhkaiyum', *Va. Subbiah Pavala Vizha Malar*, 1988, pp. 117-18; N. Ranganathan, 'The Liberation Movement', talk at Pondicherry University on 29 May 1988, p. 4; V. Subbiah. 'Puduvaiyin Pazham Perum Varalatru Pinnani', *Suthanthiram Pon Vizha Malar*, 1987, pp. 37-41; R. Ramasrinivasan, *Karaikal in Freedom Struggle*, Karaikal, 1996, p. 96; V. Subbiah, *Puduvaiyin Viduthalaiai Vendradutha Thozhilalarkalin Veera Varalaru*, Pondicherry, 1986, p. 31.
4. *Note de M. Levi*, 10 January 1950, pp. 40-1, IF 12, ADP; *Le Monde*, 13 January 1950; *Note sur la Situation dans les EF des Indes*, s.d., IF 13, ADP; *Lettre du Commissaire au Ministre de la France d'Outre-mer*, Pondicherry, 27 September 1950, pp. 208-13, IF 13, ADP.
5. Rapport au Ministre de la France d'Outre-mer, Paris, 12 February 1953, pp. 159-60, IF 62, ADP; L'Attaché financier pour le Proche-Orient au Ministre des Finances, Beyrouth, 2 February 1953, p. 75, IF 62, ADP; *Réunion tenu, sous la présidence de M. Parodi, Séc. Gén. Ministère des Affaires Etrangères*, 8 November 1952, pp. 45-6, IF 62, ADP; *Tezenas du Montcel au Gouverneur*, 16 March 1949, *Affaires Politiques*, C 449, AOM; *The HIndu*, 24 February 1950.
6. *Note de M. Levi*, 10 January 1950, p. 37, IF 12; ADP; The French Ambassador Daniel Levi still thought that France could count upon Goubert

and his party to win the referendum; *Note Ministère des Affaires Etrangères*, Paris, 27 September 1950, p. 67, IF 13, ADP.
7. *Le Monde*, 19 August 1954.
8. *Jeunesse*, 15 June 1949; Interview with Paramel Shathrugnan; Critique du rapport de Paul Devinat, Deputé sur le projet tendant à autorisé le Président de la République Française à ratifier le Traité de Cession, 28 May 1956, p. 129, no. 326, AO 1956-67, ADP; Neogy, op. cit., pp. 189, 193; Details of the life of Muthu Kumaraappa Reddiar as dictated by him in February 1968 for C.S. no. 14/67; *Note sur Mouttousamy Poullé*—Inde H 22, AOM; *Note sur Colombani*, Pondicherry, 23 June 1945—Inde H 22, AOM; Interview with Joseph Goubert and M. Husain, late Kazi of Pondicherry; Interview with Doressamy Naiker, former student leader in the 1950s.
9. *Lettre du Ministre des Affaires Etrangères à Ministre de la France d'Outremer*, Paris, 8 March 1950, pp. 127-8, no. 40, ADP.
10. Téll de Christian Belle au Ministère des Affaires Etrangères, New Delhi, 1 June 1950, p. 59, no. 43, AO, ADP; *Note pour le Séc Gén*, AO, *Ministère des Affaires Etrangères*, Paris, 7 June 1950, pp. 63-7, no. 43, ADP; G. Samboo, *Les Comptoirs Français dans l'Inde Nouvelle de la Compagnie des Indes à nos Jours*, Paris, 1950, p. 132; *Tél de Belle au Ministère des Affaires Etrangères*, New Delhi, 30 May 1950, p. 58, no. 43, ADP.
11. JO 1950, p. 26.
12. Note, *Ministère des Affaires Etrangères*, Paris, 16 January 1951, pp. 176-7, IF 13, ADP; *Note d'Ambasadde de France sur la situation dans les EF des Indes*, New Delhi, AO, 1944-55, Inde fr, no. 43, pp. 101-10, ADP; Neogy, op. cit., p. 193; *Hindustan Times*, 22 May 1951.
13. *Franc-Tireur*, 13 May 1954; *Résultat des elections du Juin 1951 en IF*, p. 33, IF 69, ADP; Neogy, op. cit., pp. 170-1; Lettre du Commissaire au Ministre de la France d'Outre-mer, Pondicherry, 23 August 1951, Affaires Politiques, E 29, AOM.
14. *Note sur la Situation Financière et Économiqe à Pondichéry*, 24 January 1951, no. 53, AO, pp. 291-300, ADP.
15. Ibid.
16. *Le Parisien Libéré*, 24 April 1954; *Note d'Ambassade de France sur la Situation dans les EF des Indes*, New Delhi, AO, 1944-55, inde fr, no. 43, pp. 101-10, ADP; *Lettre d'Ostrorog au Ministre des Affaires Etrangères*, 17 January 1952, Confdl, no. 14, pp. 16-18, AO, ADP.
17. R. Dadala, *My Struggle for the Freedom of French India*, Pondicherry, n.d., pp. 12-13.
18. Ajit Neogy, *Decolonisation of French India. Liberation Movement and*

Franco-Indian Relations 1947-54), Pondicherry, 1997, p. 201; R. Dadala, op. cit., pp. 14-15; *Renseignements par le Chef d'Escadron Guyard, Commandant les Forces Publiques*, Pondicherry, 22 November 1952, no. 53, p. 307, ADP.

19. Copy of letter of Sellane Naiker as President of Pondicherry Merger Committee to the Chief Minister of Madras, Pondicherry, 21 July 1953; copy of letter of Chief Minister of Madras to Sellane Naiker, President, Pondicherry Merger Committee, Madras, 24 July 1952; V. Subbiah, *Saga of Freedom Movement: Testament of My Life*, Madras, 1990, pp. 300-1; Copy of pamphlet by Ku. Pajanisamy titled 'Sellane Sathi Thittam', *Puduvai*, 21 January 1951; *Procés-verbal de la Réunion du 28 Février 1952 au Ministère des Affaires Etrangères, sous la présidence de Robert Schuman*, no. 42, pp. 195, 199, ADP.

20. *Lettre de Tandon au Commissaire*, Pondicherry, 12 February 1951, p. 91, no. 4, AO, ADP.

21. Rapport du Capitaine Bouhard, commandant les forces publiques sur les activities de Tandon, 12 February 1951, no. 4, pp. 95-104, AO, ADP; *Copie de la traduction d'un tract intitulé 'Dire une chose et faire une autre'*, pp. 102-4 and *Copie de la traduction d'Extrait de l'Ourimai du 10 Février 1951*, pp. 105-7, no. 4, AO, ADP.

22. Dadala, op. cit., pp. 15-16; G. Chaffard, *Les Carnets Secrets de le Décolonisation*, Paris, 1965, vol. I, pp. 223, 228.

23. Dadala, op. cit., p. 16.

24. *Rapport de la delegation du Corps des Observateurs Neutres sur sa mission dans les EF de l'Inde du sud*, March-April 1951, IF 89, ADP; *The Hindu*, 9 May 1952; AO, 1944-55, nos. 44, 46-50 *et Rapport des Observaters Neutres*, April 1951, no. 45, AO, 1944-55, Inde fr. ADP; Embassy of India to Ministry of Foreign Affairs, Paris, 13 March 1951, p. 155, IF 13, ADO; Embassy of India to Ministry of Foreign Affairrs, Paris, 20 March 1951, 31 March 1951, no. 49, ADP.

25. *French Pockets in India*, Madras, 1952; Embassy of India to Ministry of Foreign Affairs, 3 February 1950, IF 42, ADP.

26. AO à l'Ambassade de l'inde, 30 January 1952, IF 42, ADP; AO, 1944-55, Inde fr. no. 43, pp. 126-31, ADP; *Hindustan Times*, 28 October 1951; *Indian News chronicle*, 27 October 1949; *Libération*, 10 January 1950.

27. *Makkal Thalaivar Va. Subbiah Pavala Vizha Malar*, vol. III; Dadala, op. cit., pp. 18, 47; Neogy, op. cit., p. 191.

28. *Note sur la Situation Financière et Économiqe à Pondichéry*, 24 January 1951, no. 53, AO, pp. 291-300, ADP; Neogy, op. cit., pp. 192.

29. Interview with Antoine Mariadassou, Paul Radjanedassou et Doressamy Naiker.
30. *Lettre du Commissaire au Ministre de la France d'Outre-mer*, Pondicherry, 22 December 1951, AO, Inde française 1944-5, no. 14, pp. 7-8, ADP.
31. Ibid., no. 14; EF de l'Iinde, Election à l'Assemblée Répresentative, 16 December 1951, pp. 39-47, IF 69; Texte d'un tél, Pondicherry, 8 December 1951, p. 46, IF 71, ADP; Revendication de la Communauté Musulmane de Karikal, 1952—Aff. Pol. Carton 2274, Dossier 10, AOM; Lettre no. 22, 31 January 1952, *Karikal par les Notables Musulmans à Monsieur le Ministre de la France d'Outre-mer*, Paris—Aff. Pol. Carton 2274, Dossier 10, AOM.
32. *Lettre d'Ostrorog au Ministre des Affaires Etrangères*, 17 January 1952 (confld), no. 14, pp. 16-21, ADP; *Ambasadeur de France en Grande Bretagne à Robert Schuman*, London, 21 December 1951, p. 223-4, IF 13, ADP; *Times*, 21 December 1951.
33. *Discours prononcé le 29 Mars 1952 à l'Assemblée Représentative, par Ménard, Commissaire*, pp. 40-5, IF 89, ADP.
34. *Télégramme d'information, Service d'Information de l'Inde*, 2 April 1952, p. 51, no. 14, ADP.
35. *Tél du Ministre des Affaires Etrangères à AmbaFrance*, Paris, 5 June 1952, no.14, p. 66, AO, ADP; French authorities ban Indian Independence Day Celebrations, p. 58, IF 70, ADP; *Commissaire à Ministre de la France d'Outre-mer*, Pondicherry, 12 August 1952, p. 55, IF 70, ADP; Note sur la situation financière et économique à Pondichéry, 24 Janvier 1951, no. 53, AO, pp. 291-300, ADP; Crossroads, no. 9 du 6 July 1952, pp. 47-52, IF 69, ADP; Télégramme d'Information—Service d'Information de l'Inde, 2 April 1952, no. 14, p. 51, ADP.
36. Pondicherry, 20 August 1952, Reuter, no. 14, p. 188, AO, ADP.
37. *Lettre du Ministre de la France d'Outre-mer au Ministre des Affaires Etrangères*, Paris, 18 August 1952, p. 57, IF 71, ADP; *Lettre du Ministre des Affaires Etrangères au Ministre de lma France d'Outre-mer*, Paris, 8 October 1953, no. 15, p. 108, AO, ADP; Note AO, 10 April 1952, no. 14, pp. 56-7, ADP; Asie Océanie Note, 13 January 1953, pp. 14-15, no. 15, ADP.
38. 'Pirachinthiya Akathikal Maanatu Theermanankal', Villupuram, 1952; *Tél d'Ostrorog au Ministre des Affaires Etrangères*, New Delhi, 30 August 1952, p. 59, IF 71; R. Dadala, op. cit., pp. 21-2; *The Hindu*, 31 August 1952; *Pallava Nadu*, 15 May 1954; M. Padmanabhan, pamphlet, December 1954.
39. Interview with Antoine Mariadassou.

40. *Memorandum remis à Titre officieux par M. Mehta à M. Jean Roux*, 3 September 1952, no. 14, p. 95, ADP.
41. *Le Monde*, 6 November 1952; Terrorism in French Indian territory, AO, no. 14, p. 104, 29 September 1952, ADP; Inde Télégramme d'Information, Service d'Information de l'Inde, 4 November 1952, no. 14, p. 196, AO, ADP.
42. *Le Ministre de la France d'Outre-mer répond à Nehru*, Paris , 22 October 1952, no. 14, p. 147, AO, ADP; *Declaration faite par le Ministre de la France d'Outre-mer devant la Commission des Territoires d'Outre-mer de l'Assemblée Nationale*, 22 October 1952, no. 14, pp. 165-8, ADP; *Renseignements du 22 November 1952 par le chef d'escadron Guyard, Commandant des Forces Publiques*, Pondicherry, 22 November 1952, p. 307, no. 53, ADP; Commissaire au Ministre de la France d'Outremer, Pondicherry, 25 November 1952, p. 308, no. 53, AO, ADP; Note from Consul General, Pondicherry to Commissioner, Pondicherry, 10 September 1952, p. 4, no. 1, AO, ADP; *Lettre du Comissaire à Conseil Général de l'IF*, Pondicherry, 21 October 1952, pp. 12-17, no. 1, AO, ADP; *Le M.D.L. chef Sinnasamu Iyer, chief of police, Bahur à M. Le Lt. à Pondichéry, Bahur*, 11 September 1952, p. 72, IF 71, ADP.
43. *Memorandum remis à titre 'officieux' par M. Mehta à Jean Roux*, 3 September 1952, p. 95, no. 14, ADP; *Projet de Note à l'Ambassade de l'Inde, 5 November 1952, et Liste des Incidents survenus depuis fin Novembre 1951 entre franco-Indiens et Indiens*, Pondicherry, 18 October 1952, no. 14, pp. 227-40, ADP; *Indian Express*, 30 June 1952; Embassy of India, Paris, 17 December 1952, no. 14, p. 334, ADP; Note, Embassy of India to Ministry of External Affairs, Paris, 13 October 1952, p. 79, IF 71, ADP; Document remis aux Journalistes, New Delhi, 16 October 1952, pp. 98-103, IF 71, ADP; List of incidents of goondaism in Pondicherry, from 1 July to 31 October 1952, p. 112, IF 71, ADP; *The Hindu*, 24 September 1952; *Le Monde*, 24 October 1952; Cf. *Communiqué du Gouvernment Indien sur la Situation dans les Établissements Français de l'Inde*, 26 November 1952, *Affaires Politiques*, C 445, AOM.
44. *Gendarmerie Auxiliare Indienne—Plainte contre Dadala et Consorts*, Pondicherry, 12 September 1952, p. 75, IF 71, ADP; Note, Embassy of India to Ministry of Foreign Affairs, Paris, 13 October 1952, p. 79, IF 71, ADP; *Tél d'Ostrorog au Ministre des Affaires Etrangères*, New Delhi, 13 October 1952, p. 134, no. 14, AO, ADP; *Lettre du Commissaire au Ministre de la France d'Outre-mer*, Pondicherry, 30 June 1952, *Affaires Politiques*, Inde E 30, AOM.
45. *The Hindu*, 31 August, 11 October 1952; A. Ramasamy, *History of*

Pondicherry, Delhi, 1987, p. 166; Dadala, op. cit., pp. 21, 47; *Indian Express*, 22 October 1952; *The Voice*, 31 August 1955; *Déclaration de Nehru à Madras*, 9 October 1952, no. 14, p. 118, ADP.

46. *La Question des Établissements français en Inde*, Madras, 23 October 1952, Reuter, no. 14, p. 146, ADP; *Tél d'Ostrorog à Ministre des Affaires Etrangères*, New Delhi, 27 November 1952, no. 14, p. 303, AO, ADP; *Times of India*, 28 November 1952; Madras, 29 October 1952, Reuter, p. 206, no. 14, AO, ADP; Embassy of India, Paris, 24 October 1952, pp. 151, ADP.

47. Embassy of India, Note, Paris, 16 December 1952, no. 14, pp. 318-21, ADP; *Tél du Ministre des Affaires Etrangères à AmbaFrance*, New Delhi, 18 December 1952, p. 358, ADP; *Tél d'Ostrorog au Ministre des Affaires Etrangères*, New Delhi, 6 October 1952, pp. 122-3, ADP; *l'Aurore*, 23 October 1952; *Indian Express*, 17 October 1952; *Revendication de la Communauté Musulmane de Karikal*, 1952—Aff. Pol. Carton 2274, Dossier 10, AOM.

48. AO, Note, 4 May 1953, no. 15, pp. 55-60, ADP.

49. Ibid., *Note Asie Océanie, Affaires Etrangères*, 4 June 1953, pp. 62-5, ADP.

50. Ibid.

51. Embassy of India, Paris, *Aide Mémoire*, 31 March 1952, no. 14, pp. 48-9, ADP; *Indian Express*, 6 August 1953; Lettre du Commissaire au Ministre de la France d'Outre-mer, Pondicherry, 7, 22 December 1951, *Affaires Politiques*, E 29, AOM; Elections, *Circonscription de Pondichéry*—Inde Série G 8, AOM.

52. *Note sur EF de l'I'Inde*, Pondicherry, 30 November 1952, pp. 223-4, IF 65, ADP; Note of Embassy of India to Ministry of Foreign Affairs, Paris, 16 June 1952, pp. 160-1, IF 65, ADP; Note, 6 July 1953, AO, no. 15, pp. 70-3, ADP; Note sur Pakkirisamy Poullé—Inde H 22, AOM.

53. *Tél Affaires Etrangères à Ambafrance*, Paris, 8 June 1952, no. 14, AO, pp. 72-3, ADP; Note AO, 28 October 1952, no. 14, p. 177, ADP.

54. *Note pour le Séc. Gén. Affaires Etrangères*, Paris, 8 July 1953, no. 15, pp. 77-8, ADP.

CHAPTER 9

Towards Integration

EVENTS LEADING UP TO GOUBERT'S VOLTE FACE

In January 1953, Pastor Boegner, the representative of the Protestant churches in France, conveyed the message of the French president Vincent Auriol to Prime Minister Nehru, which stipulated that, according to the French constitution, no transfer of any territory could take place without ascertaining the wishes of the French citizens of that territory. But Nehru insisted that the *de facto* situation in Pondicherry be first accepted, while the *de jure* transfer could take place later after a plebiscite. He added that India had benefited from its close relationship with Anglo-Saxon culture for 150 years and there was therefore, a similar need for the maintenance of French culture in Pondicherry. He told Boegner that it was in order to acquire French culture that he had sent his daughter to study in Geneva, while he himself could also read and understand French. He, however, dismissed the idea that Pondicherry was a haven of democracy. Instead, he felt that all sorts of pressures were at play there that vitiated the democratic atmosphere. On his part, the ambassador of France in India, Count d'Ostrorog, admitted that his views were congruent with Boegner's.[1]

In some quarters, opinion was gaining ground at that time that the imperialist presence in the sub-continent through such enclaves where Nato bases could come up was a danger to India. However, the French government denied that Pondicherry would be used for strategic purposes. In the meantime, the war in French Indochina against Communist forces since 1946 had intensified and had cost France about 1900 crores of rupees until 1952. A contingent of 28,000 French troops were sent to Indochina, which included a few hundred

Pondicherrians, out of whom more than 1,000 had died. Besides, French power was being increasingly challenged in North Africa.[2]

At that time, it was also being wondered in some quarters as to why France clung to its minuscule territories in India which were of no economic value to it, and which were in fact costing it a lot financially.[3] As a matter of fact, Pondicherry was being artificially kept afloat with the help of massive aid from France to the tune of five million pounds sterling per year. Goubert was well aware of the economic pressure being exerted by the Indian Union on the French settlements. Whether France would be in a position to bail out French India permanently from the economic crisis in which it was steeped must have been a question mark on the minds of many Pondicherrians including Edouard Goubert. Earlier, the French chargé d'affaires in Delhi, Henri Roux, had considered it impossible and suggested the integration of the French territories with India. The report of M. Rivain of the Ministry of Foreign Affairs and the opinion of Mr Henry of the Ministry of Overseas France supported the setting up of a Customs Union to solve the economic problems of Pondicherry, in spite of the fact that France had refused to enter into a Customs Union with India just a few months ago in July 1952, fearing that it would lead to political union of Pondicherry with India.

Besides, it was feared that Goubert, who was all powerful in Pondicherry, would react violently if France agreed to enter into a Customs Union with India, as this would be against his personal interests and the interests of his merchant friends. Goubert himself was surprised that the French ambassador, Count d'Ostrorog, who had visited Mysore lately, had failed to visit Pondicherry, possibly fearing the authorities in Delhi. Goubert was still attached to France at that time. As for Commissioner Ménard, he wanted the installation of a radio station in Pondicherry to counter the Indian propaganda.[4] Thus it was clear at that juncture that the policy of the French establishment was to pursue the agenda of referendum to decide the future of French India, while Nehru insisted that the *de facto* transfer could take place before a plebisicite was held for the *de jure* transfer of power to the Indian Union.

There was a serious incident on the frontier of Pondicherry on 20 February 1953 in which a French Indian policeman was killed and a pro-Indian leader Tulasingam, secretary of the Merger Volunteers Dal, was arrested.[5] But Sellane Naiker accused Indian consul general, R.K. Tandon, of not actively supporting the merger movement. He accused Tandon of flirting with the 'smugglers and other French stooges', meaning Goubert and his partymen, instead. Naiker blatantly accused Tandon of having succumbed to 'certain temptations' of Pondicherry (like alcoholic drinks, etc.) under the influence of reactionary elements like Goubert and his partymen. He wrote a long letter to Prime Minister Jawaharlal Nehru asking him to replace Tandon with someone who would support the genuine mergerists. Nehru acknowledged receipt of this letter through N.R. Pillai, the secretary at the Ministry of External Affairs. This letter, however, demonstrated that Tandon was in constant touch with the Socialist Party leaders, including Goubert, during his tenure, probably with the intention of co-opting Goubert into supporting the merger.

At that time, Sellane Naiker also sent a memorandum to the Government of India on behalf of the French India Central Merger Committee on how to solve the problem of French India. In this memorandum, Sellane asked Jawaharlal Nehru to impose a total blockade of the French settlements, which would result in famine and starvation that would push the pro-French leaders like Goubert to opt for merger.[6]

In March 1953, a public meeting was held at Schoelcher Square (Odiansalai) of Pondicherry. It was presided by Nandagobalou, mayor of Mudlaiarpet. Saigon Rajamanickam, known for his pro-Goubert leanings, also spoke in this meeting. The meeting did not want integration of the French territories with India through force or pressure. It accused the government of India of offering help and protection to Communist 'bandits' who heckled French citizens. They also observed that north Indian merchants had penetrated Pondicherry and accused the 'outsiders' of carrying out smuggling activities there, contributing to the crisis of Indian currency in Pondicherry. Saigon Rajamancikam maintained that 95 per cent of the smugglers were not French citizens.[7] This statement implied that Pondicherrians were not numerous in the smuggling circuit.

In any case, the balance of trade was in India's favour during this period and there was free movement of Indian currency in the settlements, though there existed some smuggling. In 1950-1, it was Rs. 28.5 lakhs, in 1951-2 Rs. 52.2 lakhs, and in 1952-3 it was Rs. 73.8 lakhs.[8]

In July 1953, the French Foreign Ministry sent Pierre de Pimodan to study once again the economic situation in French India. He ended up declaring that the French Constitution did not permit cession of French territories without the consultation of the people living in those territories. In August 1953, a report by André Louis Gaebelé, a relative of Goubert, labelled Goubert and his men as 'gangsters' who had amassed millions of francs through illegal means, like trading contraband, with the indirect connivance of Commissioner André Ménard, as the latter had done nothing to counter them.[9] This report coming from a Frenchman of Pondicherry lent credibility to the rumour that Goubert and his associates were indeed involved in corruption and smuggling. Also that Commissioner Ménard tolerated them, either because Goubert was still pro-French in his policies or because he feared antagonising him and his men at that juncture, though he had his own misgivings and doubts about his true intentions, as seen earlier. It was at this time that the Representative Assembly opposed successfully the French Indian government's attempts to levy more taxes on the people to redress the economic and financial woes of the territories. This showed once again that Goubert's party was not a camp follower of the French establishment. Muthu Kumarappa Reddiar came down heavily on the French India government and declared that the French monetary and fiscal policies had ruined the French Indian economy.

Ménard then seems to have developed sympathy for André Gaebelé, whom he encouraged to set up the French Indian Labour Party in order to counter Goubert and his Socialist Party. It seems that Goubert unleashed his *goondas* then against the supporters of this party. But the rift between Ménard and Goubert was becoming increasingly clear. Be that as it may, the choice of André Gaebelé by Ménard at that juncture to counter Goubert proved to be a failure in the course of time.

As for establishing a French cultural centre in Pondicherry, a report by H. Deschamps ruled out a Franco-Tamil centre as it would not be welcome in Delhi.[10] It was also opined that while Britain had lost India, they had gained the respect and friendship of the subcontinent, unlike France which, by retaining its colonies in India, was compromising Indian support to it in international affairs.[11]

It was at that time that André Morisset, an old student of the Ecole Polytechnique and son of Mirra Alfassa, the Mother of the Sri Aurobindo Ashram, provided some details of the situation in Pondicherry to Maurice Schumann, member of the French Parliament. The second part of his note had mentioned the position of the Congress Party which wanted the transfer of the administration to the Government of India, even while France could retain sovereignty, but only till a final solution was arrived at by negotiations. The note also suggested that the settlements could form an autonomous unit in India, but follow a new paradigm of citizenship under which the residents would be enjoying, partly or wholly, the privilege of both Indian and French nationalities. By all accounts, it seems that the latter was the position of the Ashram, while the former was that of Nehru, Gandhi and the Congress Party.[12] Thus it is clear that the Sri Aurobindo Ashram authorities, under the guidance of Mirra Alfassa had a political agenda in Pondicherry and still held the idea of double nationality or dual citizenship for the French Indians close to their hearts. It is worthwhile to note at this juncture that Edouard Goubert had never been intimate with the Ashram and its objectives and had always steered clear of its dominant figure, Mirra Alfassa.

On 18 September 1953, Nehru declared in Parliament that the French enclaves in India were dens of intrigue and smuggling. He said that the Indian government would take measures to ameliorate this situation.[13]

On 18 and 19 October 1953, a coordinating committee of movements in favour of the integration of the French settlements with India met in Bombay. D. Jeevarathinam of Pondicherry, and C.E. Barathan and I.K. Kumaran of Mahé participated in it.[14] At that time, a Frenchman, Henri Jacquier, was elected to represent French India in the French Union Assembly, with the help of Goubert's men like Muthu Poullé and Muthu Kumarappa Reddiar. Jacquier opposed the policy of customs and economic integration with India, as it would lead to annexation in a short period. Local newspapers were quite critical of this election. They said that even after 250 years of French domination, the democratic institutions of Pondicherry were not able to designate an Indian as representative. But Goubert's men supported Jacquier. Their intention to get him elected to the French Union Assembly showed that they, including Goubert, had still not turned their back on the French Union. Besides, electing a 'white' Frenchman even after Indian Independence also showed that Goubert and his men did not adopt a racial approach in electing representatives of French India, even as late as 1953. But somehow this escaped the attention of both Commissioner Ménard and Ambassador Ostrorog.[15]

In November 1953, the French India government imposed a six per cent tax on essential food items. Traders refused to pay this tax. It also prohibited all transactions in gold through a decision adopted on 30 November 1952. On its part, the Indian government threatened to cut off water supply for irrigation and also electricity which came from Mettur under the Franco-Indian convention of 3 December 1943 which was valid for 10 years. The thermal power station established earlier in Pondicherry was old and insufficiently geared to fulfil the needs of Pondicherry. The delivery of parcels to Pondicherry was also stopped. However, the quasi-dictatorship of Goubert and his men continued as it was felt in French circles that some of them might be tempted to opt to join India very soon. Besides, Goubert and his men like Muthu Poullé and Muthu Kumarappa Reddiar controlled the market and public life of Pondicherry and made huge personal fortunes. This had been substantiated with clairity by Ajit Neogy in his work, *Decolonisation of French India.*[16]

In December 1953, Tandon was replaced by Kewal Singh, a senior member of the ICS as the consul general of India in Pondicherry. A farewell party was organised for Tandon, in which all the leading lights of Pondicherry were present. Strangely, Sellane Naiker, who had earlier asked for Tandon's recall, pronounced the vote of thanks in his favour.[17]

Even as the situation was thus in French India, the president of France, Vincent Auriol, still believed in the idea of French Union. He pronounced the following words at the assembly of the French Union:

I had a dream. . .

My dream was that during the 14th of July . . . we can witness a solemn procession of all the kings, and all the heads of state of the associated states or protected states, the representatives of the local Assemblies and territories, the indigenous chiefs—a procession without distinction of race and religion, demonstrating to all French people that France is not restricted to our native lands alone, but it envelops the whole world with its culture, arts, its efforts, its sacrifices, its radiance and its thoughts.[18]

But Vincent Auriol's dream was obviously out of step with his times, as events that were unfolding the world over would prove. A week later, C. Rajagopalachari declared that there were 1,400 refugees from French India (including 400 women and 200 children). He claimed, therefore, that the issue had become an international problem.[19]

On 8 January the same month, during a 12-party conference at Cuddalore, the French India Central Merger Congress was formed with veteran Sellane Naiker as president, under the general secretaryship of S. Lakshmanaswamy Reddiar. The other office-holders of this organisation were J. Xavéry (Karaikal), vice-president, Gnanou Ambroise and S. Perumal, secretaries, Dorai Munisamy, treasurer, and D. Jeevarathinam, S. Lakshmanaswami Reddiar, R.M.A.S. Venkatachalapathi Poullé and R. Dadala, members. They entertained the Indian consul general, Kewal Singh.[20] Later, discussions took place between the merger congress leaders like Sellane and Dadala and the Socialist Party leaders like Venkataswamy Reddiar, mayor of Thirubhuvanai, and P.A. Rathinam Chettiar, mayor of Madagadipet, to create a common front for the liberation of French India.[21]

But it seems that, at the beginning of 1954, there was a sizeable decrease in the revenue got from leasing arrack and toddy shops, in spite of an increase in its consumption, especially in the case of toddy. All fingers pointed at Goubert and his colleagues for this unusual happening. A first report was made against the associates of Goubert in February 1954. We do not know if this action infuriated Goubert and pushed him to radicalise his stand against the French in the subsequent month. But anyhow there was no follow-up action to the preceding report. Goubert asked for the recall of André Ménard. Ménard, in his turn, accused Goubert of embezzlement and opening secret communications with the Indian government. By then, stringent measures adopted by the Indian government had reduced the incidence of smuggling from French to British India. This was disadvantageous to the Pondicherry merchants and politicians, who had so far benefited from it.[22]

On 9 January 1954, Lambert Saravane released a statement highlighting the historical necessity for French India to join the Indian Union. He welcomed the growing mass support for merger in Pondicherry among certain political parties under Sellane Naiker. He wanted France to show its statesmanship by first recognising the principle of transfer of sovereignty of French India to the Indian Union and then entering negotiations with the government of India for that purpose. He dismissed the Socialist Party for deriving its strength from the colonial administration and not from the masses. He blamed the anti-merger elements who controlled the distribution of rice in Pondicherry for its shortage. He did not believe in a referendum as it would not be fair according to him. He also wondered why the French clung to these territories as they had no economic or strategic value.[23]

The French had been expecting some more stringent economic measures against their territories by the Indian government. They had not resumed negotiations since the denunciation by the Indian government of the June 1948 Agreement on 24 October 1952. They were, however, aware that the French settlements were vulnerable as they depended materially on the Indian Union. Since 14 January 1954, there was no electricity in the French enclaves of Pondicherry as the Indian government disallowed the usage of its territory to transmit electricity from Pondicherry town to the enclaves. This particularly affected the agricultural land, as the motor-driven pumps which supplied water to it did not work without electricity. Besides, the Indian government did not renew the agreement of 3 December 1943. Further, the lack of petroleum imports threatened the functioning of the electric plant in Pondicherry. The Indian government continued to complain about the smuggling of gold and precious stones into its territory from Pondicherry and pressed for a customs union.[24]

GOUBERT'S VOLTE FACE AND AFTER

In any case, it was on 5 March 1954 that Edouard Goubert organised a grand demonstration in Pondicherry, in favour of the merger. This completely contradicted his traditional stand. It was Goubert who had single-handedly prevented the French settlements from joining India through various means, including goondaism and the connivance of the French police and administration in order to silence his opponents. But in no way could one assert that Goubert did not have mass support too, especially in Pondicherry, as others, including Sellane or Subbiah or even the Congress Party, did not command much of a following in Pondicherry, especially at that time. The French still wanted to hold a referendum, while the Indian government had backed out from it because they were unsure of winning it against the power and influence wielded by Goubert. Such a man needed to be cajoled, buttressed and patronised by the French authorities. But of late, Ménard and Ostrorog were seen increasingly taking positions against him. This was a monumental error of policy committed by them. It is what pushed Goubert to connive with his close associates in order to defeat the designs of the French. The French probably thought that Goubert would never revolt against them as he was a Créole. But Goubert's volte-face had put Ménard and the French government in a very difficult position, wherein they had to find a solution without effusion of blood if they did not want to exacerbate the situation.[25]

In early March 1954, some workers of the textile mills paraded the streets of Pondicherry shouting anti-French slogans and demanding a merger. The police manhandled them. Three of their leaders who were in favour of merger were arrested. As many as 1,800 workers out of 4,000 were dismissed from their jobs at Rodier Mill. This was the time when André Ménard returned from France after obtaining some grants amounting to 5 million rupees from Paris to cover the budget deficit. Meanwhile, the Indian government considered reinforcing control on circulation of its currency between the French settlements and Indian territory.[26]

On 7 March 1954, Goubert, Karunendra Mudaliar and Sivasubramania Poullé did not participate in the council of ministers meeting, presided over by the commissioner who announced a grant of 1.5 crore rupees from France for development works in French India. At that crucial moment, Muthu Poullé and Pakkirisamy Poullé tried to patch up the differences between Goubert and Commissioner Ménard. Goubert then held talks with Kewal Singh in Madras. He was joined by Karunendra Mudaliar, Muthu Kumarappa Reddiar, Deivasikamani and P. Danaraj.[27] This showed that Goubert had came under increasing influence of landlords like Muthu Kumarappa Reddiar and Karunendra Mudaliar, who on their own did not have much political clout among the Pondicherry people. Goubert himself did not have the aristocratic lineage of a landlord. He belonged to the professional class. And he needed a sound financial backing at that time, which the landlords could provide. So it seems that he did not heed the advice of his close associates like Muthu Poullé and Pakkirisamy Poullé to patch up with the French commissioner and went ahead and radicalised his stand.

On 16 March 1954, Goubert's henchmen Bhupathi and Sandanasamy were arrested by the French police. They were accused of interfering in the auctions that took place for the sale of palm oil in Pondicherry. The mayor of Mudaliarpet, Mr Nandagopal, was arrested along with two Indians in the Indian village of Kattupalayam by French police. Since their arrests, the Indian government prohibited the usage of their territory to access the French enclaves cut off from Pondicherry.[28]

Consequently, on 19 March 1954, Edouard Goubert and four ministers of the French India government declared during a press conference that the French Indian settlements should be merged with the Indian Union without any referendum. They pointed out that a resolution was adopted by the municipal councils of eight communes demanding such a merger. Some of signatories of this resolution were Muthu Poullé, Edouard Goubert, H.M. Cassime, Virasamy Saguerre, C. Balasubramanian, Vengadasubba Reddiar, Muthu Kumarappa Reddiar and Karunendra Mudaliar. Six municipalities of Karaikal, too, adopted a similar resolution. Goubert affirmed that the French Indian Cabinet would meet by 27 March to demand such a merger unanimously and that their decision 'was irrevocable, whatever might be the consequences'. He added that the commissioner, André Ménard, had no right to dissolve the cabinet without a special decree from France.[29] Even the Socialist Party of France came out in favour of integration at that time.[30]

It is noteworthy that Goubert was still court registrar at that time.[31] The French believed that Goubert took an anti-French stand because Ménard had planned a judicial inquiry into the corrupt activities of

Goubert and his men which had cost the treasury 15,000,000 francs. Earlier, Goubert had unsuccessfully tried to get Ménard replaced using his influence in France. Goubert wanted Ménard to be replaced by Yves Perrier, the former administrator of Mahé who was his Créole relative. But the French government, as well as the French ambassador, Count d'Ostrorog, would not accept his demand. Goubert accused Ménard of trying to frame him on fabricated charges.[32] Some pro-French ex-military men, Creoles, Muslims and government servants considered Goubert's move as treacherous.[33]

At that time, the leading Indian newspaper, the *Indian Express*, known to be sympathetic to the Ashram line in French Indian politics, reported that Muthu Kumarappa Reddiar, who had somehow worked his way to become Goubert's right hand at that time, was the 'evil genius' behind Goubert's volte-face. Reddiar was accused of looting the treasury and public exchequer by the same newspaper. French records maintain that he was extremely cunning, wily, cold-blooded and calculative, and would do anything to serve his personal interests.[34] This statement was not altogether wrong because Goubert had preferred to disregard the request of Muthu Poullé and Pakkirsamy Poullé to patch up with the French commissioner and France. Instead, he seems to have taken the step of radicalising his stand. In this he had the backing of landlords and merchants like Muthu Kumarappa Reddiar and Karunendra Mudaliar, who had nothing to lose except their French masters. They did not mind the change of masters, though the new masters would be from New Delhi, to which either they or their ancestors had never owed allegiance at any point of time. But they were Indians ethnically, culturally and geographically. At that time, the Indian consul, Kewal Singh, who was from faraway Punjab and Delhi, spoke in praise of Sellane Naiker, who stood for the merger.[35] When it became obvious that Goubert had decided to radicalise his stand, Muthu Poullé fell in line with him. It would be, however, wrong to hold that Muthu Kumarappa Reddiar had influenced Goubert to radicalise his stand. It might rather have been the other way round, wherein Muthu Kumarappa Reddiar became indispensable to Goubert's strategy, as we are going to see.

K. Muthu Poullé, the mayor of Pondicherry, and C. Balasubramanian, president of the Representative Assembly, met the French commisioner and handed over a copy of the resolution passed by the municipal councils. Muthu Poullé told Ménard that the resolution stood on its own merit and had nothing to do with the rift that had developed between the French commissioner and Goubert. Copies of this resolution were also sent to Prime Minister Nehru as well as the French President and Prime Minister, and the Foreign and Overseas Ministers. During the press conference, Muthu Poullé had also asserted that the French Indians had been waiting from 1948 for the French government to settle the merger issue in consultation with the Indian government, but as they had not done anything so far, the Socialist Party had to take the initiative to merge with the mother country according to the people's wishes.

On his part, Goubert threatened that if they did not get a favourable reply from Paris to their merger demand, he would give an ultimatum to the French government to quit the settlements. He said that there would be no compromise on their demand even if Ménard was replaced with another commissioner. Goubert had gone to the point of no return. He said that he hoped to pass the merger resolution in the assembly with the support of all members from Karaikal, Mahé and Yanam and also enlist the support of all pro-merger parties in the settlements. He declared that the government had not received one-and-a-half crore rupees of subsidy for the development projects in the settlements lately announced by the commissioner. As a result, all development work had been suspended for want of funds. He added that, even if the funds were received, it would not solve the problem pertaining to the merger.[36]

Given the preceding stand of the Socialist Party leaders, Commisioner Ménard took the necessary steps to maintain law and order. He issued an order prohibiting the assembly of more than three persons in public roads. He said that the resolution of the Municipal Councils had been forwarded to the government in France and, therefore, there was no need for demonstrations.[37] The French police even arrested four pro-merger activists. Palani Doraiswamy, a correspondent of Press Trust of India was also attacked in Pondicherry. In its turn, the Indian government lodged a protest with the French ambassador in New Delhi as well as the French government in Paris against the suppression of the French India Merger Movement and the violation of Indian territory by the French police.

However, the French government still harped on holding a plebiscite to decide the future of French Indian settlements, according to Article 27, Paragraph 2, of the French Constitution, as had been done in Chandernagore, and in the presence of international observers. It also wanted India to lift the economic blockade of its enclaves to allow for free flow of goods and persons in and out of the enclaves. It decided to send the inspector general for overseas, Tezenas du Montcel, to conduct an on-the-spot study of the situation prevailing in Pondicherry. It was convinced that the rift between Goubert and Ménard had aggravated it. Henri Jacquier, representative of French India in the French Overseas Territories Council, also visited Pondichery and Karaikal to study the situation.

In a signed statement written in Tamil, issued by nine top-ranking leaders of the French Indian Socialist Party on 22 March 1954, guarantees were given to the various sections of the French Indian populace that they would continue to obtain all their present rights and privileges after the merger of the settlement with the Indian Union and the settlements would continue for a certain period as a separate administrative unit of the Indian Union. The French educated youth were assured of all opportunites of employment in the rest of India. They also assured the employees of the French Indian administration that they need not fear termination of their services and reduction in their salaries. Assurances were also given out to the pensioners of all grades that they would continue to benefit from their pensions as usual. Similar assurances were given to the traders, agriculturists and workers. The above statement was signed by:

1. P. Muthu Kumarappa Reddiar, councillor for public works and agriculture;
2. Deivasikamani, law councillor;
3. Karunendra Mudaliar, councillor for finance and education;
4. Edouard Goubert, councillor for revenue and labour;
5. P. Danaraj, councillor for health and information;
6. Subramania Poullé, councillor for food;
7. C. Balasubramnian, president of the Representative Assembly;
8. Pakkirisamy Poullé, senator and mayor of Karaikal; and
9. K. Muthu Poullé, mayor of Pondicherry.

It was announced that the Representative Assembly will inaugurate the Liberation Movement on 27 March. Commissioner Ménard retaliated by postponing indefinitely the session of the Representative Assembly. Goubert and his colleagues were dismissed from power by Ménard, on the pretext that they were not carrying out their functions. Instead of them, new ministers were nominated. Arrest warrants were issued against Goubert, Muthu Poullé and Muthu Kumarappa Reddiar. The trio threatened to join Indian Union if the cases against them were not withdrawn. The prosecuting magistrate of Pondicherry threatened to launch a case against the trio for seizing Nettapakkam. But the French governor was adamant. So, the trio planned to escape to Nettapakkam commune which comprised 12 villages and had a population of 14,000.[38]

In March 1954, Prime Minister Nehru had intervened in Parliament and condemned the arrest of Nandagopal, mayor of Mudaliarpet, and two other Indian citizens in Indian territory by the French police. A protest was lodged with the embassy of France in Delhi. On 28 March, the French Indian police dispersed a procession of about 1,000 persons in Karaikal in favour of the merger and tore the Indian flags carried by them. There were also protests in Mahé asking the French to quit. But, on the whole, the repression was never massive or drastic. In April, 300 French retired soldiers were recalled to help the local police to maintain law and order in Pondicherry. But the Indian government insisted on the direct transfer of French possesions, leaving constitutional and other matters to be settled by negotiation. The French government accused India of trying to influence the French Indians in their favour through the economic blockade. R.K. Nehru of the External Affairs Ministry claimed that essential commodities were still allowed into French India, and if petrol was no more distributed, it was because the petrol benefited only anti-merger elements.

André Ménard talked with the mayor of Karaikal, Pakkirisamy Poullé, probably to woo him over to his side. But Poullé insisted that the resolution for merger was 'irrevocable'. On 26 March, Ayyakannu Poullé, secretary of the merger committee of Karaikal, and Sellane Naiker declared their stand in favour of merger without referendum. Earlier, V. Subbiah, too, had insisted on a merger, from Kottakuppam. Now, the Socialist Party of France, SFIO, voted a resolution towards end-March 1954 in favour of the merger of French territories with India.

On 28 March 1954, the Unified Merger Committee of Karaikal, under Nagarajan decided to constitute a volunteer corps for merger. On 29 March, a mammoth procession was taken out in defiance of the ban on meetings and processions, by Venkatachalapathi Poullé, president, and Léon St Jean, general secretary of the United Merger Front. The police lathicharged the crowd and many leaders and volunteers, like Venkata Chalapathy Poullé and Srikanta Ramanujam, a Congress leader, were hurt. Some of the protesters, including Ramasrinivasan, the Karaikal National Youth Congress president, were arrested and beaten up by the police.[39]

While these events were unfolding, the Socialist leaders of French India were participating in a meeting with Henri Jacquier, member of the French Union Assembly, discussing the matter. The meeting only ended in them stressing upon the imperative of French India's integration with the Indian Union without a referendum. Tezenas du Montcel, Inspector General of the Overseas Territories of France, was received by the Indian Minister of State, R.K. Nehru. But the Government of India continued to demand the transfer of territories without referendum, as the requisite conditions according to its assessment for holding a peaceful referendum were not present.[5] The fact of the matter was that certain colonial government measures in favour of the people had dampened the pro-India feeling in the French territories since sometime. It appears that more than a genuine pro-India feeling, it was the economic pressure, and the border and custom controls, that was contributing to their wish to join the Indian Union.

In the meantime, the Communist leader and former senator, V. Subbiah, who had been holed up outside Pondicherry for a while, stated that the object of the offer of referendum by the French government was 'but a ruse to mark time and consolidate its position' and asked the Indian government to reject the idea. He added that it was ridiculous to suggest that a vote must be taken to judge whether Indians would like to throw in their lot with Indians of their own nationality or the Frenchmen who were 6,000 miles away. On 21 March 1954, he launched an appeal to all political parties from

Kottakuppam to unite to bring about the fusion of French territories with India. On his part, D. Jeevarathinam, former member of the French Parliament, opined that a referendum was not necessary and was only a delaying tactic by the French. On 29 March 1954, the United Merger Committeee of Karaikal called for direct action to effect integration of the French settlements with India.

It should be noted at this juncture that all these merger demands, and movements had never defined clearly the status of the French Indian settlements after integration with the Indian Union. The French Indians at large never agitated for the maintenance of the unique cultural and historical identity of French India, unlike Goubert and his Socialist Party which had never wanted to melt away into the Indian Union as a district or municipality of the Madras province as Chandernagore did with respect to Bengal earlier. Neither the Communist Party under Subbiah, nor the Congress Party under R.L. Purushotthama Reddiar wanted to maintain the special identity of French India. They were agreeable to getting amalgamated with the Madras Province. The members of the Sri Aurobindo Ashram who comprised migrants to Pondicherry for the large part, on the other hand, also did not want to melt away into Madras province.

Meanwhile, the Representative Assembly meeting which was to be held on 27 March 1954 was postponed *sine die* following orders emanating from Paris. This was a grave political error committed by the French establishment and its commissioner in Pondicherry at this crucial time. It drove Goubert and his associates still further, irreversibly so, into the hands of the Indian government. Of the 39 Representative Assembly members, 37 were Socialist Party members, favourable to joining India. On 27 March, Goubert and Muthu Poullé, accompanied by four vans containing 200 Congress volunteers armed with batons, passed through 16 villages of the commune of Mannadipet, raising anti-French slogans. On his part, the French Commissioner Ménard accused Goubert and his men of robbery and issued arrest warrants against them.

Ménard had always been wary of Goubert's activities at that time. He doubted his commitment to remain in the French Union. The Indian consul, Kewal Singh, seems to have manoeuvred discreetly with Goubert and his colleagues, as the others, like Sellane Naiker or

Saravane, were not strong or influential enough to counter French power. Kewal Singh seems to have succeeded in weaning Goubert and his colleagues away from the French by inviting them to Delhi. The French government, instead of acting to prevent Goubert from going over to the Indian side, accused him and others of misappropriating government funds of more than five crores which had been allotted earlier to compensate the loss suffered by the people due to a cyclone that had struck Pondicherry. Corruption cases were filed against Goubert and his colleagues. Ménard also accused him of corruption in awarding licences to sell tobacco, arrack and toddy. Goubert was willing to lift the economic blockade if the French settlements were integrated with India rapidly without referendum.[40]

FLIGHT TO NETTAPAKKAM

Till March 1954, neither Goubert nor his landlord and merchant colleagues like Muthu Kumarappa Reddiar and Muthu Poullé who was also mayor of Pondicherry, had fought outright for the Independence of French India or its merger with the Indian Union. They had instead wished to safeguard French Indian interests and identity within the French Union under certain conditions. Those conditions were never met. On top of that the French administration under Ménard wanted to arrest them. So, they had no alternative but to seek Indian support and opted for a merger under certain conditions. This decision in favour of merger was a well-calculated move by Goubert not only to further his personal interest and safety, but also to safeguard the interests of the French Indians and their unique historical and cultural identity. This was at a time when the French were dithering and unclear about the extent of autonomy they would award to French India. They even wanted to put Goubert behind bars, while Jawaharlal Nehru and the Indian government had assured him of safeguarding French Indian interests and identity in an emphatic manner especially post the Jaipur Resolution if he decided to go with India.

More than anybody else, Goubert realised that the noose was tightening around his neck, and it was just a question of time before he lost his grip over the population of French India. Increasingly, there were assaults by Subbiah and his men as well as Dadala and his men at the frontier. He knew that he could not contain endlessly the local opposition that might rear its head in Pondicherry at any opportune time. Besides, economic pressure was mounting on Pondicherry with no end to the Indian blockade in sight. He realised that the French government was not in a position to bail out Pondicherry and the other three settlements indefinitely, as they were highly dependent materially on India. Most importantly, the French, without realising the gravity of the situation, had turned against him. So Goubert, knowing that all the stakes were ranged against him, deliberately chose to ally with Muthu Kumarappa Reddiar and Muthu Poullé, with the support of the Indian high commissioner, Kewal Singh, and radicalised his stand regarding the merger. Goubert knew that his ship was sinking. He did not want to be shunted into political oblivion. So, he reacted with his uncanny cold intelligence. His reaction was a keenly thought-out move, which was actually a masterstroke that caught all unawares. It had the potential to propel him into becoming the icon of the Freedom Movement in French India, eclipsing his old rival Subbiah as well as Sellane Naiker and R.L. Purushotthama Reddiar. It would be an exaggeration to qualify this move by Goubert as a spurt of nationalist feeling in favour of India. That said, the interests of the Pondicherrians were topmost on his mind when he devised his move for the merger.

On the night of 25 March 1954, Goubert and Muthu Poullé fled to Nettapakkam where Muthu Kumarappa Reddiar was already present. They envisaged the launching of a mass satyagraha to liberate Pondicherry from Nettapakkam. Nettapakkam was actually cut off from the rest of Pondicherry by a strip of Indian territory.

Goubert left behind his properties, furniture and family and gambled his future in Nettapakkam by opting to join India. He was convinced that he would win. Otherwise, he would not have taken that step. Goubert was stocky and massive with a bull's neck, quite brutal in his behaviours and without the least subtlety. Muthu Poullé and Muthu Kumarappa Reddiar were there to support him in his adventure. The latter was quite intelligent, subtle, clear-headed and a good organiser. He spent his own money for the Liberation Movement and the administration of the liberated areas. Reddiar claimed that he had already spent Rs. 98,000 and he still had Rs. 3,00,000 at his disposal for use until total liberation. He expected the reimbursement of the money spent once Pondicherry was liberated.[41]

On 29 March, Ménard asserted that the mayor of Thirubhuvanai, Venkataswami Reddiar, was a 'traitor'. Goubert then retorted:

It does not lie in the mouth of a Frenchman to call an Indian a traitor.

No Indian who is working for the liberation of his motherland from alien rule can be called a 'traitor'.

If M. Ménard has the courage, he can call the French progressive leaders who have condemned the continuance of French rule . . . as traitors, but not Indians who are only fighting for their birthright.

If there is any traitor in the Indian soil, it is M. Ménard, the Frenchman who is trying to perpetuate foreign rule in our motherland by oppressive measures against the expressed vision and will of the people.[42]

On 31 March 1954, the French India Socialist Party members and supporters effected the peaceful capture of the Nettapakkam commune and its mayoral office. They hoisted the Indian flag on the Nettapakkam mayor's office and other public buildings. At a meeting held here on 31 March evening, a resolution was passed stating that no taxes should be paid to the French government. Goubert declared, 'Indians here have achieved Independence and they look up to India for protection and help'. Five vans with French India police stopped at Mangalam on the Indian border, while trying to cross over to Nettapakkam. Goubert established his headquarters in Nettapakkam village from where the liberation movement was being directed. He did not rule out the formation of a common pro-merger front. Goubert defiantly said:

Here I am where the French Indian commissioner's writ won't run. He is no longer of this territory. If he is a decent man, he will quit this country. . . . I was a responsible minister of French India for over five years and just now I cannot be accused of subversive activities.

Nobody, not even Commissioner Ménard nor the French police inspector of Pondicherry could foresee the flight of Goubert to Nettapakkam. They were simply taken unawares. They never knew what exactly to do as Nettapakkam was unreachable to the French police. Goubert's flight was a well-planned one. He seems to have taken advantage of his closeness to Muthu Kumarappa Reddiar in executing this plan. In this he seems to have been assisted by Muthu Poullé, the mayor of Pondicherry. This flight was most certainly conducted with the knowledge and cooperation of the consul general, Kewal Singh. Commissioner Ménard and the French establishment then realised that they had been outwitted by Goubert and his associates. By this flight, Goubert had definitely taken a giant sride towards freedom, one greater than what his counterparts and rivals like Subbiah, Sellane and Purushotthama Reddiar could accomplish.

On 1 April, Edouard Goubert at the head of 300 volunteers captured the Nettapakkam police station, guarded by 3 French Indian policemen. The Indian Union flag was hoisted on the police station, after bringing down the French flag, amidst cries of *Jai Hind*. The policemen of the station surrendered their arms and participated in the flag hoisting. The employees of the mayoral office had earlier done the same. But Ménard alleged that the French Indian officials and policemen were being held in Muthu Kumarappa Reddiar's house. This takeover of Nettapakkam was led by Edouard Goubert, K. Muthu Poullé and Muthu Kumarappa Reddiar, together with Venkata Subba Reddiar, the mayor of Nettapakkam, as well as Venkataswamy Reddiar, mayor of Mannadipet commune. The two latter men had land in Madukarai and Nettapakkam.

In the first week of April, several villages of Bahur commune were declared independent. Bahur had a population of 30,000. Goubert's forces were in the forefront of this liberation. They even set up a provisional government at Nettapakkam, led by leaders like Edouard Goubert and Muthu Kumarappa Reddiar who had become nationalists overnight. Nettapakkam was actually under the control of landlords like Muthu Kumarappa Reddiar and Venkata Subba Reddiar, who constantly supported Goubert and constituted his financial muscle. Congress leader, K. Kamaraj, visited Nettapakkam during this period to patch up the differences that might arise between the various pro-merger groups and guide them. Kamaraj moved closely with the Reddiars, who were more entrenched in the Tamil culture of the area than anyone else, but not with Goubert, who was a pure French product, culturally and by dint of his French education. It, however, appears that Kamaraj extended his support to Goubert who was bolstered by the wealthy Reddiars because he felt that Goubert had the potential to force the French outside India, rather than Sellane Naiker and his group which was made up of less wealthy individuals. Sellane, in his turn, disliked Goubert and refused to cooperate with him and his associates as they were bandits according to his opinion. Besides, Goubert was against the Merger Committee of Sellane. It also appears that though Kamaraj would have preferred uniting Sellane and Goubert on a common platform against the French, he and the high commissioner, Kewal Singh, were afraid of the Communists and Subbiah stealing a march in the Freedom Movement over the others. Probably, it was Goubert himself who informed Kamaraj of this dangerous prospect. Kamaraj being anti-Communist, naturally fell for it and started backing Goubert and the Reddiars, sacrificing Sellane and his group who were fighting their own battles for freedom from the border areas, long before Goubert entered the fray. Naturally, Sellane was infuriated by the position of Kamaraj and dismissed him in French as 'cette tête de singe et de chimpanzé' (this monkey-headed and chimpanzee-headed man). Besides, Sellane had no confidence in Lambert Saravane to speak for the Pondicherrians in France.[43]

The Socialist Party under Goubert also captured Madukarai. It adopted resolutions to join India at once. The French police did not have access to that commune as they were prevented from crossing Indian territory.[44] In fact, all the enclaves of Pondicherry region, except Bahur, were disconnected from Pondicherry proper. Bahur was accessible by sea. Nettapakkam was separated from the rest of Pondicherry by a strip of Indian territory. Indian police saw to it that the French police did not cross over to Nettapakkam through Indian territory to re-establish French control. It was actually this inaccessibility of Nettapakkam by the French Indian police and authorities, of which Muthu Kumarappa Reddiar was more conscious than anyone else, as he was from that area, that seems to have led him to induce Goubert to take the momentous decision to cross over to Nettapakkam. If it were not for this inaccessibility, Goubert would have still been in Pondicherry town.

The liberated 'areas' lacked financial resources as the French had blocked the bank balances of the various pro-merger leaders. Inspite of this, landlords like Venkata Subba Reddiar spent their own money to feed all those who came to Nettapakkam. Thus, the provisional government survived, inspite of the fact that Nehru did not openly support this secessionist government. But Nehru's police forces prevented French Indian troops from accessing Nettapakkam. Inspector Sinnasamy Iyer maintained in his report that 50 per cent of the people of Nettapakkam were still pro-French at that juncture.[45]

Goubert is known to have gone as E.G. Pillai, from now onwards and, announced that the name of the Socialist Party would hereafter be Freedom Congress. The pro-French journal, *République Française*, called him Coji E.G. The headquarters of the liberated lands was established in Nettapakkam.[46]

The Indian government had previously taken a position against Goubert citing his alleged corruption. But now the same government facilitated his activities in Nettapakkam.[47] This implied that there was some collusion between Goubert and his men and the Indian authorities prior to the former's flight to Nettapakkam.

In the beginning of April, there was an attempt by over 600 Communist volunteers to take over Tirukannur village in Thirubhuvanai commune, about 12 miles from Pondicherry. The Communists raised Indian flags on public buildings. French India police opened fire and four people were injured. A couple of days before, the inspector of colonies, Tezenas du Montcel, had assured a merchants' delegation that had approached him due to shortage of kerosene and goods in retail shops that France would not give up its enclaves.[48]

From their safe haven in Nettapakkam commune, Goubert, Muthu Poullé and Muthu Kumarappa Reddiar sent a letter/telegram asking Tezenas Du Montcel who was on an investigative fact-finding mission in Pondicherry to make an appointment with them anywhere where their security was guaranteed. They wrote in French:

How we wish we were in a position to welcome you! But two circumstances compel us to desist from expressing any feeling of happiness at your arrival. In the first place, we and our colleagues who are members of the French India Council, set up by you with good guarantee of the status, power and privilege of the ministers of the realm, are now political fugitives from the settlement, hunted out of them like common felons. Secondly, you have come on a mission which is meaningless and mysterious. Fact-finding can no longer be a bona fide object of your mission. For, what more facts does your government want than those that have been impressed on it already.

The first fact that you can never blink from is that all these pockets are of India, Indian. They are parts in a vast land and we, the residents are connected indissolubly with our brethren of the Indian soil culturally, historically and economically in such a way that no political separation could any longer be tolerated. More than these geographic and economic reasons, there is another force namely, the great impetus to freedom from colonial powers which animate the whole of South-east Asia which has also moved us towards making our present and final decision. Our decision is, as you know, we shall merge with the Indian Union without the dilatory pretext of a referendum, insisted upon by your government.

Now, Mr Factfinder, consider the greatest of all facts in recent French Indian history. It is this. We, the members of the French India Council and mayors of communes, sensing and echoing the unanimous opinion of the people of the settlements, submitted to your government at Paris a request that steps should be taken forthwith for the transfer of the settlements to the Indian Union. It was a proper request. It had universal popular backing and it was met at that moment by the commissioner's assurance that it would be conveyed to Paris in all good faith. But the commissioner who had taken an initiative to obtain a promise for us that law and order would be ensured, went out and broke law and order himself in the most flagrant manner. He signalized your government! Reaction to our just and patriotic request, by making us, the signatories, victim to police *zulum*, unwanted violence and even kidnapping as a result of which, today, some of us have had to come out almost as exiles.

If this should be the reaction to our legal and constitutional demand, what more would be the calculated violence of the French authorities in the event of a referendum? Put this justifiable fear of the French Indian citizens as another important fact in your report. Also, please explain to the government of which you are an honoured member, that the local government's response to this natural and patriotic demand of ours is proof positive that no referendum could be conceived without a recrudescence of official violence.

You yourself set up the French Indian Council. We do not know how you have taken the plight of the councillors today as reflecting on your personal honour. Be that as it may, what is the fault that we have committed? You seem to have told that you will be conducting an investigation into the real position in the French Indian settlements and would hear both sides. How can there be more than one side to this question? Probably you have made up your mind to create into being a kind of local opposition to our demand by some subsidised elements; but with all your knowledge of history, do you imagine that even if you can persuade a few people to hear false testimony against merger, this present colonial connection can last for any considerable length of time? It passes our understanding why you Frenchmen, . . . are so blind to the reading of history, so callous to the sentiments of the human heart and so indifferent to your own ultimate interests and present honour. Do not the incidents that are happening today in the French Indian territory constitute the most shameless chapter in the history of France? Frenchmen with real devotion to their tradition should feel ashamed of this foisting of Nazi methods on us even as they suffered pangs of shame and poignant feeling when they themselves were subjected to them.

Probably, political sentiments, national honour, geographical data and economic realities are not sufficient facts that could satisfy you or probably you would need more of them, in which case it is even now open to you to make an appointment with us and our colleagues anywhere where our personal safety could be guaranteed. We hear that you are being taken round at odd hours to different enclaves and shown how peaceful and presumably, therefore, pro-French the inhabitants are. If your commissioner and you could be more honest and courageous you could inform us just a while before you pass these enclaves, and we would share you quite a different picture. But in that case, you will be finding inconvenient facts.[49]

In the beginning of April 1954, V. Subbiah met Kamaraj Nadar, who succeeded Rajagopalachari as Chief Minister of Madras province. An initial attempt by Subbiah's men to capture Thirukannur was foiled by its inhabitants and its policemen. Sensing that things were accelerating in favour of merger, Subbiah, not wanting to be left behind, declared from Indian territory on Pondicherry border that his party was willing to collaborate with all pro-merger groups. He was willing to discuss the merger even with his former enemy, Goubert. On his part, Goubert had opened negotiations with Sellane Naiker, president of the Central Merger Congress, to forge a common front against the French. Subbiah declared that the Indian flag would be hoisted in Thirubhuvanai commune, an isolated enclave, 15 miles west of Pondicherry between Valavanur and Kandamangalam (Indian territories). But the mayor of Thirubhuvanai was Venkataswamy Reddiar, a Socialist Party leader. Similarly, P.A. Rathinam Chettiar, mayor of Mannadipet, also belonged to the Socialist Party. Subbiah, however, maintained that the struggle would be extended to Bahur commune. He also envisaged organising demonstrations in Pondicherry itself. He stood for the formation of a united front with the French India Socialist Party. A conference would be held in Cuddalore to create this front with the support of Sellane Naiker, the French India Youth Congress, the Students' Congress, the Pondicherry Town Congress and the French India National Congress.[50] This acceleration to the Freedom Movement, due especially to the joining of Subbiah, took place only because Goubert had set up the provisional government in Nettapakkam and was stealing the show as the foremost freedom fighter. Goubert's moves pushed Subbiah to take some action in favour of freedom. Otherwise, his men would not have resorted to capturing Thirubhuvanai.

On his part, Ménard had tried to enlist the support of Socialist Party leaders like R.M.A.S. Pakkirissamy Poullé of Karaikal, in which he signally failed. Poullé told Ménard that the merger was bound to happen. The Youth Congress leader of Karaikal, Ramasrinivasan, was arrested and released. The Congress leader of Karaikal, N. Srikantha Ramanujam, considered the idea of referendum as a fraud. R.M.A.S. Venkatachalapathy Poullé, related to Pakkirisamy, was the president of Karaikal United Front for Merger at that time.

In April 1954, the Students' Congress agitated in Pondicherry. During the agitations, one of the student leaders, B. Rangapillai, was beaten up and arrested, along with many other students. Rangapillai's finger was fractured. Sellane Naiker, president of the Central Merger Committee, defended the students in court, along with S. Perumal, and got them released. Sellane's house and that of Swamy Lourdes, *Bharat Yuva Sangam* leader, were besieged by *goondas* during this period. Sellane also released a statement in favour of the merger, claiming that French Indians were part and parcel of Mother India. On his part, A. Arulraj, president of the French Indian Youth Congress of Pondicherry, and Léon Saint Jean of Karaikal condemned police intimidation. In Karaikal, volunteers belonging to the Congress and Dravida Kazhagam who agitated for the merger were arrested.

On 14 April 1954, the Students' Congress under Dorai Munisamy agitated for freedom at the Congress headquarters in Chetty Street, Pondicherry. Sellane Naiker visited the place and spoke to the students.

Agitations were also spearheaded by the Youth Congress leaders, A. Arulraj and D. Mariappan. They were kept in lock-up for two days. B. Rangapillai, N. Damodaran, Anwar Ali Khan and others took out a students' procession on behalf of the Students' Congress. Fishermen were mobilised for the Freedom Movement by A. Arulraj, N. Ranganathan and K. Karunanidhi.

Houses of S. Perumal, president of Bar Association, Sellane Naiker and Swamy Lourdes were attacked. Earlier in Karaikal, the Youth Congress leader, A. Ramasrinivasan, and few other personalities like Shaik Madar Sahib Maracair, a leading merchant, and Nagarajan were arrested and beaten. The last two were personally attacked by the French commissioner of police of Karaikal for organising demonstrations against French rule. Some pro-French *goondas* brought down the Indian flags hoisted above some houses in Kosapalayam and Pillachavadi. The French police even arrested 60 nationalist volunteers. They took the help of ruffians to plunder the properties of Indian citizens in Kalapet.[51]

On 6 April, 46 villages of Tirubhuvanai/Mannadipet commune, which included Thirubhuvanai and Sanyasikuppam, were liberated by the Communists. A joint administration of Communists, Socialists and Congress fusionists was established. An administrative council consisting of Kalitheerthankuppam Narayanasamy, Manikka Kavundar and Manavala Reddiar came into existence and Independence was declared. Tirubhuvanai had a population of 23,000. Besides, a crowd of about 500 mergerists including Communists invaded the municipality of Tirukannur village and the police station. Two policemen who were on guard at the station refused to surrender. The head policeman called Harikrishnan, who was staunchly pro-French, threatened to open fire. A certain Tirumalai seems to have died in this operation, while four others were wounded. However, both the policemen were ultimately overpowered and taken to Nettapakkam. These men also took over the police station in Madukkarai village in the same commune, guarded by two other policemen. On 9 April, Goubert and his men captured Karaiyamputhur village.[52]

But the Indian government did not recognise the Tirubhuvanai commune takeover, until the Socialist/Congress Party backed people took credit for it. By mid-May/June 1954, the Communists were deposed by 400 of pro-Indian Goubert's men, with the backing of Muthu Kumarappa Reddiar. Over 300 volunteers of the 'Freedom Corps' formed by the French India Communist Party had been taken into custody in April earlier. Many other volunteers were arrested in and around Pondicherry on 7 April. Pro-merger processions were launched from Thengathittu, Muthirapalayam, Pakkumudayanpet and Muthialpet carrying Indian flags towards Odiansalai. Demonstrations took place in Pakkumudayanpet and Muthirapalayam under Iruchappan, Parameswaran and Ramaswami. A total of 150 people were arrested in these two places. Narayanasami and Parameswaran led the pro-merger campaign in Thengathittu, Murungapakkam, Karamanikuppam, Keerapalayam and Mudaliarpet. A total of 100 persons were arrested in these places as well. Raja and Srinivasan led the procession from Muthialpet, and the police arrested 32 persons. There was a demonstration at Dupleix Street in the heart of Pondicherry town. A procession of 18 people started from Gandhi Road. They wanted to stage a demonstration in front of the governor's palace. This procession was forcibly dispersed. Among those who participated were Namasivayam, Ranganathan, Dasarathan and Rajamanikam. Several were arrested. Besides, the French India Youth Congress volunteers had taken out a procession in Pakkumudayanpet. The volunteers were manhandled by police. Pavadai, a supporter of Lambert Saravane, was arrested. There were further demonstrations and processions on 8 April. Volunteers of the French Indian Youth Congress, the Communist Party and the Dravida Kazhagam jointly staged a demonstration by taking out a big procession. Sixty people were arrested. A procession started from Karuvadikuppam, led by Jaganatha Murugesan, an ex-serviceman of French India, who had been called to go to Indochina by the French government only a few days ago, given that there were 600 military men on leave from Saigon parading the streets of Pondicherry at that time. Subbiah attended to volunteers beaten up by the police near Kottakuppam. It is significant to note that women were not allowed to take part in these processions and demonstrations.

    N. Govindarasu Naiker, a member of the central merger committee was accused by the police of raising the Indian flag on his house. It seems that he said to the police the following:

'If what I did was a crime, I am prepared to court arrest.'

A non-violent procession and demonstration was also organised in Karaikal under the leadership of Thangaraju, Pakkirisami, Meenakshisundaram, N. Ganapathy and K. Sivaprakasam of the Jawahar Youth League. Before matters could get out of hand, Léon Saint Jean intervened and pacified the demonstrators. It was at that time that Léon Saint Jean made a crucial statement that, under Section 27 of the French Constitution, only the consent of the population was required for cession of any part of the French territory. He added the following:

> This does not mean, according to the spirit and letter of the Constitution, that there should be a referendum or plebiscite. The French government is a representative democracy and not a direct democracy like Switzerland. All decisions on behalf of the French people are taken by the elected representatives. Therefore, under the Constitution, the decision of the municipalities in the French Indian settlements and the government councillors called ministers, who are elected by secret, direct, equal and universal suffrage, is valid, lawful and sufficient for authorising France to make a treaty with the Indian government to transfer the French Indian territories to India.
>
> Only in special cases of altering the present Constitution should the people exercise their power of national sovereignty both by the vote of their elected representatives and by a referendum under Section 3 of the Constitution. In all other matters, the people can exercise their power, through their elected representatives in the National Assembly.

Manamedu, Krishnapuram and Kadavanur with a population of 3,000 declared that they were free from French rule and joined Goubert's camp. On 6 May, Coonichampet village as well as Chettypet, Thirukanur, Manadipet and Manalipet were attacked by 1,500 men led by Muthu Kumarappa Reddiar and captured. Houses were looted and the police station was set on fire. The Indian flag was raised.[53]

According to Inspector Sinnasamy Iyer, 95 per cent of the people in these places were pro-French. In Karaikal, the president of the National Congress, S. Madar Sahib, and 14 Congressmen were arrested when they went in a procession demanding the merger of Karaikal with India. In Karaikal, volunteers belonging to the Congress and Dravida Kazhagam, led by Chinnappa, M. Govindarajulu and G. Meenakshisundaram, were roughed up by the police.

P. Meenakshisundaram, A. Poyathamurthi and M. Selvaraj of the Karaikal Jawahar Youth League were also arrested and given prison sentences. Shaikh Madar Sahib, president of Karaikal Congress, Nagarajan and Darbaranya Sundaram Poullé were also attacked by the police and their Indian flags confiscated. Sellane's Central Merger committee and the Students' Congress members went door to door canvassing support for the merger. Women with babies in their arms and girls were satyagrahis in the procession of the united front led by 70-year-old, D. Mariappan. A. Arulraj who was just 27-year-old then marched in this procession. Police blocked the procession, and 40 volunteers were arrested. Leon Saint Jean of Karaikal and A. Arulraj, president of the French Indian Youth Congress, condemned the police atrocities in French India.[54]

The protests continued further in April. In Kosapalayam, 200 houses flew the tricolour, heeding the call of the Congress, Central Merger Congress, Communist Party, Bharat Yuvak Sangh, the Students' Congress and the Youth Congress. Later, 150 volunteers assembled at the Congress headquarters at Chetty Street under Dorai Munisamy. Sellane Naiker visited the students then. A total of 70 volunteers clad in khadi went in a procession led by B. Rangapillai. Police stopped the procession at Dupleix Street. They confronted about 100 anti-merger elements. The police then lathi-charged the students. Another batch of students under Dorai Munisamy took out a procession. Some students like Natarajan, Prosper and Vaidyanathan were injured by the police. Besides, Govindaraju Naiker, a leader of the Pro-Merger Movement, was kept in custody by anti-merger hooligans. The houses of Sellane Naiker, S. Perumal and Swamy Lourdes of the Bharat Yuvak Sangh and others were also attacked by the anti-merger rowdy elements. It seems that the leader of the newly formed Democratic Party, Du Tamby, accompanied by André Gaudart, an enemy of Goubert, and Mr Bleicher, openly trampled Indian flags.

Groups of ruffians terrorised the wife and children of Perumal and brought down the Indian flag. But Perumal hoisted a second flag. Sellane Naiker was kept under house arrest by ruffians for eight hours, while Swamy Lourdes escaped an attack by rowdies. Besides, 2,000 mill workers took out a procession and 20 Communist volunteers were arrested. Arul and D. Mariappan were arrested and sentenced to jail.

Four villages, Alankuppam, Alankuppampet, Tullukunpet and Chagivarayanpet, of Ozhukarai commune situated about 17 kilometres from Pondicherry to the north-west, were liberated in the month of May. It should be noted at this juncture that Muthu Kumarappa Reddiar, the deputy of Goubert, spent his personal wealth to meet the administrative expenses of the liberated areas. He earlier refuted the allegations of the prestigious French journal, *Le Monde*, that the sudden conversion of Goubert and his colleagues from anti-mergerism to pro-mergerism was motivated by personal considerations and due to the economic blockade imposed by India.[55]

For Goubert's men still in Pondicherry, like H.M. Cassime, Karunendra Mudaliar, Virasamy Saguerre, Deivasikamani and Balasubramanian, integration with India looked inevitable. In the meantime, Henri Jacquier, member of National Assembly, declared that there was no need of referendum in the French settlements and that France and India could settle the problem amicably. Nehru, on the other hand, invited France to affect the *de facto* transfer of the settlements without referendum. It was claimed then that there was no mention in Article 27, paragraph 2 of the French Constitution that a referendum or a plebiscite should be held to ascertain the wishes of the people. Instead, only the consent of the population was necessary to decide the matter of integration with India. It was thought that the consent of the elected representatives of the population alone would be more than enough for the merger to be in conformity with the Constitution.[56]

Ménard considered the takeover of Nettapakkam commune as a law and order problem, as some policemen were arrested and imprisoned in Muthu Kumarappa Reddiar's house and the official records taken away. He was extremely upset that the Indian government prohibited French police from crossing over to Nettapakkam to re-establish law and order. He accused the Indian press and media of misreporting the happenings in Nettapakkam. He refused to accept the councillors as ministers and the Government Council as a cabinet. He also refused to endorse the resolutions of 14 communes out of 16 passed in favour of the merger. He and Jacquier opened negotiations with the remaining Socialist councillors in Pondicherry, like Deivasikamani, Danaraja, Karunendra Mudaliar, Balasubramnian, president of the Representative Assembly, and Pakkirisamy Poullé, mayor of Karaikal. The negotiations were largely unsuccessful. At the same time, the commissioner issued orders suspending Venkataswamy Reddiar, mayor of Mannadipet, and Venkata Subba Reddiar, mayor of Nettapakkam. Muthu Poullé and Goubert were also suspended from their posts of mayor and deputy mayor of Pondicherry, respectively. All of them, including Muthu Kumarappa Reddiar, were to be prosecuted by Commissioner Ménard.[57]

On 6 April, demands were made to cancel the parliamentary immunity of Goubert by the Frenchman, Jules Castelanni, senator for the French colony of Madagascar. On 11 April 1954, Kewal Singh met and talked with the members of the provisional government and other leaders like Dadala at Kandamangalam outside Pondicherry. All indications point to the fact that Goubert was an extremely influential person among the people of Pondicherry at this time. Neither Muthu Kumarappa Reddiar nor Muthu Poullé could match him in popularity. In fact, without Goubert, they had no influence anywhere, except in their constituencies. They, however, were not in a position to wage a war or accomplish any sort of coup d'état against the French. Goubert's men and followers were all holed up in Nettapakkam. But Dadala at that time seems to have decided to leave for Yanam to lead the liberation struggle there.[58] By this time, however, armed military personnel from Indochina numbering 300 were patrolling the streets of Pondicherry. Subbiah recruited his militants from the weavers without jobs in Indian territory by giving each one of them six annas per day to foment trouble within Pondicherry. Commissioner Ménard accused the consul general of India of inciting the agitators who were released to take treatment in Cuddalore hospital.[59]

In the month of May, steps were taken in the French Parliament to prosecute Goubert. Goubert wrote a long letter to the president of the National Assembly in France on 26 May explaining that the reasons that led him to leave Pondicherry were the attempts to cancel his parliamentary immunity, goondaism of the French authorities and parties, false accusations against him by Ménard and the arrest warrants. Goubert regretted that France which had given the notions of liberty and human rights to the world was trampling them in their colonies through their colonial administrators who had scant regard for the rules and regulations applicable to their citizens in French India. He said that he loved the French people who had not left France, but not the colonialists who administered the overseas people. He claimed that the decree of 12 August 1947, promulgated by Governor Baron, had given executive powers to the Representative Assembly, but his successor Commissioner Ménard (commissioner since May 1950) and Commandant Guyard had done everything in their powers to undermine it. In the light of this, he was forced to demand of the French government to allow French Indians to join the Indian Union if they wanted to maintain friendship with India and prevent bloodshed. It is clear from this letter coming from Goubert himself that Commissioner Ménard and his French associates like Inspector Guyard were greatly responsible for the radicalisation of Goubert.[60]

In the month of May 1954, a conference was held at Madukarai with 300 representatives of the 60 liberated villages with a total population of 50,000 under the leadership of Edouard Goubert and the Socialist Party. An Administrative Council was formed with 19 members. This was known as the 'Council of the French Indian Liberated Areas'. It was in this conference that the dissolution of the French India Socialist Party was decided upon. A new party called the Liberation Congress of French India was formed. This party would merge with the National Congress party once French India was integrated with the Indian Union. Goubert Indianised his name as E.G. Pillai and declared that the French would not quit India unless they were pushed out. He knew the French better than anybody else due to his origins. He knew that the French would not leave even a parcel of their colonised territories if they were not forced out through violent or unconstitutional methods.[61] His assessment was perfectly right in this respect, if we take into consideration the historical struggle of the colonised people to liberate themselves from French rule. Wherever they were defeated and pushed out, due to military or economic reasons, they had left after sometimes waging bloody wars as in Indochina and Algeria. Wherever they could maintain themselves due to their superior economic and military force, they had maintained themselves as in New Caledonia or Tahiti, by making use of various methods and subterfuges, to keep the colonised people as part of France.

Towards Integration

NOTES

1. Asie-Océanie 1944-55, Inde Française, no. 15, Note du Pasteur Boegner sur son entretien avec Nehru, 10 January 1953, IF 15, pp. 2-7, ADP; Lettre d'Ostrorog au Ministre des Affaires Etrangères, New Delhi, 14 January 1953, IF 15, pp. 22-3, ADP.
2. Télégramme d'Information, Service d'Information de l'Inde, 19 March 1953, no. 15, Asie Océanie, pp. 40-1; Tél d'Ostrorog au Ministre des Affaires Etrangères, New Delhi, 18 March 1953, no. 15, Asie Océanie p. 42, ADP; Tél de Marolles au Ministre des Affaires Etrangères, New Delhi, 18 September 1953, no. 15, AO, p. 89, ADP; Tél d'Ostrorog au Ministre des Affaires Etrangères, New Delhi, 20 March 1953, no. 15, Asie Océanie, p. 46, ADP.
3. *The Eastern Economist*, 8 May 1953.
4. Note, 6 July 1953, AO, pp. 70-3, IF 15, ADP; Note pour le Ministre, Service d'Information et de Presse, 2 July 1953, p. 76, IF 15, ADP.
5. Note, AFP, New Delhi, 3 March 1953, p. 37, no. 15, ADP; *The Hindu*, 24 February 1953.
6. Letter written by Sellane Naiker as president of the French India Central Merger Committee, Pondicherry, 15 January 1953; Copy of the letter by N.R. Pillai to Sellane Naiker dated 3 February 1953 in my possession; Memorandum to the Government of India by the President, French India Central Merger Committee, Sellane Naiker, Pondicherry, 12 April 1953.
7. Rapport du M.D.L. chef R. Govindasamy, chef de poste d'Odiansalai, Odiansalai, 8 March 1953, pp. 75-80, IF 70, ADP.
8. *Indian Express*, 6 August 1953.
9. Rapport de A.L. Gaebelé, 20 August 1953, pp. 332-3, no. 53, ADP; Mémoire succinct concernant les problèmes en IF par Henri Jacquier, Conseiller à l'Union Française, November 1953, pp. 337-49, no. 53, AO, ADP; Ajit Neogy, *Decolonisation of French India*, Pondicherry, 1997, p. 220.
10. Note AO, 4 May 1953, pp. 55-60, IF 15, ADP; Note AO, Affaires Etrangères, Paris, 4 January 1953, IF 15, ADP; *The Hindu*, 8 June 1953; Neogy, op. cit., pp. 219-20.
11. *Eastern Economist*, May 1953; *Indian Express*, 17 April 1953.
12. Lettre de Maurice Schumann, Deputé du Nord à M. Jacques Roux, Direction d'Asie, Affaires Etrangères, Paris, 31 March 1953, no. 15, Asie Océanie, ADP.
13. Tél de Marolles à Ministre des Affaires Etrangères, New Delhi, 18 September 1953, p. 89, IF 15, ADP.

14. Lettre de Claude de Marolles, Chargés d'affaires de France aux Indes au Ministre des Affaires Etrangères, New Delhi, 27 October 1953, p. 123, AO, no. 15, ADP.
15. Tél de Marolle à Ministre des Affaires Etrangères, New Delhi, 21 October 1953, p. 81, IF 70, ADP; *The Hindu*, 22 November 1953.
16. Note AO, 24 February 1953, p. 35, IF 53, ADP; Rapport de M. Pimodan, 25 November 1953, pp. 350-63, no. 53, ADP; *l'Intransigeant*, 21 April 1954; Neogy, op. cit., pp. 227-8.
17. R. Dadala, *My Struggle for the Freedom of French India*, Pondicherry, n.d. p. 23; *The Hindu*, 16 November 1953; B. Mayandi Bharathi, 'Subbaiyavum Suthanthiramum Onru', *Va. Subbiah Pavala Vizha Malar*, Pondicherry, 1988, pp. 50-1; S. Lastick, 'The Role of Sellane Naicker in the Freedom Struggle of Pondicherry', M. Phil. Dissertation, University of Pondicherry, 1998, p. 74.
18. *Le Monde*, 3-4 January 1954.
19. *The Hindu*, 11 January 1954.
20. *The Hindu*, 9, 11, 25 January 1954; *Hindustan Times*, 11 January 1954.
21. *The Hindu*, 9, 25 January, 1 April 1954; Service d'info indien, 11 January 1954, p. 4, IF 54, ADP.
22. *Franc-Tireur*, 13 May 1954; Jacques Weber, *Pondichéry et les Comptoirs de l'Inde après Dupleix: La Démocratie au pays des Castes*, Paris, 1996; p. 388.
23. *Hindustan Times*, 11 January 1954; *The Hindu*, 11 January, 10 March 1954.
24. Lettre du Ministère des Affaires Etrangères au Président du Conseil, 19 February 1954, no. 16, ADP; Lettre du Commissaire au Conseil Général, Pondichéry, 12 January 1953, p. 54, IF 69, ADP; Lettre du Ministre des Affaires Etrangères au Ministre de la France d'Outre-mer, 9 January 1954, pp. 2-3, IF 54, ADP; Tél de Pondichéry au Ministère de la France d'Outre-mer, Pondicherry, 3 March 1954. Affaires Politiques, C 2276, D4, AOM.
25. Tél d'Ostrorog au Ministre des Affaires Etrangères, New Delhi, 22 March 1954, no. 16, ADP; *Le Monde*, 19 August 1954; *Franc-Tireur*, 13 May 1954; Lettre du Ministère des Affaires Etrangères au Président du Conseil, 19 February 1954, No. 16, ADP.
26. Tel d'Ostrorog au Ministre des Affaires Etrangères, 11 March 1954, 22 March 1954, pp. 11-16, no. 72, ADP; Tél à France d'Outre-mer, Pondicherry, 12 March 1954, p. 16, IF 54, ADP; Lettre d'Ostrorog au Ministre des Affaires Etrangères, New Delhi, 8 March 1954, p. 19, no. 72, ADP; Tél d'Ostrorog, New Delhi, 18 March 1954 au Ministre

des Affaires Etrangères, no. 16, AO, ADP; *Le Monde,* 12 March 1954; *The Hindu,* 9 March 1954.
27. *The Hindu,* 9 March 1954.
28. Rapport fait au nom de la Commission Etrangères, 28 May 1956, AO, Inde, 1956-7, no. 329, pp. 108-29, ADP; Tél d'Ostrorog au Ministre des Affaires Etrangères, New Delhi, 25 November 1954, p. 22, no. 72, ADP; Aide mémoire, 26 March 1954, remis à Ostrorog, p. 34, no.72, ADP; Note emis par M. Parodi, Affaires Etrangères, à M. Malik, 2 April 1954, pp. 62-4, no. 72, ADP.
29. Reuter, Pondicherry, 1 April 1954, p. 66, no. 72, ADP; Projet de déclaration, May 1954, pp. 161-2, IF 18, ADP; voir, pp. 94-101, IF 54, ADP.
30. Service d'info de l'Inde, 28 March 1954, p. 102, IF 54, ADP.
31. *L'Intransigent,* 21 March 1954, p. 34, IF 54, ADP.
32. Tél du Ministère des Affaires Etrangères à New Delhi, Paris, 30 October 1954, no. 77, p. 2, AO, ADP; Téll de Pondichéry par Landy au Ministre des Affaires Etrangères, Pondichéry, 28 October 1954, contre nomination de Perrier, originaire de Pondichéry à Pondichéry, p. 3, no. 77, ADP; Comte d'Ostrorog contre la nomination de Perrier, tél d'Ostrorog au Ministère des Affaires Etrangères, New Delhi, 29 October 1954, p. 5, no. 77, ADP; Tél de London au Ministre des Affaires Etrangères, Madras, 20 March 1954, p. 35, IF 54, ADP.
33. Tél demarqée du Gouverneur à Ministre de la France d'Outre-mer, 21 March 1954, p. 50, IF 54, ADP; Tél de Ménard au Ministre de la France d'Outre-mer, Pondicherry, 19 March 1954, p. 52, IF 54, ADP.
34. *Indian Express,* 17 April 1954; see also p. 145, IF 81, ADP.
35. Note sur Pondichéry du 13 au 15 April 1954 par M. Costilles, pp. 236-42, IF 54, ADP.
36. Ibid., *Indian Express,* 20-2 March 1954; Tél d'Ostrorog au Ministre des Affaires Etrangères, New Delhi, 22 March 1954, no. 16, AO, ADP; *The Hindu,* 20, 23 March 1954.
37. *Indian Express,* 21-3 March 1954.
38. Tél d'Ostrorog au Ministre des Affaires Etrangères, New Delhi, 22 November 1954, no. 16, AO, ADP; *Indian Express,* 23-4 March 1954; *Le Parisien Libéré,* 14 June 1954 ; Tél de Schuman, MInistre Affaires Etrangères, New Delhi, 23 March 1954, no. 16, AO, ADP; Note de l'Ambasade de l'Inde, New Delhi, 25 March 1954, no. 16, ADP; *Indian Express,* 23-5 March 1954; B. Mayandi, op. cit., pp. 47-8; *The Hindu,* 2, 7, 10 April 1954.
39. *Le Populaire,* 26, 27-8 March 1954; 7 April 1954; Tél, Ambassade de

l'Inde à M. Zarodi, 25 March 1954, no. 16, ADP; Tél. d'information, 29 March 1954, no. 16, ADP; *Eastern Economist*, 25 March 1954; Note de l'Ambassade de l'inde, New Delhi, 25 March 1954, no. 16, ADP; Tél du Comte d'Ostrorog à Ministère des Affaires Etrangères, New Delhi, 26 March 1964, no. 16, ADP; *Hindustan Times*, 19, 25 January 1952; *The Hindu*, 1 April 1954; Agence Chine Nouvelle, 21 March 1954, p. 85, IF 54, ADP; Agence Indienne de l'Info, 26 March 1954, p. 83, IF 54, ADP; La SFIO et Le problème de l'IF, 27 March 1954, p. 36, IF 86, ADP; *Hindustan Times*, 30 March 1954.

40. *Le Populaire*, 1, 7, 12 April 1954; *Eastern Economist*, 25 March 1954; *Indian Express*, 26-7, 30-1 March 1954; République Populaire de la Chine, Tél d'info, 26 March 1954, p. 36, IF 86, ADP; *Hindustan Times*, 30 March 1954; *The Hindu*, 28 March 1954; Tél d'Ostrorog à Ministère des Affaires Etrangères, New Delhi, 27 March 1954, p. 89, IF 54, ADP; Tél de London au Ministère des Affaires Etrangères, Madras, 24 March 1954, p. 77, IF 54, ADP; Tél de Comrep à France d'Outre-mer, Pondicherry, 28 March 1954, p. 109, IF 54, ADP; Tél d'Ostrorog au Ministère des Affaires Etrangères, New Delhi, 29 March 1954, p. 110, IF 54, ADP; Interview with Saraswati Subbiah; B. Mayandi, 'Subbaiyavum Suthanthiramum Onru', *Va. Subbiah Pavala Vizha Malar*, Pondicherry, 1988, pp. 47-8; *The Hindu*, 8 April 1954; Considérations qui ont determiné M. Goubert a quitter les territoires, p. 225-IF 54, ADP; Tél de M. London, Madras, 25 March 1954, à Ministère des Affaires Etrangères, no. 16, AO, ADP.

41. *Le Monde*, 20 August 1954; 2eme dépêche, de M. Nagar, correspondant de AFP, Pondicherry, June 1954, pp. 103-11, no. 73, ADP.

42. *Hindustan Times*, 30 March 1954, p. 39, IF 86, ADP; Agence indienne d'information, 30 March 1954, p. 87, IF 70, ADP.

43. Based on Interviews; Durai, Munusamy, 'Maatru Katchiyinarum Mathikum Thalaivar', *Va. Subbiah Pavala Vizha Malar*, 1988, pp. 84-5; Lettre du maire de la commune de Nettapakkam, Vengadasouba Reddiar à M. le Chef de service de ravitallement, Pondicherry, Netapakkam, 22 August 1953, p. 204, IF 62, ADP; *The Hindu*, 2 April 1954; Interview with Doressamy Naiker, former student leader of Pondicherry.

44. *Indian Express*, 26-7 March 1954.

45. *Le Monde*, 19 August 1954; *The Hindu*, 2 April 1954; Note by R.K. Nehru, 12 April 1954, p. 87, IF 18, ADP; Lettre de Sinnasamy Iyer, Commandant la brigade de Villenour à M. le s/lieutenant, Pondichéry, Villenour, 9 May 1954, pp. 285-6, IF 54, ADP; Goubert, Muthu Poullé quitte Pondichéry, pp. 174-6, IF 54, ADP; see also p. 166, AO, no. 17, ADP.

46. *Times of India*, 1 April 1954; Tél demarqué du Montcel, Pondicherry, 1 April 1954, no. 73, AO, ADP; *Répulique Française*, J.E. Sarcey (ed.), 28 May 1954.
47. *Le Monde*, 19 August 1954.
48. *The Hindu*, 2, 3, 6 April 1954; Service Indien d'Infromation, 2 April 1954, p. 10, no. 73, Asie Océanie, ADP.
49. *Indian Express*, 1-2 April 1954; *The Hindu*, 3 April 1954; *Times of India*, 1 April 1954; *Hindustan Times*, 1 April 1954.
50. Tél de London à Ministre des Affaires Etrangères, Madras, 3 April 1954, p. 127, IF 54, ADP.
51. *Indian Express*, 26-28, 31 March, 1, 2, April 1954; *The Hindu*, 1 April 1954; S. Lastick, 'The Role of Sellane Naicker in the Freedom Struggle of Pondicherry', M. Phil. Dissertation, University of Pondicherry, 1998, pp. 27-9 (taken from Sellane's personal diary); R. Ramasrinivasan. Karaikal in Freedom Struggle, Karaikal, 1996, p. 93; The Hindu, 10, 13, 14 April 1954; *The Hindu*, 1, 7, 13, 15 April 1954; Note du Ministère des Affaires Etrangères à l'Ambassade de France, 12 April 1954, p. 95, no.72, ADP; Tél d'Ostrorog au Ministère Affaires Etrangères, New Delhi, 15 April 1954, p. 101, no. 72, ADP; Note of the Ministry of External Affairs to Embassy of France, 20 April 1954, p. 111, no. 72, ADP; A. Arulraj. *Puducheri Suthanthira Poratathin Kalachuvadukal*, Pondicherry, 2005, pp. 146-7.
52. *Indian Express*, 1, 2 April 1954; *The Hindu*, 2 April 1954; Tél demarqué du Tézenas du Montcel, Pondicherry, 1 April 1954, no. 73, p. 6, AO, ADP; Agence Indienne d'information, 7 April 1954, p. 16, no. 73, AO, ADP; Projet de déclaration, May 1954, pp. 161-2, IF 18, ADP; *Hindustan Times*, 8 April 1954; Interview with A. Arulraj; A. Arulraj, *Puducheri Suthanthira Poratathin Kalachuvadukal*, Pondicherry, 2005, pp. 135-6; Interview with N. Sudarsanan, son of Narayanasamy of Kalitheerthankuppam.
53. See, p. 166, AO, no. 17, ADP; *Hindustan Times*, 1, 6, 8 April 1954; Tél demarqué, Pondicherry, 18 May 1954, p. 273, IF 54, ADP; Tél demarqué de Comrep, Pondicherry, 3 April 1954, p. 72, no. 72, ADP; *Le Populaire*, 12 April 1954; *The Hindu*, 4, 7 April 1954; V. Subbiah, *Puduvaiyin Viduthalaiai Vendradutha Thozhilalarkalin Veera Varalaru*, Pondicherry, 1986, p. 38; Agence d'information indienne, 11 April 1954, p. 20, no. 73, AO, ADP; Lettre de London à Ostrorog, Madras, 12 April 1954, no. 73, pp. 21-2, ADP; Claude de Marolle, Chargés d'affaires à Ministre des Affaires Etrangères, New Delhi, 4 June 1954, p. 41, no. 73, AO, ADP; Tél demarqué, Pondicherry, 2 April 1954, p. 69, no. 72, ADP;

Lettre de Sinnasamy Iyer, Commandant la brigade de Villenour à M. le s/lieutenant, Pondicherry, Villenour, 9 May 1954, p. 285, IF 54, ADP; *The Hindu*, 8, 9, 10 April 1954.

54. See p. 166, AO, no. 17, ADP; *Le Populaire*, 13, 14 April 1954; Lettre de Sinnasamy Iyer, Commandant la brigade de Villenour à M. le s/lieutenant, Pondicherry, Villenour, 9 May 1954, pp. 285-6, IF 54, ADP; *The HIndu*, 10, 12, 13 April 1954.

55. Claude de Marolles, charges d'affaires au Ministre des Affaires Etrangères, New Delhi, 4 June 1954, p. 41, no. 73, AO, ADP; Service d'information indienne, 2 May 1954, p. 75, no. 73, AO, ADP; *The Hindu*, 8, 15 April 1954; Note sur Mouttoukomarapparettiar, Membre de l'Assemblée Représentative—Inde H 22, AOM.

56. *Times of India*, 9 April 1954; Tél au Ministère des Affaires Etrangères, Pondicherry, 5 April 1954, pp. 139-40, IF 54, ADP; *Hindustan Times*, 8 April 1954.

57. *Hindustan Times*, 6 April 1954; *The Hindu* 3, 5, 7 April 1954; note, 14 May 1954, no. 38, p. 1, ADP.

58. R. Dadala, op. cit., pp. 24, 25; *Le Monde*, 19 August 1954; Note, 14 May 1954, pp. 21-2, no. 38, ADP.

59. *The Hindu*, 9 April 1954; Lettre du Ministre de la France d'Outre-mer au Ministre des Affaires Etrangères, Paris, 15 April 1954, no. 17, pp. 74-5, ADP.

60. Lettre de Goubert au President de l'Assemblée Nationale, Madras, 26 May 1954, pp. 177-87, no. 38, ADP.

61. Tél de London au Ministre des Affairs Etrangères, Madras, 17 May 1954, p. 239, IF 54, ADP; *The Hindu*, 10 May 1954; Paris Presse, *l'Intransigeant*, 18 May 1954, p. 74, no. 73, AO, ADP.

CHAPTER 10

Curtains Down on French Rule in India

MORE EVENTS SINCE MARCH 1954

It is noteworthy at this juncture that the responsibility of maintaining law and order was still vested in the governor. With the Socialist Party opting for merger with the Indian Union without a referendum, the French Indian administration became suspicious about the loyalty of the policemen who numbered about 650 in the four French settlements, of whom only 20 were White Frenchmen from France. Arms and ammunition were therefore delivered only to the most reliably anti-mergerist policemen. They were posted in plain clothes near the houses of the Socialist Party leaders to monitor their activities. Inspite of this Karunendra Mudaliar's office was raided by some anti-merger strongmen shouting slogans against the Socialist Party leaders. Inducements were also offered to the police in order for them to remain loyal. Thus, the total children's allowance for every policeman having more than two children was raised from Rs. 10 to Rs. 100 per month. It must be noted that till then the police force was quite loyal to the French government. It had in its ranks such loyalist officers as Sinnasamy Iyer, who was in charge of Bahur when Ramachandra Reddiar was its mayor.[1]

Ménard stepped up security operations in Pondicherry town, with the idea of arresting the pro-merger leaders. Demonstrations, processions and assembly of more than two persons were banned in all public places. Pondicherry itself was sealed off from all communication, including flow of news, ostensibly with a plan of action to round up all pro-merger leaders in the course of time. Out of eight communes in Pondicherry, three were separated from Pondicherry proper and access to them was through Indian territory, which had been sealed off by the Indian government. So French police could not go there. It seems that Commissioner André Ménard was not afraid of Eduoard Goubert who, according to him, did not have public support in Pondicherry. Instead, Ménard feared Subbiah who was then master of Thirubhuvanai village. Ménard had at his disposal, apart from the 600 policemen, some men from Indochina who were on leave in Pondicherry in order to maintain law and order. In fact, 1,000 recruits of Pondicherry were fighting France's war in Vietnam at that time.[2]

With a frame of mind that was definitely anti-Goubert and anti-Subbiah, Commissioner Ménard manoeuvred to create a new political party with a certain Franco-Indian, André Gaebelé, in the lead. He promised one-and-a-half crore rupees for the development of the people. He blatantly accused Goubert of swindling the sum of 5 crore rupees given earlier for cyclone relief measures. Goubert and his party members were openly derided and even attacked.

Commissioner Ménard made a last ditch attempt to muster some remaining support for the French regime from some French pensioners in order to set up a new pro-French political party as well as an 'interim' cabinet. Goubert, Muthu Kumarappa Reddiar and Muthu Poullé were dismissed from their posts. But Balasubramaniam, the president of the Assembly, P. Dhanaraj and Karunendra Mudaliar were still in office. They did not join Goubert in Nettapakkam.

Dutamby, a retired magistrate and pensioner (related to the student leader, Antoine Mariadassou's family) formed the pro-French Democratic Party, with the assistance of Frenchmen like Gaudart and the dental surgeon, Dr F. Bleicher. He was expected to set up the 'interim' cabinet. Mahomed Ismail, an advocate and former minister, was rumoured to take the place of Muthu Poullé.[3]

Dutamby organised pro-French demonstrations in Pondicherry on 31 March, on the very day that Nettapakkam was captured by Goubert. Rahouf of Villianur owned a fleet of buses operating in Pondicherry. It seems that Rahouf had been previously arrested for various crimes and had been released only when he gave an undertaking to lend his buses to the pro-French campaign. Rahouf was also wanted by the Indian police in connection with the arson of an old airport camp in

Indian territory. Rahouf lent a helping hand to Dutamby and collected villagers from their places in his buses and brought them to Pondicherry. The demonstrators numbering about 1,500 were escorted by French police constables on bicycles and assembled near the house of Dutamby. There they divided themselves into batches and went around Pondicherry shouting slogans like 'Long Live French India', 'Vive la France', 'Down with India' and 'Down with Indian newspapers'. A few batches were concentrated in the White town, where demonstrations were not allowed and where the Indian consulate was located.[4]

Commissioner Ménard and the inspector of colonies, Tezenas du Montcel, watched the demonstrations from the balcony of the governor's palace. Du Montcel later addressed a merchants' delegation where he declared that France would not give up its possessions in India. It is nevertheless quite strange that such demonstrations were allowed in Pondicherry at a time when there was a blanket ban on all demonstrations and the pro-merger demonstrations in Pondicherry and Karaikal were being put down with an iron hand at the same time. In the meantime, French police were posted at the Indian consulate in Pondicherry to monitor the movements there.[5]

At this juncture one could affirm that Ménard and Tézenas du Montcel were staunch colonialists who were at the service of France and French imperialism. Ménard, especially, was known to behave condescendingly towards the Pondicherrians. It seems that when Pondicherrians came to see him, he mocked them saying the following:

'VOILÀ LES FRANÇAIS QUI ARRIVENT'
(HERE COMES THE FRENCHMEN).[6]

The blockade imposed by the Indian government was also stepped up. The frequency of trains plying from Villupuram to Pondicherry was reduced to once a day. The Mettur electricity supply came just once a day. Even food items became scarce in Pondicherry. In Karaikal, the water that was much needed for irrigation was under the threat of being cut off. The French accused the Indian government of using economic pressure to gain support for the merger. They resorted to importing petrol from Djibouti into Pondicherry. Essential items were imported by sea into Pondicherry.[7]

On 6 April 1954, Prime Minister Nehru declared in Parliament that the Indian government had no intention of taking any unilateral action to take possession of the 'liberated enclaves'. He said that the takeover of Nettapakkam was a spontaneous movement of the people. However, he maintained that the ban on French police going there had to continue. He also said that except for petrol all other essential items were being supplied to Pondicherry and that certain economic measures were in place in order to prevent smuggling. He called for a *de facto* transfer of administration at once, but not the *de jure* transfer of sovereignty. He promised to safeguard the cultural and other rights of the French Indians. He also offered to open negotiations. At that time, the Praja Socialist Party of India came out in favour of the stand taken by the Socialist Party of French India under Goubert and the French Socialist Party (SFIO) in favour of a merger without plebiscite.

In April 1954, the Students' Congress agitated in Pondicherry. During the agitations, one of the student leaders, B. Rangapillai, was beaten up and arrested, along with many other students. Rangapillai's finger was fractured. Sellane Naiker, president of the Central Merger Committee, defended the students in court, along with S. Perumal, and got them released. Sellane's house and that of Swamy Lourdes, Bharat Yuva Sangam, leader were besieged by *goondas* during this period. Sellane Naiker also released a statement in favour of a merger, claiming that French Indians were part and parcel of Mother India. On their part, A. Arulraj, president of French Indian Youth Congress of Pondicherry, and Léon Saint Jean of Karaikal condemned police initimidation. In Karaikal volunteers belonging to the Congress and Dravida Kazhagam who agitated for merger were arrested.[8]

On 14 April 1954, the Students' Congress under Dorai Munisamy agitated for freedom at the Congress headquarters in Chetty Street, Pondicherry. Sellane Naiker visited the place and spoke to the students. Agitations were also spearheaded by the Youth Congress leader A. Arulraj and D. Mariappan. They were kept in lock-up for two days. B. Rangapillai, N. Damodaran, Anwar Ali Khan and others took out a students' procession on behalf of the Students' Congress.

Fishermen were mobilised for the Freedom Movement by A. Arulraj, N. Ranganathan and K. Karunanidhi.

The houses of S. Perumal, president of Bar Association, Sellane Naiker and Swamy Lourdes were attacked. Earlier in Karaikal, the Youth Congress leader, A. Ramasrinivasan, and a few other personalities, like Shaik Madar Sahib Maracair, a leading merchant and Nagarajan, were arrested and beaten. The last two were personally attacked by the French commissioner of police of Karaikal for organising demonstrations against French rule. Some pro-French *goondas* brought down the Indian flags hoisted above some houses in Kosapalayam and Pillachavadi. The French police even arrested 60 nationalist volunteers. They and some *goondas* plundered the goods of Indian citizens in Kalapet.

On his part, Tezenas du Montcel after his investigative mission in French India, arrived at certain conclusions. On the whole, he was not very optimistic about the continuance of French rule in India due to the economic pressure exerted by the Indian government. He thought that there was no military solution to the problem. He added that if the referendum was favourable to France, the Indian government would denounce it. Besides, in the then conditions, he doubted that the referendum would be favourable to France. In conclusion, he wanted to find a common solution to facilitate the cession of the French territories without violating the French Constitution, which implied painful negotiations.[9]

By the end of April, when all the major leaders of Pondicherry like V. Subbiah or Goubert were in exile, the French government accepted the proposition of Nehru for negotiations, provided the economic blockade and visa restrictions were relaxed. Ménard was kept in the dark for the moment of this evolution. In fact, it was decided to replace him. The French government wanted to complete the negotiations in one year, while the senator, Pakkirisamy Poullé, wanted to do it in ten years.[10]

Inspite of signing the merger resolution earlier, R.M.A.S. Pakkirisamy Poullé announced a plan along with Henri Jacquier to make the French territories free trade zones in order to develop trade between India and France. They even toyed with the idea of a condominium during this period. Thus they seems to have toed the earlier line of François Baron and Daniel Levi. Jacquier, on his part, tried to calm the situation and labelled Goubert's actions as superfluous by declaring that the Indian and French governments would arrive at a settlement soon. About this time, Pakkirisamy Poullé and Jacquier left for Paris from Madras to find a solution to the French settlements. It is strange to note that Goubert and Muthu Kumarappa Reddiar saw them off at the airport, though they had denounced the condominium proposal. Were they veering towards the idea of a condominium at that time? Goubert, however, declared then that the entire population was for a merger, save for some government servants.[11]

Around this time, the French Indian administration prohibited entry of Indian nationals into Pondicherry. The government of India, on its part, made it obligatory for French Indians to obtain valid identity documents with photographs delivered by the French authorities and validitated by the Indian consul general in Pondicherry in order to travel to Indian territory. There was acute scarcity of kerosene and other essential items. Petrol supplies were actually banned from entering French India. Besides, areas under cultivation in Pondicherry and Karaikal were irrigated by waters that flowed, respectively, from the Senji and Ponniar rivers and the Arsalar. If the Indian government decided to construct dams across these rivers, then Pondicherry and Karaikal would be adversely affected. Besides, sea and land customs were tightened up. Nehru, however, affirmed that the economic measures had been taken only to protect Indian interests.[12]

At this point, Subbiah took the initiative to forge a united front for merger with Sellane Naiker's Merger Congress and others. He also expressed sympathy for the movement led by Edouard Goubert.[13]

On 4 April 1954, Subbiah declared from Delhi that the struggle to drive the French out of Pondicherry would continue. He held that 'these tiny pockets are not of much economic value to the French imperialists. They were holding on to them because they were vital as ports of call and supplies on their way to their colonial empire in Indochina. He added that the Communist Party had since 1948 stood for merger with Indian Union without referendum. He then organised an all-party conference in Cuddalore. Sellane Naiker, Dadala,

Murugasamy Clemenceau, D. Mariappan, K.S. Venkatarama Iyer, A. Arulraj, Sabapathy and K. Karunanidhi participated. They decided to form an agitational group. But Sellane Naiker did not join it. Instead, he ran his own show for independence with himself as president of the Central Merger Congress.[14]

Later, V. Subbiah became president of the United Action Group, with A. Arulraj as the secretary. Subbiah wanted to step up freedom operations in Pondicherry from 7 April 1954. Subsequently, there were demonstrations and processions organised by pro-merger groups which included the Youth Congress, Communist Party and the Dravida Kazhagam, waving Indian flags. Many were arrested. Communist-sponsored volunteers which included Communist party militants, the Youth Congress and other local Left parties actively demonstrated for freedom within Pondicherry.[15]

In Karaikal, S.A. Shaikh Madar Sahib Marakkayar, member of the Karaikal United Merger Committee and Congressman, strongly refuted the statement emanating from certain quarters that the French Indian Muslims were not for a merger. Later, he was elected as president of the Karaikal National Congress. R.M.A.S. Venkatachalapathy Poullé was one of the leaders of the Merger Movement in Karaikal. Léon Saint Jean, general secretary of the United Merger Front of Karaikal, declared that a decision by the municipal and Representative Assembly members was more than enough to fulfil the conditions stipulated in the French Constitution for ruling on the merger. Later, Shaikh Madar, Pichaikannu and Nagarajan of the Congress Party were taken into custody.[16]

On 10 April 1954, one of the leaders of the Fusion Movement in Karaikal, Ramanathan Chettiar, was arrested along with Sundaramurthi, president of the Jawahar Youth League. But an anti-merger pro-French group also functioned in Karaikal at that time under the name, Progressive Party. K.T.K. Muthukumaraswami Poullé was its president, N. Appadurai Mudaliar vice-president, Robert Saint Jean general secretary and S. Hameed treasurer. There were others in Karaikal like M.S. Dawood of the 'Jeunesse Musulmane' (Muslim Youth Association) as well as a certain S. Venkataramayer who were also staunchly pro-French.

On 13 April, the merger congress under Sellane Naiker and the

French India Congress Party organised a massive pro-India demonstration in Pondicherry. The French police cracked down on the demonstration.[17]

Parisian newspapers like *l'Intransigeant* and even *Le Monde* came down heavily on Goubert for the critical situation prevailing in Pondicherry. He was derided as the most hostile racketeer, swindler, '*topas*' and 'deputy-gangster' in the whole of South Asia. He was also referred to as 'Cogi Goubert'—for his earlier love for cockfights and his lowly origins. Goubert was born of a French father, Berchin de Goubert, and a 'paria' (Pariyar) servant mother. He was brought up by his mother, according to *l'Intransigeant*. The paper attributed the current actions of Goubert against the French to his 'tumultuous childhood'. It was said that the notorious Nelly Krishnan was his right hand. With such rowdies at his command, Goubert terrorised Pondicherry and indulged in all sorts of nefarious activities to enrich himself, the paper held.[18]

During the same period, it was wrongly reported in the *Indian Express* of 15 April 1954 that the pro-French Dutamby, Gaudart and Bleicher, accompanied by policemen in a car, went to Sellane Naiker's house and asked him to haul down the Indian flag. In a letter to Sellane Naiker dated 15 April 1954, Bleicher denied any such happening.[19] In the same month of April, the French president, Joseph Laniel, sent a special representative to India, by the name of Christian Belle, to find a solution to the problem of referendum. He and the French ambassador in Delhi, Count d'Ostrorog, met R.K. Nehru and had several rounds of discussions to thrash out a solution. Further discussions took place in Paris and Delhi in which the secretary of the Ministry of Foreign Affairs, N.R. Pillai, participated. The French proposition of a mixed Franco-Indian administration was rejected, as it would be dominated by the French. But strangely, no representative from French India took part in these discussions. It showed that the French and Indian governments preferred to decide the future of French India without the concurrence of the French Indians.[20] Two major leaders of the pro-merger movement were in exile and under Indian government protection. They were not able to participate in these negotiations as representatives of the French Indians. Subbiah had been in exile for quite sometime. But it was a grave strategic error, or a calculated risk, on the part of Goubert to flee to Nettapakkam, induced by the Reddiar landlords, who had their own agendas, when he was most wanted to represent the French Indian interests during the negotiations. Lambert Saravane and Sellane Naiker were not influential enough to represent French Indian interests. Dutamy, propped up by Ménard, would never rise to the occasion. Perhaps, it was a great misfortune for French Indians that Goubert by fleeing to Nettapakkam had made himself unavailable to represent French Indian interests, when the negotiations for a settlement was on. So the negotiations would take place over and above the heads of the French Indians.

From 19 April, a system of passports and identity cards, introduced towards the end of March, were made obligatory for French Indians to cross the frontier. This created difficulties for French Indians travelling between the enclaves and to India, and also for Pondicherry to get supplies of essential food items from India. On 26 April, two Mahesians, Anandan and Achuthan, were killed in Mahé in French police firing and three others were severely wounded.[21]

In May, Bleicher complained that he and his friends had been attacked at Mortandi on the French Indian border. On 6 May 1954, Goubert's supporters attacked Koonichampattu village and ransacked it. In the process, Periathamby Gounder's house as well as his properties, which included oil engines and cattle, were destroyed. As a consequence, 50 French gendarmes and 2 officers arrived in Pondicherry to maintain law and order. The French government denied the presence of any French troops in Pondicherry. But Ménard admitted that there were some Pondicherry military personnel on leave (from Indochina), who were helping the local police to maintain order.[22]

The flight of Goubert and his associates to Nettapakkam permitted the Indian and French Governments to reopen negotiations for a settlement. R.K. Nehru, the political director, assisted by M.K.V. Padmanabhan and N.B. Nair, went to Paris to attend a Franco-Indian conference on 14 May 1954. R.K. Nehru was a cousin of the Indian Prime Minister. Sardar Malik was the Indian ambassador in Paris at that time. The French delegation was led by M. De la Tournelle, Christian Belle and Count d'Ostrorog, the French ambassador in India. During this time, opinion was gaining ground in certain quarters in France that the *de facto* transfer of territories without referendum could be first affected in exchange for a guarantee to protect French cultural and linguistic presence in Pondicherry.[23]

No Pondicherrian represented French Indians, in the high table of negotiations. Goubert and his associates had played themselves out of the negotiations at a very crucial time. Subbiah was still in exile. No other Pondicherry leader was in a position to ask for the inclusion of a French Indian representative in the negotiations. As a result, French Indian interests were no more represented by a French Indian in the ensuing negotiations between the governments of India and France. Instead, there were some individual petitions emanating from the likes of A. Senapathi Mudaliar, president of the Pondicherry General Merchants' Association, representing 1,500 trading establishments, addressed to the French commissioner and metroplitan government. Mudaliar demanded that if the French government agreed in principle to the merger of the settlements with India, a transition period of not less than 30 years should be provided for in the agreement, and all restrictions on trade lifted as well as the transit of men, postal items and goods between the French territories and the enclaves as well as with the Indian Union liberalised fully.[24]

Nehru himself announced in Parliament on 13 May 1954 that there were no plans to annex the 'liberated' villages of French India and suggested negotiations between the Indian and French governments.[25] This announcement was made without consulting Goubert or his associates. Nehru no more needed that as Goubert was no more in Pondicherry and was actually at the mercy of the Indian government in Nettapakkam and in Indian territory.

In the course of the negotiations in Paris from 17 May to 4 June 1954, R.K. Nehru insisted that the basic principles of an immediate *de facto* transfer of power to India must be admitted, especially with regard to justice, customs, finance and police, while the details could be worked out through negotiations either in Paris or in Delhi. He did not want any referendum, unlike the French, as the elected representatives had already pronounced a decision in favour of merger. R.K. Nehru did not accept the demand of the French delegation that the elected representatives' mandate should be suspended. There was no agreement on the lifting of the economic blockade or the subjection of the inhabitants of French territories to Indian police surveillance. However, the opinion gained ground in India that the Paris negotiations had failed. R.K. Nehru himself admitted it in the course of a declaration on 12 June 1954.[26]

Meanwhile the French Ambassador, Count d'Ostrorog, envisaged the immediate recall of André Ménard. He nevertheless informed Ménard that the government had decided formally to quit French India shortly. Ménard, on his part, held that any attempt to maintain French power, though it was the only honourable solution, would be costly and dangerous in the long term.[27] Besides, the failure of the Paris negotiations forced the Indian government to revert to the vexatious measures related to circulation of goods and the movement of people between French India and the Indian Union in place since April 1954. The arrival of 50 gendarmes in Pondicherry aggravated the tension. The government of India demanded their withdrawal.[28]

A new government in France, under Pierre Mendes-France, had assumed power since June 1954. R.K. Nehru met Mendes-France in June. There was then some hope that a negotiated solution would be found.[29]

In Pondicherry, Sellane Naiker, president of the Central Merger Congress, called for the immediate withdrawal of France from its territories in India. On his part, Pakkirisamy Poullé declared that a fresh French delegation would arrive in India shortly to continue with the negotiations. Later, Pakkirisamy Poullé, with the consent of the French government, seems to have even contacted Goubert in Nettapakkam, asking him to come back to Pondicherry and revive the Council of Government and occupy his place in it in such a way that he could open direct negotiations with the Indian government to determine the status of French India. But for reasons that we do not know of, Goubert refused to accept this proposition. It was a grave political error on the part of Goubert at this juncture to have neglected Pakkirisamy's proposition, which was inspired by the French government. Thus, Goubert missed the opportunity to negotiate directly with the Indian government the future status of French India once again, probably under the influence of his landlord colleagues, which left the field free for the Indian and French governments to thrash out a settlement without the direct involvement of French

Indians in it.[30] The French government, having failed in its last attempt to bring back Goubert to Pondicherry so that he might lead the negotiations with the Indian government, decided thenceforth to take matters into its own hands and step up its direct negotiations with the Indian government in its search for a constitutional solution to the French Indian problem, without involving the French Indians in any way.

In the meantime, a certain repression was unleashed both in Pondicherry and Karaikal where pro-merger meetings were dispersed and agitators were arrested and imprisoned for a few days. In Karaikal, Madar Shah Marakkayar and Nagarajan were condemned for three months in prison by the local court. They were fined heavily and banished from Karaikal for two years. Besides, Yanam was captured by the pro-mergerists. Pallur and Padakkal in Mahé were also occupied. In May 1954, the workers of Rodier Mill were laid off. This created tension in Pondicherry.[31]

In the same month, Goubert was dismissed from the UDSR group of the National Assembly in Paris, to which he belonged, on account of his separatist activities. In a long letter to the president of the National Assembly, Goubert denounced French colonialists, like Commisioner Ménard and the inspector of police, Guyard, and argued that France being the country of liberty and human rights should also consider giving freedom to French Indians. Subsequently, the National Assembly voted to cancel the parliamentary immunity of Goubert.[32]

On 8 June 1954, Goubert was summoned by the Commission of Parliamentary Immunity of the National Assembly in Paris. Goubert was accused of taking away the authority of France over a territory. On 29 June 1954, the French Parliament decided to move against Goubert legally for inciting violence and rebellion against the state. Arrest warrants had already been issued against Goubert, Muthu Kumarappa Reddiar, mayor of Nettapakkam Venkata Subba Reddiar and Muthu Poullé, the suspended mayor of Pondicherry.[33] It was rumoured then that Goubert and Muthu Kumarappa Reddiar were making preparations to invade Pondicherry with their 'volunteers'. The ire of the French was directed upon Goubert. He was recognised as the mastermind of the rebellion. The French believed that Goubert had declared war on France. They took some military measures to counter the invasion of Pondicherry by the rebels. They thought that Goubert was a gangster. Lambert Saravane remembered that in their young days they used to call him 'Coji Goubert' or 'Cock' Goubert, because he organised bloody cockfights for money. Goubert, too, disliked Ménard and wanted him replaced.[34]

At the same time, a barrage of criticism was being levelled against the consul general of India, Kewal Singh, since April 1954 by journals like *République Française*. This paper attacked the government of India, the Prime Minister of India and the consul general in the most vulgar terms. The campaign of *République Française* was reinforced by a large number of tracts and pamphlets aimed at denigrating the consul general. The Indian government brought this vilification campaign to the attention of the French authorities.[35]

But in Pondicherry, the French expected an attack by the anti-French forces in Nettapakkam. Muthu Kumarappa Reddiar, lieutenant of Goubert, threatened that he had at his disposal 15,000 men which included ex-military men and volunteers from the Indian Union and that they would attack Pondicherry once all its inhabitants were evacuated. Similar threats emanated from Tamil Nadu. A certain S.A. Rahim of the Tamil Nadu Socialist Party wanted to assemble one million men to capture Pondicherry.[36]

At this juncture, the government of India decided to accord an official status to Chandernagore, merged with India in 1951 after a people's referendum. As a result, Chandernagore would be integrated with the state of West Bengal and would have no member in the Parliament. Instead it was reduced to the status of a small municipality.[37] The question then was whether the other southern French territories would meet with the same fate or not.

In the meantime, the Dravida Kazagam and Dravida Munnetra Kazhagam, which was an offshoot of the former, joined the Freedom Movement, or rather the Merger Movement. We can never reasonably talk of a Freedom Movement in Pondicherry or French India, because the struggle was for the integration or subjection of French India to the Indian Union and never for the complete freedom of French India from both the French and Indian Unions.

However, on the eve of integration and merger, the Dravidian revolutionary poet Bharathidasan, along with a certain Lemaire Ramasamy Iyer, who was the former's neighbour, started the French Indian People's Defence Party to prevent French India going over to the Indian Union. They declared that a French warship has been sent to Pondicherry and asked the Tamilians not to trust the 'bogus' nationalists. They even printed anti-Indian tracts and distributed it among the people.[38]

In July 1954, V. Subbiah threatened from Kottakuppam to break the statue of Dupleix on 14 July, Bastille Day, which was usually celebrated with great pomp in Pondicherry. Naturally, the statue was placed under a guard by the military. But the Indian government, through its representative R.K. Nehru, denied that it was in touch with Subbiah or had any intention to annex the 'liberated' territories. At that time, in Bahur commune, a village was captured by 200 mergerists led by R. Dadala.[39]

The French Union Assembly opined that negotiations between the French and Indian governments need to be resumed in order to prevent the invasion of Pondicherry by the pro-mergerists. It was a time when the French were losing out in Indochina. In Mahé, the mayor and the municipal members had opted for a merger with the Indian Union. On 22 July 1954, French police opened fire on a group of French Indian refugees from Bahur, killing one Indian citizen.[40]

It appears that the French were no more insisting on a referendum by July. Instead they, with Pierre Mendez France in the lead, wanted to first thrash out a Franco-Indian agreement for the *de facto* and *de jure* transfers of power and then subject this agreement to a vote by elected representatives like the municipal members. The French thought that the French Constitution would not be violated in this manner. However, in the same month, there was a transfer of power in Mahé by the French administrator, Deschamps, to the joint action committee led by the Mahajana Sabha leader, I.K. Kumaran. This happened after four weeks of total economic blockade and political pressure imposed by Indians on Mahé. Accepting the reins of power, Kumaran praised France as the 'mother of democracy' and assured that French culture would be protected and promoted in Mahé.

Yanam, too, had slipped away from French control and it had happened as early as June. On 13 June 1954, Madimchetty Satyanandam, mayor of Yanam, Dadala and others marched at the head of thousands of volunteers into Yanam and overthrew the French administration there under Georges Sala, without much violence. The pro-French stalwart, Samatam Kristaya, was assassinated by the merger elements. The Nettapakkam government welcomed Yanam's 'liberation'. Muthu Kumarappa Reddiar himself went to Yanam to celebrate the 'liberation' of Yanam.[41]

In the meantime, most of the leaders at Nettapakkam had fled to Madras or Bangalore. With Dadala's return to Pondicherry, the agitation against French rule in Pondicherry gained momentum. He and his men threatened to attack Bahur and also Pondicherry. Kaatupalayam, near Tavalakuppam was penetrated by Dadala's men.[42]

By then, the French troops had suffered an ignominious defeat at Dien Bien Phu on 7 May 1954, at the hands of the Vietnamese. In July, the eight years war in Indochina of the French against the Communists led by Ho Chi Minh came to an end through the efforts of the new French president, Pierre Mendez France.[43] Pondicherry's role as a maritime link and stopover for the French between France and Indochina for more than one century thus came to an end abruptly. Given this new geopolitical scenario, wherein Pondicherry was no more needed as a link between France and Indochina, it was only to be expected that the French might abandon its territories in India shortly.

On 19 July 1954, the Democratic Party of Dutamby adopted a resolution in favour of integration with India without referendum. Dutamby submitted this resolution to the commissioner, Ménard. It was Ménard who had propped up Dutamby to counter Goubert. But now it was the turn of Dutamby to stab him in the back. Ménard accused Dutamby of being a crypto-Communist who was in constant touch with Subbiah. This he did in order to prevent Goubert from being in the good books of the consul general of India, Kewal Singh. He also admitted that he had been fooled by the posturing of Dutamby. Dutamby's pension was suspended. Later, he was wooed by the Congress Party, though he had been, in fact, sympathetic to Subbiah earlier.[44]

Meanwhile, Count d'Ostrorog thought that the time had come to act more quickly than ever to avoid a *de facto* solution being imposed on the French by the unfolding events. Besides, the Republican Party of Maurice Gaudart, ex-representative of Pondicherry in the French Union Assembly, came out in favour of a merger without referendum.[45]

When the situation was thus, on 24 July 1954, three youngsters belonging to affluent families of Pondicherry went on fast at the French India National Congress office in Chetty Street asking the French to quit Pondicherry. They were C.M. Achraff, son of H.M. Cassime, the mayor of Pondicherry, L. Balasubramaniam, son of Loganatha Iyer, head of political affairs, and the son of the magistrate Antoine Tamby, known as Prosper Tamby. Advocate S. Perumal, general secretary of the pro-merger (Sellane) Congress Party, joined them. He said that he was not averse to the holding of referendum under the control of the French and Indian governments, in which all parties must be allowed to participate. This fasting attracted the attention of the people as they belonged to three different religions—Hindu, Muslim and Christian. This sent the message that all the religious communities in Pondicherry were together in asking the French to quit India.[46]

The three students who were fasting, called off their fast after two days when many local personalities gave them their assurance that the merger would indeed take place.[47] At that time, during the course of a meeting, 150 Pondicherry merchants adopted a resolution in favour of merger. However, the Progressive Party of Karaikal, whose general secretary was Robert Saint Jean as well as ex-French military men of Karaikal, and the 'Comité de Défense des Interêts Français' of Pondicherry whose president was C. Ramasamy Iyer and vice-president Mr Valot, the 'Comité de Défense des Interêts Musulmans de Karaikal' and the 'Association Jeunesse Muslumane' of Karaikal were opposed to a merger without referendum. They considered it treason to abandon the plan without consulting the people. Some wanted the recall of Commissoner Ménard.[48]

On 9 and 15 August, a large-scale agitation took place in Pondicherry. Shops and mills were closed. Schools were closed. Police clashed with the agitators. Ansari Duraisamy and S.R. Subramaniam were arrested and let off. There were at least 200 arrests. A certain Anbarasan and 20 others were sentenced to jail for terms lasting from 3 to 6 months.[49]

In the same month, a French correspondent, Georges Gallean of *Le Monde*, met Edouard Goubert and his associates at Nettapakkam. He described Goubert as massive and slow, draped in a white shawl like a Roman senator, having a high forehead, regular features, a heavy chin, dark complexion, bad teeth and tired eyes. But he was vigorous and blunt in his speech. To Gallean, Muthu Poullé seemed silent and solid, speaking only when asked and having a sneaky sense of humour while Muthu Kumarappa Reddiar was stout, with a subtle mind, good in politics and the most intelligent of the lot. Gallean ascertained that Goubert wanted integration of French India with the Indian Union without referendum.

According to Gallean, Goubert feared that the French might turn towards Subbiah and the Communists as well as the 'Untouchables' in order to retain Pondicherry. It is noteworthy at this juncture that the French had given equal rights and privileges to the oppressed castes at par with the other castes, unlike in British India, which had endeared them to many from among this group of people. Goubert did not forget this factor. He himself was of partial 'paria' origin. He delivered a parting shot to Gallean in the following words: 'You can write whatever you want on us. I no longer read French newspapers. I have cut myself off from France'. These words show the depth of Goubert's disillusionment with France and its colonial policies and attitudes, though he had a Frenchman as father and French blood in his veins, and his increasing identification with the India of his mother of humble origins. Indians were ready to embrace him fully inspite of his partial European origin, whereas the French were unable to do the same at that time. They could not digest the fact that someone of mixed origin, who was expected to be subservient to them, had actually risen to challenge their supremacy.[50]

THE ASHRAM POSITION

There was a wrong notion prevailing in certain circles that the Sri Aurobindo Ashram was just a spiritual organisation set up with the objective of producing an elite race of 'supermen'. There was also a wrong notion that the organisation was entrenched in Hindu philosophy, tradition and belief. Nowhere in their writings had Sri

Aurobindo or Mirra Alfassa, the Mother, claimed that their organisation was a part of the Hindu religion. In fact, it was a new religion or sect, whose central figures were Sri Aurobindo and the Mother, and no one else. There is no place for Hindu idols or ceremonies in the Ashram burial complex or in the Ashram dining hall. It is rather the images of Sri Aurobindo and Mother Mirra Alfassa which were displayed everywhere.

Also, what we see in practice is that the Ashram members indulge freely in business, through which they made immense fortunes. Business was not considered as contrary to spirituality as they understood their faith. Given the immense stakes that the Ashram had in Pondicherry society, it was quite natural that the Ashram authorities tried their hands in politics, too, either directly or indirectly. We have seen that Lambert Saravane, André Zeganadan, P. Counouma and others were close to the Ashram, especially Mirra Alfassa. These personalities did play a role in French Indian politics, under the influence of the Ashram.

Sri Aurobindo had never shunned politics completely though it was said that he was meditating silently, etc. He himself had wanted the Congress leaders to accept Stafford Cripp's Mission to break the constitutional deadlock over Indian support in World War II in British India. But nobody paid attention to him at that time as his influence in Indian politics was non-existent by then. When India became Independent after Partition, he again made a political statement saying that India will be reunited again.

Coming to Pondicherry and French India, he never took a clear stand with regard to the future of French India. He put aside his meditation and freely met French politicians like Commissioner Baron and Maurice Schuman. He had a hand in the drafting of the French India Socialist Party programme, which stipulated that Pondicherry and French India would remain with the French Union. As long as he lived, he never demanded the integration of French India with the Indian Union outright. Mirra Alfassa, too, followed a similar line. Till then and even much later, she did not entertain the thought of the integration of Pondicherry with the Indian Union. Instead, she always looked at Pondicherry politics through the prism of her own Ashram interests, rather than the interest and welfare of all Pondicherrians. Her policies towards French India evolved accordingly.

Mirra Alfassa who possessed and managed immense properties in Pondicherry (White town) in her personal name and in the name of Sri Aurobindo, submitted a letter on 15 August 1954 through the French general secretary of the Ashram, Philippe Barbier Saint Hilaire, addressed to the French Ambassador, Count d'Ostrorog, expressing her desire for double nationality. Thus, even when integration with the Indian Union was round the corner, she never wanted to sever her connections with France. She still tried to salvage some connection with France for herself and the Ashramites, who were mostly mere settlers in Pondicherry and not the sons of the soil. The pro-French journal, *République Française*, which had been always critical of Goubert and his followers, came out in support of this demand.[51]

Philippe Barbier Saint Hilaire (Pavitra), Norman Dawsett, Jay Holmes Smith, Nolini Kanta Gupta, Indra Sen and K.D. Sethna, all on the staff of the Sri Aurobindo International University Centre, wrote a letter to Jawaharlal Nehru requesting him to grant them Indian nationality as well as leave room for a double nationality which, they claimed, was an inevitable step in the evolution of human unity and integration, and was viewed by Sri Aurobindo as such. In her declaration of 15 August 1954, the Mother wrote:

I want to mark this day by the expression of a long-cherished wish; that of becoming Indian citizen. From the first time I came to India in 1914, I feel that India is my true country. The country of my soul and spirit—I had decided to realize this wish as soon as India would be free—But I had to wait still longer because of my heavy responsibilities in the Ashram here in Pondicherry. Now the time has come when I can declare myself.

But in accordance with Sri Aurobindo's ideal, my purpose is to show that truth lies in union rather than in division. To reject one nationality in order to obtain another is not an ideal solution. So, I hope I shall be allowed to adopt a double nationality, that is to say, to remain French while I become Indian.

I am French by birth and early education; I am Indian by choice and predilection. In my consciousness there is no antagonism between the two; on the contrary, they combine very well and complete one another. I knew also that I can be of service to both equally, for my only aim in life is to give a concrete form to Sri Aurobindo's great teaching and in his teaching, he reveals that all the nations are essentially one and meant to express the Divine Unity upon Earth through an organized and harmonious diversity! . . .[52]

Thus, Mother Rachel Mirra Alfassa tried to justify belatedly, if unconvincingly, that her yearning was to become Indian while remaining French and fulfil the ideals of Sri Aurobindo towards human unity. Another leading French Ashramite, Bernard Enginger, published an article in *Le Monde* newspaper of France under the title 'Pondichéry doit demeurer un centre culturel Franco-Indien' (Pondicherry must remain a Franco-Indian Cultural Centre). In this article, Enginger pleaded for the grant of double nationality at least for the members of the Ashram as a sort of step towards a new union and the abolition of nationalistic antagonisms. More recently, a leading personality of the Ashram, André Morisset, the son of Mirra Alfassa, on behalf of several important members of the Ashram, had written a letter to Nehru, expressing his desire to adopt Indian nationality without giving up his original French nationality.

According to the French Overseas Minister, this demand for double nationality emanating from the Ashram was not motivated just by ideology alone, but also from material considerations, given that the Mother and the Ashram had immense properties in Pondicherry. It was believed in Ashram circles that double nationality would safeguard and protect these properties. In a meeting of the 'Conseil Superior des Français de l'étranger' (Superior Council of the Overseas French), held in November 1955, André Morisset represented Pondicherry. Here again, Morisset pleaded for double nationality. He also pleaded with the French government to support the Indian project to retain Pondicherry as a state under Group C, directly answerable to the Central Government. This would, it was thought, prevent it from being amalgamated with the 'Madrasis' who disliked anything that was French.[53]

All these attempts to procure double nationality till the last clearly demonstrated that the Ashram, under the guidance of Mirra Alfassa, never wanted a complete fusion of French India, especially Pondicherry, with the Indian Union. Instead, it wanted to maintain somehow its colonial connection with France, while remaining in Pondicherry. It never wanted to melt away into the Indian or Pondicherry society. It even used Sri Aurobindo's philosophical position and ideal of human unity to justify its demand for double nationality.

NOTES

1. *Indian Express*, 23-5 March 1954; Villianur Police Sinnasamy Iyer, pamphlet in Tamil by A. Natesa Mudaliar, editor of *Vimochanam*, 22 April 1955, Pondicherry.
2. *Daily News Release*, 25 January 1954, p. 7, IF 86, ADP; Note sur Pondichéry par M. Costilles, 13, 15 April 1954, pp. 231-6, IF 54, ADP; Copie de la Lettre du Fondateur du Centre Socialiste Franco-Asien à Ministre France d'Outre-mer, Pondicherry, 16 April 1954, pp. 251-2, IF 54, ADP.
3. *Indian Express*, 26-31 March; 1-2 April 1954; JO 1936, p. 935; Lena Tamilvanan (ed.), *Pandichery Manilam*, Madras, n.d. p. 161; *The Hindu*, 15 April 1954; *Times of India*, 1 April 1954.
4. *Indian Express*, 26-31 March, 1-2 April 1954; *The Hindu*, 2 April 1954; *Hindustan Times*, 1 April 1954; Press cuttings of French Consul, Madras, to Ministère des Affaires Etrangères, 6 April 1954, p. 81, no. 72, ADP.
5. *Indian Express*, ibid; *The Hindu*, 3, 4 April 1954; *Times of india*, 1 April 1954; Tél d'Ostrorog au Ministère des Affaires Etrangères, New Delhi, 9 April 1954, p. 84, no. 72, ADP.
6. Interview with old Pondicherrians.
7. Note Affaires Etrangères, December 1954, pp. 238-60, AO 1944-5, no. 21, ADP; *The Hindu*, 8 April 1954, Projet de Déclaration, May 1954, p. 162, IF 18, ADP.
8. Praja Socialist Party (Bengal) to the Consulate of Calcutta, 5 April 1954, p. 40, no. 17, ADP; *Hindustan Times*, 7 April 1954; Letter to Joseph Laniel, Prime Minister of France from Nehru, New Delhi, 23 April 1954, pp. 156-60, no. 17, ADP; S. Lastick, 'The Role of Sellane Naiker in the Freedom Struggle of Pondicherry', M.Phil. Dissertation, University of Pondicherry, 1998, pp. 27-9 (taken from Sellane's personal diary); R. Ramasrinivasan, *Karaikal in Freedom Struggle*, Karaikal, 1996, p. 93; *The Hindu*, 10, 13 ,14 April 1954.
9. Conclusion du rapport de M. Tézenas du Montcel au retour de sa mission dans les EF, 11 April 1954, pp. 56-61, no. 17, ADP; Ramasrinivasan, op. cit., p. 93; *The Hindu*, 1, 7, 13, 15 April 1954; Note du MInistère des Affaires Etrangères à l'Ambassade de France, 12 April 1954, p. 95, no. 72, ADP; Tél d'Ostrorog au Ministère Affaires Etrangères, New Delhi, 15 April 1954, p. 101, no. 72, ADP; Note of the Ministry of External Affairs to Embassy of France, 20 April 1954, p. 111, no. 72, ADP; A. Arulraj, *Puducheri Suthanthira Poratathin Kalachuvadukal*, Pondicherry, 2005, pp. 146-7.

10. EF de l'inde, Decision ministérielle, 27 April 1954, pp. 184-5, no. 17, O, ADP; EF de l'I nde. Réunion tenue le 28 April 1954, Affaires Etrangères, pp. 190-1, no.17, AO, ADP.
11. *The Hindu*, 7, 13 April 1954; *Hindustan Times*, 1 April 1954; Tél Comrep, Pondicherry, 14 April 1954, p. 200, IF 54, ADP; Tel d'Ostrorog au Ministère des Affaires Etrangères, New Delhi, 16 April 1954, p. 85, no. 17, ADP; *The Voice*, 31 August 1955; Ramasrinivasan, op. cit., p. 113.
12. *The Hindu*, 3, 4, 7, 15 April 1954; Mémoire redigé par une haute personalité de l'Asemblée réprésentative, 17 April 1954, pp. 221-3, IF 54, ADP.
13. Ajit Neogy, *Decolonisation of French India: Liberation Movement and Franco-Indian Relations (1947-54)*, Pondicherry, 1997, p. 225; *The Hindu*, 5 April 1954; V. Subbiah. *Saga of Freedom Movement: Testament of my Life*, Madras, 1990, p. 299.
14. Agence d'information indiene, 11 April 1954, p. 20, no. 73, AO, ADP; *The Hindu*, 5 April 1954; *Makkal Thalaivar Va. Subbiah Pavala Vizha Malar*, vol. III, 1988.
15. *Hindustan Times*, 9 April 1954; *The Hindu*, 5, 7, 8, 9 April 1954; Tél de London au Ministère des Affaires Etrangères, Madras, 30 April 1954, p. 263, IF 54, ADP.
16. *The Hindu*, 5, 9, 10, 15 April 1954; *Hindustan Times*, 9 April 1954.
17. *The Hindu*, 7, 12 April 1954; Agence d'information indienne, 11 April 1954, no. 73, p. 20, ADP; Compte rendu d'une reunion politique de la population francophone, 14 June 1954, p. 153, no. 73, ADP; *Indian Express*, 14 April 1954.
18. *l'Intransigeant*, 21 April 1954; *Le Monde*, 19 August 1954.
19. Copy of the letter of Dr F. Bleicher to Sellane Naiker, 15 April 1954; *Indian Express*, 15 April 1954.
20. *Le Populaire*, 22-5 April 1954; 7, 12-13 June 1954; *Le Parisien libéré*, 15 May, 11 June 1954; *Le Monde*, 6-7 June 1954.
21. Communiqué à la presse, EF de l'Inde, Paris, 21 April 1954, pp. 112-13, no. 17, ADP; Lettre du Ministre France d'Outre-mer à M. Le President du Conseil, Paris, 24 March 1954, p. 12, no. 17, ADP; Note du Ministère des Affaires Etrangères l'Ambassade de France, New Delhi, 29 April 1954, p. 200, no. 17, AO, ADP; *The Hindu*, 20 April 1954.
22. Bleicher, dentist, Pondichéry à Commissaire de la République, Pondicherry, 15 May 1954, pp. 131-5, no. 72, ADP; Lettre du Ministère France d'Outre-mer au Ministère des Affaires Etrangères, Paris, 15 April 1954, p. 74, no. 17, ADP; Un communiqué des Affaires Etrangères sur

les evenements de Pondichéry, AFP, Paris, 16 June 1954, no. 72, pp. 160-9, ADP; P. Padmanabhan, Pamphlet titled 'Intiya Sarkarukku Or Arivippu', Pondicherry, 22 November 1954.
23. *Le Monde*, 8 May 1954; Service d'information de 'Ambassade de l'Inde en France, 7 May 1954, IF 18, p. 48, ADP; see *Franc-Tireur*, 13 May 1954 ; *France-Soir*, 4 June 1954; *Hindustan Times*, 4 June 1954; Conversations franco-indienne, IF 18, p. 83, ADP.
24. *The Mail*, 13 May 1954.
25. AFP, Delhi, 13 May 1954, p. 36, IF 18, ADP; Neogy, op. cit., pp. 249-51.
26. Note du Ministère des Affaires Etrangères, AO, Paris, 1 June 1954, pp. 3-7, IF 19, ADP; Déclaration faite par R.K. Nehru le 12 June 1954 à propos des négociations Franco-Indiennes, 13 June 1954, pp. 87-92, IF 19, ADP; *Combat*, 4 June 1954; *The Hindu*, 16 June 1954; Neogy, op. cit., pp. 252-5.
27. Tél d'Ostrorog au Ministère d'Affaires Etrangères, New Delhi, 7 June 1954, p. 71, IF 19, ADP; Tél de André Ménard à France d'Outre-mer, Pondicherry, 17 June 1954, pp. 126-30, IF 19, ADP.
28. Note AO, 18 June 1954, pp. 136-40, IF 19, ADP; Tél de London au Ministère des Affaires Etrangères, Madras, 19 June 1954, p. 158, IF 19, ADP; Tél d'Ostrorog, New Delhi, 25 June 1954, p. 196, IF 19, ADP.
29. Lettre d'Ostrorog à Guy de la Tournelle, AO, New Delhi, 23 June 1954, pp. 102-3, IF 19, ADP.
30. Indiagram Service d'infromation de l'Ambasade de l'inde en France, 11 June 1954, pp. 82-3, IF 19, ADP; France-Soir, 13-14 June 1954; J. Weber, *Pondichéry et les Comptoirs de l'Inde après Dupleix : La Démocratie au pays desCastes*, Paris, 1996, pp. 393-4.
31. Mesures de repression prises dans les Etablissments, 1 June 1954, p. 10, IF 19, AO, ADP; Note de la Tournelle au Ministère des Affaires Etrangères, 2 June 1954, p. 17, IF 19, ADP; Conférence Franco-Indienne, séance du 3 June 1954, pp. 23-42, IF 19, ADP ; Lettre du Ministre de la France d'outre-mer à M. de Tournelle des Affaires Etrangères, Paris, 15 June 1954, p. 108, IF 19, ADP; Tél d'Ostrorog au Ministère des Affaires Etrangères, New Delhi, 8 May 1954, pp. 92-3, IF 70, ADP.
32. *Le Monde*, 8 May 1954; Lettre de E. Goubert à M. le President de l'Assemblée Nationale, Madras, 26 May 1954, pp. 113-21, IF 70, ADP; *Le Figaro*, 30 June 1952.
33. *Le Monde*, 8, 22 May 1954; Ministre France d'Outre-mer au Ministre des Affaires Etrangères, 8 July 1955, pp. 162-3; Note pour le Secretaire Général, Affaire Etrangères, 10 September 1954, AO, 1944-55, no. 21, p. 24, ADP; Note, 14 May 1954, no. 38, pp. 21-2.

34. Assemblée de l'Union Française, 7 July 1954, p. 33, IF. no. 20, ADP; Déclaration de M. Buron, Ministre des Affaires Etrangères, 14 December 1954, pp. 191-210, AO 1944-5, no. 21, ADP; Pondicherry, 1954, Pondicherry, June 1954, pp. 97-102, no. 73, ADP; *Le Monde*, 19 August 1954; Neogy, op. cit., pp. 260-1; *The Hindu*. 20 June 1954.
35. Ministry of External Affairs, New Delhi, 14 June 1954, pp. 151-2, no. 4, AO, ADP.
36. Tél de London au Ministère des Affaires Etrangères, Madras, 26 June 1954, p. 155, no. 73, ADP; *Le Monde*, 25 May 1954; Note 31 May 1954, pp. 153-5, IF 18, ADP.
37. *Le Populaire*, 10 May 1954; *The Hindu*, 1 April 1954.
38. *The Hindu*, 15 April 1954; Interview with Mannar Mannan, Saraswati Subbiah and Antoine Mariadassou; A. Arulraj, op. cit., p. 162.
39. Tél demarqué, Pondicherry, 22 July 1954, p. 180, no. 72, ADP; Tél d'Ostrorog au Ministère des Affaires Etrangères, 3 May 1954, p. 8, no. 18, ADP.
40. Tél d'Ostrorog à Ministère des Affaires Etrangères, New Delhi, 2 July 1954; L'Assemblée de Union Française, 3 July 1954, no. 20, AO, pp. 8-9, ADP; Note, Ministry of External Affairs to Embassy of France, 24 July 1954, New Delhi, p. 190, no. 72, ADP; *The Hindu*, 1 April 1954.
41. Notes rectificatives sur les evènements de Yanaon, pp. 53-66, no. 20, AO, ADP; *The Hindu*, 16, 19 June 1954; *Le Populaire*, 12-13 June 1954, 19 July 1954; *Statesman*, 17 July 1954; *Hindustan Times*, 17 July 1954; *Le Monde*, 15 June 1954; 17 July 1954; *l'Humanité*, 24 April 1954, 17 June 1954; *The Hindu*, 14 June 1954; J.B.P. More, 'Samatam Kristaya, un Yanaonais mort pour la France', *La Lettre du CIDIF*, October 2003; *The Hindu*, 12 April 1954; Interview with Madhimchetty, Georges Sala, I.K. Kumaran and Mangalat Raghavan; Neogy, op. cit., p. 263.
42. R. Dadala, *My Struggle for the Freedom of French India*, Pondicherry, n.d. pp. 30-1; *l'Aurore*, 15 June 1954; *Le Figaro*, 15, 17-18 July 1954; *Combat*, 17 July 1954; Lettre d'Escargueil, Sec-gén à Conseil Général, 23 August 1954, p. 171, no. 73, ADP.
43. *Le Populaire*, 21 July 1954; *l'Aurore*, 8-9 May 1954.
44. Tél de Ménard au Ministère des Affaires Etrangères, Pondicherry, 19 July 1954, p. 125, IF 70, ADP; Tél d'Ostrorog à l'Assemblée Répresentative, New Delhi, 20 November 1954, p. 33, IF 82, ADP; Duvauchelle à Ostrorog, Pondicherry, 10 December 1954, pp. 194-9, IF 55, ADP.
45. Tél d'Ostrorog à Ministère des Affaires Etrangères, New Delhi, 18 July

1954, p. 27, IF 55, ADP; Tél demarqué, Pondicherry, 21 July 1954, p. 36, IF 55, ADP.
46. Ramasrinivasan, op. cit., pp. 92-3; Pondicherry, 26 July 1954 (UP), IF 55, p. 38, ADP.
47. Tél démarqué, Pondicherry, 29 July 1954, p. 42, IF 55, ADP.
48. Tél de 17 Aôut 1954, du Comité de defense des intérêts Musulmans de Karikal au Président du Conseil, p. 117, IF 55, ADP; Mémoire abrégée des revendications de la population, addressée à Pierre Mendes France, 18 August 1954, pp. 110-14, IF 55, ADP; cf also pp. 133-62, IF 55, ADP for details of those who want to remain French; Tél du Parti Progressiste (Karakal) au Président de l'Union Française, 5 August 1954, pp. 70-1, IF 55, ADP; cf. also AO, IF 55, pp. 80-5, ADP.
49. Interview with A. Arulraj; Commissaire de la République au MInistre France d'outre-mer, Pondichéry, 17 August 1954, p. 94, IF 55, ADP.
50. *Le Monde*, 20, 21 August 1954.
51. Lettre de P. Landy, Conseiller diplomatique à Comte d'Ostrorog, 2 September 1954, pp. 184-5, no. 73, ADP; *République française*, 15 December 1954.
52. Sri Aurobindo Ashram, Pondicherry, 22 December 1954 to P.M. Nehru, pp. 64-8, no. 79, ADP.
53. Confidentiel, Procès-verbal de la Réunion d'information special du Bureau Permanent du Conseil Supérieur des Français de l'Etranger sur l'Inde, 19 November 1955, pp. 174-5, no. 79, ADP; Lettre du Ministre France d'Outre-mer à Ministre des Affaires Etrangères, Paris, February 1955, p. 119, no. 79, ADP; *Le Monde*, 2 October 1954.

CHAPTER 11

Merger with India

COMPROMISE AND INTEGRATION

It was in August 1954 that Diplomatic Counsellor, Pierre Landy, was sent to Pondicherry from France to assist the French Commissioner, André Ménard. He had instructions to protect the symbols of French culture in Pondicherry like the High School (Lycée Français).[1]

In the beginning of September, Edouard Goubert, along with Muthu Kumarapa Reddiar and another associate, went to Delhi, without informing the Indian Consul, Kewal Singh. They met Prime Minister Nehru. The latter gave them the assurance that an amicable settlement would be thrashed out with the French government shortly. Count d'Ostrorog, the ambassador in Delhi, who disliked Goubert, warned Nehru about 'the wiles of this individual' (Goubert). R.K. Nehru assured him that the Prime Minister did not make any commitment to Goubert.[2]

Goubert returned empty-handed. No doubt, he had earlier obtained the assurance from Nehru that French India and Pondicherry would not be part of the Madras province and the special cultural and historical characteristics of Pondicherry would be maintained. But that was all. Beyond this assurance, Goubert was in a position no more to talk of French Indian interests in greater detail and about how to safeguard them with Nehru or the Indian authorities, as he had put himself at the mercy of the Indian government by fleeing to Nettapakkam. As a result, he was not in a position of power to bargain about the interests of French Indians when the final contours of the transfer agreement would be thrashed out by the Indian and French governments without the participation of French Indians. He probably realised this fact belatedly, but could no more retrace his steps as he had gone beyond the point of no return. Even the French authorities like Count d'Ostrorog was not supportive of Goubert at this time. As a matter of fact, the question of safeguarding French Indian interests in all its aspects and details was thereafter ignored by both the French and Indian governments.

Many associations and individuals with not much influence like Ramasamy Iyer and Narayanasamy Sarcey expressed their desire to defend French interests in Pondicherry. In August 1954, a Committee for the Defence of French Interests was formed in Pondicherry, with Ramasamy Iyer as president. One of the committee members was Aziz Aboubaker, who was publishing director of the pro-French journal, *La République Française*. Islamic Committees for the Defence of French interests were also formed in Karaikal. The principal personality behind such committees was the wealthy Karaikal merchant, K.E.M. Mohamed Ibrahim Marécar. He was known in French circles to have stakes in smuggling goods. Earlier, he was a supporter of the Free Town project of Baron which had also included the promise of a separate college for Muslims. There were associations like the Muslim Welfare Society, run by S.M. Zacaria Marécar and M.A. Karime, which, conversely, favoured joining the Indian Union. There were also others like M. Jacquier, representative of French India in the French Union Assembly, and Mr Colombani of the Pondicherry Chamber of Commerce, who desired to protect French interests.[3]

On 8 September 1954, Sellane Naiker, in a report to the Government of India, accused Goubert and his men of not opting to join India until the very last moment, and having terrorised the people for the past seven years and looting the public exchequer. He opined that Goubert was waving the spectre of a 'Communist takeover' of Pondicherry to ingratiate himself with the Indian government.

The Indian National Congress did not recognise the Pondicherry Congress under Sellane Naiker. Later, Sellane issued a statement criticising even Jawaharlal Nehru for tilting towards Goubert's party and handing over power to him and his French India Socialist Party men forgetting their past misdeeds and not considering the role of the other parties.[4]

On 25 October 1954, Kewal Singh met V. Subbiah in Kottakuppam. All the cases on Subbiah were withdrawn by the Indian government and Subbiah was free to enter Pondicherry. Subbiah continued the struggle against French rule from the border areas of Pondicherry, especially from Kottakuppam, where he had immense support from the Muslims. Kottakuppam's Muslim stalwarts like Mir Nawab Sa, P.M. Hanif and Abdul Kafoor said that the celebrations on this account would start from Kottakuppam. Even Muslim women and children and elderly persons came in large numbers to felicitate Subbiah. However, most of the Muslims of French India, especially of Karaikal, were still opposed to joining the Indian Union without referendum.[5]

But by then, the French and the Indian governments represented by Count d'Ostrorog, and R.K. Nehru and Kewal Singh, respectively, as well as V.K. Krishna Menon, had resumed negotiations and reached a settlement, without any participation of the Pondicherrians or consultation with the representatives of the people of Pondicherry. A certain autonomy was guaranteed for French India. Nehru reiterated his assurance that the laws, customs, religion and languages of the foreign enclaves would be respected after integration.[6]

Georges Escargueil succeeded Commissioner André Ménard. He, too, came out in favour of merger with India against the wishes of the members of the Committee of Defence of French Interests. The French administrator of Karaikal, Boucheny, also favoured merger with India. It seemed that they were in a hurry to hand over French India to the Indian Union. The Franco-Indian journal, *République Française*, was highly critical of the French colonial authorities in Pondicherry at that juncture. Significantly, the authorities were forced to ban the journal.[7]

The French and the Indian governments signed in New Delhi a treaty of transfer on 21 October 1954. The treaty was published in Tamil and French in the *Journal Officiel* on 22 October 1954. The treaty consisted of 35 Articles and eight letters in French and Tamil. The governments also issued a joint communiqué from New Delhi. The treaty dealt with political, judicial, financial, economic and cultural matters, with special emphasis on the prevailing situation, with no clause to protect and safeguard the interests of the French Indians in the long-term after integration with India. None of the French

Indian leaders had participated in the drafting of this treaty. They never knew its contents. The people of French India were kept in the dark as well. The treaty was going to determine the fate of the French Indians, but they did not know or participate in the draft of the treaty in any way. It was purely negotiated and decided by the French government and the Indian authorities in New Delhi. In short, it could be said that the treaty was never intended to be a democratic exercise. Evidently, the treaty assumed that the French were in a sort of illegal occupation of Indian territories which needed to be simply transferred to the Indian Union without involving the French Indians who actually inhabited these territories or ascertaining their wishes and opinions.

Article 27 of the French Constitution (Fourth Republic) stipulated that no territory could be ceded, exchanged or added without the consent of the people of that territory. But as the Indian government was insisting on not holding a people's referendum, it was decided to hold a referendum of the people's representatives, i.e. the 183 members of the Municipal Councils of the four territories and the Representaive Assembly. It was a foregone conclusion that these members in their great majority would want to join the Indian Union, as most of them were supporters of Goubert.

In this way, the French thought they would have respected the referendum clause in their Constitution and saved their honour and prestige. But given that the great majority of the members were already clamouring to join the Indian Union, and that a people's referendum had already been organised in Chandernagore which had gone in India 's favour, it is quite surprising to note why the Indian government did not want to accept the organisation of a people's referendum. It is also quite perplexing as to why the French government agreed to organise a referendum of representatives and not a referendum of the people concerned as stipulated by their Constitution.

I think the Indian government did not want to take any risk as they were not sure of the mood of the people, while the French government wanted to extricate itself from a a very difficult situation that had come about due to the economic blockade and the indefensible nature of the four territories, not to speak of the fall of Indochina.

The French territories were isolated from one another by several hundreds of kilometres. If the Indian government decided to stop communications and transport connecting the territories, impose an economic blockade or discontinue the supply of water and electricity, the four territories would be completely ruined.[8] The French chargé d'affaires in New Delhi, Henri Roux, was the first to foresee this eventuality. It became inevitable in 1954. So, the French finally agreed to leave in exchange for the Indian promise to maintain Pondicherry as a centre of French culture.

Sellane Naiker was the first to react to the 21 October treaty. He, along with Dorai Munisamy and S. Perumal, founded the National Congress of Pondicherry on 26 October 1954 during an inaugural meeting held in his residence at No. 143, Mahatma Gandhi Road, Pondicherry. Those present at the meeting were Sellane Naiker, Dorai Munisamy, S. Perumal, Swamy Lourdes, N. Abdul Cader, Gnanou Ambroise, R.P. Babilonne, Tirumudy Sethurama Chettiar, A. Somasundaram Chettiar, Marie Selvanadane, A. Tiruvarasan, A. Natesa Mudaliar, B. Rangapillai, M. Lourdesamy Mudaliar, A. Rattina Mudaliar, Antoine Joseph Latour, Joseph Xavery, Obenas Thomas, S. Bapou, S. Natesa Padayachi, V. Govindaraj Naiker, M. Avanimuthu, Muthu Sittananda Mudaliar, T.S.N. Sundararaj Bhagavathar and A. Munissamy Chettiar. Among those who were absent were M. Mohamed. N. Abdul Cader presided over the meeting and Gnanou Ambroise was secretary. A provisional committee was established with A.V. Muthiah Mudaliar as president, S. Perumal, N. Abdul Cader and R.P. Babilonne as vice-presidents and Gnanou Ambroise as general secretary. Among the members, a few were for the immediate integration of Pondicherry and Karaikal with Madras state, while others wanted to maintain the status quo for at least 30 years. Sellane Naiker himself was in favour of integration. He held that steps needed to be taken for this integration thenceforth.[9]

VOTING AT KIZHUR

About 18 miles away from Pondicherry and five miles from Nettapakkam, there was a small village called Kijeour or Kizhur. One half of this village was in French India while the other half was in the Presidency of Madras of the Indian Union. Literally, Kijeour meant 'the village below'. This village was chosen by the Indian and French authorities to hold the vote of the Representative Assembly members and the municipal councillors of the 16 communes of French India to decide whether French India would remain with the French Union or not. They were 178 voters in all. Only three French journalists were present to cover this historical event. Pierre Bornecque represented the *Le Trait d'Union*, Mr Raymond who taught at the Ashram represented the *Agence France Presse* and Miss de Félice who was the only journalist who had come specially from France for the occasion on behalf of the French magazine, *Semaine du Monde*.

The pandal where the voting was to take place was in French territory, bordering the Indian territory where the Congressmen would feel safe. There was some French Indian police presence in the venue. The French Indian government bore all the expenditure related to the construction of the superb pandal, repairing of the roads, transport of the Assembly and municipal members, food, etc. The metal-frame pandal was 29 metres long, 16 metres wide and 4 metres high, planned by a Frenchman called Vion and built by four Frenchmen Aldo, Anselme Berviglieri, Lefort and Valigorski at the cost of Rs. 10,000. It was comfortable with fans, electricity, a buffet and microphones. All this was organised under the supervision of the French engineer Lemoine, who was also chief of public works.

Both the French and the Indian governments had decided to keep the treaty of cession a closely guarded secret until the voting. Pondicherrians and their representatives never knew the contents of the treaty beforehand. But they were still present at Kizhur for the voting. The treaty had been drafted without the consent of the French Parliament in almost 10 days. The president of the meeting inaugurated the conference exactly at 10 a.m. Karunendra Mudaliar, member of the Representative Assembly read the 35 clauses of the draft agreement printed out in Tamil and French. The letters exchanged between Jawaharlal Nehru, the Prime Minister of India and Count Ostrorog, Ambassador of France in India, as well as the agreement, were printed in the Government Press of Pondicherry.

Once the reading of the draft was over, the French Magistrate, Ancelin, organised the secret ballot at 11 a.m. The members had less than one hour to understand the contents of the treaty and were called to vote without the slightest discussion or deliberation. They were there just to say whether the French should quit or not by a simple 'yes' or 'no'. Each member was called by his name, and he had to choose the ballot paper marked 'yes' or 'no' and put it in an envelope. The journalists were not allowed inside, but one could see what was happening inside the tent as it was open on all sides upto a certain height. Most of the Congressmen were dressed in Tamil fashion, in a white *veshti* and shirt with a big emblem of the Indian tricolour emblazoned on it. These men had earlier assembled at Nettapakkam, where Edouard Goubert had his liberation government headquarters, on the day before the vote. The majority—of 171 out of the 178 registered members—entered the pandal from the Indian side to cast their ballot.

There were hardly a hundred spectators on the Indian side to witness the event. There were none from the French side, except 12 policemen. At exactly 1.20 p.m., the president of the conference, C. Balasubramanian, announced the results of the vote. A total of 170 members had voted to merge Pondicherry with India, while eight voted to remain with France. At that time, the journalists were allowed to enter the pandal, preceded by the secretary of the French embassy, Pierre Landy, who represented the French Ministry of Foreign Affairs and Kewal Singh, the consul general of India in Pondicherry. There was loud applause at the announcement of the result.

Balasubramanian delivered the final speech in French. He saluted first the memory of Gandhi, 'Father of the Indian nation', and thanked Nehru and Pierre Mendés France, the Prime Minister of France. He declared the pandal as a historical monument. He recalled the French principles of liberty, equality and fraternity and stressed upon the importance of safeguarding French culture in Pondicherry. He ended his speech with slogans of 'Jai Hind' and 'Vive la France'. Edouard Goubert and Muthu Kumarappa Reddiar also spoke.[10]

H.M. Cassime, the acting mayor of Pondicherry, drove back Pierre

Bornecque to Pondicherry in his car. Thus, the curtains were brought down on nearly three centuries of French rule in Pondicherry. Cassime had opted to join the Indian Union. Already in September 1954, Cassime had removed the photograph of Charles de Gaulle from the municipal building on the beach front and replaced it with that of Mahatma Gandhi.[11]

It is curious to note that the vote at Kizhur did not produce any reaction of enthusiasm or joy among the people of Pondicherry. There were no noisy demonstrations as the ones held a few months ago demanding a quick merger with India. The people appeared to be indifferent to the happenings at Kizhur, probably because they knew that integration with India had been obtained by the Indian government imposing a blockade of the French territories and not through a full referendum.[12]

Most newspapers in France did not give much importance to this transfer of power either. Some did not even report it.[13] *Le Monde* noted the transfer in one small column of the paper. The Prime Minister of India, Jawaharlal Nehru, went to Saigon on the day of the transfer.[14]

On 1 November, Pondicherry was completely free of French rule. Its first Chief Commissioner was Kewal Singh, first Chief Secretary M.V.S. Mathew and first Superintendent of Police Balakrishna Menon. None of them were Pondicherrians. The question naturally arose as to whether Pondicherrians fought for freedom in order to be governed by outsiders, though they might be Indians. It was a transfer of masters from French to Indian. On 5 November, the pro-French Progressive Party of Robert Saint Jean in Karaikal was dissolved.[15]

After the acceptance of the treaty at Kizhur, the French who had ruled Pondicherry since 1673-4 had just 10 days to prepare for their return voyage to France. The Secretary General, Georges Escargueil, had the task of winding up French affairs in Pondicherry. On the eve of their departure, two ceremonies were held by the French, one at the Monument aux Morts on the beach and the other in the Notre Dames des Anges Church in the presence of the archbishop of Pondicherry Mgr. Colas and other French dignitaries to honour those who had sacrificed their lives for France. The organisation, 'Scouts of France', in which Créoles took an active part, was dissolved.[16]

October was also the last working day before the transfer. The government servants, used to French rule until then, went about their work with great sadness. The pro-French activist, Ramasamy Iyer, president of the 'Comité de Défense des Intérêts Français' and some others presented some petitions to Escargueil to obtain certain favours like import licences.[17]

Escargueil transferred power to Pierre Landy, the last French representative of French India. Escargueil and Commandant Guyard, the chief of the French Indian police force, left Pondicherry for Madras by car on the morning of 31 October itself, leaving behind Pierre Landy. Kewal Singh accompanied them and bid farewell to Escargueil and Guyard at the frontier at Mortandi. No Pondicherrian of distinction was there at Mortandi to send them off. Escargueil reached Madras where he was received by the French consul, Roger London. When he was at the Madras airport about to embark the plane bound to France on 2 November, he told the only journalist of the Press Trust of India present there: 'We have avoided all bloodshed. But we are unable to prevent the tears flowing out'.[18]

All the French flags that flew atop the government offices had by then been brought down. But French flags still flew atop the *mairies* or municipal offices with the consent of mayors like H.M. Cassime. It was left to Pierre Landy to bring down the French flag that flew atop the governor's palace once and for all that evening. He, along with Lieutenant Meyer and the police guards, went up to the roof of the governor's palace. While the guards presented their arms, Lt Meyer brought down the flag and gave it to Pierre Landy. The flag was to be preserved at the French consulate.

That evening, C. Balasubramnian, president of the Representative Assembly, passed away all of a sudden, probably shocked at the turn of events. All Frenchmen and dignitaries were present at the funeral of Balasubramanian. Military honours were given to Balasubramanian by the last French troops. After paying his respects to Balasubramanian at his house, Pierre Landy, the last representative of France, returned to the governor's palace. The death of Balasubramanian, followed by his sister's death eight hours later, was considered a bad omen for the future of Pondicherrians by many Indians.[19]

In the meantime, R.K. Nehru, the secretary of Foreign Affairs of the Indian government, had arrived. Pierre Landy paid him a protocol visit.[20]

On 1 November 1954, at 6.45 a.m., Kewal Singh arrived at the governor's residence a few minutes before 6.45 a.m. and was welcomed by Pierre Landy. After inspecting a guard of honour by the French India police, both delegations stood for photographs. They then retired to the room of the French commissioner and signed the instrument of transfer. Power was formally transferred by Pierre Landy to the Indian commissioner, Kewal Singh, and not to any Pondicherrian or French Indian, as one would have expected. The transfer ceremony hardly lasted for three whole minutes. The transfer document was headlined, 'Documents of Transfer of Power', six copies of which were signed by the two representations. On the French side, the function was attended by Pierre Landy, M. Grangiè, director of public instruction, M. Colas, archbishop of Pondicherry and one other person. On the Indian side, there were Chief Secretary M.V.S. Mathew, K. Ramunni Menon, representative of the Madras government, Maj. Gen. Katoch, G.O.C. of the Army, and Yaswant Singh of the Air Force. Among the others present were H.M. Cassime, acting mayor of Pondicherry, and R.L. Purushotthama Reddiar.

The ceremony ended with the introduction of officials, the mayor of Pondicherry, H.M. Cassime, the Chief Justice and other judges, the archbishop of Pondicherry and prominent members of the legislature to Kewal Singh. Officials of the Government of India present were nine in number, including Secretary-General designate V.S. Mathews and Balakrishna Menon, police chief. The French flag was replaced with the Indian tricolor atop the governor's palace. A huge crowd was present in front of the palace to mark the event. Thunderous cries of 'Vande Mataram' came from the vast gathering in front of the government house. At 9 p.m., the Indian flag was hoisted at the port flagmast. At 10.30 a.m., there was a ceremony during which R.K. Nehru read the messages of the prime minister and the president of the Indian Union. It was followed by a reception at the *mairie*.

All throughout the day there were popular ceremonies organised in Pondicherry. The Ashramites showed a special interest in them. Similar ceremonies took place in Karaikal.[21]

Pierre Landy and other officials garlanded the Dupleix statue with tears in their eyes before leaving Pondicherry by ship. The commissioner spoke a few consoling words to those who were assembled there. The people of Pondicherry had not come in great numbers to wish farewell to the French. They seem to have silently accepted the decision to join India taken at Kizhur by their representatives.[22]

When Pondicherry became free of French rule, V. Subbiah, accompanied by colleagues like Gabriel Annusamy and Clemenceau Murugasamy, entered Pondicherry triumphantly, leading a procession from Kottakuppam to Muthialpet and Pondicherry. About 50,000 people from various parts of Pondicherry joined the procession. Others who accompanied the procession were N. Ranganathan, D.K. Ramanujam, Chandrasekhara Reddiar and Kavi Nara, They were welcomed by thousands of Pondicherrians with great pomp and splendour, and all the traditional ceremonies like folk dances and garlanding.[23]

It seems that Goubert and the Congress papers were not in favour of this procession. They wanted to stop it. They made use of Indian government officials and police to create obstacles even as they were still holed up in Nettapakkam while Subbiah entered Pondicherry.

There was much rejoicing all over Pondicherry. After the ceremony, a civic reception was held at the local assembly building. It was attended by the leading citizens of Pondicherry. The tricolour flew at the top of every building, amid dance dramas, songs and playing of music. The Sri Aurobindo Ashram did participate in the celebrations in its own way, guided by Mirra Alfassa, in spite of the fact that the latter had pleaded for double nationality for the adepts of the Ashram. Bernard Engenger revealed the project conceived by the French government to establish a Franco-Indian university under the control of the Sri Aurobindo Ashram which had been discussed by Maurice Schumann with Sri Aurobindo and the Mother in 1947.[24]

A similar transfer of power took place in Karaikal and other territories. The transfer took place in Karaikal at 3 p.m. A.V. Loganathan took over as first administrator of Karaikal while Jejurikar became the first administrator of Mahé.[25]

In Pondicherry, a public meeting was held to celebrate the transfer of power. After R.K. Nehru and Kewal Singh, Edouard Goubert, the chief architect of the integration of French India with the Indian Union, spoke. Perumal and Dutamby also spoke. At 9 a.m. on 1 November, during a grand all-Indian function, the French flag was again symbolically brought down and the Indian flag raised by R.K. Nehru in its stead. On the stage were present Kewal Singh, R.K. Nehru, Edouard Goubert, Muthu Poullé and Muthu Kumarappa Reddiar, as well as V. Subbiah, S. Perumal and Dutamby, in front of about one lakh people. Pierre Landy participated in the function with a broad smile on his face. Some nationalist papers like *Dinamani* tried to belittle the role played by V. Subbiah in the Freedom Movement. A total of 300 French troops left Pondicherry just after merger by chelingues to board the French ship, *Anna Salem*.[26]

At a public meeting in the town hall, H.M. Cassime welcomed R.K. Nehru and Kewal Singh. On 11 November 1954, a new municipal commission was constituted to replace the existing council. Muthu Poullé was nominated as president of the commission, with E.G. Pillai (Edouard Goubert) as vice-president. H.M. Cassime became the first deputy mayor. He was until then acting mayor.[27] Thus, Pondicherrians and French Indians became Indians, subject to Indian rule, by getting rid of French rule.

TOWARDS DE JURE TRANSFER AND AFTER

The *de facto* transfer of the French territories to India took place on 1 November 1954. But the *de jure* transfer took place through the treaty of cession of 28 May 1956 signed in New Delhi much later in 1962. Until then, French Indians were theoretically French citizens.

This treaty needed to be ratified by the French Parliament. There were some feeble and last-ditch attempts by some Pondicherrians like Joseph Bellegarde, president of the Association of the French in India and ex-soldier Mr Noël, Paul de Rozario, as well as Charles Gressieux (ex-policeman from Indochina) and his Republican Party group, to scuttle the ratification. There were also attempts to procure double nationality for Pondicherrians. This had the support of the Sri Aurobindo Ashram. The French government was never enthusiastic about such attempts.[28]

In Indian circles, it was thought that Paris would gain nothing by delaying the *de jure* transfer. The Communist leader, Subbiah, was against the 'Part C State' status conferred upon the four territories in the treaty. André Morisset, the son of Mother Mirra Alfassa, had asked for it and obtained it. The people of Pondicherry were never asked what they wanted. But the treaty was imposed upon them, and they lapped it up. The Congress leaders were not in a position to influence the treaty as they had been completely dependent on the Congress Party of Tamil Nadu and Kamaraj Nadar, the chief minister of Madras, for their survival, fearing the rise of Communism in Pondicherry. They had even abstained from combating the idea of Pondicherry joining Madras, fearing the Congress leaders of Tamil Nadu. Goubert, of course, had made himself irrelevant in the thrashing out of the treaty by fleeing to Nettapakkam and, therefore, was not in a position to defend French Indian interests to the fullest extent at the critical time of transfer of power.[29]

On 16 January 1955, Nehru visited Pondicherry. He delivered speeches at the *mairie* (municipality hall), in the French High School and at a public meeting at Lawspet. This time, he visited the Sri Aurobindo Ashram when Sri Aurobindo was no more.[30] During his stay in Pondicherry, a memorandum was submitted by the president of the Dravida Munnani (Dravidian Front) of Pondicherry against the problems faced by the south Indians due to imposition of Hindi, the penetration into Pondicherry of north Indian merchants who were a threat to the local mercantile community and the influence exerted on the local society by the 'alien' Sri Aurobindo Ashram which purportedly looked down upon Tamil culture and civilisation.[31] Nehru never responded to the petition. Nehru met Muthu Poullé, president of the municipal commission, Edouard Goubert, Pak-kirisamy Poullé, Mgr. Colas and Grangiè, director of *Collège Français*. Nehru later visited Karaikal. Later, on 4 October, Nehru came back to Pondicherry. This time, he visited the French Institute of Indology where he was welcomed by Jean Filliozat. The mayor of Pondicherry, Joseph Latour, and Edouard Goubert welcomed Nehru and delivered speeches.[32]

On 20 March 1955, the Institut Français, or the French Institute, was inaugurated by the governor-general of India, C. Rajagopalachari, in the presence of Count d'Ostrorog, to advance and propagate French culture in Pondicherry. He delivered a short speech in Tamil wherein he considered Pondicherry as a refuge for compromised politicians, criminals and aficionados of alcoholic drinks. He denounced Dupleix's bellicosity. He further said that the French Institute's utility would lie in not propagating French culture in a country which possessed already an ancient and wealthy culture but rather in propagating the culture of south India in Europe. His words were not very well received by the assembled audience.[33]

Edouard Goubert and his team and the Congress Party removed Frenchmen from all posts of responsibility. Even Pondicherrians with a French cultural background were removed. Ostrorog, the French ambassador, thought that Goubert's hostility towards the French was intended to put pressure on the French authorities to get his pension as member of the French Parliament released soon.[34]

There were also efforts by some groups like the Committee for the Defence of French Interests and individuals like Tirouvarrasan, notary Joseph Latour, former mayor of Pondicherry, J.M. Colombani, French businessman, J. Rassendran, notary and Marius Clairon, Chevalier de la Légion d'Honneur, to maintain French language and culture in Pondicherry. Lambert Saravane and Tirouvarassan founded the association 'Les Amis de la Langue et la Culture Française' in Pondicherry even before the merger. Even Goubert and Muthu Poullé were members of this association. The bi-monthly journal, *La Voix Nouvelle*, edited by Julien Adicéam, also wanted to protect French culture and language in Pondicherry. In Karaikal, there were individuals like Robert St. Jean and the lawyer, De la Flore, who stood for protecting French interests. In 1955, Solsce, president of retired military personnel, along with Lambert Saravane, Tiruvanziam, counsellor Rassendran and Mathias Clairon met Nehru and requested him to safeguard French culture in Pondicherry. Nehru did assure them on that account. But the assurance remained only in words and never translated into concrete action by the Indian government.[35]

There were others who favoured the creation of a condominium or a Franco-Indian joint administration for the four territories. Among them were Lami Symphorien of Saigon, Chevalier de la Légion d'Honneur, Dr Tiruvanziam, Manuel de Condinguy, ex-registrar in French Indochina, J.M. Colombani and R.P. Babilonne. A few were against ratification of the treaty without directly consulting the people. Among them were Manuel de Condinguy, Jules Rassendran, notary, A. Tirouvarassan, notary, J.M. Colombani, businessman, R. Doréradjou, president of the Federation of the Harijans of Pondicherry, Julien Adicéam, editor of *Voix Nouvelle*, M. Houssaine, member of Representative Assembly, R. Babilonne, Chevalier de la Légion d'Honneur, Mme Girod, doctor, Samy Abraham, principal clerk in the Indochinese court, and D. Jeevarathinam, ex-deputy of the French National Assembly.[36]

The French weekly, *République Française*, had been founded in April 1954, to protect French interests. This paper was againt the ratification of the treaty. Franco-Indian Créoles and some Renouncers like Valot, Charles Gressieux, president of the Republican Mouvement of French India, Etoile Rangassamy, president of the Dravidian Federation of Uppalam, Cheik Abdul, president of the Sports Association for the Muslim Youth, Antoine Magnifique, secretary and treasurer of 'Foyer du Soldat', Ms and Mr Pierre of Pondicherry and K.V.R. Raouf Bai (president of the Muslim League of Sultanpet) under the banner of 'Mouvement Républicain Populaire de l'Inde Française' (Popular Republican Movement of French India) fought the ratification tooth and nail. They wanted a people's referendum. They held that 'posterity will certainly blame India and France for not determining the fate of these pockets in a proper way'.

Many others regretted it that just after four months after the departure of the French, Pondicherrians had allowed themselves to be enslaved so easily by Indians through the vote at Kizhur. Some others like Samy Abraham, who had worked in the French administration of Indochina, wanted a referendum to be held to determine the *de jure* transfer of power, but also wanted a transition period of 25 years during which the institutions set up by the French would not be tampered with. Others like Mlle M. Pierre and D. Richard wanted a plebiscite to be held 30 years after being under the supervision of neutral observers. They were critical of the pro-French stand of Valot, his supporters from Indochina and his journal, *République Française*.[37] However, nothing could stop the ratification of the treaty, as the population of French India and the leaders of the main political parties that had emerged after the transfer of power had remained steadfastly against holding a people's referendum. In fact, there was no popular movement in favour of France in Pondicherry or in the other three territories.

The treaty was finally ratified by the French Parliament on 27 July 1962, just after the secession of Algeria from France. The exchange of the documents of ratification took place only on 16 August 1962, which naturally became the date of the *de jure* transfer of Pondicherry. This treaty thus saw the light of day without the participation of Pondicherrians in its drafting or signing. It can be said that by this, the Pondicherrians had given up their right to decide for themselves the course of their future.

At the time of Independence, there were 280 French families of European descent in Pondicherry. This included people of mixed blood as well. Apart from them, there were a few thousand Renouncers who had adopted the French Civil Code. But the great majority of the Pondicherry population comprised Indians with their own personal laws. During this period, many Pondicherrians, especially the Créoles and Europeans, migrated to France, selling of their properties, especially in the White town, at throwaway prices. The main beneficiary of such deals seem to have been the Sri Aurobindo Ashram, at the head of which was Mirra Alfassa. The treaty provided a period of six months starting from 16 August 1962 onwards for Pondicherrians to opt for French nationality. Those who did had the right to remain in Pondicherry as per the terms of the treaty. In 1962, there were just 6,000 people who opted for French nationality. Many of them migrated to France. It is believed that French Indians were dissuaded from opting for French nationality by the Congressmen, Communists and others, which included Goubert and Subbiah, by various means including threats and coercion.[38]

The Union Territories Act of 1963 conferred the status of a 'C' category state upon the French settlements. The Pondicherrians were bestowed with the right to have a legislative assembly and a council of ministers as well as municipal councils. The elected representatives had certain rights in the organisation of education, justice and health as well as considerable Independence in the domain of fiscality and the finances of the territories. Besides, a lieutenant governor was appointed from New Delhi, who had certain executive powers. In many respects, the arrangement was almost similar to that which prevailed in Pondicherry before its integration with India. Edouard Goubert, the architect of 'free' Pondicherry and the people in general did not oppose the 'C' status conferred upon Pondicherry, as it maintained the distinct identity and uniqueness of Pondicherrians. Even the Ashram had reasons to be happy as they were not answerable to the local government for their activities.

What the French did obtain through the treaty in exchange for some of the oldest territories of France was their formal right to preserve French culture and heritage, especially in Pondicherry. There was, of course, the Colonial College which became the *Lycée Français* and where French continued to be the medium of instruction. There was also the French consulate to cater to the needs of the French nationals. *L'Institut Français* or the French Insitute was formally inaugurated on 29 March 1955 under the presidency of Count Ostrorog, ambassador of France in India, and in the presence of C. Rajagopalachari, the last governor-general of India and an assembly of 500 persons. Jean Filliozat was the founder-director of the Insitute. This was a prime research institute with a good library and archives. A branch of the Ecole Française d'Extrême Orient was also opened in Pondicherry. Then there was the Alliance Française where the French language and culture were taught to Indians. It was revived in 1957. Finally, there was the 'Foyer du Soldat' which had its own building since 1939 when Louis Bonvin was governor of Pondicherry. Military men of Pondicherry were members of this Association. In 1947, R.P. Babilonne was the president. Dutamby Hannah was vice-president and S. Latour was secretary. Among the members were Gnana Venmani, Latour Joseph, Abdoul Soultane Cader, Titus Germain, Clairon Mathias, C.H. Dutamby and Antoine Magnifique. In 1951, its president was S. Latour and the vice-president C.H. Dutamby, while Titus was the secretary. All these institutions were established in the White town of Pondicherry.[39]

An association called the 'France-Union Indienne' was set up on 22 April 1956. André Morisset, the son of the Ashram Mother and advisor for French Foreign Commerce, was president. It had influential members like François Baron, former governor of Pondicherry, who had joined the Ashram, Henri Jacquier, and Yves Perrier, former administrator of Mahé and chief administrator of overseas affairs.[40]

Then there were about 2,000 Pondicherrians who had fought in Indochina who had returned to Pondicherry. On the whole it was estimated that there were about 1,500 French Indians serving in the French army then, who on retirement drew handsome pensions of 300 or 400 rupees per month, at a time when the average salary in Pondicherry never went beyond Rs. 110. After November 1954, there were more Pondicherrians wanting to join the French army and go to France.[41]

There were also the Renouncers who numbered about 2,000 and were faithful to France. Last but not the least were the *métis* or Franco-Indian Créoles, who spoke French, were of mixed origin and had never been to France. They numbered only a few hundreds. Most of them, assuming that there was no future for them in India, the country of their origin, migrated to France by the 1960s, disposing of their properties in the posh White town, mainly to the Ashram, at throwaway prices leaving behind their blood compatriot, Edouard Goubert, who had caused the downfall of the French singlehandedly among the Tamilians.

In 1954, it was thought that 20,000 French Indians would opt for France. But in 1961, just before the *de jure* transfer, there were just 10,000 to 20,000 Renouncers, of whom the majority were Christian. In 1960, there were 1,200 French military personnel of Pondicherry origin in activity. Pondicherrians settled and working outside French India numbered 5,438, of whom 1,120 were French government servants who worked in various other French colonies in Africa and elsewhere.[42]

When the French left, the Pondicherry wholesale trade was already in the hands of Indians, not from Pondicherry, but from Bombay, Calcutta and other Indian cities. These traders did not have a French cultural or historical background. But they controlled more or less 80 to 90 per cent of the total wholesale trade in Pondicherry.[43]

Apart from the above was the Sri Aurobindo Ashram, which had grown since the late 1920s under the guidance of the influential Mirra Alfassa. Mirra Alfassa had seen to it that French was taught in the

Ashram. Some Frenchmen thought that the core of a future Franco-Indian university existed already in Pondicherry and that core was nothing but the Sri Aurobindo Ashram.

But the Ashram was not just a spiritual centre, where the adepts engaged only in yoga and meditation. Under the guidance of Mirra Alfassa, who was the daughter of a rich banker, large properties had been acquired in the White town by the Ashram. Many rich Indians donated profusely to the Ashram. The Ashram also owned rice fields, gardens, factories, schools, a stadium, printing press, automobile workshop, carpentry workshop, guesthouses, hospitals, clinics, canteens, restaurants, and so on. To just cite an example of how wide the business interests of the Ashram were one can note that in 1954, when Pondicherry was being merged with the Indian Union, some Ashram members were setting up the Honesty Society Departmental Stores with a capital of Rs.15,000. Some of the leading members of the Ashram like Padmanabhan Counouma, Keshav Dev Poddar, Dahyabhai Patel, Hariprasad Poddar and Manoranjan Ganguly were shareholders in this venture. When the French left Pondicherry, the building on the seaside that was to serve as the French consulate was to be renovated by the Honesty Society Motor Works, an Ashram concern whose technical director was the Ashramite M. Ganguly, who resided at No.1, rue Saint Louis. In fact, Ganguly also set up the Honesty Construction Society. Others from the Ashram like Pinto owned the Honesty Engineers and Contractors, while Mirra Alfassa had set up the Ashram Printing Press. Besides, in 1955, Mirra Alfassa executed a deed by which she constituted the Sri Aurobindo Ashram Trust and transferred all properties held in her name to the board of trustees. Thus, the Ashram expanded still further as a business enterprise in various fields. Perhaps, it functioned as a sort of state within the state.[44]

Many Frenchmen had joined the Ashram including François Baron, former governor of Pondicherry, Mr Raymond of Agence France Presse who was a professor at the Ashram in 1954 and Bernard Engenger (Satprem) who was close to Mirra Alfassa. Many Pondicherry personalities like Lambert Saravane, Dr André and Counouma were also similarly close to the Ashram. The latter who came to Pondicherry from Mahé on a scholarship of Rs. 72 per year to study philosophy at Colonial College ultimately joined the Ashram and became intimate with The Mother as he could speak French and knew the affairs of Pondicherry better than anyone who had migrated to Pondicherry from other parts of India. Thus, a French cultural atmosphere prevailed in the Ashram. The French, of course, could not be anything but happy about this organisation. But according to Pierre Landy, Mirra Alfassa underwent a profound crisis of national identity during that period.[45]

Edouard Goubert, the flamboyant Franco-Indian who was despised by the French and all pro-French elements in Pondicherry as the one who finally brought down the curtains on French rule in Pondicherry, was later considered in French circles as the best guarantor for the maintenance of French culture in Pondicherry. In fact, he became the symbol of the Franco-Indian historical and cultural identity of Pondicherry. The French disliked him because he had outwitted them. Nonetheless, he had safeguarded the distinct identity of Pondicherry. But for him, and his special relationship with Jawaharlal Nehru, the other leaders including Lambert Saravane, V. Subbiah and Purushotthama Reddiar would not have resisted or been in a position to resist the persistent demand for amalgamation of Pondicherry, Karaikal, Mahé and Yanam with the provinces of the Indian Union. Pondicherry would have been merged with Tamil Nadu as Chandernagore was with West Bengal. Goubert was thus the foremost representative of Pondicherrian sub-nationalism who negotiated with great dexterity and clairvoyance, in spite of the odds stacked against him, the right of the French Indians to maintain their unique identity. Right from his entry in politics in 1946, he never swerved from his idea and objective of safeguarding the special historical and cultural character of Pondicherry. He was largely successful in achieving his objective, through his well-calculated political moves. Pondicherrians are indebted to him for that. He was also thought to be the best defender of the autonomy accorded to Pondicherry through the 1956 treaty within the Indian Union, against claims from some quarters to amalgamate the old French territories with Madras province. After the ratification of the treaty, Goubert pointed out that the four territories constituted a distinct identity, culture, administration and political history within the Indian Union.[46]

Pondicherry had its own history due to its connection with the

French. But when the freedom movement gathered steam in the Indian sub-continent, Pondicherry and its dependent territories were caught between the French Union and the Indian Union. Goubert's strategy had always been to safeguard French India's special interests. Whichever union would guarantee that, Goubert was liable to gravitate towards it. He was not worried of being a French nationalist or an Indian nationalist, but rather about how to protect the French Indian identity. It was not an accident that Goubert chose to become a freedom-fighter by opting to join the Indian Union, as Janab Husain, who became *kazi* of Pondicherry, later would hold. Instead, it was because the Indian Union under Nehru provided him a better guarantee to safeguard French Indian and Pondicherrian interests, that he with his associates, decided to throw in their lot with India. It was rather a very well-planned move that took all his political adversaries including the French by surpirise. Goubert was certain that his strategy would succeed and he won handsomely the battle for freedom wherein the French Indian identity could be safeguarded. He actually won this battle without bloodshed, as Yves Perrier, his relative and former French administrator, whom we met and interviewed in Paris, would aver, by accepting a certain dishonour for that among the French. He claimed that Pondicherrians and the French were lucky to have a person like Goubert, who facilitated the smooth and peaceful transition of power in Pondicherry from France to the Indian Union. [47]

NOTES

1. Note pour la direction générale du personnel, Paris, 10 August 1954, pp. 31, 34, no. 2, AO, ADP.
2. Tél d'Ostrorog au Ministre des Affaires Etrangères, New Delhi, 1 September 1954, pp. 128-9, IF 70, ADP; Tél à France d'Outre-mer, Pondicherry, 3 September 1954; Tél d'Ostrorog au Ministre des Affaires Etrangères, New Delhi, 14 September 1954, pp. 124-5, IF 55, ADP.
3. Pierre Landy, Conseiller diplomatique du Commissaire à Comte d'Ostrorog, Pondicherry, 14 September 1954, p. 126, IF 55, ADP; Letter, 11 September 1954, Karikal, de l'Admistrateur de Karaikal au Commissaire de la République-Constitution des comités islamiques de defense des interest Français de l'Inde Française et des interêts Musulmans de Karaikal, August 1954, Carton 838, Dossier 1042, AOM.

4. S. Lastick, 'The Role of Sellane Naiker in the Freedom Struggle of Pondicherry', M.Phil. Dissertation, University of Pondicherry, 1998, pp. 26, 80; French Indian Merger Congress: Some suggestions, 8 September 1954; National Congress, Pondicherry, Séance inaugurale (inaugural session, 26 October 1954; Statement issued by Mr Sellane Naiker, Leader of the National Congress of Pondicherry, Pondicherry, 25 December 1954, copies in my possession.
5. Tél de Pondichéry à Delhi et au France d'Outre-mer, 7 September 1954, p. 54, no. 75, Congrès de Kijéour, ADP; Tél d'Ostrorog à Ministre des Affaires Etrangères, 13 September 1954, p. 62, no. 75, ADP.
6. Tél d'Ostrorog à Ministre des Affaires Etrangères, New Delhi, 9 September 1954, p. 223, no. 75, ADP; See telegrams of Comte d'Ostrorog au Ministère des Affaires Etrangères, New Delhi, September 1954, no. 76, pp. 6, 24, 34, 174, 203, ADP; *Indian Express*, 31 August 1954; *Le Monde*, 12 August 1954.
7. *Lettre de Pierre Landy*, conseiller diplomatique au Ministre des Affaires Etrangères, Paris, 22 December 1954, no. 2, p. 88, AO, ADP; La question de l'Inde Française vue par les Pondichériens, s.d., no. 325, pp. 4-5, ADP.
8. JO 22 October 1954, pp. 565-78; no. 76, Treaty of Cession with 8 letters, pp. 371-99, no. 76, ADP; Chaffard, *Les Carnets Secrets de le Décolonisation*, Paris, 1965, vol. I, pp. 199-200.
9. National Congress, Pondicherry, Séance Inaugurale du mardi 26 October 1954; Statement of Sellane Naiker, Advisor to the National Congress, Pondicherry, n.d. (copies in my possession).
10. La question de l'Inde Française vue par les Pondichériens, s.d. no. 325, pp. 4,5, ADP; Tél de Pondichéry à France d'Outre-mer, 18 October 1954, pp. 172-4, no. 75, ADP; *Franc-Tireur*, 19 October 1954; *Combat*, 19 October 1954; Congrès des members de l'Assemblée Répresentative et des Conseils Municipaux à Kijeour, Procès-verbal, p. 176, IF 89, ADP.
11. Lettre de Ramasamy Iyer à M. Général de Gaulle, Pondicherry, 21 September 1954, AO, 1944, no. 22, p. 38, ADP.
12. D. Annoussamy, 'Les Etablissements Français en Inde', *La Lettre du CIDIF*, no. 40, 2010, p. 27; Bornecque, October 1954, *Trait d'union*; *Le Populaire*, 20 October, 2 November 1954.
13. *Le Figaro*, 1-2 November 1954; *Le Populaire*, 2 November 1954; *l'Humanité*, 2 November 1954.
14. *Combat*, 2 November 1954; *Le Monde*, 19, 20 October 1954, 2 November 1954.
15. *Ephémère*, November 1954, p. 200, IF 55, ADP.

16. Les derniers jours de Pondichéry, Pondicherry, 31 October 1954, by Georges Gallean, Intendant Militaire, p. 138, no. 74, ADP; *Lettre de Pierre Landy au Ministre des Affaires Etrangères*, 22 December 1954, Pondicherry, no. 2, pp. 94-7, AO, ADP.
17. *Lettre de Pierre Landy au Ministre des Affaires Etrangères*, 22 December 1954, Pondicherry, no. 2, p. 94, AO, ADP.
18. Roger London, Consul de France à Madras au Comte d'Ostrorog, Madras, 2 November 1954, pp. 186-7, no. 74, AO, ADP; *Lettre de Pierre Landy au Ministre des Affaires Etrangères*, 22 December 1954, Pondicherry, no. 2, pp. 99-100, AO, ADP; La question de l'Inde française vue par les Pondichériens, s.d. no. 325, pp. 4,5, ADP; Tél de Landy au Ministre Affaires Etrangères, Pondicherry, 31 October 1954, p. 136, no. 74, ADP.
19. *Lettre à Pierre Landy*, Conseiller diplomaique du Ministère des Affaires Etrangères, Pondicherry, 31 October 1954, p. 178, IF 70, ADP; Les derniers jours de Pondichéry, Pondicherry, 31 October 1954, by Georges Gallean, Intendant Militaire, pp. 138-9, no. 74, ADP.
20. *Lettre de Pierre Landy au Ministre des Affaires Etrangères*, 22 December 1954, Pondicherry, no. 2, pp. 94-101, AO, ADP.
21. Evènements de Pondichéry, 20 October-4 November 1954, pp. 171-8, no. 74, AO, ADP; *Lettre de Pierre Landy au Ministre des Affaires Etrangères*, 22 December 1954, Pondicherry, no. 2, pp. 101-19, AO, ADP; Tél de Landy au Ministre des Affaires Etrangères, Pondicherry, 31 October 1954, p. 136, no. 74, ADP.
22. Les derniers jours de Pondichéry, Pondicherry, 31 October 1954, by Georges Gallean, Intendant Militaire, pp. 138-9, no. 74, ADP; Service Indien d'Information, 1 November 1954, pp. 180-2, no. 74, ADP.
23. *Makkal Thalaivar Subbiah Pavala Vizha Malar*, vol. III; B. Mayandi, op. cit., pp. 48-9.
24. *Le Monde*, 2 October 1954; *République Française*, 8 December 1954.
25. *Indian Express*, 1, 2 November 1954; *The Hindu*, 2 November 1954; *The Mail*, 1 November 1954.
26. *Lettre de Pierre Landy à Ministre des Affaires Etrangères*, 22 December 1954, Pondicherry, no. 2, p. 105, AO, ADP; *The Mail*, 1 November 1954; B. Mayandi, op. cit., pp. 50-1; *Janasakti*, November 1954, Puratchi Malar; Les derniers jours de Pondichéry, Pondicherry, 31 October 1954, by Georges Gallean, Intendant Militaire, pp. 138-9, no. 74, ADP; *Lettre de Pierre Landy au Ministre des Affaires Etrangères*, 22 December 1954, Pondicherry, no. 2, pp. 102-4, AO, ADP.
27. Tél de Duvauchelle au Ministre des Affaires Etrangères, 11 November 1954, Pondicherry; *The Mail*, 1, 2 November 1954.

28. *Lettre d'Ostrorog au Ministre des Affaires Etrangères*, New Delhi, 18 March 1955, p. 95, no. 78, ADP; *Lettre de Charles Gressieux*, February 1962, pp. 179, 181, Asie 1944, no. 334, ADP; Treaty of Cession in English, Asie-Océanie-Inde 1956-67, no. 326, ADP; Note pour le directeur du cabinet, AO, AP, 14 May 1957, p. 104, no. 328, ADP; Note sur Bellegarde, Confidential, 29 June 1962, Asie 1944-Inde 1956-67, no. 334, p. 113, ADP.
29. Situation Générale, no. 56, Robert Duvauchelle, Représentant Français à Ministre des Affaires Etrangères, 8 January 1955, pp. 2-3, no. 56, ADP; *The Mail*, 20 July 1957; *The Hindu*, 20 July 1957; *Indian Express*, 20 July 1957; Tél de Sandou au Ministère des Affaires Etrangères, Pondicherry, 6 March 1956, Asie 1944-no. 325, ADP; Note, Affaires Etrangères, Direction Affaires Politiques, Paris, 25 November 1961, p. 40, Asie 1944-Inde 1956-67, no. 333, ADP; Jean Paul Garnier, Ambasadeur de France au Ministre affaires Etrangères, Paris, 20 December 1961, pp. 334-5, Asie 1944, no. 333, ADP; Note de Pierre Pelletier, Cabinet du Ministre, Le Directeur d'Asie Océanie, 31 December 1958, Pondicherry, pp. 188-9, Asie 1944, no. 333, ADP.
30. Tél de Duvauchelle au Ministère des Affaires Etrangères, 16 January 1955, p. 8, IF 56; *Le Trait –d'Union*, 16 January 1955.
31. Memorandum addressed to Prime Minister Jawaharlal Nehru in Pondicherry by Dravida Munnani, p. 12, IF 56, ADP.
32. Ibid., pp. 29, 54, 58, 60, 92, IF 56, ADP.
33. *République Française*, 22 March 1955; 29 March 1955; 6 May 1955.
34. *Lettre de V.L. Satyamurti du Centre Socialiste-Franco Asien à Christian Pineau*, Ministre des Affaires Etrangères, Pondicherry, 25 March 1956, no. 325, Asie 1944-January-April 1956, ADP; Count d'Ostrorog à M. Pineau, Ministre des Affaires Etrangères, 7 April 1956, New Delhi, no. 325, ADP.
35. 'Les Amis de la Langue et de la Culture Française' à M. le Premier Ministre de l'Inde, Pondicherry, 4 October 1955, p. 307, AO 1944-55, no. 21, ADP; Julien Adicéam, Directeur du journal 'La Voix Nouvelle' à M. Couve de Murville, Pondicherry, 5 September 1958, p. 119, Asie-Inde 1956-67, no. 330, ADP; Duvauchelle, représentant français à Pondichéry à Count d'Ostrorog, Pondicherry, 10 January 1954, p. 190, IF 80, ADP; Extrait de la lettre de M. Solsce, 1955, p. 211, IF 83, ADP.
36. Asie 1946-Inde 1956-67, Co-gestion Franco-Indienne, no. 331, pp. 27-9, ADP; Motion addressé au gouvernement Français, 20 July 1960, pp. 188-218, Asie 1946, no. 331, ADP; *Lettre de Samy Abraham*, commis greffier principal en Indochine, Pondicherry, 23 May 1955, AO, 1956-7, Traité de cession, pp. 21-2, no. 326, ADP.

37. Critique du rapport de Paul Devinat, Deputé sur le projet tendant à autorisé le Président de la République française à ratifier le traité de cession, signé le 28 Mai, 1956, AO 1956-67 p. 129, no. 326, ADP; *Lettre de Samy Abraham, commis-greffier*, Ancien Service Judiciaire de l'Indochine à Monsieur le Ministre, Pondicherry, 23 May 1955, Asie-Océanie, Inde 1956-67, Traité de Cession, no. 326, pp. 21-2, ADP; Groupement représentatif des interêts pondichériens, Pondicherry, 26 March 1956, Memorandum imprimé no. 325, Asie Océanie, ADP; La Question de l'Inde française vue par les Pondichériens, s.d, no. 325, p. 14, ADP; Rapport fait au nom de la commission des Affaires Etrangères, 28 May 1956, pp. 108-29, no. 329, ADP; *Times of India*, 16 July 1958; Conférence des associations civiles et militaires à Hotel Continental, 8 September 1958, Asie, Inde 1956-67, no. 330, p. 120, ADP; Mouvement Républicain Populaire de l'IF, Pondichéry, 10 Septembre 1958, Asie, Inde 1956-67, no. 330, pp. 130-7, ADP; Note sur la future organisation du Poste à Pondichéry, 5 March 1955, pp. 69, 72, no. 3, AO, ADP.

38. R. Delval, *Musulmans Français d'Origine Indienne*, Paris, 1983, pp. 143-4; A. Coret, *Le Statut Juridique Actuel des Etablissements Français de l'Inde*, Paris, 1957, p. 588.

39. Représentation Française, Pondicherry, Note sur le Foyer du Soldat, Pondicherry, 11 January 1956, pp. 175-8, no. 78, ADP; JO du 12 May 1953; Arreté fixant la compsotion du comité d'administration du Foyer du Soldat, 20 May 1947, pp. 182-5, no. 78, ADP; Tél à Affaires Etrangères, Pondicherry, 21 March 1955, 235, IF 80, ADP; Alliance Française de Pondichéry, AO, Inde 1956-67, no. 329, p. 86, ADP; Rapport fait au nom de la Commission des Affaires Etrangères, 28 May 1956, pp. 108-29, no. 329, ADP.

40. Association France Union Indienne, autorisé par arête du 12 April 1956, JO du 22 April 1956.

41. Rapport fait au nom de la Commission des Affaires Etrangères, 28 May 1956, pp. 108-30, no. 329, ADP; Rapport du lieutenant de Gendarmerie J.M. Meyer, 16 November 1954, p. 25, no. 78, ADP.

42. Asie-Océanie, Inde, 1956-67, no. 326, p. 308, ADP; Rapport fait au nom de la Commission des Affaires Etrangères, 28 May 1956, pp. 108, 129-30, no. 329, ADP; Note pour la Direction des Affaires Politiqes, Ministère des Affaires Etrangères, Paris, 1961, Pondicherry, 13 June 1960, p. 305, no. 326, ADP; Interview with Yves Perrier, Franco-Indian related to Goubert, Douglas Gressieux, Jacqueline Lernie and Anne Marie Legay.

43. Rapport fait au nom de la Commission des Affaires Etrangères, 28 May 1956, pp. 108-30, no. 329, ADP.
44. JO 1954, pp. 56-7; Letter dated 24 September 1955 re. the price of the reparation of the building, pp. 142-96, no. 3, AO, ADP; Gazette of Pondicherry, 7 April 1964.
45. *Le Monde*, 23 August 1954; A. Mariadassou, 'History of the Freedom Struggle of the French India Students Congress', *La Lettre du CIDIF*, no. 20, 1998, p. 56; *Lettre de Pierre Landy au Ministre des Affaires Etrangères*, 22 December 1954, Pondicherry, no. 2, pp. 104-5, AO, ADP; Pierre Bornecque, in *Trait d'Union*, October 1954; JO 1936, p. 952; *Inde Illustrée*, June 1933, p. 13; Ann., 1928, p. 125; JO 1934, p. 655; JO 1935, vol. I, p. 221; vol. II, p. 1172; JO 1921, p. 545.
46. Tél de Garnier, Ambassadeur à Ministre des Affaires Etrangères, New Delhi, 28 July 1962, 30 July 1962, Asie 1944, Inde. no. 334, pp. 369, 377; Asie 1944, Inde 1956-67, no. 333, p. 401; *The Mail*, 28 July 1962.
47. Interview with Yves Perrier and Anne Marie Legay; Interview with M. Husain, the late *Kazi* of Pondicherry.

Conclusions and Observations

It is obvious that it was the French who introduced their own competitive economic, administrative, educational and political system and institutions into the French Indian territories. It was within this system and the institutional structures and frameworks put in place by the French that the French Indians had to function and evolve thenceforth. The competitive system of the French brought forth in the course of time a class of landowners, the mercantile class and the professional class. These were the privileged upper-class sections of the French Indian society, while the lower classes were hierarchically below them.

The privileged upper class dominated the economic, educational, administrative and political life of the French Indian society. As the system put in place by the French was competititive in nature, the French Indians had no other altenative but to compete with one another in every field for power, position, prestige, status or profit. Therefore, competition was at the core of the French civilising mission in the parts of India that they colonised and controlled. At any rate, the educational, economic and political system put in place by the French was highly individualistic, hierarchical, competitive and centralised which was bound to throw forth its own culture, civilisation, social organization, beliefs and way of life, as it had done in France. The old cultures and religions of French India, which had been brought forth under different social conditions and systems, needed to function within this secular French system or adapt themselves to it. This system, and especially its economic content, has been legitimised and theorised by many thinkers, mainly from Europe, including Karl Marx and Friedrich Engels.

The democratic system that the French put in place in the political field was also competitive.

Naturally, the privileged classes competed for power and prestige within this system. In fact, from what we have seen earlier, it appears that democracy as introduced by the French with all its institutions was tailormade for the privileged classes to dominate politics and society in Pondicherry and French India.

Unlike in British India, the Europeans, i.e. the French, participated in this democratic process. They competed in the elections to the local, municipal and general councils, not only among themselves, but also with the Indians, for power and position in local society and politics. They also dominated the administrative, judicial and educational fields. They held most of the top posts in these fields while the subaltern posts were occupied by the Indians. But the Europeans settled in Pondicherry and French India were few in numbers. Therefore, in the type of democracy introduced by them, it was but natural that the Indians would dominate in the political field by virtue of their huge numbers. In order to offset this disadvantage, the French introduced the two-list voting system. In other words, they introduced separate electorates for the Europeans and Indians by which they elected their respective representatives to the various councils. Both the lists would have equal representation in the councils. By the creation of the two-list system on the basis of race, the Europeans vitiated the whole democratic process in French India. Later, the Creoles and the Renouncers, who were mainly Christian, were included in the European list. This electoral system was abolished only in 1945.

Right from the beginning, the democratic exercise in French India was dominated by the privileged class. From the Indian side, we have landlords like Nadou Shanmuga Velayuda Mudaliar, Gnanou Diagou Mudaliar and professionals like Ponnuthamby La Porte, as well as European industrialists and merchants like Gallois Montbrun and Henri Gaebelé, who dominated politics in Pondicherry and French India. During the later period, i.e. in the twentieth century, we have professionals like Joseph Davidu, Marie Savary and Sellane Naiker as well as the Franco-Indian Edouard Goubert and landlords and merchants like Selvarajalu Chettiar, Muthu Kumarappa Reddiar, H.M. Cassime and Muthu Poullé who dominated politics. Léon Prouchandy, who fought for Indian Independence alongside Subhas Chandra Bose in Indochina, also belonged to the privileged class. He was the first martyr from Pondicherry who suffered for the cause of Indian Independence.

The only front-ranking interloper into this class of privileged politicians was V. Subbiah. He hailed from a modest background. His education was minimal and he did not speak French. He was never a mill worker, but he successfully projected himself as the leader of mill workers and labourers. He espoused socialist views and finally founded the Communist Party of French India in 1942. On account of his radical views he had to frequently contend with harassment at the hands of the French colonial establishment as well as the Indian nationalists and the Indian government at various points of time. However, he maintained a very good relationship with some merchants and landlords like Nanayya Bhagavathar, H.M. Cassime and Muthu Poullé.

Subbiah and his associates, though they championed the causes of the working class, had never wanted to overthrow the economic system put in place by the French. His actions were always within the framework provided by the system. As a result, he is sometimes described as the quintessential symbol of 'right-wing leftism'. Such people want to improve workers' rights and conditions and implement welfare measures for the people, always within the system and never outside it. The working class is a convenient capital for them on which they build their careers.

Now the question naturally arises as to whether the preceding politicians indulged in politics only in pursuit of power, prestige, position and profit or whether principles, ideas, values and ideology had no role to play in their political forays. We should not forget, first of all, that they functioned within a democratic set-up and that democracy itself is an idea like private property, which was given a certain shape and form through institutional, administrative and legal measures. When the politicians are functioning within the parameters of this idea, how could they function solely in pursuit of power, prestige and profit, i.e. only for material reasons, as Cambridge scholars Anil Seal, Gordon Johnson and C.J. Baker had claimed? But if we take a closer look at their actions and standpoints in the course of their political evolution, the politicians were always competing with one another on the basis of a certain idea or ideas. For instance, right from the introduction of democracy in French India in 1870, Nadou Shanmuga Velayuda Mudaliar stood for the protection and upholding of Indian customs, while his rival Ponnuthamby La Porte vociferously clamoured for the adoption of French values. They both fought for power and position on the basis of such values. In the twentieth century, Henri Gaebelé and Joseph Davidu staked their claim for power on the basis of French liberal values, while the leaders of the Maha Jana Sabha Party like Marie Savary and Subbiah upheld certain Gandhian values. Much later, when the Freedom Movement gathered steam, the politicians involved themselves in it on the basis of their own ideas of how that freedom should come about. It was certainly not just for power, prestige and profit after the departure of the French. As a result, we have the Congress Party led by men like R.L. Purushot-thama Reddiar who wanted to merge the French territories with the provinces of the Indian Union, without much concern about the unique historical and cultural identity of the Pondicherrians. Sellane Naiker worked for almost the same goal. The Communist Party of French India and its leader Subbiah would also not worry about the peculiar Franco-Indian identity of the Pondicherrains in their quest for freedom. But it was Edouard Goubert alone who, right from the start, always stood for protecting the identity of the French Indians. He never swerved from this idea. Of course, one could say that he, too, was in quest for power by becoming a nationalist overnight, but his actions were motivated at the same time by his objective to safeguard the interests of the French Indians. Thus, ideas and power go hand in hand. They are parts of one and the same process. There is no idea which is not associated with power and vice-versa.

However, in order to acquire that power on the basis of an idea or a set of ideas, many French Indian politicians indulged in all sorts of illegalities like corruption, electoral fraud and rigging, embezzlement, misappropriation of public funds, abuse of power and even goondaism, because in the democratic set-up put in place by the French the privileged class was in a stronger position to dominate politics and society rather than the underprivileged and poor. In other words, the economic power of the individuals was intimately related to their political power. Thus, it would be appropriate to hold that the competitive democratic system itself spawned the corrupt activities of the French Indian politicians, right from Nadou Shanmugam to Edouard Goubert.

This brings us to the question of nationalism. Generally speaking, nationalism is the feeling of oneness on the basis of race, territory or language or some shared legacy, to the exclusion of others. The principle of oneness or the feeling of oneness, which is the basis of a nation, is shared by eminent scholars and thinkers like Ernest Renan of France, V.D. Savarkar and B.R. Ambedkar of India, according to their own understanding of what nationalism is.

Was there a feeling of oneness in the French Indian territories? They were divided on the basis of ethnicity, language, territory and geography. But they shared a common legacy due to the existence of French colonial rule there spanning over three hundred years. But this shared legacy alone was not enough to maintain Chandernagore as part of French India. Fired by the spirit of Indian nationalism, the people of Chandernagore in their large majority voted in a referendum to join the Indian Union. One could say that there was a certain oneness of feeling that pushed the Chandernagorians to join the Indian Union. But can we say that this feeling of oneness existed also in the southern French Indian territories? No, if we consider the political evolution of these territories, especially Pondicherry from at least 1945, when the two-list voter system was abolished. At the very outset, it could be said that most Pondicherrians or French Indians were never fired by the spirit of Indian nationalism in order to demand a merger with the Indian Union. In fact, there were three, or rather four, categories of politicians and their followers in French India. First, we have leaders like Lambert Saravane and Subbiah who kept alternating their opinion from being either in favour of joining the Indian Union or remaining in the newly formed French Union, according to the rapidly evolving circumstances. At one time, Subbiah even toyed with the idea of French India remaining independent of both the French and Indian Unions. Then there was the Congress group led by Purushotthama Reddiar and spearheaded by the Students' Congress who wanted a merger with the Indian Union on the basis of certain shared legacies with the rest of India and was fired by a measure of Indian nationalism. The primary worry of both Subbiah and Reddiar was not the protection of the special historical and cultural identity of Pondicherrians.

On the other hand, Edouard Goubert and his French India

Socialist Party were generally considered to be pro-French. But what the French and many others, except N.V. Rajkumar, failed to take note was that there had been no overt indication on Goubert's part that he was imbued with the French nationalist spirit or feeling of oneness with France and the French Empire or Union as was, for instance, Arthur Annasse. Neither was there any indication that he was thoroughly opposed to the rise of the spirit of Indian nationalism in French India, as promoted by the likes of Purushotthama Reddiar or Ansari Doraisamy. He also realised that Pondicherry and French India could not stand alone, independent of both the French and Indian Unions due mainly to the vulnerability of French India to the economic pressure exerted by the Indian Union. So he sat on the fence, along with some of his associates. Instead of whipping up nationalist passions of the French kind or the Indian kind, he strove to safeguard the special historical and cultural identity of the French Indians, due to their association with France. He was actually on the lookout for the best terms that the Indian government or France could offer. Whichever party would offer him the most, he would join that party. That was his gameplan. The Indian government and Jawaharlal Nehru offered him better terms to join the Indian Union than the French government who took a very ambiguous stand regarding his demand for autonomy for French India.

Goubert was actually a French Indian sub-nationalist. It was due to this that he switched sides at the last moment and announced his intention to join India. It was definitely not because he and his associates were suddenly imbued with a high sense of Indian nationalism. That never was the case. He discreetly manoeuvred his close associates like Muthu Kumarappa Reddiar and Muthu Poullé as well as the Indian Consul, Kewal Singh, and threw in his lot with India through well-calculated moves. This caught everyone, including the French and his old rivals like Subbiah, Sellane Naiker and even Lambert Saravane, by surprise.

It is quite clear from the preceding that there was no sense of oneness based on territory, ethnicity or language that bound the politicians of French India and its people to answer the call of Indian nationalism. If there was, then there would have been mass uprisings or mass non-cooperation and Civil Disobedience Movements against French rule in India. There was no such thing. There was not even a referendum like the one organised in Chandernagore to gauge the mood of the people and ascertain their views on nationalism or their desire to join the French or Indian Union. A few processions, slogans, demonstrations and fasts, such as the one by three youngsters in the aftermath of Goubert's flight to Nettapakkam, cannot be considered as a manifestation of a pervasive feeling of Indian nationalism among the people of French India. That is why there was no widespread enthusiasm among the people in favour of joining the Indian Union after the Kizhur vote of the municipals councillors and the Representative Assembly members, a majority of whom belonged to the Socialist Party of Goubert, as noted by observers. The movement towards freedom and integration with the Indian Union was certainly not because of a continuous upsurge of nationalist feelings and passions among the political leaders and people of French India, as it was the case in British India.

Besides, there was no popular uprising even in Nettapakkam. Nettapakkam was actually captured by Muthu Kumarappa Reddiar's men, and the Indian flag was raised on public buildings. Other villages and communes were 'liberated' not by any popular revolt against French rule. Instead, they were captured by Reddiar's men. Even Thirubhuvanai was captured by the Communist volunteers and 'liberated'. Inspector Sinnasamy Iyer had reported that the great majority of the people of the 'liberated' areas were actually pro-French.

The processions and demonstrations held within Pondicherry were spear-headed mostly by Students' Congress and the Youth Congress volunteers. R.L. Purushotthama Reddiar, president of the Congress Party of Pondicherry, was not involved in any struggle and was never arrested by the French police. Though Sellane Naiker and Lambert Saravane's movements in Pondicherry were never restricted, they never involved themselves directly in the agitations and never courted arrest. Even Subbiah, who was in exile, never tried to enter Pondicherry with his associates and volunteers and court arrest and imprisonment. During the Second World War, he was arrested and imprisoned for different reasons, but never for the cause of Pondicherry's Independence. Instead, he, like R. Dadala, mobilised some volunteers outside Pondicherry, for activities which were more in the nature of harassment than anything else.

However, in the dependent territories of Mahé and Yanam, there were popular revolts imbued by nationalist feelings due to the economic blockade and political pressure which forced the French to quit these territories during June-July 1954. But Pondicherry and Karaikal were relatively peaceful. Even at the last stage, there was no movement of mass non-cooperation or civil disobedience launched there in protest against French rule. No government servant ever resigned from his post and refused to serve under the French. Even Socialist party leaders like H.M. Cassime and C. Balasubramanian continued to be acting mayor/mayor and president of the Representative Assembly respectively, even after the flight of Goubert. There was no call given by them for the overthrow of the French establishment. Besides, many Muslims, especially in Karaikal, did not want to join the Indian Union for their own reasons, not to speak of the Christian populations who remained largely passive or mute spectators of the happenings in Pondicherry and Karaikal.

In the light of the above, it is difficult to concede that a genuine nationalist feeling of oneness was all pervasive among the people of Pondicherry and especially of Karaikal. They were rather conscious of their economic and material dependence on India for their very survival. The French were not able to bail them out in the long run. Goubert was most conscious of this factor when he decided to flee to Nettapakkam and fight for integration with India with the help of the Indian police and administration. He did not flee because he became a nationalist overnight or because he secretly nurtured Indian nationalist feelings right from the time he entered politics. He might have realised that it was becoming impossible to hold on to a pro-French attitude in Pondicherry in the long run, given the rising opposition to French rule from his political rivals and the continuous pressure exerted by the Indian government. He never wanted to raise the banner of revolt against French rule within Pondicherry itself and court arrest and imprisonment. So he fled because he thought that that was the only way left to him to safeguard the historical and cultural interests of the French Indians which would no doubt include his own personal interests. In this respect, Goubert and his associates can be termed as French Indian sub-nationalists who had to navigate cautiously between Indian nationalism and French colonialism or nationalism. What we have to stress here is that the freedom movement, or rather the movement towards integration with India, was never on the basis of a unified feeling of Indian nationalism, according to the definition of Ambedkar or Renan. Actually, every political leader was following his own agenda of how to incorporate the French territories in India. If the French territories were finally amalgamated with the Indian Union, it was because of the acceleration given to that process by Goubert and his men and because of technical, geographical, economic and material aspects of Pondicherry, more than because of an unadulterated upsurge of nationalism.

The nation, after all, is an idea and a feeling like religion. Neither is factual. They are based on certain beliefs and values. The politicians need the nation to function while the priest needs religion to function. Every nation and religion have its recruits and converts. The Indians or the Indian nationalist idea and feeling succeeded finally in weaning away the French Indians in their great majority towards the Indian nation, while the French could not maintain or recruit them all, except a small minority, in order to function within their national framework.

Then the question arises as to why the French finally decided to relinquish their settlements in India. The French, of course, tried their best to avoid quitting India. The talk of French empire was buried overnight, however, when nationalism reared its head in their colonies. They replaced it with the idea of French Union, where all colonised people will become equal with the French and that all of them, irrespective of caste, creed or race would be French, connected with mainland France. They considered it as a generous idea. In this way, they tried to quell the nationalism that raised its head in their colonies. In the process, they tried to nullify or deny the assertion of the historical identities of the colonised people, while keeping intact their own brand of nationalism, of which colonialism was a part. In this, they were successful only in their island colonies, whose people did not have the means to fight or even rise against French colonialism.

As a matter of fact, the French had never quit any of their colonies unless they were pushed out forcibly as in Indochina, North Africa and Madagascar. Traditionally and historically, they had the habit of walking into a country, conquering it or purchasing it or occupying it one way or the other, and then claiming that they were inalienable possessions of France and that all of their inhabitants were French, whether they liked it or not, and that they can secede only after their wishes had been officially ascertained by them.

There are several reasons which pushed the French to quit India. First of all, in May 1954, they suffered an ignominious defeat in Indochina at the hands of Vietnamese Communists, which forced them to quit the Indochinese peninsula. So, they were no more in need of Pondicherry as a halting station on their way to Indochina from France. Second, the French territories had become economically and materially dependent on the Indian Union since the time of the British. The French did nothing to extricate French Indians from this dependence. Third, the French territories in India were not islands off the Indian mainland like Réunion, New Caledonia or Guadeloupe. If they were islands, they would never have quit them. There is no such precedence in French colonial rule in the islands. Geographically speaking, the French territories were surrounded by Indian territory and, therefore, they were vulnerable, and their lands were impossible to defend if India decided to invade those territories. Besides, India was too big and important a country in the international arena for the French to afford to antagonise. Lastly, the French had antagonised Goubert, the last rampart against amalgamation with India. This led to his flight to Nettapakkam, which literally made the position of the French in their territories extremely weak and untenable. Therefore, they were pushed to negotiate with the Indian government to find a way out, even without the participation of French Indians. Besides, their strategy of using economic and cultural sops in order to keep the Indians in subservience did not work out in French India. So they chose to leave before the feeling of Indian nationalism or rather the anti-French feeling in French India, especially in Pondicherry, could gather more steam and cause a popular uprising against French rule.

The French finally chose to move out of French India and Pondicherry, given the stakes ranged against them, exactly as the British did in the rest of India. In the process, they even set aside the constitutional provisions of Article 27 of the French Constitution, which stipulated that no cession, or exchange or addition to the territories was valid without the consent of the concerned population.

Instead, they organised a vote of the members of the Municipal Council and the Representative Assembly, knowing fully well that Goubert's Socialist Party was in a majority among them and that they would vote in favour of the merger. Thus, they chose to disregard the population of French India deliberately, yet leave French India. Earlier, they had given away the loges to India even without consulting the Parliament or the people concerned, but now they threw overboard the French constitutional provision to disengage themselves from India permanently, after obtaining some guarantees for their cultural presence.

Another conclusion we can draw is that the French always believed in what they call the rapport de force or balance of power. Wherever they were in a strong position, especially in their colonies, they never relinquished their power. Wherever the rapport de force was in favour of their opponents, they gave up their power. We have seen that principle in operation in Indochina, North Africa and even in Black Africa. But wherever they were in a stronger position, they never abandoned their colonies, which they renamed as overseas territories, though there may be demands for Independence in them as in Corsica, New Caledonia and the Polynesian islands. But as far as French India was concerned, they realised in the course of time that the advantage remained with the pro-merger elements and the Indian Union. So, they made an honourable exit out of India, without effusion of blood and without losing face. They might have physically left India, but they have left behind their systems and frameworks, economic, administrative and educational, within which the Indians continue to function. They have ensured their cultural presence in India through treaties and have even appropriated physically certain Indians within their national framework and orbit, by allowing Pondicherry Indians to become French nationals. In such ways, they have sought to maintain their Indian connection, even while many Indians, including Jawaharlal Nehru, thought at the time that Pondicherry would be a window open to French culture and France.

ANNEXURE

Treaty establishing *De Jure* Cession of French Establishments in India, 28 May 1956

TREATY BETWEEN THE REPUBLIC OF FRANCE AND INDIA ESTABLISHING CESSION BY THE FRENCH REPUBLIC TO THE INDIAN UNION OF THE FRENCH ESTABLISHMENTS IN INDIA

New Delhi

Preamble

The President of the French Republic and the President of the Indian Union

CONSIDERING that their Governments, faithful to the common declaration made in 1947 and desirous of strengthening the bonds of friendship, established since then between France and India, have manifested their intention of settling amicably the problem of the French Establishments in India;

CONSIDERING that after the wish of these populations had been expressed by their representatives an agreement was concluded on 21 October 1954, transferring the powers of the Government of the French Republic to the Government of Indian Union;

HAVE DECIDED to conclude a treaty establishing the cession by the French Republic to the Indian Union of the French Establishments of Pondicherry, Karaikal, Mahe and Yanam and to settle the problems stemming therefrom and have designated thereto as their plenipotentiaries

THE PRESIDENT OF THE FRENCH REPUBLIC:

H.E. Mr STANISLAS OSTROROG,

Ambassador Extraordinary and Plenipotentiary of France in India.

THE PRESIDENT OF INDIA:

JAWAHARLAL NEHRU, Minister for External Affairs,

who, after exchanging their credentials, which having been found in legal form have agreed as follows:

Article I

France cedes to India in full sovereignty the territory of the Establishments of Pondicherry, Karaikal, Mahe and Yanam.

Article II

The Establishments will keep the benefit of the special administrative status which was in force prior to 1 November 1954. Any constitutional changes in this status which may be made subsequently shall be made after ascertaining the wishes of the people.

Article III

The Government of India shall succeed to the rights and obligations resulting from such acts of the French administrations as are binding on these Establishments.

Article IV

French nationals born in the territory of the Establishments and domiciled therein at the date of the entry into force of the Treaty of Cession shall become nationals and citizens of the Indian Union, with the exceptions enumerated under Article V hereafter.

Article V

The persons referred to in the previous Article may, by means of a written declaration drawn up within six months of the entry into force of the Treaty of Cession, choose to retain their nationality. Persons availing themselves of this right shall be deemed never to have acquired Indian nationality. The declaration of the father or, if the latter be deceased, of the mother, and in the event of the decease of both parents, of. the legal guardian shall determine the nationality of unmarried children of under 18 years of age. Such children shall be mentioned in the aforesaid declaration. But married male children of over 16 years of age shall be entitled to make this choice themselves. Persons having retained French nationality by reason of a decision of their parents, as indicated in the previous paragraph, may make a personal choice with the object of acquiring Indian nationality by means of a declaration signed in the presence of the competent Indian authorities, within six months of attaining their eighteenth birthday. The said choice shall come into force as from the date of signature of the declaration.

The choice of a husband shall not affect the nationality of the spouse. The declarations referred to in the first and second paragraphs of this Article shall be drawn up in two copies, the one in French, the other in English, which shall be transmitted to the competent French authorities. The latter shall immediately transmit to the competent Indian authorities the English copy of the aforesaid declaration.

Article VI

French nationals born in the territory of the Establishments and domiciled in the territory of the Indian Union on the date of the entry into force of the Treaty of Cession shall become nationals and citizens of the Indian Union. Notwithstanding they and their children shall be entitled to choose as indicated in Article V above. They shall make this choice under the conditions and in the manner prescribed in the aforesaid Article.

Article VII

French nationals born in the territory of the Establishments and domiciled in a country other than the territory of the Indian Union or the territory of the said Establishments on the date of entry into force of the Treaty of Cession shall retain their French nationality, with the exceptions enumerated in Article VIII hereafter.

Article VIII

The persons referred to in the previous Article may, by means of a written declaration signed in the presence of the competent Indian authorities within six months of the entry into force of the Treaty of Cession, choose to acquire Indian nationality. Persons availing themselves of this right shall be deemed to have lost French nationality as from the date of the entry into force of the Treaty of Cession. The declaration of the father, or if the latter be deceased, of the mother, and in the event of the decease of both parents, of the legal guardian shall determine the nationality of unmarried children of under 18 years of age. Such children shall be mentioned in the aforesaid declaration. But married male children of over 16 years of .age shall be entitled to make this choice themselves. Persons having acquired Indian nationality by reason of a decision of their parents, as indicated in the previous paragraph, may make a personal choice with the object of recovering French nationality by means of a declaration signed in the presence of the competent French authorities within six months of attaining their eighteenth birthday. The said choice shall come into force as from the date of signature of the declaration. The choice of a husband shall not affect the nationality of the spouse. The declarations referred to in the first and second paragraphs of this Article shall be drawn up in two copies, the one in French, the other in English and shall be signed in the presence of the competent Indian authorities who shall immediately transmit to the competent French authorities the French copy of the aforesaid declaration.

Article IX

With effect from 1 November 1954, Government of India shall take in their service all the civil servants and employees of the Establishments, other than those belonging to the metropolitan cadre or to the general cadre of the Ministry of the Overseas (France). These civil servants and employees including the members of the public forces shall be entitled to receive from the Government of India the same conditions of services, as respects remuneration, leave, and pension and the same right as respects disciplinary matter or the tenure of their posts, or similar rights as changed circumstances may permit, as they were entitled to immediately before 1 November 1954. They shall not be dismissed or their prospects shall not be damaged on account of any action done in the course of duty prior to 1 November 1954. French civil servants, magistrates and military personnel born in the Establishments or keeping their family links shall be permitted to return freely to the Establishments on leave or on retirement.

Article X

The Government of France shall assume responsibility for payment of such pensions as are supported by the Metropolitan Budget, even if the beneficiaries have acquired Indian nationality under Article IV to VII above. The Government of India shall assume responsibility for the payment of pensions, allowances and grants supported by the local budget. The system of pension of the various local Retirement Funds shall continue to be in force.

Article XI

The Government of India shall take the necessary steps to ensure that persons domiciled in the Establishments on 1 November 1954 and at present practising a learned profession therein shall be permitted to carry on their profession in these Establishments without being required to secure additional qualification, diplomas or permits or to comply with any new formalities.

Article XII

The administration's charitable institutions and loans offices shall continue to operate under their present status, and shall not be modified in the future without ascertaining the wishes of the people. The present facilities granted to the private charitable institutions shall be maintained and shall be modified only after ascertaining the wishes of the people.

Article XIII

Properties pertaining to worship or in use for cultural purposes shall be in the ownership of the missions or of the institutions entrusted by the French regulations at present in force with the management of those properties. The Government of India agree to recognise as legal corporate bodies, with all due rights attached to such a qualification, the 'Conseils de Fabrique' and the administration boards of the missions.

Article XIV

Legal proceedings instituted prior to 1 November 1954 shall be judged in conformity with the basic legislation and procedure in force at that time in the Establishments. To this end, and up to final settlement of such proceedings, the existing courts in the Establishments shall continue to function. Officers of the court shall be law graduates, habitually domiciled in the Establishments, honourably known and selected in accordance with the French regulations governing the designation of temporary judicial officers. The interested parties shall be entitled, if they so decide by common agreement, to transfer to the competent Indian Courts, the said proceedings as well as proceedings which, though already open, are not yet entered with the Registrars of the French Courts, and also proceedings which constitute an ordinary or extraordinary appeal. Judgements, decrees and orders passed by the French Courts, prior to 1 November 1954, which are final or may become so by expiration of the delays of appeal, shall be executed by the competent Indian authorities. Judgements, decrees and orders passed after 1 November 1954 in conformity with the first paragraph of the present Article shall be executed by the competent Indian authorities, irrespective of the courts which exercised the jurisdiction. Acts or deeds constitutive of rights established prior to the 1 November 1954 in conformity with French Law, shall retain the value and validity conferred at that time by the same law. The records of the French Courts shall be preserved in accordance with the rules applicable to them on the date of cession, and communication of their contents shall be given to the duly accredited representatives of the French Government whenever they apply for such communication.

Article XV

The records of the registrar offices up to the date of cession, shall be preserved in accordance with the rules applicable to them on that date and copies or extracts of the preceedings shall be issued to the parties or the authorities concerned. The personal judicial records of the Courts Registries up to the date of cession, shall be preserved in accordance with the rules applicable to them on that date and copies or extracts of these records shall be issued on request to the French authorities and likewise to the persons concerned in accordance with the legislation in force prior to 1 November 1954. The said requests on the part of the French authorities and likewise the copies addressed to them shall be drawn up in the French language and shall entail no reimbursement of costs. The French and Indian authorities shall mutually inform each other of penal sentences involving registration in the record of convictions of their own territory and pronounced either by French judicatures or by judicatures sitting in territories ceded to India concerning nationals of the other country born in the aforesaid territories.

Such information shall be sent free of charge through diplomatic channels, either in French or together with a translation into French.

Article XVI

The provisions of Article XIV of this treaty shall apply to proceedings which the 'Conseil du Contentieux Administratif' is competent to deal with. Temporary magistrates and local civil servants selected in accordance with the principles of the second paragraph of the said Article XIV shall compose this body.

Article XVII

Nationals of France and of the French Union, domiciled in the French Establishments on 1 November 1954 shall, subject to the laws and regulations in force for the time being in the Establishments, enjoy in these Establishments the same freedom of residence, movement and trade as the other inhabitants of the Establishments.

Article XVIII

All persons of French nationality acquired under Article IV to VIII or in any other manner and all French corporate bodies shall be permitted to repatriate freely their capital and properties over a period of ten years from 1 November 1954.

Article XIX

The Government of India takes the place of the territory, with effect from 1 November 1954, in respect of all credits, debts and deficits in the care of the local administration. Therefore, the Government of India shall immediately reimburse to the French Government the amount of Treasury loans and various funds placed by the latter at the disposal of the territory, as well as advances made by the 'Caisse Central de La France d'Outre-Mer', with the exception of sums remitted as grants. In addition the Government of India shall pay the indemnity agreed upon by the two Governments for the purchase of the Pondicherry power station. Simultaneously, the French Government shall reimburse to the Indian Government the equivalent value at par in pound Sterling or in Indian Rupees of the currency withdrawn from circulation from the Establishments before 1 November 1955.

Article XX

The Indian Government agree to the continuation of the French institutions of a scientific or cultural character in existence on 1 November 1954 and by agreement between the two Governments to the granting of facilities for the opening of establishments of the same character.

Article XXI

The 'College Francais de Pondicherry' shall be maintained in its present premises as a French educational establishment of the second degree with full rights. The French Government should assume the charge of its functionment as well in respect of the selection and salaries of the staff necessary for management, teaching and discipline as in respect of the organisation of studies, syllabi, and examinations and the charge of its maintenance. The premises shall be the property of the French Government.

Article XXII

Private educational institutions in existence on 1 November 1954 in French Establishments shall be allowed to continue and shall be permitted to preserve the possibility of imparting French education. They shall continue to receive from the local authorities subsidies and other facilities at least equal to those which were being granted on 1 November 1954. They will be permitted to receive without obstruction the aid which the French Government in agreement with the Government of India may desire to give them.

Article XXIII

The French Government or French recognised private organisations shall be allowed to maintain and to create by agreement between the two Governments in the former French establishments in India establishments or institutions devoted either to higher studies leading to diplomas of French language, culture and civilisation or to scientific research or to the spreading of French culture in the Sciences, Arts or Fine Arts. The Indian Government shall grant every possible facility, subject to their laws and regulations in force, for entry into and residence in India to members of French Universities sent by the French Government for a study visit or a teaching mission to India.

Article XXIV

The French Institute of Pondicherry, set up by an understanding reached between the two Governments since 21 October 1954 Agreement and inaugurated on 21 March 1955 shall be maintained as a research and advanced educational establishment. The Indian Government shall provide such suitable facilities to further the development of the activities of the said institute, as agreed upon between the two Governments from time to time.

Article XXV

Equivalences of French diplomas and degrees awarded to persons belonging to the French Establishments, namely 'Baccalaureat', 'brevet elementaire', 'brevet d'etudes du premier cycle' with diplomas and degrees awarded by Indian Universities will be accepted by the Indian Government for admission to higher studies and administrative careers. These equivalences will be fixed according to the recommendations of the Joint Educational Committee, nominated by the two Governments in accordance with the agreement of 21 October 1954. This shall apply equally to degrees in law and medicine awarded in the Establishments. Degrees of a purely local character shall be recognised under usual conditions.

Article XXIV

The French Government ceder, to the Government of India all properties owned by the local administration of the Establishments with the exception of such property as enumerated in Article VIII of the Annexed Protocol. Properties which are at present in possession of all religious authorities shall be retained by them and the Government of India agree, whenever necessary, to convey the titles to them.

Article XXVII

The French Government shall keep in their custody the records having an historical interest; the Government of India shall keep in their custody the records required for the administration of the territory. Each Government shall place at the disposal of the other lists of records in its possession and copies of such records as are of interest to the other.

Article XXVIII

The French language shall remain the official language of the Establishments so long as the elected representatives of the people shall not decide otherwise. All questions pending at the time of the ratification of the Treaty of Cession shall be examined and settled by a French Indian Commission composed of three representatives of the French Government and three representatives of the Indian Government.

Article XXX

Any disagreement in respect of the application or interpretation of the present treaty which cannot be resolved through diplomatic negotiation or arbitration shall be placed before the International Court of Justice at the request of one or other of the High Contracting Parties.

Article XXXI

The French and English texts of the present treaty shall be equally authentic. The present treaty shall be entered into force on the day of its ratification' by the two Governments concerned. The exchange of instruments of ratification shall take place at New Delhi.

The present treaty shall be deposited in the archives of the Government of India, which shall transmit an attested copy to the Government of the French Republic.

JAWAHARLAL NEHRU

Prime Minister and Ambassador Extraordinary and Minister for External Affairs.

S. OSTROROG

Plenipotentiary of France in India.

PROTOCOL

Article I

As regards the communes of Nettapacom and Tirubuvane which are part of the Establishments of Pondicherry and as regards the Establishments of Yanam and Mahe the French Government shall not be responsible, particularly in respect of Articles III, IX and XIX of the treaty, for any acts done in these communes and Establishments with effect from the date shown against each:—for Nettapacom on 31 March 1954;—for Trubuvane on 6 April 1954;—for Yanam on 13 June 1954;—for Mahe on 16 July 1954.

Article II

The sets of courses of studies at present in force shall be maintained during the appropriate transitional period in a sufficient number of educational institutions so as to ensure to the people concerned a possibility of option for the future. Transitory periods shall be provided for in every course of studies.

Article III

All pupils and students now engaged in a course of studies are given the assurance that they will be enabled to complete their studies in French according to the curricula and methods in force on 1 November 1954. They shall continue to enjoy the facilities which they enjoyed on that date, especially regarding free education and scholarships granted by local authorities, whether these scholarships be valid in the Establishments or in France.

Article IV

Regarding the organisation of the examinations of 'College Francais' and the French Institute, facilities shall be given to the representatives of the French Government concerning visas and sojourn as well as practical dispositions to be taken for holding the examinations. The French Government retains the authority to select and appoint examination boards.

Article V

Scholarships for the completion of studies leading to the 'Licence en Droit' and 'Docteur en Médecine' when begun before 1 November 1954, shall be granted on request to the students of the former Law College and of the former Medical College. If they so prefer, medical students shall have the possibility to be admitted into Indian medical colleges for completion of their studies, after being given due credits for their previous medical studies.

Article VI

The Government of India will reimburse to the personnel of education and cultural establishments whose salaries are paid by the French Government, an amount equal to the Indian income-tax paid by them unless it is covered by Double Income Tax Avoidance Agreement between India and France.

Article VII

If French books, publications and periodicals as well as educational and teaching equipment and other cultural material intended for use in French Institute and 'College Francais', are subject to import duty or other taxes, an amount equivalent to the sum so paid shall be reimbursed by the Government of India to the institutions concerned.

Article VIII

The Government of India recognise as being in the ownership of the French Government the following properties: (1) Property located in rue de la Marine (for the installation of the French Consulate); (2) Properties located on the rue Victor Simonel which are occupied by the 'College Francais de Pondicherry'; (3) the War Memorial; (4) Property No. 13 located at Karaikal so called 'Maison Lazare' (for the installation of a branch of the French Consulate); (5) Property located on the rue Saint-Louis (for the Institute).

Article IX

No one shall be prosecuted on account of political offences committed prior to 1 November 1954 and against whom no prosecution has been instituted on the said date.

Biographical Notes

ALFASSA, BLANCHE RACHEL MIRRA ALIAS LA MÈRE/THE MOTHER: Born in Paris on 21 February 1878; father's name, Maurice Alfassa; mother's name, Mathilde Ismaloun; Maurice and Mathilde married in Egypt on 18 June 1874; parents of Jewish origin; married to François Henri Morisset on 13 October 1897 in Paris; had a son through him called André; remarried Paul Antoine Richard, philosopher and lawyer, in Paris on 5 May 1911; her brother Alfassa was Governor-General of Colonies; meets Aravindha Ghose in Pondicherry in 1914; returns to Paris in 1915; returns to Pondicherry in 1920; ran the monastery or Ashram founded in Pondicherry in the name of Sri Aurobindo; she and Sri Aurobindo were founders of a new philosophy of 'supermen'; she and Sri Aurobindo supported the allied cause during the Second World War; became 'superwoman'; founder of Auroville, 1968; died on 17 November 1973 in Pondicherry; buried in the tomb of Sri Aurobindo.

ANNUSAMY, GABRIEL: Born in Pondicherry to Udayar parents; did his higher studies in France; French teacher in Calvé College; served as interim assistant director of Dupleix College of Chandernagore; an associate of Subbiah; involved in the labour movement; founded the 'Union National et Démocratique de l'Inde Française' in May 1946; was in jail during 1948-9; was suspended from service as teacher; entered Pondicherry along with Subbiah on 1 November from Kottakuppam; after merger worked as French teacher in Kapurthala.

BALASUBRAMANIAN, C.: Lawyer; representative of Yanam in the General Council, 1937; joined the Socialist Party of Goubert; president, Representative Assembly, Pondicherry; awarded the title of Chevalier de la Légion d'Honneur; presided the voting at Kijour on 31 October-1 November 1954; died at 2 a.m on 1 November 1954.

BARATHIDASAN ALIAS KANAKA SUBBU RATHINAM: Born in Pondicherry on 24 April 1891; son of Kankasabhai Mudaliar (merchant); belonged to the Senkuntha Mudaliar sub-division of weavers; Tamil teacher and poet; prolific writer and journalist; was acquainted with Barathiar and became his disciple; joined the Dravidian Movement of Periyar after Barathiar's death; contested elections to the Pondicherry Assembly as candidate of Popular Front ('Makkal Munnani') in 1955 and won; died on 21 April 1964.

BARON, CHARLES-FRANÇOIS: Born on 15 September 1900 in France; lawyer; administrator in Africa and Pondicherry, 1936; supervisor of Mont de Piété, the prison, as well as the Colonial Garden, 1936 (JO 1936, vol. I, 1449); joined the Sri Aurobindo Ashram; sent to Singapore by de Gaulle as representative of Free France; was administrator of Chandernagore, 1940; came back as governor of Pondicherry in March 1946; became high commissioner on 30 August 1947; called back to France; was close to The Mother of the Ashram; a die-hard colonialist; an admirer of Sri Aurobindo and The Mother of the Ashram; died in 1980.

BONVIN, LOUIS: Born in Montluçon, France, in 1889; studied commerce; started his colonial career in Africa in 1909; became Governor of the Colonies in 1936; appointed Governor of French India in July 1938; rallied behind De Gaulle and France Libre in 1940 and became his delegate; was against V. Subbiah, the Communist leader.

CASSIME, H.M.: Born in Pondicherry on 23 January 1900; a Tamil-speaking Muslim merchant; his grandfather's name was Isoof Sahib; his father, Mohamed Haniff, worked for the administration in French Indochina and was also Pondicherry municipal council member, merchant, landlord; had a shop called *Maison Tonkinoise* in Dupleix Street; member of Harijan Sevak Sangh, Pondicherry; was first with Subbiah; veered towards Eduoard Goubert later; was deputy mayor of Pondicherry from 1946 to 1954; imported gold and diamonds; was president of the municipal commission and acting mayor in 1954; was present during the transfer of power ceremony at the Government House; was deputy mayor in 1955-6 and 1961.

CHETTIAR, SELVARAJULU: Born on 7 December 1901; eldest son of C. Nandagobalu Chettiar, merchant; Susila Bai, wife of Selvarajulu Chettiar was born in Tiruvanmiyur; stevedore; took to his father's business at 20; landlord; fluent in French; great philanthropist; belonged to the fishing community; his only daughter was named Padmini; was interested in promoting education especially among women; spent money to develop education in Yanam; was elected to the General Council of Pondicherry from Yanam, 1928; indulged in factional quarrels in Pondicherry; wife died of fever on 22 November 1938; shot dead by a certain Ramaiya on 16 December 1938 while descending the stairs at the Government Finance Department building, located in Nehru Street, just opposite the governor's palace; his daughter was just 12 when he died, survived by brother and mother.

COUNOUMA, PADMANABHAN: Born on 17 November 1908; a Malayali of the Tiyya caste from Mahé; came to Pondicherry from Mahé on a scholarship of Rs. 72 per year to study philosophy in the Colonial College of Pondicherry in September 1921; in 1928 taught French in Calvé College; in 1933, became a fifth grade controller in Pondicherry; in 1934 was supervisor of land tax and land registry; in 1935, was supervisor of taxes; in 1936 was nominated as supervisor of mortgage in Pondicherry; elected member of the Representative Assembly of French India; was minister; joined the Sri Aurobindo Ashram in late 1940s; became a close associate of the Ashram Mother and a sort of manager of the Ashram properties; one of the pillars of the Ashram; cut himself off from his family in Mahé; his house on the seashore in Mahé was abandoned and it collapsed; died in 1990s, a bachelor.

DADALA, RAMANAYYA RAPHAEL: Born at Farompet near Yanam on 30 June 1908; son of Bairavassamy; oppressed caste Telugu; was a farm boy; converted to Catholic Christianity; educated in Andhra Pradesh and Pondicherry; studied till Baccalauréat in Pondicherry; was French teacher at Bahur for two years; became sub-inspector of police in the 1934; posted in Mudaliarpet; awarded medal of honour for his services in August 1946; dismissed by the French Indian government from the police force; became staunchly anti-French since 1951; secretary of the French India Central Merger Congress, led by

Sellane Naiker; participated actively in the Freedom Movement in Pondicherry and Yanam; was briefly administrator of Yanam after liberation; retired as excise superintendent in 1963; became landowner; a champion of scheduled castes.

GAEBELÉ, HENRI: Industrialist from Alsace; leader of the French party; Mayor of Pondicherry from 1908 to 1928; member of General Council from the 1890s till 1936; was instrumental in giving Pondicherry electricity and potable water some 28 years back; was president of the Chamber of Commerce of Pondicherry for 30 years; elected senator in December 1922 and president of General Council in 1924; died in Pondicherry in 1936; more than 15,000 people walked in his funeral procession to the Capuchin Church in Pondicherry; buried at Uppalam cemetery on the southern outskirts of Pondicherry.

GOUBERT, EDOUARD, JOSEPH ANTOINE: Born on 29 July 1894 in Pondicherry; a Franco-Tamil Créole; father was a Frenchman called Berchin de Fontaine Goubert; his mother was a 'paria' or low-caste Tamil woman of Kurusukuppam, known as Sornam to some and Muniyammal to others; First World War veteran; studied law in France: his first wife was a Créole; backed Henri Gaebelé in the municipal elections of 1928; chief registrar of Chandernagore court, 1935; chief registrar, Pondicherry; joined National Democratic Front; member of the Representative Assembly; founder of French India Socialist Party; owned a few houses, bought during his life in politics; had several children; was accused of corruption; UDSR (Union Democratique et Socialist de la Résistance) member of French National Assembly from June 1951 to June 1954; never attended parliament except to sign the register to validate his membership; revolted against French rule in late March 1954; leader of the provisional government at Nettapakkam; joined Congress Party; was Congress Chief Minister of Pondicherry until 1964; ousted from power by Venkata Subba Reddiar, his former ally; expelled from Congress; joined DMK briefly; died in Bangalore district on 14 August 1979.

GUERRE, LÉON: Born on 10 January 1834 in Pondicherry to French parents; became lawyer and proprietor in Pondicherry; was elected the first mayor of Pondicherry town in 1880; died in Pondicherry on 21 July 1895.

DAVIDU, JOSEPH VICTOR: Born in Pondicherry; hails from a modest Vellaja family; son of Tamby David; married the granddaughter of Vallabhadassou; Aravindha Ghose attended David's marriage; worked for sometime in Public Works Department; was court clerk, in 1924; became lawyer; war veteran; one of the founders of the Franco-Hindu party; interim mayor, 1934; General Council member; Tamil mayor of Pondicherry since 7 February 1935; Chevalier de la Légion d'Honneur; member of Reveil Social; escaped assassination attempt on 30 July 1936; died in 1944.

DUTAMBY, MARIE JOSEPH LOUIS: Counsellor of appeals court; was magistrate in the French colonies of West Africa; retired magistrate; president of Democratic Party; favoured Pondicherry remaining in French Union; propped up by Commissioner Ménard; in July 1954 pronounced in favour of merger with Indian Union; pension suspended by French government.

ESCARGUEIL, GEORGES: Born in Carcassone, France on 29 September 1907; 'Licencié en droit', barrister; married; spoke English; awarded the Chevalier de la Légion d'Honneur by the French government; administrator (first class) in the Ministry of the Overseas (France), Paris; was sent to Pondicherry as secretary general to wind up French settlements in India; he handed over powers to Pierre Landy and left Pondicherry on 31 October, along with Inspector Guyard towards Madras; took the flight back to Paris on 1 November 1954.

JEEVARATHINAM D.: Was the son-in-law of Muthu Poullé; was interim judge and administrator of Yanam in 1930-3; tenure in Yanam terminated due to abuse of power and disruptive activities in Yanam; member of 'Combat'; elected to the Consultative Assembly at Algiers in August 1945.

LANDY, PIERRE: Senior French diplomat of the Ministry of Foreign Affairs; representative of the French Ministry of Foreign Affairs;

effected the transfer of French India to the Indian Union; was interim representative of France in Pondicherry after the *de facto* transfer.

La Porte, Ponnouthamby: Born on 15 March 1832 in Pondicherry; belonged to the Poullé caste; rose against caste and custom since 1873; influential member of Colonial Council; leader of the Indians/Tamils who had renounced their personal laws and adopted French civil laws since 1880s; wanted fusion of castes.

Mariadassou, Antoine Hyacinthe Vallabha: Born on 10 September 1928 in Pondicherry; son of Mangaladassou and Saiva Vellaja; grandson of lawyer Vallabhadassou; brother of Dr Paramananda Mariadassou; studied in Colonial College; president of Students' Congress, 1947; fought for freedom of Pondicherry until 1952; spent some time in prison; left Pondicherry in 1953; disliked Goubert for his goondaism and for having joined the Freedom Movement in the last stages; studied engineering at the Technological Univesity of Munich; worked as engineer in Germany till 1991; married Elfriede of Germany; awarded the Tamrapatra on 26 January 1980 by the Indian government; died of a stroke on 27 June 2009; ancestors were descendants of the Tanjore royal family (according to Mariadassou himself); a person with a progressive outlook.

Marie Savary: Lawyer; belonging to the Vellaja caste; entered politics in 1923; was bailiff in Pondicherry; supported mayor Lucien Gallois Montbrun until 1933; founded the Mahajana Sabha Party in 1937 in association with V. Subbiah; was president of the muncipal commission; died in 1942.

Ménard, André: Born in France in 1907; Licenciè en droit, barrister; chief administrator of overseas France; Administrator of the Colonies, Chandernagore, 1938-9; was governor of New Hebrides, 1947-9; succeeded Charles Chambon as commissioner of French India; was governor of Pondicherry, from 31 July 1950 till October 1954; succeeded by Georges Escargueil; died in France in 1983.

MUDALIAR, LOUIS SINNAYA GNANAPREGASSA: Born in Pondicherry in 1860; father's name Sinnaya Mudaliar, he was a merchant; landlord, *dubash* and deputy director of Savanna Mill; member of General Council; member of the Chamber of Commerce; deputy to mayor of Pondicherry; his son's name was Louis Arokiassamy Mudaliar; philanthropist; died due to illness in 1920.

NADOU SHANMUGA VELAYUDA MUDALIAR: Born in 1846; son of Nadou Sidambara Mudaliar (a caste chief, agriculturist and interpreter) and Sivagamiammal; belonged to the Tondamandalavellala caste; landlord; studied law, related to Diwan Candappa Mudaliar; in politics since 1871; a jurist of French culture; leader of the Indians or Hindus and Muslims who had not renounced personal laws; accused of corruption in 1902; tall, dark and stocky; strict vegetarian; awarded Croix de la Légion d'Honneur by the French government; always dressed in white dhoti; died in Pondicherry in 1909.

NAIKER, SELLANE, RATHINA: Born in Peria Kalapet, Pondicherry, on 9 September 1884; father's name Rathina Nayagar; mother's name Irissammal; wife's name Dhanabhagyam; had four daughters; obtained law degree from University Aix Marseille (Licenciè en droit), 1913; atheist; philanthropist; son's name Manjini Naiker; promoted education among low castes; Vanniyar association leader; started as an official in the general secretariat in 1906; was arrested after a Vanniyar-Pattinava clash at Kalapet; practised law after 1913; elected to municipal council, 1919; mayor of Oulgaret, 1928; awarded Chevalier de la Légion d'Honneur, 1931; president of General Council, Pondicherry, 1933; escaped assassination attempt in 1952; founded the Pondicherry merger committee in 1949; stayed in Manjkuppam subsequently till about 1954; president of the central merger committee; founded the Pondicherry National Congress on 14 October 1954; died on 11 August 1965 at the age of 81.

OSTROROG, STANISLAS: Born in Istanbul on 20 May 1897; studied political science; French diplomat since the 1920s; was ambassador of Ireland and many Asian countries; was ambassador in New Delhi from 1951 for about a decade; the transfer of French territories in

India to the Indian Union took place when he was ambassador; Commanduer de la Légiion d'HOnneur, 1955; died on 27 September 1960.

PROUCHANDY, DARMANATHAN: Born in Pondicherry on 13 February 1847; son of Adicéanaden and Elisath; migrated to French Indochina in 1870; entered business as supplier of goods; married in Hong Kong; had two children; set up a steam navigation line in the Mekong delta; owned two steamers by the name of *Alexandre* and *Prouchandy*; wound up steam navigation business in 1900 due to stiff competition from the Messageries Fluviales, a French monopolist company and lack of support from French colonial authorities; demanded permission from the colonial authorities in Saigon in 1893-5 to run a steamer from Saigon to Thailand; permission refused; set up a fizzy drinks manufacturing factory in Saigon; was prosperous as long as the French government did not allow British soda from Singapore into French Indochina; one of his sons died in the First World War in France fighting against the Germans; died in Saigon after a terrible downturn in fortunes after the First World War; was the first Tamilian and south Indian to set up a steam navigation line; was the first Indian to attempt to run steamers by sea in 1893-5.

PROUCHANDY, LÉON: Born in Pondicherry on 1 May 1901; nephew of Chevalier Savérican Prouchandy; studied in the French College, Tabert, Saigon, Vietnam; Brevet diploma holder; married to Josephine Candappa; had a son called David; both wife and son died quite early; took care of the properties of Savérican Prouchandy, his uncle after the latter's death in 1928; resigned his lucrative job in the early 1930s in Saigon, heeding the call of Mahatma Gandhi; started the Dress Reforms among the Indians in Indochina in 1932-3; joined the Netaji movement in South-east Asia to liberate India from the British; garlanded Netaji with a gold necklace on the latter's trip to Saigon in 1943; donated generously to the INA and IIL; gave Prouchandy's family mansion, situated at 76, rue Paul Blanchy (presently Hai Bha Trung road), Saigon, free of rent, to serve as the Secretariat of the Indian Independence League and the INA; accommodated INA officials in his houses free of cost; was executive council member and last general secretary of the Indian Independence League, Saigon in 1945; close associate of Netaji; arrested by the colonial authorities after the War in September 1945; tortured in prison and rendered amnesiac; returned to Pondicherry in 1946; lived precariously until his death in 1968, at Villa Selvom, No. 5, Nehru Street, Pondicherry.

POULLÉ, MUTHU ALIAS K. MUTHUSAMY POULLÉ: Merchant; father's name, Kuppusamy; brother of Rathinavelu Pillai of the Franco-Hindu party; was member of the French India Socialist party; Mayor of Pondicherry, 1948-54; wanted Pondicherry to join the Indian Union since March 1954; fled Pondicherry with Goubert to Nettapakkam in March 1954; died in 1956.

POULLÉ, PAQUIRISSAMY, R.M.A.S.: Born on 9 August 1906 in Karaikal; son of Saminada Poullé, Nedungadu; businessman; was assistant school principal in Ambagaratur, Karaikal; rice merchant; mayor of Karaikal; elected member to the 'Conseil de la République' (Republican Council of France) in January 1947; was first Chief Minister of Pondicherry in 1955; died on 13 January 1956.

REDDIAR, MUTHU KUMARAPPA: Born on 24 September 1910; son of Visalakshi Ammal; father died in 1917; studied upto primary level; came from a modest background; had two brothers; married with two children; became a merchant, cultivator and landholder; Telugu speaker; knew some French; dealer in oil engines, sugar, gold and diamonds; moneylender and foreign money changer; became related to Venkata Subba Reddiar through marriage; municipal council member, 1914; was deputy mayor of Nettapakkam in 1933; elected mayor of Nettapakkam in 1936; president of municipal commission until 1942; Minister for Public Works and Agriculture, 1948; well-versed in the economics of Pondicherry; declared Independence of Nettapakkam along with Edouard Goubert; retired from politics after the 1955 elections in Pondicherry; indulged in business; started the Diamond Cine Corps and the Paramount Studios after Independence; entered real estate business; bought properties in Madras; died on 15 June 1968.

REDDIAR, PURUSHOTTAMA, R.L.: Born in 1906; owned some land in Irulancheri, Bahur; employee at the Pondicherry radio station; electrician; vice-president of the Harijan Sevak Sangh and Saraswati Sangam; radio mechanic; stood for workers' rights; one of the founders of Mahajana Sabha Party; treasurer of Mahajana Sabha Party; revived the Congress Party in 1946 and became its president; was member of Pondicherry assembly after 1955; died on 14 February 1979.

REDDIAR, VENKATA SUBBA: Born on 18 December 1909; son of Vaithiyalinga Reddiar, former mayor of Nettapakkam; studied upto primary level; landholder of Nettapakkam and Madukarai; Telugu Reddiar; mayor of Nettapakkam; related to Muthu Kumarappa Reddiar; was Congress Chief Minister of Pondicherry from 1965, after ousting Edouard Goubert, his former ally; died on 6 June 1982.

SAINT JEAN, LÉON: Born on 23 August 1900 at Karaikal to Christian parents; studied in Pondicherry and Karaikal; obtained the law degree from the University of Poitiers in 1927; rose up to become a writer, journalist, patriot and eminent jurist; profound scholar in Tamil and French; elected as member of Representative Assembly from Tirunallar, Karaikal in 1946; became a Congress sympathizer; wanted immediate merger with the Indian Union; refused the title of Chevalier de la Légion d'Honneur; admired French culture and language; strove for liberation in Karaikal; retired from politics from October 1954; died on 3 December 1965.

SALA, GEORGES: Born in Oran, Algeria, on 10 September 1926; passed the French law degree; posted in French Indochina for three years before being transferred to Pondicherry; administrator of Yanam, 1954; accused by pro-mergerists of mismanagement of the situation in Yanam; chief of the cabinet in Pondicherry, 1954; was posted later in Madagascar and in France until retirement; died in 2004 in his residence on the southern outskirts of Paris.

SARAVANE LAMBERT: Born in Reddiarpalalyam, Pondicherry, on 7 September 1907; ancestors migrated to Pondicherry from Tiruvannamalai; Telugu Reddiars, converted to Christianity from Pondicherry; father,

Saravane Anandou, worked as peon (customs)in French Indochina; the name, Saravane, seems to have its origin in Laos; studied at Lycée Chasseloup-Laubat, Saigon; obtained Bachelier és Lettres in Pondicherry; obtained Licence és Lettres at Aix in 1931; obtained BA in English from Loyola College, Madras; studied Sanskrit (under Sylvain Levy) and obtained Agrégation és Lettres in Paris; was assistant professor at Colonial College; married the daughter of Dr André's brother; close to Mirra Alfassa; member of the French National Assembly from Pondicherry (1946-51); was devotee of the Ashram; first wanted Pondicherry to remain in French Union; later became the first Pondicherry leader to demand integration of the French territories with India; lover of French culture and language; made some desperate attempts to protect French culture and language in Pondicherry after 1954; tried his hand in politics in Pondicherry after November 1954 for some time before settling in France; died in Paris on 18 February 1979.

SRI AUROBINDO (ARAVINDHA ACKROYD GHOSE): Born in Calcutta on 15 August 1872; son of Krishnadhan Ghose; studied in England; journalist, writer, revolutionary and nationalist; Kayastha caste; married Mrinalini Devi; accused by the British of sedition; released from Alipore Jail in May 1909; came to Pondicherry in April 1910 as refugee; welcomed to Pondicherry by Tamil nationalists like Subramania Bharathi; given refuge in Pondicherry by the wealthy Tamil Chettiars; introduced to the French couple Paul Richard and Mirra Alfassa by Tamil nationalists; founder of a new religion and monastery (Ashram) in Pondicherry in the 1920s with Mirra Alfassa; Ashram grew into a spiritual-cum-business enterprise, became recluse and 'superman'; died on 5 December 1950; buried in the Ashram house at rue de la Marine in Pondicherry with the permission of the governor of Pondicherry.

SUBBIAH, V. KAILASA: Born on 7 February 1911; born in Pondicherry; son of Varadarajulu Naidu, born in a village just outside Pondicherry in British India; mother's name V. Radja Bangarammal, French citizen; father was merchant and grandfather village munsiff in Tamil Nadu; belonged to a Telugu-speaking Balija Naidu merchant family; studied in English medium school; started as a Life Insurance Company employee; joined youth organisations; member of Harijan Seva Sangh; became labour leader; gained the support of the Valanga workers in mills; had some land in Villianur; founder of *Suthanthiram* magazine; wrote in Tamil and English; implicated in the murder of Selvarajulu Chettiar; married Saraswathi from Madras in 1943; founder of the Communist Party of French India in September 1942; joined 'Combat'; one of the founders of the National Democratic Front; was senator; first indifferent to the idea of the French enclaves joining the French Union; then wanted the enclaves to be independent of both France and India; later stood for merger of French India with India; one of the founders of Popular Front or Makkal Munnani in 1955; was member and Minister in Pondicherry Assembly; died on 12 October 1993.

SUBRAMANIAN, S.R.: Born in Valavanur on 5 July 1915; mill worker; was treasurer of the labour union (1937-8); was imprisoned for more than one year during 1938-40; one of the founders of the Communist Party of French India; president of the Rodier Labour Union (1943-6); left the Communist Party and joined the Congress Socialist Party; was an indefatigable opponent of French colonialism and cultural imperialism; died on 29 February 1992.

SAID (SYED) MOUHAMED: Born in Pondicherry in 1884; father was tailor and cloth merchant; later became prominent merchant and landlord at Hanoi, Vietnam; philanthropist; sympathetic to the All-India Muslim League; died due to illness in Pondicherry on 6 August 1945.

Bibliography

ARCHIVES AND LIBRARIES

Archives des Missions Etrangères, Paris.
Archives du Ministère des Affaires Etrangères, Paris.
Archives Nationales, Paris.
Archives d'Outre-mer, Aix-en-Provence, France.
Bharathiar Memorial Library, Puduchery.
Bharathidasan Memorial Library, Pondicherry.
Bibliothèque Internationale de Documentation Contemporaine, Paris.
Bibliothèque Nationale de France, Paris.
British Library and Records, Oriental and African Section, London.
Centre d'études de l'Inde, Paris.
Centre of South Asian Studies Library, Cambridge.
Colindale Newspaper Library, London.
Ecole Française d'Extrême Orient, Paris and Pondicherry.
Institut Français de Pondichéry, Pondicherry.
Institut National de Langues et Civilisations Orientales, Paris.
National Archives, Ho Chi Minh city (Saigon), Vietnam.
National Archives of India, Pondicherry.
Romain Roland Library, Pondicherry.
Service Historique de l'Armée, Paris.
University of Pondicherry Library, Pondicherry.

JOURNALS AND PERIODICALS

IN FRENCH

Arya, Le Mans, monthly.
Azad Hind, Saigon (weekly organ of the Netaji Movement of Saigon in French).
Combat, Alger.
Ediroli, weekly, Pondicherry; Manager: N. Narayana Vinayagam.
France-Orient, 1941.
France-Asie, Saigon, 1948.
Impartial de Pondichéry, French journal, Pondicherry, 1849.

Inde Illustrée, Pondicherry (in French).
IndeNouvelle, monthly, Pondicherry; manager, Benjamin Thiroux.
Indochine-Inde, Saigon (Franco-Tamil newspaper, formerly known as Saigon Dimanche).
Jeunesse, ed. by Dorai Munisamy/Radjanedassou; pro-Congress, nationalist.
Jeunesse de l'Empire Français, pro-French monthly, ed. by M.M. Husain (Mouhamed Houssein).
L'Aube, French newspaper, Paris.
L'Aurore, French newspaper, Paris.
Le Courrier de l'Inde Française, weekly, Paris.
Le Democrate, weekly, ed. by S. Soccalinga Poullé, 1900.
L'Echo de Pondichéry, pro-French weekly; manager, André Bayoud, 1887.
L'Epoque, French newspaper, Paris.
L'Hindou, weekly, Pondicherry; Manager: A. Arokiasamy Poullé.
L'Humanité, French daily, leftist, Paris.
L'Impartial de Pondichéry, weekly, 1849; Manager, Brün.
L'Inde Française, journal of the French party, Pondicherry.
L'Indépendant, thrice monthly, edited by A. Gnanadicom, 1897.
L'Indépendant, weekly, edited by Dartnell, Pondichéry, 1911.
L'Union Républicaine, journal of the Indian party, Pondicherry.
Le Jeune Patriote, fortnightly, pro-French, edited by Adicéam Mariasoucé Modeliar (proprietor, Tambou de Condappa).
Le Figaro, French daily, Paris.
Le Flambeau, Pondichéry.
Le Franc-Tireur, French newspaper, Paris.
Le Jeune Patriote, Pondichéry; Manager : A. Cojandéssamy Poullé, twice monthly, 1897.
Le Monde, French daily, Paris.
Le Patriote, Pondicherry; Manager, A. Cojandassamy Poullé.
Le Petit Pondichérien (Puduvai Vasi), weekly, nationalist, Manager, Kasturirangan, Pondicherry, 1911.
Le Pionnier de l'Inde Française, Manager, Ponnou Kankasabhai, February-March 1910, Pondicherry.
Le Populaire, French newspaper, Paris.
Le Progrès, journal of the Renouncers, Pondicherry; Manager, S.M. de Condinguy.
Le Progrès de l'Inde Française (in French and Tamil), Karaikal; Manager: A. Gnanapragassen.
Le Semeur, Catholic journal, Pondichéry.
Le Semeur de L'Inde Française, Pondichéry, 1913.

Le Temps de l'Inde Française, Pondicherry, Manager, P. Saligny.
Le Trait-d'Union, Pondichéry, 1944.
Libération, monthly, anti-colonial: Manager, A. Lahache.
L'Union Hindoue, weekly, Manager, Salla Balasubramanya Chetty; Editor, M.C. Radjassamy.
Messager de l'Inde, bi-weekly; Manager: Doray Eugène Savarchy.
Pages des Indes, 1936, ed. by P. Latour.
Pondichéry, Pondicherry.
Revue Historique de l'Etat de Pondichéry.
Revue Historique de l'Inde Française.
Saigon Dimanche, Saigon (Indian-owned newspaper, formerly known as *Le Reveil Saigonnais*).
Saraswati, published once every two months, Pondicherry, ed. by Saraswati Sangam; Manager, P. Joseph Latour.
Sri Soudjanarandjani, weekly, Pondicherry, ed. by Dr Paramananda Mariadassou.

IN ENGLISH

Arya, Pondicherry, philosophical journal, ed. by Paul Richard.
Indian Advertiser, Franco-Anglo-Tamil monthly, non-political, 1913, Manager, S. Rayalou Reddiar.
Indian Express, nationalist daily.
Hindustan Times, nationalist daily.
The Hindu, nationalist daily, Madras.
The Indian Advertiser, Pondicherry, 1913.
The Indian Republic, weekly, Manager, Sinnasamy Poullé, Pondicherry, 1889.
The Pondy Mail, Pondicherry, 1910.
The Voice, fortnightly, Pondicherry, ed. by A. Vincent Row.

IN TAMIL

Agni, Tamil monthly, Pondicherry, ed. by P. Bala.
Aurore (Tamil), Pondichéry, 1909-10.
Ayareru, Pondicherry, 1947; owner, V.B. Ella Pillai; Idayar caste paper.
Baradam, Pondicherry, nationalist weekly, ed. by P.R.K. Swamy; Manager, P.R. Krishnaswamynaiker.
Baratha Matha, monthly twice, edited by E.S. Reddiar, Pondicherry.
Baratha Sakthi, monthly, Pondicherry; ed. by A. Balasubramanian.
Canku, Karaikal, 1947.

Desasevagan, nationalist; Manager, Louis Sinnaya; Proprietor, Pazhani Sinnaya Rathinasamy Naidu.
Deshabandou, weekly, ed. by P.R.K. Swamy, nationalist in tone.
Desobagari, Pondicherry, pro-Franco-Hindu party, edited by Kandasamy Naiker.
Dinamani, Chennai, Tamil nationalist newspaper.
Djéasakthi, Pondicherry, ed. by Nadarajanaiker.
Djothy, ed. by P.R.K. Swamy; Manager, V. Venugobalunayakar, twice weekly.
Dupleix, Pondicherry, Franco-Tamil weekly; Manager, S.K. Ramasamy.
Frenchu Nesan. Pondichéry, weekly, 1913, ed. by V.V. Aadizhala Kramani (Nainar Mandapam).
Hindu Nesan, Pondicherry, pro-Vanniayar, weekly; Manager, P.L. Djesingh, 1890.
Ilaignar Congress, weekly, Pondicherry, ed. by Somasundaram Pillai.
India, Pondicherry, nationalist, ed. by Bharathi.
Inthiya Vikata Vinodhan, weekly, 1889, ed. by MVS Krishnamachary, Karaikal.
Janada, Pondicherry, nationalist/socialist, weekly, ed. by S.R. Subramniam.
Kalaignan, 1947, ed. by M. Naçer, Pondicherry.
Kalaimakal, pro-Tamil periodical, Pondicherry, ed. by C. Bangaru Patthar.
Kalamegam, Karaikal, nationalist, weekly, ed. by Vichur Muthukumaaswamy Mudaliar.
Karpagam, Pondichéry, monthly, 1924-7; Manager, S. Rayalu Reddiar.
Ksatriyanupalani, weekly, Karaikal, ed. by V. Narayanaswami Pillai; Nadar caste paper.
Kudiarasu, ed. by E.V. Krishnasamy, Erode.
Kudiarasu, weekly, Karaikal, nationalist; Manager, S. Chidambaram.
Kuyil, Pondicherry, Dravidian, ed. by Subburathinam alias Barathidasan.
Maanilam, Pondicherry, nationalist, ed. by P. Rangapillai; Manager, M.S. Annamalai.
Makkal Manasaatchi, weekly, Puduchery.
Maramathu Vimarsanam, monthly twice, ed. by K. Ramachandran, Pondicherry.
Muslim League, weekly, Karaikal, 1947.
NadarKulam, Pondicherry, caste-based, ed. by V. Thiagarajan, monthly.
Nyayabhimani, weekly, nationalist; Managers, Arunagirinatha Udayar, V. Subbiah Mudaliar.
Padaiyatchi, Puduchery, ed. by V. Mathurakavy, pro-Tamil and pro-Pondicherry.
Pallava Nadu, Chennai, Vannaiyar caste journal, ed. by Seyasandiran, 1954.
Parada Sakthi, Pondicherry, nationalist, ed. by A. Balasubramaniam, 1947.

Periyar, weekly, Karaikal, ed. by Tetchana.
Pittan, ed. by Tandamizhpittan (V. Srinivasan), nationalist, Pondicherry, 1947.
Podujanam, bi-monthly, Pondicherry, nationalist; ed.by C. Srinivasan.
Puduvai Murasu, Pondicherry, ed. by Ponnambalanar, pro-Self-Respect Movement.
Pudouvé Nessin, Pondicherry, 1900-5, 1910.
Puthucheriyin Kural, ed. by V. Mathurakavy, Pondicherry.
Puthuvai Mithran, weekly, ed. by S.S. Rajarathina Pillai, 1900.
Puthuvai Vinothan, weekly, ed. by C.R. Balakrishna Mudaliar, 1901.
Samudayam, Pondicherry, ed. by S.R. Subramaniam, nationalist.
Samuga Mithiran, Pondicherry, ed. by Samuthira Narayanan, 1938.
Sanmargabodhini, Pondichéry.
Sanmarka Sanku, ed. by M.M. Ali, Karaikal.
Sarva Vyapi, Pondicherry (organ of the Catholic Church); Manager, S. Mariasusai.
Sree Punitha, weekly, Karaikal, Manager, Kanakasabhai Pillai.
Sree Soudjana Ranjini, Pondicherry.
Sri Subramanya Barathi Kavitha Mandalam, 1935, monthly, ed. by Barathidasan, Pondicherry.
Sudesa Varatamani, Pondichéry, 1905-10, ed. by Mariasusai Lor.
Sukapi Viruthini, ed. by Venkatasala Nayakar.
Suryothayam, nationalist, Pondicherry, owner, Louis Chinniah Naidu.
Suthanthiram, monthy, Pondicherry, nationalist, leftist, ed. & pub., V. Subbiah.
Tay Nadu, Pondicherry, ed. by V. Venugopala Naiker.
Vennila, Pondicherry, pro-Tamil/nationalist, Pondicherry periodical, ed. by P. Sundaravadivelu.
Vidya bhi vardhani, Manager, Srinivasa Arumugam Pillai, 1897, religious-oriented.
Vijaya, Pondichéry, nationalist, ed. by Bharathi.
Vikata Prathapan, 1889-90, nationalist, ed. by S. Sinnasamy Poullé, Pondicherry.

OFFICIAL PUBLICATIONS

Annuaire des Établissements Français dans l'Inde.
Annuaire Générale de l'Indochine.
Bulletin Officiel des Etablissements Français dans l'Inde.
Journal Officiel de L'Indochine Française.
Journal Officiel des Etablissements Français dans l'Inde.

Interviews

Adhimoulame, retired sub-judge of Pondicherry, student of Lambert Saravane.

Alam, Mumtaz, daughter of J.M. Abdul Aziz, landlord of Saigon and Koothanallur, Tanjore.

Ali, A. Mohamed Maricar, Tamil journalist, originally from Karaikal, died in France.

Annoussamy, David, former Madras Court Judge, hailing from Pondicherry.

Antony, Cyril, hails from south Thamizhnadu, editor of the Gazetteer of Pondicherry.

Arago, Amalor, Professor of Mathematics in Ivory Coast, related to Joseph Davidu.

Arulraj, Anthonisamy, Muthialpet, freedom fighter of Pondicherry.

Bouchet, Jacqueline, student of Colonial College; former resident of Indochina.

Bouchet, Roland, editor of *Lettre du C.I.D.I.F.*, France.

Clemenceau, Tilakavathy, wife of Mr Murugasamy Clemenceau, communist leader, retired French soldier.

Gafoor, Abdul, prominent merchant of Pondicherry, son of N. Abdul Khader.

Georges, Sala, late administrator of French India, Paris.

Goubert, Joseph, son of Edouard Goubert.

Husain, M. M., late Kazi of Pondicherry.

Kessavaram, Jean, Pondicherrian, late employee of French Consulate, Calcutta.

Kumaran, I.K., freedom fighter, Mahé.

Kumari, Sai, late daughter of Muthu Kumarappa Reddiar, social activist.

Legay, Anne Marie, late French resident of Pondicherry, related to Maurice Gaudart, her great grand father, Mr. Léon Guerre was the first Mayor of Pondicherry; her father was the last French magistrate in Pondicherry just before 1954.

Mannan, Mannar, writer, poet and son of Tamil poet Barathidasan of Pondicherry.

Marakkayar, Farook, former Chief Minister of Pondicherry.

Mariadassou, Antoine, former Students Congress President, studied in Colonial College.

Marimuthu, N. freedom fighter, Congress leader.

Mudaliar, Govindasamy, Ananda Emporium, Pondicherry.

Muthiah, S., of Chettinad, writer, journalist and historian.

Naiker, Doressamy, Pondicherry, President of Students Congress; teacher; French pensioner.

Nallam, originally from Yanam, settled in Pondicherry, physician.

Panjab Rao More, Elenamma (Hélène), eldest daughter of Chevalier Saverikannu Prouchandy.
Perrier, Yves, late former Franco-Indian official and administrator of French Pondicherry.
Radjanedassou, Paul, President of Students Congress, 1947-8, brother of Antoine Mariadassou.
Raghavan, Mangalat, freedom-fighter, Indian Socialist party, Mahé.
Rajasekharan, retired as nursing superintendent, Pondicherry nationalist, born on 21 July 1934.
Ranganathan, N., wife of N. Ranganathan, communist leader and freedom-fighter.
Ranganathan, Seethalakshmi, wife of Dr Ranganathan, Communist party leader.
Selvaradja, Naidu, Dr. was Member of National Democratic Front, Pondicherry.
Sisupalan, Paramel, freedom-fighter, Mahajana Sabha party, Mahé, French teacher.
Sridharan, Manicoth, P. Late Professor of History, hailing from Mahé.
Subbiah, Saraswati, late Pondicherry Communist party leader V. Subbiah's wife, social activist.
Sudarsanan, N., son of S. Narayanasamy, freedom fighter of Thirubhuvanai.
Syed, Ahmed, son of Moohamed Said, prominent merchant in Indochina.
Varma, Chandra, grandson of Sellane Naiker.

Books

Adicéam, Emmanuel, *La Géographie de l'Irrigation dans le Tamilnad*, Paris, Ecole française d'Extrême Orient, 1966.
Adigal, Ilango,*Cilapatikaram*, ed. by V.V. Saminatha Iyer, Chennai: Kesari Achukootam, 1927.
Alfassa, Blanche Rachel, *Entretiens avec la Mère*, Pondichéry, Imprimerie Moderne, 1933.
Ambedkar, B.R., *The Untouchables: Who were they and Why they Became Untouchables*, New Delhi: Amrit Book Co., 1948.
Annasse, Arthur, *Les Comptoirs Français de l'Inde, Trois Siècles de Présence Française, 1664-1954*, Paris: La Pensée Universelle, 1975.
Annoussamy, David, *L'Intermède Français en Inde*, Pondichéry, Paris: l'Harmattan, 2005.
Annoussamy, David, *Pondicherry: A Social and Political History*, Pondichéry, Institut Français de Pondichéry, 2020.

Antony, Cyril, *Gazetteer of India: Union Territory of Pondicherry*, 2 vols., Pondicherry: Pondicherry Administration, 1982.

——, *Encyclopaedia of India*, Pondicherry, New Delhi: Rima, 1994.

Appadorai, A., *Documents on Political Thought in Modern India*, I, London: Oxford University Press, 1973.

Arnold, David, *The Congress in Tamilnad: Nationalist Politics in South India, 1919-37*, New Delhi: Manohar, 1977.

Arulraj, A., *Puducheri Suthanthira Poratathin Kalachuvadukal*, Puduchery: Kamarajar Desiya Viduthalia Veerar Sangam, 2005.

Aurobindo, Sri, *The Superman*, Calcutta: Arya Publishing House, 1944.

Aurobindo, Sri, *On the War, Letters of Sri Aurobindo and the Mother*, Calcutta: Arya Publishing House, 1944.

Aurobindo, Sri, *After the War*, Pondicherry: Shri Aurobindo Ashram Press, 1949.

Aurobindo, Sri, *Letters on Himself and the Ashram*, Pondicherry: Sri Aurobindo Ashram, 2011.

——, *Autobiographical Notes and Other Writings of Historical Interest*, Pondicherry: Sri Aurobindo Ashram, 2015.

Ayer, S.A., *Unto Him a Witness: The Story of Netaji Subhas Chandra Bose in East Asia*, Bombay: Thacker, 1961.

Ayyar, Narayana C.V., *Origin and Early History of Saivism in South India*. Madras: University of Madras, 1936.

Baker, C.J., *The Politics of South India, 1920-37*, Cambridge: Cambridge University Press, 1976.

Baker, C.J., Washbrook, David. *South India: Political Institution and Political Change, 1880-1940*, New Delhi: The Macmillan Company, 1975.

Baker, C.J., Gordon Johnson, Anil Seal, eds., *Power, Profit and Politics: Essays on Imperialism, Nationalism and Change in Twentieth Century India*, Cambridge: Cambridge University Press, 1981.

Bamford, P.C., *Histories of the Non-Cooperation and Khilafat Movements*, New Delhi: Deep Publications, 1974.

Barathidasan & Annadorai, *Mahakavi Bharathiar*, Pondicherry: Gnayiru Nur Padipakam, 1948.

Barnett, M.R., *The Politics of Cultural Nationalism in South India*, Princeton: Princeton University Press, 1976.

Barrington, Moore, *Social Origins of Dictatorship and Democracy*, Boston: Beacon Press, 1967.

Barros, Joao de., *Decadas da Asia*. Lisboa: na Reggia Officina, 1778.

——, *Asia. Primeira Decada*. Coimbra, Imprensa da Universidade, 1932.

Bayly, C.A., *The Local Roots of Indian Politics*, Oxford: Clarendon Press, 1975.

Bayly, C.A., *The Raj: India and the British, 1600-1947*, London: National Portrait Gallery Publication, 1990.
Bayly, Christopher & Tim Harper, *Forgotten Wars. The End of Britain's Asian Empire*, London: Allen Lane, 2007.
Begley, Vimala et al., *The Ancient Port of Arikamedu. New Excavations and Researches 1989-1992*, 2 vols., Pondicherry, Ecole Française d'Extrême Orient, 1996
Bluysen, Paul, *Notes de Voyages aux Indes. Mes Amis les Hindous*, Paris: J. Tallandier, 1914.
Bonvin, Louis (Intro.), *L'Inde Française dans la Guerre*, Pondichéry: impr. De la Mission, 1942.
Bouglé, C., *Essai sur le régime des castes*, Paris: F. Alcan, 1927.
Bourdat, Pierre, *Eighteenth Century Pondicherry*, Pondichéry: Pondicherry Museum, 1995.
Brass, Paul, *Language, Religion and Politics in North India*, London: Cambridge University Press, 1974.
Broomfield, J.H., *Elite Conflict in a Plural Society*, Berkeley, University of California Press, 1968.
Cabaton, A., *Catalogue Sommaire des Manuscrits Indiens, Indo-Chinois et Malayo-Polynésiens*, Paris: E. Leroux, 1912.
Chaffard, Georges, *Les Carnets Secrets de le Décolonisation*, 2 vols., Paris: Calmann-Levy, 1965-7.
Chand, Tara, *History of the Freedom Movement in India*, vols. I-IV, Delhi: Publications Division, Ministry of Information and Broadcasting, 1961-72.
Chandra, Bipan, *Nationalism and Colonialism in Modern India*, New Delhi: Orient Longman, 1979.
Clairon, Marcel, *La Renonciation au Statut Personnel dans l'Inde Française*, Paris: L. Tenin, 1927.
Cobban, Alfred, *A History of Modern France*. Harmondsworth: Penguin, 1965.
Cohn, Bernard, *Colonialism and its Forms of Knowledge: The British in India*, Princeton: Princeton University Press, 1996.
Coret, Alain, *Le Statut Juridique Actuel des Etablissements Français de l'Inde*, Paris: Librairie Général de Droit et de Jurisprudence, 1957.
Dadala, Ramanayya Raphael, *My Struggle for the Freedom of French India*, Pondicherry, author, n.d.
David, Georgette, *Pondichéry. Porte de l'Inde*, Paris: Publication David, 1999.
De Place, Agnès, *Dictionnaire Généalogique et Armorial de l'Inde Française, 1560-1962*, A. de Place, Versailles, 1997.
Deloche, Jean, ed., *Le papier terrier de la ville blanche de Pondichéry, 1777*, Pondichéry: Institut Français de Pondichéry, 2002.

Deloche, Jean, *Origins of the Urban Development of Pondicherry according to Seventeenth Century Dutch Plans*, Pondichéry: Institut Français de Pondichéry, 2004.

———, *Le Vieux Pondichéry 1673-1824, revisité d'après les plans anciens*, Pondichéry: Institut Français de Pondichéry, 2005.

Delval, Raymond. *Musulmans Français d'Origine Indienne*, Paris: Centre des Hautes Etudes sur l'Afrique et l'Asie Moderne, 1987.

Desai, A.R., *Social Background of Indian Nationalism*, Bombay: Popular Book Depot, 1959.

Diamond, Robert, *France under de Gaulle*, London: Facts on File, 1970.

Dianoux, Hughes Jean de, *Les Loges Françaises dans l'Inde et au Bangaldesh et les îles Spratly*, Paris: Académie des Sciences d'Outre-mer, 1986.

Dodwell, H. & Price, eds., *The Private Diary of Ananda Rangapillai – Dubash to Joseph François Dupleix, Governor of Pondicherry. A Record of Matters Political, Historical, Social and Personal from 1736 to 1761*, New Delhi: Asian Education Services, 1985.

Duperron, Anquetil, *Législation Orientale*, I, Amsterdam: M.M. Rey, 1778.

Dupuis, Jacques, *Les Ghats Orientaux et la plaine du Coromandel*, Pondichéry: Imprimerie de la Mission, 1959.

Dutt, Palme, *India Today*, Bombay: People's Publishing House, 1947.

Engels, F., *L'origine de la famille, de la propriété privée et de l'Etat*, Paris: Editions Sociales, 1983.

Esquer, A., *Essai sur les castes dans l'Inde*, Pondichéry: Imprimerie du gouvernement, 1870.

Falk, Felix, *Situation Politique de l'Inde Française*, s.l; s.d.

Fay, Peter Ward, *The Forgotten Army: India's Armed Struggle for Independence, 1942-5*, Ann Arbor: University of Michigan Press, 1993.

Franchini, Philippe, *Continental Saigon*, Paris: O. Orban, 1977.

Franchini, Philippe, *Saigon 1925-45—De la Belle Colonie à l'Eclosion Révolutionnaire ou La Fin des Dieux Blanc*, Paris: Autrement, 1993.

Francis, W., *Madras District Gazetteers, South Arcot*, Bombay: Government Press, 1906.

Froidevaux, Henri, *Bellanger de Lespinay, Vendomois – Mémoires sur son voyage aux Indes, Orientales (1670-5)*, Vendôme: Charles Huët, 1895.

Gaebelé, Yvonne Robert, *Histoire de Pondichéry de l'An 1000 à nos jours*, Pondichéry: Impr. Du gouvernement, 1960.

———, *Catalogue Général des Livres de la Bibliothèque Publique de Pondichéry*, (collaboration de K.Sadagobane) Pondichéry: Imprimerie du gouvernement, 1960.

Gallagher, John, Gordon Johnson, Anil Seal, eds., *Locality, Province and Na-*

tion: Essays on Indian Politics, 1870-1940, Cambridge: Cambridge University Press, 1973.

Gallois, Eugène, *La France dans l'Océan Indien*, Paris: Chez l'auteur, 1908.

Garstin, J.H., *Manual of South Arcot District*, Madras: Lawrence Asylum Press, 1878.

Gaudart, Edmond, *Exposition Coloniale Internationale*, Paris: Pondichéry, impr, Moderne, 1931.

Gaudart de Soulages, Michel & Philippe, Randa, *Les Dernières Années de l'Inde Française*, Paris: Dualpha, 2004.

Gaudart, Michel, *Généalogie des Familles de l'Inde Française*, XVIe-XXe siècle, Verdun, Gaudart, 1976.

Geertz, Clifford, ed., *Old Societies and New States: The Quest for Modernity in Asia and Africa*, New York: Free Press of Glancoe, 1963.

Ghose, Aurobindo, Tr. *The Wherefore of the Worlds*, by Paul Richard, Madras: Ganesan, 1923.

Ghurye. G.S., *Caste and Class in India*, Bombay: Popular Book Depot, 1950.

Giani, K.S., *Indian Independence Movement in East Asia*, 2 volumes, Lahore: Singh Brothers, 1947.

Glachant, Roger, *Historie de l'Inde des Français*, Paris: Plon, 1965.

Gnanadicom, *L'Inde Française. Sa Régénération*, Toulon: Imprimerie Cooperative, 1894.

Gnanou Diagou, *Le Droit Civil Applicable aux Musulmans de l'Inde*, I, Pondichery: Santhanam, 1984, second edition.

Gordon, Leonard, *Brothers Against the Raj*, New Delhi: Rupa, 1990.

Graf, Violette, *Les Partis Communistes Indiens*, Paris: Armand Collin, 1974.

Gressieux, Douglas, ed., *Cinquantenaire du Transfert des Comptoirs à l'Inde (1954-2004)*, Paris: Dualpha, 2005.

Gressieux, Douglas, *Les Troupes Indiennes en France, 1914-18*, Tours: Editions Sutton, 2007.

Guy, Camille, *Exposition Universelle 1900: Les Colonies française. Les Etablissements Français de l'Inde*, Paris: impr. F. Levé, 1900.

Habib, Irfan, *Essays in Indian History—Towards a Marxist Perception*, New Delhi: Tulika, 1998.

Haudrère, Philippe, *La Compagnie Française des Indes au XVIIIe siècle, 1719-1795*, 4 vols. Paris: Indes Savantes, 1989.

Hardy, Peter, *The Muslims of British India*, London: Cambridge University Press, 1972.

Heehs, Peter, *Sri Aurobindo, A Brief Biography*, New York: Oxford University Press, 1989.

Heehs, Peter, *The Bomb in Bengal: The Rise of Revolutionary Terrorism in India, 1900-10*, New Delhi: Oxford Univesity Press, 1993.

Heehs, Peter, *The Lives of Sri Aurobindo*, Columbia: Columbia University, 2008.

Hobbes, Thomas, *Leviathan*, 2 vols. London: Penguin, 2003.

Ignace, A., *Le Progrès Social dans l'Inde*, Karaikal: Saint Joseph, 1907.

Ilango, Siva, *Pirachintiyavum Dravida Iyakkamum* (Tamil), Puduchery: Gnayiru Padipakam, 2000.

Ilango, Siva, *Ettu Mani Nera Velai Aasiyavin Muthal Vetri* (Tamil), Puduchery: Gnayiru Padipakam, 2004.

Irschick, Eugene, *Politics and Social Conflict in South India: The Non-Brahman Movement and Tamil Separatism, 1916-29*, Berkeley: University of California Press, 1969.

Iyengar, Srinivasa, *Sri Aurobindo, A Biography and a History*, 2 vols., Pondicherry: Sri Aurobindo International Centre of Education, 1972.

Kalladan, ed., *Puduchery Marapum Maanpum* (Tamil), Puduchery: Puduchery Varalatru Sangam, 2002.

Kanakasabhai, V., *The Tamils Eighteen Hundred Years Ago*, Madras: Higginbothams, 1904.

Kiani, M.Z., *Indian's Freedom Struggle and the great INA*, New Delhi: Reliance Publishing House, 1994.

Knight, F., *The French Resistance*, London: Lawrence and Wishart, 1960.

Kohn, Hans, *The Age of Nationalism*, New York: Harper, 1962.

Kosambi, D.D., *An Introduction to the Study of History*, Bombay: Popular Book Depot, 1956.

Krishnamurthy, B., *Pirench Intiya Viduthalai Porattam* (Tamil), Pondicherry: Navajoti Publishers, 1991.

Krishnaswami, A., *The Tamil Country under Vijayanagar*, Annamalainagar: Annamalai University, 1964.

Kumar, Dharma, *Land and Caste in South India. Agricultural Labour in the Madras Presidency during the Nineteenth Century*, New York: Cambridge University Press, 1965.

——, *Colonialism, Property and the State*, Delhi: Oxford University Press, 1998.

Kumari, Shyam, *How they came to Sri Aurobindo and the Mother*, Pondicherry: Mother Publishing House, 1990.

Lafont, Jean Marie, *Indika. Essays on Indo-French Relations, 1630-1976*, Delhi: Manohar and Centre de Sciences Humaines, 2000.

Lafrenez, Jean, *Précis d'Histoire de la Mission de Pondichéry*, Pondichéry: publisher not specified, 1953.

Labernadie, M.V., *Le Vieux Pondichéry (1753-1815), Histoire d'une ville coloniale française*, Pondichéry: Imprimerie Moderne, 1936.

Launay, Adrien, *Histoire des Missions de l'Inde—Pondichéry, Maîssour, Coimbatore*, Paris: Ancienne Maison Charles Douniol, 1898.

Lemaire, *Election Législative de l'Inde, le 6 Mai 1906*, Saint Maur, impr. De J. Lievens, 1906.

Love, Henry Davison, *Vestiges of Old Madras*, 4 vols. London: John Murray, 1913.

Moignic, Le, *Elections Sénatoriales de l'Inde du 16 Janvier 1927*, Paris: Imprimerie Simart, 1927.

Majumdar, R.C., *History of the Freedom Movement in India*, vols. 1-3, Calcutta: K.L. Mukhopadhay, 1962-3.

Maindron, Maurice, *Dans l'Inde du Sud: Le Coromandel*, I, Paris: Lemerre, 1907; G.B. Malleson, *History of the French in India from the founding of Pondicherry in 1674 to the capture of that place in 1761*, London: Longmans Green & Co., 1893.

Mannan, Mannar, ed., *Puduvai Pukazh Manikal* (Tamil), Valavanur: Muthu Pathipagam, 1979.

Mannan, Mannar, *Karuppu Kuyilin Neruppu Kural* (Tamil), Vizhupuram, Muthu Padipagam, 2003.

Mariadassou, Paramananda, *Moeurs Médicales de l'Inde et leurs Rapports avec la Médecine Européenne*, Paris: C. Boulange, 1906.

Marx, Karl, *Capital: A Critical Analysis of Capitalist Production*, London: Lowrey & Co., 1887.

Martin, François, *Mémoire de François Martin, Fondateur de Pondichéry (1665-94)*, 3 vols., Paris: Société d'éditions, géographiques, maritimes et coloniales, 1931-4.

Martineau, Alfred, *Etablissements Français dans l'Inde*, Paris: Société d'éditions géographiques maritimes et coloniales, 1931.

———, *Inventaire des Anciennes Archives de l'Inde Française*, Pondichéry: Société de l'Histoire de l'Inde Française, 1914, 1931.

Mathew, K.S., ed., *French in India and Indian Nationalism (AD 1700-AD 1963)*, 2 vols., New Delhi: B.R. Publications, 1999.

Mathew, K.S., ed., *Maritime Malabar and the Europeans*, Gurgaon, London: Greenwich Millenium, 2003.

Mathew, K.S., *Freedom Movement in India: An Historiographical Note*, Pondicherry: *publisher not specified*, n.d.

Mathurakavi, Veera, *Puducheri I.N.A. Thyagi Léon Purushanthi Varalatru Kaiédu* (Tamil), Pondicherry: Thyagi Leon Prouchandy Sangam, 2004.

Mayer, Adrian, *Land and Society in Malabar*, Bombay, Oxford University Press, 1962.

Menon, Dilip, *Caste, Nationalism and Communism in South India: Malabar 1900-48*, Cambridge: Cambridge University Press, 1994.

Miles, William, *Imperial Burdens: Counter-colonialism in former French India*, London: Lynne Rienner publishers, 1995.

Miliband, Ralph, *The State in Capitalist Society: The Analysis of the Western System of Power*, New York: Basic Books, 1969.

Moracchini, M.D., *Les Indigènes de l'Inde Française et le Suffrage Universel*, Paris: Blot, 1883.

More, J.B.P., *The Political Evolution of Muslims in Tamilnadu and Madras, 1930-47*, Hyderabad: Orient Longman, 1997.

More J.B.P., *Freedom Movement in French India: The Mahé Revolt of 1948*, Tellicherry: IRISH, 2001.

———, *L'Inde Face à Bharati: Le Poète Rebelle*, Tellicherry: IRISH, 2003.

———, *Muslim Identity, Print Culture and the Dravidian Factor in Tamilnadu*, Hyderabad: Orient Longman, 2004.

———, Ed. *La Civilisation Indienne et les Fables Hindous du Pantchatantra*, Pondicherry: LPMC & Irish, 2004.

———, *Religion and Society in South India: Hindus, Muslims and Christians*, Nirmalagiri: IRISH, 2006.

———, *The Telugus of Yanam and Masulipatnam: From French Rule to Integration with India*, Pondicherry: S. Madhimchetty, 2007.

———, *Rise and Fall of the 'Dravidian' Justice Party, 1916-46*, Tellicherry: IRISH, 2009.

———, *Puducheri Valartha Bharathiar* (Tamil), Pondicherry: TLPMS, 2016.

———, *Indian Steamship Ventures, 1836-1910: Darmanathan Prouchandy of Pondicherry, First Steam Navigator from South India, 1891-1900*, Pondicherry: LPMS, 2013.

———, *From Arikamedu to the Foundation of Modern Pondicherry*, Pondicherry: Saindhavi, 2014.

———, *Tamil Heroes in French India, 1870-1954: Their Role in Business, Social Reforms and in Netaji's Freedom Struggle from Vietnam*, Pondicherry: TLPMS & Ilakkya, 2016.

———, *Subramania Bharathi in British and French India, Nationalist, Revivalist or Thamizh Patriot?* Chennai: Palaniappa Brothers, 2017.

———, *Bose and His Movement: From Nazi Germany to French Indochina*, New Delhi, Manohar, 2022.

Mortimer, Wheeler, *Rome Beyond the Imperial Frontiers*, Harmondsworth: Penguin Books, 1955.

Murugesan, C.S., *Viduthalai Velviyil Puduchery* (Tamil), Chennai: Sankar Pathipakam, 2004.

Narayanasamy, K., *Puduvai Thanthai Goubert* (Tamil), Puduchery: Brinda Padipagam, 1994.

Nehru, Jawaharlal, *A Bunch of Old Letters*, Delhi: Oxford University Press, 1988.

Neogy, Ajit, *Decolonization of French India: Liberation Movement and Franco-Indian Relations (1947-54)*, Pondicherry: Institut Français de Pondichéry, 1997.

Nicolas, Barry, *An Introduction to Roman Law*, Oxford: Oxford University Press, 1962.

Olagnier, Paul, *Les Jésuites à Pondichéry et l'Affaire Naniapa (1705 à 1720*, Paris: Société de l'Histoire des Colonies Françaises, 1932.

Padmanabhan, P., *Pirenchinthiya Viduthalai Poril Ithazhkal*, Pondicherry: Puduchery Tolilamurugu Pathipagam, 2004.

Pairaudeau, Natasha, *Mobile Citizens: French Indians in Indochina, 1858-1954*, Copenhagen: NIAS Press, 2016.

Pandian, P.N.S., *Ooradangu Utharavu, Puducheri Arasiyal Poratta Varalaru* (Tamil), Puduchery: Verso Pages, 2018.

Pattabiramin, P.Z., *Les fouilles d'Arikamedou (Podouké)*, Paris: Presses Universitaires de France, 1946.

———, *Quatre Vieux Temples des environs de Pondichéry*, Paris: P.U.F., 1948.

Planchais, Jean, *L'Empire Embrasé (1946-62)*, Paris: Librairie Decitre, 1990.

Poullé, Narayana, *Histoire Détaillée des Rois du Carnatic*, tr. by Gnanou Diagou, Paris: E. Leroux, 1939.

Purani, A.B., *The Life of Sri Aurobindo*, Pondicherry: Sri Aurobindo Ashram, 1978.

Pylee, M.V., *Constitutional History of India, 1600-1950*, London: Asia Publishing House, 1967.

Raja, P., *A Concise History of Pondicherry*, Pondicherry: Busybee Books, 1987.

Rajendran, N., *National Movement in Tamilnadu 1905-1914: Agitational Politics and State Coercion*, Madras: Oxford University Press, 1994.

Rajkumar, N.V., *The Problem of French India*, Delhi, New Delhi: All India Congress Committee, 1951.

Ramachandran, A., ed., *Pondicherry through the Ages*, Pondicherry: Pondicherry University, 1997.

Ramasamy, A., *History of Pondicherry*, Delhi: Sterling Publishers, 1987.

Ramasrinivasan, R., *Karaikal in Freedom Struggle*, Karaikal, Pondicherry: Qualite offset, 1998.

Renan, Ernest, *Qu'est-ce qu'une nation?* Paris: Calmann-Levy, 1882.

Renou, Louis, *La Géographie de Ptolemée*, Paris: E. Champion, 1925.

Richard, Paul, *Le Corps du Christ après sa résurrection, essai métaphysique*, Montauban: J. Granié, 1900.

Richard, Paul, *Les Dieux*, Paris: Fischbacher, 1914.

Richard, Paul, *L'Ether vivant et le Réalisme Supranerveux*, Paris: H. Daragon, 1911.

Richard, Paul, *The Scourge of Christ*, tr. into English by James Cousins, Madras: Ganesh & Co., 1921.

Richard, Paul, *The Lord of the Nations*. Madras: Ganesh, 1923.

Richard, Paul, *The Wherefore of the Worlds*, tr. from French by Aurobindo Ghose, Madras: Ganesan, 1923.

Robinson, Francis, *Separatism among Indian Muslims-The Politics of the United Provinces' Muslims, 1860-1923*, Cambridge: Cambridge University Press, 1974.

Rose, Vincent, ed., *L'Aventure des Français en Inde, xviie—xxe siècles*, Paris: Editions Kailash, 1996.

Said, Edward, *Orientalism*, London: Routledge & Kegan Paul, 1978.

Samboo, Gopaljee, *Les Comptoirs Français dans l'Inde Nouvelle de la Compagnie des Indes à nos Jours*, Paris: Fasquelle éditeurs, 1950.

Sarkar, Sumit: *Modern India, 1885-1947*, Delhi: Macmillan, 1983.

Schlatter, Richard, *Private Property, The History of an Idea*, London: Allen & Unwin, 1971.

Scholberg, Henry & Emmanuel Divi, *Bibliographie des Français dans l'Inde*, Pondichéry: The Historical Society of Pondicherry, 1973.

Seal, Anil, *The Emergence of Indian Nationalism*, Cambridge: Cambridge University Press, 1971.

Sen, Sailendra Nath, *Chandernagore: From Bondage to Freedom, 1900-55*, New Delhi: Primus Books, 2012.

Sen, S.P., *The French in India—First Establishment and Struggle*, Calcutta: University of Calcutta, 1947.

Sen, S.P., *Dictionary of National Biography*, Calcutta: Institute of Historical Studies, 1974.

Sewell, Robert, ed., *A Sketch of the Dynasties of Southern India*, Madras: E. Keys, 1883.

Sicé, Pierre-Constant, *Annuaire Statistiques des établissements français de l'Inde pour l'année 1841*, Pondichéry, (s.n.), 1841.

Sicé, E., *Un Mot sur la Représentation des Etablissements Français de l'Inde à l'Assemblée Nationale*, Pondichéry, (s.n.), 1848.

Sicé, E., *Annuaire des Etablissements Français de l'Inde. 1851, 1852, 1854*, Pondichéry, auteur, 1851, 1852, 1854.

Sidambarom, Nadour, *Les Habitants Indiens de Pondichéry à la Chambre des Deputés*, Nantes: Imprimerie Busseuil, 1846.

Sitaramayya Pattabhi, *The History of the Indian National Congress*, I, Bombay: Padma Publications, 1946.

Spengler, Oswald, *The Decline of the West*, 2 vols., New York: Alfred Knopf, 1922.
Sridharan, M.P., *Papers on French Colonial Rule in India*, Calicut: Progressive Printers and Publishers, 1997.
Srinivasachari, C.S., *Ananda Ranga Pillai: The 'Pepys' of French India*, New Delhi: Asian Educational Services, 1991.
Stein, Burton, *Peasant State and Society in Medieval South India*, Delhi: Oxford University Press, 1980.
Subbiah, V., *Saga of Freedom Movement: Testament of my Life*, Madras: New Century Book House, 1990.
Sundararajan, Saroja, *Glimpses of the History of Karaikal*, Madras: Lalitha Publications, 1985.
Tailleur, Georges, Chandernagor ou le Lit de Dupleix. Le Premier Maillon de la Chaîne, Montpellier, de Frontignan, 1979.
Tamilvanan, Lena, ed., *Pandichery Manilam*, Madras: Manimekalai Prasuram, n.d.
Thilaivanam, Su., *Puduchery Manilam Varalarum Panpadum*, Puduchery: Sivasakti Padipagam, 2008.
Thurston, Edgar, K. Rangachari, *Castes and Tribes of Southern India*, Madras: Government Press, 1909.
Tibbetts, G.R., tr. *Arab Navigation in the Indian Ocean before the coming of the Portuguese, being a translation of Kitab al-Fawa'id fi usal al-bahr wa'l-qawa'id*, London: The Royal Asiatic Society, 1981.
Tisserand, Ernest, *Les Malheurs de l'Inde Française*, Paris: S.E. Auteur, 1932.
Valmary, Jean, *Rapport sur l'Enseignement dans l'Inde Française de XVIIe siècle à nos jours*, Pondichéry: Imprimerie Moderne, 1922.
Vappala, Balachandran, *A Life in Shadow, The Secret Story of ACN. Nambiar: A Forgotten Anti-Colonial Warrior*, New Delhi: Lotus, 2016.
Varadarajan, Mu., *A History of Tamil Literature*, tr. from Tamil by E. Sa. Viswanathan, New Delhi: Sahitya Akademi, 1988.
Venkatachalapathy, A.R., *Va. Ou. Ciyum Tirunelveli Ezhuchiyum*, Chennai: Makkal Veliyeedu, 1987.
Venkatachalapathy, A.R., *V.O. Ciyum Bharathiyum*, Chennai: Makkal Veliyeedu, 1994.
Vincent, Rose, ed., *The French in India*, Bombay: Popular Prakashan, 1990.
Vinson, Julien, *Catalogue des Manuscrits Tamouls*, BNF, 1867.
Vinson, Julien, *Les Français dans l'Inde, Dupleix et Labourdonnais: 1736-48*, Paris: E. Leroux, 1894.
Viswanathan, Seeni, *Kalavarisai Paduthapatta Bharati Padaippukal*, I, Chennai: author, 1997.

Washbrook, D.A., *The Emergence of Provincial Politics, 1870-1920*, Cambridge: Cambridge University Press, 1976.
Weber, H., *La Compagnie française des Indes, 1604-1875*, Paris: A. Rousseau, 1904.
Weber, Jacques, *Les Etablissements Français en Inde au XIXe siècle (1816-1914)*, 5 vols., Paris: Librairie de l'Inde, 1988.
———, Ed. *Compagnies et Comptoirs. L'Inde des Français, xviie—xxe*, Paris: Société Française d'Histoire d'Outre-mer, 1991.
———, *Pondichéry et les Comptoirs de l'Inde après Dupleix: La Démocratie au pays des Castes*, Paris: Denoël, 1996.
Wilks, H., *Historical Sketches of South India*, 2 vols. Madras: Higginbotham's & Co., 1869.
Yule, Henry & A.C. Burnell, *Hobson-Jobson: A Glossary of Colloquial Anglo-Indian words and phrases and of kindred terms-Etymological, Historical, Geographical and Discursive*, London: John Murray, 1903.
Xavier, Thani Nayagam. *A Reference Guide to Tamil Studies*, Kuala Lumpur: University of Malaya Press, 1966.

ARTICLES

Albertelli, Mélanie, 'Les Conflits du travail à Pondichéry en 1936 sz Marie-Laure Gérart', *La Lettre du CIDIF*, no. 32-3, October 2005.
Annoussamy, David, 'L'Alliance Française de Pondichéry', *Le Trait d'Union*, April 1982.
Annoussamy, David, 'Le Rattachement de l'Inde Française à l'Union Indienne', *La Lettre du CIDIF*, no. 21, August 1999.
Annoussamy, David, 'La Population Indienne de Pondichéry et la Révolution Française', *La Lettre du CIDIF*, no. 24, 2000-1.
Annoussamy, David, 'Les Etablissements Français en Inde', *La Lettre du CIDIF*, no. 40, 2010.
Annoussamy, G., 'Thunbankallukku Tholvi Thanthavar', *Va. Subbiah Pavala Vizha Malar*, 1988, pp. 63-4.
Arumugam, S., 'Perumithathin Thiru Uruvam', *Va. Subbiah Pavala Vizha Malar*, 1988, pp. 93-7.
Arunagiri, A., 'Viduthalai Velviyil Pudamitta Pon', *Va. Subbiah Pavala Vizha Malar*, 1988, pp. 106-11.
Bornecque, Pierre, 'A Kijeour s'est joué le sourt de l'Inde Française', *Le Trait d'Union*, October 1954.
Chaffard, Georges, 'La fin des Comptoirs', *La Lettre du CIDIF*, no. 30-1, October, 2004.

David, J., 'Mémoire sur la Rénonciation au Statut Personnel', (Extract from *Sri Soudjanarandjani* (Tamil newspaper), 1920.
Dessama, Evariste, 'Tribulation de l'Inde Française', *France-Asie*, Saigon, February 1950.
Diagou, Gnanou, 'L'Affaire Savana en 1936', *La Lettre du CIDIF*, no. 28-9, October 2003.
Deloche, Jean, 'Relations Franco-Indiennes jusqu'au Transfert', *La Lettre du CIDIF*, no. 22-3, 1999-2000.
Delqueux, Juliette, 'La Cathédrale de Pondichéry et les nationalists Indiens', *La Lettre du CIDIF*, no. 37, 2007.
Dessama, Evariste, 'Tribulations de l'Inde Française', *France-Asie*, Saigon, February, 1950.
Divien, E., 'V. Subbiah' in *Va. Subbiah Pavala Vizha Malar*, 1988, pp. 39-40.
Durai, Munusamy, 'Maatru Katchiyinarum Mathikum Thalaivar', *Va. Subbiah Pavala Vizha Malar*, 1988, pp. 84-5.
Gaebelé, Robert, Yvonne, 'Ariancoupam, Terre d'Histoire et de Prière', *Revue Historique de l'Inde Française*. 8ème vol., 1952, pp. 1-10.
——, 'La Pagode de Villenour', *Revue Historique de l'Etat de Pondichéry*. 9ème vol., 1955.
Gobalakichenane, 'La Révolution Française des Tamouls de Pondichéry', *La Lettre du CIDIF*, no. 24, 2000-1.
Gupta, Nolini Kanta, 'Documents in the Life of Sri Aurobindo: Sri Aurobindo and the Mother 1914-20', *La Lettre du CIDIF*, no. 20, 1998, p. 87 (Notes ed. by Samir Kanta Gupta).
John, M.P., 'Employer-Employee Relationship', *Suthanthiram Pon Vizha Malar*, 1987, pp. 16-17.
Jouveau Dubreuil, G., 'India and the Romans', *Indian Antiquary*, 52, 1923, pp. 50-3.
——, 'Podouké—Pondichéry'. *RHIF*, pp. 151-7.
——, 'François Martin est-il Fondateur de Pondichéry? *RHIF*, no. 13, 20 Mai 1936.
——, 'Le nom de Pondichéry'. *RHEP*. 9ème vol., 1955.
——, 'Les Colonnes du Pier'. *RHEP*, 9ème vol., 1955, pp. 250-3.
——, 'Le Port de Pondichéry'. *RHEP*, 9ème vol., pp. 254-7.
——, 'Un Miracle au Large de Pondichéry'. *RHEP*, 9ème vol., pp. 304-8.
Kannappa, Siva, 'Makkal Thaliavar', *Va. Subbiah Pavala Vizha Malar*, 1988, pp. 82-3.
Larnine, Magloire, 'Le Bon Temps des Colonies' (in) *Arya*, Le Mans, 15 December 1996, no. 2.

Lafrenez, R.P., 'Précis d'Histoire de la Mission de Pondichéy', *Le Trait-d'Union*, March 1976.

Lernie-Bouchet, Jacqueline, 'Les Modeliars de la Region de Saint-Thome, Caste:SavallaVelaja: Un Essai de Généalogie', *La Lettre du C.I.D.I.F.*, no. 16-17, July 1997, pp. 99-102.

Lobligeois, Mireille, 'Ateliers Publics et Filatures Privées à Pondichéry après 1816', *BEFEO*, Tome LIX, Paris, 1972.

Malangin, Raphaël, 'Le Phare de Pondichéry'. *La Lettre du C.I.D.I.F.*, no. 32-3, October 2005, pp. 173-6.

Malangin, Raphaël, 'Le Quartier du Port à Pondichéry ou les incertitudes portuaires (1765-1954)', *La Lettre du CIDIF*, no. 38, 2008.

Mariadassou, Antoine, 'History of the Freedom Struggle of the French India Students Congress', *La Lettre du CIDIF*, no. 20, 1998, pp. 55-67.

Mariadassou, Antoine, 'Correspondance d'un jeune Pondichérien sur la situation politique en 1952', *La Lettre du CIDIF*, no. 37, 2007.

Marius, Sharmila, 'Documents sur les Premières années de Sri Aurobindo à Pondichéry', *La Lettre du Cidif*, no. 20, 1998.

Mayandi Bharathi, I., 'Subbaiyavum Suthanthiramum Onru', *Va. Subbiah Pavala Vizha Malar*, Pondicherry, 1988, pp. 46-51.

Miles, William, 'Defective Decolonization: The Pondicherry Legacy', *La Lettre du CIDIF*, no. 9, 1994, pp. 142-53.

Minattur, Joseph, *Justice in Pondicherry (1701-1960)*, Bombay, 1973.

More, J.B.P., ' The Marakkayar Muslims of Karikal, South India', *Journal of Islamic Studies*, Oxford, 2, 1, 1991.

More, J.B.P., 'Hindu-Christian Interaction in Pondicherry, 1700-1900', *Contributions to Indian Sociology*, 32, 1, 1998, pp. 97-121.

———, 'Indians in French Indochina' (in) K.S. Mathew, (ed.), *Nationalism in French India*, vol. II, New Delhi, 1999.

———, 'Muslim Evolution and Conversions in Karaikal, South India', *Islam and Christian-Muslim Relations*, 1993, 4(1), pp. 65-82.

———, 'A Tamil Muslim Sufi', *Islam and Christian-Muslim Relations*, Birmingham, 10, 1, 1999.

———, 'Pathan and Tamil Muslim Migrants in French Indochina', *Journal of Social Sciences and Humanities*, Pondicherry, vol. 1, no. 1 & 2, 2000, pp. 113-28.

———, 'A Mahesian in the French Resistance', in K.S.Mathew (ed.), *Maritime Malabar and the Europeans*, Gurgaon, London, 2003.

———, 'Samatam Kristaya, un Yanaonais mort pour la France', *La Lettre du C.I.D.I.F*, October 2003, no. 28-9.

———, 'Muslim Specificities in French India during the Nineteenth Century', *Journal of the Institute for Research in Social Sciences and Humanities*, vol. 2, no. 1, January-June 2007.

——, 'A Tamil-owned Steam Navigation Company in French Indochina, 1891-1900', *Journal of the Institute for Research in Social Sciences and Humanities*, vol. 3, no. 1, January-June 2008, pp. 19-34.

——, 'L'Evolution Socio-économique du Territoire de Pondichéry: un Aperçu', *Cinquantenaire de Transfert des Comptoirs à l'Inde (1954-2004)*, ed. by Douglas Gressieux, Coullomiers, 2005, pp. 167-82.

——, 'Léon Prouchandy. Réformateur Social de Pondichéry en Indochine Française, 1930-9', *La Lettre du C.I.D.I.F.*, Paris, November 2009.

——, 'Commerçants Musulmans tamouls en Indochine Française', *Lettres du C.I.D.I.F.*, 16 March 2011.

Nara, V., 'Varalatru Nayakanin Siraivasamum Thalaimaraivu Vazhkaiyum', *Va. Subbiah Pavala Vizha Malar*, 1988.

Ner, Marcel, 'Les Musulmans de l'Indochine Française', *Bulletin d'Ecole Française d'Extrême Orient*, XLI, 1941, pp. 151-200.

Piesse, Gabriel, 'Pondichéry de 1954 à 1963. De la République Française à l'Union Indienne: Histoire D'une Transition', *La Lettredu CIDIF*, no. 26-27, October 2002.

Pitoeff, Patrick, 'La Fin des Comptoirs de l'Inde', (M. Ménard, Governor of Pondicherry interviewed by Patrick Pitoeff on 30 August 1985 (in) *La Lettre du CIDIF*, Février, 1991.

Pattabiramin, P.Z., 'Sites Archéologiques et Préhistoriques des environs de Pondichery', *Revue Historique de l'Inde Française*. 7ème vol., 1948, pp. 145-50.

Pitoeff, Patrick, 'L'Inde Française en Sursis (1947-54)', *La Lettre du CIDIF*, December 1995-January 1996.

Ramanujam, D.K., 'Liberation Movement in French Indai', Revue Historique de Pondichéry, vol. XX, 2001, pp. 89-103.

Renault, Jean, 'Avec les Macouas de Pondichéry', *Sciences et Voyages*, March 1952.

Samy, Stéphanie, 'Une Histoire Singulière: Pondichéry de 1947 à 1954', *La Lettre du CIDIF*, Décember 1995-January 1996.

Saravane, Djea, 'Rôle Politique de Lambert Saravane lors du Transfert' *Cinquantenaire de Transfert des Comptoirs à l'Inde (1954-2004)*, ed. by Douglas Gressieux, Coullomiers, 2005, pp. 123-40.

Sebastien, A., 'Nan Kanda Imayasikaram', *Va. Subbiah Pavala Vizha Malar*, Pondicherry, 1988, pp. 100-1.

Subbiah, V., 'Naatu Viduthalai Poratathil Thozhilalar Pangum Kadamaiyum' in *Suthanthiram, Suthanthira Thina Sirappu Malar*, Pondicherry, 1980, pp. 9-14.

Subbiah, V., 'Puduvaiyin Pazham Perum Varalatru Pinnani', *Suthanthiram Pon Vizha Malar*, 1987, pp. 37-41.

Subbiah, V., 'Nan Arintha Pavendar Bharathidasan', *Suthanthiram Pon Vizha Malar*, 1987, pp. 100-3.

Subramanian, S., 'Ninaivuk Kovai', *Va. Subbiah Pavala Vizha Malar*, Pondicherry, 1988, pp. 134-8.

Vinson, Julien, 'Sur les noms de Pondichéry et de Karaikal,' *Journal Asiatique*, March-April 1918, Annexe au Procés-Verbal de la Séance du, 8 Février 1918, pp. 377-9.

Weber, Jacques, 'Chanemougam, le 'roi de l'Inde Française', *La Lettre du CIDIF*, no. 1, 1989.

Weber, Jacques, 'Chanemougam, the King of French India. Social and Political Foundations of an Absolute Power under the Third Republic', *Economic and Political Weekly*, 9 February 1991.

Weber, Jacques, 'La Rente de l'Inde: Les Origines du Monopole Britannique du sel', *La Lettre du CIDIF*, no. 22, pp. 44-64.

MISCELLANEOUS

Archival Notes: Sri Aurobindo and the Mother 1914-20, *La Lettre du CIDIF*, no. 20.

Arumugam, S. 'Puduvai Maanila Suthanthirap Poril Maanavarkalin Pangu'.

Audience Publlique correctionelle extraordinaire du Tribunal Supérieur d'appel de l'Inde Française du samedi, 9 October 1948, (in) *La Lettre du Cidif*, no. 20.

Blin, Théophile, *Etablissement de filature et tissage de Blin et Cie à Pondichéry*, Pondichéry, 1845 (copy).

Cader, Abdul, S., pamphlet protégeant avec véhémence le régime républicain des anciens temps de l'Inde Française, Pondichéry, 27 April 1948.

Certificat du Maire de Pondichéry, délivré le, 6 September 1973, concernant les fonctions civiques de H.M. Cassime (copy).

Details of the life of Muthu Kumarappa Reddiar as dictated by him in February 1968 for C.S. no. 14/67(copy in my possession, given to me by Ms. Sayeekumari, daughter of Muthu Kumarappa Reddiar).

Documents in the life of Sri Aurobindo, *La Lettre du CIDIF*, no. 20.

Etat des Services de M. Haniff en Indochine, 1927 (copy in my possession).

Exposition Coloniale Internationale de Paris, 1931.

French Indian Central Merger Congress, 'Some suggestions to the Government of India', (report), Pondicherry, 8 September 1954 (copy in my possession).

French Pockets in India, Madras, 1952.

Handbook of Statistics—Pondicherry State, Pondicherry, 1960-1.

Ini Varum aikiyam—Oru Thittam (Tamil), pamphlet of the Socialist party of French India, Pondicherry, June 1947.

Kavignar Puduvai Sivam Avarkalin Vazhkai Kurippu, Puduchery, n.d.

L'Inde Française dans la Guerre, Pondichéry, n.d.

'L'Union de l'Avenir' (Programme)—publised by the Parti Socialiste de l'Inde Française, June 1947, printed at Sri Aurobindo Ashram Press, Pondicherry.

'Lambert Saravane', *La Lettre du CIDIF,* no. 30-1, October 2004.

Lastick, S., 'The Role of Sellane Naiker in the Freedom Struggle of Pondicherry', M. Phil. Dissertation University of Pondicherry, 1998.

Leconte, Nadia, 'La migration des Pondichériens et des Karikalais en Indochine ou le combat des Indiens renonçants en Cochinchine pour la reconnaissance de leur statut (1865-1954)', Mémoire de Maîtrise, Université de Haute-Bretagne, Rennes 2, September 2001.

'Les Etablisssements Français à l'Assemblée Nationale en 1954', (Débats Parlementaire), *La Lettre du CIDIF,* no. 28-9, October 2003.

'Les Comptoirs Français de l'Inde'(1952), Le Semeur (in) *La Lettre du CIDIF,* no. 38, 2008.

Lettre d'un natif Indien aux Chambres Françaises, sur l'exécution de l'ordonnance royale du 23 Juillet 1840, concernant la représentation coloniale dna sles établissements français dans l'Inde, Paris, 1841.

Lettre du Révérend Frère Faucheux à Mme. Robert Gaebelé que lui avait demandé la situation exacte de la pagode de Vedapureeswarar, Yercaud, 20 December 1952, *Revue Historique de l'Inde Française,* vol. 9, 1955, pp. 322-3.

'Les Biens des Jésuites', Délibérations du Conseil Supérieur de Pondichéry, 25 April 1769 (in) *La Lettre du CIDIF,* no. 36, October 2007.

Les Colonies Françaises, Paris, 1889.

Les Colonies Françaises. Notice sur l'Inde, Trichinopoly, 1922.

List of Freedom Fighters of the Union Territory of Pondicherry.

Makkal Thalaivar Va. Subbiah Pavala Vizha Malar, 1988.

'Maurice Schumann à Pondichéry en 1947', (Entretien) in *La Lettre du CIDIF,* no. 38, 2008.

Mémoires adressés par les Cultivateurs français de Pondichéry, à l'Assemblée Nationale législative et à M. le Président de la République française contre la surtaxe imposé sur les terres à Adamanom des aldées par décret en faveur des Etabliseements Français dans l'Inde du 4 February 1851, par (redigé Ponnou), Paris, 1851.

Memorandum to the Government of India by the President, Sellane Naiker, French India Central Merger Committee, Pondicherry, 12 April 1953.

Ménard, André, 'La Fin des Comptoirs de l'Inde', Interview de Patrick Pitoeff du 30 Août 1985 (in) *La Lettre du CIDIF*, no. 4, 1985.

Mudaliar, Natesa A., 'Villianur Police Sinnasamy Iyer' (pamphlet), 22 April 1955, Puduchery *Mootha Thyagi A. Arulraj—84aam Aaandu Piranthathina Vizha Malar*, Puduchery, 2008.

Nara, V. Kavi, 'Udarpayirchi Isai Kalaikalil Thozhilali Varkathin Seyal'.

Narayanin, Ambady, 'Relation Culturelle entre le pays tamoul et Kerala', Conférence faite à l'occasion de l'inauguration du Kerala Samaj à Pondichéry, le 23 December 1945, Pondichéry, 1966.

Padmanabhan, M., 'The Attempt on the Life of Sellane Naiker', typescript, Pondicherry, 22 December 1954.

Padmanabhan, P., 'Intiya Sarkarukku or Arivippu', 23 November 1954, Puduchery.

Piesse, Gabriel, 'Pondichéry de 1954 à 1963, De la République Française à la'.

République Indienne: Histoire d'une Transition, Maîtrise d'Histoire, Université de Nantes, 1999, reproduced in *La Lettre du C.I.D.I.F.*, no. 26/27, 2008.

'Pirachinthiya Akathikal Maanatu Theermanankal', Villupuram, 1952.

Ponnou, Delafon, B., *Les Paysans du Territoire de Pondichéry*, doctoral dissertation, Montpellier, 1945.

'Projet d'accord établi par les gouvernments français et Indien', *La Lettre du CIDIF*, no. 21, 1999.

'Puduceriyammanperil Virutham (Strophes sur la déesse de Pondichéry) 3412' in Mss. Indien 578, BNF.

'Puthuvai Maanila Desiya Iyakkam', *50 Aandu Duthanthira Varalaru* (Souvenir in Tamil).

'Puthuvai Desiya Iyakka Varalatru NIkazchikalin Kalakurippukal', by Nara, in *Suthanthiram Pon Vizha Malar, 1934-84*, Pondicherry, 1987, pp. 41.

Ramanujam, D.K., 'Liberation Movement In French India: Its significance, Historic Importance and Special Features', paper presented at the Historical Society Seminar on 28 February 1998.

Ranganathan, N., 'The Liberation Movement', talk at Pondicherry University on 29 May 1988.

Ranganathan, N., *The Ashram in Politics*, Pondicherry, 1982 (typescript).

———, *National Movement in French India*, Pondicherry, 1988 (typescript).

Bibliography

Ranganathan, N., 'Suthithirap Poril Saka Poralikalum Naanum' (copy in my possession).

Reqûete au Roi, par les Habitants de Pondichéry, Paris, 1790.

Rouillé, Sophie, La Vie Politique et écoomique dans les Etablissements Français de l'Inde de 1914 à 1928, D.E.A., 10 September 1997.

Report on Conflict over French Enclaves in India, French India Central Merger Committee, January 1953.

Samy, Stéphanie, 'Une Historie Singulière. Pondichéry 1947 à 1954', Mémoire, Sciences-Po, Bordeaux, 1995 (in) *La Lettre du Cidif*, no. 12-13.

Sivasamy, 'The Political Struggle in French Establishments in India, 1947', (in) Fonds, Adicéam, EFEO, Pondichéry.

Socialist Party Manifesto, Pondicherry, 20 July 1948.

Subbiah, Saraswati, 'Pirenchinthiya Pakuthikalin Suthathira Porata Varalatril Communist Katchi Talaivar Thozar Va. Subbiah Avarkalin Pangu', typescript, 1998.

Subbiah, V., *Puduvaiyin Viduthalaiai Vendradutha Thozhilalarkalin Veera Varalaru*, Puduchery, 1986 (dissertation).

Suthanthiram, Suthanthira Thina Sirappu Malar, Pondicherry, 1980.

Suthanthiram Pon Vizha Malar, 1934-84, Pondicherry, 1987.

Sri Latchumi Narasimmarin Tharissanam. Singarkudin, Poovarasankuppam, Parrikal, Anthali Sthala Varalaru (Booklet in Tamil).

'Thyagi Léon Prouchandhyku Silai Vaikka Korikai' (Demand to erect a statue for Thyagi Leon Prouchandy in Pondicherry) by A. Arulraj, freedomfighter of Pondicherry, (in) *Dinamani*, Pondicherry edition, 3 November 2010.

Thyagi Na. Marimuthu Pavala Vizha Malar, Puduchery, 2003.

Traité de Cession des etablissements français de Pondichéry, de Karaikal, de Mahé et de Yanaon, *Journal Officiel des Etablissemnts Français de l'Inde* du, 23 October 1962, p. 10302; procès-verbal du 13 March 1963 (*La Lettre du CIDIF*, no. 21, Août 1999).

Translation of the Indian Socialist Party leaflet explaining party position, 1954.

'Un fiche de la police britannique sur Bharathi en 1912', *La Lettre du CIDIF*, no. 37, 2007.

Union Territory of Pondicherry—Statistical Handbook, 1981-2, Government of Pondicherry.

Va. Subbiah Pavala Vizha Malar, Pondicherry, 1988.

Vashist. M.C., 'Trade Union Movement in Pondicherry State with special reference to Mahé', M. Phil. Dissertation, University of Calicut, 1993.

Index

Adamanom 38
Agricultural Bank (*Crédit Agricole*) 37
Agricultural Credit Society 37
Alfassa, Mirra 16, 93, 94, 116, 125-8, 130, 174, 179, 188, 190-1, 193, 196, 204-5, 221, 225, 250, 275, 299, 350-2, 368, 370, 373, 375-7
Alliance Française 62
Annoussamy, G. 115
Annuaire des EtablissementsFrançais de l'Inde 29
anti-mergerist policemen 333
Archbishop Auguste-Siméon Colas 32

Baderdine Sahib, kazi of Pondicherry 33
Banqued'Indochine 37
Baradam 113
Bharathi, Subramania 90, 92, 93, 94, 118, 120, 121, 125, 130, 204; promoted Swadeshi Steam Navigation Company of Tuticorin 90
Bharathidasan 101, 104, 116, 120-3, 130, 143, 199, 219, 225-6, 247, 346; opponent of Hindi and Brahmanism 123
Brevet de Langue Indigène 58

Calvé College 60, 62, 63, 66, 115; students' strike 63
Certificat de Langue Indigène 58
Certificatd' Etudes 59
Certificatd' etudes Françaiset Indigene 61
Chamber of Agriculture 37; Robert Gaebelé 37
Chandernagore 389

Charles de Gaulle's Fourth Republic 168
Chettiar, Selvarajalu: Hindu religious festivals, celebration of 103
Civil Disobedience Movement 113
Collège Colonial of Pondicherry 57: Secondary education imparted by trained university professors 59; Valangas admitted 59
Collège Dupleix' of Chandernagore 58
Collège Calvé' of Pondicherry 58
Collège Français or French College 57, 62
Congress Party 113
Créoles, posts held 64
customs union and economic blockade 235-41; Chandernagorians 240; Customs Union Agreement of 1941 237; Customs Union Convention 235; Indian maritime customs 236; permit system 236; pro-Congress National Liberation Front 240-1

Davidu, Joseph 135
De Nourquer du Camper, Paul 33
de Richemont, Eugène Panon Desbassyns 55-6
Desasevagan 113
Deshabandhu of Pondicherry 113
Dress Reforms Movement 115

E.V. Ramasamy Naiker of Erode, 119-24; Aryan-Dravidian theory of Periyar 120; attended the *Suya Mariyathai Vaibhavam* feast 122; Bharathidasan 120-1; *Deshabandhou* criticized Periyar

and his followers 121; *Karpagam* wanted the Brahmins to adhere to the *Brahmana Dharma* 120; known as Periyar' or the Elder 120; opposition to Periyar's movement 120; Ponnuthamby La Porte 121; Self-Respect Movement 119, 130; *Sri Soudjanarandjani* 122; Vaikom Satyagraha in Travancore 119
Ecole des Arts et Métiers' in Pondicherry 60; professional courses 59
Ecole Centrale, Pondicherry 60-1
ecolecentrale or central school 56
English-medium Hindu Union Middle School, Karaikal 59
Escargueil, Georges 361
Europeanisation 35

Franc-Tireur 179
Free Town project of Baron 359
French Constitution (Fourth Republic), Article 27 361
French in Pondicherry, law studies inaugurated 59-60
French India, education in 56
French Indian economy, agriculture as mainstay 36-7
French Indian government: credit facilities for agricultural development 37; decision to teach English and Indian languages like Tamil 59; French settlements by land and sea 34; land as a chief source of revenue 34
French Indian politicians: indulged in all sorts of illegalities 388
French Indian society: landownership, institution of 35
French language 62
French rule in Pondicherry: discrimination in government employment 63; education 55

French territories, *de facto* transfer to India 369-78; creation of condominium or a Franco-Indian joint administration 371-2; France-Union Indienne 374-5; *L'Institut Français* or the French Insitute 374; Les Amis de la Langue et la Culture Française 371; *Lycée Français* 374; Pondicherry wholesale trade, in the hands of Indians 375; Union Territories Act of 1963 373-4

Gaebelé, Henri 47-9, 62, 85, 88-90, 92-3, 95-100, 103, 105-6, 142, 386, 388; General Council elections in 1906, captured power 89
Gallois-Montbrun, Armand 81
Gandhi, Mahatma 44, 94, 99, 104, 113-19, 129-31, 145, 154-5, 177, 192, 194, 204, 207, 365; all-India campaign against Untouchability 116; visit to Pondicherry 114-18; reforming Hindu society 115; philosophy, youth organisations of Pondicherry 115
Gandhian Movement 95, 99, 104, 106, 113, 115, 130; against untouchability, Léon Prouchandy of Pondicherry 115
Gauls 62
girls' boarding school (*pensionnat*) 57
Gnanadicom, M.A. 88
Goubert, Eduoard: Communist takeover' of Pondicherry 359; economic pressure and referendum 280-8; election victories 267-80; flight to Nettapakkam 311-26; French Indian sub-nationalist 390; Goubert's volte face 295-302;

rise of 217-56; trip to Paris and Delhi, and its aftermath 241-56
Goubert, Eduoard, economic pressure and referendum 280-8; criminal class of smugglers and *goondas* in the settlements 284; end to the 'plebiscite business' in Pondicherry 285; French India and India, balance of trade between 287; French intransigence in favour of respecting the Constitution 286; Houses of pro-merger leaders in the French enclaves attacked by *goondas* 283; Nehru condemned 'method of gangsters' in Pondicherry 281; Subbiah united six pro-merger groups in Cuddalore 284
Goubert, Eduoard, election victories 267-80; activities of pro-mergerists infuriated the French 275; Associatiion de la Jeuness Musulmane 279; attempt made on Goubert's life 267; awarded the grade of Chevalier de la Légion d'Honneur 270; budget of French India 269; Communists pushed out of Pondicherry 278; competitive democracy 271; council of ministers, re-organisation of 271; founded the Republican Party 272; Free Towns, status of 279; French dismissed him as a crypto-Communist 273; Jeunesse Musulmane of Karaikal and Salah Maricar 280; Poullé, Muthu 269-70; Reddiar, Muthu Kumarappa 270
Goubert, Eduoard, flight to Nettapakkam 311-26; pro-merger processions 321; *République Française* 316; Socialist Party under Goubert captured Madukarai 315; Students' Congress under Dorai Munisamy agitated for freedom 319-20
Goubert, Eduoard, rise of 217-56; 1941 Customs Agreement 232-3; Anti-Communist forces 224; Ashram angle 233-5; Ashramite, assigned to do some work in the Ashram 234; Bastille Day procession organised by French Government 233; customs union and economic blockade 235-41; de la Légiond' Honneur, Chevalier 218-19; Democratic Progressive Party candidates 226; Dravidian Pondicherrians 219; municipal elections 229-30; Munisamy, Dorai 222-3; Naiker, Sellane 220; Pondicherry Representative Assembly 220; Poullé, Muthu, mayor of Pondicherry 218; Reddiar, R.L. Purushotthama 217; referendum and elections 217-33; Socialist Party led by Goubert, Eduoard, backing of the administration 226; Socialist Party of France (SFIO) 231; Thakara Kotta theatre 219
Goubert, Eduoard, trip to Paris and Delhi, and its aftermath 241-56; Baig, Rachid Ali 246-7; Edouard Goubert and the Socialist Party 245; l'Union Républicaine de l'Inde Française 252; Municipal Councils of the French settlements 245; Pondicherrian Papusamy, 248; Students' Congress 247
Goubert's volte face 295-302; and after 302-11; balance of trade in India's favour 297-8; *de facto* situation in Pondicherry 295; French educated youth assured of opportunites of employment 307; growing mass support for merger

302; public meeting at Schoelcher Square (Odiansalai) of Pondicherry 297; relationship with Anglo-Saxon culture 295; single-handedly prevented the French settlements from joining India 303; Unified Merger Committee of Karaikal 309
Guerre, Léon 81

Hannah, Dutamby 225, 244, 334-5, 340, 347, 369, 374; organised pro-French demonstrations in Pondicherry 334
Harijan Sevak Sangh 114, 116, 118, 244; Dorairaj, R. 118; Ilayangudi Arangasamy Naiker, known as the 'Gandhi of French India' 116
health officer, five-year course in the French medical school 60
Hindu community in Pondicherry 31
Hindu Harijan Sevak Sangam 114
Hindu Nesan 88
Hindu Valanga welfare 114

Indian National Congress, 86, 114, 232, 241, 360; did not recognise Pondicherry Congress under Sellane Naiker 360; in Pondicherry 114
Iruthi Andavar Church 32

Jenma Rakini Mary Church 32
Jenmis 34
Joseph François Dupleix's governorship 29

Kanturi festivities 34
Karaikal 30-4, 37-9, 42-6, 48, 58-61, 66, 70, 76, 79-81, 85-6, 92, 120-2, 145-8, 158-60, 178-80, 226-7, 235-7, 250-3, 276-80, 308-10, 319-23, 336-9, 368-71, 392

Kizhur, voting at 363-9; *Agence France Presse* 363; *Le Trait d'Union* 363; Pondicherry became free of French rule 365, 368; *Semaine du Monde* 363

L'Inde Illustrée 113
La Porte, Ponnuthamby 83, 84-5
Land, privatisation of 36
Landownership 34; people and castes, social relations between 35
Le Gentil, Guillaume 29
Licence en Droit 59

Mahajanasabha party 145-53; General Council elections 146-7; Governor Crocicchia dissolved existing municipal commissions 149; municipal elections 146; not completely non-violent 148; stood for radical change in political system of French India 146; went for a Gandhian style Non-Cooperation Movement 148; workers' grievances 150
Manavai R. Tirumalaisami of *Swadesamitran* 125
Mass education 55
medical school in Pondicherry 60
mestrys 60
mirasdars or landlords 36
modern system of education 56
Mont de Piété 37

Naidu, Saigon Louis Sinnaya/Naidu, Mudaliar 86
Naidu, Subbiah V. 114-20, 129, 130, 135, 137, 139-40, 142-60, 172-3, 175-91, 205, 219-20, 229, 267-8, 277-80, 283-4, 288, 309-12, 318-19, 338-9, 360, 368-70, 389-91
Naiker, Sellane 117; reaction to the 21 October treaty 362
National democratic front, foundation

of 172-88; Council of Government 185; formed in September 1945 173; public opposition to reforms 185-6; Subbiah, 184-5; Subramanian, S.R. 183; Vietnam Day 182; Adicéam, Emmanuel 179; All-French India Congress 177; All-India Students' Congress 182; Balasubramanian, C. 173; Baron 179-80; Baron's governorship 174; elections held to the Representative Assembly 180; French India Students' Congress 177; Lambert, Saravane 178-9; Mariadassou, Antoine 178; Padmanabhan Counouma elected from Mahé 176; Savarinathan, Jean 176-7, 179; Socialist Party Wing of Congress party 177-8; Subbiah, V. 181-2; swept municipal elections held in June 1946 175
Nationalism 389
Nationalist Awakening in Pondicherry 168-208; Jeevarathinam, D. 168
Nehru, Jawaharlal, visit to Pondicherry 118
Netaji-Prouchandy episode 169-72; archival records attest great majority of the French Indians 170; Indian National Army, defeated on the Burmese front 171; Vichy France government in Indochina 170-1
Niyayabhimani of Karaikal 113

Pannaiyals 35, 36
paracheris (margins) 32
Paramananda Mariadassou 33
Petit Seminaire (formerly known as *Collège Colonial des Missions Etrangères*) 59
Pierre, Gaston 87

Pillai, Ananda Ranga 31
Place du Gouvernment (presently Bharathi Poonga) 33
Political institutions and early politics 76-89; 1880, French India divided into 10 communes or municipal divisions 81; 1880s, Hindu-Muslim discord and bloody riots in Pondicherry 84; All White Frenchmen 76; All-India Muslim League 86; all-White Municipality in Pondicherry 76; competition for power and prestige 87; Count André Julien Dupuy, 77; decree of 24 February 1875 80; democracy introduced into French India 86-7; educated Valangas 84; equal representation in the councils 82; French Indian government under Vicomte Desbassyns 77; French Revolution, all-White General Assembly in Pondicherry 76; General Council 80; General Council abolished in 1848 78; municipal councils and the mayors, rights and duties 81; National Assembly, elections to choose a delegate 78; Ordonnance Organique 77; Parti Libéral Renonçants' (Liberal Renouncers Party) 83; personal laws or French civil laws 85; *Place du Gouvernement* (presently Bharathi Park) 84; policy of assimilation 78-9; political consciousness among Indians 88; Ponnuthamby, caste symbolically abolished 82; Poullé caste 83; powers related to administration, vested with the governor 89; Renouncers 82-3; restricted Colonial Council 79, 80; Shanmugam 81; Third Republic

instituted in France 78; two-list voter system 82

Pondicherry (White town) 351; education secularised to a great extent 62

Pondicherry politics, 1901-35 89-106; Abdul Cader of the 4th Regiment of French Colonial Infantry of Morocco 94; anti-Christian movement 104-5; *Baradam* supported Christians 102; Bharathi, Subramania 90; Bluysen, Paul 91; Chettiar, Datchinamurthy 97; Chettiar, Nandagobalu 92-3, 96; Chettiar, Selvarajalu 99-100,103; Civil Disobedience Movement 99; Davidu, Joseph 96, 98, 102, 103-4; *Desasevagan* 97-8; *Deshabandhou* 98; Diagou, Gnanou 96; *Dupleix* criticized Hindus 102; electoral violence, arson, robbery and murder 92-3; Franco-Hindu Party 98-9, 101; Gaebelé, Henri 89, 95-6; Gandhian Movement, influence hardly felt in Pondicherry and Karaikal 95; Ghose, Aravindha (Aurobindo) 91; Guerre, Jules, elected mayor of Pondicherry 97; Le Moignic, Eugène 96; Le Moignic, Eugène 98; Louis Sinnaya, Saigon 92; Naiker, Rathina Sellane 96, 101; Naiker, Sadasiva 91-2; *Niyayabhimani* 97; November 1931, riots of 99; Poullé, Thomas Arul, elected mayor of Karaikal 97; resentment against the Christians 102; Richard, Paul 93-4; Salt Rent 101; Swadeshists of Pondicherry 89-90; Tamil Christian Renouncers 105; Uniform Civil Code 105-106; Valangas (Parayars) admitted into the police force 95

Pondicherry society: elite or upper class 38

Ponnambalam, A.: preached the egalitarian ideology in Mudaliarpet 122

Poullé, Pakkirisamy 241

primary level, no compulsory education 61

Primary schooling 58;Colonial College 58; Pensionnat de Jeunes Filles 58 primary schools or *ecolesprimaires* 56 private property 34; institution of 36 privileged upper class: democratic exercise in French India 386; dominated economic, educational, administrative and political life 385

Professional classes, emergence of: Adi Dravida/Valanga population in Pondicherry 69; administration and employment, no quota system or communal representation/ reservation 64; Alliance Educative des Vanniars 68; *Anjumane Himayat Islam* of Pondicherry 68, 70; anti-Brahmin movement 64; Appasamy, Francine 68-9; Arya Vaishya Samajam 68; Babilonne, R. 67, 68; Cercle de Pondichéry 72; Cercle Littéraire Musulman' (Muslim Literary Circle) 70; Cercle Progressiste' in Pondicherry 67; Cercle Sportif Pondichérien' 69; chery schools 64-5; chery schools' or the 'Valangamugattar' 68; Clairon, Marcel 69; *devadasi* system 72; education and culture, private effort 66-72; education and employment, open to all Indians 65; education key to employment in the French Indian administration 72; French egalitarian values 67; *French Indian Madhar Aikya Sangam* 71;

Index 453

Jawaharul Islam 70; Kalaimakal (Daughter of Arts) 66; Kalvi Kazhagam (Education Centre) 66; *Karai Muslim Sangam* 70; Kavundan, Srinivasa 68; La Solidarité des Dames de l'Inde Française 71-2; *Madjmaoul-Mousinul-Mouminine* in Pondicherry 70; Mangalavasam' at Karadikuppam 69; Mudaliar, Louis Sinnaya Gnanapragasa 69; *Muslim Kalasalai* 70; *Muslim Vidya Sangam* 70; Muslims of French India, indifferent to modern education 70; *Nangaiyar Nalvazhi Sangam* members 71; *Nangayar Nalvazhi Sangam* 71; *Neravy Muslim Educational Sangam* 70; *Nyayabhimani* of Karaikal 66; Ponnou Murugesa Poullé 67; Puduvai Kalaimakal Kazhagam (Pondicherry Daughter of Arts Association) 66; *Puduvai Tamizh Sangam* (Puduvai Tamil Sangam) 66; Refuge 69; resentment against Christians from the Hindu populace 64; Reveil Social (Social Awakening) 69; Sanror Kula Paripalana Sabhai 68; *Saraswati Sangam* 70; Self-Respect Movement in Tamil Nadu 64; Société Progressiste of the Valangamugattars 68; Société Progressiste' in Pondicherry 67-8; Society of the Ladies of Pondicherry 71; Subbiah, V. Kailasa 68; Tamil education 66-7; Tamil pundits and Brahmins, activities initiated by Bangaru Pathar 66; *Tamizh Kalvi Sabhai* (Tamil Education Society) 66; *Tamizh Tallir* 66; *Tamizhar Kalvi Kazhagam* 70; *Thanit Kalvi Koodam* 66; untouchable converts to Christianity 64; Valangamugattar caste 68; *Vigadapradapan* 66 Professional teaching 60; Ateliers de Charité 60
Prouchandy, Léon 113, 115, 121, 130, 155, 170-2, 202, 386; launched dress reforms among Indians 121
Puduvai Hindu Union School 58
Puduvai Murasu 121
Ramakrishna Reading Room 113-14

Rassendran, Louis 86
Royal College 55-7: Missionaries of the Congregation of the Holy Spirit 57

Samba Kovil 32
Sarva Vyapi 118-19
Savarinathan 114
Second World War, 1939-45 153-61; Adicéam, Emmanuel 158; *Balyan (Young Man)* 161; British Indian government, lifted the ban on the Communist Party of India 153; Clemenceau, Murugasamy 160; Combat 157, 158; *Comité Redressement Inde Française* (Recovery Committee of French India) 157; Communist Party of France 154; *Croix de la Libération* 157; Davidu, Joseph 156; *France Combattante* or Fighting France 157; Free France Movement of De Gaule 154; General Council of Pondicherry 154; Gopalan, A.K. 153; Governor Bonvin 154, 156, 158-9; Jeevarathinam, D. 158; Mouchilotte Madhavan 155; *Puduvai Thozhilali* 160; Quit India Movement, response generally muted in Pondicherry 154-5; Subbiah 153, 159-60; Tetta, Emmanuel 160

Shanmugam, Nadou 79-81, 83-93, 95-6, 98, 105-6, 130, 152, 272, 388; Brahmanical Party/Clerical Hindu Party or the Indian Party 85; favoured secular education in the pure French tradition 85; November 1901, arrested for electoral fraud and extortion 89
Sir Stafford Cripps 128-9
Socialist party of French India, foundation of 188-98; Alfassa, Mirra, the Ashram Mother 190-1; Associated State within the French Union 193; Baron's meeting with Nehru in Delhi 192; Commissioner Baron 189; Commissioner Baron's idea regarding the future of French India 193; *Français Quittez l'Inde* or French Quit India 189; free citizens under France 196; Goubert, Edouard 188; Goubert's supporters 191; Le Problème de l'Inde Française 197; Menon, Krishna 197-8; party programme 189-90; Roux, Henri 193-4; Sri Aurobindo 189; Terreur Blanche' (White Terror) 189; transfer of the *loges* to India 194-5; under Goubert 191
Socio-economic profile 38-49; Aayi Kulam 41; April 1941, customs convention of 45; Black town 38-9; Calvé Sangara Chettiar 48; Central Jail for Indians 40; Chamber of Commerce 48; charitable organisations 41; Charity Workshop ('Atelier de Charité') 40; Comité de Bienfaisance (Welfare Committee) 41; customs around Pondicherry 45; Darmanathan Prouchandy 43-4; Desbassyns Old People's Home 41; first cotton mill 1829 47; French and the British Indias, custom dispute between 44; French India, import-export trade in 42; French territories highly dependent on British India 43; Gaebelé, Henri 48; governorship of De Mellay, hospital created 40; Grand Bazar Road/Goubert Market 39-40; *Impartial* 43; Indian Tariff Act of 10 March 1894 45-6; *Kaili* manufacturing industry, destruction of 46; Karaikal port 41; Kitchi Kadai (Bazar St. Laurent) 40; La Société de Secours Musulman (Society to Help Muslims) 41; *laissez passer*, from the 'Service des Contributions' (Tax Office) 45; Madras Road 39; mortgage registries 48; Mudaliarpet Cotton Mill 47; Muthialpet *kaili* 46; oil-mills 47; Old Pondicherry, acute drinking water scarcity in 41; Pagel & Co. 47; Pala Kadai 40; Petit Bazar (Chinna Kadai/Kassim Market) 40; Pondicherry merchants 44; port of Pondicherry 42, 43; roads 39; Rodier Mill 47; Saint Louis de Gonzague 41; Sainte Elizabeth factory 48; Savanna Cotton Mill 47; saylasses (colourful loincloth or *kaili*), manufacturing of 46; sea customs of wartime 45; Sinna Supraya Poullé 41; Standard Oil Company 48; surrounded by several choultries 41; Vicomte Eugène Desbassyns, governorship of 39; White town 38-9
Sri Aurobindo Ashram 16, 116-18, 125-31, 174, 177-9, 186, 188-91, 193-4, 197, 198-200, 203-5, 207,

Index 455

218, 221, 224-6, 230, 233-5, 241, 245, 247, 250, 252, 275, 282, 299, 305, 310, 349-52, 363, 368, 370, 373-7; Ashram members indulge freely in business 350; attempts to procure double nationality 352; demand for double nationality emanating from the Ashram 352
Sri Aurobindo of Bengal in Pondicherry 124-31; French governors, participated in the activities of the Ashram 127-8; influence on Pondicherry politics and society 130; Inner Force' with the French Foreign Ministry in Paris 126; l'Idée Nouvelle' or New Idea 125; monastery or Ashram in the name of Si Aurobindo 125; *Revue de Synthèse Philosophique* 125; some Pondicherry Tamil journals held in great esteem 129
Student agitations, ashram and related events 198-208; Annusamy, G. 200; Ashram Opposition Day 204; Aurobindo Ashram 199; Baron's reforms and his concept of Free Towns 205; Dorai Munisamy (Students' Congress secretary) 201; Free Town of Chandernagore 202; Free Town project 202; Mariadassou, Antoine 199; Mudaliar, Karunendra 206; Netaji Kazhagam (Association) 202; Saravane, Lambert 205, 206; Students' Congress of Pondicherry 198; Varma, Ravindra 203
Subramanian, S.R. 115, 116, 137, 139, 145, 148, 152, 153, 173, 177, 183, 190, 191, 200
Sunnites 33
Suthanthiram 117-18
system of education 56-7

Tamil 'poyal' schools 58
Tamil *Brevet* 56
Tamil-speaking Muslims of Pondicherry 33
Tamizhar (or caste Christians) 32
Tandon, R.K. 252, 270, 273-5, 282, 284, 297, 300; consul general of India in Pondicherry 273
Telugu-speaking Reddiars 36
treaty of transfer 361

Union Socialiste Républicaine Démocratique de l'Inde Française' (Republican, Democratic Socialist Union of French India) 174
Untouchables, or the Adi Dravidas of Pondicherry 31

Valanga Christians 32, 95
Valanga marriages 32
Varnasrama Dharma, caste system 31; Chettys 31; Idayars or Yadavals 31; Kshatriyas and the Kammalars (artisans) 31; Mukkuwas in Virampattinam 31; Pallis or Vanniyars 31; Pattanavas or Mukkuwas 31; Reddiars 31; Shivaite priests 31; Shudras 31; Tamil-speaking Vellalas 31; *Tamizhars* (Tamils) 31; Telugu Komuttys 31; Telugu-speaking Kavareys 31; Valangas 31; Valluvars 31
Vijayaraghavachari 34
Vikata Prathapan 88
Voilà Les Français Qui Arrivent' (Here comes the Frenchmen) 335-49; blockade imposed by the Indian government 335; *de facto* transfer of administration 336; Democratic Party of Dutamby 347; French Socialist Party (SFIO) 336; French Union Assembly opined that

negotiations between the French and Indian governments 346; system of passports and identity cards, introduced 341

Workers' revolt of 1936 136-45; child labour was rampant 136; child labour, prevalent in the mills 137; compulsory primary education, demands for 141; Davidu, Joseph 139-40; Franco-Hindu Party, patronised by the French governors 144; French governor, measures to alleviate the sufferings of workers 139; French labour code in French India 137; Gaebelé Mill at Mudaliarpet, strike 138; Godart, Justin 143; mill workers of Pondicherry 138; Reddiar, R.L. Purushottama 140; Rodier Mill (Anglo-French Textiles) 136, 139; Savana Mill, closed for six months 140; Savana Mill, workers went on strike 137-8; trade unions 144; workers and mill owners, broad agreement between 141; workers of Gaebelé Mill went on strike 136; Workers' Protection Laws 142